Concurrent Programming

Principles and Practice

Gregory R. Andrews
The University of Arizona

The Benjamin/Cummings Publishing Company, Inc.
Redwood City, California • Menlo Park, California
Reading, Massachusetts • New York • Don Mills, Ontario
Wokingham, U.K. • Amsterdam • Bonn • Sydney
Singapore • Tokyo • Madrid • San Juan

Sponsoring editors: Alan Apt, Sally Elliott
Production supervisor: Laura Kenney
Copyeditor: Larry Olsen
Cover designer: Rudy Zehtner
Cover illustrator: Mary Ross

Library of Congress Cataloging-in-Publication Data

Andrews, Gregory R.
  Concurrent programming : principles and practice

  Includes bibliographical references and index.
  ISBN 0-8053-0086-4
  1. Parallel programming (Computer science)   I. Title.
  QA76.642.A53 1991
  004'.35–dc20   91-11435

ISBN 0-8053-0086-4

1 2 3 4 5 6 7 8 9 10—HA—95 94 93 92 91

The Benjamin/Cummings Publishing Company, Inc.
390 Bridge Parkway
Redwood City, California 94065

To Mary, Jeff, and Brad

Preface

Concurrent programming is the activity of constructing a program containing multiple processes that execute in parallel. These processes compete for access to critical resources and cooperate in performing some task. Given the specification of a problem to be solved, decisions have to be made about what and how many processes to employ and how they should interact. These decisions are affected by the application and by the underlying hardware on which the program will run. Whatever choices are made, a critical problem is ensuring that process interaction is properly synchronized.

In this book, we focus on imperative programs with explicit concurrency, communication, and synchronization. In particular, *processes* are sequential programs that execute a sequence of statements; processes communicate and synchronize by reading and writing shared variables or by sending and receiving messages. This contrasts with declarative programs—e.g., functional or logic programs—in which concurrency is mostly implicit and there is no concept of a program state. In declarative programs, independent parts of the program may execute in parallel; they communicate and synchronize implicitly when one part depends on the results produced by another.

Although the declarative approach is interesting and important, the imperative approach is much more widely used. In addition, to implement a declarative concurrent program on a traditional, von Neumann machine, one has to write an imperative concurrent program. The interested reader is referred to two excellent survey papers [Hudak 89, Shapiro 89] for descriptions of functional and concurrent logic programming.

We also focus on concurrent programs in which process execution is asynchronous; i.e., each process executes at its own rate. Such programs can be executed on a single processor (by interleaving process execution) or on a multiple instruction stream, multiple data stream (MIMD) multiprocessor. This class of multiprocessors includes ones with shared memory, ones with distributed memory (e.g., hypercubes), and networks of workstations. Although we focus on asynchronous multiprocessing, in Chapter 3 we also describe synchronous multiprocessors (so-called SIMD machines) and the associated data-parallel programming style.

Content Overview

This book contains 10 chapters organized into four parts: basic concepts, shared variables, message passing, and practice. The introduction to each part summarizes the key concepts introduced in that part and describes their relation to key concepts in previous parts. Each chapter introduces new language mechanisms and programming techniques and develops solutions to several problems. Some problems are solved in more than one chapter, which illustrates the tradeoffs between different synchronization mechanisms. Each chapter also introduces new examples. All the "classic" concurrent programming problems are covered—e.g., critical sections, producers and consumers, readers and writers, the dining philosophers, and resource allocation—as well as many important parallel and distributed programming problems. The end of each chapter contains historical notes, extensive citations to relevant literature, and numerous exercises, including several that introduce additional material.

Part I gives a concise introduction to assertional proof techniques for sequential and concurrent programming. This material is necessarily quite formal (the rest of the book is much less so). The formal treatment is important since the techniques provide the foundation and a set of tools that enable one to approach concurrent programming in a disciplined way. Chapter 1 describes our notation for sequential programming and presents an axiomatic programming logic for understanding and proving properties about sequential programs. Chapter 2 extends the sequential language with mechanisms for specifying concurrency and synchronization and extends the programming logic to address safety properties of concurrent programs.

In Part II we present a systematic method for solving synchronization problems and show how to apply this method to numerous problems in which communication and synchronization are implemented by means of shared variables. Chapter 3 covers fine-grained synchronization, in which processes interact by writing, reading, and testing shared variables. Chapter 4 describes semaphores, which obviate the need for busy waiting. Conditional critical regions (CCRs), a higher-level synchronization mechanism, are discussed in Chapter 5. Finally, Chapter 6 covers monitors, which provide more structure than CCRs yet can be implemented as efficiently as semaphores.

Part III examines concurrent programs in which processes communicate and synchronize by means of message passing. Chapter 7 describes asynchronous message passing, in which the sender of a message does not delay. That chapter also introduces and illustrates a number of paradigms for process interaction in distributed programs. Chapter 8 covers synchronous message passing, in which both the sender and receiver of a message delay. Chapter 9 covers remote procedure call (RPC) and rendezvous, both of which combine aspects of monitors and synchronous message passing. These two chapters contain additional examples illustrating the use of the process interaction paradigms.

Finally, Part IV describes the "practice" of concurrent programming. In particular, Chapter 10 gives an overview of five specific languages: Turing Plus, Occam, Ada, SR, and Linda. Together they illustrate the range of possibilities; individually they are novel and in active use. For each language, we give a complete program that solves one of the problems introduced earlier in the book. The end of Chapter 10 analyzes the performance of different synchronization mechanisms and briefly describes several additional languages.

Classroom Use

Drafts of this text have been used for concurrent programming courses at The University of Arizona and several other universities. Prerequisites for our course are undergraduate courses on operating systems and discrete mathematics, including logic. When I teach the course, I quickly review the material in Chapter 1 and then go through the other chapters in the order they appear in the text, except I combine parts of the message-passing chapters into a single lecture. In one semester it is impossible to cover everything, but I am able to cover significant parts of every chapter. I would be happy to share my syllabus and lecture notes with instructors.

Drafts of the text have also been used elsewhere for major portions of courses on advanced operating systems, distributed systems, and parallel computing. In those cases, the instructors have covered much of this material and additional topics such as database concurrency control, fault-tolerant programming, or parallel architectures. The text could also be used as the basis for a more theoretical course on the semantics of concurrent programming; in that case, it would be supplemented with material on topics such as temporal logic.

This text can be (and has been) used in "pencil and paper" courses. However, I believe that students learn more—and have more fun—if they also get to practice concurrent programming. In addition, the increasing prevalence of multiprocessors and networks of workstations means that many people will later have the opportunity to write concurrent applications. (Many of my students have in fact later written large concurrent programs in other classes and in support of their dissertation research.) There are several concurrent programming languages that could be used for programming assignments, such as those described in Chapter 10. The Historical Notes and References section of Chapter 10 gives contact information for many of these.

At The University of Arizona, we use the SR language for programming assignments. (The notation in most chapters of the book is essentially the same as SR's.) Students run some programs on a Sequent multiprocessor and some on a network of workstations. There are four or five homework assignments during the semester; each consists of exercises from the text plus a programming problem. Students also do a final project of their own choice. The SR implementation, including documentation, is available at no charge by remote file transfer or for a nominal charge on a tape or cartridge; for details, contact the SR Project, Department of Computer Science, The University of Arizona, Tucson, AZ 85721. In addition, Ron Olsson and I are writing a book entitled *Concurrent Programming in SR*, which will be published by Benjamin/Cummings in late 1991 or early 1992. That book will help students learn the SR language on their own; it will also contain numerous programming exercises.

Acknowledgments

Many people warned me that writing a textbook was a major undertaking. To an extent I believed them. Now I know for sure.

I began work on this book several years ago during a sabbatical leave spent at the University of Washington. At that time, Fred Schneider and I were planning to coauthor a text. Later, however, it became apparent that the union of everything we wanted to cover was enough for two separate books. I thank Fred for providing the challenge that led me to develop the systematic approach to solving synchronization problems that is introduced in Part II; he also provided valuable feedback on drafts of those chapters. Fred was also kind enough to share large amounts of material that I distilled into Chapters 1 and 2.

Numerous people have read, commented on, and class-tested drafts of the text. Rick Schlichting has used the materials several times at The University of Arizona, and Ron Olsson has used them several times at UC Davis. I thank them and all the students who have studied concurrent programming at Arizona and Davis the past few years. Three of my Ph.D. students have carefully read chapters: Dave Bakken, Mike Coffin, and Irv Elshoff. Ric Holt was kind enough to test the Turing Plus program in Chapter 10. Finally, several reviewers provided numerous helpful suggestions on content, organization, and technical points: Partha Dasgupta, Raphael Finkel, Andrzej Hoppe, Douglas Jones, Rod Oldehoeft, Michael Scott, Alan Shaw, John Stankovic, and Jennifer Widom. Michael Scott's comments were especially detailed and useful. Andrzej Hoppe provided the quotation in the last sentence of the introduction to Part I. And I owe Alan Shaw a major debt of gratitude since it was he who introduced me to concurrent programming when I was a student of his many years ago.

The staff of Benjamin/Cummings has been a pleasure to work with. Alan Apt has been an excellent editor; I hate to see him move on to a new position but wish him well. Jake Warde has taken this project over from Alan and has been a great help in the final stages. Laura Kenney has coordinated the production process and has gracefully accommodated my slowness in getting things finished. In a few months, she gets to repeat the process with Ron Olsson's and my book! Others who have been helpful include Gary Head (text design), Mark McCormick (writing style), Larry Olsen (copyediting), Merry Finley (drawings), Michele Carter (cover coordination), Rudy Zehtner (cover design), and Mary Ross (cover illustration).

My oldest son, Jeff, provided major assistance by preparing the bibliography. Along the way, he learned a lot about UNIX, troff, and emacs.

The National Science Foundation has supported the computing equipment used to prepare this book. The pages were generated by a Lintronic 300 phototypesetter in the Department of Computer Science at The University of Arizona. (The source files for the book contain over 1.6 million characters!) John Cropper and Dhananjay Mahajan did a masterful job producing the copy. The NSF has also supported my research over the years, most recently through grants CCR-8701516 and CCR-8811423.

Finally, and most importantly, I thank my wife, Mary, and my sons, Jeff and Brad. They have provided encouragement, support, and, above all, love. They never expressed doubt that I would eventually finish this book, but they certainly had to wonder when. When I began, my sons were in elementary school; now both are in high school. But with luck—and cooperation from readers—this book will help finance their college educations.

Greg Andrews
Tucson, Arizona

Contents

xii

Chapter 8 Synchronous Message Passing 423

## PART I

Basic Concepts

A concurrent program specifies two or more processes that cooperate in performing a task. Each process is a sequential program that executes a sequence of statements. Processes cooperate by communicating; they communicate using shared variables or message passing. When shared variables are used, one process writes into a variable that is read by another. When message passing is used, one process sends a message that is received by the other.

Concurrent programs are inherently more complex than sequential programs. In many respects, they are to sequential programs what chess is to checkers or bridge is to pinochle: Each is interesting, but the former is more intellectually intriguing than the latter. This book explores the "game" of concurrent programming, looking closely at its rules, playing pieces, and strategies. The rules are formal tools that help one to understand and develop correct programs; the playing pieces are language mechanisms for describing concurrent computations; the strategies are collections of useful programming paradigms.

The formal tools are based on assertional reasoning. The state of a program is characterized by a predicate called an assertion, and the effects of executing program statements are characterized by predicate transformers. Assertional reasoning provides the basis for a systematic method for deriving programs that satisfy specified properties. It also provides insight into tradeoffs between different language notations.

Many different language mechanisms have been proposed for specifying concurrent execution, communication, and synchronization. We describe the most important mechanisms—including semaphores, monitors, and those based on message passing—and survey programming languages that employ different combinations. For each synchronization mechanism, we show how to develop correct and efficient programs, present numerous examples, and show how to implement the mechanism. The examples illustrate how to use each mechanism effectively and point out tradeoffs with respect to ease of use and implementation cost.

Finally, this book describes important paradigms that have been identified for concurrent programming. These include solution strategies and programming techniques that are applicable to a wide variety of problems. Most concurrent programs result from combining a small number of simple structures and can be viewed as instances of a few standard problems. By learning these structures and solution techniques, one finds it easier to solve additional problems.

Hardware and Applications

The history of concurrent programming has followed the same stages as other experimental areas of computer science. The topic arose due to hardware developments and has developed in response to technological changes. Over time, the initial ad-hoc approaches have evolved into a collection of core principles and general programming techniques.

Operating systems were the first significant examples of concurrent programs and remain among the most interesting. With the advent of independent device controllers in the 1960s, it became natural to organize an operating system as a concurrent program, with processes managing devices and execution of user tasks. Processes in such a single-processor system are implemented by *multiprogramming*, with processes executed one at a time in an interleaved manner.

Technology has since evolved to produce a variety of *multiprocessor* systems. In a *shared-memory* multiprocessor, multiple processors share a common memory; memory access time is either uniform (UMA) or non-uniform (NUMA). In a *multicomputer*, several processors called nodes are connected by high-speed message-switching hardware. In a *network* system, several single or multiprocessor nodes share a communication network, e.g., an Ethernet. Several hybrid combinations also exist, e.g., networks of multiprocessor workstations. The operating systems for multiprocessors are concurrent programs in which at least some processes can execute in parallel. The processors themselves range in power from microcomputers to super-computers.

There are many examples of concurrent programs besides operating systems. They arise whenever the implementation of an application involves real or apparent parallelism. For example, concurrent programs are used to implement:

- window systems on personal computers or workstations,

- transaction processing in multiuser database systems,
- file servers in a network, and
- scientific computations that manipulate large arrays of data.

The last kind of concurrent program is often called a *parallel program* since it is typically executed on a multiprocessor. A *distributed program* is a concurrent (or parallel) program in which processes communicate by message passing.

Synchronization

As mentioned, processes in a concurrent program communicate using shared variables or messages. Communication gives rise to the need for synchronization. Two forms of synchronization occur in concurrent programs: *mutual exclusion* and *condition synchronization*. Mutual exclusion is concerned with ensuring that *critical sections* of statements that access shared objects are not executed at the same time. Condition synchronization is concerned with ensuring that a process delays if necessary until a given condition is true. For example, communication between a producer process and a consumer process is often implemented using a shared buffer. The sender writes into the buffer; the receiver reads from the buffer. Mutual exclusion is used to ensure that a sender and receiver do not access the buffer at the same time—hence a partially written message is not read. Condition synchronization is used to ensure that a message is not received before it has been sent and that a message is not overwritten before it has been received.

The *state* of a concurrent program at any point in time consists of the values of the program variables. These include explicit variables declared by the programmer and implicit variables—e.g., the program counter for each process—that contain hidden state information. A concurrent program begins execution in some initial state. Each process in the program then executes at some unknown rate. As it executes, a process transforms the state by executing statements. Each statement consists of a sequence of one or more *atomic actions* that make indivisible state transformations. Examples of atomic actions are uninterruptible machine instructions that load and store register values.

Execution of a concurrent program generates a sequence of atomic actions that is some interleaving of the sequences of atomic actions from each component process. The trace of a particular execution of a concurrent program can be viewed as a *history*:

$$s_0 \xrightarrow{\alpha_1} s_1 \xrightarrow{\alpha_2} \cdots \xrightarrow{\alpha_i} s_i \xrightarrow{\alpha_{i+1}} \cdots$$

In a history, s_0 is the initial state, the s_i's denote other states, the α_i's denote atomic actions, and $\alpha_1,$ $\alpha_2,$ ... is an interleaving of the sequences of atomic actions resulting from execution of the processes. Even parallel execution can be modeled in this way. This is because the effect of executing a set of atomic actions in parallel is equivalent to executing them in some arbitrary, serial order since the state transformation caused by an atomic action is indivisible and hence cannot be affected by atomic actions executed in parallel with it.

Each execution of a concurrent program produces a history. For all but the most trivial programs, the number of possible histories is enormous. Each process will most likely take different actions in response to different initial states. More importantly, the actions of the processes might be interleaved in a different order. This is because if atomic actions in more than one process are *eligible*—i.e., could be executed next—any one of them could be next in a history.

Given this view, the role of synchronization is to constrain the possible histories of a concurrent program to those that are desirable. Mutual exclusion is concerned with combining fine-grained atomic actions that are implemented directly by hardware into critical sections that appear to be atomic since their execution is not interleaved with other critical sections that reference the same variables. Condition synchronization is concerned with delaying a process until the state is conducive to further execution. Both forms of synchronization cause processes to be delayed and hence restrict the set of atomic actions that are eligible for execution.

Program Properties

A property of a program is an attribute that is true of every possible history of that program, and hence of all executions of the program. Every property can be formulated in terms of two special kinds of properties: safety and liveness. A *safety property* asserts that the program never enters a bad state, i.e., one in which some variables have undesirable values. A *liveness property* asserts that a program eventually enters a good state, i.e., one in which the variables all have desirable values.

Partial correctness is an example of a safety property. It asserts that if a program terminates, the final state is correct; i.e., the right result has been computed. If a program fails to terminate, it may never produce the correct answer, but there is no history in which the program has terminated without producing the correct answer. *Termination* is an example of a liveness property. It asserts that a program will eventually terminate; i.e., every history of the program is finite. *Total correctness* is a property that combines partial correctness and termination. It asserts that a program always terminates with a correct answer.

Mutual exclusion is another example of a safety property. It asserts that at most one process at a time is executing in its critical section. The bad state in this case would be one in which actions in critical sections in different processes are both eligible for execution. *Absence of deadlock* is another example of a safety property. A bad state in this case is one in which all processes are blocked; i.e., there are no eligible actions. Finally, eventual entry to a critical section is another example of a liveness property. The good state for each process is one in which its critical section is eligible.

Given a program and a desired property, how might one go about demonstrating that the program satisfies the property? A common approach is *testing* or *debugging*, which can be characterized as "kick the program and see what happens." This corresponds to enumerating some of the possible histories of a program and verifying that they are acceptable. The shortcoming of testing is that each test considers only one specific execution history; one test cannot demonstrate the absence of bad histories.

A second approach is to use *operational reasoning*, which can be characterized as "exhaustive case analysis." In this approach, all possible execution histories of a program are enumerated by considering all the ways operations of each process might be interleaved. Unfortunately, the number of histories in a concurrent program is generally enormous (hence the approach is "exhaustive"). For example, suppose a concurrent program contains n processes and that each executes a sequence of m atomic actions. Then the number of different histories of the program is $(n*m)!/(m!)^n$. (This is the number of permutations of the different atomic actions, less those that result from impossible orderings of the actions within each process.) In a program containing only three processes, each of which executes only two atomic actions, this is a total of 90 different histories!

A third approach is to employ *assertional reasoning*, which might be characterized as "abstract analysis." In this approach, formulas of predicate logic called *assertions* are used to characterize sets of states, e.g., all states in which $x > 0$. Actions are then viewed as *predicate transformers* that change the state from one satisfying one predicate to one satisfying another. The virtue of the assertional approach is that it leads to a compact representation of states and state transformations. More importantly, it leads to a way to develop and analyze programs in which the work involved is directly proportional to the number of atomic actions in the program.

In this book, we employ the assertional approach as a tool for constructing and understanding solutions to a variety of non-trivial problems. However, the other approaches also have their place. We will use operational reasoning to guide the development of many algorithms. And many of the programs in the text have been tested since that helps increase confidence in the correctness of a program. One always has to be wary of testing alone, though, since it can only reveal the presence of errors, not their absence. Moreover, concurrent programs are extremely difficult to test and debug since (1) it is difficult to stop all processes at once in order to examine their state, and (2) each execution of the same program may produce a different history because actions might be interleaved in a different order.

This part of the text presents the programming notation we will use and describes the assertional approach to program development and analysis. Chapter 1 introduces a small sequential programming language and presents a programming logic that allows one to prove properties of sequential programs. Many readers will be familiar with much of the material in this chapter; it is included so the book is self-contained. Chapter 2 extends the programming language with mechanisms for specifying concurrency and synchronization and describes the key concepts related to understanding and proving properties of concurrent programs.

The formal notation and definitions in Chapters 1 and 2 are quite detailed, and they can be intimidating and hard to grasp on first reading. Indeed, the assertional approach is too complex to use in complete detail on large programs. However, the concepts and techniques are very important since they provide the basis for a disciplined approach to developing and understanding programs. This is important for sequential programs; it is even more important for concurrent programs, as we will see in Parts II and III. Understanding the assertional approach will make you a better programmer. As one reviewer of this book said: "It is the awareness of these fundamentals that distinguishes an educated programmer from a hacker."

## CHAPTER 1

Sequential Programming

Concurrent programs extend sequential programs with mechanisms for specifying concurrency, communication, and synchronization. Our ultimate goal is to understand how to construct correct concurrent programs. This chapter shows how to construct correct sequential programs.

The first section presents the notation we will use for sequential programming. Our notation is similar to Pascal, but the control constructs, especially for iteration, are more powerful. Next we review basic concepts of formal logic, propositions, and predicates. Then we present a specific formal logical system containing axioms and inference rules for proving properties of sequential programs. Given a specification of the input assumptions and the desired final state of a program, the logic enables one to prove that the program is partially correct. Finally, the chapter presents a method—based on what are called weakest preconditions—for deriving a program and its total correctness proof hand-in-hand, starting only from a specification of the desired result. The reader familiar with these topics should find it sufficient to skim through the material, focusing on the numbered definitions and examples.

1.1 Language Notation

A sequential program contains *declarations*, *statements*, and *procedures*. Declarations define types, variables, and constants. Statements are used to assign values to variables and to control the flow of execution within the program. Procedures define parameterized subroutines and functions. In this section, we introduce and illustrate the specific programming notation that we will employ in this text. The presentation here is purposely terse, in the style of a language reference manual, since the reader should be able to understand most aspects of the notation merely by looking at sample programs.

The basic elements of a program are identifiers, keywords, literals, and operators. An identifier is a sequence of one or more letters, digits, and underscores, the first of which is a letter. Identifiers are set in *italic* type. Keywords are symbols with a fixed meaning; they are set in **boldface** type. Literals are values of the different types. Finally, operators are special characters such as = or →.

Within programs, comments begin with # and end with the end of the line on which the comment appears. We will use semicolons only to separate declarations and statements that appear on the same line. In our programming notation, semicolons are in fact optional (unlike in Pascal or C).

Declarations

The *basic types* are boolean (**bool**), integer (**int**), real (**real**), character (**char**), string (**string**), and enumeration. The boolean literals are true and false. Integer and real literals have the usual numeric values. Character literals are enclosed in single quotes; string literals are enclosed in double quotes.

An enumeration type defines an ordered collection of symbolic literals. For example,

$$\textbf{type } days = (SUN, MON, TUES, WEDS, THURS, FRI, SAT)$$

defines an enumeration type *days* whose values are the days of the week.

Variables are introduced by **var** declarations, which have the general form:

$$\textbf{var } id_1 : type_1 := value_1, \ ..., \ id_n : type_n := value_n$$

Identifier id_i is the name of a variable with data type $type_i$ and optional initial value $value_i$. For example,

$$\textbf{var } i : \textbf{int} := 0, \ x : \textbf{real}, \ s : \textbf{string}(10) := \text{"hi there"}$$

declares an integer variable i with initial value zero, a real variable x, and a variable-length string variable s with initial value "hi there" and maximum length of 10 characters. When the initial value is a value of one of the basic types, such as **int**, we will often omit the type field.

A constant is a special kind of variable; it is assigned a value only once, when it is declared. Thus, the form of a constant declaration is the same as that for a variable declaration, except **var** is replaced by **const**, and initial values must be given. For example,

> **const** $n := 100$, *today* : *days* := *FRI*

declares n to be 100 and *today* to be a *day* with value *FRI*.

   An array (subscripted variable) is declared by appending a range specification to an identifier in a variable declaration. For example,

> **var** *vector*[1:10] : **int**, *matrix*[1:n, 1:n] : **real**

declares *vector* to be an array of 10 integers and *matrix* to be an n by n array of reals (assuming n has been previously declared to be an integer and has a value of at least 1). The expression *vector*[i] references the ith element of *vector*, assuming i is an integer between 1 and 10. Similarly, *matrix*[i, j] references the element of *matrix* in row i and column j, here assuming i and j are integers between 1 and n. We will use the notation *vector*[1:5] to reference a contiguous subsection (slice) of an array, in this case the first 5 elements of *vector*. Finally, we will often use a *vector constructor* to assign to multiple elements of an array. For example,

> **var** *forks*[1:5] : **bool** := ([5] false)

declares *forks* to be a boolean array, all 5 elements of which are initially false.

   A record type defines a collection of data values of potentially different types. The fields in a record declaration have the same form as variable declarations (without the **var** keyword). For example,

> **type** *student* = **rec**(*name* : **string**(30)
> *age* : **int**
> *classes*[1:5] : **string**(15))
>
> **var** *queue* : **rec**(*front* := 1; *rear* := 1; *size* := 0; *contents*[1:n] : **int**)

declares *student* to be a record type containing three fields and *queue* to be a record variable containing four fields, three of which are initialized. We later refer to an element of a record by giving a variable name and a field name, separated by a dot; e.g., *queue.size*.

Statements

The *skip statement*, **skip**, is the "empty" statement. It terminates immediately and has no effect on any program variable. We will use **skip** in guarded statements (see below) and **await** statements (see Section 2.2) when there is no action to be taken when a boolean condition becomes true.

The *assignment statement*, $x := e$, evaluates expression e and assigns the result to target variable x. The types of e and x must be the same. For example, the following assigns $n + 2$ to the first element of *vector*:

$$vector[1] := n + 2$$

In an assignment statement, the target variable can be a scalar variable, an array or record, an element of an array, or a field of a record. If either the target or expression is undefined—e.g., an array subscript is out of range—the program terminates abnormally.

The *swap statement* is a special kind of assignment statement that interchanges the values of two variables. If *v1* and *v2* are variables of the same type, then the following swaps their values:

$$v1 :=: v2$$

A *compound statement* consists of a sequence of other statements. These are executed in sequential order. For example,

$$x := x + 1; y := y - 1$$

is a compound statement that first increments x then decrements y.

The alternative (**if**) and iterative (**do**) statements contain one or more *guarded statements* (often called guarded commands). Each has the form:

$$B \rightarrow S$$

Here, B is a boolean expression called the guard and S is a single or compound statement. Boolean expression B "guards" S in the sense that S will not be executed unless B is true.

An *alternative statement* contains one or more guarded statements:

> **if** $B_1 \rightarrow S_1$
> [] ...
> [] $B_n \rightarrow S_n$
> **fi**

The guards are evaluated in some arbitrary order. If guard B_i is found to be true, then statement S_i is executed. For example,

> **if** $x \geq y \rightarrow m := x$ [] $y \geq x \rightarrow m := y$ **fi**

sets m to the larger of x and y. If both guards happen to be true, i.e., $x = y$, the choice of which statement is executed is *non-deterministic*. If no guard is true, execution of **if** has no effect. For example,

$$\mathbf{if}\ x < 0 \rightarrow x := -x\ \mathbf{fi}$$

sets x to its absolute value. No statement is executed if x is non-negative;
otherwise the sign of x is reversed. The programmer can make this explicit
by using **skip** and writing:

$$\mathbf{if}\ x < 0 \rightarrow x := -x\ [\,]\ x \geq 0 \rightarrow \mathbf{skip}\ \mathbf{fi}$$

The *iterative statement* is similar to the alternative statement, except that
guarded statements are repeatedly evaluated and executed until all guards
evaluate to false. The form of **do** is:

$$\begin{array}{l}
\mathbf{do}\ B_1 \rightarrow S_1 \\
[\,]\quad \dots \\
[\,]\ \ B_n \rightarrow S_n \\
\mathbf{od}
\end{array}$$

As with **if**, the guards are evaluated in some arbitrary order. If at least one
guard B_i is true, then the corresponding statement S_i is executed, and the
evaluation process is repeated. Like **if**, **do** is non-deterministic if more than
one guard is true. Execution of **do** terminates when no guard is true. As an
elegant example, if X and Y are positive integers, the following implements
Euclid's algorithm for computing their greatest common divisor:

$$\begin{array}{l}
x := X;\, y := Y \\
\mathbf{do}\ x > y \rightarrow x := x - y \\
\quad [\,]\ \ y > x \rightarrow y := y - x \\
\mathbf{od}
\end{array}$$

This program employs facts about modular arithmetic and illustrates the use
of two guarded statements. The loop terminates when x and y are equal; at
that point the value of both is the greatest common divisor of X and Y.

The *for-all statement* is a special, compact form of iterative statement that
is useful for iterating across elements of an array. Its structure is:

$$\mathbf{fa}\ \text{quantifiers} \rightarrow \text{statements}\ \mathbf{af}$$

The body of **fa** is one or more statements. Each quantifier specifies a range of
values for an iteration variable:

$$\text{variable} := \text{initial\_expr}\ \mathbf{to}\ \text{final\_expr}\ \mathbf{st}\ B$$

An iteration variable is an implicitly declared integer; its scope is limited to the body of the for-all statement. The body of a for-all statement is executed once for each value of the iteration variable, beginning with the value of the initial expression and ending with the value of the final expression. If the optional such-that (**st**) clause is present, the iteration variable takes on only those values for which boolean expression B is true. If the range of a quantifier is empty, the body is not executed.

If there is more than one quantifier, they are separated by commas. In this case, the body of **fa** is executed for each combination of values of the iteration variables, with the rightmost variable varying most rapidly. Assuming each iteration of the body of **fa** terminates, the final values of the iteration variables are one more than the final values specified in the quantifier.

As an example, the following for-all statement transposes matrix m:

$$\textbf{fa } i := 1 \textbf{ to } n, j := i + 1 \textbf{ to } n \rightarrow m[i, j] :=: m[j, i] \textbf{ af}$$

A swap statement is used within the body to interchange two elements. The initial value of the second iteration variable, j, depends on that of i to avoid redundant interchanges.

As a second example, the following single statement sorts integer array $a[1:n]$ into ascending order:

$$\textbf{fa } i := 1 \textbf{ to } n, j := i + 1 \textbf{ to } n \textbf{ st } a[i] > a[j] \rightarrow a[i] :=: a[j] \textbf{ af}$$

Again the initial value of j depends on i; also, the swap statement in the body of **fa** is executed only for combinations of i and j such that $a[i] > a[j]$.

The for-all statement is simply a useful abbreviation for common cases of **do** statements. For example, the for-all statement that sorts array a is an abbreviation for:

```
var i := 1
do i ≤ n →
    j := i + 1
    do j ≤ n →
        if a[i] > a[j] → a[i] :=: a[j] fi
        j := j + 1
    od
    i := i + 1
od
```

Other instances of **fa** statements have a similar translation.

Procedures

A procedure defines a parameterized pattern for an operation. Its general form is:

> **procedure** $p(f_1 : t_1; ...; f_n : t_n)$ **returns** $r : t_r$
> > declarations
> > statements
> **end**

Identifier p is the name of the procedure. The f_i are the names of the formal parameters; the t_i are their corresponding types. The returns part is an optional specification of the name r and type t_r of the return value. The body of a procedure contains declarations of local variables and statements that implement the actions of the procedure.

A procedure declaration introduces a new block and hence a new variable scope. The formal and return parameters are accessible in the body of the procedure but not outside. Similarly, variables declared within the body of a procedure are accessible only within that procedure. The statements in a procedure can access the local variables, formal parameters, return value, and variables declared global to the procedure.

A procedure that does not have a returns part is invoked explicitly by means of the **call** statement:

> **call** $p(e_1, ..., e_n)$

A procedure that has a returns part is called a *function*. It is invoked implicitly by appearing in an expression, e.g., within an assignment statement:

> $x := p(e_1, ..., e_n)$

For both kinds of invocations, the actual parameters are expressions e_i; each must have the same type as the corresponding formal parameter. Also, the type of the value returned by a function must be appropriate for the expression in which the function call appears; e.g., in the above assignment statement, the return type of p must be the same as the type of x.

When a procedure is invoked, the actual parameters are evaluated and then passed to the procedure by value (copy in), by value/result (copy in, copy out), or by result (copy out). A value parameter is indicated by the keyword **val** in the specification of the formal parameter; this is also the default. A value/result parameter is indicated by **var**, and a result parameter is indicated by **res.**

A procedure invocation terminates when the last statement in the procedure body terminates. At this time the values of **var** and **res** parameters are assigned to the corresponding actual parameters. These actual parameters must be variables—as opposed to expressions—since they are assigned to.

As a simple example, the following procedure increments the value of its argument, which is passed by value/result:

> **procedure** *increment*(**var** x : **int**)
> $x := x + 1$
> **end**

A more realistic example is the following recursive function, which returns the factorial of its argument or –1 if the argument is negative.

> **procedure** *factorial*(i : **int**) **returns** f : **int**
>   **if** $i < 0 \rightarrow f := -1$
>   [] $i = 0$ **or** $i = 1 \rightarrow f := 1$
>   [] $i > 1 \rightarrow f := i * factorial(i - 1)$
>   **fi**
> **end** .

In this case, the argument is passed by value. Within *factorial*, f is the name of the result; it is returned when an invocation terminates.

1.2 Logic, Propositions, and Predicates

Consider the following problem called linear search. Given is array $a[1{:}n]$, with $n > 0$. Also given is that value x is in a, perhaps more than once. The problem is to compute the index i of the first occurrence of x in a, i.e., the smallest value for i such that $a[i] = x$. We can solve this problem by the following obvious program, which examines elements of a beginning with $a[1]$ and terminates when $a[i] = x$:

> **var** $i := 1$
> **do** $a[i] \neq x \rightarrow i := i + 1$ **od**

How would one *prove* that the above program correctly solves the stated problem? The point of any proof is to provide convincing evidence of the correctness of some statement. For this specific problem, the above English description and short program are probably convincing evidence to anyone who understands English and programming. But English statements are often ambiguous. Also, most real programs—especially concurrent programs—are large and complex. Thus it is necessary to have a more rigorous framework.

A *programming logic* is a formal system that supports the assertional approach to developing and analyzing programs. It includes predicates that characterize program states and relations that characterize the effect of program execution. This section summarizes relevant aspects of formal logical systems, propositional logic, and predicate logic, which is an extension of propositional logic. The next section presents a programming logic for sequential programs.

Formal Logical Systems

Any formal logical system consists of rules defined in terms of:

- a set of *symbols*,
- a set of *formulas* constructed from these symbols,
- a set of distinguished formulas called *axioms*, and
- a set of *inference rules*.

Formulas are well-formed sequences of symbols. The axioms are special formulas that are *a priori* assumed to be true. Finally, inference rules specify how to derive additional true formulas from axioms and other true formulas.

Inference rules have the form:

$$\frac{H_1, H_2, ..., H_n}{C}$$

The H_i are *hypotheses*; C is a conclusion. Both the hypotheses and conclusion are either formulas or schematic representations of formulas. The meaning of an inference rule is that if all the hypotheses are true, then we can infer that the conclusion is also true.

A *proof* in a formal logical system is a sequence of lines, each of which is an axiom or can be derived from previous lines by application of an inference rule. A *theorem* is any line in a proof. Thus, theorems are either axioms or are obtained by applying an inference rule to other theorems.

By itself, a formal logical system is a mathematical abstraction—a collection of symbols and relations between them. A logical system becomes interesting when the formulas represent statements about some domain of discourse and the formulas that are theorems are true statements. This requires that we provide an interpretation to the formulas. An *interpretation* of a logic maps each formula to true or false. A logic is *sound* with respect to an interpretation if all its axioms and inference rules are sound. An axiom is sound if it maps to true; an inference rule is sound if its conclusion maps to true, assuming all the hypotheses map to true. Thus, if a logic is sound, all theorems in the logic are true statements about the domain of discourse. In this case, the interpretation is called a *model* for the logic.

Completeness is the dual of soundness. A logic is complete with respect to an interpretation if every formula that is mapped to true is a theorem; i.e., the formula is provable in the logic. Thus, if *FACTS* is the set of true statements that are expressible as formulas in a logic and *THEOREMS* is the set of theorems of the logic, soundness means that $THEOREMS \subseteq FACTS$ and completeness means that $FACTS \subseteq THEOREMS$. A logic that is both sound and complete allows all true statements expressible in the logic to be proved. If a theorem cannot be proved in such a logic, it is not the result of a weakness of the logic.

Unfortunately, the domain of discourse of this book—properties of concurrent programs—cannot have a sound and complete axiomatization as a logical system. This is because program behavior has to include arithmetic, and a well-known result in logic—Gödel's incompleteness theorem—states that no formal logical system that axiomatizes arithmetic can be complete. However, a logic that extends another logic can be *relatively complete*, meaning that it introduces no source of incompleteness beyond that already in the logic it extends. Fortunately, relative completeness is good enough since the arithmetic properties that we will employ are certainly true, even if not all of them can be proved formally.

Propositions

Propositional logic is an instance of a formal logical system that formalizes what we usually call "common sense" reasoning. The formulas of the logic are called propositions; these are statements that are either true or false. The axioms are special propositions that are assumed to be true; e.g., "It's sunny implies it's daytime" and "It's daytime implies the stars are not visible." The inference rules allow new, true propositions to be formed from existing ones. For example, we would expect to have a transitivity rule that allows us to conclude from the two statements above that "It's sunny implies that stars are not visible."

To be more precise, in a propositional logic the propositional symbols are:

Propositional Constants: *true* and *false*

Propositional Variables: $p, q, r, \dots$

Propositional Operators: $\neg, \wedge, \vee, \Rightarrow,$ and $=$

The formulas of the logic are single propositional constants and variables, or they are constructed by using the propositional operators (connectives) to

p	q	$\neg p$	$p \wedge q$	$p \vee q$	$p \Rightarrow q$	$p = q$
false	false	true	false	false	true	true
false	true	true	false	true	true	false
true	false	false	false	true	false	false
true	true	false	true	true	true	true

Figure 1.1. Interpretations of propositional operators.

combine other formulas. There are five propositional operators: negation ($\neg$), conjunction ($\wedge$), disjunction ($\vee$), implication ($\Rightarrow$), and equivalence ($=$). Their interpretations are given in Figure 1.1.

Given a state s, we interpret a propositional formula P as follows. First, replace each propositional variable in P by its value in s. Then, use Figure 1.1 to simplify the result. When there are multiple operators in a formula, negation has the highest precedence, followed by conjunction, disjunction, implication, and finally equivalence. (This is the left-to-right order in Figure 1.1.) As in arithmetic expressions, one uses parentheses to force a different evaluation order or to make a formula clearer. For example, if p is false and q is true in a state, the interpretation of formula $p \vee (p \Rightarrow q)$ is:

$$\begin{aligned} p \vee (p \Rightarrow q) &= \text{false} \vee (\text{false} \Rightarrow \text{true}) \\ &= \text{false} \vee \text{true} \\ &= \text{true} \end{aligned}$$

Since $\vee$ has higher precedence than $\Rightarrow$, parentheses are needed in the above formula to force $\Rightarrow$ to be evaluated before $\vee$.

A formula P is *satisfied* in a state if it is true in that state; P is *satisfiable* if there is some state in which it is satisfied. Formula P is *valid* if it is satisfiable in every state. For example, $p \vee \neg p$ is valid. A valid proposition is also called a *tautology*. In a sound propositional logic, an axiom is a tautology since it is assumed to be valid.

One way to decide whether a formula is valid is to determine if its interpretation is true in every possible state. However, if the formula contains n propositional variables, this requires checking 2^n cases, one for each combination of values of the propositional variables. A much better approach is to employ tautologies that allow formulas to be simplified by transforming them into equivalent formulas.

There are many tautologies in propositional logic, just as there are many identities in trigonometry. The ones that we will employ most often are listed in Figure 1.2. These tautologies are called propositional equivalence laws since they allow a proposition to be replaced by an equivalent one. Applications of the propositional equivalence laws are transitive: In any given

Law of Negation: $P = \neg(\neg P)$

Law of Excluded Middle: $P \vee \neg P = true$

Law of Contradiction: $P \wedge \neg P = false$

Law of Implication: $P \Rightarrow Q = \neg P \vee Q$

Law of Equality: $(P = Q) = (P \Rightarrow Q) \wedge (Q \Rightarrow P)$

Laws of Or-Simplification: $P \vee P = P$
$$P \vee true = true$$
$$P \vee false = P$$
$$P \vee (P \wedge Q) = P$$

Laws of And-Simplification: $P \wedge P = P$
$$P \wedge true = P$$
$$P \wedge false = false$$
$$P \wedge (P \vee Q) = P$$

Commutative Laws: $(P \wedge Q) = (Q \wedge P)$
$$(P \vee Q) = (Q \vee P)$$
$$(P = Q) = (Q = P)$$

Associative Laws: $P \wedge (Q \wedge R) = (P \wedge Q) \wedge R$
$$P \vee (Q \vee R) = (P \vee Q) \vee R$$

Distributive Laws: $P \vee (Q \wedge R) = (P \vee Q) \wedge (P \vee R)$
$$P \wedge (Q \vee R) = (P \wedge Q) \vee (P \wedge R)$$

De Morgan's Laws: $\neg(P \wedge Q) = \neg P \vee \neg Q$
$$\neg(P \vee Q) = \neg P \wedge \neg Q$$

Figure 1.2. Propositional equivalence laws.

---

state, if $P = Q$ and $Q = R$, then $P = R$. Transitivity is often expressed by an inference rule in a propositional logic.

To illustrate the use of propositional equivalence laws, consider the following characterization of the critical section problem. Let *InA* and *InB* be the propositions:

>   *InA*: Process *A* is executing in its critical section.
>   *InB*: Process *B* is executing in its critical section.

Suppose we know that if process *A* is in its critical section, then process *B* is not in its critical section; i.e., that $InA \Rightarrow \neg InB$. Then we can rewrite this formula using two of the propositional equivalence laws as follows:

$$(InA \Rightarrow \neg\, InB) \;=\; (\neg\, InA \vee \neg\, InB) \qquad \text{by Law of Implication}$$
$$=\; \neg\,(InA \wedge InB) \qquad \text{by De Morgan's Laws}$$

Since equivalence is transitive, we thus have:

$$(InA \Rightarrow \neg\, InB) \;=\; \neg\,(InA \wedge InB)$$

Hence, it is not the case that processes A and B can be in their critical section at the same time.

As the above example illustrates, De Morgan's laws—which are the distributive laws of negation—are useful in simplifying propositional formulas. Two other tautologies will also be useful:

And-Elimination: $(P \wedge Q) \Rightarrow P$

Or-Introduction: $P \Rightarrow (P \vee Q)$

These are not equivalence laws since the left- and right-hand sides are not equivalent propositions. Instead they are laws of implication that allow one to conclude that the right-hand side is true if the left-hand side is true.

Both And-Elimination and Or-Introduction are examples of *weakening* a proposition. For example, if a state satisfies $P \wedge Q$, then it satisfies P. Thus, P is a weaker proposition than $P \wedge Q$ since in general more states satisfy just P than satisfy both P and Q. Similarly, in the Or-Introduction tautology, $(P \vee Q)$ is a weaker proposition than P (or than Q). Since *false* implies anything, *false* is the strongest proposition (no state satisfies it). Similarly, *true* is the weakest proposition (every state satisfies it).

Predicates

Propositional logic provides the basis for assertional reasoning. However, by itself it is too restrictive since the only propositional constants are the boolean values *true* and *false*. Programming languages of course have additional data types and values such as integers and reals. Thus, we need a way to manipulate any kind of boolean-valued expression. A predicate logic extends a propositional logic to support this generalization. The two extensions are as follows:

- Any expression such as $x < y$ that maps to true or false can be used in place of a propositional variable.

- Existential ($\exists$) and universal ($\forall$) quantifiers are provided to characterize sets of values.

The symbols of predicate logic are those of propositional logic plus other variables, relational operators, and quantifiers. The formulas—called *predicates*—are propositional formulas in which relational and quantified expressions can be used in place of propositional variables. To interpret a predicate in a state, we first interpret each relational and quantified expression—yielding true or false for each—and then interpret the resulting propositional formula.

A *relational expression* contains two terms separated by a relational operator such as equals (=), not equal (≠), or greater than (>). These operators are defined for characters, integers, reals, and sometimes strings, records, and so on—depending on the programming notation. We will introduce additional relational operators, such as member of (∈) and subset (⊂), as needed.

A relational expression is either true or false, depending on whether the relation holds between the arguments. We assume each relational expression is welldefined; e.g., in $x < y$ both x and y must have the same data type, and the $<$ operator must be defined for that type. In a programming language, a compiler ensures this by means of type checking.

When dealing with sets of values, we will often want to assert that some or all values of a set satisfy a property; e.g., all elements of $a[1{:}n]$ are zero. We could do this informally by using ellipses. However, *quantified expressions* provide a more precise and compact method.

The *existential quantifier* ∃, pronounced "there exists," allows one to assert that some element of a set satisfies a property. It appears in expressions of the form:

(1.1) $(\exists\, b_1, ..., b_n\colon R\colon P\,)$

The b_i following the quantifier are new variables called *bound variables*; R is a formula that specifies the set of values (range) of the bound variables; P is a predicate. The interpretation of (1.1) is true if P is true for *some* combination of the values of the bound variables. For example,

$(\exists\, i\colon 1 \le i \le n\colon a[i] = 0\,)$

is true if some element of $a[1{:}n]$ is zero. This predicate is read as "There exists some i between 1 and n such that $a[i]$ is zero."

The *universal quantifier* ∀, pronounced "for all," allows one to assert that all elements of a set satisfy a property. It appears in expressions of the form:

(1.2) $(\forall\, b_1, ..., b_n\colon R\colon P\,)$

Again, the b_i are bound variables, R specifies their values, and P is a predicate. The interpretation of (1.2) is true if P is true for *all* combinations of the values of the bound variables. For example,

$$(\forall i: 1 \le i \le n: a[i] = 0)$$

is true if all elements of $a[1{:}n]$ are zero. This predicate is read as "For all i between 1 and n, $a[i]$ is zero."

In a quantified expression, the scope of a bound variable is the expression itself. Thus, a quantified expression is like a nested block in a block-structured programming language. Most quantified expressions, such as the ones above, will also reference other variables. Thus, confusion could result if the name of a bound variable conflicts with that of another variable.

An occurrence of a variable in a predicate is said to be *free* if (1) it is not within a quantifier or (2) it is within a quantifier and is different from the name of any bound variable whose scope includes that quantifier. All occurrences of bound variables are *bound* within their scope. In the above examples, all occurrences of a are free and all occurrences of i are bound. However, in the following predicate, the first (left-most) occurrence of i is free but the others are bound:

$$i = j \wedge (\exists i, k: i, k > 0: a[i] = a[k])$$

Also, the occurrence of j is free, the occurrences of k are bound, and the occurrences of a are free.

One way to avoid potential confusion between when a variable is free in a predicate and when it is bound is to rename the bound variables. However, one has to be careful to avoid *capture*, which results if the new name for a bound variable causes occurrences of a previously free variable to become bound. In this text, we will avoid both confusion and the capture problem by always using different names for bound and free variables.

The existential and universal quantifiers are duals of each other: only one is actually needed, although both are convenient. In particular, consider the existentially quantified expression:

$$(\exists B: R: P)$$

Again, B is a collection of bound variables, R specifies their set of values, and P is a predicate. If the interpretation is true in a state, then some combination of the values of the bound variables satisfies P. Similarly, if the interpretation is false, then P is false for all combinations of values of B. In either case, the following universally quantified expression has the same interpretation:

$$\neg (\forall B: R: \neg P)$$

De Morgan's Laws for Quantifiers: $(\exists B:\ R:\ P) = \neg\,(\,\forall B:\ R:\ \neg P\,)$
$(\forall B:\ R:\ P) = \neg\,(\exists B:\ R:\ \neg P\,)$

Conjunction Law: $(\,\forall B:\ R:\ P \wedge Q\,) = (\,\forall B:\ R:\ P) \wedge (\,\forall B:\ R:\ Q\,)$

Disjunction Law: $(\exists B:\ R:\ P \vee Q\,) = (\exists B:\ R:\ P) \vee (\exists B:\ R:\ Q\,)$

Empty Range Laws: $(\,\forall B:\ \varnothing:\ P\,) = $ true
$(\exists B:\ \varnothing:\ P\,) = $ false

Figure 1.3. Laws for quantified expressions.

A similar duality exists in the other direction. Figure 1.3 gives two laws (axioms) that characterize this duality between the two quantifiers, along with a few others that we will employ.

To illustrate the use of the first Empty Range Law in Figure 1.3, consider the following predicate, which asserts that elements 1 through k of array a are sorted in ascending order:

$$(\,\forall i:\ 1 \le i \le k - 1:\ a[i] \le a[i + 1]\,)$$

If k happens to be 1—for example, at the start of a sorting program—the quantified expression is true since the range is the empty set. In other words, none of the elements of a is necessarily yet in sorted order.

Textual substitution is the final concept from predicate logic that we will employ. (The first use is in the next section in the axiom for the assignment statement.) One can also use substitution to rename variables in a predicate to avoid the capture problem mentioned above.

(1.3)   **Textual Substitution**. If no variable in expression e has the same name as any bound variable in predicate P, then P^x_e is defined to be the result of substituting e for every free occurrence of x in P.

P^x_e is pronounced "P with x replaced by e." As an example of substitution, $(x = y)^x_z$ is $(z = y)$. The names of variables in e must not conflict with bound variables in order to avoid introducing capture.

Definition (1.3) deals with substitution of one expression for one variable in a predicate. We can generalize the definition as follows to allow simultaneous substitution of several expressions for several free variables.

(1.4)   **Simultaneous Substitution**. If no variable in expressions $e1, ..., en$ has the same name as any bound variable in predicate P, and if $x1, ..., xn$ are distinct identifiers, then $P^{x1,\ \ldots\ ,\ xn}_{e1,\ \ldots\ ,\ en}$ is defined to be the result of simultaneously substituting the *e*'s for every free occurrence of the *x*'s in *P*.

The *x*'s are required to be distinct in (1.4) since otherwise more than one expression could be substituted for the same variable. However, if two identifiers *x1* and *x2* are the same, simultaneous substitution is still well defined if *e1* and *e2* are syntactically the same expression. We will make use of this latter property in the axiom for the swap statement.

1.3 A Programming Logic

A programming logic is a formal logical system that facilitates making precise statements about program execution. This section presents a specific programming logic, *PL*, for the sequential programming statements described in Section 1.1. Later chapters extend this logic to include procedures and various concurrent programming constructs.

As with any formal logical system, *PL* contains symbols, formulas, axioms, and inference rules. The symbols of *PL* are predicates, braces, and programming language statements. The formulas of *PL* are *triples* of the form:

$$\{P\}\ S\ \{Q\}$$

Above, *P* and *Q* are predicates, and *S* is a simple or compound statement.

In *P* and *Q*, the free variables are program variables and logical variables. *Program variables* are introduced in declarations. *Logical variables* are special variables that serve as placeholders for arbitrary values; they appear only in predicates, not in program statements. To distinguish between them, program variables are typeset in lower-case italics, and logical variables are typeset in upper-case Roman. For example, the predicate $x = \text{X}$ contains program variable *x* and logical variable X. It states that *x* has some value X (of the same type as *x*).

Since the purpose of *PL* is to facilitate proving properties of program execution, the interpretation of a triple characterizes the relation between predicates *P* and *Q* and the effect of executing statement *S*.

(1.5)   **Interpretation of a Triple**. Let each logical variable have some value of the correct type. Then, the interpretation of triple $\{P\}\ S\ \{Q\}$ is true if, whenever execution of *S* is begun in a state satisfying *P* and execution of *S* terminates, the resulting state satisfies *Q*.

This interpretation is called *partial correctness*, which is a safety property. It says that, if the initial program state satisfies P, then the final state in any finite history resulting from executing S will satisfy Q. The related liveness property is *total correctness*, which is partial correctness plus termination; i.e., all histories are finite. (We consider proving termination in Section 1.5.)

In a triple, predicates P and Q are often called *assertions* since they assert that the program state must satisfy the predicate in order for the interpretation of the triple to be true. Thus, an assertion characterizes an acceptable program state. Predicate P is called the *precondition* of S, denoted $pre(S)$; it characterizes the condition the state must satisfy before execution of S begins. Predicate Q is called the *postcondition* of S, denoted $post(S)$; it characterizes the state that results from executing S, if S terminates. Two special assertions are *true*, which characterizes all program states, and *false*, which characterizes no program state.

In order for interpretation (1.5) to be a model for programming logic PL, the axioms and inference rules of PL must be sound with respect to (1.5). This will ensure that all theorems provable in PL are sound. For example, the following triple should be a theorem:

$$\{\, x = 0 \,\} \;\; x := x + 1 \;\; \{\, x = 1 \,\}$$

However, the following should not be a theorem since assigning a value to x cannot miraculously set y to 1:

$$\{\, x = 0 \,\} \;\; x := x + 1 \;\; \{\, y = 1 \,\}$$

In addition to being sound, the logic should be (relatively) complete so that all triples that are true are in fact provable as theorems.

Axioms

This section and the next present the axioms and inference rules of PL along with informal justifications of their soundness and relative completeness. The historical notes at the end of the chapter give references for more detailed discussions. Throughout we assume that expression evaluation does not cause any side-effects; i.e., no variable changes value.

The skip statement does not change any variable. Thus, if predicate P is true before execution of **skip**, it remains true when **skip** terminates:

(1.6)   **Skip Axiom**: $\{P\}$ **skip** $\{P\}$

An assignment statement assigns a value e to a variable x and thus in general changes the program state. At first glance, it might seem that the axiom for assignment should start with some precondition P, and that the postcondition should be P plus a predicate to indicate that x now has value e. However, going in the other direction results in a much simpler axiom. Assume that the postcondition of an assignment is to satisfy P. Then what must be true before the assignment? First, an assignment changes only the target variable x, so all other variables have the same value before and after the assignment. Second, x has a new value e, and thus any relation pertaining to x that is to be true after the assignment has to have been true before with x replaced by e. Textual Substitution (1.3) makes exactly this transformation.

(1.7)   **Assignment Axiom**: $\{\,P_e^x\,\}\ \ x := e\ \{\,P\,\}$

To illustrate the use of this axiom, consider the following triple:

$$\{\,true\,\}\ \ x := 5\ \{\,x = 5\,\}$$

This is a theorem since:

$$(x = 5)_5^x\ =\ (5 = 5)\ =\ true$$

This indicates that starting in any state and assigning a value to a variable gives the variable that value. As a second example, consider the triple:

$$\{\,y = 1\,\}\ \ x := 5\ \{\,y = 1 \wedge x = 5\,\}$$

This is also a theorem since:

$$(y = 1 \wedge x = 5)_5^x\ =\ (y = 1 \wedge 5 = 5)\ =\ (y = 1 \wedge true)\ =\ (y = 1)$$

This illustrates that relations about variables that are not assigned to are not affected by an assignment.

Unfortunately, (1.7) is not sound for assignment to array elements or record fields. To see the problem, consider the following triple:

$$\{\,P_8^{a[3]}\,\}\ \ a[3] := 8\ \{\,P\colon\ i = 3 \wedge a[i] = 6\,\}$$

Clearly postcondition P should not be satisfied and the interpretation of the triple should be false. But what is the precondition that results from the Assignment Axiom? It should be:

$$i = 3 \wedge 8 = 6$$

This is false, but to reach this conclusion we have to realize that $a[i]$ and $a[3]$ are the same element. We cannot do this with textual substitution alone.

We can view an array as a collection of independent variables, e.g., $a[1]$, $a[2]$, and so on. Alternatively, we can view an array as a (partial) function from subscript values to array elements. (And this is in fact how arrays are typically accessed.) With this second view, an array becomes a simple variable that contains a function.

Let a be a one-dimensional array, and let i and e be expressions whose types match those of the range and base type of a, respectively. Also let $(a; i : e)$ denote the array (function) whose value is the same as a for all subscripts except i, where its value is e:

$$(1.8) \qquad (a; i : e)[j] = \begin{array}{ll} a[j] & \text{if } i \neq j \\ e & \text{if } i = j \end{array}$$

With this view, $a[i] := e$ is simply an abbreviation for $a := (a; i : e)$; i.e., we replace a by a new function that is the same as the old one, except perhaps at subscript i. Since a is now a simple variable, Assignment Axiom (1.7) applies. We can handle assignment to multidimensional arrays and records in a similar fashion.

To illustrate the functional notation for arrays, consider again the triple:

$$\{ P^{a[3]}_8 \} \; a[3] := 8 \; \{ P: \; i = 3 \wedge a[i] = 6 \}$$

Rewriting the assignment as $a := (a; 3 : 8)$ and substituting into P yields:

$$P^a_{(a; 3: 8)} = (i = 3 \wedge (a; 3 : 8)[i] = 6)$$

From definition (1.8) together with the fact that $i = 3$, the right-hand side simplifies to:

$$(i = 3 \wedge 8 = 6) = \mathit{false}$$

This is a sound interpretation since $a[3]$ cannot be equal to 6 after it is assigned 8. What has happened is that, by rewriting the array assignment, all relevant information about a was carried along in the textual substitution.

As a second example, consider:

$$\{ P^{a[i]}_5 \} \; a[i] := 5 \; \{ P: \; a[j] = 6 \wedge i \neq j \}$$

Converting the assignment to the functional notation, substituting in P, and simplifying yields:

$$\begin{aligned} P^a_{(a; i: 5)} &= ((a; i: 5)[j] = 6 \wedge i \neq j) \\ &= (a[j] = 6 \wedge i \neq j) \end{aligned}$$

This illustrates that, as expected, assigning to one array element does not affect the value of any other element.

The swap statement interchanges the values of two variables *v1* and *v2*. The effect is simultaneously to assign *v1* to *v2* and *v2* to *v1*. Hence, the axiom for swap generalizes (1.7) by employing Simultaneous Substitution (1.4).

(1.9)   **Swap Axiom**: $\{\, P^{v1,\ v2}_{v2,\ v1} \,\}\ v1 :=: v2\ \{\, P \,\}$

As an example, the following theorem follows directly from the Swap Axiom:

$$\{\, x = X \wedge y = Y \,\}\ x :=: y\ \{\, x = Y \wedge y = X \,\}$$

Above, X and Y are logical variables that stand for whatever values *x* and *y* happen to have. We handle swapping of array elements or record fields by viewing arrays and records as partial functions, as described above.

Inference Rules

The program state changes as a result of executing assignment and swap statements. Hence, the axioms for these statements use textual substitution to introduce new values into predicates. The inference rules of *PL* allow the theorems resulting from these axioms to be manipulated and combined. There is one inference rule for each of the statements that affect the flow of control in a sequential program: composition, alternation, and iteration. There is one additional inference rule that we use to connect triples to each other.

The first inference rule, the Rule of Consequence, allows us to manipulate predicates in triples. Consider the following triple:

(1.10) $\{\, x = 3 \,\}\ x := 5\ \{\, x = 5 \,\}$

Clearly this should be a theorem since *x* has value 5 after the assignment, irrespective of the value it had before. However, this does not follow directly from Assignment Axiom (1.7). As illustrated earlier, what does follow from (1.7) is the theorem:

(1.11) $\{\, true \,\}\ x := 5\ \{\, x = 5 \,\}$

Recall that *true* characterizes every program state, including $x = 3$; in particular, $(x = 3) \Rightarrow true$. The Rule of Consequence lets us make this connection and hence to conclude from the validity of (1.11) that (1.10) is also valid.

(1.12)   **Rule of Consequence**: $\dfrac{P' \Rightarrow P,\ \{P\}\ S\ \{Q\},\ Q \Rightarrow Q'}{\{P'\}\ S\ \{Q'\}}$

The Rule of Consequence allows us to strengthen a precondition, weaken a postcondition, or both.

A compound statement executes statement *S1*, then statement *S2*. The Composition Rule permits us to combine valid triples concerning *S1* and *S2*.

(1.13)   **Composition Rule**: $\dfrac{\{P\}\ S1\ \{Q\},\ \{Q\}\ S2\ \{R\}}{\{P\}\ S1; S2\ \{R\}}$

For example, consider the compound statement:

$$x := 1; y := 2$$

From the Assignment Axiom, the following are both theorems:

$$\{\,true\,\}\ x := 1\ \{\,x = 1\,\}$$
$$\{\,x = 1\,\}\ y := 2\ \{\,x = 1 \wedge y = 2\,\}$$

Hence, by the Composition Rule, the following is also a theorem:

$$\{\,true\,\}\ x := 1; y := 2\ \{\,x = 1 \wedge y = 2\,\}$$

An alternative (**if**) statement contains n guarded statements:

$$IF:\ \textbf{if}\ B_1 \rightarrow S_1\ [\,]\ ...\ [\,]\ B_n \rightarrow S_n\ \textbf{fi}$$

Recall that we assume in *PL* that guard evaluation does not have any side effects, i.e., that the B_i do not contain function calls that change result parameters or global variables. Hence, no program variable can change state as a resulting of evaluating a guard. With this assumption, if no guard is true, execution of *IF* is equivalent to **skip.** On the other hand, if at least one guard is true, then one of the guarded statements will be executed, with the choice being non-deterministic in the event more than one guard is true.

Suppose the precondition of *IF* is P and the desired postcondition is Q. Then if P is true and all the B_i are false when *IF* is executed, Q had better be true since in this case *IF* is equivalent to **skip.** However, if some B_i is true and S_i is selected for execution, then the following had better be a theorem:

$$\{P \wedge B_i\}\ S_i\ \{Q\}$$

We need theorems for each guarded statement since we cannot know in advance which one will be executed. Putting these pieces together gives the following inference rule:

(1.14)   **Alternative Rule**: $P \wedge \neg (B_1 \vee ... \vee B_n) \Rightarrow Q$
$$\frac{\{P \wedge B_i\}\ S_i\ \{Q\}, 1 \le i \le n}{\{P\}\ IF\ \{Q\}}$$

As an example of the use of the Alternative Rule, consider the following program:

$$\textbf{if } x \ge y \rightarrow m := x\ []\ \ y \ge x \rightarrow m := y\ \textbf{fi}$$

This assigns to m the maximum of x and y. Suppose initially that $x = $ X and $y = $ Y. Then, the following triple should be a theorem:

(1.15) $\{P:\ x = X \wedge y = Y\}$
$\textbf{if } x \ge y \rightarrow m := x\ []\ \ y \ge x \rightarrow m := y\ \textbf{fi}$
$\{P \wedge MAX\}$

Above, *MAX* is the predicate:

$$MAX:\ (m = X \wedge X \ge Y) \vee (m = Y \wedge Y \ge X)$$

To conclude that (1.15) is a theorem, we must satisfy the hypotheses of the Alternative Rule. The first hypothesis is trivial to satisfy for this alternative statement since at least one guard is true. To satisfy the second hypothesis, we have to consider each of the guarded statements. For the first, we apply the Assignment Axiom to statement $m := x$ with postcondition $P \wedge MAX$ and get the theorem:

$$\{R:\ P \wedge ((x = X \wedge X \ge Y) \vee (x = Y \wedge Y \ge X))\}\ m := x\ \{P \wedge MAX\}$$

If the first guarded statement is selected, then the state must satisfy:

$$(P \wedge x \ge y) = (P \wedge X \ge Y)$$

Since this implies that R is true, we can use the Rule of Consequence to get the theorem:

$$\{P \wedge x \ge y\}\ m := x\ \{P \wedge MAX\}$$

A similar theorem holds for the second guarded statement. Thus, we can use the Alternative Rule to infer that (1.15) is indeed a theorem of *PL*.

One often uses the Rule of Consequence to construct triples that satisfy the hypotheses of the Alternative Rule. Above, we used it to demonstrate that $P \wedge B_i \Rightarrow pre(S_i)$. Alternatively, we can use it with the postconditions of the S_i. Suppose the following are valid triples:

$$\{P \wedge B_i\} \ S_i \ \{Q_i\}, 1 \leq i \leq n$$

That is, each branch of an alternative statement produces a possibly different postcondition. Since we can weaken each such postcondition to the disjunction of all the Q_i, we can use the Rule of Consequence to conclude that all the following are valid:

$$\{P \wedge B_i\} \ S_i \ \{Q_1 \vee ... \vee Q_n\}, 1 \leq i \leq n$$

Hence, we can use the disjunction of the Q_i as the postcondition of **if**, assuming of course that we also satisfy the first hypothesis of the Alternative Rule.

Next consider the iterative statement. Recall that execution of **do** differs from **if** in the following way: selecting and executing one guarded statement is repeated until all guards are false. Thus, a **do** statement might iterate an arbitrary number of times, even zero. For this reason, the inference rule for **do** is based on a *loop invariant*—a predicate (assertion) I that holds both before and after every iteration of the loop. Let DO stand for the **do** statement:

$$DO: \ \mathbf{do} \ B_1 \rightarrow S_1 \ [] \ ... \ [] \ B_n \rightarrow S_n \ \mathbf{od}$$

Suppose predicate I is true before execution of DO and is to be true after every iteration. Then, if S_i is selected for execution, $pre(S_i)$ satisfies both I and B_i, and $post(S_i)$ must satisfy I. Execution of **do** terminates when all guards are false; hence $post(DO)$ satisfies both this and I. These observations yield the following inference rule:

(1.16)   **Iterative Rule**: $$\frac{\{I \wedge B_i\} \ S_i \ \{I\}, 1 \leq i \leq n}{\{I\} \ DO \ \{I \wedge \neg(B_1 \vee ... \vee B_n)\}}$$

The key to using the Iterative Rule is to come up with a loop invariant. As an example, consider the following program, which computes the factorial of integer n, assuming $n > 0$:

```
var fact := 1; i := 1
do i ≠ n → i := i + 1; fact := fact * i od
```

Before and after each iteration, *fact* contains the factorial of *i*. Hence, the following assertion is a loop invariant:

$$fact = i! \land 1 \le i \le n$$

When the loop terminates, both the invariant and the negation of the loop guard are true:

$$fact = i! \land i = n$$

Hence the program correctly computes the factorial of *n*. Section 1.5 contains additional examples of loop invariants and describes techniques for coming up with them.

The for-all statement is the final statement in our sequential programming notation. Recall that **fa** is an abbreviation for a special use of **do.** Thus, we can translate a program containing **fa** into an equivalent program containing **do**, then use the Iterative Rule to develop a partial correctness proof of the translated program. Alternatively, we could develop an inference rule for **fa** and include it in the programming logic.

1.4 Proofs in Programming Logic

Since programming logic *PL* is a formal logical system, a proof consists of a sequence of lines. Each line is an instance of an axiom or follows from previous lines by application of an inference rule. The axioms and inference rules of *PL* are those given in Section 1.3 plus ones from the underlying propositional and predicate logics. For reference, the new axioms and inference rules are summarized in Figure 1.4.

To illustrate a complete *PL* proof—in all its gory detail—consider again the linear search problem introduced at the start of Section 1.2. Given is array $a[1{:}n]$ for some positive *n*. Also given is that value *x* is an element of *a*. The problem is to compute the index of the first occurrence of *x* in *a*. More precisely, the initial state is assumed to satisfy the predicate:

$$P: \ n > 0 \land (\exists j: 1 \le j \le n: a[j] = x)$$

And the final state of the program is to satisfy:

$$LS: \ a[i] = x \land (\forall j: 1 \le j < i: a[j] \ne x)$$

The first conjunct in *LS* says that *i* is an index such that $a[i] = x$; the second says that no smaller index satisfies this property. Implicit in the problem statement is that neither *n*, *a*, nor *x* should change. We could specify this

Skip Axiom: $\{P\}$ **skip** $\{P\}$

Assignment Axiom: $\{P^x_e\}$ $x := e$ $\{P\}$

Swap Axiom: $\{P^{v1,\ v2}_{v2,\ v1}\}$ $v1 :=: v2$ $\{P\}$

Rule of Consequence: $\dfrac{P' \Rightarrow P,\ \{P\}\ S\ \{Q\},\ Q \Rightarrow Q'}{\{P'\}\ S\ \{Q'\}}$

Composition Rule: $\dfrac{\{P\}\ S1\ \{Q\},\ \{Q\}\ S2\ \{R\}}{\{P\}\ S1; S2\ \{R\}}$

Alternative Rule: $\dfrac{\begin{array}{c}P \wedge \neg(B_1 \vee ... \vee B_n) \Rightarrow Q \\ \{P \wedge B_i\}\ S_i\ \{Q\}, 1 \leq i \leq n\end{array}}{\{P\}\ IF\ \{Q\}}$

Iterative Rule: $\dfrac{\{I \wedge B_i\}\ S_i\ \{I\}, 1 \leq i \leq n}{\{I\}\ DO\ \{I \wedge \neg(B_1 \vee ... \vee B_n)\}}$

Figure 1.4. Axioms and inference rules of programming logic *PL*.

formally by including the following predicate as conjuncts in both *P* and *LS*; in the predicate N, A, and X are logical variables.

$$n = \text{N} \wedge (\ \forall i:\ 1 \leq i \leq n:\ a[i] = \text{A}[i]\ ) \wedge x = \text{X}$$

For simplicity, we omit this from the proof.

Below we give a complete proof that the following triple is valid and hence that the program is partially correct:

> $\{P\}$
> $i := 1$
> **do** $a[\text{i}] \neq x \rightarrow i := i + 1$ **od**
> $\{LS\}$

We construct the proof by first considering the effect of the first assignment, then by working from the inside of the loop to consider the effect of the loop, and finally by considering the effect of the compound statement. The loop invariant *I* is the second conjunct of *LS*; it first appears in step 4 of the proof.

1. $\{P \land 1 = 1\}$ by Assignment Axiom
    $i := 1$
    $\{P \land i = 1\}$

2. $(P \land 1 = 1) = P$ by Predicate Logic

3. $\{P\}$ by Rule of Consequence with 1 and 2
    $i := 1$
    $\{P \land i = 1\}$

4. $\{P \land (\forall j: 1 \le j < i + 1: a[j] \ne x)\}$ by Assignment Axiom
    $i := i + 1$
    $\{I: P \land (\forall j: 1 \le j < i: a[j] \ne x)\}$

5. $(I \land a[i] \ne x) =$ by Predicate Logic
    $(P \land (\forall j: 1 \le j < i + 1: a[j] \ne x))$

6. $\{I \land a[i] \ne x\}$ by Rule of Consequence with 4 and 5
    $i := i + 1$
    $\{I\}$

7. $\{I\}$ by Iterative Rule with 6
    do $a[i] \ne x \to i := i + 1$ **od**
    $\{I \land a[i] = x\}$

8. $(P \land i = 1) \Rightarrow I$ by Predicate Logic

9. $\{P\}$ by Composition Rule with 7 and 8
    $i := 1$
    do $a[i] \ne x \to i := i + 1$ **od**
    $\{I \land a[i] = x\}$

10. $(I \land a[i] = x) \Rightarrow LS$ by Predicate Logic

11. $\{P\}$ by Rule of Consequence with 9 and 10
    $i := 1$
    do $a[i] \ne x \to i := i + 1$ **od**
    $\{LS\}$

Since the triple in step 11 is a theorem, the linear search program is partially correct. Because P postulates the existence of some x such that $a[i] = x$, the loop terminates. Thus, the program also satisfies the total correctness property.

Proof Outlines

As the above example illustrates, it is tedious to construct a formal proof in
PL (or any formal logical system). The proof has the virtue that each line can
be checked mechanically. However, the form of the proof makes it hard to
read and does not convey any insight into where the steps came from.

A *proof outline*—sometimes called an *annotated program*—provides a
compact way in which to present the outline of a proof. It consists of the
statements of a program interspersed with assertions. A *complete proof
outline* contains at least one assertion before and after each statement. For
example, Figure 1.5 contains a complete proof outline for the linear search
program.

The correspondence between program execution and a proof outline is
that, when program control is at the beginning of a statement, the program
state satisfies the corresponding assertion. If the program terminates, the
final assertion eventually becomes true. Since the linear search program in
Figure 1.5 terminates, eventually program control is at the end, and the state
satisfies *LS*.

A complete proof outline encodes applications of the axioms and inference
rules for each statement in the proof outline. In particular, it represents the
steps in a formal proof in the following way.

- Each **skip**, assignment, or swap statement together with its pre- and
  postconditions forms a triple that represents an application of the
  corresponding axiom.

- The assertions before the first and after the last of a sequence of
  statements, together with the intervening statements (but not the
  intervening assertions), form a triple that represents an application of
  the Composition Rule.

- An alternative statement together with its pre- and postconditions
  represents an application of the Alternative Rule, with the hypotheses
  being represented by the assertions and statements in the guarded
  statements.

- An iterative statement together with its pre- and postconditions
  represents an application of the Iterative Rule; again the hypotheses of
  the rule are represented by the assertions and statements in the
  guarded statements.

- Finally, adjacent assertions represent applications of the Rule of
  Consequence.

The reader might find it helpful to examine the correspondence between the
components of the proof outline in Figure 1.5 and the steps in the formal
proof in the previous section.

$\{ P: \ n > 0 \wedge (\exists j: 1 \leq j \leq n: a[j] = x) \}$
$i := 1$
$\{ P \wedge i = 1 \}$
$\{ I: \ P \wedge (\forall j: \ 1 \leq j < i: \ a[j] \neq x) \}$
do $a[i] \neq x \rightarrow \{ I \wedge a[i] \neq x \}$
$\qquad\qquad i := i + 1$
$\qquad\qquad \{ I \}$
od
$\{ I \wedge a[i] = x \}$
$\{ LS: \ x = a[i] \wedge (\forall j: \ 1 \leq j < i: \ a[j] \neq x) \}$

Figure 1.5. A complete proof outline for the linear search program.

Assertions in proof outlines can be viewed as precise comments in a programming language. They characterize exactly what is true of the state at various points in the program. Just as it is neither necessary nor useful to place a comment before every statement in a program, it is usually neither necessary nor useful to place an assertion before every statement in a proof outline. Thus, we will generally place assertions only at critical points where they help provide "convincing evidence" that a proof outline in fact represents a proof. At a minimum, the critical points include the start and end of a program and the start of each loop.

Equivalence and Simulation

Occasionally it is interesting to know whether two programs are interchangeable, i.e., whether they compute exactly the same results. At other times it is interesting to know whether one program simulates another; i.e., the first computes at least all the results of the second.

In programming logic *PL*, two programs are said to be partially equivalent if, whenever they are begun in the same initial state, they end in the same final state, assuming both terminate.

(1.17)   **Partial Equivalence.** Statement lists *S1* and *S2* are partially equivalent if, for all predicates P and Q, $\{ P \} S1 \{ Q \}$ is a theorem if and only if $\{ P \} S2 \{ Q \}$ is a theorem.

This is called partial equivalence since *PL* is a logic for proving partial correctness properties only. If one of *S1* or *S2* terminates but not the other, they might be equivalent according to the above definition when in fact they are not really. In a sequential program, if *S1* and *S2* are partially equivalent and both terminate, then they are indeed interchangeable. The same is not necessarily true in a concurrent program, however, due to potential interference between processes—a topic we discuss in the next chapter.

As a simple example, the following two programs are partially equivalent:

$$S1: \ v1 :=: v2 \qquad\qquad S2: \ v2 :=: v1$$

This is because, for any postcondition P, simultaneous substitution yields the same precondition independent of the order in which the variables appear. The following statements are also partially equivalent:

$$S1: \ x := 1; y := 1 \qquad\qquad S2: \ y := 1; x := 1$$

This is because, for any predicate P, $(P_1^y)_1^x = (P_1^x)_1^y$ since x and y are distinct identifiers.

In PL, one program is said to simulate a second if, whenever they are both begun in the same initial state and terminate, the final state of the first program satisfies any assertions that apply to final state of the second. Essentially, simulation is partial equivalence in one direction.

(1.18)   **Simulation.** Statement list $S1$ simulates $S2$ if, for all predicates P and Q, $\{\,P\,\}\,S1\,\{\,Q\,\}$ is a theorem whenever $\{\,P\,\}\,S2\,\{\,Q\,\}$ is a theorem.

For example, the following statements simulate $x :=: y$, which swaps x and y:

$$t := x; x := y; y := t$$

These statements are not equivalent to $x :=: y$, however, since the simulation contains an additional variable t that could be used in the surrounding program. Even though the implementation of a swap statement on most machines would require using a temporary variable, that variable would not be visible to the programmer and hence could not be used elsewhere in the program.

1.5 Program Derivation

The examples in the previous section showed how to use programming logic PL to construct an *a posteriori* proof of partial correctness. This is important, but often a programmer is given a goal (postcondition) and initial assumption (precondition) and is asked to construct a program that meets the goal under the stated assumptions. Moreover, the program is typically expected to terminate. PL provides no guidance as to how to demonstrate this.

This section presents a systematic programming method—a programming calculus—for constructing totally correct sequential programs. The method is based on viewing statements as *predicate transformers*: functions that map predicates to predicates. It involves developing a program and its proof outline in concert, with the calculus and proof outline guiding the derivation of the program.

Weakest Preconditions

Programming is a goal-directed activity: Programmers always have some result they are trying to achieve. Suppose the goal of program S is to terminate in a state satisfying predicate Q. The weakest precondition wp is a predicate transformer that maps a goal Q into a predicate $wp(S, Q)$ according to the following definition.

(1.19)   **Weakest Precondition.** The weakest precondition of statement list S and predicate Q, denoted $wp(S, Q)$, is a predicate characterizing the largest set of states such that, if execution of S is begun in any state satisfying $wp(S, Q)$, then execution is guaranteed to terminate in a state satisfying Q.

Relation wp is called the *weakest* precondition since it characterizes the largest set of states that lead to a totally correct program.

Weakest preconditions are closely related to triples in *PL*. From the definition of wp, $\{ wp(S, Q) \} S \{ Q \}$ is a theorem of *PL*. This means that:

(1.20)   **Relation Between** wp **and** *PL*. If $P \Rightarrow wp(S, Q)$, then $\{ P \} S \{ Q \}$ is a theorem of *PL*.

The essential difference between wp and *PL* is that wp requires termination, whereas *PL* does not. This difference reduces to requiring that all loops terminate since loops are the only non-terminating statements in our programming notation (assuming all values in expressions and assignment statements are well defined).

A number of useful laws follow directly from the definition of wp. First, a program S cannot terminate in a state satisfying *false* since there is no such state. Thus,

(1.21)   **Law of the Excluded Miracle:** $wp(S, false) = false$

On the other hand, all states satisfy *true*. Thus, $wp(S, true)$ characterizes all states for which S is guaranteed to terminate, independent of the final result produced by S. (In general, $wp(S, true)$ is not computable since it requires solving what is called the halting problem.)

Suppose S is started in a state satisfying both $wp(S, Q)$ and $wp(S, R)$. Then by (1.20), S will terminate in a state satisfying $Q \wedge R$. In addition, again by (1.20), a state that satisfies $wp(S, Q \wedge R)$ satisfies both $wp(S, Q)$ and $wp(S, R)$. Thus, we have:

(1.22)   **Distributive Law of Conjunction:**
$$wp(S, Q) \wedge wp(S, R) = wp(S, Q \wedge R)$$

Next consider disjunction. Suppose a program is started in a state satisfying either $wp(S, Q)$ or $wp(S, R)$. Then by (1.20), S will terminate in a state satisfying $Q \vee R$, so we have:

(1.23)   **Distributive Law of Disjunction:**
$$wp(S, Q) \vee wp(S, R) \Rightarrow wp(S, Q \vee R)$$

However, the implication in (1.23) cannot be replaced by equality since **if** and **do** are non-deterministic statements. To see why, consider the following program, which simulates flipping a coin:

$$flip: \quad \textbf{if } true \rightarrow outcome := HEADS$$
$$\quad [] \ true \rightarrow outcome := TAILS$$
$$\quad \textbf{fi}$$

Since both guards in *flip* are true, either guarded statement may be selected. Thus, there is no starting state that guarantees a particular final value for *outcome*. In particular,

$$wp(flip, outcome = HEADS) = wp(flip, outcome = TAILS) = false$$

On the other hand, one of the guarded statements will be executed, so *outcome* will be either *HEADS* or *TAILS* when *flip* terminates, whatever the starting state. Hence,

$$wp(flip, outcome = HEADS \vee outcome = TAILS) = true$$

Although this example demonstrates that disjunction is in general distributive in only one direction, for deterministic statements the implication in (1.23) can be strengthened to equality.

(1.24)   **Distributive Law of Deterministic Disjunction:**
For deterministic S, $wp(S, Q) \vee wp(S, R) = wp(S, Q \vee R)$

This law holds for sequential programming languages, such as Pascal, that do not contain non-deterministic statements.

Weakest Preconditions of Statements

This section presents rules for computing *wp* for the various sequential statements introduced in Section 1.1. There is one rule for each kind of statement. Since *wp* is closely related to *PL*, most rules are quite similar to the corresponding axiom or inference rule of *PL*.

The **skip** statement always terminates and changes no program or logical variable. Thus,

(1.25) $wp(\textbf{skip}, Q) = Q$

An assignment statement terminates if the expression and target variable are well defined. Henceforth, we assume this to be true. If execution of $x := e$ is to terminate in a state satisfying Q, it must be started in a state in which every variable but x has the same value and x is replaced by e. As for Assignment Axiom (1.7), this is exactly the transformation provided by Textual Substitution (1.3).

(1.26) $wp(x := e, Q) = Q_e^x$

In this case, *wp* and the precondition for the Assignment Axiom are identical. Similarly, *wp* for a swap statement is the same as the precondition in Swap Axiom (1.9).

A sequence of statements *S1* and *S2* terminates in a state satisfying Q if *S2* terminates in a state satisfying Q. This requires that execution of *S2* begin in a state satisfying $wp(S2, Q)$, which in turn is the state in which *S1* must terminate. Thus, statement composition leads to composition of *wp*.

(1.27) $wp(S1; S2, Q) = wp(S1, wp(S2, Q))$

An **if** statement terminates if all expressions are well defined and the selected statement S_i terminates. Below we assume that expressions in guards are well defined. Let *IF* be the statement:

$$IF:\ \textbf{if}\, B_1 \rightarrow S_1 \,[]\, ... \,[]\, B_n \rightarrow S_n\ \textbf{fi}$$

If no guard is true, then executing *IF* is the same as executing **skip** since expression evaluation is assumed not to have side-effects. On the other hand, if S_i is executed, then guard B_i must have been true; to ensure termination in a state satisfying Q, it must be the case that $B_i \Rightarrow wp(S_i, Q)$; i.e., either B is false or execution of S terminates in a state satisfying Q. The same requirement holds for all the guarded statements. Putting all these parts together yields:

(1.28) $wp(IF, Q) = \neg(B_1 \vee ... \vee B_n) \Rightarrow Q \wedge$
                         $(B_1 \Rightarrow wp(S_1, Q) \wedge ... \wedge B_n \Rightarrow wp(S_n, Q))$

As an example of computing (1.28), consider the program and postcondition for computing the maximum of x and y given earlier in (1.15):

$$\textbf{if } x \geq y \rightarrow m := x \;\;[]\;\; y \geq x \rightarrow m := y \textbf{ fi}$$
$$\{ Q : x = X \wedge y = Y \wedge ((m = X \wedge X \geq Y) \vee (m = Y \wedge Y \geq X)) \}$$

Applying definition (1.28) to this statement and predicate—using (1.26) to compute wp of the assignments—yields:

$$\neg(x \geq y \vee y \geq x) \Rightarrow Q \wedge$$
$$(x \geq y \Rightarrow (x = X \wedge y = Y \wedge ((x = X \wedge X \geq Y) \vee (x = Y \wedge Y \geq X)))) \wedge$$
$$(y \geq x \Rightarrow (x = X \wedge y = Y \wedge ((y = X \wedge X \geq Y) \vee (y = Y \wedge Y \geq X))))$$

Since at least one of the guards is true, the first line simplifies to *true* and hence can be ignored. Rewriting the implications using the Law of Implication from Figure 1.2, the above expression simplifies to:

$$((x < y) \vee (x = X \wedge y = Y \wedge X \geq Y)) \wedge$$
$$((y < x) \vee (x = X \wedge y = Y \wedge Y \geq X))$$

Using predicate and propositional logic, this further simplifies to:

$$x = X \wedge y = Y$$

This is exactly the precondition P in the triple in (1.15). Again this points out the duality between weakest preconditions and theorems in *PL*.

The **do** statement has the most complicated weakest precondition since it is the one statement that might not terminate. Let *DO* be a **do** statement:

(1.29)   *DO*: **do** $B_1 \rightarrow S_1 \;[]\; ... \;[]\; B_n \rightarrow S_n$ **od**

And let *BB* be the predicate:

(1.30)   *BB*: $B_1 \vee ... \vee B_n$

That is, *BB* is true if some guard is true, and *BB* is false otherwise. We can rewrite *DO* in terms of IF as follows:

$$\textit{DO}: \textbf{do } BB \rightarrow IF: \textbf{if } B_1 \rightarrow S_1 \;[]\; ... \;[]\; B_n \rightarrow S_n \textbf{ fi od}$$

Now let $H_k(Q)$ be a predicate that characterizes all states from which

$$wp(\textbf{skip}, Q) \;=\; Q$$

$$wp(x := e, Q) \;=\; Q_e^x$$

$$wp(v1 :=: v2, Q) \;=\; Q_{v2,\,v1}^{v1,\,v2}$$

$$wp(S1;S2, Q) \;=\; wp(S1, wp(S2, Q))$$

$$wp(IF, Q) \;=\; \neg(B_1 \vee \ldots \vee B_n) \Rightarrow Q \;\wedge$$
$$(\, B_1 \Rightarrow wp(S_1, Q) \wedge \ldots \wedge B_n \Rightarrow wp(S_n, Q) \,)$$

$$wp(DO, Q) \;=\; (\, \exists\, k\colon\; 0 \le k\colon\; H_k(Q)\,), \text{ where}$$
$$H_0(Q) \;=\; \neg BB \wedge Q$$
$$H_k(Q) \;=\; H_0(Q) \vee wp(IF, H_{k-1}(Q))$$

Figure 1.6. Weakest preconditions of sequential statements.

---

execution of *DO* leads in k or fewer iterations to termination in a state satisfying Q. In particular,

$$H_0(Q) \;=\; \neg BB \wedge Q$$
$$H_k(Q) \;=\; H_0(Q) \vee wp(IF, H_{k-1}(Q))$$

Execution of *DO* terminates if it performs only a finite number of iterations. Thus, the weakest precondition of *DO* is:

(1.31) $wp(DO, Q) \;=\; (\, \exists\, k\colon\; 0 \le k\colon\; H_k(Q)\,)$

This and the definitions of *wp* for the other sequential programming statements are summarized in Figure 1.6.

Unfortunately, definition (1.31) does not provide any direct insight into how to compute the weakest precondition of a **do** statement. Also, the relation between (1.31) and the corresponding Iterative Rule (1.16) of *PL* is much less clear than it is for any other statement. For example, the Iterative Rule employs a loop invariant I that does not appear in (1.31). However, the following definition characterizes the relationship; it also provides a technique for establishing that a loop terminates.

(1.32)   **Relation between** $wp(DO, Q)$ **and the Iterative Rule**. Let *DO* be a **do** statement as defined in (1.29), and let *BB* represent the disjunction of the guards as defined in (1.30). Further, suppose I is a predicate and *bound* is an integer expression whose value is non-

negative. Then $I \Rightarrow wp(DO, I \land \neg BB)$ if the following three conditions are true:
(1) $(I \land B_i) \Rightarrow wp(S_i, I), 1 \leq i \leq n$
(2) $(I \land BB) \Rightarrow bound > 0$
(3) $(I \land B_i \land bound = \text{BOUND}) \Rightarrow wp(S_i, bound < \text{BOUND}), 1 \leq i \leq n$

The first condition asserts that I is invariant with respect to execution of a guarded statement. The second and third conditions deal with termination. In them, *bound* is an expression—called a *bounding expression*—whose range is the non-negative integers. The second condition in (1.32) says that the value of *bound* is positive if some guard is true. The third condition says that each loop iteration decreases the value of *bound*. Since the value of *bound* is a non-negative integer, conditions (2) and (3) together guarantee that the loop terminates.

Relation (1.32) provides insight into how to understand and develop a loop. First, identify an invariant predicate that is true before and after each loop iteration. The invariant captures *unchanging* relations between variables. Second, identify a bounding expression that is non-negative and decreases on each iteration. The bounding expression captures *changing* relations between variables, with the changes resulting from making progress toward termination.

The next two sections present examples that illustrate these ideas. They also introduce four useful techniques for developing a loop invariant.

Linear Search Revisited

Consider the linear search problem yet again. Given are array $a[1:n]$, $n > 0$, and the fact that at least one element of a has value x. The problem is to determine the index i of the first element of $a[i]$ that has value x. Thus, the final program state is to satisfy:

$$LS: \quad a[i] = x \land (\forall j: 1 \leq j < i: a[j] \neq x)$$

Since a has to be searched, a loop is required. When the postcondition of the loop is in the form of a conjunction, as above, one technique for coming up with a loop invariant is to *delete one of the conjuncts*. The conjunct to delete is typically the one that expresses the fact that the termination condition has been reached; in this case, $a[i] = x$. Thus a candidate invariant for this problem is:

$$I: \quad (\forall j: 1 \leq j < i: a[j] \neq x)$$

The negation of the deleted conjunct—in this case, $a[i] \neq x$—is then used as the guard in the loop. Variable i is initialized so that I is true before the first loop iteration. This yields the program and proof outline:

> **var** $i := 1$
> $\{\,I\!: \ (\,\forall\, j\!: \ 1 \le j < i\!: \ a[j] \ne x \,)\,\}$
> **do** $a[i] \ne x \to\ ?$ **od**
> $\{\,I \wedge a[i] = x\,\}$

The program is completed by designing an appropriate loop body. Within the body, the goals are to reestablish the invariant and to make progress toward termination. Here, this is done by incrementing i. This reestablishes the invariant since the loop guard ensures that x has not yet been found. Incrementing i also makes progress toward termination. Since there are at most n elements to examine, $n - i$ is the maximum number of elements left to examine. This is a bounding expression since its range is non-negative and its value is decreased on each iteration of the loop. Thus, the final program and proof outline are:

> **var** $i := 1$
> $\{\,I\!: \ (\,\forall\, j\!: \ 1 \le j < i\!: \ a[j] \ne x \,)\,\}$
> **do** $a[i] \ne x \to i := i + 1$ **od**
> $\{\,I \wedge a[i] = x\,\}$

The linear search problem can also be approached using a second useful technique for coming up with a loop invariant: *enlarging the range of a variable*. In the statement of the problem, it is given that x is in array a. Even though the index of its first occurrence in a is not known, there is such an index. Let *first* stand for the value of this index. Then, the goal of linear search can be expressed:

> $LS'\!: \ i = \mathit{first}$

By virtue of the interpretation attached to *first*, this is equivalent to saying:

> $LS\!: \ a[i] = x \wedge (\,\forall\, j\!: \ 1 \le j < i\!: \ a[j] \ne x\,)$

From this alternative statement of the goal, we can get an invariant from enlarging the range of i in LS'. In particular, let i range over the values from 1 to *first* until i reaches *first*. The invariant is thus:

> $I\!: \ 1 \le i \le \mathit{first}$

The appropriate loop guard in this case is $i \ne \mathit{first}$. A corresponding bounding expression is $\mathit{first} - i$. However, since *first* is not known, the guard must be expressed in terms of known quantities (the bounding expression need not be since it is not part of the program proper). Since by definition $a[first]$ is the first occurrence of x in a, $i \neq first$ and $a[i] \neq x$ have the same value. Thus, the linear search problem can be solved using the same loop guard and program as before. The only difference is how we approached the problem.

Sorting

This section develops an algorithm that sorts integer array $a[1{:}n]$ into ascending order. It illustrates the development of nested loops and also presents two additional techniques for coming up with a loop invariant: *replacing a constant by a variable* and *combining pre- and postconditions*.

For the sorting algorithm, the initial state is assumed to satisfy:

$$P: (\ \forall\ k:\ 1 \leq k \leq n:\ a[k] = A[k]\ )$$

Above, A is an array of logical variables standing for the initial values of a. The goal of the algorithm is to establish:

$$SORT: (\ \forall\ k:\ 1 \leq k < n:\ a[k] \leq a[k+1]\ ) \wedge a \text{ is a permutation of A}$$

The first conjunct asserts that the array elements are in ascending order. The second conjunct asserts that all elements of the original array are in the final array; this is necessary to include since otherwise we could establish *SORT* by, for example, setting all elements of a to zero. For clarity, the second conjunct is specified informally above; it can, however, be stated precisely as a predicate.

Obviously we have to use a loop to sort an array, so the next step is to design an appropriate loop invariant. Neither of the two previous techniques can be used, however. Deleting a conjunct from *SORT* will not yield a suitable invariant since neither conjunct can be used as a guard and neither gives any guidance on how the loop is to establish the other conjunct. Similarly, there is no single result that can be postulated to exist and thus be used as the basis for enlarging the range of a variable. Two additional techniques are needed here.

Since a loop invariant must be true initially as well as after each iteration, it is often useful to examine both the pre- and postconditions of a loop when developing an invariant. This is especially true when the input values are themselves to be modified. The question to ask is: Can the two assertions be put in the same form? Here, P is a special case of the second conjunct of *SORT* since the initial value of a is exactly A; thus a is trivially a permutation of A. Moreover, the initial state—in which the array is not sorted—is a degenerate case of the first conjunct of *SORT* if a has no elements. Thus, if either of the constants in *SORT*—1 or n—is replaced by a variable whose initial value makes the range of k empty, both P and the modified version of *SORT* will have the same form. Replacing n by variable i yields the predicate:

$$I: (\forall k: 1 \le k < i: a[k] \le a[k+1]) \land a \text{ is a permutation of A}$$

This will serve as a useful invariant if i is initialized to 1: it is true initially, will be true after each iteration if one more element of a is put in its proper place, will lead to termination if i is increased on each iteration (with bounding expression $n - i$), and suggests an easily computed loop guard of $i < n$. Pictorially, the loop invariant is:

$a[1]$ ... sorted ... $a[i-1]$	$a[i]$ ... unsorted ... $a[n]$

An outline for the sorting algorithm with this invariant is:

(1.33) **var** $i := 1$
  $\{I\}$
  do $i < n \rightarrow$ put correct value in $a[i]$; $i := i + 1$ **od**
  $\{I \land i \ge n\}$ $\{SORT\}$

At the start of each iteration, $a[1:i-1]$ is sorted; at the end, we want $a[1:i]$ to be sorted. There are two simple strategies for accomplishing this. One is to examine all the elements in $a[i:n]$, select the smallest, and swap it with $a[i]$. This approach is called *selection sort*. A second strategy is to move the value in $a[i]$ into the appropriate place in $a[1:i]$, shifting other values as necessary to make room. This is called *insertion sort*; it is analogous to the technique many bridge players employ to sort a hand of cards.

We will develop an algorithm for insertion sort since that is a somewhat better strategy, especially if a is initially close to being sorted. At the start of an insertion step, we know from loop invariant I that $a[1:i-1]$ is sorted. We need to insert $a[i]$ into the proper place so that we end up with $a[1:i]$ being sorted. A simple way to do this is first to compare $a[i]$ with $a[i-1]$. If they are in the correct order, we are done. If not, we swap them, then repeat the process by comparing $a[i-1]$ (the old $a[i]$) and $a[i-2]$. We continue until the value originally in $a[i]$ has "percolated" left to the correct position.

Again we need a loop invariant. Let j be the index of the new value that we are inserting; initially j is equal to i. At the end of the insertion loop, we then want the following predicate to be true:

$$Q: (\forall k: 1 \le k < j-1: a[k] \le a[k+1]) \land$$
$$(\forall k: j \le k < i: a[k] \le a[k+1]) \land$$
$$(j = 1 \lor a[j-1] \le a[j]) \land a \text{ is a permutation of A}$$

$\{\,P\colon (\,\forall\,k\colon\ 1 \le k \le n\colon\ a[k] = \text{A}[k]\,)\,\}$
var $i := 1,\ j : \textbf{int}$
$\{\,I\colon (\,\forall\,k\colon\ 1 \le k < i\colon\ a[k] \le a[k+1]\,)\ \wedge\ a \text{ is a permutation of A}\,\}$
do $i < n \rightarrow j := i$
               $\{\,II\colon (\,\forall\,k\colon 1 \le k < j-1\colon\ a[k] \le a[k+1]\,)\ \wedge$
                    $(\,\forall\,k\colon j \le k < i\colon\ a[k] \le a[k+1]\,)\ \wedge$
                    $a \text{ is a permutation of A}\,\}$
               do $j > 1 \textbf{ and } a[j-1] > a[j] \rightarrow$
                    $a[j-1] := a[j];\ j := j-1$
               od
               $\{\,II \wedge (\,j = 1 \vee a[j-1] \le a[j]\,)\,\}$
               $i := i+1$
               $\{\,I\,\}$
od
$\{\,I \wedge i \ge n\,\}$
$\{\,SORT\colon (\,\forall\,k\colon\ 1 \le k < n\colon\ a[k] \le a[k+1]\,)\ \wedge\ a \text{ is a permutation of A}\,\}$

Figure 1.7. Insertion sort program and proof outline.

The first conjunct says $a[1;j-1]$ is sorted; the second says $a[j;i]$ is sorted; the third says $a[j]$ is in the correct place (which might be $a[1]$). Once again we can use the technique of deleting a conjunct to get an appropriate loop invariant. We delete the third conjunct since that is the only one that might be false at the start of the insertion loop; in particular, it is the one the loop has to make true. This yields loop invariant:

$II\colon (\,\forall\,k\colon 1 \le k < j-1\colon\ a[k] \le a[k+1]\,)\ \wedge$
       $(\,\forall\,k\colon j \le k < i\colon\ a[k] \le a[k+1]\,)\ \wedge\ a \text{ is a permutation of A}$

We then use the negation of the the third conjunct in the loop guard. To maintain invariant II, the body of the inner loop swaps $a[j]$ and $a[j-1]$ and then decrements j. The corresponding bounding expression is $i-j$. Figure 1.7 contains the complete program and proof outline.

To summarize, the searching and sorting examples have described and illustrated four techniques for developing loop invariants:

- deleting a conjunct,
- enlarging the range of a variable,
- replacing a constant by a variable, and
- combining pre- and postconditions.

Each technique leads to an invariant that is easy to establish initially and that—together with the negation of the guard—ensures the desired result when the loop terminates. Even though the techniques differ, all involve starting with a precise statement of the goal of the loop. These two concepts—goal-directed programming and invariants—will play a fundamental role in the remainder of this text.

Historical Notes and References

Formal logic is concerned with the formalization and analysis of systematic reasoning methods. Its origins go back to the ancient Greeks. Although logic has since then been of interest to philosophers, it was the discovery of non-Euclidean geometries in the nineteenth century that spurred renewed, widespread interest among mathematicians. This led to a systematic study of mathematics itself as a formal logical system and hence gave rise to the field of mathematical logic—also called metamathematics (mathematics for the study of mathematics itself).

Two of the major early figures were George Boole, whose name inspired the term "boolean," and Augustus De Morgan, after whom De Morgan's Laws are named. Between 1910 and 1913, Alfred North Whitehead and Bertrand Russell published the voluminous *Principia Mathematica*, which presented what was claimed to be a system for deriving all of mathematics from logic. Shortly thereafter, David Hilbert set out to prove rigorously that the system presented in *Principia Mathematica* was both sound and complete. However, in 1931 Kurt Gödel demonstrated that there were valid statements that did not have a proof in that system or in *any* similar axiomatic system.

Although Gödel's incompleteness result brought an end to the belief that all of mathematics might be describable by a formal logical system, it did not stop interest in or work on logic. For example, in 1935 Gerhard Gentzen developed a natural deduction proof system. In contrast to the style of proof used here, which is due to Hilbert, a Gentzen-style proof involves identifying subgoals that imply the desired result, then trying to prove each subgoal, and so on. That style system is employed in many computerized theorem provers.

Formal logic is covered in all standard textbooks on mathematical logic or metamathematics. A light-hearted, entertaining introduction to the topic can be found in Douglas Hofstadter's Pulitzer Prize-winning book *Gödel, Escher, Bach: An Eternal Golden Braid* [Hofstadter 1979], which explains Gödel's result and also describes how logic is related to computability and artificial intelligence. The PQ and MIU systems in exercises 5 and 6 come from that book.

Several recent textbooks discuss formal logic specifically as it applies to programming. Constable and O'Donnell [1978] presents a natural deduction logic for programming. Gries [1981] covers in detail most of the topics presented in this chapter. Manna and Waldinger [1985] presents an axiomatization of predicates and data types as they are used in programming. Hehner [1984] presents a semantics of programming in which programs themselves are predicates manipulated according to the rules of the predicate calculus. Finally, Gallier [1986] discusses logic, Gentzen systems, and their application to automatic theorem-proving.

The programming notation used here—and in much of the rest of the book—comes from SR, a concurrent programming language designed by the author and Ronald Olsson [Andrews et al. 1988, Andrews & Olsson 1992]. The **if** and **do** statements in SR were inspired by the guarded statements (guarded commands) first introduced by Edsger W. Dijkstra [1975, 1976]. Dijkstra introduced non-deterministic control constructs to avoid over-specifying control flow. However, as we shall see, many people later realized that the concept provides an attractive basis for handling synchronization in concurrent programs, which are inherently non-deterministic.

Robert Floyd [1967] is generally credited with being the first to propose a technique for proving that programs are correct. His method involves associating a predicate with each arc in a flowchart in such a way that, if the arc is traversed, the predicate is true. A flowchart with associated assertions is thus much like a complete proof outline. Floyd credits Alan Perlis and Saul Gorn with the initial idea for his method. A similar approach based on what are called general snapshots was independently developed by Peter Naur [1966], editor of the Algol report and co-inventor (with John Backus) of the BNF notation for describing programming language syntax.

Inspired by Floyd's work, C.A.R. (Tony) Hoare [1969] developed the first formal logic for proving partial correctness properties of sequential programs. Hoare introduced the concept of a triple, the interpretation for triples, and axioms and inference rules for sequential statements (in his case, a subset of Algol). Any logical system for sequential programming that is based on this style has since come to be called a "Hoare Logic." Programming logic *PL* is an example of a Hoare Logic. In his original paper, Hoare used the notation $P \{ S \} Q$, to denote a triple, but after the introduction of Pascal in 1971, that notation was soon replaced by the one used in *PL*. The new notation is suggestive of the fact that assertions are precise comments; it is also notationally less cumbersome since predicates tend to be much shorter than statement lists.

Hoare and Nicklaus Wirth [1973]—the designer of Pascal—were the first to present a generalized form of the assignment axiom that is sound for assignment to elements of arrays and records, as well as to simple variables, entire arrays, and records. Later, Gries and Gary Levin [1980] extended the axiom to handle multiple assignment statements, in which several expressions are assigned to several target variables. Their paper also presents inference rules for procedures and procedure calls (see Section 6.2).

Proof outlines are used informally here to present the outline of a proof. They can also be formalized and treated as logical objects in their own right. Edward Ashcroft [1976] developed one of the first such formalizations. A formalization, called Generalized Hoare Logic, in which proof outlines are in fact predicates was developed by Leslie Lamport [1980]. More recently, Fred Schneider has developed a logic, called Proof Outline Logic, in which proof outlines are not just predicates but are actually properties [Schneider & Andrews 1986].

Weakest preconditions and the associated programming calculus were developed by Dijkstra [1975]; they are discussed in detail in Dijkstra [1976]. An expanded presentation of the approach, oriented towards programmers, appears in the previously cited book by Gries [1981]. That book presents and gives numerous examples of the four techniques for coming up with a loop invariant that were described in Section 1.5.

Exercises

1.1 For each of the following, state whether it is a safety or liveness property and identify the bad or good thing of interest.

(a) At most five people are in the elevator at a time.

(b) Patrons are serviced in the order they arrived.

(c) The cost of living never decreases.

(d) Two things are certain: death and taxes.

(e) All good things must come to an end.

(f) The book improves with each reading.

(g) What goes up must come down.

(h) If two or more processes are waiting to enter their critical sections, at least one succeeds.

(i) At most one person may speak at a time; any number may be listening.

(j) A hungry philosopher eventually eats.

(k) If an interrupt occurs, then a message is printed within 1 second.

1.2 Consider a chess board, which contains 64 squares organized into 8 rows and 8 columns. Squares are colored black or white; adjacent squares in the same row or column have a different color.

(a) Suppose a domino is exactly the size of two squares. Can a collection of dominos be placed on the chess board so that all squares are covered? Explain.

(b) Now suppose the upper-left and lower-right squares of the chess board are removed. Can a collection of dominos be placed on the board so that all squares are covered? Explain.

1.3 A coffee can contains black and white beans. The following process is repeated as long as possible:

> Randomly select two beans from the can. If they are the same color, throw them away but place one black bean into the can. (Assume an adequate supply of black beans.) If they are different colors, throw the black one away and place the white bean back into the can.

Determine the relation between the initial contents of the coffee can and the color of the final bean that remains.

1.4 Given is a rectangular grid of points. Two players take turns connecting any adjacent pair of points by drawing a horizontal, vertical, or diagonal line. The first player draws red lines; the second player draws blue lines. The object of the game to is to enclose a region of the grid with lines of the same color.

(a) Is there a guaranteed winning strategy the red player can follow? Explain.

(b) Is there a strategy the blue player can follow that will guarantee that the red player cannot win? Explain.

1.5 The PQ system is a formal logical system defined as follows.

    Symbols: P, Q, –

    Formulas: a P b Q c, where a, b, and c are each zero or more dashes

    Axioms: – P – Q – –

              – – P – Q – – –

    Inference Rule: Let a through f each be zero or more dashes. Then,

$$\frac{a \; P \; b \; Q \; c, \quad d \; P \; e \; Q \; f}{ad \; P \; be \; Q \; cf}$$

(a) Give a proof that "– – – P – – Q – – – – –" is a theorem of this logic.

(b) Describe why "– – P – Q – –" is not a theorem of this logic.

(c) Consider the following addition interpretation for the PQ system: A formula a P b Q c is mapped to true if and only if $|a| + |b| = |c|$, where $|x|$ denotes the length of string x. Is the logic sound with respect to this interpretation? Explain. Is the logic complete with respect to this interpretation? Explain.

(d) Consider the following subtraction interpretation for the PQ system: A formula a P b Q c is mapped to true if and only if $|a| = |c| - |b|$, where $|x|$ denotes the length of string x. Is the logic sound with respect to this interpretation? Explain. Is the logic complete with respect to this interpretation? Explain.

1.6 The MIU system is a formal logical system defined as follows.

    Symbols: M, I, U

    Formulas: Sequences of the symbols

    Axiom: M I

    Inference Rules: Let x and y be zero or more symbols.

$$I1: \quad \frac{x \, I}{x \, I \, U}$$

$$I2: \quad \frac{M \, x}{M \, x \, x}$$

$$I3: \quad \frac{x \, I \, I \, I \, y}{x \, U \, y}$$

$$I4: \quad \frac{x \, U \, U \, y}{x \, y}$$

(a) Give a proof that M U I is a theorem of the logic.

(b) Give a proof that M U I I U is a theorem of the logic.

(c) Give a proof that M I U U is a theorem of the logic.

(d) Give a convincing argument that M U is *not* a theorem of the logic.

1.7 For each of the propositional equivalence laws (Figure 1.2), demonstrate that it is a tautology by showing that its interpretation is true in every state.

1.8 Using the propositional equivalence laws (Figure 1.2), show that the following propositional formulas are valid.

 (a) And-Elimination: $(P \wedge Q) \Rightarrow P$

 (b) Or-Introduction: $P \Rightarrow (P \vee Q)$

 (c) Modus Ponens: $(P \wedge (P \Rightarrow Q)) \Rightarrow Q$

1.9 A *contradiction* is the opposite of a tautology: It is a proposition that is false in every state. For each of the following, determine whether it is a tautology, a contradiction, or neither (i.e., it is true in some states and false in others).

 (a) $P = \neg P$

 (b) $((P = Q) \wedge (Q = R)) \Rightarrow \neg(P = R)$

 (c) $(\neg P \wedge \neg Q) = \neg(P \wedge Q)$

 (d) $(\neg P \vee \neg Q) = \neg(P \vee Q)$

 (e) $(P \wedge P \Rightarrow Q) \Rightarrow Q$

1.10 A propositional formula is in *disjunctive normal form* if it is the disjunction of a set of terms, each of which is the conjunction of propositional variables or their negations. Show how the propositional equivalence laws (Figure 1.2) can be used to put any formula in disjunctive normal form.

1.11 A propositional formula is in *conjunctive normal form* if it is the conjunction of a set of terms, each of which is the disjunction of propositional variables or their negations. Show how the propositional equivalence laws (Figure 1.2) can be used to put any formula in conjunctive normal form.

1.12 Let $a[1:m]$ and $b[1:n]$ be integer arrays, $m > 0$ and $n > 0$. Write predicates to express the following properties.

 (a) All elements of a are less than all elements of b.

 (b) Either a contains a single zero or b contains a single zero.

 (c) There are not zeroes in both a and b.

 (d) All values in a are between 0 and 9, and they form a palindrome; i.e., when listed as a string, $a[1] \ldots a[n]$ reads the same in either direction.

 (e) Every element of a is an element of b.

 (f) m and n are the same, and the elements of a are a permutation of the elements of b.

 (g) m and n are the same, and the elements of a are in the reverse of the order of the elements in b.

 (h) Some element of a is larger than some element of b, and vice versa.

1.13 Define appropriate program variables, then write predicates to specify the following program properties.

(a) Processes enter their critical section in the order in which they arrived at their critical section.

(b) If all processes are waiting to enter their critical section, at least one succeeds.

(c) Within 1 second of an interrupt occurring, boolean variable b is set to true (and left set).

(d) Array a is sorted in ascending order, and all pairs of elements of the original array that have the same value are in the same relative position in a.

1.14 The existential quantifier (1.1) can be interpreted as a possibly infinite disjunction of terms

$$P_1 \vee P_2 \vee \ldots$$

where there is one term P_i for each different combination of values for the bound variables in range R. Similarly, the universal quantifier (1.2) can be interpreted as a possibly infinite conjunction of terms

$$P_1 \wedge P_2 \wedge \ldots$$

Using this interpretation and appropriate propositional equivalence laws (Figure 1.2), show that all the laws for quantified expressions (Figure 1.3) are tautologies.

1.15 For each of the following, give a complete proof outline and detailed proof in programming logic *PL* that the triple is a theorem.

(a) $\{\, a[i] = 2 \wedge a[j] = 3 \,\}\ i := j\ \{\, i = j \,\}$

(b) Given **var** $i, j, q, r :$ **int**,

> $\{\, i > 0 \wedge j > 0 \,\}$
> $q := 0; r := i$
> **do** $j \leq r \rightarrow q := q + 1; r := r - j$ **od**
> $\{\, i = q * j + r \ \wedge\ r \geq 0 \,\}$

(c) Given **var** $a[1{:}n], i, j :$ **int**,

> $\{\, true \,\}$
> $i := 2; j := 1$
> **do** $i \leq n \rightarrow$ **if** $a[i] \geq a[j] \rightarrow j := i$ **fi** **od**
> $\{\, (\, \forall\, k : 1 \leq k \leq n{:}\ a[j] \geq a[k]) \,\}$

(d) $\{\, true \,\}$ **do** true $\rightarrow$ **skip od** $\{\, x = 1 \,\}$

(e) Given **var** $n, r :$ **int**,

> $\{\, n \geq 0 \,\}$
> $r := 0$
> **do** $n \geq (r + 1)^2 \rightarrow r := r + 1$ **od**
> $\{\, r > 0 \ \wedge\ r^2 \leq n < (r + 1)^2 \,\}$

1.16   Assignment Axiom (1.7) gives the precondition as a syntactic transformation of the postcondition. Devise a "forward" assignment axiom that instead gives the postcondition as a syntactic transformation of the precondition.

1.17   (a) Generalize the functional view of one-dimensional arrays (1.8) to handle two-dimensional arrays.

(b) Generalize the functional view of one-dimensional arrays (1.8) to handle records and assignment to record fields.

1.18   Suppose the Rule of Consequence (1.12) were deleted from *PL*.

(a) Describe how to modify the axioms and other inference rules so that *PL* remains relatively complete.

(b) Is it possible to delete an axiom or any other inference rule of *PL*—making appropriate modifications to what remains—and still have a logic that is relatively complete? If so, which ones and why? If not, why not?

1.19   Suppose the **if** statement of Section 1.1 causes a program to abort rather than skip if no guard is true.

(a) Give an inference rule for this variant of **if**.

(b) Give a formula for the weakest precondition of this variant of **if**.

1.20   Suppose the **if** statement of Section 1.1 can have an optional last guard of **else**; i.e., the last guarded statement in **if** can be **else** $\rightarrow S$, where S is a statement list. The semantics of the **else** guard are that it is true if none of the other guards is true. Thus, an **if** statement with an else guard will always execute one of the guarded statements. Develop an inference rule for this kind of **if** statement.

1.21   The Alternative Rule (1.14) and Iterative Rule (1.16) assume that no variable changes state when guards are evaluated. Suppose instead that guards can contain function calls that have the side-effect of changing global variables. Devise inference rules for **if** and **do** in this case.

1.22   The **if-then-else** statement in languages such as Pascal has the form:

    if B **then** $S1$ **else** $S2$

The semantics are that $S1$ is executed if B is true, otherwise $S2$ is executed.

(a) Give an inference rule for this statement.

(b) Using your answer to (a) and Alternative Rule (1.14), give a proof outline that demonstrates that

    if B **then** $S1$ **else** $S2$

is partially equivalent to

    if $B \rightarrow S1$ [] $\neg B \rightarrow S2$ **fi**

(c) Show how to simulate the **if** statement in the text using **if-then-else** statements. Do not worry about the non-deterministic aspect of **if**. Give a proof outline that demonstrates that your implementation simulates **if**.

(d) Give a sufficient condition that would ensure that your answer to (c) is partially equivalent to **if.**

1.23 Give a proof outline that demonstrates that

$$\textbf{do } G_1 \rightarrow S_1 \text{ } [] \text{ ... } [] \text{ } G_n \rightarrow S_n \textbf{ od}$$

is partially equivalent to

$$\textbf{do } B_1 \textbf{ or } ... \textbf{ or } B_n \rightarrow$$
$$\quad \textbf{if } B_1 \rightarrow S_1 \text{ } [] \text{ ... } [] \text{ } B_n \rightarrow S_n \textbf{ fi}$$
$$\textbf{od}$$

1.24 Suppose a for-all statement has a single quantifier. Expand such a statement into one that uses assignments and a **do** statement, then use the Assignment Axiom (1.7) and Iterative Rule (1.16) to develop an inference rule for such a for-all statement.

1.25 The **while** statement

$$\textbf{while } B \rightarrow S \textbf{ end}$$

repeatedly evaluates boolean expression B and then executes statement S if B is true. The **repeat** statement

$$\textbf{repeat } S \textbf{ until } B$$

repeatedly executes statement S until boolean expression B is true at the end of some iteration.

(a) Give an inference rule for **while.**

(b) Give an inference rule for **repeat.**

(c) Using your answers to (a) and (b), give a proof outline that demonstrates that **repeat** is partially equivalent to

$$S; \textbf{ while not } B \rightarrow S \textbf{ end}$$

1.26 The **loop** statement

$$\textbf{loop } S \textbf{ end}$$

repeatedly executes statement S. The **when** statement

$$\textbf{when } B \textbf{ exit}$$

is used within S to terminate execution of **loop**; it evaluates boolean expression B and exits the loop if B is true. **loop** statements may be nested, in which case a **when** statement terminates execution only of the enclosing **loop** statement.

(a) Give inference rules for **loop** and **when.**

(b) Show how to implement the **do** statement using **loop** and **when.**

(c) Using your answer to (a) and Iterative Rule (1.16), give a proof outline that demonstrates that your answer to (b) is partially equivalent to **do.**

(d) Suppose the **when** statement is replaced by an unconditional **exit** statement. Execution of **exit** causes immediate termination of the surrounding **loop** statement. Give inference rules for **loop** and **exit** in this case.

1.27 Using predicate logic and wp laws (2.31) to (2.34), prove that for any S and Q:

(a) $wp(S, Q) \wedge wp(S, \neg Q) = false$

(b) $wp(S, Q) \vee wp(S, \neg Q) = true$

1.28 Compute the following weakest preconditions, where all variables are integers.

(a) $wp(i := 5, i = 0)$

(b) $wp(i := i + 1, i > 0)$

(c) $wp(S, i*j = 0)$, where S is $i := i + 1; j := j - 1$

(d) $wp(S, m = y)$, where S is **if** $x \geq y \to m := x \,[]\, y \geq x \to m := y$ **fi**

(e) $wp(S, x > 0)$, where S is **if** $x < 0 \to x := -x$ **fi**

(f) $wp(S, i = 2)$, where S is **if** $i < 2 \to i := i + 1 \,[]\, i > 2 \to i := 2$ **fi**

(g) $wp(S, i = 3)$, where S is **do** $i < 3 \to i := i + 1$ **od**

(h) $wp(S, a[i] = x \vee i = n + 1)$, where S is **do** $i \leq n \wedge a[i] \neq x \to i := i + 1$ **od**

1.29 For each of the following programming problems:

(1) give predicates that characterize the initial and final states,

(2) develop a loop invariant using the methods of Section 1.5,

(3) give a bounding expression, and

(4) derive a program and proof outline that solves the problem.

Develop the simplest possible predicates, and explain them in words as well as in predicate logic. The proof outline should have a level of detail comparable to that in Figure 1.7.

(a) Given integer $n > 0$, find the largest integer that is both a power of 2 and no larger than n.

(b) Determine whether integer array $a[1{:}n]$ contains all zeroes.

(c) Compute the length of the longest plateau in sorted integer array $a[1{:}n]$. A plateau is a contiguous sequence of elements having the same value.

(d) Compute the total number of plateaus in sorted integer array $a[1{:}n]$. (Don't forget plateaus of length 1.)

(e) Given integer arrays $a[1{:}n]$ and $b[1{:}m]$ that are both sorted in ascending order, compute the number of different values that appear in both a and b. Assume that values in a are distinct and that values in b are distinct.

(f) Reverse the elements of array $a[1{:}n]$ so that $a[1]$ and $a[n]$ are interchanged, $a[2]$ and $a[n-1]$ are interchanged, and so on.

(g) Given sorted integer array $a[1{:}n]$, use binary search to set i to the position of value x in a; set i to 0 if x does not occur in a. Assume a does not contain duplicate values.

(h) *Dutch National Flag*. Given character array $c[1:n]$, all elements of which are red, white, or blue, permute the array so all red elements are first, then all white elements, then all blue elements. The only way to permute c is by swapping two elements; the program should make at most n swaps.

(i) Given character array $c[1:n]$, determine whether c is a palindrome. A palindrome is string of characters that reads the same way from both the left and the right; e.g., "aha" or "able was I ere I saw elba".

(j) Given are integer p and integer arrays $value[1:n]$ and $link[1:n]$. Array *link* implements a singly-linked list; p points to the first element on the list; *value* contains the values of the elements. For example, $value[p]$ is the value of the head of the list, $value[link[p]]$ is the value of the second element on the list, and so on. The end of the list is marked by a 0 in the *link* field. Write a program that reverses the links in the list without altering the values.

(k) Given are three integer-valued functions: $f(i)$, $g(j)$, and $h(k)$. The domain of each function is the non-negative integers. The range of each is non-decreasing for increasing values of its argument; e.g., $f(i) \le f(i+1)$ for all $i \ge 0$. There is at least one value common to the range of all three functions. Find the indices i, j, and k of the smallest such value, i.e., the first point at which $f(i) = g(j) = h(k)$.

(l) Given is integer array $a[1:n]$. Rearrange a so that it is partitioned based on the value v that is initially in $a[1]$. Upon termination, your program should have rearranged a so that there is some p for which all values in $a[1:p-1]$ are less than or equal to v, $a[p] = v$, and all values in $a[p+1:n]$ are greater than or equal to v. The final values in a are to be a permutation of the initial values.

(m) Given are character arrays $str1[1:n]$ and $str2[1:n]$. Set integer *differ* to the index of the first position at which the strings in the arrays differ; if they are the same, set *differ* to 0.

(n) Given are character arrays $p[1:n]$ and $s[1:m]$, $n < m$. Set integer *first* to the index of the first position at which pattern p occurs in string s; i.e., set *first* to the smallest value such that $p[1:n] = s[first:first + n - 1]$. Set *first* to 0 if p does not occur within s.

## CHAPTER 2

Concurrency and Synchronization

Recall that a concurrent program specifies two or more cooperating processes. Each process executes a sequential program and is written using the notation introduced in the previous chapter. The processes interact by communicating, which in turn gives rise to the need for synchronization.

This chapter introduces programming notations for concurrency and synchronization. For now, processes interact by reading and writing shared variables. (We consider message passing in Part III.) This chapter also examines the fundamental semantic concepts of concurrent programming and extends Programming Logic *PL* to incorporate these concepts.

The key new problem that can arise in concurrent programs is interference, which results when one process takes an action that invalidates assumptions made by another process. Section 2.3 defines interference precisely; Section 2.4 introduces four techniques for avoiding it. These techniques will be employed extensively in the remainder of the text. The final two sections of this chapter also introduce concepts and techniques that will be used extensively in later chapters: auxiliary variables, methods for proving safety properties, scheduling policies, and liveness properties.

2.1 Specifying Concurrent Execution

When a sequential program is executed, there is a single *thread of control*: the program counter begins at the first atomic action in the process and moves through the process as atomic actions are executed. Execution of a concurrent program results in multiple threads of control, one for each constituent process.

In our programming notation, we will specify concurrent execution by the **co** statement (often called the **cobegin** statement). Let S_i be a sequential program: a sequence of sequential statements and optional declarations of local variables. The following statement executes the S_i concurrently:

(2.1)   **co** S_1 // ... // S_n **oc**

The effect is equivalent to some interleaving of the atomic actions of the S_i. Execution of **co** terminates when all of the S_i have terminated.

As a simple example, consider the following program fragment:

(2.2) $x := 0;\ y := 0$
           co $x := x + 1$ // $y := y + 1$ **oc**
           $z := x + y$

This sequentially assigns 0 to x and y, then increments x and y concurrently (or in some arbitrary order), and finally assigns the sum of x and y to z. Variables x and y are global to the processes in the **co** statement; they are declared in the enclosing process and inherited by the processes in the **co** statement following the normal scope rules of block-structured languages. A process can also declare *local* variables whose scope is limited to that process. Local variables in different processes are different variables, even if they happen to have the same name.

Often a concurrent program contains a number of processes that perform the same computation on different elements of an array. We will specify this by using quantifiers in **co** statements, with the quantifiers being identical in form to those in the for-all statement (**fa**) introduced in Section 1.1. For example, the following statement specifies n processes that in parallel initialize all elements of $a[1:n]$ to 0:

           co $i := 1$ **to** $n \rightarrow a[i] := 0$ **oc**

Each process has a local copy of i, which is an implicitly declared integer constant; the value of i is between 1 and n and is different in each process. Thus, each process has a unique identity.

As a second example, the following program multiplies n by n matrices a and b in parallel, placing the result in matrix c:

(2.3)   **co** $i := 1$ **to** $n, j := 1$ **to** $n \rightarrow$
                 var *sum* : **real** $:= 0$
                 fa $k := 1$ **to** $n \rightarrow sum := sum + a[i, k] * b[k, j]$ **af**
                 $c[i, j] := sum$
           oc

var $a[1{:}n]$, $b[1{:}n]$: **int**
Largest:: **var** max : **int**
                $max := a[1]$
                fa $j := 2$ **to** n **st** $max < a[j] \rightarrow max := a[j]$ **af**
Sum[i: $1..n$]:: $b[i] := a[1]$
                fa $j := 2$ **to** $i \rightarrow b[i] := b[i] + a[j]$ **af**

Figure 2.1. Notation for specifying larger processes.

Each of the n^2 processes has local constants i and j and local variables *sum* and k. Process (i, j) computes the inner product of row i of a and column j of b and stores the result in $c[i, j]$.

When there are several processes—or processes are lengthy—it can be awkward to specify concurrent execution using the **co** statement alone. This is because the reader can lose track of lexical context. Consequently, we will employ an alternative notation in the larger examples in this text. The alternative is used in the program in Figure 2.1. That program finds the value of the largest element of a and in parallel assigns to each $b[i]$ the sum of the elements in $a[1{:}i]$. *Largest* is the name of a single process; as shown the name is separated from the body of the process by a double colon. *Sum* is an array of n processes; each element *Sum*[i] has a different value for i, which is an implicitly declared local integer variable. The processes in Figure 2.1 are the same as if they had been specified by:

$$\textbf{co} \text{ body of } \textit{Largest} \;\; /\!/ \;\; i := 1 \textbf{ to } n \rightarrow \text{ body of } \textit{Sum} \textbf{ oc}$$

Since the notation in Figure 2.1 is merely an abbreviation for a **co** statement, the semantics of concurrent execution depend only on the semantics of **co**.

2.2 Atomic Actions and Synchronization

As mentioned earlier, we can view execution of a concurrent program as an interleaving of the atomic actions executed by individual processes. When processes interact, not all interleavings are likely to be acceptable. The role of synchronization is to prevent undesirable interleavings. This is done by combining fine-grained atomic actions into coarse-grained (composite) actions or by delaying process execution until the program state satisfies some predicate. The first form of synchronization is called *mutual exclusion*; the second, *condition synchronization*. This section examines aspects of atomic actions and presents a notation for specifying synchronization.

Fine-Grained Atomicity

Recall that an atomic action makes an indivisible state transformation. This means that any intermediate state that might exist in the implementation of the action must not be visible to other processes. A *fine-grained* atomic action is one that is implemented directly by the hardware on which a concurrent program executes.

For Assignment Axiom (1.7) to be sound, each assignment statement must be executed as an atomic action. In a sequential program, assignments appear to be atomic since no intermediate state is visible to the program (except possibly if there is a machine-detected fault). However, this is not generally the case in concurrent programs since an assignment is often implemented by a sequence of fine-grained machine instructions. For example, consider the following program, and assume that the fine-grained atomic actions are reading and writing the variables:

$$y := 0; z := 0$$
$$\textbf{co } x := y + z \text{ // } y := 1; z := 2 \textbf{ oc}$$

If $x := y + z$ is implemented by loading a register with y, then adding z to it, the final value of x could be 0, 1, 2, or 3. This is because we could see the initial values for y and z, their final values, or some combination, depending on how far the second process has executed. A further peculiarity of the above program is that the final value of x could be 2, even though $y + z$ is not 2 in any program state.

In this text, we assume that machines that execute our programs have the following realistic characteristics.

- Values of the basic and enumeration types (e.g., **int**) are stored in memory elements that are read and written as atomic actions. (Some machines have additional indivisible instructions, such as increment a memory location or move the contents of one location to another.)

- Values are manipulated by loading them into registers, operating on them there, then storing the results back into memory.

- Each process has its own set of registers. This is realized either by having distinct sets of registers or by saving and restoring register values whenever a different process is executed. (This is called a *context switch* since the registers constitute the execution context of a process.)

- Finally, any intermediate results that occur when a complex expression is evaluated are stored in registers or in memory private to the executing process—e.g., on a private stack.

With this machine model, if an expression e in one process does not reference a variable altered by another process, expression evaluation will be atomic, even if it requires executing several fine-grained atomic actions. This is because none of the values on which e depends could possibly change while e is being evaluated and because each process has its own set of registers and its own temporary storage area. Similarly, if an assignment $x := e$ in one process does not reference any variable altered by another process, execution of the assignment will be atomic. The program in (2.2) meets this requirement, and hence the concurrent assignments are atomic.

Unfortunately, most interesting concurrent programs do not meet the above disjointness requirement. However, a weaker requirement is often met. Define a *simple* variable to be a scalar variable, array element, or record field that is stored in a single memory location. Then if an expression or assignment satisfies the following property, evaluation will still be atomic.

(2.4)   **At-Most-Once Property.** An expression e satisfies the at-most-once property if it refers to at most one simple variable y that might be changed by another process while e is being evaluated, and it refers to y at most once. An assignment statement $x := e$ satisfies the at-most-once property either if e satisfies the property and x is not read by another process or if x is a simple variable and e does not refer to any variable that might be changed by another process.

This property ensures atomicity since the one shared variable, if any, will be read or written just once as a fine-grained atomic action.

For an assignment statement to satisfy (2.4), e can refer to one variable altered by another process as long as x is not read by another process (i.e., x is a local variable). Alternatively, x can be read by another process as long as e does not reference any variable altered by other processes. However, neither assignment in the following satisfies (2.4):

   co $x := y{+}1$ **//** $y := x{+}1$ **oc**

Indeed, if x and y are initially 0, their final values could both be 1. (This would result if the processes read x and y before either assigns to them.) However, since each assignment refers only once to only one variable altered by another process, the final values will be ones that actually existed in some state. This is in contrast to the earlier example in which $y + z$ referred to two variables altered by another process.

Specifying Synchronization

If an expression or assignment statement does not satisfy the At-Most-Once Property, we often need to have it executed atomically. More generally, we often need to execute sequences of statements as a single atomic action. In both cases, we need to use a synchronization mechanism to construct a *coarse-grained* atomic action, which is a sequence of fine-grained atomic actions that appears to be indivisible.

As a concrete example, suppose a database contains two values x and y, and that at all times x and y are to be the same in the sense that no process examining the database is ever to see a state in which x and y differ. Then, if a process alters x, it must also alter y as part of the same atomic action.

As a second example, suppose one process inserts elements on a queue represented as a linked list. Another process removes elements from the list, assuming there are elements on the list. Two variables point to the head and tail of the list. Inserting and removing elements requires manipulating two values; e.g., to insert an element, we have to change the link of the previously last element so it points to the new element, and we have to change the tail variable so it points to the new element. If the list contains just one element, simultaneous insertion and removal can conflict, leaving the list in an unstable state. Thus, insert and remove must be atomic actions. Furthermore, if the list is empty, we need to delay execution of remove until an element has been inserted.

We will specify atomic actions by means of angle brackets $\langle$ and $\rangle$. For example, $\langle e \rangle$ indicates that expression e is to be evaluated atomically.

We will specify synchronization by means of the **await** statement:

$$\langle\, \textbf{await}\ B\ \rightarrow\ S\, \rangle$$

Boolean expression B specifies a delay condition; S is a sequence of sequential statements that is guaranteed to terminate (e.g., a sequence of assignment statements). An **await** statement is enclosed in angle brackets to indicate that it is executed as an atomic action. In particular, B is guaranteed to be true when execution of S begins, and no internal state in S is visible to other processes. For example,

(2.5) $\langle\, \textbf{await}\ s > 0 \rightarrow s := s - 1\, \rangle$

delays until s is positive, then decrements s. The value of s is guaranteed to be positive before s is decremented.

The **await** statement is a very powerful statement since it can be used to specify arbitrary, coarse-grained atomic actions. This makes it convenient for expressing synchronization—and we will therefore use **await** to develop initial solutions to synchronization problems. This expressive power also makes **await** very expensive to implement in its most general form. However, as we shall see in this and the next several chapters, there are many special cases of **await** that can be implemented efficiently. For example, (2.5) is an example of the **P** operation on semaphore s, the topic of Chapter 4.

The general form of the **await** statement specifies both mutual exclusion and condition synchronization. To specify just mutual exclusion, we will abbreviate an **await** statement as follows:

$$\langle S \rangle$$

For example, the following increments x and y atomically:

$$\langle x := x + 1; y := y + 1 \rangle$$

The internal state in which x has been incremented but y has not is invisible to other processes that reference x or y. If S is a single assignment statement and meets the requirements of the At-Most-Once Property (2.4)—or if S is implemented by a single machine instruction—then S will be executed atomically; thus, $\langle S \rangle$ has the same effect as S.

To specify just condition synchronization, we will abbreviate an **await** statement as:

$$\langle \textbf{await } B \rangle$$

For example, the following delays the executing process until *count* > 0:

$$\langle \textbf{await } count > 0 \rangle$$

If B meets the requirements of the At-Most-Once Property, as in this example, then $\langle \textbf{await } B \rangle$ can be implemented as:

do not $B \to$ **skip od**

An *unconditional* atomic action is one that does not contain a delay condition B. Such an action can execute immediately, subject of course to the requirement that it execute atomically. Fine-grained (hardware-implemented) actions, expressions in angle brackets, and **await** statements in which the guard is the constant true or is omitted are all unconditional atomic actions.

A *conditional* atomic action is an **await** statement with a guard B. Such an action cannot execute until B is true. If B is false, it can only become true as the result of actions taken by other processes. Thus a process waiting to execute a conditional atomic action could wait for an arbitrarily long time.

2.3 Semantics of Concurrent Execution

The **co** statement in (2.2) increments both x and y. Thus, a programming logic for concurrency should enable the following to be proved:

(2.6) $\{ x = 0 \wedge y = 0 \}$
           co $x := x+1$ **//** $y := y+1$ **oc**
           $\{ x = 1 \wedge y = 1 \}$

This requires devising an inference rule for the **co** statement. Since execution of **co** results in execution of each process, the effect of **co** is the conjunction of the effects of the constituent processes. Thus, the inference rule for **co** is based on combining triples that capture the effect of executing each process.

Each process is comprised of sequential statements, plus possibly synchronization statements. Axioms and proof rules for sequential statements are those in Section 1.3. With respect to partial correctness, an **await** statement is much like an **if** statement for which the guard B is true when execution of S begins. Hence the inference rule for **await** is similar to the Alternative Rule:

(2.7)   **Synchronization Rule**: $\dfrac{\{ P \wedge B \} \; S \; \{ Q \}}{\{ P \} \; \langle \, \textbf{await} \, B \to S \, \rangle \; \{ Q \}}$

The two special forms of the **await** statement are special cases of this rule. For $\langle S \rangle$, B is true, and hence the hypothesis simplifies to $\{ P \} S \{ Q \}$. For $\langle \, \textbf{await} \, B \, \rangle$, S is **skip**, so $P \wedge B$ must imply the truth of Q.

As an example of the use of (2.7), by the Assignment Axiom the following is a theorem:

$\{ s > 0 \} \; s := s - 1 \; \{ s \geq 0 \}$

Hence, by the Synchronization Rule

$\{ s \geq 0 \} \; \langle \, \textbf{await} \, s > 0 \; \to \; s := s - 1 \, \rangle \; \{ s \geq 0 \}$

is a theorem with P and Q both being $s \geq 0$. The fact that **await** statements are executed atomically affects interaction between processes, as discussed below.

Suppose that for each process S_i in a **co** statement of form (2.1),

$\{ P_i \} \; S_i \; \{ Q_i \}$

is a theorem of Programming Logic *PL*. According to the Interpretation of

Triples (1.5), this means that, if S_i is begun in a state satisfying P_i and S_i terminates, then the state will satisfy Q_i. For this interpretation to hold when the processes are executed concurrently, the processes must be started in a state satisfying the conjunction of the P_i. If all the processes terminate, the final state will satisfy the conjunction of the Q_i. Thus, one would expect to be able to conclude that the following is a theorem:

$$\{\, P_1 \wedge ... \wedge P_n \,\} \ \textbf{co} \ S_1 \,/\!/\, ... \,/\!/\, S_n \ \textbf{oc} \ \{\, Q_1 \wedge ... \wedge Q_n \,\}$$

For program (2.6), such a conclusion would be sound. In particular, from the valid triples

$$\{\, x = 0 \,\} \ x := x + 1 \ \{\, x = 1 \,\}$$
$$\{\, y = 0 \,\} \ y := y + 1 \ \{\, y = 1 \,\}$$

the following is a sound conclusion:

$$\{\, x = 0 \wedge y = 0 \,\} \ \textbf{co} \ x = x + 1 \,/\!/\, y := y + 1 \ \textbf{oc} \ \{\, x = 1 \wedge y = 1 \,\}$$

But what about the following slightly different program?

$$\textbf{co} \ \langle\, x := x + 1 \,\rangle \,/\!/\, \langle\, x := x + 1 \,\rangle \ \textbf{oc}$$

The assignment statements are atomic, so if x is initially 0, its final value is 2. But how could this be proved? Even though the following is a theorem in isolation

$$\{\, x = 0 \,\} \ \langle\, x := x + 1 \,\rangle \ \{\, x = 1 \,\}$$

it is not generally valid when another process executes concurrently and alters shared variable x. The problem is that one process might *interfere* with an assertion in another; i.e., it might make the assertion false.

We assume that every expression or assignment statement executes atomically, either because it meets the requirements of the At-Most-Once Property (2.4) or because it is enclosed by angle brackets. An atomic action in a process is *eligible* if it is the next atomic action the process will execute. When an eligible action T executes, its precondition $pre(T)$ must be true. For example, if the next eligible action is evaluating the guards of an **if** statement, then the precondition of the **if** statement must be true. Since eligible actions in different processes execute in any order, $pre(T)$ must not become false if some other eligible action executes before T. We call predicate $pre(T)$ a *critical assertion* since it is imperative that it be true when T executes. More precisely, the following defines the set of critical assertions in a proof.

(2.8)   **Critical Assertions.** Given a proof that $\{P\} S \{Q\}$ is a theorem, the critical assertions in the proof are: (a) Q, and (b) for each statement T within S that is not within an **await** statement, the weakest predicate $pre(T)$ such that $\{pre(T)\} T \{post(T)\}$ is a theorem within the proof.

In case (b), only statements not within **await** statements need be considered since intermediate states within **await** are not visible to other processes. Also, if there is more than one valid triple about a given statement T—due to use of the Rule of Consequence—only the weakest predicate $pre(T)$ that is a precondition of T is a critical assertion. This is because any stronger assumptions are not needed to construct the entire proof.

Recall that a complete proof outline contains an assertion before and after each statement. It encodes a formal proof, presenting it in a way that makes the proof easier to understand. It also encodes the critical assertions, assuming they are the weakest ones that are required. In particular, the critical assertions of a process are the postcondition and the preconditions of every statement that is not within an **await** statement. For example, in

$$\{P_e^x\} \ \langle x := e \rangle \ \{P\}$$

P_e^x is a critical assertion since it must be true when the assignment statement is executed; P is also a critical assertion if the assignment is the last statement in a process. As a second example, in

$$\{P\} \ \langle S1; \{Q\} \ S2 \rangle \ \{R\}$$

P is a critical assertion, but Q is not since the state following execution of $S1$ is not visible to other processes.

In order for the proof of a process to remain valid according to the Interpretation for Triples (1.5), critical assertions must not be interfered with by atomic actions in other, concurrently executing processes. This is called *interference freedom*, which we define formally below.

An *assignment action* is an atomic action that contains one or more assignment statements. Let C be a critical assertion in the proof of one process. Then the only way in which C could be interfered with is if another process executes an assignment action a and a changes the state so C is false. Interference will not occur if the following conditions hold.

(2.9)   **Non-Interference.** If necessary, rename local variables in C so their names are distinct from the names of local variables in a and $pre(a)$. Then assignment action a does not interfere with critical assertion C if the following is a theorem in Programming Logic:
          $NI(a, C)$: $\{C \wedge pre(a)\} \ a \ \{C\}$

In short, C is invariant with respect to execution of assignment action a. The precondition of a is included in (2.9) since a can be executed only if the process is in a state satisfying $pre(a)$.

A collection of processes is interference-free if no assignment action in one process interferes with any critical assertion in another. If this is true, then the proofs of the individual processes remain valid in the presence of concurrent execution.

(2.10)   **Interference Freedom.** Theorems $\{\ P_i\ \}\ S_i\ \{\ Q_i\ \}$, $1 \leq i \leq n$, are interference-free if:

> For all assignment actions a in the proof of S_i,
>> For all critical assertions C in the proof of S_j, $i \neq j$,
>>> $NI(a, C)$ is a theorem.

If the proofs of n processes are interference-free, then the proofs can be combined when the processes execute concurrently. In particular, if the processes begin execution in a state that satisfies all their preconditions, and if every process terminates, then when the processes terminate the state will satisfy the conjunction of their postconditions. This yields the following inference rule for **co**.

(2.11)   **Concurrency Rule:**

$$\frac{\{\ P_i\}\ S_i\ \{\ Q_i\ \}\ \text{are interference-free theorems},\ 1 \leq i \leq n}{\{\ P_1 \wedge ... \wedge P_n\}\ \textbf{co}\ S_1\ /\!/\ ...\ /\!/\ S_n\ \textbf{oc}\ \{\ Q_1 \wedge ... \wedge Q_n\ \}}$$

In the remainder of this chapter, we give numerous examples illustrating the use of this rule.

2.4 Techniques for Avoiding Interference

To apply Concurrency Rule (2.11), we first need to construct proofs of the individual processes. Since the processes are sequential programs, these are developed using the techniques described in the previous chapter. Then we have to show that the proofs are interference-free. This is the new requirement introduced by concurrent execution.

Recall that the number of different histories of a concurrent program is exponential in the number of atomic actions that are executed. By contrast, the number of ways in which processes could interfere depends only on the number of distinct atomic actions in the program text; this number does not depend on how many actions actually get executed. For example, if there are n processes and each contains a assignment actions and c critical assertions, then in the worst case we have to prove $n * (n-1) * a * c$ non-interference theorems. Though this number is much smaller than the number of histories, it is still quite large. However, many of these theorems will undoubtedly be the same since processes are often syntactically identical or at least symmetric. More importantly, there are ways to avoid interference entirely.

In this section, we present four techniques for avoiding interference: disjoint variables, weakened assertions, global invariants, and synchronization. These techniques are employed extensively throughout the remainder of the book. All involve putting assertions and assignment actions in a form that ensures that Non-Interference formulas (2.9) are true.

Disjoint Variables

The *write set* of a process is the set of variables that it assigns to. The *reference set* of a process is the set of variables referenced in the assertions in a proof of that process. (This set will often be the same as the set of variables referenced in statements in the process but might not be; with respect to interference, the critical variables are those in assertions.)

If the write set of one process is disjoint from the reference set of a second, and vice versa, then the two processes cannot interfere. This is because Assignment Axiom (1.7) employs textual substitution, which has no effect on a predicate that does not contain a reference to the target of the assignment. (Recall that local variables in different processes are different variables, even if they happen to have the same name; thus they can be renamed before applying the Assignment Axiom.)

As an example, consider again the following program:

$$\textbf{co } x := x + 1 \textbf{ // } y := y + 1 \textbf{ oc}$$

If x and y are initially 0, then from the Assignment Axiom, both the following are theorems:

$$\{ x = 0 \} \ x := x + 1 \ \{ x = 1 \}$$
$$\{ y = 0 \} \ y := y + 1 \ \{ y = 1 \}$$

Each process contains one assignment statement and two assertions; hence there are four non-interference theorems to prove. For example, to show that $x = 0$ is not interfered with by the assignment to y,

$$NI(y := y + 1, x = 0): \ \{ x = 0 \wedge y = 0 \} \ y := y + 1 \ \{ x = 0 \}$$

must be a theorem. It is since

$$(x = 0)^y_{y+1} \ = \ (x = 0)$$

and $(x = 0 \wedge y = 0) \Rightarrow x = 0$. The other three non-interference proofs are similar since the write and reference sets are disjoint. Thus, we can apply Concurrency Rule (2.11) to conclude that the following is a theorem:

$$\{\, x = 0 \wedge y = 0 \,\}\ \ \textbf{co}\ x := x + 1\ \ /\!/\ \ y := y + 1\ \ \textbf{oc}\ \ \{\, x = 1 \wedge y = 1 \,\}$$

Technically, if an assertion in a process references an array variable, the entire array is a part of the reference set of the process. This is because the Assignment Axiom treats arrays as functions. However, assigning to one array element does not affect the value of any other. Hence if the actual array elements in the write set of a process differ from the actual array elements in the reference set of another—and the sets are otherwise disjoint—the first process does not interfere with the second. For example, in

$$\textbf{co}\ i := 1\ \textbf{to}\ n \rightarrow a[i] := i\ \ \textbf{oc}$$

the following triple is valid for each process:

$$\{\, true \,\}\ \ a[i] := i\ \ \{\, a[i] = i \,\}$$

Since the value of i is different in each process, the proofs are interference-free. Similarly, the inner-product processes in (2.3) and the *Sum* processes in Figure 2.1 would not interfere with each other as long as their proofs did not reference array elements assigned to by the other processes. In simple cases like these, it is easy to see that the array indices are different; in general, however, this can be very hard to verify, if not impossible.

Disjoint write/reference sets provide the basis for many parallel algorithms, especially those such as (2.3) that manipulate matrices. As another example, different branches of the tree of possible moves in a game-playing program can be searched in parallel. Or, multiple transactions can examine a database in parallel or they can update different relations.

Weakened Assertions

Even when the write and reference sets of processes overlap, we can sometimes avoid interference by weakening assertions to take into account the effects of concurrent execution. For example, consider the following:

(2.12) $\textbf{co}\ P1:\ \langle\, x := x + 1 \,\rangle\ /\!/\ P2:\ \langle\, x := x + 2 \,\rangle\ \textbf{oc}$

If x is initially 0, both the following triples are valid in isolation:

$$\{\, x = 0 \,\}\ \ x := x + 1\ \ \{\, x = 1 \,\}$$
$$\{\, x = 0 \,\}\ \ x := x + 2\ \ \{\, x = 2 \,\}$$

However, each assignment interferes with both assertions in the other triple. Moreover, the conjunction of the postconditions does not yield the correct result that the final value of x is 3.

If process *P1* happens to execute before *P2*, then the state will satisfy $x = 1$ when *P2* begins execution. If we weaken the precondition of *P2* to take this possibility into account, the following triple results:

(2.13) $\{ x = 0 \vee x = 1 \}$ $x := x + 2$ $\{ x = 2 \vee x = 3 \}$

Analogously, if *P2* executes before *P1*, the state will satisfy $x = 2$ when *P1* begins execution. Thus, we also need to weaken *P1*'s precondition:

(2.14) $\{ x = 0 \vee x = 2 \}$ $x := x + 1$ $\{ x = 1 \vee x = 3 \}$

These proofs do not interfere. For example, the precondition and assignment in (2.14) does not interfere with the precondition in (2.13). Applying Non-Interference definition (2.9) yields:

(2.15) $\{ (x = 0 \vee x = 1) \wedge (x = 0 \vee x = 2) \}$ $x := x + 1$ $\{ x = 0 \vee x = 1 \}$

Substituting $x + 1$ for x in the postcondition of (2.15) yields $(x = -1 \vee x = 0)$. The precondition in (2.15) simplifies to $x = 0$, which implies $(x = -1 \vee x = 0)$. Thus, by applying the Rule of Consequence to get rid of $x = -1$, (2.15) is indeed a theorem.

The other three non-interference checks are similar. Hence, we can apply Concurrency Rule (2.11) to (2.13) and (2.14), yielding the theorem:

$$\{ (x = 0 \vee x = 1) \wedge (x = 0 \vee x = 2) \}$$
$$\textbf{co } P1: \langle\, x := x + 1 \,\rangle \,\,/\!/\,\, P2: \langle\, x := x + 2 \,\rangle \textbf{ oc}$$
$$\{ (x = 2 \vee x = 3) \wedge (x = 1 \vee x = 3) \}$$

The precondition simplifies to $x = 0$, and the postcondition simplifies to $x = 3$, as desired.

Although the program in the above example is simplistic, it illustrates an important principle: In developing a proof of a process that references variables altered by other processes, take the effects of the other processes into account. The example also illustrates one way to do this: Make a weaker assertion about shared variables than could be made if a process were executed in isolation. We can always make assertions weak enough to avoid interference—e.g., every state satisfies *true*—but then the desired result probably cannot be proved. The key is to strike a balance between asserting too much and not enough.

Another application of these points is the following. Assume a process schedules operations on a moving-head disk. Other processes insert operations into a queue; when the disk is idle, the scheduler examines the queue, selects the best operation according to some criteria, and starts that operation. Although the scheduler may have selected the best operation at the time it examined the queue, it is not the case that at all times the disk is performing the best operation—or even that at the time an operation is started it is still the best one. This is because a process might have inserted another, better operation into the queue just after the selection was made— and even before the disk started to execute the selected operation. Thus, "best" in this case is a time-dependent property; however, it is sufficient for scheduling problems such as this.

As another example, many parallel algorithms for approximating solutions to partial differential equations have the following form. The problem space is approximated by a finite grid of points, say $grid[1{:}n,1{:}n]$. A process is assigned to each grid point—or more commonly, a block of grid points—as in the following program outline:

> **var** $grid[1{:}n, 1{:}n]$: **real**
> $PDE[i{:}1..n, j{:}1..n]{::}$ **do not** converged $\rightarrow$
> $\qquad\qquad grid[i,j] := f\,(\text{neighboring points})$
> **od**

The function f computed on each iteration might, for example, be the average of the four neighboring points in the same row and column. For many problems, it is imperative that the value assigned to $grid[i,j]$ on one iteration depend on the values of the neighbors from the previous iteration. Thus, the loop invariant would characterize this relation between old and new values for grid points.

In order to ensure that the invariant in each process is not interfered with, the processes must use two matrices and must synchronize after each iteration. In particular, on each iteration a *PDE* process reads values from one matrix, computes f, and then assigns the result to the second matrix. Each process then waits until all processes have computed the new value for their grid points. (The next chapter shows how to implement this kind of synchronization, which is called a barrier.) The roles of the matrices are then switched, and the processes execute another iteration.

A second way to synchronize the processes is to execute them in lock step, with each process executing the same actions at the same time. Synchronous multiprocessors, such as the Connection Machine, support this style of execution. This approach avoids interference since each process reads old values from *grid* before assigning a new value.

Occasionally a third approach is possible. For some problems, it is acceptable for f to be a function of values resulting from any prior or future iteration of neighboring processes. In effect, the loop invariant is weakened to require that f be a function of the values of the neighboring points resulting from some iteration, not necessarily just from the prior one. This technique is called *chaotic relaxation*. When it can be employed, the *PDE* processes can truly execute in parallel without synchronization.

Global Invariants

Another technique for avoiding interference is to employ a global invariant to capture the relation between shared variables. Suppose I is a predicate that references global variables. Then I is a *global invariant* with respect to a set of processes if (1) I is true when the processes begin execution, and (2) I is invariant with respect to execution of every assignment action (assignment statement or **await** statement that contains an assignment). Condition 1 is satisfied if I is true in the initial state of every process. Condition 2 is satisfied if for every assignment action a with precondition $pre(a)$,

$$\{ I \wedge pre(a) \} \ \ a \ \ \{ I \}$$

is a theorem; i.e., a does not interfere with I. Recall that $pre(a)$ is included since a can only be executed in a state in which $pre(a)$ is true.

Suppose I is a global invariant. Further suppose that every critical assertion C in the proof of a process P_j can be put in the form:

(2.16) C: $I \wedge L$

where L is a predicate about private variables. In particular, all variables referenced in L are either local to process j or are global variables that only j assigns to. (In general, L will be a different predicate in each critical assertion.)

If all assertions can be put in form (2.16), then the proofs of the processes are interference-free. This is because I is invariant with respect to every assignment action a and because no assignment action in one process can interfere with a local predicate L in another process since the targets in a are different from all the variables in L. Thus, Non-Interference requirement (2.9) is met for every pair of assignment actions and critical assertions. Moreover, we only have to check the triples in each process to verify that each critical assertion has the above form and that I is a global invariant; we do not even have to consider assertions or statements in other processes. In fact, for an array of identical processes, we only have to check one of them.

Even when we cannot put every critical assertion into form (2.16), we can sometimes use a combination of global invariants and weakened assertions to avoid interference. We will illustrate this using the producer/consumer program in Figure 2.2. That program copies the contents of *Producer* array a into *Consumer* array b using a single shared buffer *buf*. The *Producer* and

var *buf* : **int**, *p* : **int** := 0, *c* : **int** := 0

Producer:: **var** *a*[1:*n*] : **int**

      do $p < n \rightarrow \langle$ **await** $p = c \rangle$

                $buf := a[p + 1]$

                $p := p + 1$

   od

Consumer:: **var** *b*[1:*n*] : **int**

      do $c < n \rightarrow \langle$ **await** $p > c \rangle$

                $b[c + 1] := buf$

                $c := c + 1$

   od

Figure 2.2. Array copy problem using a single shared buffer.

Consumer alternate access to *buf*. First *Producer* deposits the first element of *a* in *buf*, then *Consumer* fetches it, then *Producer* deposits the second element of *a*, and so on. Variables *p* and *c* count the number of items that have been deposited and fetched, respectively. The **await** statements are used to synchronize access to *buf*. When $p = c$ the buffer is empty (the previously deposited element has been fetched); when $p > c$ the buffer is full.

Suppose the initial contents of *a*[1:*n*] is A[1:*n*], where A is an array of logical variables. The goal is to prove that, upon termination of the above program, the contents of *b*[1:*n*] are A[1:*n*]. This can be done using a global invariant as follows. Since the processes alternate access to *buf*, at all times *p* is equal to or one more than *c*. Also, when the buffer is full (i.e., $p = c + 1$), it contains A[*p*]. Finally, *a* is not altered, so it is always equal to A. Thus, a candidate global invariant is:

$$PC:\ c \leq p \leq c + 1\ \wedge\ a[1{:}n] = A[1{:}n]\ \wedge\ (p = c + 1) \Rightarrow (buf = A[p])$$

This predicate is true initially since both *p* and *c* are initially zero. It is maintained by every assignment statement, as illustrated by the complete proof outline in Figure 2.3. That proof outline contains all the critical assertions. In it, *IP* is the invariant for the *Producer* loop, and *IC* is the invariant for the *Consumer* loop.

In isolation, the proof outline for each process in Figure 2.3 follows directly from the assignment statements in the process. Assuming each process continually gets a chance to execute, the **await** statements terminate since first one guard is true, then the other, and so on. (Termination of **await** statements is considered in detail in Section 2.6.) Since the **await** statements terminate, each process terminates after *n* iterations. Thus, as

var buf : **int**, p : **int** $:= 0, c$: **int** $:= 0$
{ PC: $c \leq p \leq c + 1 \ \wedge \ a[1{:}n] = A[1{:}n] \ \wedge \ (p = c + 1) \Rightarrow (buf = A[p])$ }
Producer:: **var** $a[1{:}n]$: **int**
        { IP: $PC \wedge p \leq n$ }
        do $p < n \rightarrow$ { $PC \wedge p < n$ }
               ⟨ **await** $p = c$ ⟩
               { $PC \wedge p < n \wedge p = c$ }
               $buf := a[p + 1]$
               { $PC \wedge p < n \wedge p = c \wedge buf = A[p + 1]$ }
               $p := p + 1$
               { IP }
      od
      { $PC \wedge p = n$ }
Consumer:: **var** $b[1{:}n]$: **int**
        { IC: $PC \wedge c \leq n \wedge b[1{:}c] = A[1{:}c]$ }
        do $c \leq n \rightarrow$ { $IC \wedge c < n$ }
               ⟨ **await** $p > c$ ⟩
               { $IC \wedge c < n \wedge p > c$ }
               $b[c + 1] := buf$
               { $IC \wedge c < n \wedge p > c \wedge b[c + 1] = A[c + 1]$ }
               $c := c + 1$
               { IC }
      od
      { $IC \wedge c = n + 1$ }

Figure 2.3. Complete proof outline for array copy program.

long as the proofs underlying the proof outlines are interference-free, we can use Concurrency Rule (2.11) to combine the postconditions of the processes and hence to conclude that the program does indeed copy the contents of a into b.

Most of the critical assertions in Figure 2.3 have the form shown in (2.16): They contain the conjunction of global invariant PC and predicates that reference variables not altered by the other process. Hence those assertions cannot be interfered with. The only assertions not in form (2.16) are the two in *Producer* that assert that $p = c$ and the two in *Consumer* that assert that $p > c$. We have to check whether these are interfered with.

Consider the following assertion in *Producer*:

    A1: $PC \wedge p < n \wedge p = c$

The only variable in *A1* altered by *Consumer* is c. One assignment statement in *Consumer* alters c, and that statement has precondition:

$$A2:\ IC \wedge c < n \wedge p > c \wedge b[c+1] = A[c+1]$$

Applying Non-Interference requirement (2.9), we get the following proof obligation:

$$NI(c := c+1, A1):\ \{A1 \wedge A2\}\ c := c+1\ \{A1\}$$

Because p cannot both be equal to and greater than c, $(A1 \wedge A2)$ is false. Hence, we can use the Rule of Consequence to yield any predicate, in this case, $A1_{c+1}^{c}$. So, by the Assignment Axiom and Rule of Consequence, the above is a theorem. The other three non-interference proofs are nearly identical. Hence, the program in Figure 2.3 is interference-free.

What is happening in this array copy program is that the **await** statements ensure that the processes alternate access to the buffer; i.e., p and c alternately are the same and then differ by one. This keeps the statements that increment p and c from interfering with critical assertions in the other process.

Since each **await** statement in Figure 2.3 meets the requirements of the At-Most-Once Property (2.4), each can be implemented by a **do** loop as described in Section 2.2. For example, the $\langle$ **await** $p = c \rangle$ statement in *Producer* can be implemented by:

$$\textbf{do } p \neq c \rightarrow \textbf{skip od}$$

When synchronization is implemented in this way, a process is said to be *busy waiting* or *spinning* since it is busy doing nothing but checking the guard until it becomes false. Chapter 3 examines this kind of synchronization.

Synchronization

As described in Section 2.3, we can ignore an assignment statement that is within angle brackets when considering non-interference obligations. Since an atomic action appears to other processes to be an indivisible unit, it suffices to establish that the entire action does not cause interference. For example, given

$$\langle x := x+1; y := y+1 \rangle$$

neither assignment by itself can cause interference; only the pair of assignments might.

In addition, internal states of program segments within angle brackets are not visible. Hence, no assertion about an internal state can be interfered with by another process. For example, the middle assertion below is not a critical assertion:

$$\{ x = 0 \wedge y = 0 \} \, \langle \, x := x + 1 \, \{ x = 1 \wedge y = 0 \} \, y := y + 1 \, \rangle \, \{ x = 1 \wedge y = 1 \}$$

These two attributes of atomic actions lead to two additional techniques for avoiding interference: mutual exclusion and condition synchronization. Consider the proof outlines:

(2.17)   *P1*:: ... { *pre(a)* } *a* ...

          P2:: ... *S1* { *C* } *S2* ...

Above, *a* is an assignment statement in process *P1*, and *S1* and *S2* are statements in process *P2*. Suppose that *a* interferes with critical assertion *C*. One way to avoid interference is to use mutual exclusion to "hide" *C* from *a*. This is done by constructing a single atomic action

          ⟨ *S1*; *S2* ⟩

that executes *S1* and *S2* atomically and hence makes state *C* invisible to other processes.

Another way to eliminate interference in (2.17) is to use condition synchronization to strengthen the precondition of *a* in (2.17). Non-Interference requirement (2.9) will be satisfied if either:

- *C* is false when *a* is executed, and hence process *P2* could not be about to execute *S2*; or

- executing *a* makes *C* true, i.e., if $post(a) \Rightarrow C$.

Thus, we can replace *a* in (2.17) by the following conditional atomic action:

          ⟨ **await not** *C* **or** *B* → *a* ⟩

Here, *B* is a predicate characterizing a set of states such that executing *a* will make *C* true. From the definition of the weakest precondition, $B = wp(a, C)$ characterizes the largest set of such states.

To illustrate these techniques, consider the following example of a simplified banking system. Suppose a bank has a collection of accounts, allows customers to transfer money from one account to another, and has an auditor to check for embezzlement. Let the accounts be represented by *account*[1:*n*]. A transaction that transfers $100 from account *x* to account *y*

var *account*[1:*n*] : **int**

Transfer:: { *account*[*x*] = X ∧ *account*[*y*] = Y }
⟨ *account*[*x*] := *account*[*x*] − 100
    account[*y*] := *account*[*y*] + 100 ⟩
{ *account* [*x*] = X − 100 ∧ *account*[*y*] = Y + 100 }

Auditor:: **var** *total* := 0, *i* := 1, *embezzle* := false
    { *total* = *account*[1] + ... + *account*[*i* − 1] }
    do *i* ≤ *n* → { *C1*: *total* = *account*[1] + ... + *account*[*i* − 1] ∧ *i* ≤ *n* }
                total := *total* + *account*[*i*]; *i* := *i* + 1
                { *C2*: *total* = *account*[1] + ... + *account*[*i* − 1] }
    od
    { (*total* = *account*[1] + ... + *account*[*n*]) ∧ *i* = *n* }
    if *total* ≠ CASH → *embezzle* := true **fi**

Figure 2.4. Bank transfer and auditing problem.

could then be implemented by the *Transfer* process in Figure 2.4. In that process, we assume that *x* ≠ *y*, that there are sufficient funds, and that both accounts are valid (i.e., both *x* and *y* are between 1 and *n*). In the assertions in *Transfer*, X and Y are logical variables.

Let CASH be the total amount of cash in all accounts. The *Auditor* process in Figure 2.4 checks for embezzlement by iterating through the accounts, summing the amount in each, then comparing the total to CASH.

As programmed in Figure 2.4, *Transfer* executes as a single atomic action, so the *Auditor* will not see a state in which *account*[*x*] has been debited and then finish the audit without seeing the (pending) credit into *account*[*y*]. However, this is not sufficient to prevent interference. The problem is that, if *Transfer* executes while index *i* in *Auditor* is between *x* and *y*, the old amount in one of the accounts will already have been added to *total*, and later the new amount in the other account will be added, leading the *Auditor* incorrectly to believe funds have been embezzled. More precisely, the assignments in *Transfer* interfere with *Auditor* assertions *C1* and *C2*.

Additional synchronization is need to avoid interference between the processes in Figure 2.4. One approach is to use mutual exclusion to hide critical assertions *C1* and *C2*. This is done by placing the entire **do** loop in *Auditor* within angle brackets and hence making it atomic. Unfortunately this has the effect of making almost all of *Auditor* execute without interruption. An alternative approach is to use condition synchronization to keep *Transfer* from executing if doing so will interfere with *C1* and *C2*. In particular, we can replace the unconditional atomic action in *Transfer* by the following conditional atomic action:

$\langle$ **await** $(x < i$ **and** $y < i)$ **or** $(x > i$ **and** $y > i)$ $\rightarrow$
$account[x] := account[x] - 100; account[y] := account[y] + 100 \rangle$

This second approach has the effect of making *Transfer* delay only when *Auditor* is at a critical point between accounts x and y.

As the banking example illustrates, mutual exclusion and condition synchronization can *always* be used to avoid interference. Moreover, they are often required since the other techniques by themselves are often insufficient. Consequently, we will use synchronization extensively in the remainder of the book, often in combination with one of the other techniques, especially global invariants. However, synchronization has to be used with care since it incurs overhead and can lead to deadlock if a delay condition never becomes true. Fortunately it is possible to solve synchronization problems in an efficient and systematic way, as we will show in Part II.

2.5 Auxiliary Variables

Programming Logic *PL* extended with Concurrency Rule (2.11) is not yet a (relatively) complete logic. Some triples are valid but cannot be proven to be. The gist of the problem is that we often need to make explicit assertions about the values of the program counters in different processes. However, the program counters are part of the *hidden state*: values that are not stored in program variables. Other examples of hidden state information are queues of blocked processes and queues of messages that have been sent but not yet received.

To illustrate the problem and motivate its solution, consider the following program:

(2.18)   **co** *P1*: $\langle x := x + 1 \rangle$ **//** *P2*: $\langle x := x + 1 \rangle$ **oc**

Suppose x is initially 0. Then x will be 2 when the program terminates. But how can this be proven? In the very similar program (2.12), in which one process incremented x by 1 and the other incremented x by 2, we could weaken assertions to account for the fact that the processes could execute in either order. However, that technique will not work here. In isolation, each of the following is a valid triple:

$\{x = 0\}$ *P1*: $x := x + 1$ $\{x = 1\}$
$\{x = 0\}$ *P2*: $x := x + 1$ $\{x = 1\}$

However, *P1* interferes with both assertions in the second triple, and *P2* interferes with both assertions in the first. To account for *P2* executing before *P1*, we can try weakening the assertions in *P1* as follows:

$$\{\,x = 0 \vee x = 1\,\}\ \ P1\!:\ x := x + 1\ \ \{\,x = 1 \vee x = 2\,\}$$

But *P1* still interferes with both assertions in *P2*. So we can also try weaking the assertions in *P2*:

$$\{\,x = 0 \vee x = 1\,\}\ \ P2\!:\ x := x + 1\ \ \{\,x = 1 \vee x = 2\,\}$$

Unfortunately, interference still results, and weakening the assertions further will not help. Moreover, the assertions are already too weak to conclude that $x = 2$ in the final state of the program since the conjunction of the postconditions is $(x = 1 \vee x = 2)$.

In (2.12) the fact that the processes incremented x by different values provided enough information to distinguish which process executed first. However, in (2.18) both processes increment x by 1, and thus the state $x = 1$ does not encode which process executed first. Instead, the execution order must be encoded explicitly. This requires introducing additional variables. Let $t1$ and $t2$ be variables that are added to (2.18) in the following way:

(2.19) **var** $x := 0,\, t1 := 0,\, t2 := 0$

       co $P1\!:\langle\, x := x + 1\,\rangle;\, t1 := 1$ // $P2\!:\langle\, x := x + 1\,\rangle;\, t2 := 1$ **oc**

Process *P1* sets $t1$ to 1 to indicate that it has incremented x; *P2* uses $t2$ in a similar way.

In the initial state of (2.19), $x = t1 + t2$. The same predicate is true in the final state. Thus if this predicate were a global invariant, we could conclude that x is 2 in the final state since $t1$ and $t2$ are both 1 in that state. Unfortunately, $x = t1 + t2$ is not a global invariant since it is not true just after either process has incremented x. However, we can hide this state by combining the two assignments in each process into a single atomic action. This results in the following program and proof outline:

(2.20) **var** $x := 0,\, t1 := 0,\, t2 := 0$ $\{\,I\!:\ x = t1 + t2\,\}$

      $\{\,I \wedge t1 = 0 \wedge t2 = 0\,\}$

      co $P1\!:\ \{\,I \wedge t1 = 0\,\}\ \langle\, x := x + 1;\, t1 := 1\,\rangle\ \{\,I \wedge t1 = 1\,\}$

      // $P2\!:\ \{\,I \wedge t2 = 0\,\}\ \langle\, x := x + 1;\, t2 := 1\,\rangle\ \{\,I \wedge t2 = 1\,\}$

      oc

      $\{\,I \wedge t1 = 1 \wedge t2 = 1\,\}$

The proof outline for each process is valid in isolation. Since each assertion is the conjunction of the global invariant and a predicate about a variable not referenced by the other process, the processes are interference-free. Thus, (2.20) is a valid proof outline.

Program (2.20) is not the same as program (2.18) since it contains two extra variables. However, *t1* and *t2* are *auxiliary variables*. They were added to the program solely to record enough state information so that a proof could be constructed. Moreover, they are used in a special way. In particular, *t1* and *t2* obey the following constraint.

(2.21) **Auxiliary Variable Restriction.** Auxiliary variables appear only in assignment statements $x := e$ where x is an auxiliary variable.

An auxiliary variable cannot appear in assignments to program variables or in guards in **if**, **do**, and **await** statements. Hence it cannot affect the execution of the program to which they are added. This means that the program without the auxiliary variables has the same partial (and total) correctness properties as the program to which it is added. The following inference rule captures this fact.

Let P and Q be predicates that do not reference auxiliary variables. Let statement S be obtained from statement S' by deleting all statements that assign to auxiliary variables. Then, the following inference rule is sound.

(2.22) **Auxiliary Variable Rule:** $\dfrac{\{P\}\ S'\ \{Q\}}{\{P\}\ S\ \{Q\}}$

As an example, from (2.20) and the Rule of Consequence it follows that the following is a theorem:

$$\{x = 0\}$$
$$\textbf{co}\ P1\colon \langle\, x := x + 1;\ t1 := 1\,\rangle\ /\!/\ P2\colon \langle\, x := x + 1;\ t2 := 1\,\rangle\ \textbf{oc}$$
$$\{x = 2\}$$

Applying the Auxiliary Variable Rule to delete *t1* and *t2*, we also have the following theorem:

$$\{x = 0\}$$
$$\textbf{co}\ P1\colon \langle\, x := x + 1\,\rangle\ /\!/\ P2\colon \langle\, x := x + 1\,\rangle\ \textbf{oc}$$
$$\{x = 2\}$$

To summarize, we have proven that (2.18) has the expected effect by first introducing auxiliary variables to record control points and by then using (2.22) to delete them. In later chapters, we will see several additional uses of auxiliary variables to record hidden parts of the state.

2.6 Safety and Liveness Properties

Recall that a property of a program is an attribute that is true of every possible history of that program. Every interesting property can be formulated in terms of two kinds of properties: safety and liveness. A safety property asserts that nothing bad happens during execution; a liveness property asserts that something good eventually happens. In sequential programs, the key safety property is that the final state is correct, and the key liveness property is termination. These properties are equally important for concurrent programs. In addition, there are other interesting safety and liveness properties that apply to concurrent programs.

Two important safety properties in concurrent programs are mutual exclusion and absence of deadlock. For mutual exclusion, the bad thing is having more than one process executing critical sections of statements at the same time. For absence of deadlock, the bad thing is having some processes waiting for conditions that will never occur.

Examples of liveness properties of concurrent programs are that a request for service will eventually be honored, that a message will eventually reach its destination, and that a process will eventually enter its critical section. Liveness properties are affected by scheduling policies, which determine which eligible atomic actions are next to execute.

The next section presents a method for proving safety properties that can be expressed as a predicate characterizing a bad program state. The following section defines scheduling policies and describes their relation to liveness properties. However, a formal logic for proving liveness properties is beyond the scope of this text since our main concern is learning how to develop and understand correct programs, not with carrying out rigorous proofs of all possible properties. The reference section gives citations for the reader interested in pursuing this topic.

Proving Safety Properties

All actions a program takes must be based on its state. Even actions performed in response to reading input are based on the program's state since the input values available to a program can be thought of as part of the state. Thus, if a program fails to satisfy a safety property, there must be some sequence of states (history) that fails to satisfy the property.

For the safety properties we will be concerned with—e.g., partial correctness, mutual exclusion, and absence of deadlock—there must be some individual program state that fails to satisfy the property. For example, if the mutual exclusion property fails to hold, there must be some state in which two (or more) processes are simultaneously in their critical sections. (An example of a safety property that cannot be characterized by a single bad program state is "The value of x is non-decreasing." Just looking at one state is not sufficient to conclude that x has never decreased; rather, one must examine pairs of adjacent states.)

For safety properties that can be specified by the absence of a bad program state, there is a simple method for proving that a program satisfies the property. Let *BAD* be a predicate that characterizes a bad program state. Then a program satisfies the associated safety property if *BAD* is not true in any state in the program. Given program S, to show that *BAD* is not true in any state requires showing that it is not true in the initial state, the second state, and so on, where the state is changed as a result of executing eligible atomic actions. The critical assertions in a proof $\{P\}\,S\,\{Q\}$ characterize the initial, intermediate, and final states. This provides the basis for the following method of proving that a program satisfies a safety property.

(2.23)   **Proving a Safety Property.** Let *BAD* be a predicate characterizing a bad program state. Assume that $\{P\}\,S\,\{Q\}$ is a proof in *PL* and that the precondition P characterizes the initial state of the program. Then S satisfies the safety property specified by $\neg\,BAD$ if, for every critical assertion C in the proof, $C \Rightarrow \neg\,BAD$.

Above, P must characterize the actual initial state of the program in order to rule out the trivial proof in which every critical assertion is the constant *false* (which characterizes no state).

Recall that a global invariant I is a predicate that is true in every visible state of a concurrent program. This suggests an alternate method for proving a safety property.

(2.24)   **Proving a Safety Property Using an Invariant.** Let *BAD* be a predicate characterizing a bad program state. Assume that $\{P\}\,S\,\{Q\}$ is a proof in *PL*, that P characterizes the initial state of the program, and that I is a global invariant in the proof. Then S satisfies the safety property specified by $\neg\,BAD$ if $I \Rightarrow \neg\,BAD$.

Many interesting safety properties can be formulated in terms of predicates that characterize states that processes should not simultaneously be in. For example, in mutual exclusion, the preconditions of the critical sections of two processes should not simultaneously be true. If predicate P characterizes some state of one process and predicate Q characterizes some state of a second process, then $P \wedge Q$ will be true if both processes are in their respective states. Moreover, if $(P \wedge Q) = false$, then the processes cannot simultaneously be in the two states since no state satisfies *false*.

Suppose a safety property can be characterized by $BAD = (P \wedge Q)$ and that P and Q are not simultaneously true in a given program; i.e., $(P \wedge Q) = false$. Then the program satisfies the safety property. This is because $\neg\,BAD = \neg(P \wedge Q) = true$, and every critical assertion in a proof trivially implies this. This leads to the following very useful method for proving a safety property.

(2.25) **Exclusion of Configurations.** Given a proof of a program, one process cannot be in a state satisfying P while another process is in a state satisfying Q if $(P \wedge Q) = false$.

As an example of the use of (2.25), consider the proof outline of the array copy program in Figure 2.3. The **await** statement in each process can cause delay. The processes would deadlock if they were both delayed and neither could proceed. The *Producer* process is delayed if it is at its **await** statement and the delay condition is false; in that state, the following predicate would be true:

$$PC \wedge p < n \wedge p \neq c$$

Similarly, the *Consumer* process is delayed if it is at its **await** statement and the delay condition is false; that state satisfies:

$$IC \wedge c < n \wedge p \leq c$$

Since the conjunction of these two predicates is false, the processes cannot simultaneously be in these states; hence deadlock cannot occur.

Scheduling Policies and Fairness

Most liveness properties depend on *fairness*, which is concerned with guaranteeing that processes get the chance to proceed, regardless of what other processes do. Recall that an atomic action in a process is eligible if it is the next atomic action in the process that will be executed. When there are several processes, there are several eligible atomic actions. A *scheduling policy* determines which one will be executed next.

Since atomic actions can be executed in parallel only if they do not interfere, parallel execution can be modeled by interleaved, serial execution. Hence to define the formal attributes of scheduling policies, we emphasize in this section scheduling on a single processor. Later chapters discuss practical aspects of scheduling on shared- and distributed-memory multiprocessors.

A low-level scheduling policy, such as the processor allocation policy in an operating system, is concerned with performance and hardware utilization. This is important, but equally important are global attributes of scheduling policies and their effect on termination and other liveness properties of concurrent programs. Consider the following program with two processes, *Loop* and *Stop*:

var *continue* := true

Loop:: **do** *continue* → **skip od**

Stop:: *continue* := false

Suppose a scheduling policy assigns a processor to a process until that process either terminates or delays. If there is only one processor, the above program will not terminate if *Loop* is executed first. However, the program will terminate if eventually *Stop* gets a chance to execute.

(2.26) **Unconditional Fairness.** A scheduling policy is unconditionally fair if every unconditional atomic action that is eligible is eventually executed.

For the above program, round-robin would be an unconditionally fair policy on a single processor, and parallel execution would be unconditionally fair on a multiprocessor.

When a program contains conditional atomic actions, we need to make stronger assumptions to guarantee that processes will make progress. This is because a conditional atomic action, even if eligible, is delayed until the guard is true.

(2.27) **Weak Fairness.** A scheduling policy is weakly fair if it is unconditionally fair and every conditional atomic action that becomes eligible is eventually executed if its guard becomes true and thereafter remains true.

In short, if ⟨ **await** $B → S$ ⟩ is eligible and B becomes true and remains true, then the atomic action eventually executes. Round-robin and timeslicing are weakly fair scheduling policies if every process gets a chance to execute. This is because any delayed process will eventually see that its delay condition is true.

Weak fairness is not, however, sufficient to ensure that any eligible **await** statement eventually executes. This is because the guard might well change value—from false to true and back to false—while a process is delayed. In this case, we need a stronger scheduling policy.

(2.28) **Strong Fairness.** A scheduling policy is strongly fair if it is unconditionally fair and every conditional atomic action that becomes eligible is eventually executed if its guard is infinitely often true.

A guard is infinitely often true if it is true an infinite number of times in every execution history of a (non-terminating) program. To be strongly fair, a scheduling policy cannot happen only to consider selecting an action when the guard is false; it must sometime select the action when the guard is true.

To see the difference between weakly and strongly fair policies, consider the following program:

(2.29)   **var** *continue* := true, *try* := false

       Loop:: **do** *continue* → *try* := true; *try* := false **od**

       Stop:: ⟨ **await** *try* → *continue* := false ⟩

With a strongly fair policy, this program will eventually terminate since *try* is infinitely often true. However, with a weakly fair policy, the program might not terminate since *try* is also infinitely often false.

Unfortunately, it is impossible to devise a general processor scheduling policy that is both practical and strongly fair. Consider program (2.29) again. On a single processor, a scheduler that alternates the actions of the two processes would be strongly fair since *Stop* would see a state in which *try* is true; however, such a scheduler is impractical to implement. On the other hand, round-robin and timeslicing are practical but not strongly fair in general. A multiprocessor scheduler that executes the processes in (2.29) in parallel is also practical, but it too is not strongly fair. In the latter cases, *Stop* might always examine *try* when it is false. This is unlikely, of course, but theoretically possible.

There are, however, special instances of practical, strongly fair policies. For example, suppose two processes repeatedly execute

$$\langle \text{ await } s > 0 \rightarrow s := s - 1 \rangle$$

and that other processes repeatedly increment *s*. Further suppose that the two processes are scheduled in first-come/first-served (FCFS) order—i.e., every time both are trying to execute **await**, the one that has waited the longest is scheduled first. Then each process will continually make progress. FCFS is a special instance of round-robin scheduling that we will often use in this way to ensure progress when processes compete for access to shared resources.

To further clarify the different kinds of scheduling policies, consider again the array copy program in Figure 2.2. As noted, that program is deadlock-free. Thus, the program will terminate as long as each process continues to get a chance to make progress. Each will as long as the scheduling policy is weakly fair. This is because, when one process makes the delay condition of the other true, that condition remains true until the other process continues and changes shared variables.

Both **await** statements in Figure 2.2 have the form ⟨ **await** *B* ⟩, and *B* refers to only one variable altered by the other process. Consequently, both

await statements can be implemented by busy-waiting loops. For example, ⟨ **await** $p = c$ ⟩ in the *Producer* can be implemented by:

do $p \neq c \rightarrow$ **skip od**

In this case, the program will terminate if the scheduling policy is unconditionally fair since there are now no conditional atomic actions and the processes alternate access to the shared buffer. It is not in general the case, however, that an unconditionally fair scheduling policy will ensure termination of a busy waiting loop; e.g., see (2.29). This is because an unconditionally fair policy might always schedule the atomic action that examines the loop guard when the guard is true. When a busy waiting loop never terminates, a program is said to suffer from *livelock*, the busy-waiting analog of deadlock. Absence of livelock is a liveness property—the good thing being eventual loop termination—since with busy waiting a process always has some action it can execute.

Historical Notes and References

Concurrent programming has been studied for the past three decades. One of the first, and most influential, papers on the subject was by Edsger W. Dijkstra [1965]. That paper introduced the **parbegin** statement, which was the precursor of the **co** (**cobegin**) statement. The name for the statement was inspired by the **begin** block of Algol 60, a language that was in vogue at the time. The Dijkstra paper also introduced the critical section and producer/consumer problems and several others that are examined in later chapters. Variants of **cobegin** have been included in the programming languages Algol 68 [van Wijngaarden et al. 1975], Communicating Sequential Processes (CSP) [Hoare 1978], Edison [Brinch Hansen 1981], Argus [Liskov & Scheifler 1983], and SR [Andrews et al. 1988]. The form of **co** and the use of quantifiers come from SR; the notation for larger processes is similar to a notation introduced in CSP.

The effects of implementing assignment statements using registers and fine-grained atomic actions are discussed in most operating systems texts, where they are used to motive the critical section problem (see Chapter 3 for discussion of that problem). An interesting discussion of the consequences of having data that cannot be read or written as a single atomic action—and how to deal with this situation—appears in Lamport [1977b]. (See also Peterson [1983a].)

The angle bracket notation for specifying coarse-grained atomic actions was invented by Leslie Lamport and formalized in Lamport [1980]. However, it was popularized by Dijkstra, with the first published use being Dijkstra [1977]. A different notation was employed by Owicki and Gries [1976]. In particular, they used "**await** B **then** S **end**" to specify conditional atomic actions; an unconditional atomic action was specified by "**await** true **then** S **end**." The specific notation used here combines angle brackets and a variant of **await**. The terms *unconditional* and *conditional atomic actions* are due to Fred Schneider [Schneider & Andrews 1986].

The first work on proving properties of concurrent programs was based on a flowchart representation of the program [Ashcroft & Manna 1971, Levitt 1972, Ashcroft 1975]. Thus it was a direct outgrowth of Floyd's original approach to proving properties of sequential programs.

At about the same time, Tony Hoare [1972] extended his partial correctness logic for sequential programs to include inference rules for concurrency and synchronization, with synchronization specified by conditional critical regions (the topic of Chapter 5). However, that logic was incomplete since assertions in one process could not reference variables in another, and global invariants could not reference local variables.

Susan Owicki, in a dissertation supervised by David Gries, was the first to develop a complete logic for proving partial correctness properties of concurrent programs [Owicki 1975, Owicki & Gries 1976]. The logic covered concurrency and synchronization by means of shared variables, semaphores, or conditional critical regions. That work also introduced and formalized the concept of interference freedom and illustrated several of the techniques for avoiding interference described in Section 2.4. (The technique of using disjoint sets of variables first appeared in a different context in Bernstein [1966].) On a personal note, the author had the good fortune to be at Cornell while this research was being done.

The need in a Hoare-style programming logic for auxiliary variables that record hidden parts of the program state was independently recognized by many people. The first paper that employs them is Clint [1973]. (Clint called them ghost variables.) They were later used in Hoare [1975], Owicki [1975] and Owicki and Gries [1976]. Owicki was the first to formalize an inference rule for deleting them. Recently, however, McCurley [1989] has shown that Auxiliary Variable Rule (2.22) is unsound if assignments to auxiliary variables might cause a program to abort; e.g. due to an array subscript being out of bounds or division by zero.

Lamport [1977a] later formulated an alternative way to reason about the program counter using three control predicates to indicate whether a program is at the beginning of (*at*), inside (*in*), or immediately after (*after*) a statement. Although auxiliary variables and control predicates are equally powerful for reasoning about the program counter, Lamport [1988] argues that control predicates are sometimes easier to use. However, auxiliary variables are often needed to reason about other aspects of the hidden state, such as the contents of message queues.

The Owicki-Gries work addresses only three safety properties: partial correctness, mutual exclusion, and absence of deadlock. Lamport independently developed an idea similar to interference freedom—monotone assertions—as part of a general method for proving both safety and liveness properties [Lamport 1977a]. That paper in fact introduced the terms *safety* and *liveness*. Methods (2.23) and (2.24) for proving safety properties are based on Lamport's method. The Exclusion of Configurations method (2.25) is due to Schneider [Schneider & Andrews 1986]; it is a generalization of the Owicki-Gries method for proving mutual exclusion and absence of deadlock.

In 1980, Lamport [1980] developed Generalized Hoare Logic (GHL), which permits one to verify arbitrary safety properties of concurrent programs using a Hoare-style logic. A GHL formula describes a program in terms of an invariant rather than as a relation between a pre- and postcondition. A triple is in fact a special case of a GHL formula. The relations between GHL, Floyd's original method, and the Owicki-Gries method are described in Lamport and Schneider [1984].

Lamport [1990] has also recently developed two predicate transformers for concurrency: *win* (weakest invariant) and *sin* (strongest invariant). This work ties together aspects of weakest preconditions and global invariants. As an example, Lamport's paper presents a correctness proof of the bakery algorithm for solving the critical section problem. (The algorithm is presented in Section 3.4.)

A book by Nissim Francez [1986] contains a thorough discussion of fairness and its relation to termination, synchronization, and guard evaluation. The terminology for *unconditionally*, *weakly*, and *strongly fair* schedulers comes from that book, which contains an extensive bibliography. These scheduling policies were first defined and formalized in Lehman et al. [1981], although with somewhat different terminology.

Programming Logic *PL* is a logic for proving safety properties. One way to construct formal proofs of liveness properties is to extend *PL* with two temporal operators: henceforth and eventually. These enable one to make assertions about sequences of states and hence about the future. Such a *temporal logic* was first introduced by Amir Pnueli [1977]. Owicki and Lamport [1982] show how to use temporal logic and invariants to prove liveness properties of concurrent programs. Schneider [1987] gives formal definitions of safety and liveness properties and shows how to specify them in Predicate Logic.

All texts on operating systems contain some coverage of concurrent programming, especially as it applies to that application. In addition, several survey papers and textbooks are devoted to aspects of concurrent programming. Horning and Randell [1973] give several formalizations of the notion of process and discuss ways of controlling process interaction. Brinch Hansen [1972] and Presser [1975] illustrate the use of various synchronization primitives by giving solutions to some standard concurrent programming problems. Difficulties associated with organizing an operating system as a concurrent program are described in Atwood [1976]. A general survey of concurrent programming concepts and the most important language notations (as of 1983) appears in Andrews and Schneider [1983]. Language mechanisms specifically suited for distributed programming—the subject of Part III of this text—are surveyed in Bal et al. [1989].

Per Brinch Hansen [1977] wrote the first textbook devoted exclusively to concurrent programming. It describes the design of three operating systems and contains Concurrent Pascal programs for them. Holt et al. [1978] and its successor Holt [1983] cover those aspects of concurrent programming most closely related to operating systems. Another undergraduate text [Ben-Ari 1982] covers important synchronization mechanisms and shows how to construct informal correctness proofs for concurrent programs. Fillman and Friedman [1984] cover models, languages, and heuristics for concurrent programming. Perrott [1987] surveys a number of languages for parallel programming. Whiddet [1987] and Burstard et al. [1988] examine engineering aspects of constructing concurrent programs. Gehani and McGettrick [1988] is an anthology of twenty-four important papers on concurrent programming. Finally, several advanced texts discuss formal logics and methodologies for concurrent programs: Barringer [1985] surveys verification techniques; Chandy and Misra [1988] present Unity, an architecture-independent approach to parallel program design; de Bakker et al. [1986] contains a collection of survey articles and tutorials on formal aspects of concurrency; and Hoare [1985] discusses the theory of communicating sequential processes. Several additional books are in preparation.

The titles of the papers and books cited above reveal a curious evolution of terminology. In the 1960s, programs containing multiple processes were called concurrent programs. Beginning in the 1970s, many started to call them *parallel programs* since that phrase better indicates how such programs are executed. However, with the advent of parallel processing machines in the 1980s, the term parallel program has come to be used mainly to refer to programs that are specifically intended for execution on machines containing numerous processors. Thus, the field has come full circle, and the term *concurrent program* is once again used to refer to any program that contains multiple processes, independent of how the program is executed. Parallel programs are a subclass of concurrent programs. *Distributed programs* are another subclass—those that can be executed on processors that do not share memory. To make matters even more confusing, parallel programs for distributed-memory machines such as hypercubes are in fact distributed programs! Whatever the terminology, however, the essential concepts are the same: processes, communication, and synchronization.

Exercises

2.1   Consider a concurrent program with the following two processes:

$$P1::\ x := x + 1 \qquad P2::\ x := x + 2$$
$$ y := y + x \qquad y := y - x$$

Assume that x and y are initially 0.

(a) Suppose the above assignment statements are implemented by single machine instructions and hence are atomic. How many possible histories are there? What are the possible final values of x and y?

(b) Suppose each assignment statement is implemented by three atomic actions that load a register, add or subtract a value from that register, then store the result. How many possible histories are there now? What are the possible final values of x and y?

2.2   Consider the concurrent program:

$$\textbf{var}\ u := 0, v := 1, w := 2, x : \textbf{int}$$
$$\textbf{co}\ x := u + v + w\ /\!/\ u := 3\ /\!/\ v := 4\ /\!/\ w := 5\ \textbf{oc}$$

Assuming that the atomic actions are reading and writing individual variables, what are the possible final values of x?

2.3   Suppose a concurrent program contains N processes and each process executes M distinct atomic actions. Prove that

$$\frac{(N\,M)!}{(M!)^N}$$

different histories (interleavings) are possible.

2.4   In many cases, a for-all statement (**fa**) and a concurrent statement (**co**) are partially equivalent, as defined in (1.17). Determine a set of conditions on the body of a for-all statement such that it is partially equivalent to the corresponding concurrent statement. For example,

$$\textbf{fa } i := 1 \textbf{ to } n \rightarrow a[i] := 0 \textbf{ fa}$$

is partially equivalent to:

$$\textbf{co } i := 1 \textbf{ to } n \rightarrow a[i] := 0 \textbf{ oc}$$

Your set of conditions should be ones that could be checked by a compiler, but they should be as general as possible.

2.5 For each of the following, show whether the precondition and statement

$$\{ x \geq 4 \} \ \langle x := x - 4 \rangle$$

interferes with the given triple.

(a) $\{ x \geq 0 \} \ \langle x := x + 5 \rangle \ \{ x \geq 5 \}$

(b) $\{ x \geq 0 \} \ \langle x := x + 5 \rangle \ \{ x \geq 0 \}$

(c) $\{ x \geq 10 \} \ \langle x := x + 5 \rangle \ \{ x \geq 11 \}$

(d) $\{ x \geq 10 \} \ \langle x := x + 5 \rangle \ \{ x \geq 12 \}$

(e) $\{ x \text{ is odd} \} \ \langle x := x + 5 \rangle \ \{ x \text{ is even} \}$

(f) $\{ x \text{ is odd} \} \ \langle y := x + 1 \rangle \ \{ y \text{ is even} \}$

(g) $\{ y \text{ is odd} \} \ \langle y := y + 1 \rangle \ \{ y \text{ is even} \}$

(h) $\{ x \text{ is a multiple of } 3 \} \ y := x \ \{ y \text{ is a multiple of } 3 \}$

2.6 Consider the program:

$$\textbf{var } x, y : \textbf{int}$$
$$S: \ \textbf{co } x := x - 1; x := x + 1 \ /\!/ \ y := y + 1; y := y - 1 \textbf{ oc}$$

Prove that $\{ x = y \} \ S \ \{ x = y \}$ is a theorem. Show all non-interference proofs in detail.

2.7 Consider the program:

$$\textbf{var } x := 0$$
$$S: \ \textbf{co } \langle x := x + 2 \rangle \ /\!/ \ \langle x := x + 3 \rangle \ /\!/ \ \langle x := x + 4 \rangle \textbf{ oc}$$

Using the technique of weakened assertions, prove that $\{ x = 0 \} \ S \ \{ x = 9 \}$ is a theorem.

2.8 (a) Show how to simulate the general iterative statement **do** using the concurrent statement **co** to evaluate all guards in parallel and non-deterministically select a true guard, if there is one. Other statements you may use are assignment, **if**, and single-guard **do** statements. You may not use **await** statements.

(b) Develop a complete proof outline that shows that your implementation correctly simulates **do**. Demonstrate that the concurrent processes are interference-free.

2.9 Using **co** to examine all array elements in parallel, write a program that sets boolean variable *allzero* to true if integer array $a[1:n]$ contains all zeroes; otherwise, the program should set *allzero* to false.

2.10 (a) Develop a program to find the maximum value in integer array $a[1:n]$ by searching even and odd subscripts of a in parallel.

(b) Develop a complete proof outline that demonstrates that your solution is partially correct. Demonstrate that the processes are interference-free.

2.11 Given are three integer-valued functions: $f(i)$, $g(j)$, and $h(k)$. The domain of each function is the non-negative integers. The range of each is non-decreasing for increasing values of its arguments; e.g., $f(i) \leq f(i+1)$ for all $i \geq 0$. There is at least one value common to the range of the three functions. (This has been called the earliest common meeting time problem, with the ranges of the functions being the times at which three people can meet.)

(a) Write a concurrent program to set i, j, and k to the smallest integers such that $f(i) = g(j) = h(k)$. Use **co** to do comparisons in parallel.

(b) Develop a complete proof outline to show that your solution is partially correct. Demonstrate that the concurrent processes are interference-free.

2.12 Assume that $\{ P_1 \} S_1 \{ Q_1 \}$ and $\{ P_2 \} S_2 \{ Q_2 \}$ are both theorems and that they are interference-free. Prove that

$$\textbf{co } S_1 \; / \! / \; S_2 \textbf{ oc}$$

is partially equivalent both to $S_1; S_2$ and to $S_2; S_1$.

2.13 Assume that $\{ P_1 \} S_1 \{ Q_1 \}$ and $\{ P_2 \} S_2 \{ Q_2 \}$ are both theorems and that they are interference-free. Assume that S_1 contains an **await** statement $\langle \textbf{ await } B \rightarrow T \rangle$. Let S_1' be S_1 with the **await** statement replaced by:

$$\textbf{do not } B \rightarrow \textbf{skip od}; T$$

Answer the following as independent questions.

(a) Will $\{ P_1 \} S_1' \{ Q_1 \}$ still be a theorem? Carefully explain your answer. Is it always a theorem? Sometimes? Never?

(b) Will $\{ P_1 \} S_1' \{ Q_1 \}$ and $\{ P_2 \} S_2 \{ Q_2 \}$ still be interference-free? Again, carefully explain your answer. Will they always be interference-free? Sometimes? Never?

2.14 Consider the program:

$$\textbf{co } \langle \textbf{ await } x \geq 3 \rightarrow x := x - 3 \rangle$$
$$/ \! / \; \langle \textbf{ await } x \geq 2 \rightarrow x := x - 2 \rangle$$
$$/ \! / \; \langle \textbf{ await } x = 1 \rightarrow x := x + 5 \rangle$$
$$\textbf{oc}$$

Let P be a predicate that characterizes the weakest deadlock-free precondition for the program, i.e., the largest set of states such that, if the program is begun in a state satisfying P, then it will terminate if scheduling is weakly fair. Determine P. Explain your answer.

92   Concurrency and Synchronization

2.15 Consider the program:

> **var** s : **int** := 1, i : **int**
> **co** i := 1 **to** 2 → **do** true → ⟨ **await** $s > 0 \to s := s - 1$ ⟩
> $\qquad\qquad\qquad\qquad\qquad S_i$
> $\qquad\qquad\qquad\qquad\qquad ⟨\, s := s + 1 \,⟩$
> $\qquad\qquad$**od**
> **oc**

Above, S_i is a statement list that is assumed not to modify shared variable s.

(a) Develop complete proof outlines for the two processes. Demonstrate that the proofs of the processes are interference-free. Then use the proof outlines and the method of Exclusion of Configurations (2.25) to show that S_1 and S_2 cannot execute at the same time and that the program is deadlock-free. (Hint: You will need to introduce auxiliary variables to the program and proof outlines.)

(b) What scheduling policy is required to ensure that a process delayed at its first **await** statement will eventually be able to proceed? Explain.

2.16 Using the method of Exclusion of Configurations (2.25), prove that the *Producer* and *Consumer* processes in Figure 2.3 cannot access *buf* at the same time.

2.17 Consider the following solution to the array copy problem:

> **var** buf : **int**, $empty$: **bool** := true, $full$: **bool** := false
> *Producer*:: **var** $a[1{:}n]$: **int**, p : **int** := 1
> $\qquad\qquad$**do** $p \le n$ → ⟨ **await** $empty \to empty$:= false ⟩
> $\qquad\qquad\qquad\quad buf := a[p];\ full$:= true
> $\qquad\qquad\qquad\quad p := p + 1$
> $\qquad$**od**
> *Consumer*:: **var** $b[1{:}n]$: **int**, c : **int** := 1
> $\qquad\qquad$**do** $c \le n$ → ⟨ **await** $full \to full$:= false ⟩
> $\qquad\qquad\qquad\quad b[c] := buf;\ empty$:= true
> $\qquad\qquad\qquad\quad c := c + 1$
> $\qquad$**od**

Prove that access to *buf* is mutually exclusive and that the program is deadlock-free. Do so by first developing complete, interference-free proof outlines for each process. Use the technique of a global invariant in developing your proof outlines; you will also want to use some auxiliary variables (two boolean variables are sufficient).

2.18 Quicksort is a recursive sorting method that works as follows. Given array $a[1{:}n]$, first select a partition value, e.g., $a[1]$. Second, partition the elements of a into two smaller arrays, *left* and *right*, such that all elements in *left* are less than $a[1]$ and all elements in *right* are greater than or equal to $a[1]$. Third, recursively sort *left* and *right*.

Write a recursive quicksort procedure; use parallelism whenever possible. Give a proof outline for the procedure body. Show clearly what you assume to be true before and after each recursive call. (You might want to look at the inference rules for procedures, which are given in Chapter 6.)

2.19 The 8-queens problem is concerned with placing 8 queens on a chess board in such a way that none can attack another. One queen can attack another if they are in the same row or column or are on the same diagonal.

Write a parallel program to generate all 92 solutions to the 8-queens problem. (Hint: Use a recursive procedure to try queen placements and a second procedure to check whether a given placement is acceptable.) Give a proof outline for your program. Show clearly what you assume to be true at the start and end of each procedure body and before and after each recursive call.

2.20 The stable marriage problem is the following. Let *Man* and *Woman* each be arrays of n processes. Each man ranks the women from 1 to n, and each woman ranks the men from 1 to n. A *pairing* is a one-to-one correspondence of men and women. A pairing is *stable* if, for two men m_1 and m_2 and their paired women w_1 and w_2, both the following conditions are satisfied:

(1) m_1 ranks w_1 higher than w_2, or w_2 ranks m_2 higher than m_1; and

(2) m_2 ranks w_2 higher than w_1, or w_1 ranks m_1 higher than m_2.

Put differently, a pairing is unstable if a man and woman would both prefer each other to their current pair. A solution to the stable marriage problem is a set of n pairings, all of which are stable.

Give a predicate that specifies the goal, and then write a parallel program to solve the stable marriage problem. Be sure to explain your solution strategy. Also give a proof outline for your solution. At a minimum, include pre- and postconditions for each process and invariants for each loop.

2.21 The quadrature problem is to approximate the area under a curve, i.e., to approximate the integral of a function. Given is a continuous, non-negative function $f(x)$ and two endpoints l and r. The problem is to compute the area of the region bounded by $f(x)$, the x axis, and the vertical lines through l and r. The typical way to solve the problem is to subdivide the regions into a number of smaller ones, use something like a trapezoid to approximate the area of each smaller region, and then sum the areas of the smaller regions.

Write a recursive function that implements a parallel, adaptive solution to the quadrature problem. Also give a proof outline for the procedure body. Show clearly what you assume to be true before and after each recursive call. The function should have four arguments: two points a and b and two function values $f(a)$ and $f(b)$. It first computes the midpoint between a and b, then computes three areas: from a to m, m to b, and a to b. If the sum of the smaller two areas is within EPSILON of the larger, the function returns the area. Otherwise it recursively and in parallel computes the areas of the smaller regions. Assume EPSILON is a global constant.

2.22 Gaussian elimination with partial pivoting is a method for reducing real matrix $m[1{:}n, 1{:}n]$ to upper-triangular form. It involves iterating across the columns of m and zeroing out the elements in the column below the diagonal element $m[d, d]$. This is done by performing the following three steps for each column.

First, select a pivot element, which is the element in column d having the largest absolute value. Second, swap row d and the row containing the pivot element. Finally, for each row r below the new diagonal row, subtract a multiple of row d from row r. The multiple to use for row r is $m[r, d]/m[d, d]$; subtracting this multiple of row d has the effect of setting $m[r, d]$ to zero.

Write a program that implements the above algorithm. Use parallelism whenever possible. Assume every divisor is non-zero; i.e., assume the matrix is non-singular. Also give a proof outline for your program. Show enough detail to provide convincing evidence that your program is correct.

## PART II

Shared Variables

Loops are the most complex statements in sequential programs. As described in Chapter 1, the key to developing and understanding a loop is to come up with a loop invariant. Getting a suitable invariant involves focusing on what does not change each time the loop is executed. The same viewpoint provides a useful basis for solving synchronization problems, which are the key problems that arise in concurrent programs.

The role of synchronization is to avoid interference, either by making sets of statements atomic and thus hiding intermediate states (mutual exclusion) or by delaying a process until a required condition holds (condition synchronization). We can always avoid interference by using **await** statements, as described in Section 2.4. However, **await** statements in their full generality cannot be implemented efficiently. In this part of the text we show how to use lower-level synchronization primitives that can be implemented efficiently in hardware or software. Since will be using lower-level primitives, we need to use the other techniques introduced in Section 2.4: disjoint variables, weakened assertions, and global invariants. Disjoint variables and global invariants are the most generally useful of these techniques. Global invariants also aid in proving safety properties, as described in (2.24).

A major purpose of Part II is to illustrate a method for solving synchronization problems in a systematic way. The basis of the method is to view processes as *invariant maintainers*. In particular, for each synchronization problem we define a global invariant that characterizes key relations between global and local variables. With respect to synchronization, the role of each process is then to ensure that the invariant is maintained. We will also partition variables used to solve different problems into disjoint sets, with each set having its own invariant. Our solution method consists of the following four four steps:

1. Define the Problem Precisely. Identify the processes and specify the synchronization problem. Introduce variables as needed and write a predicate that specifies the invariant property that is to be maintained.

2. Outline a Solution. Annotate the processes with assignments to the variables. Initialize the variables so the invariant is initially true. Enclose sequences of assignments in angle brackets when they must be executed atomically in order for the variables to satisfy their definition.

3. Ensure the Invariant. When necessary, guard the unconditional atomic actions to ensure that each action maintains the global invariant. Given action S and intended invariant I, this involves computing $wp(S, I)$ to determine the set of states from which execution of S is guaranteed to terminate with I true. Since S is a sequence of assignment statements, it will terminate once begun.

4. Implement the Atomic Actions. Transform the atomic actions resulting from steps 2 and 3 into code that employs only sequential statements and available synchronization primitives.

The first three steps are essentially independent of the synchronization primitives that are available. The starting point is coming up with an appropriate invariant. Since all interesting safety properties can be expressed as a predicate on program states, this suggests two ways to come up with an invariant: specify a predicate *BAD* that characterizes a bad state, then use ¬*BAD* as the global invariant; or directly specify a predicate *GOOD* that characterizes good states and use it as the invariant.

Given an invariant, the second and third steps are essentially mechanical. The creative step is the last one, which involves using some specific synchronization mechanism to implement the atomic actions. How one does this depends on the synchronization mechanism that is employed. Different mechanisms give rise to different programming techniques.

In this part of the book, we show how to solve synchronization problems for programs in which processes communicate by means of shared variables. A variety of synchronization mechanisms are examined, and the above solution method is applied to a variety of different problems. Chapter 3 examines the use of fine-grained atomic actions that are directly implemented by machine instructions. Chapters 4 to 6 describe semaphores, conditional critical regions, and monitors. Throughout, we introduce numerous interesting and practical problems, give techniques for coming up with global invariants, illustrate important programming paradigms, discuss implementation issues, and identify tradeoffs between the various synchronization mechanisms.

## CHAPTER 3

Fine-Grained Synchronization

Recall that *busy waiting* is a form of synchronization in which a process repeatedly checks a condition until it becomes true. The virtue of busy waiting synchronization is that we can implement it using only the machine instructions available on contemporary processors. Although busy waiting is inefficient when processes are executed by multiprogramming, it can be quite acceptable and efficient when each process executes on its own processor. This is possible in multiprocessors, which are becoming increasingly common. Hardware itself also employs busy waiting synchronization; e.g., it is used to synchronize data transfers on memory busses and local networks.

This chapter examines several practical problems and shows how to solve them using busy waiting. The first is the classic critical section problem. We develop four solutions that use different techniques and have different properties; the techniques are also applicable to other problems. Solutions to the critical section problem are also important since they can be used to implement **await** statements and hence arbitrary atomic actions. We show how to do this at the end of Section 3.1.

Sections 3.5 and 3.6 examine an interesting class of parallel programs and an associated synchronization mechanism. Many problems can be solved by parallel iterative algorithms in which several processes repeatedly manipulate a shared array. This kind of algorithm is called a *data parallel algorithm* since the shared data is manipulated in parallel. In such an algorithm, each iteration typically depends on the results of the previous iteration. Hence, at the end of an iteration, every process needs to wait for the others before beginning the next iteration. This kind of synchronization point is called a *barrier*. We show how to implement barrier synchronization in Section 3.5 and then give several examples of data parallel algorithms in

Section 3.6. In Section 3.6 we also describe synchronous multiprocessors (SIMD machines), which are especially suited to implementing data parallel algorithms. This is because SIMD machines execute instructions in lock step on every processor; hence, they provide automatic barrier synchronization.

Section 3.7 examines the problem of garbage collection in a list-processing environment and develops a parallel garbage-collection algorithm that has essentially no synchronization overhead. The solution is quite subtle; its derivation illustrates the importance of employing a systematic problem-solving method.

We conclude the chapter by showing how to implement processes using a software kernel. First we present a single-processor kernel. Then we extend that kernel to allow processes to execute concurrently on a shared-memory multiprocessor. The multiprocessor kernel employs critical section protocols, such as those developed earlier in the chapter, to protect kernel data structures. We also describe some of the performance implications of multiprocessors, such as the effects of caches.

3.1 The Critical Section Problem

The *critical section* problem is one of the classic concurrent programming problems. It was the first problem to be studied extensively and remains of interest since solutions can be used to implement arbitrary **await** statements. This section defines the problem and systematically develops a solution. Then we show how to use the solution to implement both unconditional and conditional atomic actions.

In the critical section problem, n processes repeatedly execute a critical section of code, then a non-critical section. The critical section is preceded by an entry protocol and followed by an exit protocol.

(3.1) $P[i: 1..n]$:: **do** true →
                        entry protocol
                        critical section
                        exit protocol
                        non-critical section
          od

Each critical section is a sequence of statements that access some shared object. Each non-critical section is another sequence of statements. We assume that a process that enters its critical section will eventually exit; thus, a process may terminate only outside its critical section. Our task is to design entry and exit protocols that satisfy the following four properties.

(3.2)   **Mutual Exclusion.** At most one process at a time is executing its critical section.

(3.3)   **Absence of Deadlock.** If two or more processes are trying to enter their critical sections, at least one will succeed.

(3.4)   **Absence of Unnecessary Delay.** If a process is trying to enter its critical section and the other processes are executing their non-critical sections or have terminated, the first process is not prevented from entering its critical section.

(3.5)   **Eventual Entry.** A process that is attempting to enter its critical section will eventually succeed.

The first property is a safety property, with the bad state being one in which two processes are in their critical section. In a busy-waiting solution, (3.3) is a liveness property called *absence of livelock*. This is because processes never block—they are alive, but they may loop forever trying to make progress. (If processes block while waiting to enter their critical section, (3.3) is a safety property.) The third property is a safety property, the bad state being one in which the one process cannot proceed. The last property is a liveness property since it depends on the scheduling policy.

In this section, we develop a solution that satisfies the first three properties. This is sufficient for most applications since it is highly unlikely that a process would not eventually be able to enter its critical section. The next two sections develop additional critical section protocols that satisfy all four properties.

A trivial way to solve the problem is to enclose each critical section in angle brackets, i.e., use unconditional **await** statements. Mutual exclusion follows immediately from the semantics of angle brackets. The other three properties would be satisfied if scheduling is unconditionally fair since that scheduling policy ensures that a process attempting to execute the atomic action corresponding to its critical section would eventually get to do so, no matter what the other processes did. However, this "solution" begs the issue of how to implement angle brackets.

A Coarse-Grained Solution

For the critical section problem, all four properties are important, but mutual exclusion is the most critical. Thus, we focus on it first and then consider how also to achieve the other properties.

To specify the mutual exclusion property, we need to have some way to indicate that a process is in its critical section. Thus, we need to introduce additional variables. To simplify notation, we develop a solution for two processes; the solution generalizes readily to one for n processes.

var *in1* := false, *in2* := false
{ *MUTEX*: ¬(*in1* ∧ *in2*) }
P1:: **do** true → *in1* := true   # entry protocol
                     critical section
                     in1 := false   # exit protocol
                     non-critical section
       od
P2:: **do** true → *in2* := true   # entry protocol
                     critical section
                     in2 := false   # exit protocol
                     non-critical section
       od

Figure 3.1. Critical section problem: solution outline.

Let *in1* and *in2* be boolean variables. When process *P1* is in its critical section, *in1* is true; otherwise *in1* is false. Process *P2* and *in2* are related similarly. Then we can specify the mutual exclusion property by:

$$MUTEX: \neg(in1 \wedge in2)$$

This predicate has the form of a safety property, where the bad thing is that both *in1* and *in2* are true. Adding these new variables to (3.1) so they satisfy their definition, we have the solution outline shown in Figure 3.1.

The program in Figure 3.1 clearly does not yet solve the problem. To ensure that *MUTEX* is invariant, we need it true before and after each assignment to *in1* or *in2*. From the initial values assigned to these variables, *MUTEX* is true initially. Now consider the entry protocol in *P1*. If *MUTEX* is to be true after this assignment, before the assignment the state must satisfy:

$$wp(in1 := true, MUTEX) \ = \ \neg(true \wedge in2) \ = \ \neg in2$$

Hence, we need to strengthen the entry protocol in *P1* by replacing the unconditional assignment by the conditional atomic action:

$$\langle \textbf{await not } in2 \rightarrow in1 := true \rangle$$

The processes are symmetric, so we use the same kind of conditional atomic action for the entry protocol for *P2*.

var *in1* := false; *in2* := false
{ *MUTEX*: ¬(*in1* ∧ *in2*) }
P1:: **do** true → { *MUTEX* ∧ ¬*in1* }
                  ⟨ **await not** *in2* → *in1* := true ⟩   # entry protocol
                  { *MUTEX* ∧ *in1* }
                  critical section
                  in1 := false   # exit protocol
                  { *MUTEX* ∧ ¬*in1* }
                  non-critical section
      od
P2:: **do** true → { *MUTEX* ∧ ¬*in2* }
                  ⟨ **await not** *in1* → *in2* := true ⟩   # entry protocol
                  { *MUTEX* ∧ *in2* }
                  critical section
                  in2 := false   # exit protocol
                  { *MUTEX* ∧ ¬*in2* }
                  non-critical section
      od

Figure 3.2. Critical section problem: coarse-grained solution.

What then about the exit protocols? In general, it is never necessary to delay when leaving a critical section. More formally, if *MUTEX* is to be true after the exit protocol in *P1*, the precondition of the exit protocol must satisfy:

$$wp(in1 := \text{false}, MUTEX) \ = \ \neg(\text{false} \wedge in2) \ = \ true$$

This is, of course, satisfied by every state. The same situation exists for the exit protocol for *P2*. Thus, we do not need to guard the exit protocols.

Replacing the entry protocols in Figure 3.1 by conditional atomic actions, we have the coarse-grained solution and proof outline shown in Figure 3.2. By construction, the solution satisfies the mutual exclusion property. Absence of deadlock and unnecessary delay follow from the method of Exclusion of Configurations (2.25). If the processes are deadlocked, each is trying to enter its critical section but cannot do so. This means the preconditions of the entry protocols are both true, but neither guard is true. Thus, the following predicate characterizes a deadlock state:

$$\neg in1 \wedge in2 \wedge \neg in2 \wedge in1$$

Since this predicate is false, deadlock cannot occur in the above program.

var *lock* := false

P1:: **do** true → ⟨ **await not** *lock* → *lock* := true ⟩   # entry protocol
                  critical section
                  lock := false   # exit protocol
                  non-critical section
    od

P2:: **do** true → ⟨ **await not** *lock* → *lock* := true ⟩   # entry protocol
                  critical section
                  lock := false   # exit protocol
                  non-critical section
    od

Figure 3.3. Critical section solution using locks.

Next consider absence of unnecessary delay. If process *P1* is outside its critical section or has terminated, then *in1* is false. If *P2* is trying to enter its critical section but is unable to do so, then the guard in its entry protocol must be false. Since

$$\neg in1 \wedge in1 = false$$

P2 cannot be delayed unnecessarily. The analogous situation holds for *P1*.

Finally, consider the liveness property that a process trying to enter its critical section eventually is able to do so. If *P1* is trying to enter but cannot, *P2* is in its critical section and hence *in2* is true. By the assumption that a process in its critical section eventually exits, *in2* will eventually become false and hence *P1*'s entry guard will become true. If *P1* is still not allowed entry, it is either because the scheduler is unfair or because *P2* again gains entry to its critical section. In the latter situation, the above scenario repeats, so eventually *in2* becomes false. Thus, *in2* becomes true infinitely often—or *P2* halts, in which case *in2* becomes and remains true. A strongly fair scheduling policy is sufficient to ensure that *P1* gains entry in either case. The argument that *P2* eventually gains entry is symmetric.

Spin Locks: A Fine-Grained Solution

The coarse-grained solution in Figure 3.2 employs two variables. To generalize the solution to *n* processes, we would have to use *n* variables. However, there are only two states we are interested in: some process is in its critical section or no process is. One variable is sufficient to distinguish between these two states, independent of the number of processes.

var *lock* := false
P1:: **var** *cc* : **bool**
    do true → *TS(lock, cc)*   # entry protocol
          do *cc* → *TS(lock, cc)* **od**
          critical section
          lock := false   # exit protocol
          non-critical section
    od
P2:: **var** *cc* : **bool**
    do true → *TS(lock, cc)*   # entry protocol
          do *cc* → *TS(lock, cc)* **od**
          critical section
          lock := false   # exit protocol
          non-critical section
    od

Figure 3.4. Critical section solution using test-and-set.

For this problem, let *lock* be a boolean variable that indicates when a process is in a critical section. That is, *lock* is true when either *in1* or *in2* is true, and is false otherwise:

$$lock = (in1 \lor in2)$$

Using *lock* in place of *in1* and *in2*, the entry and exit protocols in Figure 3.2 can be implemented as shown in Figure 3.3.

The significance of this change of variables is that almost all machines, especially multiprocessors, have some special instruction that can be used to implement the conditional atomic actions in Figure 3.3. Examples are Test-and-Set, Fetch-and-Add, and Compare-and-Swap. Here we define and use Test-and-Set (*TS*); the other two are defined later in the chapter.

The *TS* instruction takes two boolean arguments: a shared *lock* and a local condition code *cc*. As an atomic action, *TS* sets *cc* to the value of *lock*, then sets *lock* to true:

(3.6)   *TS(lock, cc)*: ⟨ *cc* := *lock*; *lock* := true ⟩

Using *TS*, we can implement the coarse-grained solution in Figure 3.3 by the algorithm in Figure 3.4. In particular, we replace the conditional atomic actions in Figure 3.3 by loops that do not terminate until *lock* is false, and hence *TS* sets *cc* to false.* If both processes are trying to enter their critical section, only one can succeed in being the first to set *lock* true; hence, only one will terminate its entry protocol. When a lock variable is used in this way, it is typically called a *spin lock* since the processes spin while waiting for the lock to be cleared.

The programs in both Figures 3.3 and 3.4 correctly solve the critical section problem. Mutual exclusion is ensured because, as noted, only one of the two processes can see that *lock* is false. Absence of deadlock results from the fact that, if both processes are in their entry protocols, *lock* is false, and hence one of the processes will succeed in entering its critical section. Unnecessary delay is avoided because, if both processes are outside their critical section, *lock* is false, and hence one can successfully enter if the other is executing its non-critical section or has terminated. In addition, a process trying to enter its critical section will eventually succeed if scheduling is strongly fair since *lock* will become true infinitely often (or will become and remain true).

The solution in Figure 3.4 has one additional attribute that the solution in Figure 3.2 does not have: It solves the critical section problem for any number of processes, not just two. This is because there are only two states of interest, independent of the number of processes. Thus, any number of processes could share *lock* and execute the same protocols.

A solution to the critical section problem similar to the one in Figure 3.4 can be employed on any machine that has some instruction that tests and alters a shared variable as a single atomic action. For example, some machines have an increment instruction that increments an integer value and also sets a condition code indicating whether the result is positive or non-negative. Using this instruction, the entry protocol can be based on the transition from zero to one. The exercises consider several representative instructions. (This kind of question is a favorite of exam writers!) One thing to remember when constructing a busy waiting solution to the critical section problem is that in most cases the exit protocol should return the shared variables to their initial state. In Figure 3.2, this is a state in which *in1* and *in2* are both false; in Figures 3.3 and 3.4, this is a state in which *lock* is false.

Although the solution in Figure 3.4 is correct, experiments on multiprocessors have shown that it can lead to poor performance if several processes are competing for access to a critical section. This is because *lock* is a shared variable and every delayed process continuously references it. This "hot spot" causes *memory contention*, which degrades the performance of memory units and processor-memory interconnection networks.

---

*The *TS* instruction is often a function in which *cc* is the return value. In this case, *TS* can be called just once in the loop guard in each process. We have not defined or used *TS* in this way since our programming notation and logic do not permit side-effects in guard evaluation.

In addition, the *TS* instruction writes into *lock* every time it is executed, even when *lock*'s value does not change. Since most shared-memory multiprocessors employ caches to reduce traffic to primary memory, this makes *TS* significantly more expensive than an instruction that merely reads a shared variable. (When a value is written by one processor, the caches on other processors might need to be invalidated or altered.) Cache invalidation overhead can be reduced by modifying the entry protocol to use a test-and-test-and-set protocol as follows:

(3.7)   **do** *lock* → **skip od**   # spin while lock is set
            TS(*lock*, *cc*)
            do *cc* → **do** *lock* → **skip**   # spin again
                   TS(*lock*, *cc*)
            od

Here, a process merely examines *lock* until there is the possibility that *TS* can succeed. Since *lock* is only examined in the two additional loops, its value can be read from a local cache without affecting other processors. Memory contention is still a problem, however. When *lock* is cleared, at least one and possibly all delayed processes will execute *TS*, even though only one can proceed. The next section presents a way to reduce memory contention; the exercises consider additional techniques.

Implementing Await Statements

Any solution to the critical section problem can be used to implement an unconditional atomic action ⟨ *S* ⟩ by hiding internal control points from other processes. Let CSenter be a critical section entry protocol, and let CSexit be the corresponding exit protocol. Then ⟨ *S* ⟩ can be implemented by:

    CSenter
    S
    CSexit

This assumes that critical sections in all processes that examine variables altered in *S* are also protected by similar entry and exit protocols. In essence, ⟨ is replaced by CSenter, and ⟩ is replaced by CSexit.

The above code skeleton can also be used as a building block to implement any conditional atomic action ⟨ **await** *B* → *S* ⟩. Recall that a conditional atomic action delays the executing process until *B* is true, then executes *S*. Also, *B* must be true when execution of *S* begins. To ensure that the entire action is atomic, we can use a critical section protocol to hide intermediate states in *S*. We can then use a loop to repeatedly test *B* until it is true. Thus, a code skeleton for implementing ⟨ **await** *B* → *S* ⟩ is:

CSenter
do not $B \rightarrow$? **od**
S
CSexit

Here we assume that critical sections in all processes that alter variables referenced in B or S or that reference variables altered in S are protected by similar entry and exit protocols.

The remaining concern is how to implement the loop body. If the body is executed, B was false. Hence, the only way B will become true is if some other process alters a variable referenced in B. Since we assume that any statement in another process that alters a variable referenced in B must be in a critical section, we have to exit the critical section while waiting for B to become true. But to ensure atomicity of the evaluation of B and execution of S, we must reenter the critical section before reevaluating B. Hence a candidate refinement of the above protocol is:

(3.8)   CSenter
do not $B \rightarrow$ CSexit; CSenter **od**
S
CSexit

This implementation preserves the semantics of conditional atomic actions, assuming the critical section protocols guarantee mutual exclusion. If scheduling is weakly fair, the process executing (3.8) will eventually terminate the loop, assuming B eventually becomes true and remains true. Weakly fair scheduling is also sufficient to ensure eventual entry into a critical section. If scheduling is strongly fair, the loop will terminate if B becomes true infinitely often.

Although (3.8) is correct, it is inefficient—even granting that busy waiting is often inefficient in any event. This is because a process executing (3.8) is spinning in a "hard" loop—continuously exiting, then reentering its critical section—even though it cannot possibly proceed until at least some other process alters a variable referenced in B. This leads to memory contention since every delayed process continuously accesses the variables used in the critical section protocols and the variables in B.

To reduce memory contention, it is preferable for a process to delay for some period of time before reentering the critical section. Let Delay be some code that "slows" a process down. Then we can replace (3.8) by the following protocol for implementing a conditional atomic action:

(3.9)   CSenter
         do not $B \rightarrow$ CSexit; Delay; CSenter **od**
         S
         CSexit

The Delay code might, for example, be an empty loop that iterates a random number of times. (To avoid memory contention in this loop, the Delay code should access only local variables.) This kind of back-off protocol is also useful within the CSenter protocols themselves; e.g., it can be added to the delay loop in the simple test-and-set entry protocol given in Figure 3.4.

If S is simply the **skip** statement, protocol (3.9) can of course be simplified by omitting S. If in addition, B satisfies the requirements of the At-Most-Once Property (2.5), the statement $\langle$ **await** B $\rangle$ can be implemented as:

   do not $B \rightarrow$ **skip od**

This implementation is also sufficient if B remains true once it becomes true.

As mentioned at the start of the chapter, busy waiting synchronization is often used within hardware. In fact, a protocol similar to (3.9) is used by Ethernet controllers to synchronize access to an Ethernet—a common, local-area communication network. In particular, to transmit a message, an Ethernet controller first sends it on the Ethernet, then listens to see if it collided with another message sent at about the same time by another controller. If no collision is detected, the transmission is assumed to have been successful. If a collision is detected, the controller delays, then attempts to resend the message. To avoid a race condition in which two controllers repeatedly collide because they always delay about the same amount of time, the delay is randomly chosen from an interval that is doubled each time a collision occurs. Hence, this is called the "binary exponential back-off" protocol. Experiments have shown that this kind of back-off protocol is also useful in (3.9) and in critical section entry protocols.

3.2 Critical Sections: Tie-Breaker Algorithm

When a solution to the critical section problem employs an instruction like Test-and-Set, scheduling must be strongly fair to ensure eventual entry. This is a strong requirement since—as observed in Section 2.6—practical scheduling policies are only weakly fair. Although it is unlikely that a process trying to enter its critical section will never succeed, it could happen if two or more processes are always contending for entry. This is because the spin lock solution in Figure 3.4 does not control the order in which delayed processes enter their critical sections if two or more are trying to do so.

The *tie-breaker algorithm*—also called Peterson's algorithm—is a critical section protocol that requires only unconditionally fair scheduling to satisfy the eventual entry property. It also does not require special hardware instructions such as Test-and-Set. However, the algorithm is consequently much more complex than the spin lock solution. This section develops the tie-breaker algorithm, first for 2 processes and then for $n \geq 2$.

A Coarse-Grained Solution

To motivate the tie-breaker algorithm, consider again the coarse-grained program in Figure 3.2. The goal now is to implement the conditional atomic actions using only simple variables and sequential statements. For example, we want to implement the entry protocol in process *P1*,

$$\langle\ \textbf{await not}\ in2 \rightarrow in1 := \text{true}\ \rangle$$

in terms of fine-grained atomic actions.

As a starting point, consider implementing each **await** statement in Figure 3.2 by first looping until the guard is true, then executing the assignment. Then the entry protocol for *P1* would be:

> **do** $in2 \rightarrow$ **skip od**   # entry protocol for *P1*
> $in1 := \text{true}$

Similarly, the entry protocol for *P2* would be:

> **do** $in1 \rightarrow$ **skip od**   # entry protocol for *P2*
> $in2 := \text{true}$

The corresponding exit protocol for *P1* would set $in1$ to false, and that for *P2* would set $in2$ to false.

The problem with this "solution" is that the two actions in the entry protocols are not executed atomically. Consequently, mutual exclusion is not ensured. For example, the desired postcondition for the delay loop in *P1* is that $in2$ is false. Unfortunately this is interfered with by the assignment $in2 := \text{true}$. Operationally it is possible for both processes to evaluate their delay conditions at about the same time and to find that they are true.

Since each process wants to be sure that the other is not in its critical section when the **do** loop terminates, consider switching the order of the statements in the entry protocols. Namely, the entry protocol in *P1* becomes:

> $in1 := true$ # entry protocol in *P1*
> **do** $in2 \rightarrow$ **skip od**

var *in1* := false; *in2* := false; *last* := 1

P1:: **do** true → *in1* := true; *last* := 1   # entry protocol
            ⟨ **await not** *in2* **or** *last* = 2 ⟩
            critical section
            in1 := false   # exit protocol
            non-critical section
     od

P2:: **do** true → *in2* := true; *last* := 2   # entry protocol
            ⟨ **await not** *in1* **or** *last* = 1 ⟩
            critical section
            in2 := false   # exit protocol
            non-critical section
     od

Figure 3.5. Two-process tie-breaker algorithm: coarse-grained solution.

Similarly, the entry protocol in *P2* becomes:

      in2 := true   # entry protocol in *P2*
      do *in1* → **skip od**

This helps but still does not solve the problem. Mutual exclusion is ensured, but deadlock can now result: If *in1* and *in2* are both true, neither delay loop will terminate. However, there is a simple way to avoid deadlock: Use an additional variable to break the tie if both processes are delayed.

Let *last* be an integer variable that indicates which of *P1* or *P2* was last to start executing its entry protocol. Then if both *P1* and *P2* are trying to enter their critical sections—hence, both *in1* and *in2* are true—the last process to start its entry protocol delays. This yields the coarse-grained solution shown in Figure 3.5.

A Fine-Grained Solution

The algorithm in Figure 3.5 is very close to a fine-grained solution that does not require **await** statements. In particular, if each **await** statement satisfied the requirements of the At-Most-Once Property (2.4), then we could implement them by busy-waiting loops. Unfortunately, each **await** references two variables altered by the other process. However, in this case it is not necessary that the delay conditions be evaluated atomically. Informally this is true for the following reasons.

var *in1* := false; *in2* := false; *last* := 1

P1:: **do** true → *in1* := true; *last* := 1   # entry protocol
                  do *in2* **and** *last* = 1 → **skip od**
                  critical section
                  in1 := false   # exit protocol
                  non-critical section
    od

P2:: **do** true → *in2* := true; *last* := 2   # entry protocol
                  do *in1* **and** *last* = 2 → **skip od**
                  critical section
                  in2 := false   # exit protocol
                  non-critical section
    od

Figure 3.6. Two-process tie-breaker algorithm: fine-grained solution.

Consider the **await** statement in *P1*. If the delay condition is true, either *in2* is false or *last* is 2. The only way *P2* could then make the delay condition false is if it executes the first statement in its entry protocol, which sets *in2* to true. But then the next action of *P2* is to make the condition true again by setting *last* to 2. Thus, when *P1* is in its critical section, it can be assured that *P2* will not be in its critical section. The argument for *P2* is symmetric.

Since the delay conditions need not be evaluated atomically, each **await** can be replaced by a **do** loop that iterates as long as the negation of the delay condition is false. This yields the fine-grained tie-breaker algorithm shown in Figure 3.6.

To prove formally that the fine-grained algorithm is correct, we can introduce two auxiliary variables to record when each process is between the first two assignments in its entry protocol. For example, we can replace the first two assignments in *P1* by:

$$\langle\, in1 := \text{true};\, mid1 := \text{true}\, \rangle$$
$$\langle\, last := 1;\, mid1 := \text{false}\, \rangle$$

Making a comparable change to *P2*, the following assertion is true when *P1* is in its critical section:

$$\{\, in1 \wedge \neg mid1 \wedge (\neg in2 \vee last = 2 \vee mid2)\, \}$$

With this and the corresponding assertion before *P2*'s critical section, we can use Exclusion of Configurations (2.25) to conclude that *P1* and *P2* cannot

```
var in[1:n] := ([n] 0); last[1:n] := ([n] 0)
P[i: 1..n]:: do true →
            fa j := 1 to n-1 →          # entry protocol
                # record that process i is in stage j and is last
                in[i] := j; last[j] := i
                fa k := 1 to n st i ≠ k →
                    # wait if process k is in higher numbered stage and
                    # process i was the last to enter this stage
                    do in[k] ≥ in[i] and last[j] = i → skip od
                af
            af
            critical section
            in[i] := 0                   # exit protocol
            non-critical section
      od
```

Figure 3.7. The n-process tie-breaker algorithm.

---

execute their critical sections simultaneously. We leave to the reader the tasks of developing a complete proof outline and proving that the tie-breaker algorithm also satisfies the other three properties of a solution to the critical section problem.

An *N*-Process Solution

The tie-breaker algorithm in Figure 3.6 solves the critical section problem for two processes. We can use the basic idea to solve the problem for any number of processes. In particular, if there are n processes, the entry protocol in each process consists of a loop that iterates through $n - 1$ stages. In each stage, we use instances of the two-process tie-breaker algorithm to determine which processes get to advance to the next stage. If we ensure that at most one process at a time is allowed to get through all $n - 1$ stages, then at most one at a time can be in its critical section.

Let $in[1:n]$ and $last[1:n]$ be integer arrays, where $n > 1$. The value of $in[i]$ indicates which stage $P[i]$ is executing; the value of $last[j]$ indicates which process was the last to begin stage j. These variables are used as shown in Figure 3.7. The outer for-all loop executes $n - 1$ times. The inner for-all loop in process $P[i]$ checks every other process. In particular, $P[i]$ waits if there is some other process in a higher or equal numbered stage and $P[i]$ was the last process to enter stage j. Once another process enters stage j or all processes "ahead" of $P[i]$ have exited their critical section, $P[i]$ can proceed to the next stage. Thus, at most $n - 1$ processes can be past the first stage, $n - 2$ past the second stage, and so on. This ensures that at most one process at a time can complete all $n-1$ stages and hence be executing its critical section.

The n-process solution is livelock-free, avoids unnecessary delay, and ensures eventual entry. These properties follow from the fact that a process delays only if some other process is ahead of it in the entry protocol, and from the assumption that every process eventually exits its critical section. We leave to the reader developing a formal proof of the correctness of the n-process algorithm (see exercise 3.1).

In the solution in Figure 3.7, the entry protocol executes $O(n^2)$ instances of the two-process tie-breaker algorithm. This is because the inner for-all loop is executed $n-1$ times on each of the $n-1$ iterations of the outer for-all loop. This happens even if only one process is trying to enter its critical section. There is a variation of the n-process algorithm that requires executing only $O(n*m)$ instances of the two process tie-breaker if only m processes are contending for entry to the critical section (see exercise 3.10). However, the other algorithm has a much larger variance in potential delay time when there is contention.

3.3 Critical Sections: Ticket Algorithm

The n-process tie-breaker algorithm is quite complex and consequently is hard to understand. This is in part because it was not obvious how to generalize the two-process algorithm to n processes. Here we develop an n-process solution to the critical section problem that is much easier to understand. The solution also illustrates how integer counters can be used to order processes. The algorithm is called a *ticket algorithm* since it is based on drawing tickets (numbers) and then waiting turns.

Coarse-Grained Solution

Some stores—such as ice cream stores and bakeries—employ the following method to ensure that customers are serviced in order of arrival. Upon entering the store, a customer draws a number that is one larger than the number held by any other customer. The customer then waits until all customers holding smaller numbers have been serviced. This algorithm is implemented by a number dispenser and by a display indicating which customer is being served. If the store has one employee behind the service counter, customers are served one at a time in their order of arrival. We can use this idea to implement a fair critical section protocol.

Let *number* and *next* be integers that are initially 1, and let *turn*[1:n] be an array of integers, each of which is initially 0. To enter its critical section, process $P[i]$ first sets *turn*[i] to the current value of *number* and then increments *number*. These are a single atomic action to ensure that

var *number* := 1, *next* := 1, *turn*[1:*n*] : **int** := ([*n*] 0)
{ *TICKET*: (*P*[*i*] is in its critical section) ⟹ (*turn*[*i*] = *next*) ∧
           (∀ *i, j*: 1 ≤ *i, j* ≤ *n*, *i* ≠ *j*: *turn*[*i*] = 0 ∨ *turn*[*i*] ≠ *turn*[*j*]) }

P[*i*: 1 .. *n*]:: **do** true →
                ⟨ *turn*[*i*] := *number*; *number* := *number* + 1 ⟩
                ⟨ **await** *turn*[*i*] = *next* ⟩
                critical section
                ⟨ *next* := *next* + 1 ⟩
                non-critical section
          od

Figure 3.8. The ticket algorithm: coarse-grained solution.

---

customers draw unique numbers. Process *P*[*i*] then waits until the value of *next* is equal to the number it drew. In particular, we want the following predicate to be invariant:

$$\{ \textit{TICKET}:\ (P[i] \text{ is in its critical section}) \Rightarrow (turn[i] = next) \land$$
$$(\forall i, j:\ 1 \le i, j \le n, i \ne j:\ turn[i] = 0 \lor turn[i] \ne turn[j]) \}$$

The second conjunct says that non-zero values of *turn* are unique; hence at most one *turn*[*i*] is equal to *next*. Upon completing its critical section, *P*[*i*] increments *next*, again as an atomic action.

This protocol results in the algorithm shown in Figure 3.8. Predicate *TICKET* is a global invariant since *number* is read and incremented as an atomic action and *next* is incremented as an atomic action. Hence at most one process can be in its critical section. Absence of deadlock and unnecessary delay also follow from the fact that non-zero values in *turn* are unique. Finally, if scheduling is weakly fair, the algorithm ensures eventual entry since once a delay condition becomes true, it remains true.

Unlike the tie-breaker algorithm, the ticket algorithm has one potential shortcoming that is common in algorithms that employ incrementing counters: the values of *number* and *next* are unbounded. If the ticket algorithm runs for a long time, incrementing a counter will eventually cause arithmetic overflow. For this algorithm, however, we can overcome this problem by resetting the counters to a small value, say one, any time they get too large (see exercise 3.11). If the largest value is at least as large as *n*, then the values of *turn*[*i*] are guaranteed to be unique.

var *number* := 1, *next* := 1, *turn*[1:*n*] : **int** := ([*n*] 0)
{ *TICKET*: (*P*[*i*] is in its critical section) ⇒ (*turn*[*i*] = *next*) ∧
         (∀ *i*, *j*: 1 ≤ *i*, *j* ≤ *n*, *i* ≠ *j*: *turn*[*i*] = 0 ∨ *turn*[*i*] ≠ *turn*[*j*]) }

P[*i*: 1 .. *n*]:: **do** true →
                    turn[*i*] := *FA*(*number*, 1)
                    do *turn*[*i*] ≠ *next* → **skip od**
                    critical section
                    next := *next* + 1   # need not be atomic; see text
                    non-critical section
          od

Figure 3.9. The ticket algorithm using fetch-and-add.

Fine-Grained Solutions

The algorithm in Figure 3.8 employs three coarse-grained atomic actions. It is easy to implement the **await** statement using a busy-waiting loop since the boolean expression references only one shared variable. Even though the last atomic action, which increments *next*, references *next* twice, it too can be implemented using regular load and store instructions. This is because at most one process at a time can execute the exit protocol. Unfortunately, it is hard in general to implement the first atomic action, which reads *number* and then increments it.

Some machines, such as the BBN Butterfly and NYU Ultracomputer, have instructions that return the old value of a variable and increment or decrement it as a single indivisible operation. This kind of instruction does exactly what is required for the ticket algorithm. As a specific example, Fetch-and-Add is an instruction with the following effect:

$$FA(\textit{var}, \textit{incr}): \langle \textit{temp} := \textit{var}; \textit{var} := \textit{var} + \textit{incr}; \textbf{return}(\textit{temp}) \rangle$$

Figure 3.9 gives the ticket algorithm implemented using *FA*. As in the coarse-grained algorithm, we can avoid counter overflow by resetting the counters when they reach a limit larger than *n*.

On machines that do not have Fetch-and-Add or a comparable instruction, we have to use another approach. The key requirement in the ticket algorithm is that every process draw a unique number. If a machine has an atomic increment instruction, we might consider implementing the first step in the entry protocol by:

$$turn[i] := \textit{number}; \langle \textit{number} := \textit{number} + 1 \rangle$$

This ensures that *number* is incremented correctly, but it does not ensure that processes draw unique numbers. In particular, every process could execute the first assignment above at about the same time and draw the same number! Thus, it is essential that both assignments be executed as a single atomic action.

We have already seen two other ways to solve the critical section problem: spin locks and the tie-breaker algorithm. Either of these could be used within the ticket algorithm to make number drawing atomic. In particular, let CSenter be a critical section entry protocol, and let CSexit be the corresponding exit protocol. Then we could replace the *FA* statement in Figure 3.9 by:

(3.10)   CSenter; *turn*[*i*] := *number*; *number* := *number* + 1; CSexit

Although this might seem like a curious approach, in practice it would actually work quite well, especially if an instruction like Test-and-Set is available to implement CSenter and CSexit. With Test-and-Set, processes might not draw numbers in exactly the order they attempt to—and theoretically a process could spin forever—but with very high probability every process would draw a number, and most would be drawn in order. This is because the critical section within (3.10) is very short, and hence a process is not likely to delay in CSenter. The major source of delay in the ticket algorithm is waiting for *turn*[*i*] to be equal to *next*.

3.4 Critical Sections: Bakery Algorithm

The ticket algorithm can be implemented directly on machines that have an instruction like Fetch-and-Add. If only less powerful instructions are available, we can simulate the number drawing part of the ticket algorithm using (3.10). But that requires using another critical section protocol, and the solution might not be fair. Here we present a ticketlike algorithm—called the *bakery algorithm*—that is fair and that does not require any special machine instructions. The algorithm is consequently more complex than the ticket algorithm in Figure 3.9. However, it illustrates a way to break ties when two processes draw the same number.

Coarse-Grained Solution

In the ticket algorithm, each customer draws a unique number and then waits for its number to be equal to *next*. The bakery algorithm takes a different approach that does not require an atomic number dispenser and does not use a *next* counter. In particular, when a customer enters the store, it first looks around at all the other customers in the store and sets its

var $turn[1:n]$: **int** := ([n] 0)
{ $BAKERY$: ($P[i]$ is executing its CS) $\Rightarrow$ ($turn[i] \neq 0 \wedge$
                    ($\forall j$: $1 \leq j \leq n, j \neq i$: $turn[j] = 0 \vee turn[i] < turn[j]$)) }

$P[i: 1 .. n]$:: **do** true $\rightarrow$
                    $\langle$ $turn[i] := max(turn[1:n]) + 1$ $\rangle$
                    fa $j := 1$ **to** n **st** $j \neq i \rightarrow$
                        $\langle$ **await** $turn[j] = 0$ **or** $turn[i] < turn[j]$ $\rangle$
                    af
                    critical section
                    $\langle$ $turn[i] := 0$ $\rangle$
                    non-critical section
         od

Figure 3.10. The bakery algorithm: coarse-grained solution.

---

number to one larger than any that it sees. Then it waits for its number to be smaller than that of any other customer. As in the ticket algorithm, the customer with the smallest number is the one that gets serviced next. The difference is that customers check with each other rather with a central *next* counter to decide on the order of service.

As in the ticket algorithm, let $turn[1:n]$ be an array of integers, each of which is initially zero. To enter its critical section, process $P[i]$ first sets $turn[i]$ to one more than the maximum of the other values of *turn*. Then $P[i]$ waits until $turn[i]$ is the smallest of the non-zero values of *turn*. Thus, the bakery algorithm keeps the following predicate invariant:

$BAKERY$: ($P[i]$ is executing its CS) $\Rightarrow$ ($turn[i] \neq 0 \wedge$
                    ($\forall j$: $1 \leq j \leq n, j \neq i$: $turn[j] = 0 \vee turn[i] < turn[j]$))

Upon completing its critical section, $P[i]$ resets $turn[i]$ to zero.

Figure 3.10 contains a coarse-grained bakery algorithm meeting these specifications. The first atomic action guarantees that non-zero values of *turn* are unique. The for-all statement ensures that the consequent in predicate $BAKERY$ is true when $P[i]$ is executing its critical section. The algorithm satisfies the mutual exclusion property since $turn[i] \neq 0$, $turn[j] \neq 0$, and $BAKERY$ cannot all be true at once. Deadlock cannot result since non-zero values of *turn* are unique, and as usual we assume that every process eventually exits its critical section. Processes are not delayed unnecessarily since $turn[i]$ is zero when $P[i]$ is outside its critical section. Finally, the bakery algorithm ensures eventual entry if scheduling is weakly fair since once a delay condition becomes true, it remains true.

The values of *turn* in the bakery algorithm can get arbitrarily large. Unlike the ticket algorithm, this problem cannot be solved by cycling through a finite set of integers. However, the *turn[i]* continue to get larger only if there is *always* at least one process trying to get into its critical section. This is not likely to be a practical problem, however, since it means that processes are spending way too much time trying to enter critical sections. In this case, it is inappropriate to use busy waiting.

A Fine-Grained Solution

The coarse-grained bakery algorithm in Figure 3.10 cannot be implemented directly on contemporary machines. The assignment to *turn[i]* requires computing the maximum of *n* values, and the **await** statement references a shared variable twice. These actions could be implemented atomically by using another critical section protocol such as the tie-breaker algorithm, but that would be quite inefficient. Fortunately, there is a simpler approach.

When *n* processes need to synchronize, it is often useful first to develop a solution for *n* = 2 and then to generalize that solution. This was the case earlier for the tie-breaker algorithm and is again useful here since it helps illustrate the problems that have to be solved. Thus, consider the following two-process version of the coarse-grained bakery algorithm.

(3.11)   **var** *turn1* := 0, *turn2* := 0
     P1:: **do** true → *turn1* := *turn2* + 1
                 do *turn2* ≠ 0 **and** *turn1* > *turn2* → **skip od**
                 critical section
                 turn1 := 0
                 non-critical section
         od
     P2:: **do** true → *turn2* := *turn1* + 1
                 do *turn1* ≠ 0 **and** *turn2* > *turn1* → **skip od**
                 critical section
                 turn2 := 0
                 non-critical section
         od

Above, each process sets its value of *turn* by an optimized version of (3.10), and the **await** statements are tentatively implemented by a busy-waiting loop.

The problem with the above "solution" is that neither the assignment statements in the entry protocols nor the **do** loop guards satisfy the At-Most-Once Property (2.4); hence they will not be evaluated atomically. Consequently, the processes could start their entry protocols at about the same

var *turn1* := 0, *turn2* := 0

P1:: **do** true → *turn1* := 1; *turn1* := *turn2* + 1
                do *turn2* ≠ 0 **and** *turn1* > *turn2* → **skip od**
                critical section
                turn1 := 0
                non-critical section
    od

P2:: **do** true → *turn2* := 1; *turn2* := *turn1* + 1
                do *turn1* ≠ 0 **and** *turn2* ≥ *turn1* → **skip od**
                critical section
                turn2 := 0
                non-critical section
    od

Figure 3.11. Bakery algorithm: fine-grained for two processes.

time, and both could set *turn1* and *turn2* to 1. If this happens, both processes could be in their critical section at the same time.

The two-process tie-breaker algorithm in Figure 3.6 suggests a partial solution to the problem in (3.11): If both *turn1* and *turn2* are 1, let one of the processes proceed and have the other delay. For example, let the lower-numbered process proceed by strengthening the second conjunct in the delay loop in *P2* to *turn2* ≥ *turn1*.

Unfortunately, it is still possible for both processes to enter their critical section. For example, suppose *P1* reads *turn2* and gets back 0. Then suppose *P2* starts its entry protocol, sees that *turn1* is still 0, sets *turn2* to 1, and then enters its critical section. At this point, *P1* can continue its entry protocol, set *turn1* to 1, and then proceed into its critical section since both *turn1* and *turn2* are 1 and *P1* takes precedence in this case. This kind of situation is called a *race condition* since *P2* "raced by" *P1* and hence *P1* missed seeing that *P2* was changing *turn2*.

To avoid this race condition, we can have each process set its value of *turn* to 1 (or any non-zero value) at the start of the entry protocol. Then it examines the other's value of *turn* and resets its own. The solution is shown in Figure 3.11. One process cannot now exit its **do** loop until the other has finished setting its value of *turn* if it is in the midst of doing so. The solution gives *P1* precedence over *P2* in case they both have the same (non-zero) value for *turn*. When *P1* is in its critical section, the following predicate is true:

$$turn1 > 0 \land (turn2 = 0 \lor turn1 \leq turn2)$$

```
var turn[1:n] := ([n] 0)
{ BAKERY: (P[i] is executing its CS) ⇒ ( turn[i] ≠ 0 ∧
                    ( ∀ j: 1 ≤ j ≤ n, j ≠ i:  turn[j] = 0 ∨ turn[i] < turn[j]
                          ∨ (turn[i] = turn[j] ∧ i < j) ) ) }
P[i: 1 .. n]::  var j : int
            do true →
                turn[i] := 1; turn[i] := max(turn[1:n]) + 1
                fa j := 1 to n st j ≠ i →
                    do turn[j] ≠ 0 and (turn[i], i) > (turn[j], j) → skip od
                af
                critical section
                turn[i] := 0
                non-critical section
            od
```

Figure 3.12. Bakery algorithm: fine-grained for n processes.

Similarly, when *P2* is in its critical section,

$$turn2 > 0 \land (turn1 = 0 \lor turn2 < turn1)$$

Mutual exclusion of the critical sections follows from the method of Exclusion of Configurations (2.25) since the conjunction of the preconditions of the critical sections is false. The two-process bakery algorithm also satisfies the other critical section properties.

The processes in Figure 3.11 are not quite symmetric since the delay conditions in the second loop are slightly different. However, we can rewrite them in a symmetric form as follows. Let (a, b) and (c, d) be pairs of integers, and define the *greater than* relation between such pairs as follows:

$$(a, b) > (c, d) = \begin{matrix} true & \text{if } a > c \text{ or if } a = c \text{ and } b > d \\ false & \text{otherwise} \end{matrix}$$

Then we can rewrite $turn1 > turn2$ in *P1* as $(turn1, 1) > (turn2, 2)$ and can rewrite $turn2 \geq turn1$ in *P2* as $(turn2, 2) > (turn1, 1)$.

The virtue of a symmetric specification is that it is now easy to generalize the two-process bakery algorithm to an n-process algorithm, as shown in Figure 3.12. The solution employs a for-all loop as in the coarse-grained solution so that a process delays until it has precedence over all other processes. Predicate *BAKERY* is a global invariant that is almost identical to the global invariant in Figure 3.10. The difference is the third line, which reflects the fact that, in the fine-grained solution, two processes might have the same value for their element of *turn*. Here we give precedence to the lower-numbered process.

3.5 Barrier Synchronization

Many problems can be solved using iterative algorithms that successively compute better approximations to an answer, terminating when either the final answer has been computed or—in the case of many numerical algorithms—when the final answer has converged. Typically such an algorithm manipulates an array of values, and each iteration performs the same computation on all array elements. Hence, we can often use multiple processes to compute disjoint parts of the solution in parallel. The grid computation in Section 2.4 for approximating a solution to a partial differential equation is one example of a parallel, iterative algorithm. We will examine several others in the next section and in later chapters.

A key attribute of most parallel iterative algorithms is that each iteration typically depends on the results of the previous iteration. One way to structure such an algorithm is to implement the body of each iteration using one or more **co** statements. Ignoring termination, and assuming there are n parallel tasks on each iteration, this approach has the general form:

> **do** true $\rightarrow$
>   **co** $i := 1$ **to** $n \rightarrow$ code to implement task i **oc**
> **od**

Unfortunately, the above approach is quite inefficient since **co** spawns n processes on each iteration. It is much more costly to create and destroy processes than to implement process synchronization. Thus, an alternative structure will result in a more efficient algorithm. In particular, create the processes once at the beginning of the computation, then have them synchronize at the end of each iteration:

> *Worker*[i: 1 .. n]:: **do** true $\rightarrow$
>   code to implement task i
>   wait for all n tasks to complete
>   **od**

This type of synchronization is called *barrier synchronization* since the delay point at the end of each iteration represents a barrier that all processes have to arrive at before any are allowed to pass.

Below we develop several busy-waiting implementations of barrier synchronization. Each employs a different process interaction technique. We also describe when each kind of barrier is appropriate to use.

Shared Counter

The simplest way to specify the requirements for a barrier is to employ a shared integer, *count*, which is initially zero. Assume there are *n* worker processes that need to meet at a barrier. When a process arrives at the barrier, it increments *count*. Hence, when *count* is *n*, all processes can proceed. To specify this precisely, let *passed[i]* be a boolean variable that is initially false; *Worker[i]* sets *passed[i]* to true when it has passed the barrier. Then the required property that no worker passes the barrier until all have arrived is ensured if the following predicate is a global invariant:

$$COUNT:: (\,\forall\, i:\ 1 \le i \le n:\ passed[i]\ \Rightarrow\ count = n\,)$$

Annotating the processes with uses of *count* and *passed* as defined, and guarding the assignments to *passed* to ensure that *COUNT* is invariant, yields the following partial solution:

(3.12) **var** *count* := 0, *passed*[1:*n*] : **bool** := ([*n*] false)

$\qquad$ *Worker*[*i*: 1 .. *n*]:: **do** true $\rightarrow$
$\qquad\qquad\qquad\qquad\qquad$ code to implement task *i*
$\qquad\qquad\qquad\qquad\qquad$ ⟨ *count* := *count* + 1 ⟩
$\qquad\qquad\qquad\qquad\qquad$ ⟨ **await** *count* = *n* $\rightarrow$ *passed*[*i*] := true ⟩
$\qquad\qquad$ **od**

Above, *passed* is an auxiliary variable that is used merely to specify the barrier property. After deleting it from the program, we can implement the **await** statement by a busy-waiting loop. Also, many machines have an indivisible increment instruction. For example, using the Fetch-and-Add instruction defined in Section 3.3, we can implement the above barrier by:

$\qquad$ *FA*(*count*, 1)
$\qquad$ **do** *count* ≠ *n* $\rightarrow$ **skip od**

The above program does not fully solve the problem, however. The difficulty is that *count* must be 0 at the start of each iteration. Hence, *count* needs to be reset to 0 each time all processes have passed the barrier. Moreover, it has to be reset before any process again tries to increment *count*.

It is possible to solve this "reset" problem by employing two counters, one that counts up to *n* and another that counts down to 0, with the roles of the counters being switched after each stage (see exercise 3.13). However, there are additional, pragmatic problems with using shared counters. First, they have to be incremented and/or decremented as atomic actions. Second, when a process is delayed in (3.12), it is continuously examining *count*. In the worst case, *n* − 1 processes might be delayed waiting for the *n*th process to arrive at the barrier. This could lead to severe memory contention, except on multiprocessors with coherent caches. But even then, the value of *count* is continuously changing, so every cache needs to be updated. Thus, it is appropriate to implement a barrier using counters only if the target machine has atomic increment instructions, coherent caches, and efficient cache update. Moreover, n should be relatively small (e.g., at most 30).

Flags and Coordinators

One way to avoid the memory contention problem is to distribute the implementation of *count* by using n variables that sum to the same value. In particular, let *arrive*[1:n] be an array of integers initialized to zeroes. Then replace the increment of *count* in (3.12) by *arrive*[i] := 1. With this change, the following predicate is a global invariant:

(3.13) $count = arrive[1] + ... + arrive[n]$

Memory contention is avoided if the elements of *arrive* are stored in different memory banks. (We could also implement *arrive* by a boolean array, but a packed boolean array could also cause memory contention.)

With the above change, the remaining problems are implementing the **await** statement in (3.12) and resetting the elements of *arrive* at the end of each iteration. Using relation (3.13) and ignoring auxiliary variable *passed*, the **await** statement could obviously be implemented as:

$$\langle\, \textbf{await } (arrive[1] + ... + arrive[n]) = n \,\rangle$$

However, this reintroduces memory contention. Moreover it is inefficient since the sum of the *arrive*[i] is continually being computed by every waiting *Worker*.

We can solve both the memory contention and reset problems by using an additional set of shared values and by employing an additional process, *Coordinator*. Instead of having each *Worker* sum and test the values of *arrive*, let each worker wait for a single value to become true. In particular, let *continue*[1:n] be another array of integers, initialized to zeroes. After setting *arrive*[i] to 1, *Worker*[i] delays by waiting for *continue*[i] to be set to 1:

(3.14) $arrive[i] := 1$
            $\langle\, \textbf{await } continue[i] = 1 \,\rangle$

The *Coordinator* process waits for all elements of *arrive* to become 1, then sets all elements of *continue* to 1:

(3.15)   **fa** $i := 1$ **to** $n \rightarrow \langle$ **await** $arrive[i] = 1 \rangle$ **af**
          fa $i := 1$ **to** $n \rightarrow continue[i] := 1$ **af**

Thus, *arrive* and *continue* have the following interpretation:

$$(\, \forall \, i \colon \, 1 \leq i \leq n \colon \, (arrive[i] = 1) \Rightarrow Worker[i] \text{ has reached the barrier}) \, \wedge$$
$$(\, \forall \, i \colon \, 1 \leq i \leq n \colon \, (continue[i] = 1) \Rightarrow Worker[i] \text{ may pass the barrier})$$

The **await** statements in (3.14) and (3.15) can be implemented by **do** loops since each references a single shared variable. Also, the *Coordinator* can use a for-all statement to wait for each element of *arrive* to be set; since all must be set before any *Worker* is allowed to continue, the *Coordinator* can test the *arrive[i]* in any order. Finally, memory contention is not a problem since the processes wait for different variables to be set and these variables could be stored in different memory units.

Variables used the way *arrive* and *continue* are used in (3.14) and (3.15) are called *flag variables*. This is because each variable is raised by one process to signal that a synchronization condition is true. The remaining problem is augmenting (3.14) and (3.15) with code to clear the flags by resetting them to 0 in preparation for the next iteration. Here two general principles apply.

(3.16)   **Flag Synchronization Principles.** The process that waits for a synchronization flag to be set is the one that should clear that flag. A flag should not be set until it is known that it is clear.

The first part of the principle ensures that a flag is not cleared before it has been seen to be set. Thus, in (3.14) *Worker[i]* should clear *continue[i]*, and in (3.15) *Coordinator* should clear all elements of *arrive*. The second part of the principle ensures that another process cannot again set the same flag before it is cleared, which could lead to deadlock if the first process later waits for the flag to be set again. In (3.15) this means *Coordinator* should clear *arrive[i]* before setting *continue[i]*. The *Coordinator* can do this by executing another for-all statement after the first one in (3.15). Alternatively, *Coordinator* can clear *arrive[i]* immediately after it has waited for it to be set. Adding flag clearing code, we get the full solution shown in Figure 3.13.

Although Figure 3.13 implements barrier synchronization in a way that avoids memory contention, the solution has two undesirable attributes. First, it requires an extra process. Since busy-waiting synchronization is inefficient unless each process executes on its own processor, the *Coordinator* should execute on its own processor, which is not then available for execution of another process that might be doing useful work.

The second shortcoming of using a coordinator is that the execution time of each iteration of *Coordinator*—and hence each instance of barrier

var *arrive*[1:*n*] : **int** := ([*n*] 0), *continue*[1:*n*] : **int** := ([*n*] 0)

Worker[*i*: 1 .. *n*]:: **do** true →

      code to implement task *i*

      arrive[*i*] := 1

      ⟨ **await** *continue*[*i*] = 1 ⟩

      continue[*i*] := 0

   od

Coordinator:: var *i* : **int**

   do true →

      fa *i* := 1 **to** *n* → ⟨ **await** *arrive*[*i*] = 1 ⟩; *arrive*[*i*] := 0 **af**

      fa *i* := 1 **to** *n* → *continue*[*i*] := 1 **af**

   od

Figure 3.13. Barrier synchronization using a coordinator process.

---

synchronization—is proportional to the number of *Worker* processes. In iterative algorithms, the code executed by each *Worker* is typically identical, and hence each is likely to arrive at the barrier at about the same time if every *Worker* is executed on its own processor. Thus, all *arrive* flags should get set at about the same time. However, *Coordinator* cycles through the flags, waiting for each one to be set in turn.

We can overcome both these problems by combining the actions of the coordinator and workers so that each worker is also a coordinator. In particular, we can organize the workers into a tree, as shown in Figure 3.14. Then we can have workers send arrival signals up the tree and continue signals back down the tree. In particular, a worker node first waits for its children to arrive, then tells its parent node that it too has arrived. When the root node learns that its children have arrived, it knows that all other workers have also arrived. Hence the root can tell its children to continue; they in turn can tell their children to continue, and so on. The specific actions of each kind of worker process are listed in Figure 3.15. The **await** statements can of course be implemented by spin loops.

The implementation in Figure 3.15 is called a *combining tree barrier*. This is because each process combines the results of its children, then passes them on to its parent. Since the height of the tree is $\lceil \log_2 n \rceil$, the approach scales very well. In particular, it uses the same number of variables as the centralized coordinator, but it is much more efficient for large *n*..

On multiprocessors that use broadcast to update caches, we can make the combining tree barrier even more efficient by having the root node broadcast a single message that tells all other nodes to continue. In particular, the root sets one *continue* flag, and all other nodes wait for it to be set. This *continue*

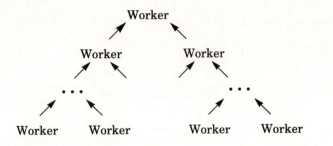

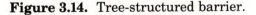

Figure 3.14. Tree-structured barrier.

---

leaf node l: $arrive[l] := 1$
           $\langle$ **await** $continue[l] = 1 \rangle$; $continue[l] := 0$

interior node i: $\langle$ **await** $arrive[left] = 1 \rangle$; $arrive[left] = 0$
           $\langle$ **await** $arrive[right] = 1 \rangle$; $arrive[right] = 0$
           $arrive[i] := 1$
           $\langle$ **await** $continue[i] = 1 \rangle$; $continue[i] := 0$
           $continue[left] := 1$; $continue[right] := 1$

root node r: $\langle$ **await** $arrive[left] = 1 \rangle$; $arrive[left] = 0$
           $\langle$ **await** $arrive[right] = 1 \rangle$; $arrive[right] = 0$
           $continue[left] := 1$; $continue[right] := 1$

Figure 3.15. Barrier synchronization using a combining tree.

---

flag can later be cleared in either of two ways. One is to use double buffering; i.e., use two continue flags and alternate between them. The other way is to alternate the sense of the continue flag; i.e., on odd-numbered rounds wait for it to be set to 1, and on even-numbered rounds wait for it to be set to 0.

Symmetric Barriers

In the combining-tree barrier, processes play different roles. In particular, those at interior nodes in the tree execute more actions than those at the leaves or root. Moreover, the root node needs to wait for arrival signals to propagate up the tree. If every process is executing on a different processor and is executing the same algorithm—which is often the case in parallel iterative algorithms—then all processes should arrive at the barrier at about the same time. Thus, if every process takes the exact same sequence of actions when it reaches a barrier, then all might be able to proceed in parallel

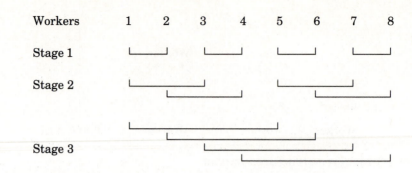

Figure 3.16. Butterfly barrier for 8 processes.

through it. This section presents two symmetric barriers. These are especially suitable for shared-memory multiprocessors with non-uniform memory access time (e.g., the BBN Butterfly or Monarch).

A symmetric n-process barrier is constructed from pairs of simple, two-process barriers. To construct a two-process barrier, we could use the coordinator/worker technique. However, the actions of the two processes would then be different. Instead, we can construct a fully symmetric barrier as follows. Let each process have a flag that it sets when it arrives at the barrier. It then waits for the other process to set its flag and finally clears the other's flag. If $P[i]$ is one process and $P[j]$ is the other, the symmetric two-process barrier is then implemented as follows:

(3.17) $P[i]$:: $\langle$ **await** $arrive[i] = 0 \rangle$ $P[j]$:: $\langle$ **await** $arrive[j] = 0 \rangle$
              $arrive[i] := 1$ $arrive[j] := 1$
              $\langle$ **await** $arrive[j] = 1 \rangle$ $\langle$ **await** $arrive[i] = 1 \rangle$
              $arrive[j] := 0$ $arrive[i] := 0$

The second, third, and fourth lines in each process follow the Flag Synchronization Principles (3.16). The first line is needed to guard against one process racing back to the barrier and setting its flag before the other process has cleared the flag. (Alternatively, the processes could use two sets of flag variables and alternate between them.)

The question now is how to combine two-process barriers to construct an n-process barrier. Let $Worker[1{:}n]$ be the n processes. If n is a power of 2, we could combine them as shown in Figure 3.16. This kind of barrier is called a *butterfly barrier* due to the shape of the interconnection pattern, which is similar to the interconnection pattern for the Fourier transform.

A butterfly barrier has $\log_2 n$ stages. Each *Worker* synchronizes with a different other *Worker* at each stage. In particular, in stage s a *Worker*

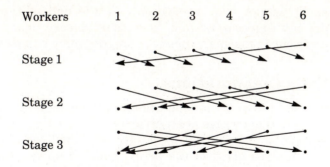

Figure 3.17. Dissemination barrier for 6 processes.

synchronizes with a *Worker* at distance 2^{s-1} away. Each two-process barrier is implemented as shown in (3.17), and different flag variables are used for each different two-process barrier. When every *Worker* has passed through $\log_2 n$ stages, all *Workers* must have arrived at the barrier and hence all can proceed. This is because every *Worker* has directly or indirectly synchronized with every other one.

When n is not a power of 2, a butterfly barrier can be constructed by using the next power of 2 greater than n and having existing *Worker* processes substitute for the missing ones at each stage. This is not very efficient, however. In general, it is better to use what is called a *dissemination barrier*, as shown in Figure 3.17. Again there are stages, and in stage s a *Worker* synchronizes with one at distance 2^{s-1} away. However, each two-process barrier is implemented slightly differently than in a butterfly barrier. In particular, each *Worker* sets its arrival flag for a *Worker* to its right (modulo n) and waits for, then clears, the arrival flag of a *Worker* to its left (modulo n). This kind of barrier is called a dissemination barrier since it is based on a technique for disseminating information to n processes in $\lceil \log_2 n \rceil$ rounds. In this case, each *Worker* disseminates notice of its arrival at the barrier.

3.6 Data Parallel Algorithms

A *data parallel algorithm* is an iterative algorithm that repeatedly and in parallel manipulates a shared array. This kind of algorithm is most closely associated with synchronous multiprocessors, i.e. single instruction stream, multiple data stream (SIMD) machines. However, data parallel algorithms are also useful on asynchronous multiprocessors.

This section develops data parallel solutions to three problems: partial sums of an array, finding the end of a linked list, and region labeling. These illustrate the basic techniques that arise in data parallel algorithms and illustrate uses of barrier synchronization. At the end of the section we describe SIMD multiprocessors and how they remove many sources of interference and hence remove the need for programming barriers.

Parallel Prefix Computations

It is frequently useful to apply an operation to all elements of an array. For example, to compute the average of an array of values $a[1:n]$, we first need to sum all the elements, then divide by n. Or we might want to know the averages for all prefixes $a[1:i]$ of the array, which requires computing the sums of all prefixes. Because of the importance of this kind of computation, the APL language provides special operators called reduction and scan. The Connection Machine, a massively parallel SIMD machine, also provides reduction operators in hardware for combining values in messages.

In this section, we show how to compute in parallel the sums of all prefixes of an array. This is thus called a *parallel prefix* computation. The basic algorithm can be used for any associative binary operator, such as addition, multiplication, logic operators, or maximum. Consequently, parallel prefix computations are useful in many applications, including image processing, matrix computations, and parsing a regular language. (See Historical Notes and References and Exercises.)

Suppose we are given array $a[1:n]$ and are to compute $sum[1:n]$, where $sum[i]$ is to be the sum of the first i elements of a. The obvious way to solve this problem sequentially is to iterate across the two arrays:

> $sum[1] := a[1]$
> **fa** $i := 2$ **to** $n \rightarrow sum[i] := sum[i-1] + a[i]$ **af**

In particular, each iteration adds $a[i]$ to the already computed sum of the previous $i-1$ elements.

Now consider how we might parallelize this approach. If our task were merely to find the sum of all elements, we could proceed as follows. First, add pairs of elements in parallel; e.g., add $a[1]$ and $a[2]$ in parallel with adding other pairs. Second, combine the results of the first step, again in pairs; e.g., add the sum of $a[1]$ and $a[2]$ to the sum of $a[3]$ and $a[4]$ in parallel with computing other partial sums. If we continue this process, in each step we would double the number of elements that have been summed. Thus, in $\lceil \log_2 n \rceil$ steps we would have computed the sum of all elements. This is the best we can do if we have to combine all elements two at a time.

To compute the sums of all prefixes in parallel, we can adapt this technique of doubling the number of elements that have been added. First, set all the $sum[i]$ to $a[i]$. Then, in parallel add $sum[i-1]$ to $sum[i]$, for all $i > 1$. In particular, add elements that are distance 1 away. Now double the distance, adding $sum[i-2]$ to $sum[i]$, in this case for all $i > 2$. If we continue

var $a[1{:}n]$: **int**, $sum[1{:}n]$: **int**, $old[1{:}n]$: **int**
$Sum[i{:}\,1..n]$::   **var** $d := 1$
               $sum[i] := a[i]$ # initialize elements of *sum*
               barrier
               $\{SUM\!:\ sum[i] = a[i-d+1] + ... + a[i]\,\}$
               do $d < n \rightarrow$
                    $old[i] := sum[i]$ # save old value
                    barrier
                    if $(i - d) \geq 1 \rightarrow sum[i] := old[i - d] + sum[i]$ **fi**
                    barrier
                    $d := 2 * d$
         od

Figure 3.18. Computing all partial sums of an array.

---

to double the distance, then after $\lceil \log_2 n \rceil$ rounds we will have computed all partial sums. As a specific example, the following table illustrates the steps of the algorithm for a six-element array:

initial values of $a[1{:}6]$	1	2	3	4	5	6
sum after distance 1	1	3	5	7	9	11
sum after distance 2	1	3	6	10	14	18
sum after distance 4	1	3	6	10	15	21

Figure 3.18 gives an implementation of this algorithm. Each process first initializes one element of *sum*. Then it repeatedly computes partial sums. In the algorithm, **barrier** represents a barrier synchronization point implemented using one of the algorithms in the previous section. (For this problem, the barriers can be optimized since only pairs of processes need to synchronize in each step; see exercise 3.19.)

The barriers in Figure 3.18 are needed to avoid interference. For example, all elements of *sum* need to be initialized before any process examines them. Also, each process needs to make a copy of the old value in $sum[i]$ before it updates that value. Loop invariant *SUM* specifies how much of the prefix of a each process has summed on each iteration.

As mentioned, we can modify this algorithm to use any associative binary operator. All that we need to change is the operator in the statement that modifies *sum*. Since we have written the expression in the combining step as $old[i - d] + sum[i]$, the binary operator need not be commutative. We can also adapt the algorithm in Figure 3.18 to use fewer than n processes. In this case, each process would be responsible for computing the partial sums of a slice of the array.

Operations on Linked Lists

When working with linked data structures such as trees, programmers often use balanced structures such as binary trees in order to be able to search for and insert items in logarithmic time. Using data parallel algorithms, however, even many operations on linear lists can be implemented in logarithmic time. Here we show how to find the end of a serially linked list. The same kind of algorithm can be used for other operations on serially linked lists; e.g., computing all partial sums of data values, inserting an element in a priority list, or matching up elements of two lists.

Suppose we have a linked list of up to n elements. The links are stored in array $link[1:n]$, and the data values are stored in array $data[1:n]$. The head of the list is pointed to by another variable, $head$. If element i is part of the list, then either $head = i$ or $link[j] = i$ for some j, $1 \leq j \leq n$. The $link$ field of the last element on the list is a null pointer, which we will represent by zero. We also assume that the $link$ fields of elements not on the list are null pointers and that the list is already initialized. Following is a sample list:

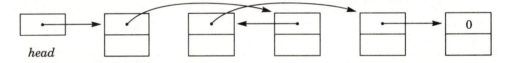

The problem is to find the end of the list. The standard sequential algorithm starts at list element $head$ and follows links until finding a null link; the last element visited is the end of the list. The execution time of the sequential algorithm is thus proportional to the length of the list. However, we can find the end of the list in time proportional to the logarithm of the length of the list by using a data parallel algorithm and the technique of doubling that was introduced in the previous section.

We assign a process $Find$ to each list element. Let $end[1:n]$ be a shared array of integers. If element i is a part of the list, the goal of $Find[i]$ is to set $end[i]$ to the index of the end of the last element on the list; otherwise $Find[i]$ should set $end[i]$ to zero. To avoid special cases, we will assume that the list contains at least two elements.

Initially each process sets $end[i]$ to $link[i]$, i.e., to the index of the next element on the list (if any). Thus, end initially reproduces the pattern of links in the list. Then the processes execute a series of rounds. In each round, a process looks at $end[end[i]]$. If both it and $end[i]$ are non-zero, then the process sets $end[i]$ to $end[end[i]]$. After the first round, $end[i]$ will thus

var *link*[1:*n*] : **int**, *end*[1:*n*] : **int**

Find[*i*: 1..*n*]::   **var** *new* : **int**, *d* := 1
                end[*i*] := *link*[*i*]   # initialize elements of *end*
                barrier
                { *FIND*:   *end*[*i*] = the index of the end of the list
                        at most 2^{d-1} links away from element *i* }
                do $d < n \rightarrow$
                    new := 0   # see if *end*[*i*] should be updated
                    if *end*[*i*] $\neq$ 0 **and** *end*[*end*[*i*]] $\neq$ 0 $\rightarrow$ *new* := *end*[*end*[*i*]] **fi**
                    barrier
                    if *new* $\neq$ 0 $\rightarrow$ *end*[*i*] := *new* **fi**   # update *end*[*i*]
                    barrier
                    $d := 2 * d$
                af

Figure 3.19. Finding the end of a serially linked list.

---

point to a list element two links away (if there is one). After two rounds, *end*[*i*] will point to a list element four links away (again, if there is one). After $\lceil \log_2 n \rceil$ rounds, every process will have found the end of the list.

Figure 3.19 gives an implementation of this data parallel algorithm. Since the programming technique is the same as in the parallel prefix computation, the algorithm is structurally identical to that in Figure 3.18. Again, **barrier** specifies barrier synchronization points, and these are needed to avoid interference. Loop invariant *FIND* specifies what *end*[*i*] points to before and after each iteration. If the end of the list is fewer than 2^{d-1} links away from element *i*, then *end*[*i*] will not change on further iterations.

To illustrate the execution of this algorithm, consider a 6-element list linked together as follows:

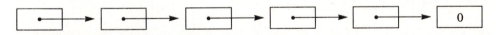

At the start of the for-all loop in *Find*, the *end* pointers will contain these links. After the first iteration of the for-all loop, *end* will contain the following links:

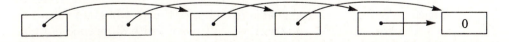

Notice that the *end* links for the last two elements have not changed since they are already correct. After the second round, the *end* links will be:

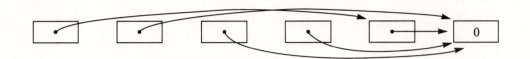

After the third and final round, the *end* links will have their final values:

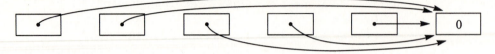

As with the parallel prefix computation, we can adapt this algorithm to use fewer than *n* processes. As before, each would then be responsible for computing the values for a subset of the *end* pointers.

Grid Computations

Many problems in image processing or involving partial differential equations can be solved using what are called *grid computations* or *mesh computations*. The basic idea is to employ a matrix of points that superimposes a grid or mesh on a spatial region. In an image processing problem, the matrix is initialized to pixel values, and the goal is to do something like find sets of neighboring pixels having the same intensity. For partial differential equations, the edges of the matrix are initialized to boundary conditions, and the goal is to compute an approximation for the value of each interior point, which corresponds to finding a steady state solution to the equation. In either case, the basic outline of a grid computation is:

> initialize the matrix
> **do** not yet terminated →
>   compute a new value for each point
>   check for termination
> **od**

On each iteration, the new values of points can typically be computed in parallel.

As a specific example, this section presents a solution to Laplace's equation in two dimensions: $\Delta^2(\Phi) = 0$. Let $grid[0{:}n + 1, 0{:}n + 1]$ be a matrix of points. The edges of *grid* represent the boundary of a two-dimensional region. The interior elements of *grid* correspond to a mesh that is superimposed on the region. The goal is to compute the steady state values of interior points. For Laplace's equation, we can use a finite difference method such as Jacobi iteration. In particular, on each iteration we compute a new value for each interior point by taking the average of the previous values of its four closest neighbors. This method is stationary, so we can terminate the

var *grid*[0:*n* + 1, 0:*n* + 1], *newgrid*[0:*n* + 1, 0:*n* + 1] : **real**
var *converged* : **bool** := false

Grid[*i*: 1..*n*, *j*: 1..*n*]::
    do not *converged* →
        newgrid[*i*, *j*] :=
            (*grid*[*i* − 1, *j*] + *grid*[*i* + 1, *j*] + *grid*[*i*, *j* − 1] + *grid*[*i*, *j* + 1]) / 4
        barrier
        check for convergence
        barrier
        grid[*i*, *j*] := *newgrid*[*i*, *j*]
        barrier
    od

Figure 3.20. Grid computation for solving Laplace's equation.

---

computation when the new value for every point is within some constant EPSILON of its previous value.

Figure 3.20 presents a grid computation that solves Laplace's equation. Once again we use barriers to synchronize steps of the computation. In this case, there are three steps per iteration: update *newgrid*, check for convergence, and then move the contents of *newgrid* into *grid*. Two matrices are used so that new values for grid points depend only on old values. The computation terminates when values in *newgrid* are all within EPSILON of those in *grid*. These differences can of course be checked in parallel, but the results need to be combined. This can be done using a parallel prefix computation. We leave the details to the reader (see exercise 3.23).

Although there is a great deal of potential parallelism in a grid computation, on most machines there is way too much. Consequently, it is typical to partition the grid into blocks and to assign one process (and processor) to each block. Each process manages its block of points; the processes interact as in Figure 3.20.

Synchronous Multiprocessors

On an asynchronous multiprocessor, each processor executes a separate process and the processes execute at potentially different rates. Asynchronous multiprocessors are examples of MIMD machines, which means they have multiple instruction streams and multiple data streams, i.e., multiple independent processes. This is the execution model we have assumed.

Although MIMD machines are the most widely used and flexible multiprocessors, commercial SIMD machines have recently become available, e.g., the Connection Machine. An SIMD machine has multiple data streams but only a single instruction steam. In particular, every processor executes exactly the same sequence of instructions, and they do so in lock step. This makes SIMD machines especially suited to executing data parallel algorithms. For example, on an SIMD machine, the algorithm in Figure 3.18 for computing all partial sums of an array simplifies to:

$$\textbf{var } a[1{:}n] : \textbf{int}, sum[1{:}n] : \textbf{int}$$

$$Sum[i{:}1..n]{::} \textbf{ var } d := 1$$
$$\quad sum[i] := a[i] \qquad \text{\# initialize elements of } sum$$
$$\quad \textbf{do } d < n \rightarrow$$
$$\qquad \textbf{if } (i - d) \geq 1 \rightarrow sum[i] := sum[i - d] + sum[i] \textbf{ fi}$$
$$\qquad d := 2 * d$$
$$\quad \textbf{od}$$

We do not need to program barriers since every process executes the same instructions at the same time; hence every instruction and indeed every memory reference is followed by an implicit barrier. In addition, we do not need to use extra variables to hold old values. In the assignment to $sum[i]$, every process(or) fetches the old values from sum before any assigns new values. Hence an SIMD machine reduces some sources of interference by making parallel expression evaluation appear to be atomic.

It is technologically much easier to construct an SIMD machine with a massive number of processors than it is to construct a massively parallel MIMD machine. This makes SIMD machines attractive for large problems that can be solved using data parallel algorithms. The challenge for the programmer, however, is to keep the processors busy doing useful work. In the above algorithm, for example, fewer and fewer processors update $sum[i]$ on each iteration. Those processors for which the guard on the **if** statement is false simply delay until the others complete the **if** statement. Although conditional statements are necessary in most algorithms, they reduce efficiency on SIMD machines.

3.7 On-The-Fly Garbage Collection

This section develops a parallel algorithm for garbage collection in a list-processing environment. The problem is important and the solution is practical, even on a single processor. The solution is also subtle, due to the fine degree of interaction between the list manipulation and garbage collection processes. To manage this intricacy, one has to use a systematic approach. In fact, several purported "solutions" to this problem have contained subtle synchronization errors.

A list consists of a sequence of atoms and/or lists. For example, $(a, (b, c))$ is a list consisting of the atom a followed by the list (b, c), which in turn consists of a sequence of two atoms. Lists are the basic data type in Lisp and are one of the main data types in Icon. They are also employed in many applications—e.g., symbolic computation—written in languages such as C and Pascal.

The data structure commonly used in implementations of LISP is a rooted, directed graph in which each node contains two fields. The first field contains either an atom or a pointer to the head of a list. The second field contains either a null pointer or a pointer to the head of a list. (A tag field is used to indicate whether the first field contains an atom or a pointer.) For example, the list $(a, (b, c))$ would be represented as follows:

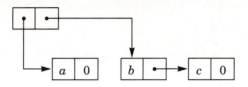

Above, a null pointer is represented by a zero.

Associated with each graph is one distinguished root node. A node is *reachable* if it can be reached from the root by following a series of links. In general, a graph is allowed to contain cycles.

List processing actions add or delete links to existing nodes or add links to new nodes. For this reason, we will call the process that manipulates a list the *Mutator*. New nodes are taken from a free list of unused nodes as needed. Nodes are called *garbage* if they were part of a list but have become unreachable because links were deleted. One way to reclaim garbage is to have the programmer explicitly place it back on the free list. A far better way is to employ a *garbage collector*.

In a sequential environment, garbage collection is typically triggered when *Mutator* needs a new node but the free list is empty. The garbage collector is then activated. It marks all nodes that are reachable and then reclaims unmarked nodes by appending them to the free list. *Mutator* then resumes execution.

The disadvantage of the sequential approach is that it results in unpredictable interruptions in *Mutator*'s actions. This can be particularly annoying in an interactive environment. Thus it is attractive to employ a second process, *Collector*, that finds and collects garbage "on the fly." In particular, *Collector* executes concurrently with *Mutator*, repeatedly marking reachable nodes, then collecting unmarked nodes. This approach can of course readily be implemented on a shared-memory multiprocessor. It can also be implemented efficiently on a single processor by executing *Collector* whenever *Mutator* is blocked waiting for input or output to complete.

Problem Specification

We now define the parallel garbage collection problem more precisely. This requires deciding on a representation for nodes and lists and specifying the invariant relations the processes are to maintain. For simplicity, we assume there are only two lists: one representing *Mutator*'s graph and one containing the free list. Let variable *root* point to the root of the graph, and let *free* point to the head of the free list. We also ignore the tag field that indicates whether a field contains an atom or a pointer.

The *Collector* process repeatedly executes three phases:

- a marking phase that marks all reachable nodes,
- a collecting phase that appends unreachable nodes to the free list, and
- an unmarking phase.

To distinguished marked from unmarked nodes, let each node have a "color." In particular, at the start of the marking phase, all nodes are white (ignoring the actions of *Mutator* for now). During the marking phase, *Collector* colors all reachable nodes black; at the end of this phase, unreachable nodes will still be white. During the collecting phase, white nodes are appended to the free list. During the unmarking phase, black nodes are again whitened. *Collector* thus has the following outline:

> *Collector*:: **do** true →
>   mark: color all reachable nodes black
>   collect: append all white nodes to free list
>   unmark: whiten all black nodes
>   **od**

Mutator takes three kinds of actions that interact with *Collector*: It adds new links to already reachable nodes, deletes links to nodes, or takes nodes off the free list and adds links to them. *Mutator* actions on the data in a node do not affect garbage collection and hence are not of concern here. Similarly, whether *Mutator* terminates or not is of no concern. Thus, *Mutator* will be modeled as follows:

> *Mutator*:: **do** true → add link to reachable node
>   [] true → delete link
>   [] true → take free node and add link to it
>   **od**

Figure 3.21 illustrates a sequence of *Mutator* actions.

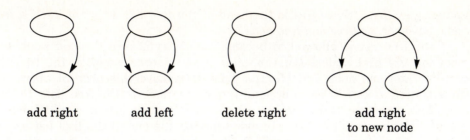

add right   add left   delete right   add right
to new node

Figure 3.21. A sequence of *Mutator* actions.

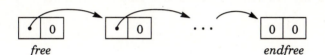

free   *endfree*

Figure 3.22. Representation of the free list.

Ignoring the data fields, we will represent the graph and free list by three arrays* and three auxiliary variables:

var *left*[0:n], *right*[0:n] : **int**
var *color*[0:n] : (white, black)
var *root*, *free*, *endfree* : **int**

Variable *root* contains the index of the root of the *Mutator*'s graph; *free* contains the index of the head of the free list. These nodes are in fixed places in the array and do not change. We will represent a null link by 0 and hence will not use the 0th elements of the arrays for regular nodes. Since the free list and "null" node are stored in the arrays, they will be marked and unmarked by *Collector*, just like other nodes.

We will represent the free list as shown in Figure 3.22. The value in *left*[*free*] points to the first free node, and the *left* fields of free nodes are used to link free nodes together. The *right* fields of free nodes are null pointers (i.e., 0). Variable *endfree* is the index of the end of the free list. When *Mutator* needs a free node, it uses *left*[*free*] and then updates *free*. *Collector* appends a node to the free list by making node *endfree* point to it, then

*This representation makes the algorithms easier to read than the alternative of representing each node by a record. The latter representation could, however, result in better memory utilization since the fields of each node would be in adjacent memory locations.

updating *endfree*. Since *free* is the head of the free list, it is not itself a free node; however, *endfree* is a free node.

If the free list is allowed to become empty, removing the last node and inserting the first node become special cases. Worse, suppose the free list contains just one node and *Mutator* tries to remove this node at about the same time *Collector* tries to append a garbage node to the free list. In this case, *free* points to node *endfree*, so removal and insertion would have to execute with mutual exclusion to avoid having the end of the free list linked to a node that was just removed! Both problems are avoided if the free list always contains at least one node; i.e., a node is removed only if there will be at least one node left on the free list. This requirement is reasonable, given that in practice the number of nodes will be quite large. It is captured by ensuring that the following predicate is a global invariant:

(3.18)   *FREE*: $left[free] \neq 0$

The critical requirement for a garbage collector is that only unreachable nodes are collected as garbage. In other words, nodes that are appended to the free list must not be reachable from *root*. Thus, the following predicate must be a global invariant:

(3.19)   *GC*: node *endfree* is not reachable from *root*

This predicate could be stated formally, but the informal characterization is easier to understand, provided care is taken when dealing with it.

Solution Outline

In a *Mutator/Collector* system, the initial state has all but one node on the free list, with the other node being the *root* of the *Mutator* graph. If node 1 is the initial *root*, the following code initializes the shared variables:

$$left[0] := 0; right[0] := 0$$
$$root := 1; left[root] := 0; right[root] := 0; color[root] := \text{white}$$
$$\textbf{fa } i := 2 \textbf{ to } n - 1 \rightarrow left[i] := i + 1; right[i] := 0; color[i] := \text{white } \textbf{af}$$
$$left[n] := 0; right[n] := 0; color[n] := \text{white}$$
$$free := 2; endfree := n$$

After initialization, predicates *FREE* and *GC* are indeed true, assuming that n is at least 2.

In the collecting phase, *Collector* appends white nodes to the free list. To ensure that *GC* is true, such a node must not be reachable from *root*. Hence, at the start of the collecting phase, all white nodes must be unreachable. Since *Collector* blackens reachable nodes during the marking phase—

including *root*, *free*, and the null node (0)—white nodes are not reachable if, at the end of the marking phase, the successors of each black node are also black. In short, there should be no edges from black to white nodes. Thus the goal of the marking phase is to make the following predicate true:

(3.20)   *MARK1*: (∀ i: $1 \leq i < n + 1$: (*color*[i] = black) ⇒
    (*color*[*left*[i]] = black ∧ *color*[*right*[i]] = black))

One way to achieve *MARK1* is first to color *root* and *free* black, then to color reachable nodes in waves spreading out from *root* and *free*. In a sequential environment, the most efficient way to mark reachable nodes would be to follow links, say, in a depth-first manner. However, parallel execution of *Mutator* could interfere with this since *Mutator* might add and delete links. Thus, the marking phase needs repeatedly to search for black nodes with white successors, then color the successors. An appropriate loop invariant results by replacing the constant $n + 1$ in *MARK1* by variable k:

(3.21)   *I1*: (∀ i: $1 \leq i < k$: (*color*[i] = black) ⇒
    (*color*[*left*[i]] = black ∧ *color*[*right*[i]] = black))

To make *I1* true initially, we need to initialize k to 1 so the range is empty.

On each loop iteration in the marking phase, if node k is white or is black and has no white successors, k is increased. On the other hand, if node k is black and has a white successor, k's successors are colored black. Since the index of a successor might be less than k, to reachieve loop invariant *I1*, we set k to the minimum of *left*[k], *right*[k], and $k + 1$. The resulting algorithm for the marking phase is shown in Figure 3.23. Assuming *Mutator* does not color nodes white, the marking loop terminates since eventually every reachable node is black and there are only a finite number of such nodes.

The collecting phase can be implemented by iterating through the nodes, placing all white ones at the end of the free list. The unmarking phase can also be implemented by iterating through the nodes, whitening all black nodes. Since every node is either black or white, these two phases are disjoint; hence they can be combined as shown in Figure 3.23.

There are six *Mutator* actions that affect garbage collection: delete a left or right link, add a left or right link to an existing node, and add a left or right link to a new node. Since the actions on the left and right links are symmetric, we will consider only those on the left links. Ignoring for now potential interference with *Collector*, the actions on the left link can be implemented as shown in Figure 3.24.

```
# marking phase — blacken reachable nodes
color[0] := black; color[root] := black; color[free] := black; k := 1
{ I1 }
do k ≤ n and color[k] = black and ( (color[left[k]] = white
      or color[right[k]] = white ) →
            color[left[k]] := black; color[right[k]] := black
            k := min(left[k], right[k], k + 1)
 [] k ≤ n and color[k] = black and color[left[k]] = black
      and color[right[k]] = black → k := k + 1
 [] k ≤ n and color[k] = white → k := k + 1
od
{ I1 ∧ k = n + 1 }  { MARK1 }
# collect white nodes and unmark black nodes
fa k := 0 to n →
      if color[k] = white → left[k] := 0; right[k] := 0
                                  left[endfree] := k; endfree := k
      [] color[k] = black → color[k] := white
      fi
af
```

Figure 3.23. Initial version of body of *Collector* process.

A Coarse-Grained Solution

We now need to examine the actions of *Collector* and *Mutator* to see which need to be grouped into larger atomic actions in order to ensure the invariance of predicates *FREE* (3.18) and *GC* (3.19). The marking phase of *Collector* does not reference *free* or *endfree* and does not alter any links; hence it does not interfere with either *FREE* or *GC*. The collecting phase of *Collector* adds nodes to the free list but does so in a way that cannot interfere with the invariance of either *FREE* or *GC*. In particular, at the end of the marking phase, *MARK1* is true, and hence no white node is reachable from either *root* or *free*. Thus, adding white node k to the free list does not invalidate *GC*. Moreover, since node k was not reachable, k was not on the free list, and hence $left[free] \neq k$. Thus, setting *endfree* to k cannot invalidate the invariance of *FREE*. The end result of these observations is that we do not need to change the *Collector* from that in Figure 3.23.

Next consider the *Mutator* actions in Figure 3.24. Deleting a link cannot affect either *FREE* or *GC*; it might make a node unreachable, but, if so, *Collector* will eventually determine that and collect the node. However, adding a link to a new or existing node makes it reachable from *root* and hence would interfere with *GC* if the node were to be collected as garbage.

DeleteLeft: # delete the left link of node *i*
                  left[*i*] := 0
AddLeft: # add a left link from node *i* to already reachable node *j*
                  left[*i*] := *j*
NewLeft: # get free node *f* and add a left link from node *i* to *f*
                  f := *left*[*free*]
                  left[*i*] := *f*
                  left[*free*] := *left*[*f*]
                  left[*f*] := 0

Figure 3.24. Outline of *Mutator* actions on left links.

Collector leaves *GC* invariant as long as *MARK1* (3.20) is true at the end of the marking phase. This in turn requires that *Mutator* not interfere with loop invariant *I1* (3.21) of the marking phase. Consider *Mutator* action *AddLeft*, which adds a link from node *i* to an already reachable node *j*. If node *i* was white, then adding a link to *j* cannot interfere with *I1* since the antecedent of the implication is false for node *i*. Similarly, if nodes *i* and *j* are both black, adding a link from *i* to *j* cannot interfere with *I1* since the consequent of the implication is already true. However, if node *i* is black and node *j* is white, then node *j* needs to be blackened when *Mutator* adds an edge to it. Thus, it appears that *AddLeft* should be:

> *AddLeft*: ⟨ *left*[*i*] := *j*; *color*[*j*] := black ⟩

This ensures that *I1* is true for node *i*. But what about node *j*? If *j* happens to be less than *Collector* loop index *k*, then *j* is now black, but there is no assurance that *j*'s successors are black. Either the value of *k* has to be decreased to at most *j* or assertion *I1* has to be weakened. The *Mutator* cannot alter *k* without interfering with *Collector*, so we have to consider ways to weaken *I1*.

One way to weaken *I1* to take account of the above situation is to have *Mutator* set a variable to indicate that it has just blackened *j* (*left*[*i*]), then have *Mutator* wait until *Collector* blackens *j*'s successors and clears the variable. However, this delays *Mutator*, which undermines the purpose of parallel garbage collection. A second approach is to use a third color, gray, to "shade" a white node when a link is added to it. We thus modify the declaration of *color*:

> **var** *color*[1:*n*] : (white, gray, black)

And we change *AddLeft* as follows:

$$AddLeft: \langle\ left[i] := j;\ \textbf{if}\ color[j] = \text{white} \rightarrow color[j] := \text{gray}\ \textbf{fi}\ \rangle$$

Now *I1* will not be interfered if we weaken it as follows:

(3.22)   *I2*: ($\forall\ i$: $1 \le i < k$: $(color[i] = \text{black}) \Rightarrow$
            $(color[left[i]] \ne \text{white} \wedge color[right[i]] \ne \text{white}))$

In short, the successors of black nodes are never white.

At the end of the marking phase, it is imperative that white nodes not be reachable. When there were only two colors—white and black—predicate *MARK1* (3.20) ensures that white nodes are unreachable. This predicate in turn follows from the marking phase loop invariant *I1* together with termination of the marking phase ($k = n + 1$). Unfortunately, the weaker loop invariant *I2* (3.22) is not strong enough to ensure that all nodes are black or white; there could now also be gray nodes. We cannot strengthen the loop invariant since the stronger loop invariant *I1* (3.21) is interfered with. Thus we have to strengthen the loop termination condition.

What we require at the end of the marking phase is that no successor of a black node be white and that there be no gray nodes:

(3.23)   *MARK2*: ($\forall\ i$: $1 \le i < n + 1$: $(color[i] = \text{black}) \Rightarrow$
                $(color[left[i]] \ne \text{white} \wedge color[right[i]] \ne \text{white}))$
            $\wedge$ ($\forall\ i$: $1 \le i < n + 1$: $color[i] \ne \text{gray})$

The first conjunct above follows from *I2*. To satisfy the second requirement, we need to augment the marking phase to ensure that there are no gray nodes when the phase terminates. Clearly one modification is to blacken a gray node whenever one is seen; if k is not changed at this point, the next iteration of the marking loop will if necessary blacken k's successors and reset the value of k. This is not sufficient to ensure *MARK2*, however, since k could be larger than the index of a gray node and *Mutator* actions could prevent the *Collector* from ever seeing a link to the gray node (see exercise 3.31). Thus, when all nodes have been examined (i.e., $k = n + 1$), *Collector* needs to make one last pass over the entire array to ensure that there are no gray nodes. Adding these two modifications, we get the *Collector* algorithm shown in Figure 3.25. The collecting and unmarking phases of the *Collector* are the same as before.

In Figure 3.25, the last arm of the marking loop checks the colors of all nodes. If all are black or white, variable *possible_gray* is set to false. If a gray node is found, k is set to point to that node, which will get blackened on the next iteration of the marking loop. When the marking phase terminates, all nodes are black or white, and white nodes are not reachable. Since

```
# marking phase — blacken reachable nodes
color[0] := black; color[root] := black; color[free] := black
possible_gray := true; k := 1
{ I2 }
do k ≤ n and color[k] = black and
        (color[left[k]] ≠ black or color[right[k]] ≠ black) →
                color[left[k]] := black; color[right[k]] := black
                k := min(left[k], right[k], k + 1)
[] k ≤ n and color[k] = black and color[left[k]] = black
        and color[right[k]] = black → k := k + 1
[] k ≤ n and color[k] = gray → color[k] := black
[] k ≤ n and color[k] = white → k := k + 1
[] k = n + 1 and possible_gray →
                j := 1; do j ≤ n and color[j] ≠ gray → j := j + 1 od
                if j = n + 1 → possible_gray := false
                [] j < n + 1 → k := j
                fi
od
{ I2 ∧ k = n + 1 ∧ ¬possible_gray } { MARK2 }
# collect white nodes and unmark black nodes
fa k := 0 to n →
        if color[k] = white → left[k] := 0; right[k] := 0
                                left[endfree] := k; endfree := k
        [] color[k] = black → color[k] := white
        fi
af
```

Figure 3.25. Final version of body of *Collector* process.

Mutator adds links only to already reachable nodes, which are now black, *Mutator* will not color any node gray, at least not until after it has already been whitened in the collecting/unmarking phase. Thus, *Mutator* will not interfere with *MARK2*.

The final thing we have to consider is *Mutator*'s *NewLeft* action. As in *AddLeft*, if the node f taken off the free list is white, it should be colored gray when it is linked to node i, again to avoid interference with *I2*. Thus, the second assignment in *NewLeft* needs to be replaced by:

$$\langle \; left[i] := f; \textbf{if } color[f] = \text{white} \rightarrow color[f] := \text{gray } \textbf{fi} \; \rangle$$

Similarly, when *left[free]* is changed, the node at the front of the free list needs to be made at least gray. To ensure that *FREE* is not interfered with,

DeleteLeft: # delete the left link of node i
                $left[i] := 0$

AddLeft: # add a left link from node i to node j
                $\langle\, left[i] := j;$ **if** $color[j] =$ white $\rightarrow color[j] :=$ gray **fi** $\rangle$

NewLeft: # get free node f and add a left link from node i to f
                $f := left[free]$
                $\langle\, left[i] := f;$ **if** $color[f] =$ white $\rightarrow color[f] :=$ gray **fi** $\rangle$
                $\langle\,$ **await** $f \neq endfree \rightarrow$
                $\qquad left[free] := left[f]$
                $\qquad$ **if** $color[left[free]] =$ white $\rightarrow color[left[free]] :=$ gray **fi** $\rangle$
                $left[f] := 0$

Figure 3.26. Coarse-grained *Mutator* actions on left links.

---

we also need to guard the assignment to $left[free]$. In particular, since

$$wp(left[free] := left[f],\ FREE) = (left[f] \neq 0) = (f \neq endfree)$$

we replace the assignment to $left[free]$ by the conditional atomic action:

$\langle\,$ **await** $f \neq endfree \rightarrow$
$\quad left[free] := left[f]$
$\quad$ **if** $color[left[free]] =$ white $\rightarrow color[left[free]] :=$ gray **fi** $\rangle$

With these changes to *NewLeft* and the earlier change to *AddLeft*, the *Mutator*'s actions are as shown in Figure 3.26.

A Fine-Grained Solution

Although the coarse-grained solutions in Figures 3.25 and 3.26 are correct, *Mutator* has three composite atomic actions: one in *AddLeft* and two in *NewLeft*. These could be implemented using a critical section protocol, but the resulting overhead would make parallel garbage collection little if any better than traditional, sequential garbage collection. Fortunately it is possible to implement these specific atomic actions in an efficient way using simple machine instructions.

First consider the atomic action in *AddLeft* in Figure 3.26. This adds a link from node i to node j, then colors node j gray if it was previously white. Suppose we separate this into two atomic actions:

(3.24) $\langle \mathit{left}[i] := j \rangle$
          $\langle \textbf{if } \mathit{color}[j] = \mathit{white} \rightarrow \mathit{color}[j] := \text{gray } \textbf{fi} \rangle$

We can implement the first atomic action above by load and store instructions available on any processor since i is a reachable node, and hence *Collector* will not assign to *left*[i]. We can also implement the **if** statement atomically if a machine has an "or to memory" instruction, which most do. Let white be represented by the bit string 00, gray by 01 and black by 11. Then executing 01 **or** *color*[k] will make node k gray if it was white but will not change node k's color if it was gray or black.

Although each action in (3.24) can be implemented atomically, executing the first by itself interferes with *Collector*'s marking invariant *I2* (3.22). In particular, interference occurs if the color of a node (i above) is black but the color of a successor (j above) is white. However, the situation is temporary; as soon as the second action is executed, *I2* will again be true. Moreover, since j is already reachable, it is now pointed to by two nodes; hence, *Collector* cannot complete the marking phase without coloring j black. As seen earlier with the tie-breaker algorithm (Section 3.3), we can address this problem in a formal proof of correctness by using an auxiliary variable. Here we need to indicate that *Mutator* has just added a link and is at the control point between the two statements in (3.24); then we need to weaken *I2* to account for this situation.

Now consider the atomic actions in *NewLeft* in Figure 3.26. The first is similar to the one in *AddLeft*, so it too can be implemented as in (3.24). The second, conditional atomic action in *NewLeft* is more complex. However, once the guard becomes true, it remains true since the *Collector* appends nodes to the end of the free list and hence only makes *endfree* point to nodes farther away from *free*. Thus, the guard and assignments can be put in separate actions as follows:

(3.25) $\langle \textbf{await } f \neq \mathit{endfree} \rightarrow \textbf{skip} \rangle$
          $\langle \mathit{left}[\mathit{free}] := \mathit{left}[f]$
          $\textbf{if } \mathit{color}[\mathit{left}[\mathit{free}]] = \text{white} \rightarrow \mathit{color}[\mathit{left}[\mathit{free}]] := \text{gray } \textbf{fi} \rangle$

Now the conditional action can be implemented by a loop since it references only one variable that is altered by *Collector*. The second atomic action in (3.25) is similar to the other actions that add a link to a node and then color it gray. Thus, it too can be implemented as in (3.24).

To summarize, the parallel garbage collector consists of the *Collector* shown in Figure 3.25 and the *Mutator* actions shown in Figure 3.26. The atomic actions in *Mutator* are in turn implemented using (3.24) and (3.25), with coloring a node being implemented by an "or-to-memory" instruction.

3.8 Implementing Processes

We have used the **co** statement and processes throughout this chapter and will use them throughout the remainder of the book. This section shows how to implement them. First, we give an implementation for a single processor. Then we generalize the implementation to support execution of processes on a shared-memory multiprocessor. (We describe implementations for distributed memory machines in Part III.)

Both implementations employ a collection of data structures and routines called a *kernel*.* The role of the kernel is to provide a virtual processor for each process so that the process has the illusion that it is executing on its own processor. Since our focus is just on implementing processes, we do not cover many operating system issues that arise in practice, e.g., dynamic storage allocation, priority scheduling, virtual memory, device control, file access, or protection. The Historical Notes section cites references that discuss these issues and their relation to a kernel; also see the exercises.

Recall that processes are merely abbreviations for **co** statements. Thus, it is sufficient to show how to implement **co** statements. Consider the following program fragment:

(3.26)   **var** shared variables
           S_0
           co P_1: S_1 // ... // P_n: S_n **oc**
           S_{n+1}

The P_i are process names. The S_i are statement lists and optional declarations of variables local to the P_i. We need three different mechanisms to implement (3.26):

- one to create processes and start them executing,
- one to stop a process,
- and a third to determine that the **co** statement has completed.

A *primitive* is a routine that is implemented by a kernel in such a way that it appears to be an atomic instruction. We will create and destroy processes by two kernel primitives: **fork** and **quit.** When one process invokes **fork**, another process is created and made eligible for execution. Arguments to **fork** indicate the address of the first instruction to be executed by the new process and any other data needed to specify its initial state (e.g., parameters). When a process invokes **quit**, it ceases to exist.

---

*A kernel is sometimes called a *nucleus*. In either case, the name indicates that this software is common to every processor and is the core software module.

A kernel usually provides a third primitive to enable a process to delay until another process terminates. However, since in this chapter processes synchronize by means of busy waiting, we will detect process termination by using a global array of boolean variables. (Later chapters describe other mechanisms.) In particular, we can use these global variables, **fork**, and **quit** to implement (3.26) as follows:

(3.27)   **var** $done[1{:}n]$: **bool** := ($[n]$ false), other shared variables
$\quad\quad$ S_0
$\quad\quad$ # create the processes, then wait for them to terminate
$\quad\quad$ **fa** $i := 1$ **to** $n \to$ **fork**(P_i) **af**
$\quad\quad$ **fa** $i := 1$ **to** $n \to$ **do not** $done[i] \to$ **skip od af**
$\quad\quad$ S_{n+1}

Each of the P_i executes the following code:

$\quad\quad$ P_i: S_i; $done[i]$:= true; **quit**( )

We assume that the main process in (3.27) is created implicitly so that it automatically begins execution. We also assume that the code and data for all the processes are already stored in memory when the main process begins.

We now present a single-processor kernel that implements **fork** and **quit.** We also describe how to schedule processes so that each gets a periodic chance to execute.

A Single-Processor Kernel

Any kernel contains data structures that represent processes and three basic kinds of routines: interrupt handlers, the primitives themselves, and a dispatcher. The kernel may also contain other data structures and functionality, e.g., file descriptors and file access routines. We focus here just on the parts of a kernel that implement processes.

There are three basic ways to organize a kernel:

- as a monolithic unit in which each kernel primitive executes as an atomic action;

- as a collection of specialized processes that interact to implement kernel primitives; e.g., one may handle file I/O, and another, memory management; or

- as a concurrent program in which more than one user process may be executing a kernel primitive at the same time.

We use the first approach here since that is the simplest for a small, single-processor kernel. We will use the third later in the multiprocessor kernel.

Each process is represented in the kernel by a *process descriptor*. When a process is idle, its descriptor contains all the information needed to execute the process. This includes the address of the next instruction the process will execute and the contents of processor registers.

The kernel starts executing when an interrupt occurs. Interrupts can be divided into two broad categories: external interrupts from peripheral devices and internal interrupts (also called traps) triggered by the executing process. When an interrupt occurs, the processor automatically saves enough state information so that the interrupted process can be resumed. Then the processor enters an *interrupt handler*; there is typically one handler for each kind of interrupt.

To invoke a kernel primitive, a process causes an internal interrupt by executing a machine instruction variously named a supervisor call (SVC) or trap. The process passes an argument with the SVC instruction to indicate what primitive is to be executed and passes other arguments in registers. The SVC interrupt handler first saves the full state of the executing process. Then it calls the appropriate primitive, which is implemented within the kernel by a procedure. When the primitive completes, it in turn calls the *dispatcher* (processor scheduler). The dispatcher selects a process for execution and then loads its state.

To ensure that the primitives are executed atomically, the first action of an interrupt handler is to inhibit further interrupts; the last action of the dispatcher is to enable interrupts.* When an interrupt occurs, further interrupts are inhibited automatically by the hardware; the kernel reenables interrupts as a side-effect of loading a process state. Figure 3.27 illustrates the kernel components and shows the flow of control through the kernel. As shown, control flows in one direction: from interrupt handlers through the primitives to the dispatcher and then back out to one active process.

We will represent the process descriptors by an array:

var *process_descriptors*[1:*n*] : *process_type*

The *process_type* is a record type describing the fields in a process descriptor. When the kernel is asked to create a new process, it allocates and initializes an empty descriptor. When the kernel's dispatcher schedules a process, it needs to find the descriptor of a process that is eligible to execute. Both functions could be implemented by searching through the *process_descriptors* array, assuming each record contains a field indicating whether the entry is

---

*Some machines have multiple interrupt classes or levels. In this case, each interrupt handler need inhibit only those interrupts that could interfere with the one being processed.

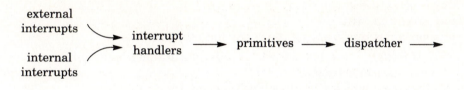

Figure 3.27. Kernel components and flow of control.

free or in use. More commonly, however, two lists are maintained: a *free list* of empty descriptors and a *ready list* of descriptors of processes that are waiting a turn to execute. We use the list representation below. An additional kernel variable, *executing*, contains the index of the descriptor of the process that is currently executing.

With this representation for the kernel data structures, the *fork* primitive takes a descriptor off the free list, initializes it, and inserts it on the end of the ready list. The *quit* primitive puts the descriptor of the executing process on the free list and sets *executing* to zero to indicate to the dispatcher that the process no longer wants to execute.

When the dispatcher is called at the end of a primitive, it checks the value of *executing*. If it is zero, the dispatcher removes the first descriptor from the ready list and sets *executing* to point to it. (If *executing* is not zero, the currently executing process is to continue executing.) The dispatcher then loads the state of the process that is to execute next. We assume here that the ready list is a first-in, first-out (FIFO) queue.

Our remaining concern is to ensure fairness of process execution. If the executing process were always to terminate in finite time, the above implementation of the kernel would ensure fairness since we assume the ready list is a FIFO queue. However, if any process—such as the main process in (3.27)—waits for a condition that is not yet true, it will spin forever unless it is forced to relinquish the processor. We can use an interval timer to ensure that processes periodically release control of the processor, assuming of course that such a timer is provided by the hardware. This, plus the fact that the ready list is a FIFO queue, will guarantee each process periodic chances to execute.

An *interval timer* is a device that, when initialized with a positive integer value, decrements the value at a fixed rate and triggers a timer interrupt when the value becomes zero. The kernel uses such a timer as follows. First, before loading the state of the process that is to execute next, the dispatcher initializes the timer. Then, if the timer interrupts occurs, the timer interrupt handler places the descriptor of *executing* at the end of the ready list, sets *executing* to 0, and then calls the dispatcher. This causes processes to take turns executing in round-robin fashion.

var *process_descriptors*[1:*n*] : *process_type*
var *executing* : **int**
var variables representing the ready list and free lists
SVC_Handler: # entered with interrupts automatically inhibited
    save state of *executing*
    determine which primitive was invoked, then call it
Timer_Handler: # entered with interrupts automatically inhibited
    insert descriptor of *executing* at end of ready list; *executing* := 0
    call *dispatcher*( )
procedure *fork*(initial process state)
    remove a descriptor from the free list
    initialize the descriptor
    insert the descriptor on the end of the ready list
    call *dispatcher*( )
end
procedure *quit*( )
    insert descriptor of *executing* at end of free list; *executing* := 0
    call *dispatcher*( )
end
procedure *dispatcher*( )
    if *executing* = 0 → remove descriptor from front of ready list
                          set *executing* to point to it
    fi
    start the interval timer
    load state of *executing*   # interrupts automatically enabled
end

Figure 3.28. Outline of a single-processor kernel.

Putting all these pieces together, we have the outline for a single-processor kernel shown in Figure 3.28. We assume that when the kernel is initialized—which happens as a result of "booting" a processor—one process is created and made the executing process. We also assume that a side-effect of starting the interval timer in *dispatcher* is to disable any interrupt that might have been pending as a consequence of the timer reaching zero while the kernel is executing. With this latter, reasonable assumption, the process that is selected for execution will not immediately get interrupted and lose control of the processor.

The kernel in Figure 3.28 ignores exceptions that might occur, such as the free list being empty when *fork* is called. This implementation also assumes that there is always at least one ready process. In practice, a kernel would always have one "do nothing" process that is dispatched when there is no useful work to be done (this is often directly supported in hardware). As noted earlier, we have also ignored several other issues that have to be addressed in practice, e.g., I/O interrupt handling, device control, file access, and memory management.

A Multiprocessor Kernel

A shared-memory multiprocessor has two or more processors and at least some memory that is accessible to every processor. It is relatively straightforward to extend the single-processor kernel to a multiprocessor kernel. The main changes we need to make are to store kernel procedures and data structures in shared memory, to access the data structures with mutual exclusion when that is needed to avoid interference, and to change *dispatcher* to exploit the multiple processors. There are some subtleties, however, that result from the special characteristics of multiprocessors.

We assume that internal interrupts (traps) are serviced by the processor that was executing the process that caused the trap and assume that every processor has an interval timer. For now, we also assume that each kernel operation and process can be executed by any processor. (At the end of the section, we describe how to deal with binding kernel operations and processes to processors and how to deal with effects of caches and non-uniform memory access time.)

When a processor is interrupted, it enters the kernel and inhibits further interrupts on that processor. This makes execution in the kernel indivisible on that processor, but it does not prevent other processors from simultaneously executing in the kernel. To preclude interference between the processors, we could make the entire kernel a critical section. However, this is a poor choice for two reasons. First, it unnecessarily precludes some safe concurrent execution. In particular, only access to shared data structures such as the free and ready lists is critical. Second, making the entire kernel into a critical section results in unnecessarily long critical sections. This decreases performance because it delays processors trying to enter the kernel, and it increases memory contention for the variables that implement the kernel critical section protocol. The following principle elucidates a much better choice.

(3.28) **Multiprocessor Locking Principle.** Make critical sections short by individually protecting each critical data structure. Use separate critical sections—with separate variables for the entry and exit protocols—for each critical data structure.

In our kernel, the critical data are the free and ready lists. To protect access to these, we can use any of the critical section protocols given earlier in this chapter. On a particular multiprocessor, the choice of which to use will be affected by which special instructions are available. For example, if there is a Fetch-and-Add instruction, we can use the simple and fair ticket algorithm in Figure 3.9.

Because we assume that traps are handled by the processor on which the trap occurs and that each processor has its own interval timer, the trap and timer interrupt handlers are essentially the same as in the single-processor kernel. The two differences are that *executing* is an array, with one entry per processor, and that *Timer_Handler* needs to lock and unlock the ready list.

The code for the three kernel primitives is also essentially the same. Again, the differences are that *executing* is an array and that the free and ready lists need to be accessed in critical sections.

The greatest changes are to the code for the dispatcher. Before, we had one processor and assumed it always had a process to execute. Now there could be fewer processes than processors, and hence some processors could be idle. When a new process is forked (or awakened after an I/O interrupt), it needs to be assigned to an idle processor, if there is one. This functionality can be provided in three different ways:

- Have each processor, when idle, execute a special process that periodically examines the ready list until it finds a ready process.

- Have a processor executing *fork* search for an idle processor and assign the new process to it.

- Use a separate dispatcher process that executes on its own processor and continuously attempts to assign ready processes to idle processors.

Because idle processors have nothing else to do until they find some process to execute, we will use the first approach. In particular, when the dispatcher finds that the ready list is empty, it sets *executing*[i] to point to the descriptor of an idle process. That process on processor i executes the code shown in Figure 3.29.

In essence, *Idle* is a self-dispatcher. It first spins until the ready list is not empty, then it removes a process descriptor and begins executing that process. To avoid memory contention, *Idle* should not continuously examine the ready list or continuously lock and unlock it. Thus, we use a test-and-test-and-set protocol similar to the ones shown earlier in (3.7) and (3.9). Since the ready list might be empty again before *Idle* acquires the ready-list lock, it needs to retest whether the list is empty.

Our remaining concern is to ensure fairness. Again, we will employ timers to ensure that processes executing outside the kernel are forced to relinquish processors. We assume each processor has its own timer, which it uses as in the single-processor kernel. However, timers alone are not sufficient since processes can now be delayed within the kernel waiting to

```
Idle:: do executing[i] = Idle process →
            do ready list empty → Delay od
            lock ready list
            if ready list not empty →      # need to check it again
                remove descriptor from front of ready list
                set executing[i] to point to it
            fi
            unlock ready list
        od
        start the interval timer on processor i
        load state of executing[i]      # with interrupts enabled
```

Figure 3.29. Code for the idle process.

---

acquire access to the shared kernel data structures. Thus, we need to use a fair solution to the critical section problem such as the tie-breaker, ticket, or bakery algorithms given earlier. If instead we use the test-and-set protocol, there is the possibility that processes might starve. This is not very likely, however, since the critical sections in the kernel are very short.

Figure 3.30 outlines a multiprocessor kernel that incorporates all these assumptions and decisions. Variable i is the index of the processor executing the routines, and lock and unlock are critical section entry and exit protocols. Again, we have ignored possible exceptions and have not included code for I/O interrupt handlers, memory management, and so on.

The multiprocessor kernel in Figure 3.30 employs a single ready list that is assumed to be a FIFO queue. If processes have different priorities, the ready list needs to be a priority queue. However, this will cause a processor to take longer when accessing the ready list, at least when doing an insertion. Thus the ready list might become a bottleneck. If there are a fixed number of priority levels, one solution is to employ a set of queues and give each its own set of locks. This way a descriptor can be inserted at the end of the appropriate queue without having to search for the appropriate place. If there is not a fixed number of priority levels, they could be grouped into classes, and there could be one ready list per class.

The kernel in Figure 3.30 also assumes that a process can execute on any processor. In particular, the dispatcher always schedules the first ready process. On some multiprocessors, some processes—such as device drivers or file servers—might have to execute on a specific processor because a peripheral device is attached only to that processor. In this case, each such processor should have its own ready list and perhaps its own dispatcher. (The situation gets more complicated if a special processor can also execute regular processes since it then needs to be able to schedule them, too.)

var *process_descriptors*[1:*n*] : *process_type*
var *executing*[1:*p*] : **int**   # one entry per processor
var variables representing the ready and free lists and their locks

SVC_Handler: # entered with interrupts inhibited on processor *i*
    save state of *executing*[*i*]
    determine which primitive was invoked, then call it

Timer_Handler: # entered with interrupts inhibited on processor *i*
    lock ready list; insert *executing*[*i*] at end; unlock ready list
    executing[*i*] := 0
    call *dispatcher*( )

procedure *fork*(initial process state)
    lock free list; remove a descriptor; unlock free list
    initialize the descriptor
    lock ready list; insert descriptor at end; unlock ready list
    call *dispatcher*( )
end

procedure *quit*( )
    lock free list; insert *executing*[*i*] at end; unlock free list
    executing[*i*] := 0
    call *dispatcher*( )
end

procedure *dispatcher*( )
    if *executing*[*i*] = 0 →
        lock ready list
        if ready list not empty → remove descriptor from ready list
                                        set *executing*[*i*] to point to it
        [] ready list empty → set *executing*[*i*] to point to *Idle* process
        fi
        unlock ready list
    fi
    if *executing*[*i*] not *Idle* process → start timer on processor *i* **fi**
    load state of *executing*[*i*]   # interrupts automatically enabled
end

Figure 3.30. Outline of a kernel for a shared-memory multiprocessor.

Even if a process can execute on any processor, it may be very inefficient
to schedule it on an arbitrary processor. On a non-uniform memory access
machine, for example, processors can access local memory more rapidly than
remote memory. Hence, a processor should preferably execute processes
whose code and data are stored locally or at least those whose code is local.

This suggests having a separate ready list per processor and assigning processes to processors depending on where their code is stored. Having separate ready lists, however, raises the issue of *load balancing*, i.e., having each processor handle about the same amount of computational load. It is not sufficient to assign the same number of processes to each processor; different processes in general generate different loads, and this can vary dynamically.

Regardless of whether memory access time is uniform or not, it is common for processors to have cache memories or virtual memory translation buffers. In this case, a process should be rescheduled on the processor where it last executed, assuming part of its state is in the cache or translation buffers. Moreover, if two processes share data and that data is in a cache, they might execute most efficiently if they are multiplexed on the same processor rather than executed on different processors; this is called *co-scheduling*. Again this suggests having a separate ready list per processor, which in turn raises the issue of load balancing.

Historical Notes and References

The systematic method for solving synchronization problems described in the introduction to Part II and employed in Chapters 3 to 6 was developed by the author [Andrews 1989]. It was inspired by Edsger Dijkstra's seminal work [1976] on a calculus for deriving sequential programs (see Section 1.6) and by two Dijkstra notes [1979, 1980] on programming with semaphores (see Chapter 4). The method was also inspired by Leslie Lamport and Fred Schneider's observation [1980] that synchronization can be viewed as the problem of maintaining a global invariant.

The critical section problem was introduced by Dijkstra [1965]. It is the first of several synchronization problems that have become classics. (The others are introduced in subsequent chapters.) Because the problem is fundamental, it has been studied by scores of people, who have published literally hundreds of papers on the topic. This chapter has presented four of the most important solutions; the exercises give several additional ones; and M. Raynal [1986] has written an entire book on various algorithms for mutual exclusion. Although devising busy-waiting solutions was early on mostly an academic exercise—since busy waiting is inefficient on a single processor—the advent of multiprocessors has spurred renewed interest in such solutions. Indeed, contemporary multiprocessors all contain some instruction that facilitates at least one busy-waiting solution.

Dijkstra's original paper presented the first *n*-process software solution. It is an extension of the first two-process solution, which was designed by Dutch mathematician T. Dekker (see exercise 3.2 and Bic and Shaw [1988]). However, Dijkstra's original formulation of the problem did not require the eventual entry property (3.5). Donald Knuth [1966] was the first to publish a solution that also ensures eventual entry; deBruijn [1967] and Eisenberg and McGuire [1972] reduce the worst-case entry delay time in Knuth's solution.

The tie-breaker algorithm was discovered by Gary Peterson [1981]; it is often called Peterson's algorithm as a result. This algorithm is particularly simple for two processes, unlike the earlier solutions of Dekker, Dijkstra, et al. Peterson's algorithm also generalizes much more readily to an *n*-process solution, as shown in Figure 3.7. That solution requires that a process go through all *n*–1 stages, even if no other process is trying to enter its critical section. Block and Woo [1990] present a variation that requires only *m* stages if just *m* processes are contending for entry. However, this variation has a much higher bound on the amount of time a process could delay before getting permission to enter (see exercise 3.10).

The bakery algorithm was devised by Lamport [1974]. The version in Figure 3.12 appeared in Lamport [1979]; it is an improvement over the original algorithm. In addition to being much more intuitive than earlier critical section solutions, the bakery algorithm allows processes to enter in essentially FIFO order. It also has the interesting property that it is tolerant of some hardware failures. First, if one process reads *turn*[*i*] while another process is setting it in the entry protocol, the read can return any value between 1 and the value being written. Second, a process *P*[*i*] may fail at any time, assuming it immediately sets *turn*[*i*] to 0; i.e., *P*[*i*] appears to have failed outside its critical section. However, the value of *turn*[*i*] can become unbounded in Lamport's solution if there is always at least one process in its critical section. Several people have developed variations on the bakery algorithm that use only bounded numbers of values (e.g., Peterson [1983b].)

The coarse-grained ticket algorithm is the simplest of the *n*-process solutions to the critical section problem; it also allows processes to enter in the order in which they draw numbers. The ticket algorithm can in fact be viewed as an optimization of the bakery algorithm. However, it requires a Fetch-and-Add instruction to be implemented directly, and only a few experimental machines currently provide such an instruction (e.g., the NYU Ultracomputer and IBM RP3—see Almasi and Gottlieb [1989] for descriptions of these machines).

Harry Jordan [1978] was one of the first to recognize the importance of barrier synchronization in parallel iterative algorithms; he is credited with coining the term *barrier*. Although barriers are not nearly as commonplace as critical sections, they too have been studied by dozens of people who have developed several different implementations. Lubachevsky [1984] presents a centralized barrier that uses two counters, with processes alternating use of the counters. As discussed in the text, such a barrier requires a Fetch-and-Add instruction to be implemented efficiently.

The combining tree barrier in Figures 3.14 and 3.15 is similar to ones devised by Yew, Tzeng, and Lawrie [1987] and by Mellor-Crummey and Scott [1991]. The butterfly barrier was devised by Brooks [1986]. Hensgen, Finkel, and Manber [1988] developed the dissemination barrier; their paper also describes a tournament barrier, which is similar in structure to a combining tree (see exercise 3.15). Gupta [1989] describes a "fuzzy barrier," which includes a region of statements a process can execute while it waits for a barrier; his paper also describes a hardware implementation of fuzzy barriers.

As described in several places in the text, busy-waiting implementations of locks and barriers can lead to memory and interconnection-network contention. Thus it is important for delayed processes to spin on the contents of local memory, e.g., cached copies of variables. Hill and Larus [1990] summarize the kinds of multiprocessor caches and how they affect performance. Goodman et al [1989] describe efficient synchronization primitives for cache-coherent multiprocessors. Eggers and Katz [1989] use traces of parallel programs to examine the effects of sharing on cache and bus performance. Anderson [1989] examines the performance implications of several lock protocols and presents a new, array-based lock protocol. Finally, an excellent paper by Mellor-Crummy and Scott [1991] analyzes the performance of several lock and barrier protocols, including Anderson's and most of those described in the text. That paper also presents a new, list-based lock protocol and a scaleable, tree-based barrier with only local spinning. The conclusions in the text about which barriers are best on which machines are based on Mellor-Crummy and Scott's experiments.

Data parallel algorithms are most closely associated with massively parallel machines since those machines permit thousands of data elements to be operated on in parallel. Many of the earliest examples of data parallel algorithms were designed for the NYU Ultracomputer [Schwartz 1980]; all have the characteristic attribute that execution time is logarithmic in the size of the data. The Ultracomputer is a MIMD machine, and its designers realized the importance of efficient critical section and barrier synchronization protocols. Consequently, they implemented a Replace-and-Add operation in an early hardware prototype [Gottlieb et al. 1983]; this instruction adds a value to a memory word and then returns the result. However, more recent versions of the Ultracomputer provide a Fetch-and-Add operation instead [Almasi & Gottlieb 1989], which returns the value of a memory word before adding to it. This change was made because Fetch-and-Add, unlike Replace-and-Add, generalizes to any binary combining operator, e.g., Fetch-and-Max or Fetch-and-And. This general kind of instruction is called a Fetch-and-Φ operation. (The BBN Butterfly and Monarch and IBM RP3 also provide Fetch-and-Φ instructions.)

The commercial introduction of the massively parallel Connection Machine in the mid 1980s spurred renewed interest in data parallel algorithms. That machine was designed by Daniel Hillis [1985] as part of his Ph.D. dissertation at MIT. (Precious few dissertations have been as influential!) The Connection Machine can have up to 64K processing elements; it also has a virtual processor mechanism that supports the illusion of have many times more processors. This enables a data parallel algorithm to have a very fine granularity; e.g., a processor can be assigned to every element of an array. The Connection Machine is also a SIMD machine, which means barrier synchronization does not have to be programmed since it is automatically provided after every machine instruction. Hillis and Steele [1986] give an overview of the original Connection Machine and describe several data parallel algorithms. Tucker and Robertson [1988] describe the most recent machine, the CM-2, and several applications. Skillicorn and Barnard [1989] look in particular at using the Connection Machine to parse programming languages in logarithmic time.

The first garbage-collection algorithms were designed in the early 1960s in support of early implementations of LISP (see Cohen [1981] for a general survey). Guy Steele [1975] wrote one of the earliest papers on parallel garbage collection; the paper was written while Steele was a Harvard undergraduate, and it won an ACM student paper competition. The garbage-collection algorithm developed in Section 3.7 is very similar to one designed by Dijkstra, et al. [1978]. A detailed proof outline for that algorithm is given in Gries [1977a], which curiously appeared in print before the algorithm itself! Kung and Song [1977] give a more efficient algorithm that uses four colors, and Ben-Ari [1984] gives additional algorithms that require only two colors. Appel et al. [1988] describe a new algorithm that is both concurrent and real-time; i.e., the mutator is never interrupted for more than a small, constant amount of time.

The **fork** and **quit** primitives used in the kernel implementations were first introduced in Dennis and Van Horn [1966]. That paper also introduced a **join** primitive that can be used to wait for a process to quit. Variants of **fork**, **join**, and **quit** are used in most operating systems kernels; e.g., they are used in UNIX [Ritchie & Thompson 1974] where they are named **fork**, **wait**, and **exit.** Similar primitives have been included in PL/I, Mesa [Mitchell et al. 1979], and most recently Modula-3 [Cardelli et al. 1989].

In Modula-3, process management and lock primitives are provided by a special threads package rather than being part of the language proper. A *thread* is an independent thread of control within a larger process. It is not a true process since it does not have its own address space; also, execution of a thread is often interleaved with that of other threads. Several operating systems, e.g. Mach [Young et al. 1987], provide threads to support pseudo-concurrency in applications.

Several operating system texts describe implementations of single-processor kernels. Bic and Shaw [1988], Holt et al. [1978], and Holt [1983] contain particularly good descriptions. Those books also describe the other functions an operating system must support—such as a file system and memory management—and how they relate to the kernel. Thompson [1978] describes the implementation of the UNIX kernel; Holt [1983] describes a UNIX-compatible system called Tunis.

Unfortunately, operating systems texts do not yet describe multiprocessor kernels in any detail. However, an excellent report on experience with some of the early multiprocessors developed at Carnegie-Mellon appears in Jones and Schwarz [1980]; the Multiprocessor Locking Principle (3.28) comes from that paper. Several more recent multiprocessors and aspects of their operating systems and low-level primitives are discussed in Almasi and Gottlieb [1989]. Tucker and Gupta [1989] describe process control and scheduling issues for shared-memory multiprocessors with uniform memory access time. Scott et al. [1990] discuss kernel issues for non-uniform memory access (NUMA) multiprocessors, including the use of multiple ready lists. In general, the proceedings of the following three conferences are excellent sources for much of the best recent work on language and software issues related to multiprocessors: Architectural Support for Programming Languages and Operating Systems (ASPLOS), Symposium on Operating Systems Principles (SOSP), and Principles and Practice of Parallel Programming (PPoPP).

If there are a large number of processors, a shared ready list can be a source of contention. The designers of the Ultracomputer operating system have developed parallel implementations of queue insert and delete routines [Gottlieb et al. 1983, Almasi & Gottlieb 1989]. The algorithms use Fetch-and-Add to manipulate queue pointers and counters and use critical sections to protect access to individual queue elements.

Herlihy and Wing [1990] present a non-blocking implementation of concurrent queues. An implementation is *non-blocking* if some process will complete an operation in a finite number of steps, regardless of the execution speed of other processes. In Herlihy and Wing's implementation, the insert operation is also *wait free*; i.e., every insert operation will complete in a finite number of steps, again regardless of execution speeds. Herlihy [1990] presents a general methodology for implementing highly concurrent data structures. The method employs the Compare-and-Swap instruction (see exercise 3.6). Herlihy [1991] contains a comprehensive discussion of wait-free synchronization, and shows that Compare-and-Swap is the only commonly available instruction powerful enough to transform the implementation of any sequential object into one that is non-blocking or wait free.

Exercises

3.1 For each of the following solutions to the critical section problem, construct a complete proof outline. Demonstrate that the proof outline is interference-free. Finally, using the proof outline and the method of Exclusion of Configurations (2.25), prove that the solution ensures mutual exclusion and avoids deadlock.

(a) The Test-and-Set solution in Figure 3.4.

(b) The tie-breaker algorithm in Figure 3.7.

(c) The ticket algorithm in Figure 3.9.

(d) The bakery algorithm in Figure 3.12.

3.2 Following is Dekker's algorithm for solving the critical section problem for two processes:

> **var** *enter1* := false, *enter2* := false, *turn* := 1
>
> *P1*:: **do** true →
>   *enter1* := true
>   **do** *enter2* → **if** *turn* = 2 →
>   *enter1* := false
>   **do** *turn* = 2 → **skip od**
>   *enter1* := true
>   **fi**
>   **od**
>   critical section
>   *enter1* := false; *turn* := 2
>   non-critical section
>   **od**
>
> *P2*:: **do** true →
>   *enter2* := true
>   **do** *enter1* → **if** *turn* = 1 →
>   *enter2* := false
>   **do** *turn* = 1 → **skip od**
>   *enter2* := true
>   **fi**
>   **od**
>   critical section
>   *enter2* := false; *turn* := 1
>   non-critical section
>   **od**

(a) Explain clearly how the program ensures mutual exclusion, avoids deadlock, avoids unnecessary delay, and ensures eventual entry. For the eventual entry property, how many times can one process that wants to enter its critical section be bypassed by the other before the first gets in? Explain.

(b) Construct a complete, interference-free proof outline. Using the proof outline, prove that the program ensures mutual exclusion and avoids deadlock.

3.3   Consider the following protocol for the critical section problem:

$$\textbf{var } turn := 1$$

P1:: **do** true →   *P2*:: **do** true →
           do *turn* = 2 → **skip od**   **do** *turn* = 1 → **skip od**
           critical section   critical section
           turn := 2   *turn* := 1
           non-critical section   non-critical section
      od   **od**

Develop a complete, interference-free proof outline and demonstrate that this program ensures mutual exclusion and avoids deadlock. Describe why the program does not avoid unnecessary delay or ensure eventual entry.

3.4   Suppose a computer has atomic decrement and increment instructions that also return the value of the sign bit of the result. In particular, the decrement instruction has the following effect:

$$DEC(variable, sign): \langle \; variable := variable - 1$$
$$\textbf{if } variable \geq 0 \rightarrow sign := 0$$
$$[] \; variable < 0 \rightarrow sign := 1$$
$$\textbf{fi} \,\rangle$$

INC is similar, the only difference being that it adds 1 to *variable*.

(a) Using *DEC* and/or *INC*, develop a solution to the critical section problem for *n* processes. Do not worry about the eventual entry property. Describe clearly how your solution works and why it is correct.

(b) Develop a complete, interference-free proof outline for your answer to (a). Using the proof outline, prove that your solution ensures mutual exclusion and avoids deadlock.

3.5   Suppose a computer has an atomic swap instruction, defined as follows:

$$Swap(var1, var2): \langle \; var1 :=: var2 \,\rangle$$

(a) Using *Swap*, develop a solution to the critical section problem for *n* processes. Do not worry about the eventual entry property. Describe clearly how your solution works and why it is correct.

(b) Develop a complete, interference-free proof outline for your answer to (a). Using the proof outline, prove that your solution ensures mutual exclusion and avoids deadlock.

3.6   IBM mainframes have an atomic Compare-and-Swap instruction, which has the following effect:

$$CSW(a, b, c, cond): \langle \; \textbf{if } a = c \rightarrow c := b; cond := 0$$
$$[] \; a \neq c \rightarrow a := c; cond := -1$$
$$\textbf{fi} \,\rangle$$

Parameters *a*, *b*, and *c* are simple variables, e.g., integers.

(a) Using *CSW*, develop a solution to the critical section problem for *n* processes. Do not worry about the eventual entry property. Describe clearly how your solution works and why it is correct.

(b) Develop a complete, interference-free proof outline for your answer to (a). Using the proof outline, prove that your solution ensures mutual exclusion and avoids deadlock.

3.7 The tie-breaker algorithm for two processes uses three shared variables. The following algorithm uses only two [Burns 81]:

> **var** *lock1* := false, *lock2* := false
>
> *P1*:: **var** *res1* : **bool**
>   **do** true →
>   ⟨ *res1* := *lock1*; *lock1* := true ⟩
>   **if** *res1* → ⟨ **await not** *lock2* → *lock2* := true ⟩
>   ⟨ **await not** *lock1* → *lock1* := true ⟩
>   *lock2* := false
>
>   **fi**
>   critical section
>   *lock1* := false
>   ⟨ **await not** *lock2* ⟩
>   non-critical section
>   **od**
>
> *P2*:: **var** *res2* : **bool**
>   **do** true →
>   ⟨ *res2* := *lock1*; *lock1* := true ⟩
>   **if** *res2* → ⟨ **await not** *lock2* → *lock2* := true ⟩
>   ⟨ **await not** *lock1* → *lock1* := true ⟩
>   *lock2* := false
>
>   **fi**
>   critical section
>   *lock1* := false
>   ⟨ **await not** *lock2* ⟩
>   non-critical section
>   **od**

(a) Explain clearly how this program ensures mutual exclusion, avoids deadlock, avoids unnecessary delay, and ensures eventual entry. (Hint: What are the roles of the two lock variables?)

(b) Construct a complete, interference-free proof outline. Using the proof outline, prove that the program ensures mutual exclusion and avoids deadlock.

(c) Show how to implement each of the atomic actions. Assume that the Test-and-Set instruction (3.6) is available.

3.8 In the critical section protocols in the text, every process executes the same algorithm. It is also possible to solve the problem using a coordinator process. In particular, when a regular process *P[i]* wants to enter its critical section, it tells the coordinator, then waits for the coordinator to grant permission.

(a) Develop protocols for the regular processes and the coordinator. Do not worry about the eventual entry property. (Hint: See the barrier synchronization algorithm in Figure 3.13).

(b) Modify your answer to (a) so that it also ensures eventual entry.

(c) Develop a complete, interference-free proof outline for your answer to (a). Then show that the solution ensures mutual exclusion and avoids deadlock.

3.9 Consider the following critical section protocol [Lamport 87]:

> **var** *lock* := 0
>
> *P*[*i*: 1..*n*]:: **do** true →
> $\quad$ ⟨ **await** *lock* = 0 ⟩; *lock* := *i*
> $\quad$ **do** *lock* ≠ *i* → Delay
> $\qquad\qquad$ ⟨ **await** *lock* = 0 ⟩; *lock* := *i*
> $\quad$ **od**
> $\quad$ critical section
> $\quad$ *lock* := 0
> $\quad$ non-critical section
> **od**

(a) Explain how the program ensures mutual exclusion, avoids deadlock, and avoids unnecessary delay. Explain why this program does not ensure eventual entry; in particular, give a scenario that shows how one process can loop forever in its entry protocol. Explain the role of Delay.

(b) Construct a complete, interference-free proof outline. Using the proof outline, prove that the program ensures mutual exclusion and avoids deadlock.

3.10 Consider the following variation on the *n*-process tie-breaker algorithm:

> **var** *in* := 0, *last*[1:*n*] : **int**
>
> *P*[*i*: 1..*n*]:: **var** *stage* : **int**
> $\quad$ **do** true →
> $\qquad$ ⟨ *in* := *in* + 1 ⟩; *stage* := 1; *last*[*stage*] := *i*
> $\qquad$ ⟨ **await** *last*[*stage*] ≠ *i* **or** *in* ≤ *stage* ⟩
> $\qquad$ **do** *last*[*stage*] ≠ *i* →   # go to next stage
> $\qquad\quad$ *stage* := *stage* + 1; *last*[*stage*] := *i*
> $\qquad\quad$ ⟨ **await** *last*[*stage*] ≠ *i* **or** *in* ≤ *stage* ⟩
> $\qquad$ **od**
> $\qquad$ critical section
> $\qquad$ ⟨ *in* := *in* − 1 ⟩
> $\qquad$ non-critical section
> $\quad$ **od**

(a) Explain clearly how this program ensures mutual exclusion, avoids deadlock, and ensures eventual entry.

(b) Develop a complete, interference-free proof outline. Using the proof outline, prove that the program ensures mutual exclusion and avoids deadlock.

(c) Show that in the worst case a process $P[i]$ might have to wait for other processes to enter and exit critical sections up to $n * (n - 1) / 2$ times before $P[i]$ gets to enter its critical section. Compare this delay with the worst-case delay of the algorithm in Figure 3.7.

(d) Convert the coarse-grained solution above to a fine-grained solution in which the only atomic actions are reading and writing variables. Do not assume increment and decrement are atomic. (Hint: Change *in* to an array.)

3.11   (a) Modify the coarse-grained ticket algorithm in Figure 3.8 so *next* and *number* do not overflow. (Hint: Pick a constant MAX greater than n, and use modular arithmetic.)

(b) Using your answer to (a), modify the fine-grained ticket algorithm in Figure 3.9 so *next* and *number* do not overflow. Assume the Fetch-and-Add instruction is available.

3.12   In the bakery algorithm (Figure 3.12), the values of *turn* are unbounded if there is always at least one process in its critical section. Assume reads and writes are atomic. Is it possible to modify the algorithm so that values of *turn* are always bounded? If so, give a modified algorithm. If not, explain why not.

3.13   Display (3.12) shows how to use a shared counter for barrier synchronization, but that solution does not solve the problem of resetting the counter to zero. Develop a complete solution by using two counters. First specify your approach, then develop a coarse-grained solution, and finally develop a fine-grained solution. Assume the Fetch-and-Add instruction is available. (Hints: The "increment" in Fetch-and-Add can be negative. Be careful about a process coming back around to the barrier before all others have left it.)

3.14   Develop a complete, interference-free proof outline that demonstrates the correctness of the barrier synchronization algorithm in Figure 3.13.

3.15   A *tournament barrier* has the same kind of tree structure as in Figure 3.14, but the worker processes interact differently than they do in the combining-tree barrier of Figure 3.15. In particular, each worker is a leaf node. Pairs of adjacent workers wait for each other to arrive. One "wins" and proceeds to the next level up the tree; the other waits. The winner of the "tournament" at the top of the tree announces that all workers have reached the barrier; i.e., it tells all of them that they can continue.

(a) Write programs for the workers, showing all details of how they synchronize. Assume that the number of workers, n, is a power of 2. Either use two sets of variables or reset their values so that the worker processes can use the tournament barrier again on their next loop iteration.

(b) Compare your answer to (a) with the combining-tree barrier in Figure 3.15. How many variables are required for each kind of barrier? If each assignment and **await** statement takes one unit of time, what is the total time required for barrier synchronization in each algorithm? What is the total time for the combining-tree barrier if it is modified so that the root broadcasts a single *continue* message, as described in the text?

3.16 Construct a complete, interference-free proof outline that demonstrates that the two-process symmetric barrier in (3.17) is correct and reusable.

3.17 (a) Give complete details for a butterfly barrier for 8 processes. Show all variables that are needed, and give the code that each process would execute. The barrier should be reusable.

(b) Repeat (a) for a dissemination barrier for 8 processes.

(c) Compare your answers to (a) and (b). How many variables are required for each kind of barrier? If each assignment and **await** statement takes one unit of time, what is the total time required for barrier synchronization in each algorithm?

(d) Repeat (a), (b), and (c) for a 6-process barrier.

(e) Repeat (a), (b), and (c) for a 14-process barrier.

3.18 Modify each of the following algorithms to use only k processes instead of n processes. Assume that n is a multiple of k.

(a) The parallel prefix computation in Figure 3.18;

(b) The linked-list computation in Figure 3.19; and

(c) The grid computation in Figure 3.20.

3.19 In the parallel prefix algorithm in Figure 3.18, there are three barrier synchronization points. Some of these can be optimized since it is not always necessary for all processes to arrive at a barrier before any can proceed. Identify the barriers that can be optimized, and give the details of the optimization. Use the smallest possible number of two-process barriers.

3.20 One way to to sort n integers is to use an odd/even exchange sort (also called an odd/even transposition sort). Assume there are n processes $P[i: 1..n]$ and that n is even. In this kind of sorting method, each process executes a series of rounds. On odd-numbered rounds, odd-numbered processes $P[odd]$ exchange values with $P[odd + 1]$ if the values are out of order. On even-numbered rounds, even-numbered processes $P[even]$ exchange values with $P[even + 1]$, again if the values are out of order. ($P[1]$ and $P[n]$ do nothing on even numbered rounds.)

(a) Determine how many rounds have to be executed in the worst case to sort n numbers. Then write a data parallel algorithm to sort integer array $a[1:n]$ into ascending order.

(b) Modify your answer to (a) to terminate as soon as the array has been sorted (e.g., it might initially be in ascending order).

(c) Modify your answer to (a) to use k processes; assume n is a multiple of k.

3.21 Assume there are n processes $P[1:n]$ and that $P[1]$ has some local value v that it wants to broadcast to all the others. In particular, the goal is to store v in every entry of array $a[1:n]$. The obvious sequential algorithm requires linear time. Write a data parallel algorithm to store v in a in logarithmic time.

3.22 Assume $P[1:n]$ is an array of processes and $b[1:n]$ is a shared boolean array.

(a) Write a data parallel algorithm to count the number of $b[i]$ that are true.

(b) Suppose the answer to (a) is *count*, which will be between 0 and n. Write a data parallel algorithm that assigns a unique integer index between 1 and *count* to each $P[i]$ for which $b[i]$ is true.

3.23 Add convergence-checking code to the grid computation in Figure 3.20. Use a parallel prefix computation to combine the results of the individual processes.

3.24 Modify the data parallel algorithm for finding the end of a linked list (Figure 3.19) so that it works correctly if the list has zero or one elements.

3.25 Suppose you are given two serially linked lists. Write a data parallel algorithm that matches corresponding elements. In particular, when the algorithm terminates, the ith elements on each list should point to each other. (If one list is longer that the other, extra elements on the longer list should have null pointers.) Define the data structures you need. Do not modify the original lists; instead store the answers in additional arrays.

3.26 Suppose that you are given a serially linked list and that the elements are linked together in ascending order of their data fields. The standard sequential algorithm for inserting a new element in the proper place takes linear time (on average, half the list has to be searched). Write a data parallel algorithm to insert a new element into the list in logarithmic time.

3.27 Consider a simple language for expression evaluation with the following syntax:

> *expression* ::= *operand* | *expression operator operand*
> *operand* ::= *identifier* | *number*
> *operator* ::= + | *

An identifier is as usual a sequence of letters or digits, beginning with a letter. A number is a sequence of digits. The operators are + and *.

Given is an array of characters $ch[1:n]$. Each character is either a letter, a digit, a blank, +, or *. The sequence of characters from $ch[1]$ to $ch[n]$ represents a sentence in the above expression language.

Write a data parallel algorithm that determines for each character in $ch[1:n]$ the token (non-terminal) to which it belongs. Assume you have n processes, one per character. The result for each character should be one of ID, NUMBER, PLUS, TIMES, or BLANK. (Hints: A regular language can be parsed by a finite-state automaton, which can be represented by a transition matrix. The rows of the matrix are indexed by states, the columns by characters; the value of an entry is the new state the automaton would enter, given the current state and next character. The composition of state transition functions is associative, which makes it amenable to a parallel prefix computation.)

3.28 The following region-labeling problem arises in image processing. Given is integer array $image[1:n, 1:n]$. The value of each entry is the intensity of a pixel. The neighbors of a pixel are the four pixels that surround it, i.e., the elements of *image* to the left, right, above, and below it. Two pixels belong to the same region if they are neighbors and they have the same value. Thus, a region is a maximal set of pixels that are connected and that all have the same value.

The problem is to find all regions and assign every pixel in each region a unique label. In particular, let *label*[1:*n*, 1:*n*] be a second matrix, and assume that the initial value of *label*[*i*, *j*] is $n * i + j$. The final value of *label*[*i*, *j*] is to be the largest of the initial labels in the region to which pixel [*i*, *j*] belongs.

Write a data parallel grid computation to compute the final values of *label*. The computation should terminate when no *label* changes value on an iteration.

3.29 Using a grid computation to solve the region-labeling problem of the previous exercise requires worst case execution time of $O(n^2)$. This can happen if there is a region that "snakes" around the image. Even for simple images, the grid computation requires $O(n)$ execution time.

The region-labeling problem can be solved as follows in time $O(\log n)$. First, for each pixel, determine whether it is on the boundary of a region and, if so, which of its neighbors are also on the boundary. Second, have each boundary pixel create pointers to its neighbors that are on the boundary; this produces doubly linked lists connecting all pixels that are on the boundary of a region. Third, using the lists, propagate the largest label of any of the boundary pixels to the others that are on the boundary. (The pixel with the largest label for any region will be on its boundary.) Finally, use a parallel prefix computation to propagate the label for each region to pixels in the interior of the region.

Write a data parallel program that implements this algorithm. Analyze its execution time, which should be $O(\log n)$.

3.30 On a synchronous (SIMD) multiprocessor, every processor executes the same sequence of machine instructions in lock step. In particular, every read, write, and test occurs at the same time. If a processor evaluates a guard in an **if** or **do** statement and the guard is false, that processor does not execute the guarded statement, but it does stay synchronized with the other processors until they finish executing the guarded statement. Then all processors proceed to the next statement.

Assume you have a simple programming language. The sequential statements are assignment, **if**, and **do**, and **do** contains only one guarded statement. The concurrent statement is **cosynch**; this is like **co**, except that processes execute synchronously as described above. For example, the following program shifts the elements of *a*[1:*n*] left one position, leaving *a*[*n*] alone:

> **var** $a[1{:}n]$
> **cosynch** $i := 1$ **to** $n - 1 \rightarrow a[i] := a[i+1]$ **oc**

Because execution is synchronous, the assignments do not interfere; all processes read a value from *a* before any assign to *a*.

Develop a programming logic for this language. In particular, design an assignment axiom and inference rules for **if**, **do**, and **cosynch.** Do not worry about sequential statements outside of **cosynch**; concentrate on synchronous concurrency. (This is a hard enough problem as is!) To get started, consider how to simulate synchronous execution using asynchronous processes (**co**) plus barriers.

3.31 The following problems address aspects of the parallel garbage collector developed in Section 3.7.

(a) In the marking phase of the *Collector* (Figure 3.25), the last arm of the **do** loop goes over the entire set of nodes to determine whether there are any gray ones. Suppose this arm is removed. Explain what can go wrong, and find an example of *Mutator* and *Collector* actions that illustrates the problem.

(b) The various *Mutator* actions in Figure 3.26 that add a link to a node color the node at least gray *after* adding a link to it. Suppose instead that a node is colored at least gray *before* a link is added to it and that these are separate actions. In particular, suppose the statements in (3.24) are executed in the other order. Explain what can go wrong, and find an example of *Mutator* and *Collector* actions that illustrates the problem.

(c) In the garbage collector, the head of the free list, *free*, is not actually on the list. Hence, *Collector* never colors it. Suppose instead that *free* were stored in the array *Collector* examines. Would the solution still work correctly? If so, explain carefully why. If not, explain why not and find a counter-example.

(d) As programmed in Figure 3.23, the marking phase of *Collector* is very inefficient since it might have to go back over nodes whenever it blackens one and since it makes a last pass checking for gray nodes. Consider various ways to make *Collector* more efficient, e.g., blacken nodes by directly following links, keep a count of the number of gray nodes, or have *Mutator* record when it has colored a node gray. Reprogram *Collector* (and *Mutator* if necessary) to implement your choices. Justify your choices, and also justify that the resulting algorithm is correct.

(e) As discussed in the text, the two actions in (3.24) interfere with *Collector*'s marking invariant *I2*. Add an auxiliary variable to record when *Mutator* is between the actions in (3.24), and weaken *I2* so it is not interfered with. However, the weaker predicate must still be strong enough to conclude that all reachable nodes are black at the end of the marking phase.

3.32 Develop a parallel garbage collector that uses only two colors, black and white. Do not worry about efficiency of the marking phase of *Collector*. Develop a proof outline that demonstrates the correctness of your algorithm. (Hint: Have *Collector* color reachable nodes black, count the number of black nodes, and then repeat the process if there are more black nodes than before [Ben-Ari 84].)

3.33 Two primitives in the UNIX kernel are similar to the following:

> **sleep**(*value*): block the executing process on *value*
> **wakeup**(*value*): awaken all processes blocked on *value*

Above, *value* is any integer, e.g., the address of a child process.

Process *P1* is to execute statements *S1* and *S2*; process *P2* is to execute statements *S3* and *S4*. Statement *S4* must be executed after *S1*. A colleague gives you the following program:

> *P1*:: *S1*; **wakeup**(1); *S2*   *P2*:: *S3*; **sleep**(1); *S4*

Is the solution correct? If so, explain why. If not, explain how it can fail, and describe how to change the primitives so that it is correct.

3.34 The program in (3.27) uses busy waiting to have the main process wait for the P_i to quit. Suppose instead that the kernel's **fork** primitive returns a unique process identifier (e.g., the address of the process's descriptor) and that the kernel provides a primitive **wait**(process_id). The **wait** primitive blocks the executing process until the named process has executed **quit.**

Add **wait** to the single-processor kernel in Figure 3.28.

3.35 In the multiprocessor kernel described in the text, a processor executes the *Idle* process when it finds the ready list empty (Figure 3.29). On some machines, there is a bit in the processor status word that, if set, causes a processor to do nothing until it is interrupted. Such machines also provide interprocessor interrupts; i.e., one processor can interrupt a second, which causes the second processor to enter a kernel CPU interrupt handler.

Modify the multiprocessor kernel in Figure 3.30 so that a processor sets its idle bit if it finds the ready list empty. Hence another processor will need to awaken it when there is a process for it to execute.

3.36 Suppose process dispatching is handled by one master processor. In particular, all the master does is execute a dispatcher process. Other processors execute regular processes and kernel routines.

Design the dispatcher process, and modify the multiprocessor kernel in Figure 3.30 as appropriate. Define any data structures you need. Remember that an idle processor must not block inside the kernel since that prevents other processors from entering the kernel.

3.37 In a multiprocessor system, assume each processor has its own ready list and that it executes only those processes on its ready list. As discussed in the text, this raises the issue of load balancing since a new process has to be assigned to some processor.

There are numerous load-balancing schemes—e.g., assign to a random processor, assign to a "neighbor," or keep ready lists roughly equal in length. Pick some scheme, justify your choice, and modify the multiprocessor kernel to use multiple ready lists and the load-balancing scheme you choose. Also show how to handle idle processors. Try to minimize overhead due to extra code or lock contention. (For example, if each processor is the only one that accesses its own ready list, ready lists do not need to be locked.)

3.38 Modify the multiprocessor kernel (Figure 3.30) so that a process is generally executed by the same processor that executed it last. However, your solution should avoid starving processes; i.e., every process should periodically get a chance to execute. Also consider what to do about idle processors. Define any data structures you need. Explain the rationale for your solution.

3.39 Add an additional primitive, **multifork**([*] initial process state), to the multiprocessor kernel (Figure 3.30). The argument is an array of initial process states; **multifork** creates one process for each argument. In addition, **multifork** specifies that all of the newly created processes are to be co-scheduled on the same processor, e.g., because the processes share cached data.

Modify the other parts of the kernel as needed to implement co-scheduling. Your solution should avoid starving processes; i.e., every process should periodically get a chance to execute. Also consider what to do about idle processors.

3.40 A concurrent queue is a queue in which insert and delete operations can execute in parallel. Assume the queue is stored in array *queue*[1:*n*]. Two variables *front* and *rear* point to the first full element and the next empty slot, respectively. The delete operation delays until there is an element in *queue*[*front*], then removes it and increments *front* (modulo *n*). The insert operation delays until there is an empty slot, then puts a new element in *queue*[*rear*] and increments *rear* (modulo *n*).

Design algorithms for queue insertion and deletion that maximize parallelism. In particular, except at critical points where they access shared variables, inserts and deletes ought to be able to proceed in parallel with each other and with themselves. You will need additional variables. You may also assume the Fetch-and-Add instruction is available.

## CHAPTER 4

Semaphores

Synchronization protocols that use only busy waiting can be difficult to design, understand, and prove correct. As we saw in the last chapter, most busy-waiting protocols are quite complex. Also, there is no clear separation between variables that are used for synchronization and those that are used for computing results. A consequence of these attributes is that one has to be very careful to ensure that processes are correctly synchronized.

A further deficiency of busy waiting is that it is inefficient when processes are implemented by multiprogramming. A processor executing a spinning process can usually be more productively employed executing another process. This is even true on a multiprocessor since there are usually more processes than processors.

Because synchronization is fundamental to concurrent programs, it is desirable to have special tools that aid in the design of correct synchronization protocols and that can be used to block processes that must be delayed. *Semaphores* are one of the first such tools and certainly one of the most important. They make it easy to protect critical sections and can be used in a disciplined way to implement condition synchronization. Semaphores can also be implemented in more than one way. In particular, they can be implemented using busy waiting, but they also have implementations that interact with a process scheduler to achieve synchronization without busy waiting.

The concept of a semaphore—and indeed the very term—is motivated by one of the ways in which railroad traffic is synchronized to avoid train collisions. A railroad semaphore is a signal flag that indicates whether the track ahead is clear or is occupied by another train. As a train proceeds, semaphores are set and cleared, with semaphores remaining set far enough behind the train so that another train has time to stop if necessary. Thus, railroad semaphores can be viewed as mechanisms that signal conditions in order to ensure mutually exclusive occupancy of critical sections of track. Semaphores in concurrent programs are similar: They provide a basic signaling mechanism and are used to implement mutual exclusion and condition synchronization.

This chapter defines the syntax and semantics of semaphores and then illustrates how to use them to solve synchronization problems. For comparison purposes, we examine again some of the problems considered in previous chapters, including critical sections, producers and consumers, and barriers. In addition, we introduce several interesting new problems: bounded buffers, dining philosophers, readers and writers, and shortest-job-next resource allocation. Solutions are developed following the derivation method introduced at the start of Part II. We also describe three important programming techniques: changing variables, split binary semaphores, and one called passing the baton. The latter method is a very general one; we will in fact use variations on it in several subsequent chapters.

4.1 Notation and Semantics

A semaphore is an instance of an abstract data type: it has a representation that is manipulated only by two special operations, **P** and **V**. The **V** operation signals the occurrence of an event; the **P** operation is used to delay a process until an event has occurred. In particular, the two operations must be implemented so that they preserve the following property for every semaphore in a program.

(4.1)   **Semaphore Invariant.** For semaphore s, let nP be the number of completed **P** operations, and let nV be the number of completed **V** operations. If *init* is the initial value of s, then in all visible program states, $nP \leq nV + init$.

Thus, execution of a **P** operation potentially delays until an adequate number of **V** operations have been executed.

The simplest way to provide the required synchronization is to represent each semaphore by a non-negative integer s that records the initial value plus the difference between the number of completed **V** and **P** operations; in particular, $s = init + nV - nP$. With this representation, the Semaphore Invariant becomes:

$$SEM: \ s \geq 0$$

Since a successful **P** operation implicitly increments nP, it decrements s. For

SEM to be a global invariant, the decrement must be guarded since:

$$wp(s := s - 1, s \geq 0) \ = \ s - 1 \geq 0 \ = \ s > 0$$

A **V** operation implicitly increments nV so also increments s. Unlike the decrement in the **P** operation, however, the increment need not be guarded since:

$$s \geq 0 \ \Rightarrow \ wp(s := s + 1, s \geq 0)$$

These observations yield the following definitions for the **P** and **V** operations:

$$\mathbf{P}(s): \ \langle \ \mathbf{await} \ s > 0 \to s := s - 1 \ \rangle$$
$$\mathbf{V}(s): \ \langle \ s := s + 1 \ \rangle$$

Note that **P** and **V** are both atomic actions. Also note that **P** and **V** are the *only* operations on semaphores; i.e., the value cannot be examined directly.

Semaphores as defined above are called *general semaphores:* the value of s can be any non-negative integer. A *binary semaphore* is a semaphore whose value is only 0 or 1. In particular, a binary semaphore b satisfies a stronger global invariant:

$$BSEM: \ 0 \leq b \leq 1$$

Maintaining this invariant requires guarding the **V** operation as well as the **P** operation (or causing the program to abort if the **V** operation is executed when b is 1). Thus, the operations on a binary semaphore have the following definitions:

$$\mathbf{P}(b): \ \langle \ \mathbf{await} \ b > 0 \to b := b - 1 \ \rangle$$
$$\mathbf{V}(b): \ \langle \ \mathbf{await} \ b < 1 \to b := b + 1 \ \rangle$$

As long as a binary semaphore is used in such a way that a **V** operation is executed only when b is 0, **V**(b) will not cause delay. (This is often assumed, and hence **V**(b) is often defined simply to be $\langle \ b := b + 1 \ \rangle$. However, this simpler definition is incorrect if **V** is inadvertently executed when b is 1 since then *BSEM* will not be invariant.)

We will declare semaphores in programs by using a special type **sem.** The default initial value of each semaphore is 0. When we want a different initial value, we will use an assignment in the declaration, as in:

var *mutex* : **sem** := 1

This is the same as implicitly executing the appropriate number of **V** operations. For a general semaphore, the initial value is required to be non-negative; for a binary semaphore, it must be 0 or 1. We will also use arrays of semaphores, as in:

var *forks*[1:5] : **sem** := ([5] 1)

In this case, each element of *forks* is initialized to 1.

Since the semaphore operations are defined in terms of **await** statements, their formal semantics follow directly from applications of Synchronization Rule (2.7). Recall that inference rule:

Synchronization Rule: $\dfrac{\{P \wedge B\}\ S\ \{Q\}}{\{P\}\ \langle\,\textbf{await}\ B \to S\,\rangle\ \{Q\}}$

Let g be a general semaphore. Substituting $g > 0$ for B and $g := g - 1$ for S, the hypothesis above becomes:

$$\{P \wedge g > 0\}\ g := g - 1\ \{Q\}$$

Using the Assignment Axiom, this simplifies to:

$$(P \wedge g > 0) \Rightarrow Q^{g}_{g-1}$$

Making the same substitutions in the conclusion of the Synchronization Rule, we get the inference rule shown in Figure 4.1. The inference rule for $\mathbf{V}(g)$ follows similarly: substitute *true* for B and $g := g + 1$ for S in the Synchronization Rule, and simplify the hypothesis. In practice, P and Q in the inference rules are usually the same predicate and usually include the global invariant $g \geq 0$ as a conjunct. As we will see, however, they occasionally are different when assignments to auxiliary variables are added to the **P** and **V** operations to record that they have been executed.

Figure 4.1 also contains inference rules for binary semaphores. These are nearly identical to those for general semaphores. The one difference results from the fact that $\mathbf{V}(b)$ is a conditional atomic action, and hence the hypothesis for $\mathbf{V}(b)$ includes the condition $b < 1$ in the antecedent of the implication.

Fairness attributes of semaphore operations also follow from the fact that they are defined in terms of **await** statements. Let s be a binary or general semaphore. Using the terminology of Section 2.6, if $s > 0$ becomes true and remains true, execution of $\mathbf{P}(s)$ will terminate if the underlying scheduling policy is weakly fair. If $s > 0$ is infinitely often true, execution of $\mathbf{P}(s)$ will terminate if the underlying scheduling policy is strongly fair. The **V**

General Semaphore Rules:

$$\frac{(P \wedge g > 0) \Rightarrow Q^g_{g-1}}{\{P\}\ \mathbf{P}(g)\ \{Q\}}$$

$$\frac{P \Rightarrow Q^g_{g+1}}{\{P\}\ \mathbf{V}(g)\ \{Q\}}$$

Binary Semaphore Rules:

$$\frac{(P \wedge b > 0) \Rightarrow Q^b_{b-1}}{\{P\}\ \mathbf{P}(b)\ \{Q\}}$$

$$\frac{(P \wedge b < 1) \Rightarrow Q^b_{b+1}}{\{P\}\ \mathbf{V}(b)\ \{Q\}}$$

Figure 4.1. Inference rules for semaphore operations.

operation on a binary semaphore has similar fairness attributes. Since the **V** operation on a general semaphore is an unconditional atomic action, it will terminate if the underlying scheduling policy is unconditionally fair. As we will see in Section 4.6, we can implement semaphores so that delayed processes are awakened in the order they delayed. In this case, a process delayed at a **P** operation will be able to proceed if other processes execute an adequate number of **V** operations.

4.2 Basic Uses and Programming Techniques

Semaphores directly support the implementation of critical section protocols. They also directly support simple forms of condition synchronization in which conditions represent the occurrence of events. This section illustrates these uses by deriving solutions to four problems: critical sections, barriers, producers/consumers, and bounded buffers. The solutions illustrate additional ways to specify synchronization properties. They also illustrate two important programming techniques: changing variables and split binary semaphores. Subsequent sections show how to use these techniques to construct solutions to more complex synchronization problems.

Critical Sections: Changing Variables

Recall that, in the critical section problem, each of n processes $P[1:n]$ repeatedly executes a critical section of code, in which it requires exclusive access to some shared resource, and then a non-critical section, in which it

var $in[1{:}n]$: **int** := $([n]\ 0)$
$\{\ CS{:}\ in[1] + ... + in[n] \le 1\ \}$
$P[i{:}\ 1..n]{::}$ **do** true $\rightarrow$ $\{\ in[i] = 0\ \}$
$\qquad\qquad\qquad\qquad in[i] := 1$
$\qquad\qquad\qquad\qquad \{\ in[i] = 1\ \}$
$\qquad\qquad\qquad\qquad$ critical section
$\qquad\qquad\qquad\qquad in[i] := 0$
$\qquad\qquad\qquad\qquad \{\ in[i] = 0\ \}$
$\qquad\qquad\qquad\qquad$ non-critical section
$\qquad$ **od**

Figure 4.2. Solution outline for critical section problem.

computes using only local objects. A global invariant specifying the mutual exclusion property was specified in several different ways in Chapter 3. Since semaphore operations manipulate integers, when they are ultimately used for synchronization, it is always best to specify invariant properties using integers. This is because, as will be seen here and in later sections, atomic actions can then often be turned directly into semaphore operations.

Let $in[i]$ be 1 when $P[i]$ is in its critical section, and 0 otherwise. (As before, we assume that in is not altered within any critical or non-critical section.) The required property is that at most one process at a time is within its critical section. We can specify this directly by the predicate:

$$CS{:}\ in[1] + ... + in[n] \le 1$$

Alternatively, we can specify the bad state in which more than one process is in its critical section by:

$$BAD{:}\ in[1] + ... + in[n] > 1$$

Since all $in[i]$ are 0 or 1, $CS = \neg BAD$, so the specifications are the same.

Given the above specification, we get the solution outline shown in Figure 4.2. The processes share array $in[1{:}n]$, with each process setting and clearing its element of in before and after executing its critical section. Initially all elements of in are zero, so predicate CS is initially true. Each process contains assertions about the element of in manipulated by that process. These assertions follow from the actions of the process; they are not interfered with since each process manipulates a different element of in. Thus, the solution outline is also a valid proof outline. However, it is not yet strong enough to conclude that execution of the critical sections is mutually exclusive. For this, we must include invariant CS in the proof outline.

var $in[1:n] : $ **int** $:= ([n]\ 0)$
$\{\ CS:\ in[1] + ... + in[n] \leq 1\ \}$
$P[i: 1..n]::$ **do** true $\rightarrow \{\ in[i] = 0 \wedge CS\ \}$
$\qquad\qquad\qquad \langle$ **await** $in[1] + ... + in[n] = 0 \rightarrow in[i] := 1\ \rangle$
$\qquad\qquad\qquad \{\ in[i] = 1 \wedge CS\ \}$
$\qquad\qquad\qquad$ critical section
$\qquad\qquad\qquad in[i] := 0$
$\qquad\qquad\qquad \{\ in[i] = 0 \wedge CS\ \}$
$\qquad\qquad\qquad$ non-critical section
$\qquad$ **od**

Figure 4.3. Coarse-grained solution for the critical section problem.

The third derivation step is to guard assignments to ensure that CS is true after each atomic action. (Since CS is true initially, this will ensure that it is a global invariant.) Consider the first assignment, which sets $in[i]$ and thus establishes $in[i] = 1$. Computing the weakest precondition yields:

$$wp(in[i] := 1, in[i] = 1 \wedge CS) = (1 + in[1] + ... + in[n] \leq 1)$$

Since all elements of in are either 0 or 1, this simplifies to:

$$in[1] + ... + in[n] = 0$$

We use this to guard the first atomic action in each process since no weaker predicate suffices. For assignments that clear $in[i]$, computing wp we get:

$$wp(in[i] := 0, in[i] = 0 \wedge CS) = (in[1] + ... + in[n] \leq 1)$$

Since precondition $in[i] = 1 \wedge CS$ implies that this is true, we do not need to guard the second atomic action. Adding the guard to the first atomic action, we get the coarse-grained solution shown in Figure 4.3.

Since the derivation of the solution in Figure 4.3 has ensured that CS is invariant, the proof outline is valid. Thus we can use it and the method of Exclusion of Configurations (2.25) to prove that the solution ensures mutual exclusion (3.2), is deadlock-free (3.3), and avoids unnecessary delay (3.4). For example, mutual exclusion follows from:

$$(in[i] = 1 \wedge in[j] = 1 \wedge i \neq j \wedge CS) = \textit{false}$$

If scheduling is strongly fair, the solution also ensures eventual entry into a critical section (3.5).

The remaining derivation step is to use semaphores to implement the atomic actions in Figure 4.3. Here we can do this by *changing variables* so that each atomic statement becomes a semaphore operation. Let *mutex* be a semaphore whose value is:

$$mutex = 1 - (in[1] + ... + in[n])$$

We use this change of variables since it makes *mutex* a non-negative integer, as required for a semaphore. With this change, we can replace the first atomic action in the coarse-grained solution by:

$$\langle \textbf{await } mutex > 0 \to mutex := mutex - 1; in[i] := 1 \rangle$$

And we can replace the last atomic action by:

$$\langle mutex := mutex + 1; in[i] := 0 \rangle$$

After making these changes, *in* has become an auxiliary variable—it is used only in assignments to itself. Thus the program has the same properties after we use Auxiliary Variable Rule (2.22) to delete the auxiliary variables. What is left are atomic statements that are simply the **P** and **V** operations on semaphore *mutex*. Thus, we have the final solution shown in Figure 4.4. This solution works for any number of processes, and it is much simpler than any of the busy-waiting solutions in Chapter 3.

The technique of changing variables that we used above leads to a compact solution. This is because it permits **await** statements to be implemented directly by semaphore operations. In fact, the technique can be used whenever the following conditions are true.

(4.2)   **Conditions for Changing Variables.** Atomic actions can be implemented by semaphore operations if the following conditions hold:

(a) Different guards reference disjoint sets of variables, and these variables are referenced only in atomic statements.

(b) Each guard can be put in the form *expr* > 0, where *expr* is an integer expression.

(c) Each guarded atomic statement contains one assignment that decrements the value of the expression in the transformed guard.

(d) Each unguarded atomic statement increments the value of the expression in one transformed guard.

var *mutex* : **sem** := 1

P[*i*: 1..*n*]:: **do** true → **P**(*mutex*)

                    critical section

                    V(*mutex*)

                    non-critical section

       od

Figure 4.4. Semaphore solution to the critical section problem.

When these conditions hold, one semaphore is used for each different guard. The variables that were in the guards then become auxiliary variables, and the atomic statements simplify to semaphore operations. We will use this technique in several additional examples in this chapter.

Barriers: Signaling Events

We introduced barrier synchronization in Section 3.5 as a means to synchronize stages of parallel iterative algorithms, such as the data parallel algorithms in Section 3.6. The busy-waiting implementations given in Section 3.5 used flag variables that processes set and cleared as they arrived at and left a barrier. This section shows how to implement barriers using semaphores. The basic idea is to use one semaphore for each synchronization flag. A process sets a flag executing a **V** operation; a process waits for a flag to be set and then clears it by executing a **P** operation.

Consider first the problem of implementing a two-process barrier. Recall that two properties are required. First, neither process can get past the barrier until both have arrived. Second, the barrier must be reusable since in general the same processes will need to synchronize after each stage of the computation. For the critical section problem, we needed only one variable per process to specify the required synchronization since the only concern was whether a process was inside or outside its critical section. Here, however, we need to know each time a process arrives at or departs from the barrier, and then we need to relate the states of the two processes.

The way to specify barrier synchronization—and similar kinds of synchronization as we will see in the next and later sections—is to use incrementing counters. Each counter records when a process reaches a critical execution point. Let *arrive1* and *depart1* count the number of times process *P1* arrives at and departs from the barrier, and let *arrive2* and *depart2* serve a similar role for process *P2*. All four counters are initially zero. Then barrier synchronization is specified by the predicate:

var *arrive1* := 0, *depart1* := 0, *arrive2* := 0, *depart2* := 0
{ *BARRIER*: *depart1* ≤ *arrive2* ∧ *depart2* ≤ *arrive1* }
P1:: **do** true → { *arrive1* = *depart1* }
                        ⟨ *arrive1* := *arrive1* + 1 ⟩
                        { *arrive1* = *depart1* + 1 }
                        ⟨ *depart1* := *depart1* + 1 ⟩
                        { *arrive1* = *depart1* }
        od
P2:: **do** true → { *arrive2* = *depart2* }
                        ⟨ *arrive2* := *arrive2* + 1 ⟩
                        { *arrive2* = *depart2* + 1 }
                        ⟨ *depart2* := *depart2* + 1 ⟩
                        { *arrive2* = *depart2* }
        od

Figure 4.5. Solution outline for barrier synchronization.

BARRIER: *depart1* ≤ *arrive2* ∧ *depart2* ≤ *arrive1*

This says that *P1* cannot get past the barrier any more times than *P2* has arrived and, symmetrically, that *P2* cannot get past the barrier any more times than *P1* has arrived. The corresponding solution and proof outline is shown in Figure 4.5.

The next step is to ensure that *BARRIER* is a global invariant. We do not need to guard the assignments to *arrive1* or *arrive2*, but we do need to guard the assignments to *depart1* and *depart2* since these values need to be bounded. As usual, we could use *wp* to calculate the guard. However, by inspection it is clear that *depart1* must be less than *arrive2* before being incremented, and similarly *depart2* must be less than *arrive1*. Adding the guards yields the solution and proof outline shown in Figure 4.6.

As usual, the final step in solving the problem is to implement the **await** statements. Here, we can again use the technique of changing variables since the required conditions (4.2) are met: the guards are disjoint, each can be put in the form *expr* > 0, guarded statements decrement the expression in their guard, and unguarded statements increment the expression in some guard. In particular, we introduce two new variables with the following definitions:

$$barrier1 = arrive1 - depart2$$
$$barrier2 = arrive2 - depart1$$

These variables are initially 0. Next we change the guards in the **await**

var *arrive1* := 0, *depart1* := 0, *arrive2* := 0, *depart2* := 0
{ *BARRIER*: *depart1* ≤ *arrive2* ∧ *depart2* ≤ *arrive1* }
P1:: **do** true → { *BARRIER* ∧ *arrive1* = *depart1* }
        ⟨ *arrive1* := *arrive1* + 1 ⟩
        { *BARRIER* ∧ *arrive1* = *depart1* + 1 }
        ⟨ **await** *depart1* < *arrive2* → *depart1* := *depart1* + 1 ⟩
        { *BARRIER* ∧ *arrive1* = *depart1* }
    od
P2:: **do** true → { *BARRIER* ∧ *arrive2* = *depart2* }
        ⟨ *arrive2* := *arrive2* + 1 ⟩
        { *BARRIER* ∧ *arrive2* = *depart2* + 1 }
        ⟨ **await** *depart2* < *arrive1* → *depart2* := *depart2* + 1 ⟩
        { *BARRIER* ∧ *arrive2* = *depart2* }
    od

Figure 4.6. Coarse-grained barrier synchronization.

---

statements in Figure 4.6 to use these variables, and we add assignments to them to the atomic actions that change the original counters. For example, we replace the increment of *arrive1* in *P1* by:

⟨ *barrier1* := *barrier1* + 1; *arrive1* := *arrive1* + 1 ⟩

And we replace the guarded **await** statement in *P1* by:

⟨ **await** *barrier2* > 0 →
    barrier2 := *barrier2* − 1; *depart1* := *depart1* + 1 ⟩

After making this change of variables, the four original variables become auxiliary variables. Deleting the auxiliary variables, the actions on *barrier1* and *barrier2* are simply semaphore operations. Thus, we have the final solution shown in Figure 4.7.

In Figure 4.7, the semaphores are used as *signals* that indicate when events occur. When a process arrives at the barrier, it signals that event by executing a **V** operation on a semaphore. The other process waits for the event by executing a **P** operation on the same semaphore. Since barrier synchronization is symmetric, each process takes the same actions—they just signal and wait on different semaphores. When semaphores are used in this way, they are much like flag variables, and their use follows the Flag Synchronization Principles (3.16).

var *barrier1* : **sem** := 0, *barrier2* : **sem** := 0

P1:: **do** true → **V**(*barrier1*)
　　　　　　　　P(*barrier2*)
　　　　od

P2:: **do** true → **V**(*barrier2*)
　　　　　　　　P(*barrier1*)
　　　　od

Figure 4.7. Barrier synchronization using semaphores.

We can use two-process barriers as shown in Figure 4.7 to implement an *n*-process butterfly barrier having the structure shown in Figure 3.16. Or we can use the same idea to implement an *n*-process dissemination barrier having the structure shown in Figure 3.17. In that case, each process signals the barrier semaphore of another process, then waits for its barrier semaphore to be signaled. Alternatively, we can use semaphores as signal flags to implement *n*-process barrier synchronization using a central coordinator process (Figure 3.13) or a combining tree (Figure 3.15). In fact, since **V** operations are remembered, we only need one semaphore for the *Coordinator* in Figure 3.13. This is another virtue of semaphores relative to boolean flags.

Producers and Consumers: Split Binary Semaphores

This section reexamines the producers/consumers problem introduced in Section 2.4. There we assumed that there was one producer and one consumer; here we consider the general situation in which there are multiple producers and consumers. The solution illustrates another use of semaphores as signaling flags. It also introduces the important concept of a split binary semaphore.

In the producers/consumers problem, producers send messages that are received by consumers. The processes communicate using a single shared buffer, which is manipulated by two operations: *deposit* and *fetch*. Producers insert messages into the buffer by calling *deposit*; consumers receive messages by calling *fetch*. To ensure that messages are not overwritten before being received and are only received once, execution of *deposit* and *fetch* must alternate, with *deposit* executed first.

As with barrier synchronization, the way to specify the required alternation property is to use incrementing counters to indicate when a process reaches critical execution points. Here the critical points are starting and completing execution of *deposit* and *fetch*. Thus, let *inD* and *afterD* be integers that count the number of times producers have started and finished executing *deposit*. Also, let *inF* and *afterF* be integers that count the number of times consumers have started and finished executing *fetch*. Then the following predicate specifies that *deposit* and *fetch* alternate:

$$PC: \ inD \leq afterF + 1 \ \wedge \ inF \leq afterD$$

In words, this says that *deposit* can be started at most one more time than *fetch* has been completed and that *fetch* can be started no more times than *deposit* has been completed. (Again, we could specify this property by characterizing the bad state, then negate that predicate. Here the bad state is one in which two or more deposits or fetches are executed in a row.)

For this problem, the shared variables are the above counters and a variable *buf* that holds one message of some type T. Since our main concern is how producers and consumers synchronize, each process simply executes a loop; producers repeatedly deposit messages, and consumers repeatedly fetch them. Producers deposit messages into the buffer by executing:

$$deposit: \ \langle \ inD := inD + 1 \ \rangle$$
$$buf := m$$
$$\langle \ afterD := afterD + 1 \ \rangle$$

Consumers fetch messages from the buffer by executing:

$$fetch: \ \langle \ inF := inF + 1 \ \rangle$$
$$m := buf$$
$$\langle \ afterF := afterF + 1 \ \rangle$$

To get a correct implementation of *deposit* and *fetch*, we need to guard assignments to ensure the invariance of synchronization property *PC*. Again using *wp* to compute the guards, we see that we need to guard the increments of *inD* and *inF* but not the increments of *afterD* and *afterF* since they clearly preserve the invariant. (Also recall that it is never necessary to delay when leaving a critical section of code.) Adding guards that ensure the invariance of *PC* yields the solution shown in Figure 4.8.

To implement the statements that access the counters using semaphores, we can once again use the technique of changing variables since again the conditions in (4.2) are met. In particular, let *empty* and *full* be semaphores whose values are:

$$empty = afterF - inD + 1$$
$$full = afterD - inF$$

With this change, the four counters become auxiliary variables, so they can be

var *buf* : T   # for some type T
var *inD* := 0, *afterD* := 0, *inF* := 0, *afterF* := 0
{ *PC*: *inD* ≤ *afterF* + 1 ∧ *inF* ≤ *afterD* }

Producer[*i*: 1..*M*]:: **do** true →
                          produce message *m*
                          deposit: ⟨ **await** *inD* ≤ *afterF* → *inD* := *inD* + 1 ⟩
                                        buf := *m*
                                        ⟨ *afterD* := *afterD* + 1 ⟩
                  od
Consumer[*j*: 1..*N*]:: **do** true →
                          fetch: ⟨ **await** *inF* < *afterD* → *inF* := *inF* + 1 ⟩
                                   m := *buf*
                                   ⟨ *afterF* := *afterF* + 1 ⟩
                          consume message *m*
                  od

Figure 4.8. Coarse-grained producers and consumers.

---

deleted. Thus, the first statements in *deposit* and *fetch* become **P** operations, and the last statements become **V** operations. This yields the final solution shown in Figure 4.9.

In Figure 4.9, *empty* and *full* are both binary semaphores. Moreover, together they form what is called a split binary semaphore: at most one of them is one at a time, as specified in predicate *PC'*.

(4.3)   **Split Binary Semaphore.** Binary semaphores b_1, ..., b_n form a split binary semaphore in a program if the following assertion is a global invariant in the program: *SPLIT*: $0 \le b_1 + ... + b_n \le 1$.

The term *split binary semaphore* comes from the fact that the b_i can be viewed as a single binary semaphore b that has been split into n binary semaphores. These n semaphores are used in such a way that *SPLIT* is invariant.

Split binary semaphores are important because of the way in which they can be used to implement mutual exclusion. Given a split binary semaphore, suppose that one of the constituent semaphores has an initial value of 1 (hence the others are initially 0). Further suppose that, in the processes that use the semaphores, every execution path alternately executes a **P** operation on one of the semaphores, then a **V** operation on a possibly different one of the semaphores. Then all statements between any **P** and the next **V** execute with mutual exclusion. This is because, while one process is between a **P** and

var *buf* : T   # for some type T
var *empty* : **sem** := 1, *full* : **sem** := 0
{*PC'*: 0 ≤ *empty* + *full* ≤ 1 }
Producer[*i*: 1..*M*]:: **do** true → produce message *m*
                                    deposit: **P**(*empty*)
                                                buf := *m*
                                                V(*full*)
                  od
Consumer[*j*: 1..*N*]:: **do** true → *fetch*: **P**(*full*)
                                            m := *buf*
                                            V(*empty*)
                            consume message *m*
               od

Figure 4.9. Producers and consumers using semaphores.

---

a **V**, the semaphores are all 0, and hence no other process can complete a **P** until the first process executes a **V**. The solution to the producers/consumers problem in Figure 4.9 illustrates this: each *Producer* alternately executes **P**(*empty*) then **V**(*full*); each *Consumer* alternately executes **P**(*full*) then **V**(*empty*). In Section 4.4, we will use this property to construct a general method for implementing **await** statements.

Bounded Buffers: Resource Counting

The previous section showed how to synchronize access to a single communication buffer. If messages are produced at approximately the same rate at which they are consumed, a single buffer provides reasonable performance since a process would not generally have to wait very long to access to the buffer. Commonly, however, producer and consumer execution is bursty. For example, a process writing an output file might produce several lines at once, then do more computation before producing another set of lines. In such cases, a buffer capacity larger than one can significantly increase performance by reducing the number of times processes block. (This is an example of the classic time/space tradeoff in computer systems.)

   This section develops a solution to the *bounded buffer* problem, namely, the problem of implementing a multislot communication buffer. The solution builds upon the solution in the previous section. It also illustrates the use of general semaphores as resource counters.

   Assume for now that there is just one producer and just one consumer. The producer deposits messages in a shared buffer; the consumer fetches them. The buffer contains a queue of messages that have been deposited but not yet fetched. This queue can be represented by a linked list or by an array. We will use the array representation since it is somewhat simpler to program. In particular, let the buffer be represented by $buf[1:n]$, where n is greater than 1. Let *front* be the index of the message at the front of the queue, and let *rear* be the index of the first empty slot past the message at the rear of the queue. Initially, *front* and *rear* are set to the same value, say 0. Then the producer deposits message m into the buffer by executing:

$$deposit:\ buf[rear] := m;\ rear := rear \bmod n + 1$$

And the consumer fetches a message into its local variable m by executing:

$$fetch:\ m := buf[front];\ front := front \bmod n + 1$$

The **mod** (modulo) operator is used to ensure that the values of *front* and *rear* are always between 1 and n. The queue of buffered messages is thus stored in slots from $buf[front]$ up to but not including $buf[rear]$, with *buf* treated as a circular array in which $buf[1]$ follows $buf[n]$. As an example, one possible configuration of *buf* is shown below:

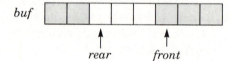

The shaded slots are full; the blank ones are empty.

When there is a single buffer—as in the producers/consumers problem—execution of *deposit* and *fetch* must alternate. When there are multiple buffers, *deposit* can execute whenever there is an empty slot, and *fetch* can execute whenever there is a stored message. We can specify this synchronization requirement by a straightforward generalization of producers-consumers predicate *PC*. As before, let *inD* and *afterD* indicate the number of times the producer has started and finished executing *deposit*, and let *inF* and *afterF* indicate the number of times the consumer has started and finished executing *fetch*. Then access to *buf* needs to be synchronized so that the following predicate is a global invariant:

$$BUFFER:\ inD \le afterF + n \ \wedge\ inF \le afterD$$

The only difference between this predicate and predicate *PC* in the previous section is that *deposit* can be started up to n times more than *fetch* has finished, rather than just one time more. Inserting assignments to these variables at the start and end of *deposit* and *fetch* and guarding those

var *buf*[1:*n*] : T   # for some type T
var *front* := 0, *rear* := 0
var *inD* := 0, *afterD* := 0, *inF* := 0, *afterF* := 0
{ *BUFFER*: *inD* ≤ *afterF* + *n* ∧ *inF* ≤ *afterD* }

Producer:: **do** true →
                produce message *m*
                deposit: ⟨ **await** *inD* < *afterF* + *n* → *inD* := *inD* + 1 ⟩
                        buf[*rear*] := *m*; *rear* := *rear* **mod** *n* + 1
                        ⟨ *afterD* := *afterD* + 1 ⟩
        od
Consumer:: **do** true →
                fetch: ⟨ **await** *inF* < *afterD* → *inF* := *inF* + 1 ⟩
                        m := *buf*[*front*]; *front* := *front* **mod** *n* + 1
                        ⟨ *afterF* := *afterF* + 1 ⟩
                consume message *m*
        od

Figure 4.10. Coarse-grained bounded buffer.

---

assignments to ensure that *BUFFER* is invariant, we get the solution to the bounded buffer problem shown in Figure 4.10. In the solution, *Producer* and *Consumer* can in fact access *buf* at the same time—unlike in Figure 4.8, where they alternate access. This is perfectly acceptable since, if *deposit* and *fetch* execute concurrently, then *front* ≠ *rear*, so the processes will be accessing different elements of array *buf*.

Once again we can use the technique of changing variables to implement the atomic actions in Figure 4.10 using semaphores. Again let *empty* and *full* be semaphores that indicate the number of empty and full slots, respectively. They are related to the incrementing counters by:

$$empty = afterF - inD + n$$
$$full = afterD - inF$$

With this change of variables, the atomic actions again become semaphore operations, and we get the final solution shown in Figure 4.11. The semaphores are used in the same way as in Figure 4.9. The only difference is that *empty* is initially *n*; hence *empty* and *full* range in value from 0 to *n*.

In Figure 4.11, the semaphores serve as *resource counters*: each counts the number of units of a resource. In this case, *empty* counts the number of empty buffer slots, and *full* counts the number of full slots. When neither process is executing *deposit* or *fetch*, the sum of the values of the two

var *buf*[1:*n*] : T   # for some type T
var *front* := 0, *rear* := 0
var *empty* : **sem** := *n*, *full* : **sem** := 0   # $n - 2 \leq empty + full \leq n$
Producer:: **do** true →
                    produce message *m*
                    deposit: **P**(*empty*)
                                    buf[*rear*] := *m*; *rear* := *rear* **mod** *n* + 1
                                    V(*full*)
            od
Consumer:: **do** true →
                    fetch: **P**(*full*)
                                    m := *buf*[*front*]; *front* := *front* **mod** *n* + 1
                                    V(*empty*)
                                consume message *m*
            od

Figure 4.11. Bounded buffer using semaphores.

---

semaphores is *n*, the total number of buffer slots. Resource counting semaphores are useful whenever processes compete for access to multiple-unit resources such as buffer slots or memory blocks.

In Figure 4.11, we assumed that there is only one producer and only one consumer since this ensures that *deposit* and *fetch* execute as atomic actions. Suppose, however, that there are two (or more) producers. Then each could be executing *deposit* at the same time if there are at least two empty slots. In that case, both processes could try to deposit their message into the same slot! (This will happen if both assign to *buf*[*rear*] before either increments *rear*.) Similarly, if there are two (or more) consumers, both could execute *fetch* at the same time and retrieve the same message. In short, *deposit* and *fetch* become critical sections. Each must be executed with mutual exclusion—but they can execute concurrently with each other since *empty* and *full* are used in such a way that producers and consumers access different buffer slots. We can implement the required exclusion using the solution to the critical section problem shown in Figure 4.4, with separate semaphores being used to protect each critical section. The complete solution is shown in Figure 4.12.

Here we have solved the two problems separately—first the synchronization between the producer and consumer, then the synchronization between producers and between consumers. This made it simple to combine the solutions to the two subproblems to get a solution to the full problem. We will use the same idea in solving the readers/writers problem in

```
var buf[1:n] : T        # for some type T
var front := 0, rear := 0
var empty : sem := n, full : sem := 0        # n − 2 ≤ empty + full ≤ n
var mutexD : sem := 1, mutexF : sem := 1
Producer[1:M]::  do true →
                        produce message m
                        deposit:  P(empty)
                                  P(mutexD)
                                  buf[rear] := m; rear := rear mod n + 1
                                  V(mutexD)
                                  V(full)
                 od
Consumer[1:N]::  do true →
                        fetch:  P(full)
                                P(mutexF)
                                m := buf[front]; front := front mod n + 1
                                V(mutexF)
                                V(empty)
                        consume message m
                 od
```

Figure 4.12. Multiple producers and consumers using semaphores.

Section 4.3. When there are multiple kinds of synchronization, it is generally useful to examine them separately and then combine the solutions.

4.3 Selective Mutual Exclusion

The last section showed how to use semaphores to implement critical sections. This section builds upon that technique to implement more complex forms of mutual exclusion. We consider two classic synchronization problems: the dining philosophers and readers and writers. The solution to the dining philosophers illustrates how to implement mutual exclusion between processes that compete for access to overlapping sets of shared variables. The solution to the readers/writers problem illustrates how to implement a combination of concurrent and exclusive access to shared variables. These problems are representative of such selective mutual exclusion problems; other examples are in the exercises.

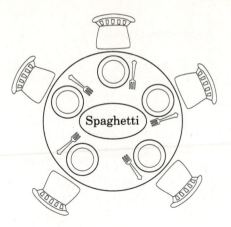

Figure 4.13. The dining philosophers.

Dining Philosophers

Although the dining philosophers problem is more whimsical than practical, it is similar to realistic problems in which a process requires simultaneous access to more than one resource. Consequently, the problem is often used to illustrate and compare different synchronization mechanisms.

(4.4)   **Dining Philosophers Problem**. Five philosophers sit around a circular table. Each philosopher spends his life alternately thinking and eating. In the center of the table is a large platter of spaghetti. Because the spaghetti is long and tangled—and the philosophers are not mechanically adept—a philosopher must use two forks to eat a helping. Unfortunately, the philosophers can only afford five forks. One fork is placed between each pair of philosophers, and they agree that each will use only the forks to the immediate left and right. The problem is to write a program to simulate the behavior of the philosophers. The program must avoid the unfortunate (and eventually fatal) situation in which all philosophers are hungry but none is able to acquire both forks; e.g., each holds one fork and refuses to give it up.

The setting for this problem is depicted in Figure 4.13. Clearly, two neighboring philosophers cannot eat at the same time. Also, with only five forks, at most two philosophers at a time can be eating.

We will simulate the actions of the philosophers as follows:

> *Philosopher*[*i*: 1..5]:: **do** true →
>   think
>   acquire forks
>   eat
>   release forks
> **od**

We assume that the lengths of the thinking and eating periods of the philosophers vary; this could be simulated by using random delays.

To solve the problem requires programming the actions of acquiring and releasing forks. As usual, the first step is to specify the required synchronization precisely. Since the forks are the shared resource, we will focus upon the actions of acquiring and releasing them. (Alternatively, we could specify the required synchronization in terms of whether or not philosophers are eating; see exercise 4.17.)

To specify the states of philosophers and forks, we could record for each philosopher and fork whether or not a philosopher has a fork. This is similar to specifying whether or not a process is in a critical section. Or we can again use incrementing counters; this results in a simpler specification since it uses fewer variables. Let $up[i]$ count the number of times that fork i has been picked up, and let $down[i]$ count the number of times it has been put down. Clearly a fork cannot be put down more times than it has been picked up. Also, a fork can be picked up by at most one philosopher at a time. These constraints are specified by the predicate:

$$FORKS: (\ \forall i:\ 1 \leq i \leq 5:\ down[i] \leq up[i] \leq down[i] + 1)$$

This must be a global invariant.

Each philosopher first picks up two forks, then eats, then puts the forks down. Assume philosopher i picks up forks i and $(i \bmod 5) + 1$, as shown in Figure 4.13. With the above representation, picking up a fork involves incrementing the appropriate element of up, and putting the fork down involves incrementing the appropriate element of $down$. Guarding the increments to the counters to ensure the invariance of *FORKS* yields the coarse-grained solution shown in Figure 4.14. In the solution, we use $i \oplus 1$ as shorthand for $(i \bmod 5) + 1$.

Once again the atomic statements meet the requirements for changing variables, so up and $down$ can be replaced by a new array *fork* satisfying:

$$fork[i] = 1 - (up[i] - down[i])$$

As before, up and $down$ become auxiliary variables, and *fork* becomes an array of semaphores. *Philosopher*[*i*] picks up both forks by executing:

var $up[1{:}5] : \textbf{int} := ([5]\, 0),\ down[1{:}5]\ \textbf{int} := ([5]\, 0)$
$\{\ FORKS{:}\ (\ \forall i{:}\ 1 \le i \le 5{:}\ down[i] \le up[i] \le down[i] + 1)\ \}$

$Philosopher[i{:}\ 1..5]{::}\ \textbf{do}\ \text{true} \rightarrow$

$\qquad\qquad\qquad \langle\ \textbf{await}\ up[i] = down[i] \rightarrow up[i] := up[i] + 1\ \rangle$

$\qquad\qquad\qquad \langle\ \textbf{await}\ up[i \oplus 1] = down[i \oplus 1] \rightarrow$

$\qquad\qquad\qquad\qquad up[i \oplus 1] := up[i \oplus 1] + 1\ \rangle$

$\qquad\qquad\qquad \text{eat}$

$\qquad\qquad\qquad \langle\ down[i] := down[i] + 1\ \rangle$

$\qquad\qquad\qquad \langle\ down[i \oplus 1] := down[i \oplus 1] + 1\ \rangle$

$\qquad\qquad\qquad \text{think}$

$\qquad \textbf{od}$

Figure 4.14. Coarse-grained solution to the dining philosophers problem.

$\qquad \textbf{P}(fork[\text{i}]);\ \textbf{P}(fork[i \oplus 1])$

Similarly, *Philosopher[i]* puts the forks down by executing:

$\qquad \textbf{V}(fork[i]);\ \textbf{V}(fork[i \oplus 1])$

Although the above approach correctly ensures that neighboring philosophers do not eat at the same time, the solution can result in deadlock. In particular, if all philosophers have picked up one fork, then none can pick up a second fork. A necessary condition for deadlock is that there is circular waiting, i.e., one process is waiting for a resource held by a second, which is waiting for a resource held by a third, and so on up to some process that is waiting for a resource held by the first process. Thus, to avoid deadlock it is sufficient to ensure that circular waiting cannot occur. For this problem, one approach is to have one of the processes, say *Philosopher[5]*, pick up its forks in the other order. Figure 4.15 gives this solution. (The Historical Notes and the Exercises discuss other approaches.) Formally proving that the solution is deadlock-free requires adding auxiliary variables to indicate which philosopher holds each fork, and then using the method of Exclusion of Configurations (2.25).

Readers and Writers

The readers/writers problem is another classic synchronization problem. Like the dining philosophers, it is often used to compare and contrast synchronization mechanisms. It is also an eminently practical problem.

var *forks*[1:5] : **sem** := ([5] 1)

Philosopher[*i*: 1..4]:: **do** true →
$\qquad\qquad$ **P**(*fork*[*i*]); **P**(*fork*[*i* + 1])
$\qquad\qquad$ eat
$\qquad\qquad$ **V**(*fork*[*i*]); **V**(*fork*[*i* + 1])
$\qquad\qquad$ think
$\qquad$ **od**

Philosopher[5]:: **do** true →
$\qquad\qquad$ **P**(*fork*[1]); **P**(*fork*[5])
$\qquad\qquad$ eat
$\qquad\qquad$ **V**(*fork*[1]); **V**(*fork*[5])
$\qquad\qquad$ think
$\qquad$ **od**

Figure 4.15. Dining philosophers solution using semaphores.

(4.5) $\qquad$ **Readers/Writers Problem.** Two kinds of processes—readers and writers—share a database. Readers execute transactions that examine database records; writer transactions both examine and update the database. The database is assumed initially to be in a consistent state (i.e., one in which relations between data are meaningful). Each transaction, if executed in isolation, transforms the database from one consistent state to another. To preclude interference between transactions, a writer process must have exclusive access to the database. Assuming no writer is accessing the database, any number of readers may concurrently execute transactions.

This is another example of a selective mutual exclusion problem. In the dining philosophers problem, pairs of processes competed for access to forks. Here, classes of processes compete for access to the database. Individual writer processes compete for access with each other, and readers as a class compete with writers.

Here we derive a solution to the problem that illustrates how to implement this kind of exclusion. As usual, the starting point is to specify the required synchronization. Since writers need to exclude each other, we can specify their interaction as in the critical section problem. In particular, let *writing*[*j*] be 1 when a writer is accessing the database, and let *writing*[*j*] be 0 otherwise. Then the sum of the *writing*[*j*] must be at most 1. Since the readers as a class need to exclude individual writers, it suffices to employ one variable, *reading*, that is 1 when any reader is reading the database and is 0

var *reading* := 0, *nr* := 0, *writing*[1:*n*] := ([*n*] 0)
{ *RW*: *reading* + *writing*[1] + ... + *writing*[*n*] ≤ 1 }
Reader[*i*: 1..*m*]:: **do** true →
⟨ *nr* := *nr* + 1
   if *nr* = 1 → *reading* := *reading* + 1 **fi** ⟩
read the database
⟨ *nr* := *nr* − 1
   if *nr* = 0 → *reading* := *reading* − 1 **fi** ⟩
od
Writer[*j*: 1..*n*]:: **do** true →
⟨ *writing*[*j*] := *writing*[*j*] + 1 ⟩
write the database
⟨ *writing*[*j*] := *writing*[*j*] − 1 ⟩
od

Figure 4.16. Readers and writers solution outline.

---

otherwise. Initially all the variables are 0. The following predicate specifies the required synchronization:

$$RW:\ reading + writing[1] + ... + writing[n] \le 1$$

This as usual is to be a global invariant.

The above specification says that *reading* is 1 when any reader is reading the database and is 0 otherwise. This is different than in previous mutual exclusion problems. Before, there was a constraint on every individual process. Here, only the first reader should increment *reading* before accessing the database, and only the last reader should decrement it when all readers are done. To implement this, let *nr* be the number of active readers, i.e., those trying to access the database. Then *reading* should be incremented when *nr* is 1 and decremented when *nr* is back to 0. Ignoring the actual representation of the database—which is most likely stored in files—and ignoring other actions of the processes, we thus get the solution outline shown in Figure 4.16. In readers, altering and examing *nr* and *reading* are made into composite atomic actions in order to preserve the specified relation between these actions. In particular, outside the atomic actions, the following predicate is also invariant:

$$(nr > 0 \land reading = 1)\ \lor\ (nr = 0 \land reading = 0)$$

var *reading* := 0, *nr* := 0, *writing*[1:*n*] := ([*n*] 0)
{ *RW*: *reading* + *writing*[1] + ... + *writing*[*n*] ≤ 1 }
below *SUM* is *reading* + *writing*[1] + ... + *writing*[*n*]

Reader[*i*: 1..*m*]:: **do** true →
$\quad\quad\quad\quad$ ⟨ *nr* := *nr* + 1
$\quad\quad\quad\quad\quad$ **if** *nr* = 1 →
$\quad\quad\quad\quad\quad\quad\quad$ **await** *SUM* ≤ 0 → *reading* := *reading* + 1
$\quad\quad\quad\quad\quad$ **fi** ⟩
$\quad\quad\quad\quad$ read the database
$\quad\quad\quad\quad$ ⟨ *nr* := *nr* − 1
$\quad\quad\quad\quad\quad$ **if** *nr* = 0 → *reading* := *reading* − 1 **fi** ⟩
$\quad\quad$ **od**

Writer[*j*: 1..*n*]:: **do** true →
$\quad\quad\quad\quad$ ⟨ **await** *SUM* ≤ 0 → *writing*[*j*] := *writing*[*j*] + 1 ⟩
$\quad\quad\quad\quad$ write the database
$\quad\quad\quad\quad$ ⟨ *writing*[*j*] := *writing*[*j*] − 1 ⟩
$\quad\quad$ **od**

Figure 4.17. Coarse-grained readers and writers solution.

To refine the outline in Figure 4.16 into a solution that uses semaphores, we first need to guard assignments to *reading* and *writing* to ensure that *RW* is invariant. Then we need to implement the resulting atomic actions. To ensure *RW*, when *reading* is incremented, the sum of *writing*[*j*] must be 0. When *writing*[*j*] is incremented, the sum of *reading* and the other *writing*[*k*] must be 0. As usual, decrementing *reading* and *writing*[*j*] need not be guarded. Adding appropriate guards to Figure 4.16 yields the coarse-grained solution shown in Figure 4.17. There the **await** statement in readers is in the middle of an atomic action. This is the first time this has occurred. Consequently, we need to ensure that the entire enclosing action is indivisible, even if **await** causes delay. Below we show how to do this.

Recall that, if two atomic actions reference disjoint sets of variables, then they can execute concurrently since they will appear to be indivisible with respect to each other. In Figure 4.17, *nr* is referenced only by reader processes. The only actions within readers that reference variables accessed by writers are the **await** statement and the decrement of *reading*. Hence, the composite actions in readers can be subdivided into the parts that are critical with respect to other readers and the parts that are also critical with respect to writers. We showed earlier how to use semaphores to implement critical sections. Let *mutexR* be a semaphore that is used to implement critical sections between readers. Using this semaphore, the reader's entry protocol in Figure 4.17 becomes:

> $\mathbf{P}(mutexR)$
> $\quad nr := nr + 1$
> $\quad \mathbf{if}\ nr = 1 \rightarrow \langle\ \mathbf{await}\ SUM \leq 0 \rightarrow reading := reading + 1\ \rangle\ \mathbf{fi}$
> $\mathbf{V}(mutexR)$

The corresponding reader's exit protocol is:

> $\mathbf{P}(mutexR)$
> $\quad nr := nr - 1$
> $\quad \mathbf{if}\ nr = 0 \rightarrow \langle\ reading := reading - 1\ \rangle\ \mathbf{fi}$
> $\mathbf{V}(mutexR)$

In essence, we have replaced the angle brackets in Figure 4.17 by semaphore operations as in Figure 4.4. After doing this, we need to enclose the actions that reference variables shared with writers—*reading* and the *writing[j]*—within angle brackets to indicate that they must also be atomic.

To get a complete solution, we now need to use semaphores to implement the above reader actions above and the writer actions in Figure 4.17. Since these actions implement reader/writer exclusion—as specified by keeping predicate *RW* invariant—again we can use the technique of changing variables. In particular, let *rw* be a semaphore whose value is:

$$rw = 1 - (reading + writing[1] + ... + writing[n])$$

Making this change, the remaining atomic actions become semaphore operations, so the final solution is as shown in Figure 4.18. In the solution, *mutexR* protects the critical section between readers, and *rw* protects the critical section between readers and writers. Variable *nr* is used so that only the first reader to arrive executes $\mathbf{P}(rw)$, and the last reader to leave executes $\mathbf{V}(rw)$. These could of course be different reader processes.

The algorithm in Figure 4.18 is called a *readers' preference* solution to the readers/writers problem. This term denotes the fact that, if some reader is accessing the database and both another reader and a writer arrive at their entry protocols, then the new reader gets preference over the writer. Actually, the solution gives readers "weak" preference. A "strong" readers' preference solution is one in which a reader *always* gets preference over a writer when both kinds of processes are at their entry protocols—in particular, if both a reader and a writer are delayed executing $\mathbf{P}(rw)$.

Since the algorithm in Figure 4.18 gives readers preference over writers, the solution is not fair. This is because a continual stream of readers can permanently prevent writers from accessing the database. The next section develops a different solution that is fair.

var *nr* := 0, *mutexR* : **sem** := 1, *rw* : **sem** := 1

Reader[*i*: 1..*m*]:: **do** true →

        P(*mutexR*)

          nr := *nr* + 1

          if *nr* = 1 → **P**(*rw*) **fi**

        V(*mutexR*)

        read the database

        P(*mutexR*)

          nr := *nr* − 1

          if *nr* = 0 → **V**(*rw*) **fi**

        V(*mutexR*)

    od

Writer[*j*: 1..*n*]:: **do** true →

        P(*rw*)

        write the database

        V(*rw*)

    od

Figure 4.18. Readers and writers solution using semaphores.

4.4 General Condition Synchronization

The previous section approached the readers/writers problem as a mutual exclusion problem. The focus was on ensuring that writers excluded each other, and that readers as a class excluded writers. The resulting solution (Figure 4.18) thus consisted of overlapping solutions to critical section problems: one between readers and one between writers.

This section develops a different solution to the problem by starting from a different—and simpler—specification of the required synchronization. The solution introduces a general programming technique called *passing the baton*. This technique employs split binary semaphores to provide exclusion and to control which delayed process is next to proceed. It can be used to implement arbitrary **await** statements and thus to implement arbitrary condition synchronization. The technique can also be used to control precisely the order in which delayed processes are awakened.

Readers and Writers Revisited

As defined in (4.5), readers examine a shared database, and writers both examine and alter it. To preserve database consistency, a writer requires exclusive access, but any number of readers may execute concurrently. A simple way to specify this synchronization is to count the number of each kind of process trying to access the database, then to constrain the values of the counters. In particular, let nr and nw be non-negative integers that respectively record the number of readers and writers accessing the database. The bad state to be avoided is one in which both nr and nw are positive or nw is greater than one. The inverse set of good states is characterized by the predicate:

$$RW: \ (nr = 0 \lor nw = 0) \land nw \leq 1$$

The first term says readers and writers cannot access the database at the same time; the second says there is at most one active writer. With this specification of the problem, an outline of the reader processes is:

$$Reader[i: 1..m]:: \ \textbf{do} \ \text{true} \rightarrow \langle \ nr := nr + 1 \ \rangle$$
$$\text{read the database}$$
$$\langle \ nr := nr - 1 \ \rangle$$
$$\textbf{od}$$

The corresponding outline for writer processes is:

$$Writer[j: 1..n]:: \ \textbf{do} \ \text{true} \rightarrow \langle \ nw := nw + 1 \ \rangle$$
$$\text{write the database}$$
$$\langle \ nw := nw - 1 \ \rangle$$
$$\textbf{od}$$

To refine this outline into a coarse-grained solution, we need to guard the assignments to the shared variables to ensure that RW is invariant. From

$$wp(nr := nr + 1, RW) \ = \ (nr = -1 \lor nw = 0)$$

and the fact that nr and nw are non-negative, we need to guard $nr := nr + 1$ by $nw = 0$. Similarly, we need to guard $nw := nw + 1$ by $nr = 0 \land nw = 0$. We do not, however, need to guard either decrement. Informally, it is never necessary to delay a process that is giving up use of a resource. More formally,

$$wp(nr := nr - 1, RW) \ = \ ((nr = 1 \lor nw = 0) \land nw \leq 1)$$

This is true since $(nr > 0 \land RW)$ is true before nr is decremented. The reasoning for nw is analogous. Inserting the guards yields the coarse-grained solution in Figure 4.19.

var $nr := 0$, $nw := 0$
$\{\,RW\!:\ (nr = 0 \lor nw = 0) \land nw \leq 1\,\}$
$Reader[i: 1..m]$:: **do** true $\to \langle$ **await** $nw = 0 \to nr := nr + 1\,\rangle$
                      read the database
                      $\langle\ nr := nr - 1\,\rangle$
           od
$Writer[j: 1..n]$:: **do** true $\to \langle$ **await** $nr = 0$ **and** $nw = 0 \to nw := nw + 1\,\rangle$
                     write the database
                     $\langle\ nw := nw - 1\,\rangle$
          od

Figure 4.19. A second coarse-grained readers/writers solution.

The Technique of Passing the Baton

In Figure 4.19, the two guards in the **await** statements overlap. Hence, we cannot use the technique of changing variables to implement the atomic statements. This is because no one semaphore could discriminate between the guards. Thus we require a different technique. The one introduced here is called *passing the baton*, for reasons explained below. This technique is powerful enough to implement any **await** statement.

After the third step of our derivation method, the solution will contain atomic statements having either of two forms:

$$F_1: \langle\, S_i \,\rangle \quad \text{or} \quad F_2: \langle\, \textbf{await}\ B_j \to S_j \,\rangle$$

We can use split binary semaphores as follows to implement both the mutual exclusion and condition synchronization in these statements. First, let e be a binary semaphore whose initial value is one. It is used to control entry into the atomic statements. Second, associate one semaphore b_j and one counter d_j with each semantically different guard B_j; these are all initially zero. Semaphore b_j is used to delay processes waiting for B_j to become true; d_j is a count of the number of processes delayed on (or about to delay on) b_j.

The entire set of semaphores—e and the b_j—are used as follows so they form a split binary semaphore (4.3). Statements of the form F_1 are replaced by the program fragment:

(4.6) F_1: **P**(e) $\{\,I\,\}$
               S_i $\{\,I\,\}$
               SIGNAL

Statements of the form F_2 are replaced by the program fragment:

(4.7) F_2: **P**(e) $\{\,I\,\}$
                 if not $B_j \rightarrow d_j := d_j + 1;\, \mathbf{V}(e);\, \mathbf{P}(b_j)$ **fi** $\{\,I \wedge B_j\,\}$
                 S_j $\{\,I\,\}$
                 SIGNAL

We have annotated the above program fragments with assertions that are true at critical points; I is the synchronization invariant. In both fragments, *SIGNAL* is the following statement:

(4.8)   *SIGNAL*: **if** B_1 **and** $d_1 > 0 \rightarrow \{\,I \wedge B_1\,\}$ $d_1 := d_1 - 1;\, \mathbf{V}(b_1)$
                     [] ...
                     [] B_n **and** $d_n > 0 \rightarrow \{\,I \wedge B_n\,\}$ $d_n := d_n - 1;\, \mathbf{V}(b_n)$
                     [] **else** $\rightarrow \{\,I\,\}$ $\mathbf{V}(e)$
                 fi

The first n guards in *SIGNAL* check whether there is some process waiting for a condition that is now true. The last guard, **else**, is an abbreviation for the negation of the disjunction of the other guards (i.e., **else** is true if none of the other guards is true). If the **else** guard is selected, the entry semaphore e is signaled. Again, *SIGNAL* is annotated with assertions that are true at critical points.

With these replacements, the semaphores form a split binary semaphore since at most one semaphore at a time is 1, and every execution path starts with a **P** and ends with a single **V**. Hence the statements between any **P** and **V** execute with mutual exclusion. The synchronization invariant I is true before each **V** operation, so it is true whenever one of the semaphores is 1. Moreover, B_j is guaranteed to be true whenever S_j is executed. This is because, either the process checked B_j and found it to be true, or the process delayed on b_j, which is signaled only when B_j is true. In the latter case, the predicate B_j is effectively transferred to the delayed process. Finally, the transformation does not introduce deadlock since b_j is signaled only if some process is waiting on or is about to be waiting on b_j. (A process could have incremented the counter and executed **V**(e) but might not yet have executed the **P** operation on the condition semaphore.)

This programming technique is called *passing the baton* because of the way in which semaphores are signaled. When a process is executing within a critical region, think of it as holding a baton that signifies permission to execute. When that process reaches a *SIGNAL* fragment, it passes the baton to one other process. If some process is waiting for a condition that is now true, the baton is passed to one such process, which in turn executes the critical region and passes the baton to another process. When no process is waiting for a condition that is true, the baton is passed to the next process

var $nr := 0, nw := 0$ $\{$ *RW*: $(nr = 0 \lor nw = 0) \land nw \leq 1$ $\}$
var e : **sem** $:= 1, r$: **sem** $:= 0, w$: **sem** $:= 0$ $\{$ *SPLIT*: $0 \leq (e + r + w) \leq 1$ $\}$
var $dr := 0, dw := 0$ $\{$ *COUNTERS*: $dr \geq 0 \land dw \geq 0$ $\}$

Reader[i: 1..*m*]:: **do** true $\rightarrow$
                    $\mathbf{P}(e)$
                    if $nw > 0 \rightarrow dr := dr + 1$; $\mathbf{V}(e)$; $\mathbf{P}(r)$ **fi**
                    $nr := nr + 1$
                    $SIGNAL_1$
                    read the database
                    $\mathbf{P}(e)$
                    $nr := nr - 1$
                    $SIGNAL_2$
          od
Writer[j: 1..*n*]:: **do** true $\rightarrow$
                    $\mathbf{P}(e)$
                    if $nr > 0$ **or** $nw > 0 \rightarrow dw := dw + 1$; $\mathbf{V}(e)$; $\mathbf{P}(w)$ **fi**
                    $nw := nw + 1$
                    $SIGNAL_3$
                    write the database
                    $\mathbf{P}(e)$
                    $nw := nw - 1$
                    $SIGNAL_4$
          od

Figure 4.20. Readers and writers outline with passing the baton.

---

that tries to enter the critical region for the first time—i.e., a process that executes $\mathbf{P}(e)$.

Readers and Writers Solution

We can use the passing-the-baton technique as follows to implement the coarse-grained solution to the readers/writers problem given in Figure 4.19. In that solution, there are two different guards, so we need two condition semaphores and associated counters. Let semaphore r represent the reader delay condition $nw = 0$, and let w represent the writer delay condition $nr = 0$ $\land nw = 0$. Let dr and dw be the associated counters. Finally, let e be the entry semaphore. Performing the baton-passing replacements given in (4.6) and (4.7) yields the solution shown in Figure 4.20. In the solution, $SIGNAL_i$ is an abbreviation for:

$$\textbf{if } nw = 0 \textbf{ and } dr > 0 \rightarrow dr := dr - 1; \textbf{V}(r)$$
$$[] \; nr = 0 \textbf{ and } nw = 0 \textbf{ and } dw > 0 \rightarrow dw := dw - 1; \textbf{V}(w)$$
$$[] \; (nw > 0 \textbf{ or } dr = 0) \textbf{ and } (nr > 0 \textbf{ or } nw > 0 \textbf{ or } dw = 0) \rightarrow \textbf{V}(e)$$
$$\textbf{fi}$$

Here, $SIGNAL_i$ ensures that nw is zero when semaphore r is signaled and ensures that both nr and nw are zero when semaphore w is signaled. Semaphore e is signaled only when there are no delayed readers or writers that could proceed.

In Figure 4.20—and in general—the preconditions of the $SIGNAL$ fragments allow many of the guards to be simplified or eliminated. In reader processes, both $nr > 0$ and $nw = 0$ are true before $SIGNAL_1$. Hence that signal fragment simplifies to:

$$\textbf{if } dr > 0 \rightarrow dr := dr - 1; \textbf{V}(r) \; [] \; dr = 0 \rightarrow \textbf{V}(e) \textbf{ fi}$$

Before $SIGNAL_2$ in readers, both nw and dr are 0. In writer processes, $nr = 0$ and $nw > 0$ before $SIGNAL_3$, and $nr = 0$ and $nw = 0$ before $SIGNAL_4$. Using these facts to simplify the signal protocols yields the final solution shown in Figure 4.21.

In Figure 4.21, the last **if** statement in writers is non-deterministic: If there are both delayed readers and delayed writers, either could be signaled when a writer finishes its exit protocol. Also, when a writer finishes, if there is more than one delayed reader and one is awakened, the others are awakened in cascading fashion. The first reader increments nr, then awakens the second, which increments nr and awakens the third, and so on. The baton keeps getting passed from one delayed reader to another until all are awakened.

Alternative Scheduling Policies

Like the readers/writers solution given earlier in Figure 4.18, the solution in Figure 4.21 gives readers preference over writers. Unlike the earlier solution, however, we can readily modify the new solution to schedule processes in other ways. For example, to give writers preference, it is necessary to ensure that:

- new readers are delayed if a writer is waiting, and

- a delayed reader is awakened only if no writer is waiting.

We can meet the first requirement by strengthening the delay condition in the first **if** statement in readers:

var $nr := 0$, $nw := 0$ { RW: $(nr = 0 \lor nw = 0) \land nw \leq 1$ }
var e : **sem** $:= 1$, r : **sem** $:= 0$, w : **sem** $:= 0$ { $SPLIT$: $0 \leq (e + r + w) \leq 1$ }
var $dr := 0$, $dw := 0$ { $COUNTERS$: $dr \geq 0 \land dw \geq 0$ }

$Reader[i: 1..m]$::   **do** true →
                          P(e)
                          if $nw > 0 → dr := dr + 1$; **V**(e); **P**(r) **fi**
                          $nr := nr + 1$
                          if $dr > 0 → dr := dr - 1$; **V**(r) [] $dr = 0 → $ **V**(e) **fi**
                          read the database
                          P(e)
                          $nr := nr - 1$
                          if $nr = 0$ **and** $dw > 0 → dw := dw - 1$; **V**(w)
                          [] $nr > 0$ **or** $dw = 0 → $ **V**(e)
                          fi
             od

$Writer[j: 1..n]$::   **do** true →
                          P(e)
                          if $nr > 0$ **or** $nw > 0 → dw := dw + 1$; **V**(e); **P**(w) **fi**
                          $nw := nw + 1$
                          V(e)
                          write the database
                          P(e)
                          $nw := nw - 1$
                          if $dr > 0 → dr := dr - 1$; **V**(r)
                          [] $dw > 0 → dw := dw - 1$; **V**(w)
                          [] $dr = 0$ **and** $dw = 0 → $ **V**(e)
                          fi
             od

Figure 4.21. Readers and writers solution using passing the baton.

---

      if $nw > 0$ **or** $dw > 0 → dr := dr + 1$; **V**(e); **P**(r) **fi**

To meet the second requirement, we can strengthen the first guard in the last **if** statement in writers:

      if $dr > 0$ **and** $dw = 0 → dr := dr - 1$; **V**(r)
      [] $dw > 0 → dw := dw - 1$; **V**(w)
      [] $dr = 0$ **and** $dw = 0 → $ **V**(e)
      fi

This eliminates the non-determinism that was present in that statement, which is always safe to do. Neither of these changes alters the structure of the solution. This is a virtue of the passing-the-baton technique: Guards can be manipulated to alter the order in which processes are awakened without affecting the basic correctness of the solution.

We can also alter the solution in Figure 4.21 to ensure fair access to the database, assuming the semaphore operations are themselves fair. For example, we could force readers and writers to alternate turns when both are waiting. In particular, when a writer finishes, all waiting readers get a turn; and when the readers finish, one waiting writer gets a turn. We can implement this alternation by adding a boolean variable *writer_last* that is set to true when a writer starts writing and is cleared when a reader starts reading. Then we change the last **if** statement in writers to:

> **if** $dr > 0$ **and** $(dw = 0$ **or** *writer_last*$) \rightarrow dr := dr - 1; \mathbf{V}(r)$
> $[]\ dw > 0$ **and** $(dr = 0$ **or** **not** *writer_last*$) \rightarrow dw := dw - 1; \mathbf{V}(w)$
> $[]\ dr = 0$ **and** $dw = 0 \rightarrow \mathbf{V}(e)$
> **fi**

Again the structure of the solution is unchanged.

This technique of passing the baton can also be used to provide finer-grained control over the order in which processes use resources. The next section illustrates this. The only thing we cannot control is the order in which processes delayed on the entry semaphore e are awakened. This depends on the underlying implementation of semaphores.

4.5 Resource Allocation

Resource allocation is the problem of deciding when a process can be given access to a resource. In concurrent programs, a resource is anything that a process might be delayed waiting to acquire. This includes entry to a critical section, access to a database, a slot in a bounded buffer, a region of memory, use of a printer, and so on. We have already examined several specific resource allocation problems. In most, the simplest possible allocation policy was employed: If some process is waiting and the resource is available, allocate it. For example, the solution to the critical section problem in Section 4.2 ensured that *some* waiting process was given permission to enter; it did not attempt to control *which* process was given permission if there was a choice. Similarly, the solution to the bounded buffer problem in Section 4.2 made no attempt to control which producer or which consumer next got access to the buffer. The only more complex allocation policy considered so far was in the readers/writers problem. However, our concern there was giving preference to classes of processes, not to individual processes.

This section shows how to implement general resource allocation policies and in particular shows how to control explicitly which process gets a resource when more than one is waiting. First we describe the general solution pattern. Then we implement one specific allocation policy—shortest job next. The solution employs the technique of passing the baton. It also introduces the concept of private semaphores, which provide the basis for solving other resource allocation problems.

Problem Definition and General Solution Pattern

In any resource allocation problem, processes compete for use of units of a shared resource. A process requests ones or more units by executing the *request* operation, which is often implemented by a procedure. Parameters to *request* indicate how many units are required, identify any special characteristics such as the size of a memory block, and give the identity of the requesting process. Each unit of the shared resource is either free or in use. A request can be satisfied when all the required units are free. Hence *request* delays until this condition is true, then returns the requested number of units. After using allocated resources, a process returns them to the free pool by executing the *release* operation. Parameters to *release* indicate the identity of the units being returned. Ignoring the representation of resource units, the *request* and *release* operations have the following general outline:

$$request(\text{parameters}): \langle \textbf{await } request \text{ can be satisfied} \rightarrow \text{take units} \rangle$$
$$release(\text{parameters}): \langle \text{return units} \rangle$$

The operations need to be atomic since both need to access the representation of resource units. As long as this representation uses variables different from other variables in the program, the operations will appear to be atomic with respect to other actions and hence can execute concurrently with other actions.

This general solution pattern can be implemented using the passing-the-baton technique introduced in Section 4.4. In particular, *request* has the form of F_2 so it is implemented by a program fragment similar to (4.7):

(4.9) $request(\text{parameters}): \mathbf{P}(e)$
$\qquad\qquad\qquad\qquad\qquad$ **if** request cannot be satisfied $\rightarrow DELAY$ **fi**
$\qquad\qquad\qquad\qquad\qquad$ take units
$\qquad\qquad\qquad\qquad\qquad$ *SIGNAL*

Similarly, *release* has the form of F_1 so it is implemented by a program fragment similar to (4.6):

(4.10)   *release*(parameters): **P**(*e*)
                                               return units
                                               SIGNAL

As before, *e* is a semaphore that controls entry to the operations, and *SIGNAL* is a code fragment like (4.8); *SIGNAL* either awakens a delayed process—if some pending request can be satisfied—or executes **V**(*e*). The *DELAY* code is a program fragment similar to that shown in (4.7): record that there is a delayed request, execute **V**(*e*), then delay on a condition semaphore. The exact details of how *SIGNAL* is implemented for a specific problem depend on what the different delay conditions are and how they are represented. In any event, the *DELAY* code needs to save the parameters describing a delayed request so that they can be examined in the *SIGNAL* fragments. Also, there needs to be one condition semaphore for each different delay condition.

The next section develops a solution to one specific resource allocation problem. The solution illustrates how to solve any such problem. Several additional resource allocation problems are given in the exercises.

Shortest-Job-Next Allocation

Shortest-job-next is an allocation policy that occurs in many guises and is used for many different kinds of resources. Assume the shared resource has a single unit (the general case is considered at the end of this section). Then this policy is defined as follows.

(4.11)   **Shortest-Job-Next (SJN) Allocation**. Several processes compete for use of a single shared resource. A process requests use of the resource by executing *request*(*time*, *id*), where *time* is an integer that specifies how long the process will use the resource and *id* is an integer that identifies the requesting process. When a process executes *request*, if the resource is free, it is immediately allocated to the process; if not, the process delays. After using the resource, a process makes it free by executing *release*( ). When the resource is freed, it is allocated to the delayed process (if any) that has the minimum value for *time*. If two or more processes have the same value for *time*, the resource is allocated to the one that has waited the longest.

For example, the SJN policy can be used for processor allocation (in which case *time* is execution time), for spooling files to a printer (in which case *time* is printing time), or for remote file transfer (ftp) service (in which case *time* is the estimated file-transfer time). The SJN policy is attractive because it minimizes average job completion time. However, it is inherently unfair: a process can be delayed forever if there is a continual stream of requests specifying shorter usage times. (Such unfairness is extremely unlikely in practice unless a resource is totally overloaded. If unfairness is of concern, the SJN policy can be modified slightly so that a process that has been delayed a long time is given preference; this technique is called aging.)

If a process makes a request and the resource is free, the request can be satisfied immediately since there are no other pending requests. Thus, the SJN aspect of the allocation policy comes into play only if more than one process has a pending request. Since there is a single resource, it is sufficient to use a single variable to record whether the resource is available. Let *free* be a boolean variable that is true when the resource is available and false when it is in use. To implement the SJN policy, pending requests need to be remembered and ordered. Let *P* be a set of pairs (*time*, *id*), ordered by the values of *time* fields. If two pairs have the same value for *time*, let them occur in *P* in the order in which they were inserted. With this specification, the following predicate is to be a global invariant:

$$SJN:\ P \text{ is an ordered set } \wedge\ free \Rightarrow (P = \varnothing)$$

In short, *P* is ordered, and, if the resource is free, *P* is the empty set. Initially, *free* is true and *P* is empty, so *SJN* is trivially true.

Ignoring the SJN policy for the moment, a request can be satisfied exactly when the resource is available. This results in the coarse-grained solution:

> **var** *free* := true
>
> *request*(*time*, *id*): ⟨ **await** *free* → *free* := false ⟩
>
> *release*( ): ⟨ *free* := true ⟩

With the SJN policy, however, a process executing *request* needs to delay until the resource is free and the process's request is the next one to be honored according to the SJN policy. From the second conjunct of *SJN*, if *free* is true at the time a process executes *request*, set *P* is empty. Hence the above delay condition is sufficient to determine whether a request can be satisfied immediately. The *time* parameter comes into play only if a request must be delayed, i.e., if *free* is false. Based on these observations, we can implement *request* as shown in (4.9):

> *request*(*time*, *id*): **P**(*e*)
>
>   **if not** *free* → *DELAY* **fi**
>
>   *free* := false
>
>   *SIGNAL*

And we can implement *release* as shown in (4.10):

> *release*( ): **P**(*e*)
> *free* := true
> *SIGNAL*

In *request*, we assume that **P** operations on the entry semaphore *e* complete in the order in which they are attempted; i.e., **P**(*e*) is FCFS. If this is not the case, requests will not necessarily be serviced in SJN order.

The remaining concern is to implement the SJN aspect of the allocation policy. This involves using set *P* and semaphores to implement *DELAY* and *SIGNAL*. When a request cannot be satisfied, it needs to be saved so it can be examined later when the resource is released. Thus, in *DELAY* a process needs to:

- insert its parameters in *P*,
- release control of the critical section protecting *request* and *release* by executing **V**(*e*), then
- delay on a semaphore.

When the resource is freed, if set *P* is not empty, the resource needs to be allocated to exactly one process in accordance with the SJN policy. In this case, inserting parameters in *P* corresponds to incrementing a counter c_j in (4.7). In both cases, a process indicates that it is about to delay and indicates what condition it is waiting for.

In earlier examples—such as the readers/writers solution developed in Section 4.4—there were just a few different delay conditions, and hence just a few condition semaphores were needed. Here, however, each process has a different delay condition, depending on its position in *P*: the first process in *P* needs to be awakened before the second, and so on. Thus, each process needs to wait on a different delay semaphore. Assume there are *n* processes that use the resource. Let *b*[1:*n*] be an array of semaphores, each entry of which is initially 0. Also assume the values of process *id*s are unique and are in the range from 1 to *n*. Then process *id* delays on semaphore *b*[*id*]. Augmenting *request* and *release* above with uses of *P* and *b* as specified, we get the solution to the SJN allocation problem shown in Figure 4.22.

In Figure 4.22, the insert in *request* is assumed to place the pair in the proper place in *P* in order to maintain the first conjunct in *SJN*. Hence, *SJN* is indeed invariant outside *request* and *release*; i.e., *SJN* is true just after each **P**(*e*) and just before each **V**(*e*). The first guarded statement in the signal code in *release* awakens exactly one process if there is a pending request, and hence *P* is not empty. The "baton" is passed to that process, which sets *free* to false. This ensures that the second conjunct in *SJN* is true if *P* is not empty. Since there is only a single resource, no further requests could be satisfied, so the signal code in *request* is simply **V**(*e*).

var *free* := true, *e* : **sem** := 1, *b*[1:*n*] : **sem** := ([*n*] 0)
var *P* : **set of** (**int**, **int**) := ∅
{ *SJN*: *P* is an ordered set ∧ *free* ⇒ (*P* = ∅) }

request(*time*, *id*): **P**(*e*) { *SJN* }
                    if not *free* → insert (*time*, *id*) in *P*; **V**(*e*); **P**(*b*[*id*]) **fi**
                    free := false { *SJN* }
                    V(*e*)   # optimized since *free* is false at this point

release( ): **P**(*e*) { *SJN* }
          free := true
          if *P* ≠ ∅ → remove first pair (*time*, *id*) from *P*; **V**(*b*[*id*])
          [] *P* = ∅ → { *SJN* } **V**(*e*)
          fi

Figure 4.22. Shortest-job-next allocation using semaphores.

Semaphores *b*[*id*] in Figure 4.22 are examples of what are called private semaphores.

(4.12)   **Private Semaphore.** Semaphore *s* is called a private semaphore if exactly one process executes **P** operations on *s*.

Private semaphores are useful in any situation in which it is necessary to be able to signal individual processes. For some allocation problems, however, there may be fewer different delay conditions than there are processes that compete for a resource. In that case, it can be more efficient to use one semaphore for each different condition than to use private semaphores for each process. For example, if memory blocks are allocated in a few sizes only—and it does not matter what order blocks are allocated to processes competing for the same size—then it would be sufficient to have one delay semaphore for each different block size.

We can readily generalize the solution in Figure 4.22 to resources having more than one unit. In this case, each unit would either be free or allocated, and *request* and *release* would have a parameter, *amount*, to indicate how many units a process requires or is returning. We would then modify the solution in Figure 4.22 as follows:

- Replace boolean variable *free* by an integer *avail* that records the number of available units.

- In *request*, test whether *amount* units are free, i.e., whether *amount* ≤ *avail*. If so, allocate them; if not, record how many units are required before delaying.

- In *release*, increase *avail* by *amount*, then determine whether the oldest delayed process that has minimum value for *time* can have its request satisfied. If so, awaken it; if not, execute **V**(*e*).

The other modification is that it might now be possible to satisfy more than one pending request when units are released. For example, there could be two delayed processes that together require fewer units than were released. In this case, the one that is awakened first needs to signal the second after taking the units it requires. In short, the signaling protocol at the end of *request* needs to be the same as the one at the end of *release*.

4.6 Implementation

Since the semaphore operations are special cases of **await** statements, we can implement them using busy waiting and the techniques of Chapter 3. However, the only reason one might want to do so is to be able to write programs using semaphores rather than lower-level spin locks and flags. Consequently, we will just show how to add semaphores to the kernel described in Section 3.8. This involves augmenting the kernel with semaphore descriptors and three additional primitives: *create_sem*, *P*, and *V*.

A semaphore descriptor contains the value of one semaphore; it is initialized by invoking *create_sem*. The *P* and *V* primitives implement the **P** and **V** operations. We assume here that all semaphores are general semaphores; hence the **V** operation never blocks. In this section, we describe how these components are included in a single-processor kernel and how to change the resulting kernel to support multiple processors.

Recall that, in the single-processor kernel described earlier, one process at a time was executing, and all others were ready to execute. As before, the index of the descriptor of the executing process is stored in variable *executing*, and the descriptors for all ready processes are stored on the ready list. When semaphores are added to the kernel, there is a third possible process state: blocked. In particular, a process is blocked if it is waiting to complete a **P** operation. To keep track of blocked processes, each semaphore descriptor contains a linked list of the descriptors of processes blocked on that semaphore. On a single processor, exactly one process is executing, and its descriptor is on no list; every other process descriptor is either on the ready list or is on the blocked list of some semaphore.

For each semaphore declaration in a concurrent program, one call to the *create_sem* primitive is generated; the semaphore's initial value is passed as an argument. The *create_sem* primitive finds an empty semaphore descriptor, initializes the semaphore's value and blocked list, and returns a "name" for the descriptor. This name is typically either the descriptor's address or an index into a table that contains the address.

procedure *create_sem*(initial value) **returns** *name*
    get an empty semaphore descriptor
    initialize the descriptor
    set *name* to the name (index) of the descriptor
    call *dispatcher*( )
end

procedure *P*(*name*)
    find semaphore descriptor of *name*
    if value > 0 → value := value − 1
    [] value = 0 → insert descriptor of *executing* at end of blocked list
                    executing := 0   # indicate *executing* is now blocked
    fi
    call *dispatcher*( )
end

procedure *V*(*name*)
    find semaphore descriptor of *name*
    if blocked list empty → value := value + 1
    [] blocked list not empty →
          remove process descriptor from front of blocked list
          insert the descriptor at end of ready list
    fi
    call *dispatcher*( )
end

Figure 4.23. Semaphore primitives for a single-processor kernel.

After a semaphore is created, it is used by invoking the *P* and *V* primitives. Both have a single argument that is the name of a semaphore descriptor. The *P* primitive checks the value in the descriptor. If the value is positive, it is decremented; otherwise, the descriptor of the executing process is inserted on the semaphore's blocked list. Similarly, *V* checks the semaphore descriptor's blocked list. If it is empty, the semaphore's value is incremented; otherwise one process descriptor is removed from the blocked list and inserted on the ready list. It is common for each blocked list to be implemented as a FIFO queue since this ensures that the semaphore operations are fair.

Outlines of these primitives are given in Figure 4.23. They are added to the routines in the single processor kernel given earlier in Figure 3.28. Again, the *dispatcher* procedure is called at the end of each primitive; its actions are the same as before.

For simplicity, the implementation of the semaphore primitives in Figure 4.23 does not reuse semaphore descriptors. This would be sufficient if all semaphores are global to processes, but in general this is not the case. Thus it is usually necessary to reuse semaphore descriptors as well as process descriptors (as was done in Figure 3.28). One approach is for the kernel to provide an additional *destroy_sem* primitive; this would then be invoked by a process when it no longer needs a semaphore. An alternative is to record in the descriptor of each process the names of all semaphores that process created. Then, the semaphores it created could be destroyed by the kernel when the process invokes the *quit* primitive. With either approach, it is imperative that a semaphore not be used after it has been destroyed. Detecting misuse requires that each descriptor have a unique name that is validated each time P or V is used. This can be implemented by letting the name of a descriptor be a combination of an index—which is used to locate the descriptor—and a unique sequence number.

We can extend the single-processor implementation of the semaphore primitives in Figure 4.23 into one for a multiprocessor in the same way as described in Section 3.8 and shown in Figure 3.30. Again, the critical requirement is to lock shared data structures, but only for as long as absolutely required. Hence, there should be a separate lock for each semaphore descriptor. A semaphore descriptor is locked in P and V just before it is accessed; the lock is released as soon as the descriptor is no longer needed. As in the prior multiprocessor kernel, locks are acquired and released by a busy-waiting solution to the critical section problem.

In a multiprocessor kernel, the same issues arise that were discussed at the end of Section 3.8. In particular, a process might need to execute on a specific processor, it may be important to execute a process on the same processor that it last executed on, or it may be important to co-schedule processes on the same processor. To support this functionality—or to avoid contention for a shared ready list—each processor might well have its own ready list. In this case, when a process is awakened in the V primitive, the process needs to be put on the appropriate ready list. Thus, either the V primitive needs to lock a possibly remote ready list, or it needs to inform another processor and let that processor put the unblocked process on its ready list. The first approach requires remote locking; the second requires using something like interprocessor interrupts to send a message from one processor to another.

Historical Notes and References

In the mid 1960s, Edsger Dijkstra and five colleagues developed one of the first multiprogrammed operating systems at the Technological University of Eindhoven in The Netherlands. (The designers humbly named it "THE" multiprogramming system, after the Dutch initials of the institution!) The system has an elegant structure, which consists of a kernel and layers of virtual machines implemented by processes [Dijkstra 1968a]. It also introduced semaphores, which Dijkstra invented in order to have a useful tool for implementing mutual exclusion and for signaling the occurrence of events such as interrupts. Dijkstra also invented the term *private semaphore*.

Because Dijkstra is Dutch, **P** and **V** stand for Dutch words. In particular, **P** is the first letter of the Dutch word *passeren*, which means "to pass"; **V** is the first letter of *vrygeven*, which means "to release." (Note the analogy to railroad semaphores.) Dijkstra and his group later observed that **P** might better stand for *prolagen*—formed from the Dutch words *proberen* ("to try") and *verlagen* ("to decrease")—and that **V** might better stand for *verhogen* ("to increase").

At about the same time, Dijkstra [1968b] wrote an important paper on cooperating sequential processes. His paper showed how to use semaphores to solve a variety of synchronization problems such as producers and consumers. The paper introduced the problems of the dining philosophers and the sleeping barber (Section 6.3).

In his seminal paper on monitors (discussed in Chapter 6), Tony Hoare [1974] introduced the concept of a split binary semaphore and showed how to use it to implement monitors. However, Dijkstra [1979, 1980] was the one who later named the technique and illustrated its general utility. In particular, Dijkstra [1979] showed how to use split binary semaphores to solve the readers/writers problem; Dijkstra [1980] showed how to implement general semaphores using only split binary semaphores. Dijkstra's readers/writers solution is similar to the one shown in Figure 4.21, but it has a lengthier protocol before reading and before writing.

The author developed the technique of changing variables to convert a coarse-grained solution using integers to a fine-grained one using semaphores [Andrews 1989]. That paper also introduced the technique of passing the baton. It was inspired by Dijkstra's papers on split binary semaphores. In fact, the technique of passing the baton is basically an optimization of the algorithms in Dijkstra [1979, 1980].

The solution to the dining philosophers problem in Figure 4.15 uses asymmetry to avoid deadlock. In particular, one philosopher picks up the forks in a different order than the others. Equivalently, we could have odd-numbered philosophers pick up forks in one order, and even-numbered philosophers pick them up in the other order. A second way to avoid deadlock is to allow at most four philosophers at a time to start to acquire forks; i.e., allow at most four at a time to sit at the table (see exercise 4.16). In essence, this uses an outside agent. A third approach is to have philosophers pick up both forks at once, inside a critical section; however, this can lead to starvation. Mani Chandy and Jay Misra [1984] have proposed an interesting fourth approach, which passes tokens between philosophers. Since this is most appropriate in distributed programs, we present their algorithm in Section 8.5.

All the above approaches to the dining philosophers problem are deterministic; i.e., every process takes a predictable set of actions. Lehman and Rabin [1981] have shown that any deterministic solution has to use asymmetry or an outside agent if it is to be deadlock- and starvation-free. They then present an interesting probabilistic algorithm that is perfectly symmetric (see exercise 4.19). The basic idea is that philosophers use coin flips to determine the order in which to try to pick up forks—which introduces asymmetry—and the philosopher who has most recently used a fork defers to a neighbor if they both want to use the same fork.

Courtois, Heymans, and Parnas [1971] introduced the readers/writers problem and presented two solutions using semaphores. The first is the readers' preference solution we developed in Section 4.4 (Figure 4.18). The second solution gives writers preference; it is much more complex than their readers' preference solution and uses five semaphores and two counters (see exercise 4.20). Their writers' preference solution is also quite difficult to understand. In contrast, as shown in Section 4.5 and Andrews [1989], by using the technique of passing the baton we can readily modify the readers' preference solution to give writers preference or to get a fair solution.

Scheduling properties of algorithms often depend on the semaphore operations being strongly fair, namely, a process delayed at a **P** operation eventually proceeds if enough **V** operations are executed. The kernel implementation in Figure 4.23 provides strongly fair semaphores since blocked lists are maintained in FIFO order. However, if blocked processes were queued in some other order—e.g., by their execution priority—then the **P** operation might be only weakly fair. Morris [1979] shows how to implement a starvation-free solution to the critical section problem using weakly fair binary semaphores. Martin and Burch [1985] present a somewhat simpler solution to the same problem. Finally, Udding [1986] solves the same problem in a systematic way that makes clearer why his solution is correct. All three papers use split binary semaphores and a technique quite similar to passing the baton.

Many people have proposed variations on semaphores. For example, Patil [1971] proposed a **PMultiple** primitive, which waits until a set of semaphores are all non-negative and then decrements them (see exercise 4.26). Reed and Kanodia [1979] present mechanisms called eventcounts and sequencers, which can be used to construct semaphores but can also be used directly to solve additional synchronization problems (see exercise 4.33). Recently, Faulk and Parnas [1988] have examined the kinds of synchronization that arise in hard-real-time systems, which have critical timing deadlines. They propose two sets of synchronization mechanisms: high-level ones based on relations and state transitions and low-level ones based on semaphores and regions of mutual exclusion. Application programmers use the high-level primitives, which are in turn implemented using the low-level ones. Faulk and Parnas argue that in real-time systems, the **P** operation on semaphores should be replaced by two more primitive operations: **pass**, which waits until the semaphore is non-negative; and **down**, which decrements it.

Although semaphores are much easier to use than busy waiting and provide a mechanism for blocking processes, they are still fairly low-level mechanisms. They are often used within operating systems and are sometimes provided in system call libraries (e.g., Sequent's parallel programming library). However, semaphores have not been included in many concurrent programming languages, at least not as the primary synchronization mechanism. There are better higher-level mechanisms, as we will see in later chapters. Still, semaphores have been very influential, and they are widely used to implement higher-level mechanisms.

Exercises

4.1 Develop a simulation of general semaphores using only binary semaphores. Specify a global invariant, then develop a coarse-grained solution, and finally develop a fine-grained solution. (Hint: Use the technique of passing the baton.)

4.2 Consider the following proposed simulation of general semaphores using binary semaphores. Integer s is the value of the semaphore or the number of delayed processes, semaphore *mutex* is used for mutual exclusion, and semaphore *delay* is used to delay processes trying to execute **P** operations.

> \# simulation of **P**(s)
> **P**(*mutex*); $s := s - 1$
> **if** $s < 0 \rightarrow$ **V**(*mutex*); **P**(*delay*) $[]$ $s \geq 0 \rightarrow$ **V**(mutex) **fi**
>
> \# simulation of **V**(s)
> **P**(*mutex*); $s := s + 1$
> **if** $s \leq 0 \rightarrow$ **V**(*delay*) **fi**
> **V**(*mutex*)

Assume binary semaphores have the semantics defined in Section 4.1; i.e., both **P** and **V** can block. Is the above solution correct? If so, give a proof outline and convincing argument. If not, explain and illustrate what can go wrong.

4.3 Recall that Fetch-and-Add, *FA(var, increment)*, is an atomic function that returns the old value of *var* and adds *increment* to it. Using *FA*, develop a simulation of the **P** and **V** operations on general semaphore s. Assume that memory reads and writes are atomic but that *FA* is the only more powerful atomic operation.

4.4 Suppose a machine has atomic increment and decrement instructions, *INC(var)* and *DEC(var)*. These respectively add 1 to or subtract 1 from *var*. Assume that memory reads and writes are atomic but that *INC* and *DEC* are the only more powerful atomic operations.

(a) Is it possible to simulate the **P** and **V** operations on a general semaphore s? If so, give a simulation and a proof outline that demonstrates its correctness. If not, explain carefully why it is not possible to simulate **P** and **V**.

(b) Suppose *INC* and *DEC* both have a second argument, *sign*, that is set to the sign bit of the final value of *var*. In particular, if the final value of *var* is negative, *sign* is set to 1; otherwise, *sign* is set to 0. Is it now possible to simulate the **P** and **V** operations on a general semaphore s? If so, give a simulation and a proof outline that demonstrates its correctness. If not, explain carefully why it is still not possible to simulate **P** and **V**.

4.5 If scheduling is strongly fair, the solution to the critical section problem in Figure 4.4 ensures eventual entry; i.e., it is starvation-free. However, if scheduling is weakly fair, a process could wait forever trying to enter its critical section if other processes are always trying to enter.

(a) Assume scheduling is weakly fair and hence that semaphores are so-called weak semaphores. Develop a solution to the critical section problem that ensures eventual entry using weak semaphores and other variables.

(b) Give a proof outline that demonstrates that your solution ensures mutual exclusion and avoids deadlock. Give a careful explanation of how it ensures eventual entry.

4.6   A precedence graph is a directed, acyclic graph. Nodes represent tasks, and arcs indicate the order in which tasks are to be accomplished. In particular, a task can execute as soon as all its predecessors have been completed. Assume that the tasks are processes and that each process has the following outline:

>   *P*:: wait for predecessors, if any
>   body of *P*
>   signal successors, if any

(a) Using semaphores, show how to synchronize five processes whose permissible execution order is specified by the following precedence graph:

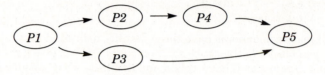

Minimize the number of semaphores that you use, and do not impose constraints not specified in the graph. For example, *P2* and *P3* can execute concurrently after *P1* completes.

(b) Describe how to synchronize processes, given an arbitrary precedence graph. In particular, devise a general method for assigning semaphores to edges or processes and for using them. Do not try to use the absolute minimum number of semaphores since determining that is an NP-hard problem for an arbitrary precedence graph!

4.7   The UNIX kernel provides two primitives similar to the following:

>   **sleep**(*value*): block the executing process on *value*
>   **wakeup**(*value*): awaken all processes blocked on *value*

Assume *value* is an integer between 1 and *n*. Develop an implementation of these primitives. First specify a global invariant, then develop a coarse-grained solution, and finally develop a fine-grained solution that uses semaphores for synchronization.

4.8   Give all possible final values of variable *x* in the following program. Explain how you got your answer.

>   **var** $x := 0$, $s1$: **sem** $:= 1$, $s2$: **sem** $:= 0$
>
>   **co** $\mathbf{P}(s2); \mathbf{P}(s1); x := x * 2; \mathbf{V}(s1)$
>   // $\mathbf{P}(s1); x := x * x; \mathbf{V}(s1)$
>   // $\mathbf{P}(s1); x := x + 3; \mathbf{V}(s2); \mathbf{V}(s1)$
>   **oc**

4.9   (a) Using semaphores for synchronization, give the actions of leaf nodes, interior nodes, and the root node for a combining tree barrier. (See Figures 3.14 and 3.15.) Make sure the barrier can be reused by the same set of processes.

(b) If there are n processes, what is the total execution time for one complete barrier synchronization as a function of n? Assume each semaphore operation takes one time unit. Illustrate your answer by showing the structure of the combining tree and giving the execution time for a few values of n.

4.10　(a) Give complete details for a butterfly barrier for 8 processes. Use semaphores for synchronization, and show the code that each process would execute. The barrier should be reusable.

(b) Repeat (a) for a dissemination barrier for 8 processes.

(c) Compare your answers to (a) and (b). How many variables are required for each kind of barrier. If each semaphore operation takes one unit of time, what is the total time required for barrier synchronization in each algorithm.

(d) Repeat (a), (b), and (c) for a 7-process barrier.

(e) Repeat (a), (b), and (c) for a 12-process barrier.

4.11　Two kinds of processes, A's and B's, enter a room. An A process cannot leave until it meets two B processes, and a B process cannot leave until it meets one A process. A process leaves the room—without meeting any other processes— once it has met the required number of the other kind of process.

(a) Develop a solution to this problem. First specify a global invariant, then develop a coarse-grained solution, and finally develop a fine-grained solution that uses semaphores for synchronization.

(b) Modify your answer to (a) so that the first of the two B processes that meet an A process does not leave the room until after the A process meets a second B process.

4.12　Develop a complete proof outline for the multiple producers and consumers program in Figure 4.12. Prove that, if a producer and a consumer are accessing *buf* at the same time, then they are accessing different slots; i.e., *front ≠ rear*.

4.13　Develop a concurrent implementation of a bounded buffer with multiple producers and multiple consumers. In particular, modify the solution in Figure 4.12 so that deposits can execute concurrently and fetches can execute concurrently. Each deposit must place a message into a different empty slot. Fetches must retrieve messages from different full slots.

4.14　In the producer/consumer problem, let *count* be an integer bounded by 0 and n. Then coarse-grained actions for *deposit* and *fetch* into an n slot buffer are:

$$deposit: \langle \textbf{await } count < n \rightarrow$$
$$buf[rear] := m; rear := rear \textbf{ mod } n + 1; count := count + 1 \rangle$$
$$fetch: \langle \textbf{await } count > 0 \rightarrow$$
$$m := buf[front]; front := front \textbf{ mod } n + 1; count := count - 1 \rangle$$

Implement these **await** statements using semaphores. (Hint: Use a variation of passing the baton.)

4.15   *Atomic Broadcast.* Assume that one producer process and n consumer processes
        share a bounded buffer having b slots. The producer deposits messages in the
        buffer; consumers fetch them. Every message deposited by the producer is to be
        received by all n consumers. Furthermore, each consumer is to receive the
        messages in the order they were deposited. However, different consumers can
        receive messages at different times. For example, one consumer could receive
        up to b more messages than another if the second consumer is slow.

        Develop a solution to this problem. First specify a global invariant, then
        develop a coarse-grained solution, and finally develop a fine-grained solution
        that uses semaphores for synchronization.

4.16   Modify the dining philosophers solution in Figure 4.15 so that every philo-
        sopher first picks up his left fork, then his right. Avoid deadlock by allowing at
        most four philosophers to try to pick up their forks at the same time. Explain
        why this avoids deadlock.

4.17   Solve the dining philosophers problem by focusing on the state of each philo-
        sopher rather than the state of the forks. In particular, let *eating*[1:5] be a
        boolean array; *eating*[i] is true if *Philosopher*[i] is eating, and is false otherwise.

        (a) Specify a global invariant, then develop a coarse-grained solution, and
        finally develop a fine-grained solution that uses semaphores for synchro-
        nization. Your solution should be deadlock-free, but an individual philosopher
        might starve. (Hint: Use the technique of passing the baton.)

        (b) Modify your answer to (a) to avoid starvation. In particular, if a philo-
        sopher wants to eat, eventually he gets to.

4.18   Solve the dining philosophers problem using a centralized coordinator process.
        In particular, when a philosopher wants to eat, he informs the coordinator and
        then waits for permission (i.e., the philosopher waits to be given both forks).

        (a) Specify a global invariant, then develop a coarse-grained solution, and
        finally develop a fine-grained solution that uses semaphores for synchro-
        nization. Your solution should be deadlock-free, but an individual philosopher
        might starve.

        (b) Modify your answer to part (a) to avoid starvation. In particular, if a
        philosopher wants to eat, eventually he gets to.

4.19   In the dining philosophers problem, assume that a philosopher flips a perfect
        coin to determine which fork to pick up first.

        (a) Develop a fully symmetric solution to this problem. In particular, every
        philosopher should execute the same algorithm. Specify a global invariant,
        then develop a coarse-grained solution, and finally develop a fine-grained
        solution. Use busy waiting, semaphores, or both for synchronization. Your
        solution should be deadlock-free, but an individual philosopher might starve
        (with low probability). (Hint: Have a philosopher put his first fork back down
        and flip the coin again if the second fork is unavailable.)

        (b) Extend your answer to (a) to guarantee absence of starvation. Clearly
        explain your solution. (Hint: Use extra variables to preclude one philosopher

from eating again if a neighbor wants to eat.)

4.20 Consider the following writers' preference solution to the readers/writers problem [Courtois et al. 1971]:

> **var** $nr := 0$, $nw := 0$
> **var** $m1$: **sem** := 1, $m2$: **sem** := 1, $m3$: **sem** := 1
> **var** $read$ **sem** := 1, $write$: **sem** := 1

# reader process	# writer process
P($m3$)	**P**($m2$)
P($read$)	$nw := nw + 1$
P($m1$)	**if** $nw = 1 \rightarrow$ **P**($read$)
$nr := nr + 1$	**V**($m2$)
if $nr = 1 \rightarrow$ **P**($write$) **fi**	**P**($write$)
V($m1$)	write the database
V($read$)	**V**($write$)
V($m3$)	**P**($m2$)
read the database	$nw := nw - 1$
P($m1$)	**if** $nw = 0 \rightarrow$ **V**($read$)
$nr := nr - 1$	**V**($m2$)
if $nr = 0 \rightarrow$ **V**($write$) **fi**	
V($m1$)	

The code executed by reader processes is similar to that in Figure 4.18, but the code for writer processes is much more complex.

Explain the role of each semaphore. Develop assertions that indicate what is true at critical points. In particular, show that the solution ensures that writers have exclusive access to the database and a writer excludes readers. Give a convincing argument that the solution does indeed give writers preference over readers.

4.21 (a) Alter the readers/writers solution in Figure 4.21 to give writers preference over readers.

(b) Compare your answer to (a) with the writers preference solution given in the previous exercise. How many semaphore operations are executed by readers and by writers in each solution? In the best case? In the worst case?

4.22 Assume there are n reader processes in the readers/writers problem. Let rw be a semaphore with initial value n. Suppose the reader's protocol is:

> **P**(rw)
> read the database
> **V**(rw)

Develop a protocol for writer processes that ensures the required exclusion, is deadlock-free, and avoids starvation (assuming the **P** operation is strongly fair).

4.23 Modify the readers/writers solution in Figure 4.21 so that the exit protocol in *Writer* awakens all waiting readers, if there are any. (Hint: You will also need to modify the entry protocol in *Reader* processes.)

4.24   Suppose the **P** and **V** operations on semaphores are replaced by the following:

> **PChunk**(*s*, *amt*): ⟨ **await** *s* ≥ *amt* → *s* := *s* − *amt* ⟩
> **VChunk**(*s*, *amt*): ⟨ *s* := *s* + *amt* ⟩

The value of *amt* is a positive integer. These primitives generalize normal **P** and **V** by allowing *amt* to be other than 1.

(a) Use **PChunk** and **VChunk** to construct a simple reader's preference solution to the readers/writers problem. First give a global invariant, then develop a coarse-grained solution, and finally develop a fine-grained solution. (Hint: Use the technique of changing variables.)

(b) Identify other problems that could benefit from the use of these two primitives and explain why. (Hint: Consider other problems in the text and in these exercises.)

(c) Modify the *P* and *V* kernel primitives in Figure 4.23 to implement **PChunk** and **VChunk** instead of **P** and **V**.

4.25   *Cigarette Smokers Problem* [Patil 1971, Parnas 1975]. Suppose there are three smoker processes and one agent process. Each smoker continuously makes a cigarette and smokes it. Making a cigarette requires three ingredients: tobacco, paper, and a match. One smoker process has tobacco, the second paper, and the third matches. Each has an infinite supply of these ingredients. The agent places a random two ingredients on the table. The smoker who has the third ingredient picks up the other two, makes a cigarette, then smokes it. The agent waits for the smoker to finish. The cycle then repeats.

Develop a solution to this problem. First specify a global invariant, then develop a coarse-grained solution, and finally develop a fine-grained solution that uses semaphores.

4.26   Suppose the **P** and **V** operations on semaphores are replaced by the following:

> **PMultiple**(*s1*, ..., *sN*):
>   ⟨ **await** *s1* > 0 **and** ... **and** *sN* > 0 → *s1* := *s1* − 1; ...; *sN* := *sN* − 1 ⟩
> **VMultiple**(*s1*, ..., *sN*): ⟨ *s1* := *s1* + 1; ...; *sN* := *sN* + 1 ⟩

The arguments are one or more semaphores. These primitives generalize normal **P** and **V** by allowing a process to simultaneously do a **P** or **V** operation on multiple semaphores.

(a) Use **PMultiple** and **VMultiple** to construct a simple solution to the cigarette smokers problem.

(b) Identify other problems that could benefit from the use of these two primitives and explain why. (Hint: Consider other problems in the text and in these exercises.)

(c) Does **VMultiple** provide any additional expressive power over a sequence of normal **V** operations? Explain.

(d) Show how to simulate these primitives using the normal semaphore primitives **P** and **V** (and other variables).

(e) Modify the kernel primitives in Figure 4.23 to implement **PMultiple** and **VMultiple** instead of **P** and **V**.

4.27 *The Unisex Bathroom.* Suppose there is one bathroom in your department. It can be used by both men and women, but not at the same time.

(a) Derive a solution to this problem. First specify a global invariant, then develop a coarse-grained solution, and finally develop a fine-grained solution. Allow any number of men or women to be in the bathroom at the same time. Your solution should ensure the required exclusion and avoid deadlock, but it need not be fair.

(b) Modify your answer to (a) so that at most four people are in the bathroom at the same time.

(c) Modify your answer to (a) to ensure fairness. You might want to solve the problem differently. (Hint: Use the technique of passing the baton.)

4.28 *Search/Insert/Delete.* Three kinds of processes share access to a singly-linked list: searchers, inserters, and deleters. Searchers merely examine the list; hence they can execute concurrently with each other. Inserters add new items to the end of the list; insertions must be mutually exclusive to preclude two inserters from inserting new items at about the same time. However, one insert can proceed in parallel with any number of searches. Finally, deleters remove items from anywhere in the list. At most one deleter process can access the list at a time, and deletion must also be mutually exclusive with searches and insertions.

(a) This problem is an example of selective mutual exclusion. Derive a solution using semaphores that is similar in style to the readers/writers solution in Figures 4.16 and 4.17. First specify the synchronization property as a global invariant, then develop a coarse-grained solution, and finally develop a fine-grained solution.

(b) This is also an example of a general condition synchronization problem. Derive a solution that is similar in style to the readers/writers solution in Figures 4.19 to 4.21. First specify the synchronization property as a global invariant. Use three counters: *ns*, the number of active searchers; *ni*, the number of active inserters; and *nd*, the number of active deleters. Then develop a coarse-grained solution. Finally, develop a fine-grained solution using the technique of passing the baton.

4.29 Consider the following memory allocation problem. Suppose there are two operations: *request(amount* : **int**) and *release(amount* : **int**). When a process calls *request*, it delays until at least *amount* free pages of memory are available, then takes *amount* pages. A process returns *amount* pages to the free pool by calling *release*. (Pages may be released in different quantities than they are acquired.)

(a) Develop implementations of *request* and *release* that use the shortest-job-next (SJN) allocation policy. In particular, smaller requests take precedence over larger ones. First specify a global invariant, then develop a coarse-grained solution, and finally develop a fine-grained solution that uses semaphores.

(a) Develop implementations of *request* and *release* that use a first-come, first-served (FCFS) allocation policy. This means that a pending request might have to delay, even if there is enough memory available. First specify a global invariant, then develop a coarse-grained solution, and finally develop a fine-grained solution that uses semaphores.

4.30 Suppose *n* processes *P*[1:*n*] share three printers. Before using a printer, *P*[*i*] calls *request*(*printer*). This operation returns the identity of a free printer. After using that printer, *P*[*i*] returns it by calling *release*(*printer*).

(a) Develop implementations of *request* and *release*. First specify a global invariant, then develop a coarse-grained solution, and finally develop a fine-grained solution that uses semaphores for synchronization.

(b) Assume each process has a priority stored in global array *priority*[1:*n*]. Modify *request* and *release* so that a printer is allocated to the highest priority waiting process. You may assume that each process has a unique priority.

4.31 *The Dining Savages.* A tribe of savages eats communal dinners from a large pot that can hold M servings of stewed missionary. When a savage wants to eat, he helps himself from the pot, unless it is empty. If the pot is empty, the savage wakes up the cook and then waits until the cook has refilled the pot. The behavior of the savages and cook is specified by the following processes:

> *Savage*[1:*n*]:: **do** true → get serving from pot; eat **od**
>
> *Cook*:: **do** true → sleep; put M servings in pot **od**

Develop code for the actions of the savages and cook. Use semaphores for synchronization. Your solution should avoid deadlock and awaken the cook only when the pot is empty.

4.32 *The Roller Coaster Problem* [Herman 1989]. Suppose there are *n* passenger processes and one car process. The passengers repeatedly wait to take rides in the car, which can hold C passengers, C < *n*. However, the car can go around the tracks only when it is full.

(a) Develop code for the actions of the passenger and car processes. First specify a global invariant, then develop a coarse-grained solution, and finally develop a fine-grained solution using semaphores.

(b) Generalize your answer to (a) to employ *m* car processes, *m* > 1. Since there is only one track, cars cannot pass each other; i.e., they must finish going around the track in the order in which they started. Again, a car can go around the tracks only when it is full.

4.33 An eventcount is used to record the number of times an event has occurred. It is represented by an integer initialized to zero and is manipulated by the following primitives:

> **advance**(*ec*): ⟨ *ec* := *ec* + 1 ⟩
> **read**(*ec*): ⟨ **return**(*ec*) ⟩
> **wait**(*ec*, *value*): ⟨ **await** *ec* ≥ *value* ⟩

A sequencer dispenses unique values. It is also represented by an integer initialized to zero and is manipulated by the following atomic function:

$$\textbf{ticket}(seq): \langle\, temp := seq;\ seq := seq + 1;\ \textbf{return}(temp)\,\rangle$$

The **ticket** primitive is identical to the Fetch-and-Add instruction with an increment of 1. A sequencer is often used in the second argument to the **wait** primitive.

(a) Using eventcounts, develop a solution to the single producer, single consumer problem (see Figure 4.11). Assume the communication buffer contains n slots.

(b) Using eventcounts and sequencers, extend your answer to (a) to permit multiple producers and multiple consumers (see Figure 4.12).

(c) Using eventcounts and sequencers, develop a simulation of the **P** and **V** operations on a general semaphore.

(d) Using eventcounts and sequencers, develop a simulation of the **PMultiple** primitive defined in exercise 4.26. First show how to handle two arguments, then show how to generalize your answer to handle any number of arguments.

(e) Add the eventcount and sequencer primitives to the kernel in Figure 4.23. Define any additional data structures that you need.

4.34 Modify the kernel primitives and data structures in Figure 4.23 to implement binary rather than general semaphores. (Recall that the **V** operation on a binary semaphore blocks the executing process if the semaphore's value is 1.)

4.35 (a) Extend the single-processor kernel in Figure 4.23 to a kernel for a shared-memory multiprocessor. See Figure 3.30 for ideas.

(b) In a multiprocessor kernel, critical data structures need to be accessed with mutual exclusion. Explain why locks in such a kernel should be implemented using busy waiting rather than semaphores.

4.36 Suppose input and output on a terminal are supported by two procedures:

> *get*(**var** *ch* : **char**)
> *put*(*ch* : **char**)

An application process calls *get* to receive the next input character; it calls *put* to send a character to the display.

Assume both input and output are buffered; i.e., up to n input characters can be stored waiting to be retrieved by *get*, and up to n output characters can be stored waiting to be printed.

(a) Develop implementations of *get* and *put*, assuming that they are procedures that execute outside of the kernel. These procedures should use semaphores for synchronization. Define any additional processes you need, and show the actions the kernel should take when an input or output interrupt occurs. Use *startread* to initiate reading from the keyboard, and use *startwrite* to initiate writing to the display.

(b) Develop implementations of *get* and *put*, assuming that they are kernel primitives. Again, specify the actions the kernel should take when an input or output interrupt occurs, use *startread* to initiate reading from the keyboard, and use *startwrite* to initiate writing to the display.

(c) Analyze and compare the efficiency of your answers to (a) and (b). Consider factors such as the number of statements that get executed in each case, the number of context switches, and the time the kernel is locked.

(d) Extend your answer to (a) to support echoing of input characters. In particular, each character that is input from the keyboard should automatically be written to the display.

(e) Extend your answer to (c) to support echoing of input characters.

4.37 Suppose input and output on a terminal are supported by two procedures:

$$getline(\textbf{var } str : \textbf{string}(MAXLINE); \textbf{var } count : \textbf{int})$$
$$putline(str : \textbf{string}(MAXLINE))$$

An application process calls *getline* to receive the next line of input; it calls *putline* to send a line to the display. A call of *getline* returns when there is another line of input. Result argument *str* is set to the contents of the line, and *count* is set to its actual length. A line contains at most MAXLINE characters; it is terminated by a newline character, which is not part of the line itself.

Assume both input and output are buffered; i.e., up to n input lines can be stored waiting to be retrieved by *getline*, and up to n output lines can be stored waiting to be printed. Also assume that input lines are echoed to the display; i.e., each complete input line is also sent to the display. Finally, assume that input lines are "cooked"; i.e., backspace and line-kill characters are processed by *getline* and do not get returned to the application process.

(a) Develop implementations of *getline* and *putline*, assuming that they are procedures that execute outside of the kernel. These procedures should use semaphores for synchronization. Define any additional processes you need, and show the actions the kernel should take when an input or output interrupt occurs. Use *startread* to initiate reading from the keyboard, and use *startwrite* to initiate writing to the display.

(b) Develop implementations of *getline* and *putline*, assuming that they are kernel primitives. Again, specify the actions the kernel should take when an input or output interrupt occurs, use *startread* to initiate reading from the keyboard, and use *startwrite* to initiate writing to the display.

4.38 Some machines provide instructions that implement the **P** and **V** operations on semaphores. These instructions manipulate the value of the semaphore, then trap into the kernel if a process needs to be blocked or awakened. Design implementations for these machine instructions, and give the kernel code for the associated interrupt handlers. (Hint: Let the value of the semaphore become negative; if a semaphore is negative, its absolute value indicates the number of blocked processes.)

## CHAPTER 5

Conditional Critical Regions

Semaphores are a fundamental synchronization mechanism. As shown in the previous chapter, they can be used systematically to solve any synchronization problem. However, solving a mutual exclusion problem requires finding the right change of variable to use. Also, solving a condition synchronization problem requires using several semaphores and additional variables in a relatively complex protocol.

A worse difficulty with semaphores is that the low-level nature of **P** and **V** makes it quite easy to err when using them. The programmer must be careful not to omit a **P** or **V** accidentally, not to execute one too many **P** or **V** operations, to employ the wrong semaphore, or to fail to protect all critical sections.

A final problem with semaphores is that one programs both mutual exclusion and condition synchronization using the same pair of primitives. This makes it difficult to identify the purpose of a given **P** or **V** without looking at other operations on the same semaphore. Since mutual exclusion and condition synchronization are distinct concepts, they should ideally be programmed in different ways.

Conditional critical regions (CCRs) overcome these difficulties by providing a structured notation for specifying synchronization. With CCRs, shared variables that need to be accessed with mutual exclusion are declared together in resources. Variables in a resource are accessed only in **region** statements that name the resource. Mutual exclusion is provided by guaranteeing that execution of **region** statements that name the same resource is not interleaved. Condition synchronization is provided by boolean conditions in **region** statements.

With CCRs, mutual exclusion is implicit, and condition synchronization is programmed explicitly. This makes CCRs generally easier to use than semaphores. It also leads to a simpler proof system. However, **region** statements are more expensive to implement than semaphore operations. This is because delay conditions in **region** statements have to be re-evaluated either every time a shared variable changes or every time a kernel needs to decide if some blocked process can now execute.

Because CCRs are relatively inefficient, they have not been as widely used as other mechanisms. Still, they are worth studying for several reasons:

- CCRs are the historical "stepping stone" from semaphores to monitors, the topic of Chapter 6;

- they illustrate how the use of structured synchronization statements can eliminate interference; and

- they introduced the use of boolean synchronization conditions, which have subsequently been employed in many language notations, as we shall see in later chapters.

The remainder of this chapter defines the syntax and semantics of CCRs and gives several examples illustrating their use. The examples illustrate the expressive power of CCRs relative to semaphores. The last section describes how to implement CCRs and points out their inefficiency relative to semaphores.

5.1 Notation and Semantics

The programming notation for conditional critical regions imposes compiler-enforceable restrictions on the use of shared variables. These restrictions make programs more structured and lead to a simpler proof system in which interference is automatically precluded.

The CCRs notation employs two mechanisms: **resource** declarations and **region** statements. A **resource** is a named collection of shared variables to which mutually exclusive access is required. The form of a **resource** declaration is:

> **resource** r (variable declarations)

Identifier r is the name of the resource; the name can be either a simple or subscripted identifier. The components of r are one or more variable declarations. These are declared like record fields (see Section 1.1), with the **var** keyword being omitted.

Every shared variable in a program must belong to a resource. The variables in a resource may be accessed *only* within **region** statements that name the resource. A **region** statement has the form

region r **when** $B \rightarrow S$ **end**

where r is the resource name, B is a boolean guard, and S is a statement list. Both B and S can reference the variables in r as well as variables local to the executing process. The **when** phrase is optional; it may be omitted if B is not needed.

Execution of a **region** statement delays the executing process until B is true; then S is executed. Execution of **region** statements that name the same resource is mutually exclusive; in particular, B is guaranteed to be true when execution of S begins. Thus, a **region** statement is very similar to an **await** statement. The differences are that a **region** statement explicitly names the collection of shared variables that it will access and the delay condition can only depend on these variables. As we will see, this makes the semantics of CCRs simpler than the semantics of programs that use **await** statements; it also makes **region** statements simpler to implement than arbitrary **await** statements.

Two **region** statements may be nested as long as they name different resources. When executing the nested **region** statement, a process has exclusive access to the variables in both resources. Also, a process retains exclusive access to the outer resource even if the process is delayed waiting to execute the nested **region** statement. Thus, deadlock could occur if two processes nest **region** statements in a different order.

A compiler for a language containing CCRs can check that all shared variables are within resources and that they are accessed only within **region** statements. Thus a compiler can ensure that shared variables are accessed with mutual exclusion. By contrast, such compile-time checks cannot be made for arbitrary programs that employ semaphores.

Examples

Before defining the formal semantics of CCRs, we give two basic examples to illustrate how they are used and interpreted. The first example shows how to simulate semaphores using CCRs. In Section 5.6 we will show how to simulate CCRs using semaphores. Thus, semaphores and **region** statements are equally powerful in terms of the problems they can be used to solve.

Let s be a (general) semaphore with initial value $n \geq 0$. Using CCRs, a semaphore with initial value n is represented by a resource:

resource *sem*(s : **int** := n)

The **P** and **V** operations on s are then simulated by:

> $P(s)$: **region** *sem* **when** $s > 0 \to s := s - 1$ **end**
>
> $V(s)$: **region** *sem* $\to s := s + 1$ **end**

Note the similarity between this implementation and the earlier implementation in terms of **await** statements (Section 4.1).

As a second example—which better illustrates how semaphores and CCRs differ—consider how to implement a single-slot buffer. Recall that such a buffer has one slot that can contain a message and that the slot is accessed by two operations: *deposit* and *fetch*. As before, execution of *deposit* and *fetch* must alternate. To represent the buffer, two variables are needed: one for the buffer itself and one to synchronize execution of *deposit* and *fetch*. For synchronization, it suffices to use a boolean variable that indicates whether the buffer is full or empty. The buffer is thus represented by the resource

> **resource** *buffer*(b : T; *full* : **bool** := false)

where T is some data type. Given this representation, *deposit* and *fetch* are programmed as:

> *deposit*: **region** *buffer* **when not** *full* $\to b$:= data; *full* := true **end**
>
> *fetch*: **region** *buffer* **when** *full* $\to$ result := b; *full* := false **end**

Here both synchronization and access to the buffer are combined into a single **region** statement. Note how this implementation differs from that in Figure 4.8, in which **await** statements were used to implement synchronization only. The approach taken in Figure 4.8 was necessary in order to use semaphores to implement the **await** statements, as shown in Figure 4.9. In general, CCRs lead to more compact solutions to synchronization problems because fewer statements are required. Also, **region** statements allow synchronization conditions to be express directly as boolean expressions; with semaphores, synchronization conditions are implicit.

Inference Rules

The structure provided by CCRs—specifically that all shared variables must belong to resources and that resource variables are accessible only within **region** statements—leads to a proof system that is simpler than the one introduced in Section 2.3. The main simplification is that interference is automatically precluded, and hence it is not necessary to prove noninterference.

The order in which processes execute **region** statements that name the same resource is non-deterministic if the guards in both statements are true. Either could be executed before the other. Thus, to specify the acceptable states of the resource variables, it is necessary to use a predicate that is a global invariant: it must be true initially and must be true before and after each **region** statement. With CCRs, the predicate associated with a resource is called a *resource invariant*. There is one such invariant for each resource.

To preclude interference, all variables referenced in a resource invariant must belong to the associated resource. To relate the states of different processes to each other, it is usually necessary to use auxiliary variables. These may be added to resources and included in resource invariants. Like program variables, such variables must then be referenced and altered only within **region** statements. An auxiliary variable may also appear in assertions in the proof of a process, as long as the variable is not changed by any other process. This permits process states to be related without introducing potential interference.

Let r be a resource, and let RI be the associated resource invariant. Assume RI is initially true. Then, any **region** statement

> **region** r **when** $B \rightarrow S$ **end**

can assume that both RI and B are true when execution of S begins as long as execution of every such S reestablishes RI. The leads to the following inference rule for **region** statements:

(5.1) **Region Rule:**
$$\frac{\{\,P \wedge RI \wedge B\,\}\ S\ \{\,Q \wedge RI\,\} \quad \text{no variable free in } P \text{ or } Q \text{ is changed in another process}}{\{\,P\,\}\ \textbf{region}\ r\ \textbf{when}\ B \rightarrow S\ \textbf{end}\ \{\,Q\,\}}$$

As usual, P and Q are assertions local to the process executing a **region** statement. These assertions can reference shared variables that are not changed by other processes, but only RI can reference shared variables that might be changed by other processes.

The Region Rule is similar to Synchronization Rule (2.7). The difference is that resource invariant RI explicitly appears in the hypothesis but does not appear in the conclusion. Thus, resource invariants do *not* appear in proofs of individual processes. (If they could appear in proofs, we would have to prove non-interference. This is because a resource invariant is not necessarily true while a process is executing a **region** statement.) Instead, resource invariants are introduced in the proof of a program by employing a different inference rule for the **co** statement.

Suppose a concurrent program contains m resources, with associated invariants RI_1, ..., RI_m. Assume processes synchronize only by means of **region** statements. Also assume that all shared variables belong to resources and are accessed only within **region** statements. Then when using CCRs, Concurrency Rule (2.11) is replaced by:

(5.2)   **CCRs Rule:** $\{P_i\}\ S_i\ \{Q_i\}, 1 \le i \le n$
                                      no variable free in P_i or Q_i is changed in $S_j, i \ne j$
                                      all variables in RI_k are local to resource $r_k, 1 \le k \le m$

$$\{RI_1 \wedge ... \wedge RI_m \wedge P_1 \wedge ... \wedge P_n\}$$
$$\textbf{co } S_1\ //\ ...\ //\ S_n\ \textbf{oc}$$
$$\{RI_1 \wedge ... \wedge RI_m \wedge Q_1 \wedge ... \wedge Q_n\}$$

This inference rule requires that the resource invariants are initially true. Then—as a result of Region Rule (5.1)—the resource invariants will always be true, except perhaps when a **region** statement is being executed. Since **region** statements are mutually exclusive by definition, resource invariants cannot be interfered with. Moreover, assertions in processes cannot reference variables changed by other processes. For these reasons, processes cannot interfere.

This absence of the need to prove non-interference is the important difference between CCRs Rule (5.2) and Concurrency Rule (2.11). It results from the compiler-enforceable requirement that shared variables all belong to resources that are accessed only by mutually exclusive **region** statements. Subsequent sections give examples of the use of (5.1) and (5.2).

Safety and Liveness Properties

Even though **region** statements can be used to ensure mutually exclusive access to a resource, there are situations in which mutual exclusion is required but cannot be programmed directly using **region** statements. For example, it is sometimes necessary that statements not inside a **region** statement execute as a critical section; the readers/writers problem is an example. In such a program, it might be necessary to prove mutual exclusion. Similarly, it is often necessary to prove that a program is deadlock-free.

Safety properties such as mutual exclusion and absence of deadlock can be proved using a variation on the method of Exclusion of Configurations (2.25). The variation results from the fact that resource invariants are not included directly in proofs of individual processes. However, resource invariants are true whenever no process is in the midst of executing a **region** statement. Moreover, if a process is in the middle of executing a **region** statement, there was a possible program state in which the process had not yet begun executing the **region** statement; in that state, the associated resource invariant was true. This observation yields a sufficient condition for mutual exclusion.

(5.3)   **Mutual Exclusion for Conditional Critical Regions.** Let S_1 and S_2 be statements in different processes in a concurrent program, and assume neither S_1 nor S_2 is within a **region** statement. Let $pre(S_1)$ and $pre(S_2)$ be the corresponding preconditions in a proof of the program. Let RI_1, ..., RI_m be the the resource invariants in the proof, and assume the initial state $P_1 \wedge ... \wedge P_n$ is true when execution of the program begins. Then S_1 and S_2 are mutually exclusive if:

$$pre(S_1) \wedge pre(S_2) \wedge RI_1 \wedge ... \wedge RI_m = \text{false}$$

In short, if the conjunction of all the predicates is false, then the program cannot be in a state in which S_1 and S_2 are both eligible for execution.

We can prove absence of deadlock in a similar way. However, deadlock is a *global* safety property in the sense that a program is deadlocked only if *no* process can proceed. Hence, we have to consider the states of all processes.

A program employing CCRs is deadlocked if every process has terminated or is blocked and at least one process is blocked. If a process i has terminated, its postcondition Q_i is true. If a process is blocked, it is trying to execute **region** r **when** $B \to S$ **end** and either B is false or another process is using resource r. Finally, if all processes are blocked or terminated, no **region** statement is being executed; hence, all resource invariants are true. This yields the following sufficient condition for absence of deadlock.

(5.4)   **Absence of Deadlock for Conditional Critical Regions.** Assume that a concurrent program contains one **co** statement and that **region** statements in the program are not nested. Let RI_1, ..., RI_m be the resource invariants in a proof of the program, and assume that the initial state $P_1 \wedge ... \wedge P_n$ of the program is true when execution begins. Let D_1 be a predicate that characterizes the state in which every process has terminated or is blocked. Let D_2 be a predicate that characterizes the state in which at least one process is blocked. Then the program is deadlock-free if:

$$D_1 \wedge D_2 \wedge RI_1 \wedge ... \wedge RI_m = \text{false}$$

The above definition assumes that **region** statements are not nested. If they are nested in a program, then a process could also be blocked trying to execute a **region** statement that is locked by another process that is blocked trying to execute a nested **region** statement. The conditions in (5.4) can be generalized to handle this situation. Definition (5.4) also assumes there is only one **co** statement. Again, the conditions can be generalized to handle programs with multiple **co** statements.

A concurrent program with CCRs will terminate as long as each process terminates. This will be the case if the program is deadlock-free and if the sequential statements—particularly loops—in each process terminate.

Many concurrent programs contain perpetual loops and hence do not terminate. Liveness properties for such programs—such as eventual entry into a critical section or eventual acquisition of a shared resource—depend on how **region** statements are scheduled. As discussed in Section 2.6, scheduling policies can be unconditionally fair, weakly fair, or strongly fair. These policies have the same definitions for **region** statements as they do for **await** statements. For example, an eligible **region** statement will eventually be executed with a weakly fair scheduling policy if the boolean guard B becomes true and remains true.

5.2 Dining Philosophers Revisited

With CCRS, solutions to synchronization problems are derived in much the same way as before. The first three steps are identical: specify a global invariant, outline a solution, then guard assignments to shared variables to ensure the invariant is true. Again, we will program coarse-grained solutions using **await** statements.

The last derivation step is implementing the **await** statements. With CCRs, this is straightforward since **region** statements are very similar to **await** statements. Shared variables that are used together are placed in the same resource, and **await** statements are replaced by **region** statements. That's all there is to it! Because **region** statements directly provide mutual exclusion and condition synchronization, no intricate steps using fine-grained synchronization or semaphores are required.

This approach can always be used. The only complication is that variables in the same resource are always accessed with mutual exclusion, and this may overly constrain possible concurrency. To achieve maximal concurrency requires using more resources or removing some shared variables from resources. Doing this, however, may make it harder to ensure required synchronization properties.

This section derives a new solution to the dining philosophers problem. The solution also illustrates various aspects of the formal semantics of CCRs. Section 5.4 examines a problem—a bounded buffer with concurrent access—that requires splitting a resource.

Recall that, in the dining philosophers problem (4.4), five philosophers compete for the use of five forks, which are set on the table between each pair of philosophers. In order to eat, a philosopher needs to acquire two forks, one on each side. In Section 4.3, the synchronization requirement was specified

```
var eating[1:5] : bool := ([5] false)
EAT:  ( ∀ i:  1 ≤ i ≤ 5:  eating[i] ⇒ ¬(eating[i ⊖ 1] ∨ eating[i ⊕ 1]) )

Philosopher[i: 1..5]::
    do true →    { ¬eating[i] }
        think
        〈 await not (eating[i ⊖ 1] or eating[i ⊕ 1]) → eating[i] := true 〉
        { eating[i] }
        eat
        〈 eating[i] := false 〉
    od
```

Figure 5.1. Coarse-grained dining philosophers solution.

---

in terms of the states of the forks: Each fork could be picked up at most one more time than it had been put down. This specification led to the semaphore-based solution in Figure 4.15. Here, we will express the synchronization requirement in terms of the state of the philosophers. Either specification is perfectly acceptable, but different solutions result.

As before, we simulate the actions of the philosophers as follows:

```
Philosopher[i: 1..5]::  do true → think
                            acquire forks
                            eat
                            release forks
                        od
```

A bad state for this program is one in which neighboring philosophers are eating at the same time. Let $eating[i]$ be true if *Philosopher*[i] is eating, and false otherwise. Then the good states of the program are characterized by:

$$EAT: (\forall i: 1 \le i \le 5: eating[i] \Rightarrow \neg(eating[i \ominus 1] \vee eating[i \oplus 1]))$$

In *EAT*, ⊖ denotes the left neighbor, and ⊕ denotes the right neighbor. (The value of $i \ominus 1$ is actually $((i + 3) \bmod 5) + 1$ and the value of $i \oplus 1$ is actually $(i \bmod 5) + 1$.)

Acquiring forks involves setting $eating[i]$ to true; releasing forks involves setting $eating[i]$ to false. To ensure that *EAT* is an invariant, we need to guard setting $eating[i]$ to true; the appropriate guard is the consequent of the implication in *EAT*. However, we do not need to guard setting $eating[i]$ to false since that action makes the antecedent of an implication false.

Figure 5.1 contains the coarse-grained solution resulting from this specification. Assertions about the value of *eating* for each philosopher are

resource *table*(*eating*[1:5] : **bool** := ([5] false))

EAT: (∀ *i*: 1 ≤ *i* ≤ 5: *eating*[*i*] ⇒ ¬(*eating*[*i* ⊖ 1] ∨ *eating*[*i* ⊕ 1]))

Philosopher[*i*: 1..5]::
    do true →   { ¬*eating*[*i*] }
        think
        region *table* **when not** (*eating*[*i* ⊖ 1] **or** *eating*[*i* ⊕ 1]) →
            eating[*i*] := true **end**
        { *eating*[*i*] }
        eat
        region *table* → *eating*[*i*] := false **end**
    od

Figure 5.2. Dining philosophers solution using CCRs.

---

included at appropriate points. Recall that this is permissible since *eating*[*i*] is only changed by *Philosopher*[*i*].

The program for each philosopher is now in a form that can be converted directly into one that uses CCRs. Array *eating* becomes a resource, and the statements that reference the values in *eating* become **region** statements. Making these changes, we get the final solution shown in Figure 5.2.

In Figure 5.2, all shared variables are in the one resource *table*, and the resource invariant references only these variables. The assertions follow from the initialization of *eating* and from applications of Region Rule (5.1). Moreover, as noted, the assertions in each process satisfy the requirement that they not reference variables changed by another process. Thus, the proof outline in Figure 5.2 satisfies the hypotheses of the CCRs Rule (5.2).

Since we constructed the solution to ensure the invariance of *EAT*, it has the required exclusion property that neighboring philosophers cannot eat at the same time. We can also prove this formally by applying the conditions for mutual exclusion given in (5.3). Assume two neighboring philosophers *i* and *i* ⊕ 1 are both trying to eat; i.e, they are both at the section of code labeled "eat." Then the preconditions of these two statements are true. This together with the invariance of *EAT* yields a contradiction:

$$(eating[i] \wedge eating[i \oplus 1] \wedge EAT) = false$$

Hence, the philosophers cannot be eating at the same time.

The solution is also deadlock-free. Informally, this is because if all processes are delayed at their first **region** statements, then all values of *eating* are false; hence at least one philosopher can proceed. Formally, this follows by applying the conditions for Absence of Deadlock for Conditional Critical Regions. Following (5.4), predicate D_1 asserts that every process has terminated or is blocked, and predicate D_2 asserts that at least one process is blocked. Since the processes in Figure 5.2 do not terminate, these conditions simplify to asserting that every process is blocked:

$$(\forall\, i\colon\ 1 \leq i \leq 5\colon\ \neg eating[i] \wedge (eating[i \ominus 1] \vee eating[i \oplus 1]))$$

The first conjunct specifies that philosopher i is at its first **region** statement; the second specifies that the guard on that statement is false. Even without *EAT*, this simplifies to *false*. Hence the solution is deadlock-free.

The solution in Figure 5.2 is not fair, however, even with a strongly fair scheduling policy. This is because one philosopher could be blocked and its neighbors could "conspire" so that one or the other is always eating. Even though each neighbor would periodically not be eating, the state in which neither is eating might never occur. This is highly unlikely—assuming the philosophers are in fact "thinkers"—but it is theoretically possible.

5.3 Readers/Writers Revisited

In Chapter 4, we introduced the readers/writers problem and developed two solutions using semaphores for synchronization. Those solutions could instead employ CCRs by simulating the semaphore operations as shown in Section 5.1. However, we can use CCRs to achieve much more succinct solutions. This section develops two such solutions. The first gives readers preference. The second gives writers preference and illustrates the use of two **region** statements in the entry protocol.

Readers' Preference Solution

Recall the definition of the readers/writers problem given in (4.5): Reader processes examine a shared database, and writers both examine and alter it. Readers may access the database concurrently, but writers require exclusive access. Following the specification given in Section 4.4, let *nr* be the number of readers accessing the database, and let *nw* be the number of writers. Then the required synchronization is specified by:

$$RW\colon\ (nr = 0 \vee nw = 0) \wedge nw \leq 1$$

Modeling the actions of the processes by perpetual loops as before, this specification resulted in the coarse-grained solution shown earlier in Figure 4.19. For example, before accessing the database, a reader process executes:

$$\langle\ \textbf{await}\ nw = 0 \rightarrow nr := nr + 1\ \rangle$$

resource $rw(nr := 0; nw := 0)$
$\{ RW: (nr = 0 \lor nw = 0) \land nw \leq 1 \}$
Reader$[i: 1..m]$:: **do** true $\rightarrow$ **region** rw **when** $nw = 0 \rightarrow nr := nr + 1$ **end**
                                      read the database
                                      region $rw \rightarrow nr := nr - 1$ **end**
          od
Writer$[j: 1..n]$:: **do** true $\rightarrow$ **region** rw **when** $nr = 0$ **and** $nw = 0 \rightarrow$
                              $nw := nw + 1$ **end**
                          write the database
                          region $rw \rightarrow nw := nw - 1$ **end**
      od

Figure 5.3. Readers and writers using CCRs.

We can directly convert the solution in Figure 4.19 into a program that uses CCRs. Again we place the shared variables in a resource and replace each **await** statement by a **region** statement. Making these substitutions yields the program shown in Figure 5.3. The solution is much more compact than any of the semaphore-based solutions. This results from the implicit exclusion of **region** statements and the use of boolean guards to specify synchronization conditions.

Because the solution in Figure 5.3 is merely a recoding of an already correct solution, it is correct. However, the program does not contain enough information to prove formally that the solution has the required exclusion and is deadlock-free. For example, to prove that two writers cannot simultaneously access the database, it is necessary to know that both are trying to, and then to use (5.3) to establish a contradiction. Formally proving mutual exclusion and absence of deadlock requires adding auxiliary variables and relating their values to the values of nr and nw.

Writers' Preference Solution

The solution in Figure 5.3 gives preference to readers: If some reader is in his critical section, another reader can enter his critical section, but a writer is delayed. Essentially this is because the entry condition for writers is stronger than that for readers: A writer has to wait until there are no readers or writers, whereas a reader only has to wait for no writers. To give writers preference, we could use CCRs to simulate the semaphore method of passing the baton, as shown in Section 4.4. However, we can use CCRs directly to implement a writers' preference solution. The basic idea is to strengthen the entry condition for readers.

resource $rw(nr := 0; nw := 0; ww := 0)$
$\{\, RW\!: (nr = 0 \lor nw = 0) \land nw \leq 1\,\}$
$Reader[i\!: 1..m]$:: **do** true $\rightarrow$ **region** rw **when** $nw = 0$ **and** $ww = 0 \rightarrow$
                        $nr := nr + 1$ **end**
                    read the database
                    region $rw \rightarrow nr := nr - 1$ **end**
        od
$Writer[j\!: 1..n]$:: **do** true $\rightarrow$ **region** $rw \rightarrow ww := ww + 1$ **end**
                    region rw **when** $nr = 0$ **and** $nw = 0 \rightarrow$
                        $nw := nw + 1; ww := ww - 1$ **end**
                    write the database
                    region $rw \rightarrow nw := nw - 1$ **end**
        od

Figure 5.4. Writers' preference solution using CCRs.

Recall that a writers' preference solution is one that ensures that writers get to access the database as soon as possible. In particular, a reader who wants to access the database is delayed if a writer is already accessing the database *or* if any writer is delayed. To express the preference property, let ww indicate the number of waiting writers. Then if ww is positive, no new reader can start reading the database, which is to say that nr cannot be incremented. This is specified by:

$$ww \geq 0 \land (ww > 0 \Rightarrow nr \text{ does not increase})$$

Unfortunately, the second conjunct cannot be expressed easily in predicate logic. This is because it expresses a relation between pairs of states rather than a property that is true of a single state. However it can still be used as an informal specification since it specifies a safety property, the bad thing being a state transition in which ww is positive but nr is increased.

To get a writers' preference solution, we need to modify the readers' preference solution in Figure 5.3 to include the additional requirement specified above. In particular, we add ww to resource rw. Writers increment ww to indicate that they wish to access the database; a writer decrements ww once he has acquired access. Finally, the guard in the reader's entry protocol is strengthened to include the conjunct $ww = 0$; this ensures that nr is not increased if $ww > 0$.

Figure 5.4 contains a solution incorporating these changes. The solution uses two **region** statements, one after the other, in the entry protocol for writers. The first records that a writer has arrived. The second is used to delay until it is safe to access the database. We will employ this technique again in Section 5.5; it is often used to solve scheduling problems using CCRs.

5.4 Interprocess Communication

Recall that a bounded buffer is a multislot buffer used for communication between producer and consumer processes. In particular, a bounded buffer is a FIFO queue accessed by *deposit* and *fetch* operations. Producers place messages in the buffer by executing *deposit*, delaying if necessary until there is a free buffer slot. Consumers retrieve messages by executing *fetch*, delaying if necessary until there is a full buffer slot.

Section 4.2 showed how to implement a bounded buffer using semaphores for synchronization. Here, we use conditional critical regions to implement two solutions. In the first, *deposit* and *fetch* have exclusive access to the buffer. In the second, *deposit* and *fetch* may execute concurrently. In both solutions, we use CCRs directly to achieve the required synchronization.

Bounded Buffer with Exclusive Access

As in Section 4.2, we will represent the buffer by an array *buf*[1:*n*] and two index variables, *front* and *rear*. Messages that have been deposited but not yet fetched are stored in the circular queue beginning at *buf*[*front*]. Unless the buffer is full, *buf*[*rear*] is the first empty slot past the deposited messages. Earlier, we synchronized access to the buffer by using counters that recorded the number of times *deposit* and *fetch* had been executed. That approach is appropriate when semaphores are used to implement synchronization. However, it is simpler to specify the required synchronization by using a single variable, *count*, that records the number of full buffer slots. The values of all these variables are related by the predicate:

$BUFFER$: $1 \le front \le n \wedge 1 \le rear \le n \wedge 0 \le count \le n \wedge$
$rear = (front + count - 1) \bmod n + 1 \wedge$
count slots in the circular queue beginning at *buf*[*front*] contain the most recently deposited items in the order in which they were deposited

This predicate is to be invariant. The ordering relationship in *BUFFER* could be specified formally by introducing something like timestamps to record when each item was deposited. However, the informal specification is easier to understand.

Initially *count* is zero. It is incremented in *deposit* and decremented in *fetch*. Given the bounds on *count* specified in *BUFFER*, *deposit* must delay until *count* is less than *n*, so the actions of *deposit* are:

resource *buffer*(*buf*[1:*n*] : T; *front* := 1; *rear* := 1; *count* := 0)
{ *BUFFER* }

deposit: **region** *buffer* **when** *count* < *n* →
$\qquad$ *buf*[*rear*] := data; *rear* := *rear* **mod** *n* + 1; *count* := *count* + 1
$\quad$ **end**

fetch: **region** *buffer* **when** *count* > 0 →
$\qquad$ result := *buf*[*front*]; *front* := *front* **mod** *n* + 1; *count* := *count* − 1
$\quad$ **end**

Figure 5.5. Bounded buffer with exclusive access.

$\langle$ **await** *count* < *n* → *buf*[*rear*] := data
$\qquad\qquad$ *rear* := *rear* **mod** *n* + 1; *count* := *count* + 1 $\rangle$

Similarly, *fetch* must delay until *count* is positive, so its actions are:

$\langle$ **await** *count* > 0 → result := *buf*[*front*]
$\qquad\qquad$ *front* := *front* **mod** *n* + 1; *count* := *count* − 1 $\rangle$

Once again, it is straightforward to implement these code fragments using CCRs. As before, the shared variables are placed in a resource, *BUFFER* becomes the resource invariant, and the **await** statements are replaced by **region** statements. This yields the implementation shown in Figure 5.5.

Clearly the solution in Figure 5.5 preserves invariant *BUFFER*. It is also deadlock-free, assuming the buffer has at least one slot. However, the solution imposes more exclusion than is necessary. In particular, both *deposit* and *fetch* have exclusive access to the buffer, even though they can safely execute in parallel when there are both empty slots and available messages. In general, there may be more exclusion than necessary when all shared variables are in the same resource. Avoiding excessive exclusion requires either removing some of the shared variables from resources or separating them into disjoint resources. The next section shows how to do this.

Bounded Buffer with Concurrent Access

In the semaphore-based implementation of a bounded buffer given in Figure 4.11, one producer and one consumer can concurrently access *buf*. That solution could be programmed using CCRs to simulate semaphores. However, the buffer itself would not be within a resource. This violates the requirement imposed by CCRs that all shared variables belong to resources, and it is that requirement that obviates the need to prove that processes do not interfere.

This section develops a CCR-based implementation in which all shared variables are within resources. The solution also illustrates the use of nested **region** statements. The key to the new solution is to respecify the buffer invariant in a different way that does not require an implementation with exclusive access.

Independently of how a bounded buffer is represented, the essential requirements are that *deposit* not overwrite an unfetched message, that *fetch* only read deposited messages and only read them once, and that *fetch* read messages in the order in which they were deposited. If the buffer is represented by a circular queue, these requirements are met if the full slots are contiguous, *deposit* writes into the next empty slot—which then becomes full—and *fetch* reads from the first full slot—which then becomes empty. In particular, let the buffer be represented by:

> **var** *slot*[1:n] : T, *full*[1:n] : **bool** := ([n] false)
> **var** *front* := 1, *rear* := 1

Here, *full* is an array that records for each slot whether it is full or empty. Now *deposit* and *fetch* must maintain the invariant:

> *CONCBUF*: $1 \le front \le n \wedge 1 \le rear \le n \wedge$ the full slots in the
> circular queue beginning at *slot*[*front*] contain the most
> recently deposited messages in chronological order

As before, execution of *deposit* needs to delay if the buffer is full. With the earlier representation, as specified in *BUFFER*, the buffer was full if *count* was n. Here, the buffer is full if all slots are full; this simplifies to checking whether *full*[*rear*] is true. Thus, we get the following implementation of *deposit* using an **await** statement:

> ⟨ **await not** *full*[*rear*] → *slot*[*rear*] := data; *full*[*rear*] := true
> *rear* := *rear* **mod** $n + 1$⟩

Similarly, execution of *fetch* needs to delay if the buffer is empty. With the above representation, this occurs if *full*[*front*] is false, so we get the following implementation of *fetch*:

> ⟨ **await** *full*[*front*] → result := *slot*[*front*]; *full*[*front*] := false
> *front* := *front* **mod** $n + 1$ ⟩

As usual, we could convert this solution directly into one using CCRs by placing all shared variables in one resource and implementing *deposit* and *fetch* by **region** statements. The resulting implementation would be essentially equivalent to the one in the previous section. However, we can implement the above solution in a different way that allows concurrent access to different buffer slots.

To allow more concurrency in a program, we need to look for ways to make atomic actions finer-grained without introducing interference. First consider the **await** statement in *deposit*. Only the first two assignments need be guarded. The last statement, which modifies *rear*, need not be since incrementing *rear* modulo n ensures that *rear* stays between 1 and n, as specified in *CONCBUF*. Thus the **await** statement in *deposit* can be separated into two atomic actions—one to manipulate *slot* and *full*, the other to increment *rear*:

(5.5)　　$\langle$ **await not** *full*[*rear*] $\rightarrow$ *slot*[*rear*] := data; *full*[*rear*] := true $\rangle$
　　　　$\langle$ *rear* := *rear* **mod** $n + 1 \rangle$

The same observations apply to the *fetch* operation. We do not need to guard the assignment to *front*, so it can be placed in a separate atomic action:

(5.6)　　$\langle$ **await** *full*[*front*] $\rightarrow$ result := *slot*[*front*]; *full*[*front*] := false $\rangle$
　　　　$\langle$ *front* := *front* **mod** $n + 1 \rangle$

When a producer process is between the two atomic actions in *deposit*, one more slot has been filled, but *rear* has not yet been updated. At this point, *full*[*rear*] is true, and hence a second producer will delay until *rear* is incremented. This ensures that *CONCBUF* is invariant since it ensures that all full slots are contiguous and that messages are deposited in chronological order.

In (5.5), the first **await** statement in *deposit* references only one buffer slot, and the last references only one of the pointer variables; the **await** statements in *fetch* (5.6) are similar. As observed earlier, the way to increase concurrency with CCRs is to place shared variables in different resources. Here we can employ several disjoint resources: one for each slot, one for *front*, and one for *rear*. It would then appear that we could implement (5.5) and (5.6) by using four different **region** statements, one for each atomic action. However, the rules for using CCRs require that the variables in a resource be accessed only within **region** statements that name the resource. Both actions in *deposit* in (5.5) require access to *rear*; similarly, both actions in *fetch* in (5.6) require access to *front*. To program this using CCRs, we merely nest a **region** statement to access a buffer slot within a **region** statement that accesses one of the pointers.

Based on these considerations, we get the CCR-based program shown in Figure 5.6. The solution is correct, independent of the number of producers or consumers. However, at most one producer and consumer at a time can be

resource *buffer*[1:*n*] (*slot* : T; *full* : **bool** := false)
resource *f* (*front* : **int** := 1)
resource *r* (*rear* : **int** := 1)
{ *CONCBUF* }

deposit: **region** *r* →
                region *buffer*[*rear*] **when not** *full* →
                    slot := data; *full* := true
                end
                rear := *rear* **mod** *n* + 1
            end
fetch: **region** *f* →
                region *buffer*[*front*] **when** *full* →
                    result := *slot*; *full* := false
                end
                front := *front* **mod** *n* + 1
            end

Figure 5.6. Bounded buffer with concurrent access.

accessing the buffer. If it is not imperative that messages be deposited and fetched in strictly chronological order, the solution can be converted into one in which all buffer slots may be accessed concurrently (see exercise 5.21).

Although the implementation in Figure 5.6 permits producers and consumers to access the buffer concurrently, it will generally be less efficient than the implementation in Figure 5.5. This is because Figure 5.6 contains two **region** statements in both *deposit* and *fetch*. As we shall see in Section 5.6, **region** statements are relatively expensive to implement. Thus, Figure 5.6 is preferable to Figure 5.5 only if the time spent accessing the buffer is at least as great as the synchronization overhead imposed by **region** statements. This will be the case only if it takes a long time to fill or empty a buffer slot, either because slots are large or because they are stored on external storage (and hence the buffer assignment statements in Figure 5.6 are actually file transfers).

5.5 Scheduling and Resource Allocation

In Section 4.5, we described the general nature of resource allocation problems and showed how semaphores could be used to solve them. In particular, we derived a solution to the shortest-job-next allocation problem (4.11). Again, we could reprogram that semaphore-based solution using conditional critical regions to simulate semaphores. As with the other problems considered in this chapter, however, there is a more straightforward solution using CCRs. The basic idea is the same as that used in the writers' preference solution to the readers/writers problem: Have each process wait for a distinct condition.

Recall that, in the shortest-job-next (SJN) allocation problem, several processes compete for access to a shared resource. Processes request use of the resource, use it once their request has been granted, and eventually return it. If more than one process is delayed waiting for its request to be satisfied, when the resource is released it is given to the delayed process that will use it for the shortest length of time. As in Section 4.5, let *free* be a boolean variable that indicates whether the resource is free or in use, and let P be a set of (*time*, *id*) pairs ordered by the values of *time*, with pairs having the same value for *time* occurring in P in the order in which they were inserted. Then, as before, the following predicate expresses the requirements of an SJN allocation policy:

$$SJN: \ P \text{ is an ordered set} \land free \Rightarrow (P = \varnothing)$$

Ignoring the SJN allocation policy for the moment, the corresponding coarse-grained solution is:

> **var** *free* := true
>
> *request*(*time*, *id*): ⟨ **await** *free* → *free* := false ⟩
>
> *release*( ): ⟨ *free* := true ⟩

We could use CCRs to implement the above solution directly, but then no scheduling would occur: When the resource is released, it would be acquired by an arbitrary delayed requester. With semaphores, we used the method of passing the baton to implement the above program fragments so that the SJN allocation policy was followed. That approach cannot be used with CCRs, however, unless we merely use CCRs to simulate semaphores. There are two reasons. First, a process is not permitted to delay in the middle of a **region** statement; it can only delay before entering. Using a second, nested **region** statement—as in Figure 5.6—will not help since a process delayed at the nested statement would retain exclusive control of the resource named in the outer statement. Second, when a process exits a **region** statement, it releases control of the resource to any other process that is delayed at a **region** statement whose guard is true. CCRs do not directly provide any analog of split binary semaphores, which provide the basis of passing the baton. Still, the idea behind the method of passing the baton suggests how to solve the SJN allocation problem using CCRs. The key is to assign a unique delay condition to each process.

resource *sjn*(*free* : **bool** := true; *next* := 0; *P* : **set of** (**int**, **int**) := ∅)
{ *SJN*: *P* is an ordered set ∧ *free* ⇒ (*P* = ∅) }

request(*time*, *id*): **region** *sjn* →
                    if *free* → *free* := *false*; *next* := *id*
                    [] **not** *free* → insert (*time*, *id*) in *P*
                fi
         end
         region *sjn* **when** *next* = *id* → **skip end**

release( ): **region** *sjn* →
        if *P* ≠ ∅ → remove first pair (*time*, *id*) from *P*; *next* := *id*
        [] *P* = ∅ → *free* := true; *next* := 0
        fi
    end

Figure 5.7. Shortest-job-next allocation using CCRs.

A requesting process first needs to check if the resource is free. If it is, the process can take it; if not, the process needs to save its (*time*, *id*) arguments in set *P* and then delay. Since *P* is shared, it must belong to a resource and hence can only be accessed using **region** statements. Thus, we need to use one **region** statement to store the arguments into *P*, and a second **region** statement to delay. Because the state of the resource might change between execution of the two **region** statements, the outcome of the first—whether the process can take the resource or needs to delay—needs to be recorded. We can program this by using a variable *next* that is assigned the *id* of the next process to be allocated the resource. In particular, if a requesting process finds that the resource is *free*, it sets *next* to its *id*; otherwise it stores (*time*, *id*) in the proper place in *P*. A requesting process then delays at the second **region** statement until *next* is equal to its *id*.

Next consider *release*. The key requirement is to "pass the baton" to one delayed request or to make the resource free if no requests are delayed. Since CCRs use boolean guards on **region** statements, we have to "pass the baton" using a boolean expression rather than a semaphore. Again, we can use variable *next*. When the resource is released and *P* is not empty, the first pending request is removed, and *next* is set to the *id* of that request. Otherwise, *next* is set to some value that is not a process identity, and *free* is set to true. We will assume that process identities are positive, and hence we will set *next* to zero when the resource is free.

The CCRs solution using this approach is shown in Figure 5.7. The reader might find it instructive to compare the solution with the semaphore-based solution in Figure 4.22. The structure of the two solutions is similar.

However, the CCRs solution uses *next* and boolean conditions rather than semaphores to indicate which process is next to use the resource. A second difference is the need for two **region** statements in *request*. This results from the fact that a process cannot delay within a **region** statement. On the other hand, the use of **region** statements ensures that the shared variables are accessed with mutual exclusion. With semaphores, care has to be taken to ensure that the split binary semaphore property is maintained.

We can employ this same basic pattern for any resource allocation problem (see the exercises). We can implement different scheduling policies by imposing different orders on the request queue and by using multiple request queues if there are multiple resources being allocated at once. The key to solving any scheduling problem is to use unique values as the basis for delay conditions.

5.6 Implementations

As in Chapters 3 and 4, we assume that processes have private copies of local variables and share global variables. In the case of CCRs, global variables are grouped into resources. However, nothing special need be done to implement this grouping—such as putting each resource into a protected memory area—since the requirement that a **resource** be accessed only by **region** statements that name that resource can be enforced by the compiler for a language that employs CCRs. Thus, the key to implementing CCRs is to implement **region** statements.

This section presents four different implementations. Each employs a different combination of techniques presented in earlier chapters. The first employs busy waiting, the second and third employ semaphores, and the fourth extends the kernel of Section 3.6.

Using Busy Waiting

Since **region** statements are very similar to **await** statements, they can be implemented in the same way using busy waiting. In particular, the statement **region** r **when** $B \rightarrow S$ **end** can be implemented as in (3.9) by the code sequence:

(5.7)   CSenter
          do not $B \rightarrow$ CSexit; Delay; CSenter **od**
          S
          CSexit

The entry and exit protocols in (5.7) can be implemented using any of the protocols for the critical section problem—e.g., spin locks, the tie-breaker algorithm, the bakery algorithm, or semaphores. One set of critical section variables is used for each different resource.

As usual, a busy-waiting protocol such as (5.7) is inefficient if process execution is multiplexed on one or more processors. In this case, it is better to employ a blocking implementation of **region** statements—i.e., one in which a process releases control of a processor if it must be delayed awaiting entry to a **region** statement. either because the resource is in use or because the boolean guard is false. Below we present three such implementations.

Using Semaphores with Passing the Baton

In a program that uses CCRs, all **region** statements will have one of two forms:

$$F_1: \textbf{region } r \to S \textbf{ end}$$
$$F_2: \textbf{region } r \textbf{ when } B \to S \textbf{ end}$$

These are nearly identical to the two different kinds of **await** statements. Hence, we can implement **region** statements using the method of passing the baton, as introduced in Section 4.4. Following that method, we need one entry semaphore per resource and one delay semaphore and one delay counter for each *semantically* different guard B in **region** statements that name the same resource. (Two boolean conditions might syntactically be the same but have different values in different processes because the conditions reference local variables.) For example, in the readers' preference solution to the readers/writers problem (Figure 5.3), there are two different guards: one for delayed readers and one for delayed writers. By contrast, in the solution to the shortest-job-next allocation problem (Figure 5.7), each requesting process waits for a different condition.

Assume $B_1, ..., B_m$ are the different conditions in **region** statements for one resource. For that resource, let e be the entry semaphore, $b[1{:}m]$ be the delay semaphores, and $d[1{:}m]$ be the delay counters. Semaphores e and $b[1{:}m]$ form a split binary semaphore, with e initially 1 and the others initially 0. The $d[i]$ record the number of processes delayed on each of the $b[i]$; these counters are initially 0. Following the transformation in (4.6), **region** statements of form F_1 are then implemented by:

(5.8) F_1: **P**(e)
                    S
                    SIGNAL

Similarly, **region** statements of form F_2 with guard B_i are implemented by the transformation in (4.7):

(5.9) F_2: **P**(e)
          if not $B_i \rightarrow d[i] := d[i] + 1;$ **V**(e); **P**($b[i]$) **fi**
          S
          SIGNAL

Finally, as in (4.8), the *SIGNAL* code fragment is:

(5.10)   *SIGNAL*: **if** B_1 **and** $d_1 > 0 \rightarrow d_1 := d_1 - 1;$ **V**(b_1)
          [] ...
          [] B_n **and** $d_n > 0 \rightarrow d_n := d_n - 1;$ **V**(b_n)
          [] **else** $\rightarrow$ **V**(e)
          fi

We could always implement CCRs using this method of passing the baton. However, there are three potential shortcomings. First, it can require a large number of semaphores. In general, one is required for each different guard in **region** statements.

Second, in general, every condition needs to be reevaluated in every *SIGNAL* fragment. In Chapter 4, we showned how it is often possible to simplify the *SIGNAL* fragments. But those simplifications were done by hand and were based on knowledge of the state of the program at *SIGNAL* points. If a language provides **region** statements, the compiler writer needs to write *one* algorithm that translates an arbitrary **region** statement into code that uses semaphores. It is very difficult in general to automate optimizations, especially those based on the program state.

The third shortcoming of the above approach is that it requires that each process be able to evaluate the guards of all other processes. This can be difficult to implement since guards in **region** statements are allowed to reference variables local to the executing process. Local variables were used, for example, in the solution to the shortest-job-next allocation problem in Figure 5.7. In general, it is necessary to place code to evaluate the guards in shared storage so that all processes can execute it. Also, such code must be able to reference the values of local variables used for synchronization or global copies of such values.

The busy-waiting implementation of **region** statements given in (5.7) does not have these shortcomings since processes evaluate their own guards (but that implementation does of course employ busy waiting). The passing-the-baton implementation above blocks processes until it is certain they can proceed to execute a **region** statement. Our challenge now is to combine the simplicity of the busy-waiting implementation with the better performance (in general) of the blocking implementation.

Using Semaphores with Rem's Algorithm

There are two potential sources of spinning in (5.7). First, a process might spin in the CSenter protocol if that is implemented using busy waiting. This is easily overcome by using (blocking) semaphores to implement CSenter and CSexit, as in Figure 4.4. The second source of spinning is repeated execution of the **do** loop until B becomes true. Most of this spinning can be eliminated if a process blocks until it is at least *possible* that its guard is true. These observations suggest the following outline for an implementation of **region** r **when** $B \to S$ **end**:

(5.11)   **P**(e)
         do not $B \to EXIT1$; *DELAY* **od**
         S
         EXIT2

Above, e is an entry semaphore as in (5.9); it protects initial entry into the critical section that must be associated with resource r. After gaining entry, a process evaluates its own guard B. If it is true, the process can then execute S and exit. However, if B is false, the process releases mutual exclusion at *EXIT1* and then delays until the guard might have changed.

The key to refining (5.11) is of course implementing the exit and delay code. There are two requirements:

- Processes must evaluate B and possibly execute S one at a time since variables in resource r must be accessed with mutual exclusion.

- When resource variables change, if the guards for one or more of the delayed processes become true, one of the delayed processes must be next to acquire access to r. In short, processes should not be delayed unnecessarily.

The guard of a delayed process can become true only as the result of some other process executing a **region** statement on the same resource and changing a shared variable. (If the guard is false and references only local variables, it will never become true; hence the process will deadlock.) Thus, a delayed process should block until some other process reaches *EXIT2*. Moreover, when a process reaches *EXIT2*, it needs to awaken *all* processes that are waiting to access the resource. This is because the other processes must reevaluate their own guards, and any—perhaps all—such guards might now be true.

These two requirements imply that *DELAY* must consist of two stages: First a process waits until its guard could possibly be true, then it waits a turn to reevaluate the guard. Delayed processes move from the first to the second stage as a result of another process reaching *EXIT2*. These two stages cannot be combined because then it would be impossible to distinguish between processes that have not yet reevaluated their guard and processes that have reevaluated their guard but found it still to be false and hence need to delay again.

Based on the above observations, there are three conditions for which a process could be waiting: initial entry to a **region** statement, potential change to its guard, and a turn to reevaluate the guard. As in the method of passing the baton, we associate one split binary semaphore with each condition. Let e (entry), d (delay), and g (guard) be these semaphores, respectively. We also need to record the number of processes waiting for each of the last two conditions. Let nd be the number of processes delayed because their guards are false and let ng be the number of processes waiting to reevaluate a guard that could be true. Associated with each resource being simulated, we thus have the following shared variables:

$$\textbf{var } e : \textbf{sem} := 1, d : \textbf{sem} := 0, g : \textbf{sem} := 0, nd : \textbf{int} := 0, ng : \textbf{int} := 0$$

Informally, these variables are used as described above. More precisely, to ensure that execution of **region** statements is mutually exclusive, the simulation must preserve the invariance of the split binary semaphore property:

$$0 \le (e + d + g) \le 1$$

To avoid introducing unnecessary delay in the implementation, e must not be signaled if there is any delayed process whose guard could be true or if there is any process waiting to reevaluate its guard. Also, neither d nor g should be signaled unless some process is waiting for the associated condition. Finally, processes wanting to reevaluate their guard must wait until all delayed processes have been awakened and moved to the second stage. These properties require the invariance of:

$$REM: (e = 1 \;\Rightarrow\; (ng = 0 \wedge B \text{ is false for all } nd \text{ delayed processes})) \;\wedge$$
$$(d = 1 \;\Rightarrow\; nd > 0) \;\wedge\; (g = 1 \;\Rightarrow\; ng > 0)$$

If we refine (5.11) to use these variables in the ways described, guard **V** operations to ensure the above invariants, and then simplify the guarded commands, we have the solution shown in Figure 5.8. That algorithm is often called Rem's algorithm, after the person who first discovered it.

In Figure 5.8, each execution path has alternating **P** and **V** operations, beginning with a **P** and ending with a **V**. Since the semaphores are initialized so that e is 1 and d and g are 0, they thus satisfy the split binary semaphore property. This ensures the first requirement of the solution, that processes evaluate B and execute S with mutual exclusion.

```
P(e)
do not B →
    nd := nd + 1
    if ng > 0 → V(g)          # let another process reevaluate its guard;
    [] ng = 0 → V(e)          # open entry gate when all have done so
    fi
    P(d); nd := nd − 1        # delay until guard could possibly be true
    ng := ng + 1             # move to guard evaluation (second) stage
    if nd > 0 → V(d)          # let another process move to second stage;
    [] nd = 0 → V(g)          # when all moved, let first reevaluate guard
    fi
    P(g); ng := ng − 1       # wait turn to reevaluate guard
od
S
if nd > 0 → V(d)                      # move one process from delay stage;
[] nd = 0 and ng > 0 → V(g)          # if all moved, let one reevaluate guard;
[] nd = 0 and ng = 0 → V(e)          # otherwise open entry gate.
fi
```

Figure 5.8. Implementation of CCRs using semaphores.

The second requirement—avoiding unnecessary delay—results from the use of two delay stages and a passing-the-baton form of signaling to move processes from one stage to the next. In particular, when one process executes its statement S, it awakens the first delayed process, which awakens the next, and so on until all delayed processes have been awakened; then one process is allowed to reevaluate its guard. This cascading wakeup continues until all delayed processes have completed their **region** statement or delayed again because their guard is still false. At this time e is finally signaled. Thus, delayed processes all get the chance to proceed before any other process gets the chance to execute a **region** statement for the first time.

Although this solution uses fewer semaphores than the one using passing the baton—and it does not require that processes be able to evaluate the guards of other processes—it is clearly quite complex. This solution is also less efficient since numerous semaphore operations are executed if many processes are delayed, and each could cause a context switch. Moreover, *all* delayed processes are awakened every time one process successfully completes executing S. In contrast, with passing the baton, a delayed process is awakened only when its guard is true.

The solution in Figure 5.8 can, however, be simplified in some cases. For example, when there is no guard in a **region** statement, the **do** loop can be deleted. The solution can also be simplified if we relax the requirement that delayed processes take precedence over new arrivals. Unfortunately, even with these simplifications, **region** statements are inherently costly, especially relative to semaphores. This is because it is necessary to reevaluate all delay conditions.

Using a Kernel

The least expensive way to provide a blocking implementation of **region** statements is by means of kernel primitives. The essential idea is to mimic one of the semaphore implementations by using primitives for each of the key steps: entry to a **region** statement, delay in the event the associated guard is false, and exit from a **region** statement. We also need a primitive to create a resource descriptor. Thus, we require four primitives: *create_resource*, *enter*, *delay*, and *exit*. These are added to a kernel that implements processes, such as that described in Chapter 3.

A compiler needs to generate one call to *create_resource* for each resource in a program. This primitive allocates and initializes a resource descriptor, then returns a name r for it. For now assume that processes evaluate their own guards in **region** statements. Then each such statement is translated into a fragment similar to (5.11):

$$
\begin{aligned}
&enter(r) \\
&\textbf{do not } B \rightarrow delay(r) \textbf{ od} \\
&S \\
&exit(r)
\end{aligned}
$$

Above, r is the resource name returned by *create_resource*, B is the guard in the **region** statement, and S is the statement in the **region** statement.

To implement the synchronization required for **region** statements, each resource descriptor contains a mutual exclusion lock and three queues. The lock is set if some process is executing a **region** statement that names that resource. The queues contain descriptors of processes waiting to access the resource. The entry queue contains processes waiting to begin executing a **region** statement, the delay queue contains processes delayed because their guards were false, and the retry queue contains processes that were delayed but are now waiting a turn to reevaluate their guard. (These queues serve the roles of the blocked lists for semaphores e, d, and g, respectively, in Figure 5.8.)

Figure 5.9 gives code outlines for the four primitives. When a process calls *enter(r)*, it either acquires the resource lock or is placed at the end of the entry queue, depending on whether the lock is clear or set. A process is placed on the delay queue when it calls *delay(r)*. Finally, when a process calls *exit*(*r*), the kernel moves all processes on the delay queue to the retry queue.* If the retry queue is not empty, *exit* moves one process from the retry queue to the ready list. Otherwise, *exit* either moves one process from the entry queue to the ready list or clears the resource lock. The ready list and *dispatcher* routine are the same as in the kernels in Chapters 3 and 4.

This kernel-based implementation of **region** statements is more efficient than one built on top of semaphores, mainly because it avoids the cascading wakeup of the semaphore-based implementation. This is because when one process exits a **region** statement, all delayed processes are moved as a group to the retry queue. This kernel also ensures that delayed processes get a chance to reevaluate their guards in a FIFO order. Hence the implementation is strongly fair since a delayed process will eventually get to the front of the retry queue, and thus it will eventually get to proceed if its guard is infinitely often true (assuming no process terminates inside a **region** statement).

The kernel in Figure 5.9 has processes reevaluate their own delay conditions. If instead the kernel were to evaluate delay conditions, it would be even more efficient since we could eliminate the *delay* primitive and the retry and entry queues. In particular, we could change *enter* and *exit* as follows. First, add a parameter to *enter* that points to code that evaluates the guard in the associated **region** statement. When *enter* is called, the kernel first checks the resource's lock. If it is not set, the kernel evaluates the guard by calling the process's evaluation code. If the guard is true, the kernel sets the lock and allows the executing process to proceed. If the guard is false, or if the lock is already set, the kernel blocks the process on the delay queue.

The second change is to *exit*, which a process calls after executing the body of a **region** statement. This primitive now scans the delay queue, evaluating the guards of delayed processes.† As soon as the kernel finds one process whose guard is true, it moves that process to the ready list and calls the *dispatcher*. If the kernel finds no true guard—or if the delay queue is empty—the kernel clears the resource's lock. Essentially, then, *enter* and *exit* are now be like **P** and **V** operations on a binary semaphore, with the extra constraint that a process returns from *enter* only if the guard on its **region** statement is true.

This second kernel would be more efficient than the one in Figure 5.9. First, it is entered only twice per **region** statement rather than three times; this reduces overhead. More importantly, the second kernel awakens a process only when its guard is true. The down side is that the kernel must be

---

*Alternatively, the kernel could employ multiple delay queues, one for each different delay condition. In this case, *exit* would need to move only one process from each delay queue to the retry queue. Other processes would be moved to the retry queue on subsequent calls of *exit*.

†Again the kernel could employ multiple delay queues, one for each different delay condition. If more than one process is waiting for the same condition, the kernel would then need to evaluate the condition only once.

procedure *create_resource*( ) **returns** *name*
    get empty resource descriptor and initialize it
    set *name* to the identity (index) of the descriptor
    call *dispatcher*( )
end

procedure *enter*(*name*)
    find resource descriptor of *name*
    if *lock* set → insert *executing* at end of entry queue; *executing* := 0
    [] *lock* clear → set *lock*   # acquire exclusive access to *name*
    fi
    call *dispatcher*( )
end

procedure *delay*(*name*)
    find resource descriptor of *name*
    insert *executing* at end of delay queue; *executing* := 0
    if retry queue not empty →
        move process from front of retry queue to end of ready list
    [] retry queue empty **and** entry queue not empty →
        move process from front of entry queue to end of ready list
    [] retry queue empty **and** entry queue empty → clear *lock*
    fi
    call *dispatcher*( )
end

procedure *exit*(*name*)
    find resource descriptor for *name*
    move all descriptors on delay queue to retry queue
    if retry queue not empty →
        move process from front of retry queue to end of ready list
    [] retry queue empty **and** entry queue not empty →
        move process from front of entry queue to end of ready list
    [] retry queue empty **and** entry queue empty → clear *lock*
    fi
    call *dispatcher*( )
end

Figure 5.9. Kernel primitives for CCRs.

---

able to evaluate guards, which means that it needs to be able to access user data and code. Moreover, the kernel must trust the user's code. If the kernel supports programs written only in one or more trusted languages—e.g., it is part of the run-time library for an implementation of a high-level language—

then the safety of user-written code will not be an issue. However, safety is an important issue in a multiuser, multiapplication environment.

Either single-processor kernel can readily be extended to a multiprocessor kernel. As before, the main change is to protect shared data structures so that they are accessed with mutual exclusion. Again, however, we would also need to address the issues discussed at the ends of Section 3.8 and 4.6: avoiding memory contention, exploiting cached data, binding processes to processors, and co-scheduling of processes on processors. In addition, if memory-access time is non-uniform, it is important to reduce the number of remote memory references that have to be made to evaluate delay conditions. Doing so is a non-trivial problem. If processes evaluate their own guards—as in Figure 5.9—then resource variables are likely to be remote. If the kernel evaluates guards—as in the second kernel—then the evaluation code is likely to be remote from the processor executing the kernel.

Historical Notes and References

Conditional critical regions were first proposed by Tony Hoare [1972]. They were popularized by Per Brinch Hansen in two much more widely circulated articles [1972b, 1973b] and in his operating systems text [1973a]. The notation used here combines aspects of those proposed by Hoare and Brinch Hansen.

Hoare [1972] also proposed inference rules for **region** statements. However, his programming logic was incomplete since assertions in one process could not reference variables in another and since resource invariants could not reference variables local to processes. The first set of (relatively) complete inference rules was developed by Susan Owicki in a dissertation supervised by David Gries [Owicki 1975, Owicki & Gries 1976b]. Inference rules (5.1) and (5.2) are due to them, as are the sufficient conditions for mutual exclusion (5.3) and absence of deadlock (5.4).

Variants of CCRs are the primary synchronization mechanism in two languages designed by Brinch Hansen: DP [1978] and Edison [1981a, 1981b]. They are also used in Argus [Liskov & Scheifler 1982] and Lynx [Scott 1987, 1991] for synchronizing access to local variables. The use of structured synchronization statements and boolean conditions—which originated with CCRs—has also heavily influenced several additional languages, including Ada [Dept. of Defense 1983], CSP [Hoare 1978, 1985], Occam [May 1983, Burns 1988], and SR [Andrews 1981, Andrews et al. 1988]. All these languages are described in later chapters.

In [1972a], Brinch Hansen compares CCRs to semaphores and argues that CCRs are much simpler to use and more directly express synchronization conditions. He uses the readers/writers problem as his main example. Shortly after that paper appeared, the originators of the readers/writers problem wrote a rebuttal [Courtois et al. 1972]. The rebuttal points out that Brinch Hansen's solution does not give writers preference if both readers and writers are waiting to access the database. The crux of the problem is that, with CCRs, if two processes are trying to access the same resource, the semantics of **region** statements do not specify the order in which they will be granted access. The rebuttal by Courtois et al. also makes the interesting, and valid, point that "an efficient implementation has never been published." Indeed, this tradeoff between expressive power and implementation efficiency is at the heart of many arguments about the relative merits of different programming language mechanisms (e.g., declarative vs. imperative languages).

The first published implementation of CCRs of which the author is aware is in a paper by H.A. Schmid [1976]. More widely known is Rem's algorithm (Figure 5.8), which was designed by Martin Rem in early 1977. Rem sent a note describing his algorithm to his mentor Edsger Dijkstra, who subsequently wrote it up and distributed it as part of his EWD series [Dijkstra 1982]. Rem also sent his note to David Gries, who developed an assertional proof showing that Rem's algorithm correctly simulates the **region** statement [Gries 1977].

Rem's algorithm uses three semaphores. Two additional implementations, which use only two binary semaphores, are described in Kessels and Martin [1979]. Exercise 5.28 gives one of their algorithms.

Exercises

5.1 Prove that the conditions in (5.3) are sufficient to ensure mutual exclusion. Explain why the conditions are not necessary.

5.2 (a) Prove that the conditions in (5.4) are sufficient to ensure absence of deadlock. Explain why the conditions are not necessary.

(b) Generalize the conditions in (5.4) to permit **region** statements to be nested.

5.3 (a) Develop a program that copies the contents of array $a[1:n]$ in a producer process to array $b[1:n]$ in a consumer process. Use a single-slot buffer.

(b) Develop a complete proof outline that demonstrates that your answer to (a) is correct. (Hint: You will need to use auxiliary variables.)

5.4 Modify the solution to the dining philosophers problem (Figure 5.2) so that it is fair, assuming scheduling is strongly fair. In particular, if a philosopher wants to eat, eventually he is able to do so.

5.5 Develop a complete proof outline for the readers/writers solution in Figure 5.3. Using your proof outline and (5.3), prove that the solution guarantees reader/writer exclusion and writer/writer exclusion. Using your proof outline and (5.4), prove that the solution is deadlock-free. (Hint: You will need to use auxiliary variables.)

5.6 (a) Modify the readers/writers solution in Figure 5.3 so that readers have strong preference; i.e., if both readers and writers are waiting to access the database when a writer finishes, the readers get preference.

(b) Modify the readers/writers solution in Figure 5.3 so that it is fair; i.e., neither readers nor writers get starved. (Hint: Have readers and writers alternate turns if both are trying to access the database.)

5.7 Implement the solution to the readers/writers problem given in Figure 4.18 using CCRs rather than semaphores. Use as few **region** statements as possible.

5.8 Develop a first-come, first-served solution to the critical section problem that uses CCRs for synchronization. (Hint: Use incrementing counters as in the ticket algorithm of Section 3.3.)

5.9 *The One-Lane Bridge.* Cars coming from the north and the south arrive at a one-lane bridge. Cars heading in the same direction can cross the bridge at the same time, but cars heading in opposite directions cannot.

(a) Develop a solution to this problem. First specify a global invariant, then develop a coarse-grained solution, and finally develop a fine-grained solution using CCRs for synchronization. Do not worry about fairness, and do not give preference to any one kind of car.

(b) Develop a complete proof outline, and then use (5.3) and (5.4) to demonstrate that your answer to (a) ensures mutual exclusion and avoids deadlock.

(c) Modify your answer to (a) to ensure fairness. (Hint: Allow at most C cars to cross in one direction if cars are waiting to cross in the other direction.)

5.10 In many database applications, database records can be locked in either exclusive or shared mode. If a process holds an exclusive lock, it is the only one permitted to access the record. However, several processes can hold a shared lock.

Develop routines to implement record locking and unlocking. First specify a global invariant, then develop a coarse-grained solution, and finally develop a fine-grained solution using CCRs for synchronization.

5.11 Develop an implementation of a counter barrier using CCRs (see Section 3.5). The barrier should be reusable, so you need to worry about resetting the counter(s).

5.12 Two kinds of processes, A's and B's, enter a room. An A process cannot leave until it meets two B processes, and a B process cannot leave until it meets one A process. Either kind of process leaves the room—without meeting any other processes—once it has met the required number of other processes.

(a) Develop a solution to this problem. First specify a global invariant, then develop a coarse-grained solution, and finally develop a fine-grained solution that uses CCRs for synchronization.

(b) Modify your answer to (a) so that the first of the two B processes that meets an A process does not leave the room until after the A process meets a second B process.

5.13 *Atomic Broadcast.* Assume that one producer process and n consumer processes share a bounded buffer having b slots. The producer deposits messages in the buffer; consumers fetch them. Every message deposited by the producer is to be received by all n consumers. Furthermore, each consumer is to receive the messages in the order they were deposited. However, different consumers can receive messages at different times. For example, one consumer could receive up to b more messages than another if the second consumer is slow.

Develop a solution to this problem. First specify a global invariant, then develop a coarse-grained solution, and finally develop a fine-grained solution that uses CCRs for synchronization.

5.14 *Search / Insert / Delete*. Three kinds of processes share access to a singly-linked list: searchers, inserters, and deleters. Searchers merely examine the list; hence they can execute concurrently with each other. Inserters add new items to the end of the list; insertions must be mutually exclusive to preclude two inserters from inserting new items at about the same time. However, one insert can proceed in parallel with any number of searches. Finally, deleters remove items from anywhere in the list. At most one deleter process can access the list at a time, and deletion must also be mutually exclusive with searches and insertions.

Derive a solution to this problem. First specify the synchronization property as a global invariant. Use three counters: ns, the number of active searchers; ni, the number of active inserters; and nd, the number of active deleters. Then develop a coarse-grained solution. Finally, develop a fine-grained solution using CCRs for synchronization.

5.15 *Memory Allocation*. Suppose there are two operations: *request*(*amount* : **int**) and *release*(*amount* : **int**). When a process calls *request*, it delays until at least *amount* free pages of memory are available, then takes *amount* pages. A process returns *amount* pages to the free pool by calling *release*. (Pages may be released in different quantities than they are acquired.)

(a) Develop implementations of *request* and *release*. First specify a global invariant, then develop a coarse-grained solution, and finally develop a fine-grained solution that uses CCRs for synchronization. Do not worry about the order in which requests are serviced.

(b) Modify your answer to (a) to use the shortest-job-next (SJN) allocation policy. In particular, smaller requests take precedence over larger ones.

(c) Modify your answer to (a) to use a first-come, first-served (FCFS) allocation policy. This means that a pending request might have to delay, even if there is enough memory available.

(d) Suppose *request* and *release* acquire and return contiguous pages of memory; i.e., if a process requests two pages, it delays until two adjacent pages are available. Develop implementations of these version of *request* and *release*. First choose a representation for the status of memory pages and specify a global invariant. Then develop a coarse-grained solution, and finally develop a fine-grained solution that uses CCRs for synchronization.

5.16 Suppose n processes $P[1{:}n]$ share three printers. Before using a printer, $P[i]$ calls *request*(*printer*). This operation returns the identity of a free printer. After using that printer, $P[i]$ returns it by calling *release*(*printer*).

(a) Develop implementations of *request* and *release*. First specify a global invariant, then develop a coarse-grained solution, and finally develop a fine-grained solution that uses CCRs for synchronization.

(b) Assume each process has a priority stored in global array *priority*[1:*n*]. Modify *request* and *release* so that a printer is allocated to the highest priority waiting process. You may assume that each process has a unique priority.

5.17 Suppose a computer center has two printers, A and B, that are similar but not identical. Three kinds of processes use the printers: those that must use A, those that must use B, and those that can use either A or B.

Derive code that each kind of process executes to request and release a printer. First specify a global invariant, then develop a coarse-grained solution, and finally develop a fine-grained solution using CCRs for synchronization. Your solution should be fair, assuming **region** statements are strongly fair and assuming a process using a printer eventually releases it.

5.18 *The Roller Coaster Problem* [Herman 1989]. Suppose there are *n* passenger processes and one car process. The passengers repeatedly wait to take rides in the car, which can hold C passengers, C < *n*. However, the car can go around the tracks only when it is full.

(a) Develop code for the actions of the passenger and car processes. First specify a global invariant, then develop a coarse-grained solution, and finally develop a fine-grained solution using CCRs for synchronization.

(b) Generalize your answer to (a) to employ *m* car processes, *m* > 1. Since there is only one track, cars cannot pass each other; i.e., they must finish going around the track in the order in which they started. Again, a car can go around the tracks only when it is full.

5.19 *Interval Timer.* Assume a special clock process maintains approximate time in a shared variable that records the number of milliseconds since the processor was booted. The clock process uses a kernel primitive *waitclock(msecs)*. This primitive sets a hardware timer so that it will cause an interrupt in *msecs* milliseconds and then delays the executing process until the timer interrupt occurs.

(a) Give the code for the clock process. Also design an implementation of a procedure *nap(interval)* that delays the executing process until at least *interval* milliseconds have expired. Use CCRs for synchronization between the clock process and application processes that call *nap*.

(b) Modify your answer to (a) so that the clock process and application processes are awakened only when necessary. For example, if one application process wants to nap for 10 milliseconds, the clock process should set the hardware timer to 10 milliseconds, and both it and the application process should block until 10 milliseconds have expired. However, another application process might then want to nap for 5 milliseconds. Define any additional kernel primitives you need and any additional assumptions you need to make. For example, you might need to allow application processes to read and/or reset the hardware timer.

5.20 Suppose a producer process has local array *a*[1:*m*] and a consumer process has local array *b*[1:*m*]. The producer and consumer use the bounded buffer with concurrent access shown in Figure 5.6 to copy the contents of *a* to *b*.

Write code for the producer and consumer, and give a complete proof outline that demonstrates that your program is correct. Be careful to meet all the requirements of Region Rule (5.1) and CCRs Rule (5.2).

5.21   Modify the bounded buffer with concurrent access (Figure 5.6) to permit concurrent *deposits* and *fetches*. In particular, up to n producers should be able to deposit items simultaneously, and up to n consumers should be able to fetch items simultaneously. As usual, a producer should only deposit an item into an empty slot, and a consumer should only fetch from a full slot. It is permissible for items to be fetched in a different order than they are deposited.

5.22   Suppose the **region** statement is modified to allow a delay anywhere within the body of the statement [Brinch Hansen 1972b, 1973b]. In particular, the form of this generalized **region** statement is:

region $r \to S1$; **await** B; $S2$ **end**

Either or both of $S1$ and $S2$ could be empty; there could also be multiple **await** statements. The semantics of **await** B are to delay until B is true; a process releases control of r while it is delayed and regains exclusive control when B is true.

(a) Rewrite the shortest-job-next allocator (Figure 5.7) to use the generalized **region** statement in *request*.

(b) Develop an inference rule for this generalized **region** statement.

(c) Is the generalized **region** statement more powerful than a series of normal **region** statements? If so, describe how and why. If not, show how to translate the generalized **region** statement into normal **region** statements.

(d) Give an implementation of the generalized **region** statement using semaphores.

(e) Modify the kernel primitives in Figure 5.9 to implement the generalized **region** statement.

5.23   Consider the shortest-job-next allocation problem discussed in Section 5.5. Suppose *request* and *release* are implemented as follows:

resource $sjn(P :$ **set of** (**int**, **int**) $:= \varnothing$)

request(*time*, *id*):
   region $sjn \to$ insert (*time*, *id*) in P **end**
   region sjn **when** (*time*, *id*) at front of $P \to$ **skip end**

release( ):   **region** $sjn \to$ remove first pair (*time*, *id*) from P **end**

As before, P is ordered by increasing values of *time*.

Is this implementation correct? Either give a convincing argument that it is or give an example illustrating what can go wrong.

5.24 Consider the shortest-job-next allocation problem discussed in Section 5.5. Suppose *request* and *release* are implemented as follows:

> **resource** *sjn*(*free* : **bool** := true; *P* : **set of** (**int**, **int**) := ∅)
>
> *request*(*time*, *id*):
>   **region** *sjn* → insert (*time*, *id*) in *P* **end**
>   **region** *sjn* **when** *free* **and** (*time*, *id*) at front of *P* →
>   remove (*time*, *id*) from *P*; *free* := false
>   **end**
>
> *release*( ): **region** *sjn* → *free* := true **end**

As before, *P* is ordered by increasing values of *time*.

Is this implementation correct? Either give a convincing argument that it is or give an example illustrating what can go wrong.

5.25 Prove the correctness of the implementation of a **region** statement using semaphores with passing the baton, as given in (5.8) to (5.10). Namely, develop a complete proof outline that demonstrates that the implementation simulates a **region** statement. The **region** statement has inference rule (5.1).

5.26 Prove that Rem's algorithm (Figure 5.8) is correct. Namely, develop a complete proof outline that demonstrates that Rem's algorithm simulates a **region** statement. The **region** statement has inference rule (5.1).

5.27 Suppose we remove the second requirement in Rem's algorithm. Namely, delayed processes do not necessarily get to reevaluate their delay condition before processes executing a **region** statement for the first time. Simplify Rem's algorithm in this case.

5.28 Consider the following proposal for implementing a **region** statement using semaphores [Kessels & Martin 1979]:

> **P**(*e*)
> **do not** *B* → *nd* := *nd* + 1; **V**(*e*) →
>   **P**(*d*); *nd* := *nd* − 1
>   **if** *nd* = 0 → **V**(*e*) [] *nd* > 0 → **V**(*d*) **fi**
>   **P**(*e*)
> **od**
> *S*
> **if** *nd* = 0 → **V**(*e*) [] *nd* >0 → **V**(*d*) **fi**

Semaphore *e* is initially 1; semaphore *d* and counter *nd* are initially 0.

Develop a complete proof outline that demonstrates that this algorithm correctly simulates a **region** statement. Demonstrate that, if no process is blocked on a **P** operation, then the delay condition *B* is false for all processes blocked on *d*.

5.29 Consider the following proposal for implementing a **region** statement using semaphores:

$$\mathbf{P}(e)$$
$$\mathbf{do\ not\ } B \rightarrow nd := nd + 1; \mathbf{V}(e); \mathbf{P}(d); \mathbf{P}(e) \mathbf{\ od}$$
$$S$$
$$\mathbf{do\ } nd > 0 \rightarrow nd := nd - 1; \mathbf{V}(d) \mathbf{\ od}$$
$$\mathbf{V}(e)$$

Semaphore e is initially 1; semaphore d and counter nd are initially 0.

Does this solution work correctly? If so, annotate the solution with assertions, and give a convincing argument that it correctly simulates a **region** statement. If not, clearly explain what the problem is, and give an example of an execution sequence that causes problems.

5.30   Consider the following proposal for implementing a **region** statement using semaphores [Gries 1977]:

$$\mathbf{P}(e)$$
$$\mathbf{do\ not\ } B \rightarrow nd := nd + 1$$
$$\qquad \mathbf{if\ } ng > 0 \rightarrow \mathbf{V}(g) \ [] \ ng = 0 \rightarrow \mathbf{V}(e) \mathbf{\ fi}$$
$$\qquad \mathbf{P}(d)$$
$$\qquad \mathbf{P}(g); ng := ng - 1$$
$$\mathbf{od}$$
$$S$$
$$\mathbf{do\ } nd > 0 \rightarrow \mathbf{V}(d); nd := nd - 1; ng := ng + 1 \mathbf{\ od}$$
$$\mathbf{if\ } ng > 0 \rightarrow \mathbf{V}(g) \ [] \ ng = 0 \rightarrow \mathbf{V}(e) \mathbf{\ fi}$$

Semaphore e is initially 1; semaphores g and d and counters ng and nd are initially 0.

Does this solution work correctly? If so, annotate the solution with assertions, and give a convincing argument that it correctly simulates a **region** statement. If not, clearly explain what the problem is, and give an example of an execution sequence that causes problems.

5.31   Consider the dining philosophers program in Figure 5.2 and the kernel implementation of CCRs given in Figure 5.9.

(a) Translate the **region** statements executed by each philosopher into code that uses the kernel primitives.

(b) Consider the following sequence of events in the philosophers program:

> *Philosopher*[1] begins to eat
> *Philosopher*[3] begins to eat
> *Philosopher*[2] wants to eat and delays
> *Philosopher*[4] wants to eat and delays
> *Philosopher*[3] finishes eating
> *Philosopher*[3] again wants to eat
> *Philosopher*[1] finishes eating

Show the contents of the delay queue, retry queue, ready list, and *lock* before and after each of the above events. Describe the specific actions that cause changes to these variables. For simplicity, assume that processing for each event is completed before the next event occurs.

CHAPTER 6

Monitors

With semaphores and conditional critical regions, shared variables are global to all processes. Statements that access shared variables might be grouped into procedures, but such statements can be dispersed throughout a program. Thus, to understand how shared variables are used, one must examine an entire program. Also, if a new process is added to the program, the programmer must verify that the process uses the shared variables correctly.

Conditional critical regions are more structured than semaphores since related variables are declared together in a resource with an associated invariant and resource variables can be accessed only by means of **region** statements. However, **region** statements are much more costly to implement than semaphore operations.

Monitors are program modules that provide more structure than conditional critical regions yet can be implemented as efficiently as semaphores. First and foremost, monitors are a data abstraction mechanism: they encapsulate the representations of abstract resources and provide a set of operations that are the *only* means by which the representation is manipulated. In particular, a monitor contains variables that store the resource's state and procedures that implement operations on the resource. A process can access the variables in a monitor only by calling one of the monitor procedures. Mutual exclusion is provided by ensuring that execution of procedures in the same monitor is not overlapped. This is similar to the implicit mutual exclusion provided by **region** statements. However, unlike in **region** statements, condition synchronization in monitors is provided by a low-level mechanism called *condition variables*. As we shall see, condition variables are used for signaling in much the same way as semaphores.

When monitors are used for synchronization, a concurrent program contains two kinds of modules: active processes and passive monitors. Assuming all shared variables are within monitors, two processes can interact only by calling procedures in the same monitor. The resulting modularization has two important benefits. First, a process that calls a monitor procedure can ignore how the procedure is implemented; all that matters are the visible effects of calling the procedure. Second, the programmer of a monitor can ignore how or where the monitor's procedures are used. Once a monitor is implemented correctly, it remains correct, independent of the number of processes that use it. Also, the programmer of a monitor is free to change the way in which the monitor is implemented, so long as the visible procedures and their effects are not changed. Together, these benefits make it possible to design each process and monitor relatively independently. This in turn makes a concurrent program easier to develop and understand.

This chapter describes monitors, discusses their semantics and implementation, and illustrates their use with several examples. Several new problems are introduced and solved, including two classic problems: the sleeping barber and disk head scheduling. Because of their utility and efficiency, monitors have been employed in several concurrent programming languages, including Concurrent Pascal, Modula, Mesa, Pascal Plus, Concurrent Euclid, and Turing Plus.

6.1 Programming Notation

A monitor places a wall around both the variables and the procedures that implement a shared resource. A monitor declaration has the form:

(6.1)   **monitor** *Mname*
             declarations of permanent variables; initialization code
             procedure op_1(*formals*$_1$) body of op_1 **end**
             ...
             procedure op_n(*formals*$_n$) body of op_n **end**
          end

The permanent variables represent the state of the resource. They are called permanent variables because they exist and retain their values as long as the monitor exists. The procedures implement the operations on the resource. As usual, these procedures may have formal parameters and local variables.

A monitor has three properties that are a consequence of its being an abstract data type. First, only the procedure names are visible outside the monitor—they provide the only gates through the monitor wall. Thus, to alter the resource state represented by the permanent variables, a process must call one of the monitor procedures. Syntactically, monitor calls have the form:

call *Mname.op$_i$*(arguments)

where *op$_i$* is one of the procedures in *Mname.* The second property is that the procedures within a monitor may access only the permanent variables and their parameters and local variables. They may not access variables declared outside the monitor. Third, permanent variables are initialized before any procedure body is executed.

One of the attractive attributes of a monitor—or any abstract data type—is that it can be developed in relative isolation. As a consequence, however, the programmer of a monitor cannot know *a priori* the order in which the monitor's procedures might be called. As usual, whenever execution order is indeterminate, it is incumbent upon the programmer to define an invariant. Here the invariant is a *monitor invariant* that specifies the "reasonable" states of the permanent variables when no process is accessing them. The initialization code in a monitor must establish the invariant. Each procedure must maintain it. (Axioms and inference rules for monitors are described in Section 6.2.)

What distinguishes a monitor from a data abstraction mechanism in a sequential programming language is that a monitor is shared by concurrently executing processes. Thus, processes executing in monitors may require mutual exclusion—to avoid interference—and may require condition synchronization—to delay until the monitor state is conducive to continued execution. We now turn attention to how processes synchronize within monitors.

Synchronization in Monitors

Monitor synchronization could be provided in several ways. Here, we describe an attractive, reasonably widely used method that is employed in the Mesa and Turing Plus languages and in the UNIX operating system. In Section 6.5, we examine and compare alternative methods.

Synchronization is easiest to understand and hence to program if mutual exclusion and condition synchronization are provided in different ways. It is best if mutual exclusion is implicitly provided since this precludes interference. By contrast, condition synchronization must be explicitly programmed since different programs require different synchronization conditions. Although it is easiest to synchronize by means of boolean conditions as in **region** statements, lower-level mechanisms can be implemented much more efficiently. They also provide the programmer with finer control over execution order, which aids in solving allocation and scheduling problems.

Based on these considerations, mutual exclusion in monitors is implicitly provided and condition synchronization is explicitly programmed using mechanisms called condition variables. In particular, at most one process at a time may be executing within any procedure in a monitor. Two processes may, however, execute concurrently outside monitors or in different monitors. Because execution within a monitor is mutually exclusive, processes cannot interfere with each other when accessing permanent monitor variables.

A *condition variable* is used to delay a process that cannot safely continue executing until the monitor's state satisfies some boolean condition. It is also used to awaken a delayed process when the condition becomes true. The declaration of a condition variable has the form:

var c : **cond**

An array of condition variables is declared in the usual way by appending range information to the variable's name. The value of c is a queue of delayed processes, but this value is not directly visible to the programmer. The boolean delay condition is implicitly associated with the condition variable by the programmer; we will follow the convention of specifying it in a comment attached to the variable's declaration. Since condition variables are used to synchronize access to permanent variables in a monitor, they may be declared and used only within monitors.

To delay on condition variable c, a process executes:

wait(c)

Execution of **wait** causes the executing process to delay at the rear of c's queue. So that some other process can eventually enter the monitor to awaken the delayed process, execution of **wait** also causes the process to relinquish exclusive access to the monitor. (If a process executing in one monitor calls a procedure in a second monitor and then waits in that procedure, it releases exclusion only in the second monitor. The process retains exclusive control of the first monitor. Section 6.5 contains further discussion of this topic of nested monitor calls.)

Processes delayed on condition variables are awakened by means of **signal** statements. If c's delay queue is not empty, execution of

signal(c)

awakens the process at the front of the delay queue and removes it from the queue. That process executes at some future time when it can reacquire exclusive access to the monitor. If c's delay queue is empty, execution of **signal** has no effect; i.e., it is equivalent to **skip.** Independent of whether a delayed process is awakened, the process executing **signal** retains exclusive

monitor *Bounded_Buffer*

    var *buf*[1:*n*] : *T*   # for some type *T*
    var *front* := 1, *rear* := 1, *count* := 0
    var *not_full* : **cond**   # signaled when *count* < *n*
    var *not_empty* : **cond**   # signaled when *count* > 0
    { *BUFFER*: $1 \le front \le n \wedge 1 \le rear \le n \wedge 0 \le count \le n \wedge$
                $rear = (front + count - 1) \bmod n + 1 \wedge$
                count slots in the circular queue beginning at *buf*[*front*]
                    contain the most recently deposited items in the order
                    in which they were deposited }

  procedure *deposit*(*data* : *T*)
    do *count* = *n* → **wait**(*not_full*) **od**
    buf[*rear*] := *data*; *rear* := (*rear* **mod** *n*) + 1; *count* := *count* + 1
    signal(*not_empty*)
  end

  procedure *fetch*(**var** *result* : *T*)
    do *count* = 0 → **wait**(*not_empty*) **od**
    result := *buf*[*front*]; *front* := (*front* **mod** *n*) + 1; *count* := *count* − 1
    signal(*not_full*)
  end

end

Figure 6.1. Monitor implementation of a bounded buffer.

---

control of the monitor; thus it can continue executing. For this reason, **signal** is said to have *signal-and-continue* semantics. (Section 6.5 discusses alternative signaling semantics.)

The **wait** and **signal** operations on condition variables are similar to the **P** and **V** operations on semaphores: **wait**, like **P**, delays a process; and **signal**, like **V**, awakens a process. However, there are three important differences. First, **signal** has no effect if no process is delayed on the condition variable; the fact that it was executed is not remembered. Second, **wait** always delays a process until a later **signal** is executed. Third, the process executing **signal** always executes (at least in the monitor) before a process awakened as a result of the **signal**. These differences cause condition synchronization to be programmed differently with condition variables than with semaphores.

Figure 6.1 illustrates how a monitor encapsulates shared variables and operations on them. It also illustrates how **wait** and **signal** are used. The monitor implements a bounded buffer having the specification given in Section 5.4. In particular, the monitor invariant is the same predicate,

BUFFER, that was earlier used as a resource invariant. The reader might find it instructive to compare this solution with the one in Figure 5.5.

In Figure 6.1, both **wait** statements are enclosed in loops. This is always a safe way to ensure that the desired condition is true before the permanent variables are accessed. Here it is necessary if there are multiple producers and consumers. When a process executes **signal**, it merely gives a hint that the signaled condition is now true. Because the signaler and possibly other processes may execute in the monitor before a process awakened by **signal**, the awaited condition may no longer be true when the awakened process resumes execution. For example, a producer could be delayed waiting for an empty slot, then a consumer could fetch a message and awaken the delayed producer. However, before the producer gets a turn to execute, another producer could enter *deposit* and fill the empty slot. An analogous situation could occur with consumers. Thus, in general it is necessary to recheck the delay condition.

The **signal** statements in *deposit* and *fetch* are executed unconditionally since in both cases the signaled condition is true at the point of the **signal.** In fact, as long as **wait** statements are enclosed in loops that recheck the awaited condition, **signal** statements can be executed *at any time* since they merely give hints to delayed processes. A program will execute more efficiently, however, if **signal** is executed only if it is certain—or at least likely—that some delayed process could proceed. In short, it is usually safe to execute **signal** more often than necessary, as long as it is executed often enough to avoid deadlock and unnecessary delay.

Additional Operations on Condition Variables

A few additional operations on condition variables are useful. All have simple semantics and can be implemented efficiently since they merely provide additional operations on the queue associated with a condition variable.

To determine whether at least one process is delayed on condition variable c, a process in a monitor can invoke the boolean-valued function:

> **empty**(c)

This function is true if the delay queue is empty; otherwise, it is false.

With **wait** and **signal** as defined, delayed processes are awakened in the order in which they delayed; i.e., the delay queue is a first-in, first-out (FIFO) queue. The *priority* **wait** statement allows the programmer to exert more control over the order in which delayed processes are queued, and hence awakened. This statement has the form:

> **wait**(c, *rank*)

monitor *Shortest_Job_Next*

> **var** *free* := true
> **var** *turn* : **cond**   # signaled when resource available
> { *SJN*: *turn* is ordered by *time* ∧ *free* ⇒ *turn* is empty }
> **procedure** *request*(*time* : **int**)
> > **if** *free* → *free* := false [] **not** *free* → **wait**(*turn*, *time*) **fi**
> **end**
> **procedure** *release*( )
> > **if** **empty**(*turn*) → *free* := true [] **not** **empty**(*turn*) → **signal**(*turn*) **fi**
> **end**

end

Figure 6.2. Shortest-job-next allocation with monitors.

Here, *c* is a condition variable and *rank* is an integer-valued expression. Processes delayed on *c* are awakened in ascending order of *rank*; the process delayed the longest is awakened in the case of a tie. To avoid potential confusion resulting from using both regular and priority **wait** on the same condition variable, we shall always use one kind of **wait** or the other.

Using **empty** and priority **wait**, it is straightforward to implement a monitor that provides shortest-job-next allocation for a single unit resource, as shown in Figure 6.2. That monitor has two operations: *request* and *release*. When a process calls *request*, it delays until the resource is free or is allocated to it. After acquiring and using the resource, a process calls *release*. The resource is then allocated to the requesting process that will use it the shortest length of time; if there are no pending requests, the resource is freed.

In Figure 6.2, priority **wait** is used to order delayed processes by the amount of time they will use the resource; **empty** is used to determine if there are delayed processes. When the resource is released, if there are delayed processes, the one with minimal rank is awakened; otherwise, the resource is marked as being free. In this case the **wait** statement is not placed in a loop since the decision as to when a delayed process can proceed is best made by the process releasing the resource.

With priority **wait**, it is sometimes useful to be able to determine the rank of the process at the front of a delay queue, i.e., the value of the minimum delay rank. Assuming the delay queue associated with *c* is not empty and all **wait** statements that reference *c* are priority **wait** statements,

minrank(*c*)

is an integer-valued function that returns the minimum delay rank. If the

wait(c)	wait at end of queue
wait(c, *rank*)	wait in order of increasing value of rank
signal(c)	awaken process at front of queue then continue
signal_all(c)	awaken all processes on queue then continue
empty(c)	true if wait queue is empty; false otherwise
minrank(c)	value of rank of process at front of wait queue

Figure 6.3. Operations on condition variables.

---

delay queue is empty, **minrank** returns some arbitrary integer value.

Broadcast **signal** is the final operation on condition variables. It is used if more than one delayed process could possibly proceed or if the signaler does not know which delayed processes might be able to proceed (because they themselves need to recheck delay conditions). This operation has the form:

signal_all(c)

Execution of **signal_all** awakens all processes delayed on c. In particular, its effect is the same as executing:

do not empty(c) → **signal**(c) **od**

Each awakened process resumes execution in the monitor at some time in the future, subject to the usual mutual exclusion constraint. Like **signal**, **signal_all** has no effect if no process is delayed on c. Also, the signaling process continues execution in the monitor.

As long as all **wait** statements that name a condition variable are enclosed in loops that recheck the awaited condition, **signal_all** can be used in place of **signal.** Because awakened processes execute with mutual exclusion and recheck their delay conditions, ones that find the condition no longer true simply go back to sleep. For example, **signal_all** could be used in place of **signal** in the *Bounded_Buffer* monitor given earlier in Figure 6.1. In this case, however, it is more efficient simply to use **signal** since at most one awakened process could proceed; any others will need to go back to sleep. Other examples in which **signal_all** is quite useful are given later.

For reference, Figure 6.3 summarizes the six different operations on condition variables.

6.2 Formal Semantics and Program Proofs

A concurrent program employing monitors will contain both processes and monitors. To develop a formal proof of such a program, we need to develop proofs for each process and each monitor and then tie the separate proofs together. Process proofs are developed as before. Monitor proofs are developed by employing axioms and inference rules for the various monitor mechanisms. The separate proofs are tied together by using an inference rule for procedure call.

This section presents axioms and inference rules for monitors and procedure calls. We then describe how to prove safety properties, such as absence of deadlock, and also discuss liveness properties. Finally, we illustrate the various concepts by presenting an algorithm and proof for a monitor-based solution to the readers/writers problem.

Axioms and Proof Obligations

As noted in Section 6.1, the programmer of a monitor cannot know *a priori* the order in which the monitor's procedures might be called. Hence the key to developing a proof of a monitor is to specify a monitor invariant that is true when no process is accessing the monitor's permanent variables. The statements that initialize the permanent variables must establish the monitor invariant. Assuming that the invariant is true when a procedure begins execution, the procedure must reestablish the invariant before returning. In addition, a monitor procedure can delay by executing **wait**. Since exclusion is released when a process delays, the monitor invariant must also be true at all delay points.

Let *MI* be the invariant for a monitor having the general form shown in (6.1). To establish that *MI* is true after initialization, we need to show that the following triple is a theorem:

(6.2)   { true } initialization { *MI* }

The initialization code includes any assignments statements in the declarations of permanent variables.

For each procedure op_i, we assume that *MI* is true when the procedure is called. In addition, the procedure might require that initial values of value and value/result parameters satisfy some predicate *IN*. When the procedure terminates, the result and value/result parameters might then satisfy some potentially different predicate *OUT*. Thus, the proof obligation for each monitor procedure op_i is to show that the following triple is a theorem:

(6.3)   { *IN* ∧ *MI* } body of op_i { *OUT* ∧ *MI* }

The body of a monitor procedure will in general use condition variables to block and awaken processes. Thus to prove that triples like (6.3) are theorems, we need axioms for the four **wait** and **signal** operations given in Figure 6.2. (The **empty** and **minrank** operations are functions that simply return a value without causing side-effects.)

The axioms given below deal with the *visible* program state as recorded in program variables and possibly auxiliary variables. They do not take into account the queue manipulation that results from **wait** and **signal** operations and hence the order in which delayed processes are awakened. With these axioms, auxiliary variables would have to be used to simulate the contents of delay queues. Alternatively, it is possible to devise more powerful axioms. (See the References and Exercises).

Execution of **wait**(c) causes the executing process to release exclusive control of the monitor and then to delay. Because exclusion is released, the delaying process must ensure that the monitor invariant MI is true when **wait** is executed. After the process is awakened, it can assume that MI is again true since all other processes will either be executing outside the monitor, delayed waiting to enter, or delayed on a condition variable. The values of some of the permanent variables will no doubt have changed, but the permanent variables as a group will still satisfy MI. These considerations lead to the following axiom for **wait**:

(6.4)   **Wait Axiom**: $\{ L \wedge MI \}$ **wait**(*cond*) $\{ L \wedge MI \}$

Here L is an assertion that references only the formal parameters or local variables of the procedure containing **wait**. Thus, L characterizes the private state (within the monitor) of the executing process while it is delayed.

With respect to visible program variables, the priority wait statement has the same effect as **wait**. The difference between the two kinds of **wait** is the order in which delayed processes are queued and hence the order in which they will be awakened. This can affect liveness properties such as individual starvation. For example, with priority wait, some process might delay forever if there is always a higher-priority process waiting whenever a **signal** is executed.

Delayed processes are awakened as a result of execution of **signal** or **signal_all**. Recall that **signal**(c) awakens one process delayed on condition variable c; if there is none, **signal** is equivalent to **skip**. In either case, the signaling process continues executing in the monitor (although it may be about to return). Also, no program variable changes as a result of executing **signal**. Thus, **signal** has the same axiom as **skip**:

(6.5)   **Signal Axiom**: $\{ P \}$ **signal**(c) $\{ P \}$

If **signal** is the last statement executed in a monitor procedure, then P must imply that the monitor invariant is true.

Broadcast signal—**signal_all**(*c*)—awakens zero or more processes, depending on how many are delayed on *c*. Like **signal**, it does not change any program variables. Hence **signal_all** has the same axiom as (6.5).

To summarize, developing a proof of a monitor requires meeting two proof obligations: first showing that initialization code establishes the monitor invariant *MI* (6.2) and then showing that each procedure body in the monitor satisfies a theorem of form (6.3). Developing proofs of procedure bodies in general requires applying the axioms for **wait** (6.4) and **signal** (6.5). A simple example will help illustrate these concepts.

Consider the problem of using a monitor to implement a general semaphore.* Let *s* be an integer that records the value of the semaphore and let *P* and *V* be procedures that implement the **P** and **V** operations on the semaphore. As usual, *P* and *V* must preserve the semaphore invariant $s \geq 0$, which in this case serves as a monitor invariant; hence *P* must delay until *s* is positive. One implementation of such a monitor follows:

(6.6)   **monitor** *Semaphore*   # Invariant *SEM*: $s \geq 0$
       var *s* := 0, *pos* : **cond**   # *pos* is signaled when $s > 0$
       procedure *P*( ) **do** $s = 0 \rightarrow$ **wait**(*pos*) **od**; $s := s - 1$ **end**
       procedure *V*( ) $s := s + 1$; **signal**(*pos*) **end**
   end

The **do** loop in *P* ensures that *s* is positive before it is decremented. The **signal** in *V* awakens one delayed process, if there is one.

The only initialization code in *Semaphore* is within the declaration of *s*. This satisfies proof obligation (6.2) since the following is clearly a theorem in programming logic *PL*:

$$\{\text{ true }\}\ s := 0\ \{\ SEM\ \}$$

Next consider procedure *P*. Since there are no arguments, nothing needs to be asserted about their values. Hence we need to show that

$$\{\ SEM\ \}\ \text{body of } P\ \{\ SEM\ \}$$

is a theorem. It is since the following is a valid proof outline:

---

*Later we show how to implement monitors using semaphores. Hence the two mechanisms are equally powerful, in the sense that they can solve the same synchronization problems. They differ in the ways discussed at the start of this chapter.

$$\{\,\text{SEM}\,\}$$
$$\textbf{do}\ s = 0 \rightarrow \{\text{SEM} \land s = 0\,\}\ \{\,SEM\,\}\ \textbf{wait}(pos)\ \{\,SEM\,\}\ \textbf{od}$$
$$\{\,SEM \land s \neq 0\,\}$$
$$s := s - 1$$
$$\{\,SEM\,\}$$

Here *SEM* serves as the loop invariant as well as the monitor invariant. (The monitor invariant will always be part of the loop invariant for any delay loop at the start of a monitor.)

The remaining proof obligation for monitor *Semaphore* is to show that procedure *V* satisfies (6.3). As with *P* there are no parameters, so there is no local assertion *L*. Thus, we need to show that

$$\{\,SEM\,\}\ \text{body of}\ V\ \{\,SEM\,\}$$

is a theorem. It is since the following is a valid proof outline:

$$\{\,SEM\,\}\ s := s + 1\ \{\,s > 0\,\}\ \textbf{signal}(pos)\ \{\,s > 0\,\}\ \{\,SEM\,\}$$

A Procedure Call Inference Rule

Proofs—or proof outlines—of monitors can be developed in relative isolation. A monitor invariant is ensured solely by the monitor since permanent variables cannot be referenced except by calling a monitor procedure. The only two parts of the proof of a monitor that depend on its use are the parts, *IN* and *OUT*, of the preconditions and postconditions of procedure bodies that make assertions about the formal parameters. These requirements must be met by processes that call the monitor's procedures.

This section presents an inference rule for the procedure **call** statement. The rule is not complete since we make some simplifying assumptions—such as no aliasing—that might not hold in general. However, the rule is sufficient for most programs and illustrates the general principles. (See the Historical Notes for a discussion of procedure call rules and citations to relevant work.)

Recall that each monitor procedure *op* must satisfy a theorem of form (6.3):

$$\{\,IN \land MI\,\}\ \text{body of}\ op\ \{\,OUT \land MI\,\}$$

As before, *IN* is a predicate specifying initial requirements on the value parameters, *MI* is the monitor invariant, and *OUT* is a predicate specifying the final values of result parameters. Let *x*, *y*, and *z* be vectors of value, value/result, and result formals, respectively. For notational convenience, we assume that all value parameters appear first in the procedure heading, followed by the value/result parameters, then the result parameters. Now consider a call of *op*:

(6.7)   **call** *op*(*a*, *b*, *c*)

Here *a*, *b*, and *c* are vectors of value, value/result, and result arguments, respectively. Recall from the definition of procedures and the **call** statement in Section 1.1 that the value/result and result arguments must be variables, not expressions, since they will be assigned to when the **call** terminates.

What we desire is an inference rule that allows us to make a conclusion about the effect of executing (6.7). Below we will use the term *value arguments* (formals) to refer to both the value and value/result arguments (formals). Similarly, we will use *result arguments* (formals) to refer to both the value/result and result arguments (formals).

Execution of (6.7) causes three things to happen. First, value arguments *a* and *b* are evaluated and assigned to the corresponding formals *x* and *y*. Second, the procedure body is executed. Finally, when the procedure terminates, result formals *y* and *z* are copied back into the corresponding arguments *b* and *c*.

In a procedure declaration, value formals are required to be distinct. If a procedure body assumes that value formals initially satisfy predicate *IN*, the effect of evaluating the value arguments and assigning them to the value formals is captured by simultaneous substitution (1.4) into *IN*:

(6.8) $IN \, {}^{x,\,y}_{a,\,b}$

This must be true at the start of execution of **call**; i.e., it must be true in the precondition. Similarly, when the procedure returns, the result formals will satisfy *OUT*, and the values of these formals are copied into the corresponding arguments. Outside the procedure, the result formals are simply renamed to use the result arguments. If the result arguments are distinct identifiers—i.e., there is no parameter aliasing—the effect of this renaming is also captured by simultaneous substitution:

(6.9) $OUT \, {}^{y,\,z}_{b,\,c}$

This predicate will be true in the postcondition of a **call**.

When the body of *op* is executing, no variables local to the calling process will change value except for those passed as result arguments. Let *PR* be a predicate that specifies the state of the calling process at the time of a **call** of *op*. Further, assume that *PR* does not contain references to the result arguments or to any variable changed by the body of *op*. In the case of a monitor procedure, the second assumption means that *PR* does not reference permanent monitor variables or auxiliary variables that might be changed by *op*. With these assumptions, *PR* will remain true throughout execution of *op*. In particular, it will be true when *op* returns.

Putting these pieces together, if the state of a process satisfies *PR* and (6.8) before execution of **call**, then when the **call** terminates, the process's state will satisfy *PR* and (6.9). This will be true if the stated assumptions are met. These assumptions become hypotheses, and we get the following inference rule for the **call** statement:

(6.10)   **Call Rule:** $\{\,IN\,\}$ body of *op* $\{\,OUT\,\}$
   IN references value formals only
   OUT references result formals only
   result arguments *b* and *c* are distinct identifiers
   PR does not reference result arguments or any
      variable changed by the body of *op*

$$\{\,PR \wedge IN\,_{a,\,b}^{x,\,y}\,\}\ \ \textbf{call}\ op(\,a,\,b,\,c\,)\ \{\,PR \wedge OUT\,_{b,\,c}^{y,\,z}\,\}$$

A simple example will illustrate the use of (6.10). Consider the following procedure, which swaps the values of its two value/result arguments:

(6.11)   **procedure** *swap*(**var** *x, y* : **int**)
      $\{\,x = \mathrm{X} \wedge y = \mathrm{Y}\,\}$
      $x :=: y$
      $\{\,x = \mathrm{Y} \wedge y = \mathrm{X}\,\}$
   end

In the pre- and postconditions, X and Y are logical variables that stand for any fixed values of *x* and *y*. The pre- and postconditions are related by application of the axiom for the swap statement (1.12).

Now suppose a process calls *swap*(*a, b*) in a state in which *a* is 1, *b* is 2, and *c* is 3. Then applying (6.10), the following theorem will be true:

$\{\,a = 1 \wedge b = 2 \wedge c = 3\,\}$
call *swap*(*a, b*)
$\{\,a = 2 \wedge b = 1 \wedge c = 3\,\}$

Here *PR* in (6.10) is the predicate *c* = 3. The relation between the initial and final values of *a* and *b* follows from substituting into and out of the pre- and postconditions of (6.11), with logical variable X standing for 1 and logical variable Y standing for 2. As required by (6.10), the arguments *a* and *b* are distinct identifiers and are not referenced in *PR*.

Safety and Liveness Properties

When monitors are used for communication and synchronization, the inference rule for a **co** statement is similar to the inference rule for conditional critical regions (5.2). This is because the permanent variables in a monitor can be accessed only within that monitor, just as the permanent variables in a resource can be accessed only within **region** statements. Also, monitors preclude interference, as long as assertions within processes do not reference variables changed in other processes. This is because monitors then provide the only means to access shared variables, and monitor procedures execute with mutual exclusion.

Suppose a concurrent program contains m monitors, with associated invariants MI_1, ..., MI_m. Assume processes interact only by means of monitors. Also assume that all shared variables belong to monitors and hence are accessed only by monitor procedures. Then the semantics of concurrent execution are specified by the following inference rule:

(6.12)   **Monitors Rule:**

$$\{ P_i \} \ S_i \ \{ Q_i \}, 1 \le i \le n$$
no variable free in P_i or Q_i is changed in $S_j, i \ne j$
all variables in MI_k are local to monitor m_k

$$\frac{}{\begin{array}{l} \{ MI_1 \wedge ... \wedge MI_m \wedge P_1 \wedge ... \wedge P_n \} \\ \textbf{co } S_1 \ /\!/ \ ... \ /\!/ \ S_n \ \textbf{oc} \\ \{ MI_1 \wedge ... \wedge MI_m \wedge Q_1 \wedge ... \wedge Q_n \} \end{array}}$$

This inference rule requires that the monitor invariants are initially true. Then—as a result of proof obligations (6.3) for monitor procedures—the monitor invariants will always be true, except perhaps when a process is executing within a monitor procedure. Since monitor procedures are mutually exclusive by definition, monitor invariants cannot be interfered with. Moreover, assertions in processes are not permitted to reference variables changed by other processes. Hence, processes cannot interfere.

To prove safety properties such as mutual exclusion and absence of deadlock, we can use a variation on the method of Exclusion of Configurations (2.25). As with CCRs, the variation again results from the fact that monitor invariants cannot appear directly in proofs of individual processes. However, they are true whenever no process is executing a monitor procedure. Moreover, if a process is executing a monitor procedure, there was a program state in which either the process had not yet entered the procedure or it was waiting on a condition variable; in either case, the associated monitor invariant was true. This leads to the following sufficient condition for mutual exclusion of statements in two different processes.

(6.13)   **Mutual Exclusion for Monitors.** Let S_1 and S_2 be statements in different processes in a concurrent program, and assume neither S_1 nor S_2 is within a monitor. Let $pre(S_1)$ and $pre(S_2)$ be the corresponding preconditions in a proof of the program. Let MI_1, ..., MI_m be the the monitor invariants in the proof, and assume the initial state $P_1 \wedge ... \wedge P_n$ is true when execution of the program begins. Then S_1 and S_2 are mutually exclusive if:

$$pre(S_1) \wedge pre(S_2) \wedge MI_1 \wedge ... \wedge MI_m = \text{false}$$

This condition is nearly identical to the corresponding one for CCRs (5.3).

We can prove absence of deadlock in a similar way. Since a program is deadlocked only if *no* process can proceed, the states of all processes have to be considered. A program employing monitors is deadlocked if every process has terminated or is blocked, and at least one process is blocked. If a process i has terminated, its postcondition Q_i is true. Assuming that procedures in monitors do not call other monitors—i.e., that there are no nested monitor calls—a process is blocked only if it is delayed at a **wait** statement in some monitor. Hence the precondition of that **wait** statement is true. Finally, if all processes are blocked or terminated, no monitor procedures are being executed, so all monitor invariants are true. These observations yield the following sufficient condition for absence of deadlock.

(6.14)   **Absence of Deadlock for Monitors.** Assume that a concurrent program contains one **co** statement and that monitor procedures do not call procedures in other monitors. Let MI_1, ..., MI_m be the the monitor invariants in a proof of the program, and assume that the initial state $P_1 \wedge ... \wedge P_n$ of the program is true when execution begins. Let D_1 be a predicate that characterizes the state in which every process has terminated or is blocked. Let D_2 be a predicate that characterizes the state in which at least one process is blocked. Then the program is deadlock-free if:

$$D_1 \wedge D_2 \wedge MI_1 \wedge ... \wedge MI_m = \text{false}$$

Again, this condition is similar to the corresponding one for CCRs (5.4). It too can be generalized to allow nested **co** statements and nested monitor calls.

As usual, a concurrent program will terminate as long as each process terminates. This will be the case if the program is deadlock-free and if the sequential statements in each process terminate. For programs that employ monitors, other liveness properties such as absence of individual starvation depend on how entry into monitor procedures is scheduled, on the execution of adequate numbers of **signal** statements, and on the effect of priority wait statements.

A process is eligible to execute within a monitor procedure when it calls such a procedure or when it is signaled after waiting on a condition variable. (Of course, execution must be mutually exclusive, but this does not affect when a process is eligible to execute.) Assuming monitor procedures all terminate, then a process waiting to execute in a monitor will eventually be able to do so if scheduling is unconditionally fair. Thus eventual entry into a monitor depends on the underlying scheduling policy.

On the other hand, eventual wakeup after waiting on a condition variable depends on the actions of the program itself. If a program employs priority wait, it is possible that a process might block forever, even if the program does not deadlock. Also, if a program places **wait** statements in loops that recheck delay conditions, a process might never find its delay condition true if some other process always "beats it to the punch." All an underlying scheduling policy can do is ensure that the process gets a chance to recheck the condition. Only the programmer can ensure that it is eventually seen to be true. (Later examples will show how to ensure that an awakened process sees that its delay condition is true.)

An Example: Readers and Writers

This section presents a solution to the readers/writers problem using monitors and then uses the solution to illustrate how to prove program properties with monitors. Recall that, in the readers/writers problem, reader processes query a database and writer processes examine and alter it. Readers may access the database concurrently, but writers require exclusive access.

Although the database is shared, we cannot encapsulate it by a monitor because then readers could not access the database concurrently. Instead, we use a monitor merely to arbitrate access to the database. The database itself is global to the readers and writers—e.g., it is stored in an external file. As we shall see, this same basic structure is often employed in monitor-based programs.

For the readers/writers problem, the arbitration monitor grants permission to access the database. To do so, it requires that processes inform it when they desire access and when they have finished access. Since there are two kinds of processes and two actions per process, the monitor has four procedures: *request_read*, *release_read*, *request_write*, and *release_write*. These procedures are used in the obvious ways. For example, a reader calls *request_read* before reading the database and calls *release_read* after reading the database.

To synchronize access to the database, we need to record how many processes are reading and how many are writing. Thus, as before, let nr be the number of readers, and let nw be the number of writers. These are the permanent variables of the monitor. For proper synchronization, these

monitor *RW_Controller*   # Invariant *RW*

   var *nr* := 0, *nw* := 0
   var *oktoread* : **cond**   # signaled when *nw* = 0
   var *oktowrite* : **cond**   # signaled when *nr* = 0 ∧ *nw* = 0
   procedure *request_read*( )
     do *nw* > 0 → **wait**(*oktoread*) **od**
     nr:= *nr* + 1
   end
   procedure *release_read*( )
     nr:= *nr* − 1
     if *nr* = 0 → **signal**(*oktowrite*) **fi**
   end
   procedure *request_write*( )
     do *nr* > 0 ∨ *nw* > 0 → **wait**(*oktowrite*) **od**
     nw := *nw* + 1
   end
   procedure *release_write*( )
     nw := *nw* − 1
     signal(*oktowrite*)
     signal_all(*oktoread*)
   end
end

Figure 6.4. Readers/writers solution using monitors.

---

variables must satisfy the monitor invariant:

$$RW: \ (nr = 0 \lor nw = 0 \ ) \land nw \leq 1$$

Initially, both *nr* and *nw* are 0. Each variable is incremented in the appropriate request procedure and decremented in the appropriate release procedure.

Figure 6.4 contains a monitor that meets this specification. Condition variables and **wait** and **signal** statements are used to ensure that *RW* is invariant. At the start of *request_read*, a reader process needs to delay until *nw* is not zero. Let *oktoread* be the condition variable on which readers delay. Similarly, writers need to delay at the start of *request_write* until both *nr* and *nw* are zero. Let *oktowrite* be the condition variable on which they delay. When *nr* becomes zero in *release_read*, one delayed writer can proceed, if there is one. We awaken a delayed writer by signaling *oktowrite*. When *nw* becomes zero in *release_write*, either one delayed writer or all delayed readers can proceed. We awaken a delayed writer by signaling *oktowrite*; we awaken all delayed readers by a broadcast signal of *oktoread*.

In Figure 6.4, writers are signaled in *release_read* only if *nr* is zero. Since writers recheck their delay condition, the solution would still be correct if writers were always signaled. However, the solution would then be less efficient since a signaled writer would have to go right back to sleep if *nr* were zero. On the other hand, at the end of *release_write*, it is known that both *nr* and *nw* are zero. Hence any delayed process could proceed. The solution in Figure 6.4 does not arbitrate between readers and writers. Instead it awakens all delayed processes and lets the underlying scheduling policy determine which executes first and hence which gets to access the database.

We now show how to prove formally that the monitor in Figure 6.4 provides the required exclusion and ensures absence of deadlock. To prove these properties, we need to use auxiliary variables to keep track of the various execution stages of each process. Let $read[i]$ be 1 when *Reader[i]* is reading, and 0 otherwise. Similarly, let $write[j]$ indicate whether *Writer[j]* is writing. These variables are set in request procedures in the monitor and cleared in release procedures. In order to include assertions in the proof of each process about the value of its auxiliary variable, that variable is passed as a value/result parameter to the monitor procedures. We also need to relate the values of monitor variables *nr* and *nw* to the sums of the $read[i]$ and $write[j]$. In particular, we require the invariance of:

$$AV: \ nr = read[1] + ... + read[m] \wedge nw = write[1] + ... + write[n]$$

This assertion is conjoined to the previous monitor invariant *RW*.

Proof outlines for the reader and writer processes and the monitor are given in Figure 6.5. Using these proof outlines, the mutual exclusion and absence of deadlock properties follow directly from application of (6.13) and (6.14). For example, a reader i and a writer j cannot simultaneously access the database since:

$$(read[i] = 1 \wedge write[j] = 1 \wedge RW \wedge AV) = false$$

Similarly, two writers j and k have mutually exclusive access to the database since:

$$(write[j] = 1 \wedge write[k] = 1 \wedge j \neq k \wedge RW \wedge AV) = false$$

We can prove absence of deadlock in a similar way. Since the processes in Figure 6.4 execute permanent loops, the program will be in a deadlock state only if all processes are blocked. Hence we need to come up with a predicate that characterizes this state. If reader process i is blocked, it is delayed at

var *read*[1:*m*] := ([*m*] 0), *write*[1:*n*] := ([*n*] 0)   # auxiliary variables

Reader[*i*: 1..*m*]:: **do** true →
                         { *read*[*i*] = 0 }
                         RW_Controller.request_read(read[*i*])
                         { *read*[*i*] = 1 }
                         read the database
                         RW_Controller.release_read(read[*i*])
          od

Writer[*j*: 1..*n*]:: **do** true →
                         { *write*[*j*] = 0 }
                         RW_Controller.request_write(write[*j*])
                         { *write*[*j*] = 1 }
                         write the database
                         RW_Controller.release_write(write[*j*])
          od

Figure 6.5 (b). Proof outlines of reader and writer processes.

---

the **wait** statement in *request_read*. Hence the precondition of that
statement is true. This precondition includes the value of formal parameter
reader as well as monitor invariants *RW* and *AV*. In particular, *reader* is 0 at
this point, so *read*[*i*] is also 0. Similarly, if writer process *j* is blocked, it is
delayed at the **wait** statement in *request_write*; in this case *writer* is 0, so
write[*j*] is also 0. If all processes are blocked, all *read*[*i*] and *write*[*j*] are 0 and
RW and *AV* are true. So far we have determined the following:

$$((\forall i: 1 \leq i \leq m: \ read[i] = 0) \land$$
$$(\forall j: 1 \leq j \leq n: \ write[j] = 0) \land RW \land AV) \ = \ (nr = 0 \land nw = 0)$$

But if the program is deadlocked, *some* process had to be the last one to block.
If it was a reader, then $nw > 0$ when the process blocked; if it was a writer,
then either $nr > 0$ or $nw > 0$. This, together with the above predicate, yields a
contradiction. Hence, the solution is deadlock-free.

The above analysis reveals a curious fact about monitors: Nowhere did we
consider whether **signal** statements were executed. In fact, the program in
Figure 6.5 will not have global deadlock, even if all **signal** statements are
deleted!* This will not be the case in all monitors, but **signal** statements

---

*From *RW*, at least one of *nr* or *nw* would always be zero. Hence either readers or writers
would always be able to proceed, assuming as usual that code that accesses the database terminates.

monitor *RW_Controller*   # Invariant $RW \wedge AV$

   var $nr := 0$, $nw := 0$
   var *oktoread* : **cond**   # signaled when $nw = 0$
   var *oktowrite* : **cond**   # signaled when $nr = 0 \wedge nw = 0$

   procedure *request_read*(**var** *reader* : **int**) $\{ RW \wedge AV \wedge reader = 0 \}$
     do $nw > 0 \rightarrow$ **wait**(*oktoread*) **od**
     $nr := nr + 1$; *reader* := 1
   end $\{ RW \wedge AV \wedge reader = 1 \}$

   procedure *release_read*(**var** *reader* : **int**) $\{ RW \wedge AV \wedge reader = 1 \}$
     $nr := nr - 1$; *reader* := 0
     if $nr = 0 \rightarrow$ **signal**(*oktowrite*) **fi**
   end $\{ RW \wedge AV \wedge reader = 0 \}$

   procedure *request_write*(**var** *writer* : **int**) $\{ RW \wedge AV \wedge writer = 0 \}$
     do $nr > 0 \vee nw > 0 \rightarrow$ **wait**(*oktowrite*) **od**
     $nw := nw + 1$; *writer* := 1
   end $\{ RW \wedge AV \wedge writer = 1 \}$

   procedure *release_write*(**var** *writer* : **int**) $\{ RW \wedge AV \wedge writer = 1 \}$
     $nw := nw - 1$; *writer* := 0
     signal(*oktowrite*)
     signal_all(*oktoread*)
   end $\{ RW \wedge AV \wedge writer = 0 \}$

end

Figure 6.5 (a). Proof outline for readers/writers monitor.

---

mainly affect whether individual processes are able to proceed. This is the case for other explicit signaling mechanisms such as semaphores. In contrast, signaling is implicit in higher-level mechanisms such as CCRs; i.e., a process delayed at a **region** statement is guaranteed to be able to proceed if the resource is not in use and the boolean guard is true. As observed earlier, explicit signaling mechanisms are more efficient to implement; however, they require that the programmer take greater care.

6.3 Synchronization Techniques

In this section, we develop monitor-based solutions to three synchronization problems. In doing so, we will illustrate several different programming techniques. The derivation method employs the same basic steps used for previous synchronization mechanisms: define the problem and the structure of a solution, annotate the solution, guard assignments, and implement the resulting solution using monitor mechanisms. However, each step is realized in a slightly different way due to the unique characteristics of monitors.

Because monitors are an abstraction mechanism, the starting point in designing a monitor is to define the abstract resource it implements. The best place to start is with the monitor procedures. In particular, first define the procedure names, their parameters, the pre- and postconditions of their bodies, and any assumptions about the order in which the procedures will be called by processes. Then, specify the permanent variables of the monitor and the associated monitor invariant. Finally, outline the procedure bodies and add initialization code so that the monitor invariant is initially true.

After outlining the procedure bodies, we next need to add condition synchronization when that is necessary to ensure the monitor invariant or to ensure the desired postcondition of a procedure. When developing a coarse-grained solution, we will use a variant of the **await** statement to specify condition synchronization. In particular, we will use **await** B, where B is a boolean condition. Execution of this form of **await** delays the executing process until B is true. While delayed, the process releases exclusive control of the monitor; hence the monitor invariant must be true when **await** B is executed. When the process continues, the monitor invariant will again be true, as will B. The axiom for **await** within monitors is thus:

(6.15)   **Await Axiom**: $\{\, L \wedge MI \,\}$ **await** B $\{\, L \wedge MI \wedge B \,\}$

As in the Wait Axiom (6.4), L is an assertion about parameters and local variables, and MI is the monitor invariant.

To complete the implementation of a monitor, we need to use condition variables to implement **await** statements. In general, we will use one condition variable for each different condition appearing in **await** statements. Let c_B be the condition variable associated with **await** B. Then, we will generally implement **await** B by the following loop:

> **do not** $B \rightarrow$ **wait**(c_B) **od**

As we shall see, however, sometimes we can represent related conditions by the same condition variable, and sometimes we can use priority **wait** to order delayed processes. Also, it is sometimes useful to implement **await** using an **if** statement rather than a **do** loop.

To awaken processes delayed on condition variables, we also need to add **signal** statements to procedure bodies. In particular, we add them after assignments to permanent variables whenever some delay condition could now be true and some process might be waiting for that condition. Failure to execute an adequate number of **signals** could result in permanent blocking of some processes. As noted earlier, execution of superfluous **signals** is harmless when **wait** statements are embedded in loops as shown above.

However, a program will execute more efficiently if **signal** statements are executed only when it is likely that waiting processes could proceed.

To summarize, the monitor-specific aspects of the general derivation method are the initial focus on the abstraction provided by a monitor, the use of **await** B to delay execution when necessary, and the use of condition variables to implement **await** statements. Although the experienced programmer will often add condition variables directly to the annotated procedure bodies, we will first guard assignments using **await** and then use condition variables to implement **await.** In this way, we focus first on the boolean conditions required for correct synchronization and then consider how to implement the synchronization efficiently using condition variables.

Interval Timer: Covering Conditions and Priority Wait

We now turn attention to a new problem: the design of an interval timer that makes it possible for processes to delay for a specified number of time units. Such a facility is often provided by operating systems to enable users to do such things as periodically execute utility commands.

Although a timer monitor is interesting in its own right, the derivation will illustrate three techniques that often arise in the design of monitors. First, we will see how the postcondition of a monitor procedure—and not just the monitor invariant—can lead to the need to delay a process. Second, we will introduce the concept of a covering condition variable. Finally, we will see when priority **wait** can be used to provide a compact, efficient delay mechanism.

A monitor that implements an interval timer is another example of a resource controller. In this case, the resource is a logical clock. Such a resource has two operations: *delay(interval)*, which delays the calling process for *interval* ticks of the clock, and *tick*, which increments the value of the logical clock. (Other operations might also be provided. For example, there might be operations to return the value of the clock or to delay a process until the clock has reached a specific value.)

We assume *interval* is non-negative. We also assume *tick* is called by a single process that is periodically awakened by a hardware timer. (Typically this process has a high execution priority, so the value of the logical clock remains fairly accurate.) Other processes may call *delay*. To represent the value of the logical clock, we use integer variable *tod* (time of day). Initially, *tod* is 0; it satisfies the simple invariant:

$$CLOCK: \ tod \geq 0 \land tod \text{ increases monotonically by } 1$$

Thus, we have the outline shown in Figure 6.6 for a monitor that implements an interval timer. In the assertions in the figure, TOD is a logical constant. The postcondition of *delay* requires only that *tod* be at least as large as

```
monitor Timer          # Invariant CLOCK
    var tod := 0
    procedure delay( interval : int )
        { interval ≥ 0 ∧ tod = TOD ∧ CLOCK }
        body of delay
        { tod ≥ TOD + interval ∧ CLOCK }
    end
    procedure tick( )
        { tod = TOD ∧ CLOCK }
        body of tick
        { tod = TOD + 1 ∧ CLOCK }
    end
end
```

Figure 6.6. Outline of an interval-timer monitor.

TOD + *interval*; we do not insist on exact equality since a delayed process might not execute before the high-priority process that calls *tick* has done so again.

To realize the postcondition of *delay* in Figure 6.6, a process that calls *delay* first needs to compute the desired wakeup time. This is accomplished in the obvious way by executing:

$$wake\_time := tod + interval$$

Here, *wake_time* is a variable local to the body of *delay*. Next the process waits until *tick* has been called often enough to make the postcondition true. This is accomplished by executing:

$$\textbf{await } wake\_time \leq tod$$

The body of the *tick* procedure is even simpler: it merely increments *tod*.

The remaining step is to implement the **await** statement in *delay* using condition variables. One approach is to employ one condition variable for each different condition. Here, each delayed process could be waiting for a different time, so each process would need a private condition variable. Before delaying, a process would record in permanent variables the time it wishes to be awakened. When *tick* is called, the permanent variables would be consulted, and, if some processes were due to be awakened, their private condition variables would be signaled. Although certainly feasible, and for some problems necessary, this approach is much more cumbersome and

```
monitor Timer        # Invariant CLOCK
   var tod := 0
   var check : cond       # signaled when tod has increased
   procedure delay( interval : int )
      var wake_time : int
      wake_time := tod + interval
      do wake_time > tod → wait(check) od
   end
   procedure tick( )
      tod := tod + 1
      signal_all(check)
   end
end
```

Figure 6.7. Interval timer with a covering condition.

---

inefficient than necessary for the *Timer* monitor.

A much simpler way to implement **await** in *Timer* is to employ a single *covering condition*. Such a condition variable is one for which the associated boolean condition "covers" the actual conditions for which different processes are waiting. When any of the covered conditions could be true, all processes delayed on the covering condition variable are awakened. Each such process rechecks its specific condition and either continues or waits again. In the *Timer* monitor, we can employ one covering condition variable, *check*, with associated boolean condition "*tod* has increased." Processes wait on *check* in the body of *delay*; every waiting process is awakened each time *tick* is called. In particular, we get the *Timer* monitor shown in Figure 6.7. In *tick*, a broadcast signal, **signal_all**, is used to awaken all delayed processes.

Although the solution in Figure 6.7 is compact and simple, it is not very efficient for this problem. Using a covering condition variable is appropriate only if the expected cost of false alarms—i.e., awakening a process that finds that its delay condition is false so immediately goes back to sleep—is lower than the cost of maintaining a record of the conditions of all waiting processes and only awakening a process when its condition is true. Often this is the case (see the exercises), but here it is likely that processes delay for relatively long intervals and hence would be needlessly awakened numerous times.

By using priority **wait**, we can transform the solution into one that is equally simple, yet highly efficient. In particular, priority **wait** can be used whenever there is a static order between the conditions for which different processes are waiting; i.e., one will become true before the other or both will become true at the same time. Here, waiting processes can be ordered by

```
monitor Timer        # Invariant CLOCK
    var tod := 0
    var check : cond        # signaled when minrank(check) ≤ tod
    procedure delay( interval : int )
        var wake_time : int
        wake_time := tod + interval
        if wake_time > tod → wait(check, wake_time) fi
    end
    procedure tick( )
        tod := tod + 1
        do not empty(check) and minrank(check) ≤ tod → signal(check) od
    end
end
```

Figure 6.8. Interval timer with priority wait.

their wakeup times. Then, when *tick* is called, **minrank** is used, so delayed processes are signaled exactly when their delay condition is true. Incorporating these refinements, we have the final version of the *Timer* monitor shown in Figure 6.8. A **do** loop is no longer needed in *delay* since *tick* ensures that a process is awakened only when its delay condition is true. However, the **signal** in *tick* is embedded in a loop since there may be more than one process waiting for the same *wake_time*.

To summarize, there are three basic ways to implement **await** B when B references variables local to the waiting process. The preferred choice—because it leads to compact, efficient solutions—is to use priority **wait**, as here or in the *Shortest_Job_Next* monitor given in Figure 6.2. This approach can be used whenever there is a static order between waiting conditions.

The second best choice, because it also leads to compact solutions, is to use a covering condition variable. This approach can be used whenever it is possible for waiting processes to recheck their own conditions; however, it cannot be used when waiting conditions depend on a function of the states of other waiting processes. Use of covering condition variables is appropriate as long as the cost of false alarms is less than the cost of maintaining in permanent variables exact records of waiting conditions.

The third choice is to record in permanent variables the waiting conditions of delayed processes and to employ private condition variables to awaken such processes when appropriate. This approach leads to more complex solutions but is required if neither of the other choices can be employed or if the second choice is not efficient enough. Examples of problems whose solutions employ the latter two choices are given in the exercises.

A Fair Semaphore: Passing the Condition

At times it is necessary to ensure that a process awakened by **signal** takes precedence over other processes that call a monitor procedure before the awakened process gets a chance to execute. This is done by passing a condition directly to an awakened process rather than making it globally visible. We illustrate the technique here by deriving a monitor that implements a fair semaphore: a semaphore in which processes are able to complete **P** operations in first-come, first-served order. (In fact, we used the same technique earlier in the *Shortest_Job_Next* monitor in Figure 6.2.)

Recall the *Semaphore* monitor given earlier in (6.6):

> **monitor** *Semaphore*　　# Invariant *SEM*: $s \geq 0$
> 　　**var** $s := 0$, *pos* : **cond**　　# *pos* is signaled when $s > 0$
> 　　**procedure** $P(\ )$　**do** $s = 0 \rightarrow$ **wait**(*pos*) **od**; $s := s - 1$　**end**
> 　　**procedure** $V(\ )$　$s := s + 1$; **signal**(*pos*)　**end**
> **end**

In this implementation of a semaphore, it may appear that processes are able to complete P in the order in which they called P. Condition variable queues are FIFO queues in the absence of priority **wait** statements. Consequently, delayed processes are certainly awakened in the order in which they waited. However, since **signal** is not preemptive, before an awakened process gets a chance to execute, some other process could call P, find $s > 0$, and thus complete P before the awakened process. In short, calls from outside the monitor can "steal" signaled conditions. (This cannot happen with preemptive signaling disciplines, as we shall see in Section 6.5.)

To preclude conditions from being stolen, the signaling process needs to pass the condition directly to the awakened process rather than make it globally visible. We can implement this as follows. First, change the body of V to an alternative statement. If some process is delayed on pos when V is called, awaken one but do *not* increment s; otherwise increment s as usual. Second, replace the delay loop in P by an alternative statement that checks the condition $s > 0$. If s is positive, the process decrements s and proceeds; otherwise, the process delays on *pos*. When a process delayed on *pos* is awakened, it simply returns from P; it does not decrement s in this case to compensate for the fact that s was not incremented before **signal** was executed in the V operation. Incorporating these changes yields the monitor shown in Figure 6.9.

In Figure 6.9, the condition associated with *pos* has changed to reflect the different implementation. Also, s is no longer the difference between the number of completed V and P operations. Rather, the value of s is now $nV - nP - pending$, where nV is the number of completed V operations, nP is

monitor *Semaphore*   # Invariant $s \geq 0$
  var $s := 0$
  var *pos* : **cond**   # signaled in V when *pos* is not empty
  procedure $P(\ )$
    if $s > 0 \rightarrow s := s - 1$
    [] $s = 0 \rightarrow$ **wait**(*pos*)
    fi
  end
  procedure $V(\ )$
    if empty(*pos*) $\rightarrow s := s + 1$
    [] **not empty**(*pos*) $\rightarrow$ **signal**(*pos*)
    fi
  end
end

Figure 6.9. A FIFO semaphore.

---

the number of completed P operations, and *pending* is the number of processes that have been awakened by execution of **signal** but have not yet completed executing P. (Essentially, *pending* is an implicit auxiliary variable that is incremented before **signal** and decremented after **wait**.)

This technique of passing a condition directly to a waiting process can be applied to many other problems. For example, we will use it in Section 6.4, where we show how to schedule a moving head disk. One has to use this technique with care, however, since **wait** statements are no longer in loops that recheck the condition. Instead, the burden of establishing the condition and ensuring that it will remain true is on the signaler. In addition, **signal** statements can no longer be replaced by **signal_all**.

The Sleeping Barber Problem: Rendezvous

In this section, we consider another classic synchronization problem: the sleeping barber. Like the dining philosophers problem, this one has a colorful definition. Moreover, the sleeping barber is representative of practical problems, such as the disk head scheduler described in Section 6.4. In particular, the problem illustrates the important client/server relationship that often exists between processes. Also, it contains an important type of synchronization called a rendezvous. Finally, the problem is an excellent illustration of the utility of and need for a systematic approach to solving synchronization problems. Ad-hoc techniques are far too error-prone for solving a problem such as this.

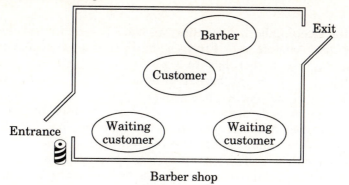

Figure 6.10. The sleeping barber problem.

(6.16) **Sleeping Barber Problem.** An easy-going town contains a small barber shop having two doors and a few chairs. Customers enter through one door and leave through the other door. Because the shop is small, at most one customer or the barber can move around in it at a time. The barber spends his life serving customers, one at a time. When none are in the shop, the barber sleeps in the barber's chair. When a customer arrives and finds the barber sleeping, the customer awakens the barber, sits in the barber's chair, and sleeps while the barber cuts his hair. If the barber is busy when a customer arrives, the customer goes to sleep in one of the other chairs. After giving a haircut, the barber opens the exit door for the customer and closes it when the customer leaves. If there are waiting customers, the barber then awakens one and waits for the customer to sit in the barber's chair. Otherwise, the barber goes back to sleep until a new customer arrives.

The customers and barber are processes, and the barber's shop is a monitor within which the processes interact, as shown in Figure 6.10. Customers are *clients* that request a service from the barber, in this case, haircuts. The barber is a *server* who repeatedly provides the service. This type of interaction is an example of a *client/server* relationship.

To implement these interactions, we can model the barber shop by a monitor with three procedures: *get_haircut*, *get_next_customer*, and *finished_cut*. Customers call *get_haircut*; they return from this procedure after receiving a haircut. The barber repeatedly calls *get_next_customer* to wait for a customer to sit in the barber's chair, then gives the customer a haircut, and finally calls *finished_cut* to allow the customer to leave the shop. Permanent variables are used to record the status of the processes and to represent the various chairs in which processes sleep.

Within the sleeping barber monitor, we need to synchronize the actions of the barber and customers. First, a barber and a customer need to *rendezvous*; i.e., the barber has to wait for a customer to arrive, and a customer has to wait for the barber to be available. Second, the customer needs to wait until the barber has finished giving him a haircut, which is indicated by the barber's opening the exit door. Finally, before closing the exit door, the barber needs to wait until the customer has left the shop. In short, both the barber and customer proceed through a series of synchronized stages, starting with a rendezvous.

A rendezvous is similar to a two-process barrier since both parties must arrive before either can proceed. (It differs from a two-process barrier, however, since the barber can rendezvous with any customer.) As with barriers, the most straightforward way to specify synchronization stages such as these is to employ incrementing counters that record the number of processes that have reached each stage.

Customers have two important stages: sitting in the barber's chair and leaving the barber shop. Let *cinchair* and *cleave* be counters for these stages. The barber repeatedly goes through three stages: becoming available, giving a haircut, and finishing a haircut. Let *bavail*, *bbusy*, and *bdone* be the counters for these stages. All counters are initially zero. Since the processes pass sequentially through these stages, the counters must satisfy the invariant:

$$C1:\ cinchair \geq cleave \ \wedge\ bavail \geq bbusy \geq bdone$$

To ensure that the barber and a customer rendezvous before the barber starts cutting the customer's hair, a customer cannot sit in the barber's chair more times than the barber has become available. In addition, the barber cannot become busy more times than customers have sat in the barber's chair. Thus, we also require the invariance of:

$$C2:\ cinchair \leq bavail \ \wedge\ bbusy \leq cinchair$$

Finally, customers cannot leave the shop more times than the barber has finished giving haircuts, which is expressed by the invariant:

$$C3:\ cleave \leq bdone$$

The monitor invariant for the barber shop is the conjunction of these three invariants:

$$BARBER:\ C1 \wedge C2 \wedge C3$$

We need to add these five counters to the bodies of the *Barber_Shop* procedures. We also need as usual to use **await** to guard assignments to the

```
monitor Barber_Shop        # Invariant BARBER
    var cinchair := 0, cleave := 0
    var bavail := 0, bbusy := 0, bdone := 0
    procedure get_haircut( )      # called by customers
        await cinchair < bavail; cinchair := cinchair + 1
        await cleave < bdone; cleave := cleave + 1
    end
    procedure get_next_customer( )      # called by the barber
        bavail := bavail + 1
        await bbusy < cinchair; bbusy := bbusy + 1
    end
    procedure finished_cut( )       # called by the barber
        bdone := bdone + 1
        await bdone = cleave
    end  { bdone = cleave }
end
```

Figure 6.11. Sleeping barber monitor with **await** statements.

---

counters in order to ensure the monitor invariant. Finally, we need to insert an **await** at the end of *finished_cut* to ensure that the barber cannot return from *finished_cut* until the just-serviced customer has left the shop. The net result of adding assignments to the counters and **await** statements is the monitor shown in Figure 6.11. That monitor—unlike others we have considered—has a procedure, *get_haircut*, containing more than one **await** statement. This is because a customer proceeds through two stages, waiting for the barber, then waiting for the barber to finish giving a haircut.

Although incrementing counters are useful for recording stages through which processes pass, their values can increase without bound. As with several examples in earlier chapters, however, we can avoid this problem by changing variables. We can do this whenever, as here, synchronization depends only on the differences between counter values. In particular, we use one new variable to record each difference that appears in the **await** statements in Figure 6.11. Let *barber*, *chair*, and *open* be these variables. They are related to the counters as follows:

$$barber = bavail - cinchair$$
$$chair = cinchair - bbusy$$
$$open = bdone - cleave$$

With these substitutions, the new variables satisfy the invariant:

```
monitor Barber_Shop        # Invariant BARBER′
    var barber := 0, chair := 0, open := 0
    var barber_available : cond        # signaled when barber > 0
    var chair_occupied : cond          # signaled when chair > 0
    var door_open : cond               # signaled when open > 0
    var customer_left : cond           # signaled when open = 0
    procedure get_haircut( )        # called by customers
        do barber = 0 → wait(barber_available) od
        barber := barber − 1
        chair := chair + 1; signal(chair_occupied)
        do open = 0 → wait(door_open) od
        open := open − 1; signal(customer_left)
    end
    procedure get_next_customer( )        # called by the barber
        barber := barber + 1; signal(barber_available)
        do chair = 0 → wait(chair_occupied) od
        chair := chair − 1
    end
    procedure finished_cut( )        # called by the barber
        open := open + 1; signal(door_open)
        do open > 0 → wait(customer_left) od
    end
end
```

Figure 6.12. Sleeping barber monitor using condition variables.

$BARBER'$: $0 \leq barber \leq 1 \ \wedge \ 0 \leq chair \leq 1 \ \wedge \ 0 \leq open \leq 1$

The value of *barber* is 1 when the barber is waiting for a customer to sit in the barber's chair, *chair* is 1 when the customer has sat in the chair but the barber has not yet become busy, and *open* is 1 when the exit door has been opened but the customer has not yet left.

In addition to changing variables, we also need to implement the **await** statements using condition variables. As in the readers/writers problem, the synchronization conditions reference only permanent variables; they do not reference variables local to processes. Thus, we use four condition variables, one for each of the four different boolean conditions. We also replace the **await** statements by **wait** statements embedded in loops. Finally, we add **signal** statements at points where conditions are made true. Making these changes, we have the final solution shown in Figure 6.12.

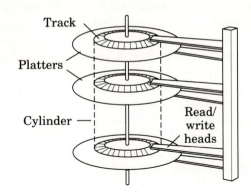

Figure 6.13. A moving-head disk.

6.4 Disk Scheduling: Program Structures

In this section, we examine another important problem—scheduling access to a moving head disk—and show how the techniques described in the previous section can be applied to develop a solution. Equally important, we examine two different ways in which the solution can be structured. The disk-scheduling problem is representative of numerous scheduling problems. Also, each of the solution structures is applicable in numerous other situations. We begin by summarizing the relevant characteristics of moving-head disks, which are used to store data files.

Figure 6.13 shows the structure of a moving-head disk. The disk contains several platters that are connected to a central spindle and that rotate at constant speed. Data is stored on the surfaces of the platters. Each platter is like a phonograph record, except that the recording tracks form separate, concentric circles rather than being connected in a spiral. The tracks in the same relative position on different platters form a cylinder. Data is accessed by positioning a read/write head over the appropriate track, then waiting for the platter to rotate until the desired data passes by the head. Normally there is one read/write head per platter. These heads are connected to a single arm, which can move in and out so that read/write heads can be placed at any cylinder and hence over any track.

The physical address of any piece of data stored on a disk consists of a cylinder, a track number, which specifies the platter, and an offset, which specifies the distance from a fixed clock point that is the same on every track. To access the disk, a program executes a machine-specific input/output instruction. The parameters to such an instruction are a physical disk address, a count of the number of bytes to transfer, an indication of the kind of transfer to perform (read or write), and the address of a primary buffer containing the data to write or into which the data will be read.

As a consequence of these disk characteristics, disk access time depends on three quantities: *seek time* to move a read/write head to the appropriate cylinder, *rotational delay*, and data *transmission time*. Transmission time depends totally on the number of bytes to be transferred, but the other two quantities depend on the state of the disk. In the best case, a read/write head is already at the requested cylinder, and the requested track area is just beginning to pass under the read/write head. In the worst case, read/write heads have to be moved clear across the disk, and the requested track has to make a full revolution. A characteristic of moving-head disks is that the time required to move the read/write heads from one cylinder to another is an increasing function of the distance between the two cylinders. Also, the time it takes to move a read/write head even one cylinder is much greater than platter rotation time. Thus, the most effective way to reduce the average disk access time is to minimize head motion and hence to reduce seek time. (It also helps to reduce rotational delay, but this is harder to accomplish since rotational delays are typically quite short.)

We assume there are several clients that use a disk. For example, in a multiprogrammed operating system, these could be processes executing user commands or system processes implementing virtual memory management. Whenever only one client at a time wants to access the disk, nothing can be gained by not allowing the disk to be accessed immediately since we cannot in general know when another client may also want to access the disk. Thus, disk scheduling is applied only if two or more clients want to access the disk.

An attractive scheduling strategy is always to select the pending request that wants to access the cylinder closest to the one at which the read/write heads are currently positioned. This is called the *shortest-seek-time* (SST) strategy since it minimizes seek time. However, SST is an unfair strategy since a steady stream of requests for cylinders close to the current position could starve requests farther away. Although such starvation is extremely unlikely, there is no bound on how long a request might be delayed.

An alternative, fair scheduling strategy is to move the disk heads in only one direction until all requests in that direction have been serviced. In particular, select the client request closest to the current head position in the direction the disk heads last moved. If there is no pending request in the current search direction, reverse directions. This strategy is variously called SCAN, LOOK, or—more colorfully—the *elevator algorithm* since it is analogous to the way in which an elevator visits floors, picking up and unloading customers. The only problem with this strategy is that a pending request just behind the current head position will not be serviced until the head moves away and then back. This leads to a large variance in the expected waiting time before a request is serviced.

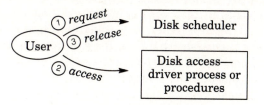

Figure 6.14. Disk scheduler as separate monitor.

A third strategy is similar to the second but greatly reduces the variance in expected waiting time. In this strategy, which is called CSCAN or CLOOK (C for circular), requests are serviced in only one direction, e.g., from outermost cylinder to innermost. In particular, there is only one search direction, and the request closest to the current head position in that direction is selected. When there are no further requests ahead of the current head position, searching starts over from the outermost cylinder. This is analogous to an elevator that only takes passengers up. (They presumably either walk down or jump!) CSCAN is nearly as efficient as the elevator algorithm with respect to reducing seek time because for most disks it takes only approximately twice as long to move the heads across all cylinders as it does to move them from one cylinder to the next. Moreover, the CSCAN strategy is fair as long as a continual stream of requests for the current head position is not allowed to starve other pending requests.

In the remainder of this section, we develop two structurally different solutions to the disk-scheduling problem. In the first, the scheduler is implemented by a distinct monitor, as in the solution to the readers/writers problem (Figure 6.4). In the second, the scheduler is implemented by monitor that acts as an intermediary between users of the disk and a process that performs actual disk access; this structure is similar to that of the solution to the sleeping barber problem (Figure 6.12). Both monitors implement the CSCAN strategy, but they can easily be modified to implement any of the scheduling strategies.

Scheduler as a Separate Monitor

One way to organize a solution to the disk-scheduling problem is to have the scheduler be a monitor that is separate from the resource being controlled, in this case, a disk. This structure is depicted in Figure 6.14. The solution has three kinds of components: user processes, the scheduler, and the procedures or process that performs disk transfers. The scheduler is implemented by a monitor so that scheduling data is accessed only by one user process at a time. The monitor provides two operations: *request* and *release*.

A user process wishing to access cylinder *cyl* first calls *request(cyl)*; the process returns from *request* when the scheduler has selected its request. The user process then accesses the disk, for example, by calling a procedure or by communicating with a disk driver process. After accessing the disk, the user calls *release* so that another request can be selected. The user interface to the scheduler is thus:

> *Disk_Scheduler.request(cyl)*
> access the disk
> *Disk_Scheduler.release*()

Disk_Scheduler has the dual roles of scheduling requests and ensuring that at most one process at a time uses the disk. Thus, all users *must* follow the above protocol.

We assume that disk cylinders are numbered from 0 to *MAXCYL* and that scheduling is to employ the CSCAN strategy with a search direction from 0 to *MAXCYL*. As usual, the critical step in deriving a correct solution is to state precisely the properties the solution is to have. Here, at most one process at a time can be allowed to use the disk, and pending requests are to be serviced in CSCAN order.

Let *position* indicate the current head position, i.e., the cylinder being accessed by the process using the disk. When the disk is not being accessed, we will set *position* to –1. (Any invalid cylinder number would do, or we could use an additional variable.)

To implement CSCAN scheduling, we need to distinguish between pending requests to be serviced on the current scan across the disk and those to be serviced on the next scan across the disk. Let *C* and *N* be disjoint sets that contain these requests. In particular, the contents of *C* and *N* are:

> $C: \{ cyl_i \mid cyl_i \geq position \}$
> $N: \{ cyl_i \mid cyl_i \leq position \}$

where the cyl_i are the arguments of pending requests. (Since more than one process could request the same cylinder, the different values of cyl_i need to be distinguishable. Here, we subscript *cyl* by user process index *i*.)

A pending request for which $cyl_i = position$ is stored in only one of the sets, as described below. Since the CSCAN strategy services requests in ascending order, both sets are ordered by increasing value of cyl_i; requests for the same cylinder are ordered by set insertion time. *C*, *N*, and *position* are the monitor's permanent variables. For correct scheduling, they must satisfy the invariant:

> *DISK*: *C* and *N* are ordered sets $\wedge$
> $(\forall\, cyl_i:\ cyl_i \in C:\ position \le cyl_i)\ \wedge$
> $(\forall\, cyl_j:\ cyl_j \in N:\ position \ge cyl_j)\ \wedge$
> $(position = -1)\ \Rightarrow\ (C = \varnothing \wedge N = \varnothing)$

When a process P_i calls *request*, it takes one of three actions. If *position* is -1, the disk is free; thus, the process sets *position* to cyl_i and proceeds to access the disk. If the disk is not free and if $cyl_i > position$, the process inserts cyl_i in set *C*; otherwise, it inserts cyl_i in set *N*. We use *N* rather than *C* when $cyl_i = position$ to avoid potential unfairness; in this case, the request waits until the next scan across the disk. After recording cyl_i in the appropriate set, the process delays until it is granted access to the disk, i.e., until *position* = cyl_i as described below.

When a process calls *release*, it updates the permanent variables so as to maintain *DISK*. If *C* is not empty, there are pending requests for the current scan. In this case, the releasing process removes the first element of *C* and sets *position* to its value. If *C* is empty but *N* is not, we need to start the next scan; i.e., it needs to become the current scan. The releasing process accomplishes this by swapping *C* and *N* (which sets *N* to the null set), removing the first element of *C*, and setting *position* to its value. Finally, if both *C* and *N* are empty, the releasing process sets *position* to -1 to indicate that the disk is free.

Putting these parts together, we have the monitor shown in Figure 6.15. There, *insert(set, value)* places *value* in the proper position in ordered *set*; *delete(set)* removes the first element from *set* and returns its value.

The final step in deriving a solution is as usual to implement **await** using condition variables. We have here a situation like that in the interval timer problem: There is a static order between waiting conditions, and thus it is possible to use priority **wait** to implement each **await**. In particular, requests in sets *C* and *N* are both serviced in ascending order of cyl_i. We also have a situation like that in the FIFO semaphore: When the disk is released, permission to access the disk is transferred to one specific waiting process. In particular, we set *position* to the value of the pending request that is to be serviced next. Because of these two attributes, we can implement **await** efficiently by combining aspects of the *Timer* and *Semaphore* monitors in Figures 6.8 and 6.9.

To represent sets *C* and *N*, let *scan*[0:1] be an array of condition variables indexed by integers *c* and *n*. When a requesting process needs to insert its parameter *cyl* in set *C* and then wait for *position* to be equal to *cyl*, it simply executes **wait**(*scan*[*c*], *cyl*). Similarly, a process inserts its request in set *N* and then delays by executing **wait**(*scan*[*n*], *cyl*). Because condition variables are ordered queues and only one process gets awakened when **signal** is executed, it is no longer necessary to distinguish between equal values of *cyl*.

monitor *Disk_Scheduler*   # Invariant *DISK*

   var *position* : **int** := −1
   var *C*, *N* : **ordered set of int** := ∅
   procedure *request*(cyl_i : **int**)
     if *position* = −1 → *position* := cyl_i
     [] *position* ≠ −1 **and** cyl_i > *position* →
         insert(*C*, cyl_i)
         await *position* = cyl_i
     [] *position* ≠ −1 **and** cyl_i ≤ *position* →
         insert(*N*, cyl_i)
         await *position* = cyl_i
    fi
   end
   procedure *release*()
     if *C* ≠ ∅ → *position* := *delete*(*C*)
     [] *C* = ∅ **and** *N* ≠ ∅ → *C* :=: *N*; *position* := *delete*(*C*)
     [] *C* = ∅ **and** *N* = ∅ → *position* := −1
    fi
   end
end

Figure 6.15. Separate disk scheduler using **await** statements.

We also change the body of *release* to use this representation of the sets *C* and *N*. In particular, we use **empty** to test whether a set is empty, use **minrank** to determine its smallest value, and use **signal** to remove the first element and at the same time awaken the appropriate requesting process. Also, we swap the sets when needed simply by swapping the values of *c* and *n*. (This is why *scan* is an array.)

Incorporating these changes, we have the final solution shown in Figure 6.16. Since *c* is the index of the current scan at the end of *release*, it is sufficient to include just one **signal** statement. If in fact *position* is −1 at this point, *scan*[*c*] will be empty, and thus **signal** will have no effect.

Scheduling problems such as this are among the most difficult to solve correctly, whatever synchronization mechanism is employed. The critical step is specifying exactly the order in which processes are to be served. When the relative service order is static—as it is here—we can use ordered sets. This leads to a solution that can make use of priority **wait** statements. Unfortunately, the relative service order is not always static; e.g., a process that is delayed a long time might have its service priority increased to avoid starvation. Implementing a dynamic scheduling strategy requires either

```
monitor Disk_Scheduler        # Invariant DISK
    var position := -1, c := 0, n := 1
    var scan[0:1] : cond      # scan[c] is signaled when disk is released
    procedure request(cyl : int)
        if position = -1 → position := cyl
        [] position ≠ -1 and cyl > position → wait(scan[c], cyl)
        [] position ≠ -1 and cyl ≤ position → wait(scan[n], cyl)
        fi
    end
    procedure release( )
        if not empty(scan[c]) → position := minrank(scan[c])
        [] empty(scan[c]) and not empty(scan[n]) →
                    c :=: n; position := minrank(scan[c])
        [] empty(scan[c]) and empty(scan[n]) → position := -1
        fi
        signal(scan[c])
    end
end
```

Figure 6.16. Separate disk scheduler using condition variables.

---

using private condition variables to awaken individual processes or using covering conditions to let delayed processes schedule themselves (see the exercises).

Scheduler as an Intermediary

Implementing *Disk_Scheduler*, or any resource controller, as a separate monitor is a viable way to structure a solution to a scheduling/allocation problem. Because the scheduler is separate, it can be designed independently of the other components. However, this very separation introduces two potential problems:

- The presence of the scheduler is visible to the processes that use the disk; if the scheduler is deleted, user processes change.

- All user processes must follow the required protocol of requesting the disk, then using it, then releasing it. If any process fails to follow this protocol, scheduling is defeated; also, exclusive disk access might not be ensured.

Figure 6.17. Disk scheduler as an intermediary.

Both these problems can be alleviated if the disk-use protocol is embedded in a procedure and user processes do not directly access either the disk or the disk scheduler. However, this introduces another layer of procedures and some attendant inefficiency.

In addition to the above two problems, there is a third problem, if the disk is accessed by a disk driver process rather than by procedures that are called directly by user processes. In particular, after being granted access to the disk, a user process must communicate with the driver to pass arguments and to receive results (see Figure 6.14). These communication paths could be implemented by two instances of the bounded buffer monitor of Figure 6.1. But the user interface would then consist of three monitors—the scheduler and two bounded buffers—and the user would have to make a total of four monitor calls every time it uses the device. Since the disk users and disk driver have a client/server relationship, we could implement the communication interface using a variant of the solution to the sleeping barber problem. But we would still have two monitors—one for scheduling and one for interaction between user processes and the disk driver.

When a disk is controlled by a driver process, the best possible approach is to combine the scheduler and communication interface into a single monitor. Essentially, the scheduler becomes an intermediary between the user processes and the disk driver, as shown in Figure 6.17. The monitor forwards user requests to the driver in the desired order of preference. The net result is that the disk interface employs only one monitor, and the user must make only one monitor call per disk access. Also, the presence or absence of scheduling is transparent. Moreover, there is no multistep protocol the user can fail to follow. Thus, this approach overcomes all three difficulties caused by the scheduler being a separate monitor.

In the remainder of this section, we show how to transform the solution to the sleeping barber problem (Figure 6.12) into a disk driver interface that both provides communication between clients and the disk driver and implements CSCAN scheduling. We need to make several changes to the sleeping barber solution. First, we need to rename the processes, monitor, and monitor procedures as described below and shown in Figure 6.17.

monitor *Disk_Interface*
    permanent variables for status, scheduling, and data transfer
    procedure *use_disk*(*cyl* : **int**, transfer and result parameters)
        wait for turn to use driver
        store transfer parameters in permanent variables
        wait for transfer to be completed
        retrieve results from permanent variables
    end
    procedure *get_next_request*(**res** transfer parameters)
        select next request
        wait for transfer parameters to be stored
    end
    procedure *finished_transfer*(results)
        store results in permanent variables
        wait for results to be retrieved by client
    end
end

Figure 6.18. Outline of disk interface monitor.

Second, we need to parameterize the monitor procedures to transfer requests from users (customers) to the disk driver (barber) and to transfer results back; in essence, we need to turn the "barber's chair" and "exit door" into communication buffers. Finally, we need to add scheduling to the user/disk-driver rendezvous so that the driver services the preferred user request. These changes yield a disk interface with the outline shown in Figure 6.18.

To refine the outline in Figure 6.18 into an actual solution, we employ the same basic synchronization as in the sleeping barber solution (Figure 6.12). However, we add scheduling as in the *Disk_Scheduler* monitor (Figure 6.16) and add parameter passing as in a single-slot buffer (Figure 6.1). Essentially, the monitor invariant for *Disk_Interface* becomes the conjunction of barber shop invariant *BARBER'*, disk scheduler invariant *DISK*, and bounded buffer invariant *BB* (simplified to the case of a single-slot buffer).

A user process waits its turn to access the disk by executing the same actions as in the *request* procedure of the *Disk_Scheduler* monitor in Figure 6.16. Similarly, the driver process indicates it is available by executing the same actions as in the *release* procedure of the *Disk_Scheduler* monitor. Initially, however, we will set *position* to −2 to indicate that the disk is neither available nor in use until after the driver makes its first call to *get_next_request*; hence, users need to wait for the first scan to start.

monitor *Disk_Interface*   # Invariant combines *BARBER'*, *DISK*, and *BB*
  var *position* := –2, *c* := 0, *n* := 1, *scan*[0:1] : **cond**
  var *arg_area* : *arg_type*, *result_area* : *result_type*, *args* := 0, *results* := 0
  var *args_stored*, *results_stored*, *results_retrieved* : **cond**

  procedure *use_disk*(*cyl* : **int**; transfer and result parameters)
      if *position* = –1 → *position* := *cyl*
      [] *position* ≠ –1 **and** *cyl* > *position* → **wait**(*scan*[*c*], *cyl*)
      [] *position* ≠ –1 **and** *cyl* ≤ *position* → **wait**(*scan*[*n*], *cyl*)
      fi
      arg_area := transfer parameters
      args := *args*+1; **signal**(*args_stored*)
      do *results* = 0 → **wait**(*results_stored*) **od**
      result parameters := *result_area*
      results := *results*–1; **signal**(*results_retrieved*)
  end

  procedure *get_next_request*(**res** transfer parameters)
      if not empty(*scan*[*c*]) → *position* := **minrank**(*scan*[*c*])
      [] **empty**(*scan*[*c*]) **and not empty**(*scan*[*n*]) →
                  c :=: *n*; *position* := **minrank**(*scan*[*c*])
      [] **empty**(*scan*[*c*]) **and empty**(*scan*[*n*]) → *position* := –1
      fi
      signal(*scan*[*c*])
      do *args* = 0 → **wait**(*args_stored*) **od**
      transfer parameters := *arg_area*; *args* := *args*–1
  end

  procedure *finished_transfer*(result parameters)
      result_area := result parameters; *results* := *results*+1
      signal(*results_stored*)
      do *results* > 0 → **wait**(*results_retrieved*) **od**
  end
end

Figure 6.19. Disk interface monitor.

When it becomes a user's turn to access the disk, the user process deposits its transfer arguments in permanent variables, then waits to fetch results. After selecting the next user request, the driver process waits to fetch the user's transfer arguments. The driver then performs the requested disk transfer. When it is done, the driver deposits the results, then waits for them to be fetched. The deposits and fetches are implemented as for a single-slot buffer. These refinements lead to the monitor shown in Figure 6.19.

Although this user/disk-driver interface is quite efficient, it can be made even more efficient by two relatively simple changes. First, the disk driver can begin servicing the next user request sooner if *finished_transfer* is modified so that the driver does not wait for results from the previous transfer to be retrieved. We must be careful, however, to ensure that the results area is not overwritten in the event the driver completes another transfer before the results from the previous one have been retrieved. The second change is to combine the two procedures called by the disk driver. This eliminates one monitor call per disk access. Implementing this change requires slightly modifying the initialization of *results*. We leave incorporating both of these changes to the reader (see exercise 6.29).

6.5 Alternative Approaches to Synchronization

Monitors, as we have defined them, have three distinguishing characteristics. First, a monitor encapsulates its permanent variables; such variables can be accessed only by calling a monitor procedure. Second, procedures in a monitor execute with mutual exclusion. These two characteristics imply that permanent variables are not subject to concurrent access. Third, condition synchronization is provided by means of condition variables and the **wait** and **signal** operations. Execution of **wait** delays the executing process and temporarily releases monitor exclusion; this is the only way—other than returning from a monitor procedure—in which a process releases exclusion. Execution of **signal** awakens one delayed process, if there is one, but the signaling process retains exclusive access to the monitor; the awakened process resumes executing at some future time when it can reacquire exclusive access.

Monitors with these characteristics have been included in the Mesa programming language, and this approach to condition synchronization is also used within the UNIX operating system. There are, however, other ways in which condition synchronization could be provided. Also, mutual exclusion is not always required within monitors. In this section, we first describe and compare alternative mechanisms for condition synchronization. Then we describe alternatives to mutual exclusion. Finally, we describe how both condition synchronization and exclusion could be provided by means of what are called path expressions.

Alternative Signaling Disciplines

In this section, we assume that monitor procedures execute with mutual exclusion, and we focus on different ways in which condition synchronization can be realized. We have already seen two techniques for specifying such synchronization. In deriving monitors, we first used **await** to delay execution when necessary. We then implemented **await** using condition variables and **wait** and **signal** operations. In fact, **await** could be used directly to specify condition synchronization, thereby avoiding the last derivation step at the expense of a more costly underlying implementation (similar to that for **region** statements).

The two approaches are similar, in that delay points are programmed explicitly. They differ in the way signaling is done. With **await**, signaling is implicit; it is provided by a kernel or by compiler-generated code. For this reason, **await** is called an *automatic signaling* (AS) mechanism. By contrast, with condition variables, signaling is explicit. Furthermore, **signal**, as we have defined it, is *non-preemptive* since the signaling process continues executing. Another process is not given control of the monitor until the signaler waits or returns. (The same is true for automatic signaling.) This kind of explicit signaling is therefore called *signal and continue* (SC).

Three other mechanisms for condition synchronization in monitors have also been incorporated in concurrent programming languages. All employ condition variables and the **wait** and **signal** operations, but they attach different semantics to **signal.** In all three cases, **signal** is *preemptive*: If a process executes **signal** and awakens another, the signaling process is forced to delay, and the awakened process is the next to execute in the monitor. Thus, permission to execute in the monitor is transferred from the signaler to the awakened process, which might signal yet another process and pass permission to it, etc. The rationale for preemptive signaling is that the signaled condition is guaranteed to be true at the time the awakened process resumes execution, just as in the baton-passing method for using semaphores. By contrast, with signal and continue either the signaler or some other process could invalidate the condition before the signaled process resumes execution.

The three preemptive signaling mechanisms differ from each other with respect to what happens to the signaling process. The first possibility is that the signaling process is forced to exit the monitor, i.e., to return from the procedure being executed. This is called *signal and exit* (SX) or sometimes signal and return; it has been included in the language Concurrent Pascal. Another possibility is that the signaling process is allowed to continue executing in the monitor, but that it must first wait until it can re-acquire exclusive access. This is called *signal and wait* (SW) and has been included in Modula and Concurrent Euclid. The final possibility is a variation on signal and wait: the signaling process is forced to wait, but it is assured that it will be given control of the monitor before any new calls of the monitor procedures. This discipline is called *signal and urgent wait* (SU) and has been included in Pascal-Plus.

All told, then, there are five different signaling disciplines:

- Automatic Signaling (AS): implicit and non-preemptive.

- Signal and Continue (SC): explicit and non-preemptive.

- Signal and Exit (SX): explicit, preemptive, and signaler exits monitor.

- Signal and Wait (SW): explicit, preemptive, and signaler waits.

- Signal and Urgent Wait (SU): explicit, preemptive, and signaler waits, but signaler executes again before new monitor entries.

Even though they appear to be quite different, each signaling discipline can be used to simulate the others. Thus they can solve the same problems, although signal and exit can require changing the interface to a monitor. Moreover, in many cases the explicit signaling disciplines can be used interchangeably—the syntactically same monitor is correct, independently of the semantics of **signal**, the only difference being that processes execute in different orders in the monitor. The disciplines differ mainly with respect to their ease of use in developing correct solutions and with respect to their implementation cost. Below we examine these similarities and differences.

Equivalence of the Signaling Disciplines

To show that two mechanisms are equally powerful, it is sufficient to show that each can simulate the other. As defined in (1.18), one mechanism simulates another if any program that uses the first mechanism has the same properties as a program that uses the other. In this section, we outline how the various signaling mechanisms can simulate each other. We also describe situations in which the explicit signaling disciplines are interchangeable.

We have already seen several examples that showed how to simulate automatic signaling using signal and continue. In particular, we can always replace **await** B by:

$$\textbf{do not } B \rightarrow \textbf{wait}(c_B) \textbf{ od}$$

This is correct as long as we add sufficient **signals** to procedures that could make B true. We used a different simulation in those cases where we could use priority **wait** to gain increased efficiency or when we needed to control exactly which delayed process should be signaled.

Signal and continue can also be simulated using automatic signaling. The idea is to replace **wait**(c) by an **await** and other statements that simulate waiting on the condition variable and to replace **signal**(c) by statements that simulate signaling the condition variable. Let condition variable c be represented by an explicit queue CQ. Also, let each process i have a boolean variable *waiting*[i] that is true when the process is waiting on some condition variable queue. Initially, CQ is empty and all *waiting*[i] are false. Then

wait(c) in process i can be simulated by:

> insert i at end of CQ; waiting[i] := true
> **await** (**not** waiting[i])

And **signal**(c) can be simulated by:

> **if** CQ not empty →
> > remove first element j from CQ; waiting[j] := false
>
> **fi**

The other operations on condition variables—e.g., priority **wait** and **empty**—can be simulated in a similar fashion.

Automatic signaling can also be simulated using the signal and wait (SW) discipline. To show this, we need first to specify the semantics of signal and wait more precisely. With SW, the proof of the body of a monitor procedure has the same form as for SC and AS. As with the SC discipline, before waiting, a process releases control of the monitor in which it is executing; thus monitor invariant *MI* must be true before execution of **wait.** Once a process is signaled, however, it is the next to execute in the monitor. Thus, the monitor state is the same as it was at the time the process was signaled. Let *T* be a predicate that characterizes this state. Then, the axiom for **wait** with the SW discipline is:

(6.17)   **SW Wait Axiom:** $\{ MI \wedge L \}$ **wait**(c) $\{ T \wedge L \}$

Again, *L* is an assertion about parameters and variables local to the monitor procedure.

Given the above axiom for **wait**, it is necessary that the permanent variables satisfy *T* whenever **signal**(c) is executed and the queue associated with c is not empty. After execution of **signal**(c), the signaling process leaves the monitor and waits to reenter. When it reenters, the permanent variables will again satisfy *MI*. Thus, when the signaled queue is not empty, the axiom for **signal** is:

(6.18)   **SW Signal Axiom:** $\{ T \wedge L \wedge \neg \mathbf{empty}(c) \}$ **signal**(c) $\{ MI \wedge L \}$

Once again, *L* is an assertion about parameters and variables local to the executing process. An additional proof obligation with the signal and wait discipline is to show that the same predicate *T* is used for all **wait** and **signal** operations on a given condition variable.

We can now show how to simulate automatic signaling using signal and wait. The simplest approach is to embed **wait** in a loop:

do not $B \rightarrow$ **wait**(c_B) **od**

Since the waiting process rechecks its own condition when it is awakened, we only require that monitor invariant *MI* be true after **wait**; i.e., $T = MI$ in the SW axioms. Therefore, we add **signal**(c_B) statements to monitor procedures any time B could be true, but add them only when the monitor invariant is also true. By doing so, the simulation has the same partial correctness properties as the program being simulated. As long as an adequate number of **signal** statements are executed, the simulation is also deadlock-free, assuming the program being simulated is deadlock-free.

Signal and wait can also be simulated using automatic signaling. The simulation is basically the same as the simulation of SC using AS. However, with SW, a signaler must delay after awakening a process, and the awakened process must be the next to execute in the monitor. Pre-emptive signaling can be simulated as follows. Let *pending* be a boolean variable that is set to true by a signaler when a process is awakened and to false by the awakened process when it resumes execution. After setting *pending* to true, the signaler then delays by executing **await** (**not** *pending*). Also, at the entry to each monitor procedure, a process delays until *pending* is false. In this way, a signaled process is assured of being the next process to make progress in a monitor procedure, even if it is not the next process actually to get to execute.

From the above four simulations, it follows that SC and SW can simulate each other. For example, SC can be simulated using AS, then AS can be simulated using SW. Thus, SC and SW are equally powerful. The main difference between the SC and SW disciplines is that processes execute in different orders within monitors. Another difference is that broadcast **signal** is not well defined for the SW discipline or for either of the other preemptive signaling disciplines. This is because it is not possible preemptively to transfer control of the monitor to more than one process since they must execute in the monitor with mutual exclusion. Instead, broadcast **signal** must be simulated by awakening processes one at a time in a cascading fashion; i.e., one process signals a second, which signals a third, and so on.

In addition to being equally powerful, SC and SW are in many cases interchangeable, in the sense that a monitor that uses one discipline has the same safety properties as a *syntactically identical* monitor that uses the other. Informally, this is because we can simulate AS in the same way using SC and SW. More precisely, the following definition gives sufficient conditions to ensure that a monitor has the same properties, independently of whether the SC or SW signaling discipline is used.

(6.19)   **Conditions for Interchangeability of SC and SW.** A program will have the same safety properties for both the signal and continue (SC) and signal and wait (SW) disciplines if every monitor satisfies the following conditions:

(1) The monitor invariant is true before every **signal**, and no stronger assertion about the permanent variables is required after any **wait**; i.e., waiting processes require only that the invariant is true when they resume execution.

(2) All **signal** operations are executed immediately before **wait** statements or before ends of procedures; they are not immediately followed by assignments that alter permanent variables.

(3) Broadcast **signal** is not used.

The first requirement ensures that SC and SW are interchangeable with respect to partial correctness because either set of proof rules is then applicable. The second requirement ensures that, if a condition has become true, a signaled process will be able to see that it is true whether or not the signaler continues. The third requirement avoids the fact that broadcast **signal** is defined for SC but not for SW.

All monitors in this chapter that do not use **signal_all** meet these requirements and are therefore correct for both the SW and SC disciplines. The two monitors that use **signal_all**—*RW_Controller* (Figure 6.4) and *Timer* with covering conditions (Figure 6.7)—meet the first two requirements and therefore can be changed to employ the SW discipline merely by simulating **signal_all** using repeated signals.

When the first two requirements in (6.19) are not met, monitors that are syntactically identical have different properties, depending on whether the SC or SW signaling discipline is used. For example, consider the following monitor, which implements a FIFO semaphore for the SW but not for the SC discipline:

> **monitor** *Semaphore1*   # Invariant $s \geq 0$
>   **var** $s := 0, pos$: **cond**   # *pos* signaled when $s > 0$
>   **procedure** $P(\ )$ **if** $s = 0 \rightarrow$ **wait**(*pos*) **fi**; $s := s - 1$ **end**
>   **procedure** $V(\ )$ $s := s + 1$; **signal**(*pos*) **end**
> **end**

This monitor does not meet the first requirement for SW and SC to be interchangeable. Although the monitor invariant is true before the **signal** in V, a waiting process in P requires the stronger assertion $s > 0$ when it reenters the monitor; otherwise, the semaphore invariant would not hold at the end of P. This assumption is valid if SW is used but not if SC is used.

With SC, s can become negative if a waiting process is awakened, but another process calls P before the awakened process reenters the monitor.

As an example of the necessity of the second requirement in (6.19)—that signals follow statements that change permanent variables—consider the following monitor, which also implements a (non-FIFO) semaphore:

monitor *Semaphore2*   # Invariant $s \geq 0$
    var $s := 0, pos : $ **cond**   # *pos* signaled when $s > 0$
    procedure $P(\ )$ **do** $s = 0 \rightarrow$ **wait**(pos) **od**; $s := s - 1$ **end**
    procedure $V(\ )$ **signal**(pos); $s := s + 1$ **end**
end

This monitor is identical to one given earlier in (6.6), except that in procedure V, **signal** is executed before s is incremented rather than after. This is irrelevant when the SC discipline is used because a process awakened by **signal** cannot execute until after the signaler increments s. However, this monitor can lead to deadlock when SW is used. Suppose a process is waiting within P, s is 0, and V is called. With the SW discipline, the waiting process will be awakened and begin executing before s is incremented; thus, this process will again wait when it should be able to proceed. The process will in fact wait forever if V is never again called.

Signal and urgent wait (SU) is also as powerful as the other signaling disciplines. Because SU and SW are quite similar, the simulations are quite similar to those for signal and wait (see exercise 6.31). In fact, *any* monitor that uses signal and wait can use signal and urgent wait. If it does not matter whether a delayed signaler reenters the monitor before or after new calls—as in SW—then the signaler can be forced to reenter before new calls. Thus, all monitors in this chapter that use signal and continue and do not employ **signal_all** are also correct if signal and urgent wait is used. There are, however, monitors that are correct for signal and urgent wait but not for the other disciplines. This occurs in the rare situations where it is imperative that a delayed signaler execute before new monitor entries. Any such monitor can, however, be reprogrammed so that it works correctly without this requirement.

The final signaling discipline, signal and exit (SX), can also be used to simulate the others. However, SX is less expressive and can be more difficult to use since a process is forced to return from a monitor procedure if it executes **signal.** Thus, each monitor procedure that uses SX can execute at most one **signal**, and there cannot be other statements that should be executed afterwards. When this is the case, it is trivial to simulate SX using SW or SU because the three disciplines are then interchangeable. If the requirements for SC and SW to be interchangeable are also met, a monitor that uses SX can also use SC. For example, several of the monitors given earlier—e.g., *Bounded_Buffer* (Figure 6.1) and *Shortest_Job_Next* (Figure 6.2)—are correct for all of the explicit signaling disciplines. Again, the only difference between the disciplines is the order in which processes execute.

Using SX, it is, however, more difficult to simulate other signaling disciplines. If a monitor procedure contains statements to be executed after a **signal**, it must be divided into multiple smaller procedures. For example, the *get_haircut* procedure in the *Barber_Shop* monitor (Figure 6.12) would have to be divided into three procedures, such that each contains one **signal** as its last statement. Unfortunately, this alters the interface to the monitor since it requires that a customer call each procedure. (However, the different interface could be encapsulated in a shared, non-monitor procedure so that customer processes would not have to be aware of the change.)

Differences Between the Signaling Disciplines

We have shown that the various signaling disciplines are equally powerful, in that any one can be used to simulate the others. They differ, however, with respect to ease of use and implementation cost. Since condition synchronization involves delaying a process until the state satisfies a boolean condition, such synchronization is normally easiest to program when synchronization statements employ explicit boolean conditions. Thus, automatic signaling is generally easier to use than condition variables and explicit signaling, just as conditional critical regions are generally easier to use than semaphores. However, when the delay conditions can be encoded using priority **wait**, using explicit signaling results in a much more compact program because the priority queue need not be programmed explicitly.

Of the explicit signaling disciplines, SX is the most difficult to use because it often requires subdividing monitor procedures into smaller than ideal units; this increases the number of procedures and affects the user interface. The other explicit signaling disciplines—SC, SW, and SU—do not have this difficulty, and they are approximately equal with respect to ease of use. There are, however, two reasons to prefer SC over the other explicit signaling disciplines.

The main reason for preferring SC is that it is not preemptive. This results in simpler proof rules for **wait** and **signal.** In particular, it means that each monitor procedure can be developed independently of the others, the only caveat being that an adequate number of **signal** statements need to be included at appropriate points. By contrast, with the SW and SU disciplines, the programmer must ensure that the permanent variable component T is the same in the preconditions of all **signal** statements and the postconditions of all **wait** statements that name the same condition variable. This requires designing the monitor procedures as a group. Using SC sometimes requires that **wait** be embedded in a loop, but this is a small price to pay.

The second reason to prefer SC is that it provides a broadcast **signal** primitive. This operation is often useful, as shown in the solutions to the readers/writers and interval timer problems. Such an operation can be simulated using SU or SW, but the simulation must be done with care. For example, if any of the awakened processes might again need to wait on c, then it is not correct to simulate **signal_all**(c) by:

$$\textbf{do not empty}(c) \rightarrow \textbf{signal}(c) \textbf{ od}$$

This is because c might never become empty, and hence the above loop will not terminate. Instead, one process must be signaled, then this process must signal the next before returning from the monitor or waiting, and so on until all waiting processes have been awakened. The result is a program that is lengthier and more complex than one programmed using **signal_all.**

The different signaling disciplines also differ with respect to implementation cost. The factors that affect implementation cost are the time it takes to execute **wait** and **signal** and the number of context switches required. (Space requirements are virtually identical for all disciplines.) With respect to implementation cost, SX and SC are approximately equal, SW and SU are slightly more expensive, and AS is the most expensive. To substantiate this claim, below we outline how to implement monitors for the various disciplines. Section 6.6 describes in detail how to implement the SC discipline.

Independent of the signaling discipline used, we must implement monitor exclusion. This can be accomplished by means of a lock and an entry queue for each monitor. The lock is held by at most one ready process at a time. When a process calls a monitor procedure, it delays on the entry queue until it can acquire the lock. When a process returns from a monitor, it releases the lock. The lock is then either passed on to one waiting process—which then becomes ready to execute—or the lock is made free if no processes are waiting.

For all the explicit signaling disciplines, we also need one queue for each condition variable. When a process executes **wait**(c), it blocks on the queue associated with c and releases the monitor lock. When a process executes **signal**(c), one process on the c queue is awakened, if there is one. With the SC discipline, this newly awakened process rejoins the monitor entry queue and waits for the lock to be released. By contrast, with the preemptive signaling disciplines, the newly awakened process is given control of the lock and is made ready to execute.

The three preemptive disciplines differ with respect to what happens to the signaling process. With SX, it simply returns from the procedure in which it was executing; with SW, the signaler rejoins the entry queue; with SU, it joins a special queue, called the urgent queue. SC, SX, and SW are similar, in that all processes waiting to acquire the monitor lock are on one queue, the entry queue. With SU, there are two queues of such processes—the urgent queue and the entry queue—and processes on the urgent queue have priority. (These queues can be merged by inserting signalers on the front of the entry queue and processes just entering the monitor at the end; in this case, the urgent queue becomes an urgent stack.)

Each of the explicit signaling disciplines thus requires an entry queue and condition variable queues; SU also requires an urgent queue. These queues are manipulated in virtually identical ways. However, with SX and SC, only one condition variable queue is affected when **signal** is executed. With SW and SU, both a condition variable queue and the entry or urgent queue are affected since the signaler blocks. Because two queues are manipulated, **signal** takes slightly longer to execute for SW or SU than for SC or SX.

All signaling disciplines, explicit or implicit, require a context switch when a process calls a monitor procedure and finds the monitor locked or when a process executes **wait** or **await.** Also, with all signaling disciplines, a context switch is optional when a process exits a monitor; if there is a process on the entry queue, it is awakened and given the monitor lock, but both this process and the one exiting the monitor are ready, so either could execute next. However, SC and SX do not require a context switch when **signal** is executed, whereas SW and SU do. This absence of a required context switch is especially important on a multiprocessor. At exit points with the SC and SX disciplines, both a signaler *and* an awakened process can execute, the signaler outside the monitor and the awakened process inside. For all these reasons, SC and SX are the least expensive preemptive disciplines to implement, and SW and SU are slightly more expensive.

Automatic signaling has the most expensive implementation. With automatic signaling, there are no explicit condition variable queues. Such queues could be implicitly associated with each semantically different boolean condition B in **await** statements, but this is not feasible when B references local variables, which it often does. Thus, in general, each process needs its own delay queue.

The main difficulty in implementing **await** is providing the automatic signaling. Whenever a process exits a monitor by returning or waiting, some waiting process might be able to proceed. The problem is determining which one. (This problem does not exist with the other signaling disciplines since the programmer explicitly signals processes.) One approach is for the exiting process to evaluate the conditions of waiting processes. If the exiting process finds a waiting process whose condition is true, that process is awakened and given control of the monitor lock; otherwise, one process on the entry queue, if there is one, is given control of the monitor lock. The problem with this approach is that it requires that each process be able to evaluate the waiting conditions of others; this is difficult if the conditions depend on the values of local variables, which they often do. A second approach is to let each process reevaluate its own waiting condition. This is accomplished by placing all delayed processes on the entry queue and letting them enter the monitor one at a time. Unfortunately, this second approach results in numerous context switches, many of which might be unproductive.

To summarize, the various signaling disciplines are equally powerful, but they differ with respect to ease of use and implementation cost. Automatic signaling is the easiest to use for solving problems that do not require distinguishing between processes waiting for the same condition; otherwise explicit signaling is easier to use. Of the explicit signaling disciplines, SC is the easiest to use, followed by SW and SU, then SX. With respect to implementation cost, SC and SX are least costly, followed by SW and SU, then the much costlier AS. Thus, on balance, SC is the preferred signaling discipline. This is why it is the one emphasized in this chapter.

Alternatives to Mutual Exclusion

With monitors, as we have defined them, the permanent variables of a monitor can be accessed by at most one process at a time. Consequently, assertions within a monitor cannot be interfered with. This absence of interference results from three attributes of monitors. First, only procedure names are visible outside a monitor; variables names are not. Second, procedures in a monitor execute with mutual exclusion. Third, if a process executing a procedure in one monitor calls a procedure in another, it retains exclusive control of the first monitor, even if it waits to gain entry to or waits within the second monitor. The first two attributes are clearly necessary to guarantee that interference will not occur. The third attribute is not strictly necessary, however.

When a process executing within a monitor calls a procedure outside the monitor, it is said to have made a *nested call*. If monitor exclusion is retained when a nested call is made—which we have assumed—the call is termed a *closed call*. The alternative is to release monitor exclusion when a nested call is made and to reacquire exclusion when the call returns; this kind of nested call is termed an *open call*.

Permanent monitor variables are clearly protected from concurrent access on a closed call since no other process can enter the monitor while the nested call is being executed. Permanent variables are also protected from concurrent access on an open call, as long as such variables are not passed by reference as arguments on the call. However, since an open call releases exclusion, the monitor invariant must be true before the call.

Thus, open calls have slightly more complex semantics than closed calls. On the other hand, a closed call is more prone to deadlock. In particular, if a process is delayed at a **wait** statement in a closed call, it cannot be awakened by another process that has to make the same set of nested calls. This is because the delayed process retains exclusive control of outer monitors. To eliminate this source of deadlock, some people have proposed that a process should release mutual exclusion in all monitors when it delays. This semantics requires the monitor invariant to be true before every nested call. It also requires a process to reacquire exclusive access to all monitors before it continues executing, which introduces execution overhead.

Any concurrent program can be structured so that nested calls are never used. In fact, none of the examples in this chapter employs them. However, nested calls are useful when a program is structured as a hierarchically organized collection of modules.

As an example, consider again the disk-scheduling problem. Assume that the disk is accessed directly by client processes. When the scheduler is a separate monitor, as in Figure 6.14, clients have to call the monitor's *request* procedure, then access the disk, then call the *release* procedure. To hide this protocol from clients and ensure that they follow it, the protocol could be packaged in a shared procedure that the client calls. A different approach is to replace *Disk_Scheduler* by two monitors, as shown in Figure 6.20. Clients make one call to the *doIO* operation of the *Disk_Access* monitor. That monitor schedules access as in Figure 6.16. When it is a process's turn to access the disk, it makes a second call to the *read* or *write* operation of a second monitor, *Disk_Transfer*. In particular, *Disk_Access* is programmed as:

> **monitor** *Disk_Access*
>
> > **var** permanent variables as in *Disk_Scheduler*
> >
> > **procedure** *doIO(cyl* **int**; transfer and result arguments)
> > actions of *Disk_Scheduler.request*
> > call either *Disk_Transfer.read* or *Disk_Transfer.write*
> > actions of *Disk_Scheduler.release*
> > **end**
>
> **end**

Here, the calls to *Disk_Transfer* are both nested calls. In fact, for disk scheduling to take place, they must be open calls. Otherwise, at most one process at a time could ever be within *doIO*, making the request and release actions superfluous. Open calls can be used here since the requirements are met: only local variables (parameters to *doIO*) are passed as arguments to *Disk_Transfer*, and the disk scheduler invariant, *DISK*, will be true before *read* or *write* is called.

Often, as above, nested calls need to be open calls. However, closed calls are needed if a process must retain exclusive control while making a nested call. Since closed calls have somewhat simpler semantics, on balance they are slightly preferable. But either choice is reasonable since a program can always be structured to employ whichever semantics is provided. In fact, a language could provide both open and closed calls, at the expense of providing two mechanisms for specifying which kind of call to use.

Figure 6.20. Disk access using nested monitors.

Independent of the semantics of nested calls, there is the issue of mutual exclusion within a monitor. By having monitor procedures execute one at a time, permanent variables cannot be accessed concurrently. However, this is not always necessary to avoid interference. If a procedure reads but does not alter permanent variables, different calls of the procedure could execute concurrently. Or, if a procedure merely returns the value of some permanent variable and this value can be read atomically (e.g., it is a simple variable), then the procedure can be allowed to execute concurrently with any monitor procedure. By the time the calling process examines the returned value, it might not be the same as the permanent variable's current value. But this can happen even if procedures execute with mutual exclusion since the order in which processes execute is unpredictable in general. For example, we could add a procedure *read_clock* to the *Timer* monitor in Section 6.3 to return the value of *tod*, thus turning the monitor into a software clock as well as a timer. Whether or not *read_clock* executes with mutual exclusion, a process that calls *read_clock* could only assert that the return value is no greater than the current value of *tod*.

A program will execute more efficiently if procedures that could execute concurrently without introducing interference are actually allowed to do so. This is because a process calling such a procedure would never have to delay waiting for the monitor lock, would not delay other processes while it holds the lock, and would not have to release the lock on return. In the *Timer* example mentioned above, this means that processes executing the *tick* procedure would never be delayed by processes executing *read_clock*. In fact, even the overhead of a procedure call can be avoided by allowing permanent variables such as *tod* to be read but not written outside a monitor. In general, however, allowing permanent variables to be visible outside a monitor introduces the possibility that assertions outside the monitor could be interfered with.

Even in situations where different monitor procedures alter permanent variables, they can sometimes safely execute in parallel. For example, we have seen in previous chapters that a producer and a consumer can concurrently access different slots of a bounded buffer (e.g., see Section 5.4). If monitor procedures must execute with mutual exclusion, it is awkward to program such a buffer. Either each buffer slot has to be encapsulated by a separate monitor, or the buffer has to be global to processes, which then synchronize using monitors that implement semaphores. Fortunately, such situations are rare.

Path Expressions

We have now considered several signaling disciplines. Independent of the discipline, one programs condition synchronization using statements within monitor procedures. We have also examined issues related to exclusion in monitors. Again, independent of the choice of the semantics of nested calls or whether some procedures might be allowed to execute concurrently, implicit in monitors is the assumption that procedures do not interfere with each other.

There are, however, two other ways in which synchronization could be programmed within a modular construct that provides the same data-encapsulation facilities as monitors. The first approach is to employ semaphores for all synchronization. In particular, change the semantics of monitors so that by default procedures execute concurrently. Then, the programmer explicitly programs *both* mutual exclusion and condition synchronization using semaphores in the ways shown in Chapter 4. (See Section 9.1 for examples.) This provides flexibility since any combination of exclusive and concurrent execution of monitor procedures can be programmed. For example, one can directly program a bounded buffer with concurrent access. Also, the programmer is free to retain or release exclusion before a nested call. Unfortunately, this extra flexibility makes solutions to most problems, which require exclusion, longer and more error-prone. Also, interference is not automatically precluded; instead, the programmer must be careful to use semaphores correctly to implement exclusion when necessary. The encapsulation provided by monitors helps in this regard since assertions about permanent variables cannot be interfered with by statements outside a monitor, assuming such variables are not visible outside the monitor and are not passed by reference on nested calls.

A second, quite different approach to synchronization in monitors employs what are called *path expressions*. As above, the semantics of monitors are changed so that by default procedures execute concurrently. However, instead of using semaphores to program mutual exclusion and condition synchronization, all synchronization is specified by path expressions declared at the beginning of the monitor.

A path expression is like a regular expression in which the operands are procedure names and the operators specify whether the procedures are to execute exclusively, concurrently, or sequentially. For example, in one of the notations that has been proposed, the following path expression specifies that each *fetch* must be preceded by a *deposit* (the semicolon) and that only one of *deposit* or *fetch* can execute at a tim

(6.20)   **path** 1 : (*deposit*; *fetch*) **e**

Such a path expression might be   plements a single-
slot buffer, in which case the bodi   procedures would
only contain code to access the b   le, synchronization
constraints for a bounded buffer   uld be specified by:

(6.21)   **path** N : (1: (*deposit*);

This path expression specifie   *posit* are mutually
exclusive, activations of *fetch*   , each *fetch* must be
preceded by a corresponding   of completed *deposit*
operations is never more tha   number of completed
fetch operations. In both ca   e that implements the
constraints specified by the   ld be generated automatically by a compiler.

Path expressions provi   for specifying synchronization that can be express   procedure names. They
are ill suited, however, f   ation that depends on
procedure parameters or t   us, they are ill suited for
most scheduling problem   path expressions have
addressed this deficiency   flexibility of conventional
monitor synchronization   let alone semaphore-based
synchronization. Also, n   hown when procedures are
allowed to execute concu   ns, path expressions have
not proven popular for programming sy   ion constraints. They have,
however, proven useful for high-level specification of the permissible orders
in which events can occur in a concurrent program. The Historical Notes
mention some of these applications and give citations to relevant literature.

6.6 Implementations

In the previous section, we briefly described how to implement monitors.
Here we develop two complete implementations. First, we show how
monitors can be implemented using semaphores. Then, we describe a kernel
implementation. We assume the monitor semantics defined in Section 6.1. In
particular, procedures execute with mutual exclusion, and condition
synchronization uses the signal and continue discipline.

For both implementations, we assume a monitor's permanent variables
are stored in memory accessible to all processes that call the monitor's
procedures. Code that implements the procedures can be stored in shared

memory, or copies of the code can be stored in local memory on each processor that executes processes that use the monitor. We also assume the permanent variables are initialized before the procedures are called. This can be accomplished by, for example, allocating and initializing permanent variable storage before creating any processes that will access it. (Alternatively, initialization code could be executed on the first call of a monitor procedure. This is, however, less efficient since every call would have to check to see if it were the first.)

Given these assumptions, our concerns are implementing mutual exclusion of monitor procedures and condition synchronization between monitor procedures. In particular, we need to develop (1) entry code that is executed after a process calls a monitor procedure but before the process begins executing the procedure body, (2) exit code that is executed just before a process returns from a procedure body, and (3) code that implements **wait**, **signal** and the other operations on condition variables.

Using Semaphores

To implement monitor exclusion, we use one entry semaphore for each monitor. Let e be the semaphore associated with monitor M. Since e is to be used for mutual exclusion, its initial value is 1, and its value is always 0 or 1. The purpose of the entry protocol of each procedure in M is to acquire exclusive access to M; as usual with semaphores, this is implemented by $\mathbf{P}(e)$. Similarly, the exit protocol of each procedure releases exclusive access, so it can be implemented by $\mathbf{V}(e)$.

Execution of **wait**($cond$) releases monitor exclusion and delays the executing process on condition variable $cond$. The process resumes execution in the monitor when it has been signaled and can regain exclusive control of the monitor. Assume for now that processes delayed on a semaphore are awakened in the order in which they delayed, i.e., semaphore queuing is FIFO. Then the queue for $cond$ can be represented by a semaphore c, and the length of the queue can be represented by an integer counter nc. Initially c and nc are both 0 since no process is waiting; at all times their values are non-negative.

Given this representation for $cond$, a process indicates it is about to delay by incrementing nc and then delays by executing $\mathbf{P}(c)$. However, just before executing $\mathbf{P}(c)$, the process must release monitor exclusion; as in the exit protocol, this is accomplished by executing $\mathbf{V}(e)$. After being awakened, the process must reacquire exclusion; as in the entry protocol, this is accomplished by executing $\mathbf{P}(e)$.

With the above representation for condition variables, implementation of **signal** is straightforward. Execution of **signal**($cond$) has no effect if no process is waiting; i.e., if $nc = 0$. Otherwise, one process delayed on $cond$ is awakened; i.e., nc is decremented, then $\mathbf{V}(c)$ is executed.

shared variables: $e : \textbf{sem} := 1$ # Invariant $0 \leq e \leq 1$
$\qquad\qquad\qquad\quad c : \textbf{sem} := 0$ # Invariant $c \geq 0$
$\qquad\qquad\qquad\quad nc : \textbf{int} := 0$ # Invariant $nc \geq 0$

monitor entry: $\textbf{P}(e)$

wait(*cond*): $nc := nc + 1; \textbf{V}(e); \textbf{P}(c); \textbf{P}(e)$

signal(*cond*): $\textbf{if } nc > 0 \rightarrow nc := nc - 1; \textbf{V}(c) \textbf{ fi}$

monitor exit: $\textbf{V}(e)$

Figure 6.21. Implementing monitors using semaphores.

To summarize, Figure 6.21 shows how to implement monitor synchronization using semaphores. Mutual exclusion is ensured since e is initially 1 and every execution path executes alternate $\textbf{P}(e)$ and $\textbf{V}(e)$ operations. Also, nc is positive when at least one process is delayed or is about to delay on c.

Given the above representation for condition variables, it is straightforward to implement the **empty** primitive. In particular, **empty** returns true if $nc > 0$, and it returns false if $nc = 0$. It is also straightforward to implement **signal_all**: execute $\textbf{V}(c)$ nc times and then set nc to zero.

However, we cannot implement priority **wait** and **minrank** without changing the representation of the condition queue. In particular, we need to use a priority queue to store the ranks of delayed processes, and we need to replace the single delay semaphore by an array of private semaphores. Then, when a process waits, it stores its delay rank and identity on the priority queue, exits the monitor by executing $\textbf{V}(e)$, and finally delays by executing $\textbf{P}$ on its private semaphore. When a process executes **signal** and the priority queue is not empty, it removes the smallest rank from the priority queue and then signals the corresponding process's private semaphore. This same technique can also be used to implement non-priority **wait** if semaphore queuing is not FIFO.

Using a Kernel

Monitors can also be implemented directly by a kernel. By combining the actions required to implement **wait** and **signal** into single primitives, the implementation is more efficient than the semaphore-based one. Also, it is straightforward to implement the other operations on condition variables in a kernel, as will be shown.

We assume that processes are implemented as described in Chapter 3. In particular, each process has a descriptor, and the descriptors of processes that are ready to execute on a processor are linked together on a ready list. To also implement monitors, we add primitives for monitor entry, monitor exit, and each of the operations on condition variables. Primitives are also needed to create descriptors for each monitor and each condition variable (unless these are created when the kernel itself is initialized). These are not shown here; they are analogous to the primitives to create semaphores (Figure 4.23) or resources (Figure 5.9).

Each monitor descriptor contains a lock and an entry queue of descriptors of processes waiting to enter (or reenter) the monitor. The lock is used to ensure mutual exclusion. When the lock is set, exactly one process is executing in the monitor; otherwise, no process is executing in the monitor.

The descriptor for a condition variable contains the head of a queue of descriptors of processes waiting on that condition variable. Thus, every process descriptor—except perhaps those of executing processes—is linked to either the ready list, a monitor entry queue, or a condition variable queue. Condition variable descriptors are commonly stored adjacent to the descriptor of the monitor in which the condition variables are declared. This is done to avoid excessive fragmentation of kernel storage and to allow the run-time identity of a condition variable simply to be an offset from the start of the appropriate monitor descriptor.

The monitor entry primitive *enter(name)* finds the descriptor for monitor *name*, then either sets the monitor lock and allows the executing process to proceed or blocks the process on the monitor entry queue. To enable the descriptor to be found quickly, the run-time identity of *name* is typically the address of the monitor descriptor. The monitor exit primitive *exit(name)* either moves one process from the entry queue to the ready list or clears the monitor lock. Figure 6.22 gives code outlines for these primitives. As in previous kernels, the primitives are entered as a result of a supervisor call, *executing* points to the descriptor of the executing process or is set to 0 when the executing process blocks, and each primitive calls *dispatcher* as its last action. Also, *lock* and entry queue are the components of the descriptor of monitor *name*.

The **wait**(c) statement is implemented by invoking the kernel primitive *wait(name, cname)*, and the **signal**(c) statement is implemented by invoking the kernel primitive *signal(name, cname)*. In both primitives, *name* is the name of the descriptor of the monitor within which the primitive is invoked, and *cname* is the name of the descriptor of the appropriate condition variable. Execution of *wait* delays the executing process on the specified condition variable queue and then either awakens some process on the monitor entry queue or clears the monitor lock. Execution of *signal* checks the condition variable queue. If it is empty, the primitive simply returns; otherwise, the descriptor at the front of the condition variable queue is moved to the end of the monitor entry queue. Figure 6.22 also gives code outlines for these primitives. There, delay queue is the queue in the condition variable descriptor. Since a process that calls *wait* exits the monitor, the *wait* primitive simply calls the *exit* primitive after blocking the executing process.

procedure *enter(name : monitor_index)*
  find descriptor for monitor *name*
  if *lock* = 1 → insert descriptor of *executing* at end of entry queue
              executing := 0
  [] *lock* = 0 → *lock* := 1   # acquire exclusive access to *name*
  fi
  call *dispatcher*( )
end

procedure *exit(name : monitor_index)*
  find descriptor for monitor *name*
  if entry queue not empty → move process descriptor from front of
                  entry queue to rear of ready list
  [] entry queue empty → *lock* := 0   # clear the lock
  fi
  call *dispatcher*( )
end

procedure *wait(name : monitor_index; cname : condvar_index)*
  find descriptor for condition variable *cname*
  insert descriptor of *executing* at end of delay queue; *executing* := 0
  call *exit(name)*
end

procedure *signal(name : monitor_index; cname : condvar_index)*
  find descriptor for monitor *name*
  find descriptor for condition variable *cname*
  if delay queue not empty → move process descriptor from front of
                  delay queue to rear of entry queue
  fi
  call *dispatcher*( )
end

Figure 6.22. Monitor kernel primitives.

It is straightforward to implement the other operations on condition variables. For example, implementing **empty**(*c*) involves testing whether *c*'s delay queue is empty. However, if the delay queue is directly accessible to processes, it is not necessary to use a kernel primitive to implement **empty**. This is because the executing process already has the monitor locked, so the contents of the condition queue cannot be changed by another process. By implementing **empty** in this way, we avoid the overhead of a supervisor call and return.

We can also make the implementation of *signal* more efficient than is shown in Figure 6.22. In particular, we could modify *signal* so that it *always* moves a descriptor from the front of the appropriate delay queue to the end of the appropriate entry queue. Then, **signal** is translated into code that tests the delay queue and only invokes *signal* if the delay queue is not empty. By making these changes, the overhead of kernel entry and exit is avoided when **signal** has no effect. Independent of how **signal** is implemented, **signal_all** is implemented by a kernel primitive that moves all descriptors from the specified delay queue to the end of the ready list.

Priority **wait** is implemented analogously to non-priority **wait.** The only difference is that the descriptor of the executing process needs to be inserted at the appropriate place on the delay queue. To keep that queue ordered, the rank of each waiting process needs to be recorded; the logical place to store the rank is in the process's descriptor. This also makes implementation of **minrank** trivial. In fact, **minrank**—like **empty**—can be implemented without entering the kernel, as long as the minimum rank can be read directly by the executing process.

This kernel can be extended to one for a multiprocessor using the techniques described in Section 3.6. Again, the key requirement is to protect kernel data structures from being accessed simultaneously by processes executing on different processors. And again, one has to worry about avoiding memory contention, exploiting caches, co-scheduling processes, and balancing processor load.

On a single processor, monitors can in some cases be implemented even more efficiently without using a kernel. If there are no nested monitor calls—or if nested calls are all open calls—and all monitor procedures are short and guaranteed to terminate, it is both possible and reasonable to implement mutual exclusion by inhibiting interrupts. This is done as follows. On entry to a monitor, the executing process inhibits all interrupts. When it returns from a monitor procedure, it enables interrupts. If the process has to wait within a monitor, it blocks on a condition variable queue, and the fact that the process was executing with interrupts inhibited is recorded. (This is often encoded in a processor status register that is saved when a process blocks.) When a waiting process is awakened as a result of **signal**, it is moved from the condition variable queue to the ready list; the signaling process continues to execute. Finally, whenever a ready process is dispatched, it resumes execution with interrupts inhibited or enabled, depending on whether interrupts were inhibited or enabled at the time the process blocked. (Newly created processes begin execution with interrupts enabled.)

This implementation does away with kernel primitives—they become either in-line code or regular subroutines—and does away with monitor descriptors. Since interrupts are inhibited while a process is executing in a monitor, it cannot be forced to relinquish the processor. Thus, the process has exclusive access to the monitor until it waits or returns. Assuming monitor procedures terminate, eventually the process will wait or return. If the process waits, when it is awakened and resumes execution, interrupts are again inhibited, so the process again has exclusive control of the monitor in which it waited. Nested monitor calls cannot be allowed, however, or else, while a process is waiting in a second monitor, another process might start executing in the monitor from which the nested call was made.

Monitors are implemented in essentially this way within the UNIX operating system. In fact, on entry to a monitor procedure in UNIX, interrupts are inhibited only from those devices that could cause some other process to call the same monitor before the interrupted process waits or returns from the monitor. In general, however, a kernel implementation is needed since not all monitor-based programs meet the requirements for this specialized implementation. In particular, only in a "trusted" program such as an operating systems is it likely that all monitor procedures can be guaranteed to terminate. Also, the specialized implementation only works on a single processor. On a multiprocessor, locks of some form are still required to ensure mutual exclusion of processes executing on different processors.

Historical Notes and References

The concept of data encapsulation originated with the **class** construct of Simula-67 [Dahl 1972]. Edsger W. Dijkstra [1972] is generally credited with being the first to advocate using data encapsulation to control access to shared variables in a concurrent program. He called such a unit a "secretary" but did not propose any syntactic mechanism for programming secretaries. Per Brinch Hansen [1972] advocates the same idea and presents a specific language proposal called a **shared class** in Brinch Hansen [1973a]. The one example given in that book uses the **await** statement for condition synchronization.

Monitors were named and popularized by Tony Hoare.* They first appear as a programming tool in a paper that describes a structured paging system [Hoare 1973]. The most influential paper on monitors is the excellent [Hoare 1974]. Condition synchronization in Hoare's proposal employs the signal and urgent wait (SU) signaling discipline. Hoare [1974] gives proof rules for monitors. That paper also contains numerous interesting examples, including a bounded buffer, interval timer, and disk head scheduler (elevator algorithm). The reader might find it instructive to compare Hoare's solutions, which use SU signaling, with those in this chapter, which use SC signaling. Hoare [1974] also introduced the concept of a split binary semaphore and showed how to use it to implement monitors.

Concurrent Pascal [Brinch Hansen 1975] was the first concurrent programming language to include monitors. Its three structuring components are processes,

*Recall that a year earlier Brinch Hansen and Hoare concurrently developed conditional critical regions. In the late 1970s they would again concurrently develop quite similar message passing mechanisms: communicating sequential processes [Hoare 1978] (see Chapter 8) and distributed processes [Brinch Hansen 1978] (see Chapter 9).

monitors, and classes. Signaling in monitors employs the signal and exit (SX) discipline. Classes are like monitors, except they cannot be shared by processes and hence have no need for mutual exclusion or condition synchronization. Concurrent Pascal has been used to write several operating systems [Brinch Hansen 1976a, 1976b, 1977]. In Concurrent Pascal, I/O devices and the like are treated as special monitors that are implemented by the language's run-time system, which thus hides the notion of an interrupt. Loehr [1977] and Keedy [1978] examine the use of the language for programming operating systems and analyze its approach to I/O.

Modula is another influential monitor-based language.* It was developed by Nicklaus Wirth, the designer of Pascal, as a systems language for programming dedicated computer systems, including process control applications [Wirth 1977a, 1977b, 1977c, 1977d]. Modula extends a modified Pascal with processes, interface modules, which are like monitors, and device modules, which are special interface modules for programming device controllers. Condition variable signaling in Modula usually employs the signal and wait (SW) discipline. The exception is within device modules, in which signal and continue (SC) is used when a device driver process signals a lower-priority user process. The run-time system for Modula is very small and efficient, and device modules provide a useful set of mechanisms for programming device controllers. Thus Modula gives the programmer more low-level control than Concurrent Pascal; but in doing so it requires the programmer to be more careful. Modula's strengths and weaknesses have been evaluated by Andrews [1979], Holden and Wand [1980], and Bernstein and Ensor [1981].

Monitors have been included in several additional languages. These differ in terms of their mechanisms for sequential programming, mechanisms for creating and naming processes, monitors, and other modules, and the signaling discipline they use for condition variables. SIMONE [Kaubisch et al. 1976] was another early language based on Pascal; it uses the signal and urgent wait (SU) discipline.

Mesa was developed at Xerox PARC [Mitchell et al. 1979]; it uses the signal and continue discipline. Lampson and Redell [1980] give an excellent description of experience with processes and monitors in Mesa. That paper discusses the technique of using a *covering condition* to awaken delayed processes, which we illustrated in Figure 6.7. Lampson [1983] describes Cedar, a descendant of Mesa.

Pascal Plus [Welsh & Bustard 1979] uses the signal and urgent wait (SU) discipline. It also introduced the **minrank** primitive, which is called the PRIORITY function. Two books, Welsh and McKeag [1980] and Bustard et al. [1988], give several large examples of systems programs written in Pascal Plus.

Ric Holt and his colleagues at the University of Toronto have designed a series of monitor-based languages. The first, CSP/k [Holt et al. 1978], is a superset of SP/k, which is in turn a structured subset of PL/I. Concurrent Euclid [Holt 1983] extends Euclid [Lampson et al. 1977]; it has been used to implement a UNIX-compatible nucleus called Tunis. Holt [1983] contains an excellent overview of concurrent

---

*Wirth later developed Modula-2 [Wirth 1982], and others have recently developed Modula-3 [Cardelli et al. 89]. Despite the similar names, these are quite different from the original Modula. In particular, neither Modula-2 nor Modula-3 contains processes or monitors. Instead, they provide co-routines and a powerful data-abstraction mechanism that can be used to program modules that implement (pseudo) processes and monitors as well as other concurrent programming mechanisms.

programming as well as very readable descriptions of Concurrent Euclid, UNIX, and operating system and kernel design. Holt's most recent language is Turing Plus [Holt & Cordy 1985], which extends the sequential programming language Turing [Holt & Cordy 1988]. All of CSP/k, Concurrent Euclid, and Turing Plus employ the signal and wait (SW) discipline. However, Turing Plus also supports the signal and continue (SC) discipline and requires its use within device monitors so that interrupt handlers are not preempted. Section 10.1 gives an overview of Turing Plus and an example program.

Emerald is a different kind of language than the above. It is not based on monitors but rather includes them as a synchronization mechanism. In particular, Emerald is an object-oriented distributed programming language [Black et al. 1986, Black et al. 1987, Raj et al. 1991]. As in other object-oriented languages, an object has a representation and is manipulated by invoking operations. However, objects in Emerald can execute concurrently, and, within an object, invocations can execute concurrently. When mutual exclusion and condition synchronization are required, variables and the operations that access them can be defined within a monitor. Objects in Emerald can also be mobile; i.e., they can move during program execution.

As mentioned, Hoare's classic paper [1974] introduced proof rules for monitors. However, Hoare confessed in his paper that his proof rules seem incapable of handling the more complex examples. One problem is that he required the monitor invariant to be true before executing **signal.** John Howard [1976a] developed a stronger set of axioms and also examined the effects of queueing and priorities. That paper contains a correctness proof for a disk scheduler. In a second paper, Howard [1976b] presents formal proof rules for each of the five signaling disciplines and shows how each can simulate the other. (However, Howard's semantics for signal and continue are somewhat more complex than the semantics used in this chapter since he requires awakened processes to execute before new callers.) The procedure call rule given in (6.10) was adapted from Gries and Levin [1980].

The idea of using automatic signaling (**await**) rather than condition variables was first mentioned at the end of Hoare [1974]. Although it is attractive to use explicit boolean synchronization conditions for many problems, they have the same problems as conditional critical regions. In particular, it is awkward to solve many scheduling problems, and **await** is costly to implement in general. Kessels [1977] proposes an efficient variant of **await** in which a boolean expression is explicitly declared with each condition variable. However, Kessels does not permit delay conditions to depend on parameters to operations—only on permanent variables—and hence his approach cannot be used to solve most scheduling problems.

Dijkstra [1968b] introduced the sleeping barber problem in his important paper on using semaphores. Teory and Pinkerton [1972] and Geist and Daniel [1987] discuss and analyze a variety of different disk scheduling algorithms. Section 6.4 uses the the circular scan algorithm. Later we will show how to implement shortest seek time (Section 7.4). Hoare's paper [1974] illustrates the elevator algorithm.

Lister [1977] raised the problem of what to do about nested monitor calls. This led to a flurry of follow-up papers [Haddon 1977, Parnas 1978, Wettstein 1978] and other letters in *Operating Systems Review*, the quarterly newsletter of the ACM Special Interest Group on Operating Systems (SIGOPS). These papers discussed four possibilities:

- Prohibit nested calls, as was done in SIMONE [Kaubisch et al. 1976], or permit them but only to monitors that are not lexically nested, as was done in Modula [Wirth 1977a].

- When a process blocks in a monitor, release exclusion only in that monitor; this is the approach taken in Concurrent Pascal [Brinch Hansen 1975].

- Use open calls so that a process releases exclusion whenever it leaves a monitor; Haddon [1978] argues that this approach is best.

- Use closed calls, but when a process blocks in a monitor, release exclusion in all monitors on the call chain and reacquire it before the process continues; Wettstein [1978] gives a nice implementation of this approach that works with signal and continue semantics.

Subsequent papers suggested other possibilities. One is to provide special-purpose constructs that can be used for particular situations in which nested calls arise. The manager construct [Silberschatz et al. 1977] and the scheduler monitor [Schneider & Bernstein 1978] are two examples. An even more attractive possibility is to let the programmer specify whether a specific call is open or closed. This was first proposed in Andrews and McGraw [1977]. The SB-Mod language—a modification of Modula— also takes this approach [Bernstein & Ensor 1981].

In reaction to Lister's paper, David Parnas [1978] argued that the issue is not mutual exclusion per se but data integrity, which does not necessarily require mutual exclusion. In particular, concurrent execution of monitor procedures is fine as long as processes in a monitor do not interfere with each other. Andrews and McGraw [1977] define a monitor-like construct that permits the programmer to specify which procedures can execute in parallel. Mesa [Mitchell et al. 1979] also provides mechanisms that give the programmer control over the granularity of exclusion.

Roy Campbell and Nico Habermann [1974] developed the idea of path expressions while Campbell was a Ph.D. student. Campbell and a Ph.D. student of his own, Robert Kolstad, subsequently developed an extension called open path expressions [Campbell & Kolstad 1979, 1980], which they incorporated into a language called Path Pascal. Equations (6.20) and (6.21) are examples of open path expressions. As noted at the end of Section 6.5, path expressions are ill suited for solving scheduling problems. Andler [1979] presents an extension, called predicate path expressions, that partially addresses this problem. (A textbook by Maekawa et al. [1987] gives examples of both open and predicate path expressions and also describes how to implement them.)

Although path expressions are not as powerful as one would like for expressing all synchronization, they are useful for specify permissible execution sequences. For example, Kieburtz and Silberschatz [1983] show how to use simple path expressions to specify the permissible orders in which monitor procedures can be called. This is useful for ensuring that a user process obeys the protocol intended by the designer of the monitor; e.g., the user calls *request* before using a disk and calls *release* afterwords. Gehani [1990b] presents a fairly elaborate synchronization mechanism called a capsule that combines aspects of monitors, path expressions, boolean condition synchronization, and scheduling functions.

Several papers and books describe kernel implementations of monitors. Wirth [1977c] describes the Modula kernel. Holt et al. [1978] describe both single and multiple processor kernels for CSP/k. That book's successor [Holt 1983] describes kernels for Concurrent Euclid. Joseph et al. [1984] present the design and implementation of a complete operating system for a shared-memory multiprocessor. They use monitors within the operating system and show how to implement them using a kernel. Thompson [1978] and Holt [1983] describe the implementation of UNIX.

The UNIX kernel implements mutual exclusion by performing context switches only when user processes block or exit the kernel and by inhibiting external interrupts at critical points. The UNIX equivalent of a condition variable is called an event. An event is an arbitrary integer, which is typically the address of a descriptor, e.g., a process or file descriptor. A process blocks by executing **sleep**(*e*). It is awakened when another process executes **wakeup**(*e*). The **wakeup** primitive has signal and continue semantics. It is also a broadcast primitive; namely, **wakeup**(*e*) awakens all processes blocked on event *e*. UNIX has no equivalent of the **signal** primitive to awaken just one process. Thus, if more than one process could be waiting for an event, each has to check if the condition it was waiting for is still true and go back to sleep if it is not.

Exercises

6.1 Suppose the **empty** primitive is not available. Develop a simulation of it. In particular, show the code you would need to add before and after each **wait** and **signal** statement. (Do not worry about **signal_all**.) Your solution should work for any of the four explicit signaling disciplines.

6.2 Consider the bounded buffer monitor in Figure 6.1.

(a) Develop a complete proof outline for the monitor.

(b) Write a producer process and a consumer process that use the bounded buffer to copy the contents of producer array $a[1{:}m]$ into consumer array $b[1{:}m]$. Develop complete proof outlines for the producer and consumer. You will need to use Call Rule (6.10) and Monitors Rule (6.12). Using (6.14), prove that your answer program is deadlock-free.

6.3 Consider the *Shortest_Job_Next* monitor in Figure 6.2. For each of the three preemptive signaling disciplines—SX, SW, and SU—determine whether the monitor is correct if that signaling discipline is used. If so, explain why. If not, modify the monitor so it is correct.

6.4 Consider the following monitor with the indicated invariant:

```
monitor foo      # Invariant: sum ≥ 0
   var sum : int := 0
   procedure add( val a, b : int; var c, d : int; res e : int )
      if a ≤ b → sum := sum + b − a
      [] a ≥ b → sum := sum + a − b
      fi
      c := c + 1; d := sum; e := a + b
   end
end
```

(a) Develop a proof outline for the body of *add*.

(b) Using Call Rule (6.10), show that each of the following is a theorem:

$$\{\, u = 10 \wedge v = 20 \wedge w = 4 \,\}$$
call *foo.add*(u, v, w, x, y)
$$\{\, u = 10 \wedge v = 20 \wedge w = 5 \wedge x \geq 0 \wedge y = 30 \,\}$$

$$\{\, u = 11 \wedge v = 3 \wedge w = 11 \wedge x < y \wedge x \leq -3 \,\}$$
call *foo.add*(u, v, w, x, y)
$$\{\, x \geq 0 \wedge y = u + v \,\}$$

6.5   (a) Prove that the conditions in (6.13) are sufficient to ensure mutual exclusion. Explain why the conditions are not necessary.

(b) Prove that the conditions in (6.14) are sufficient to ensure absence of deadlock. Explain why the conditions are not necessary.

6.6   Develop axioms for **wait** and **signal** for each of the preemptive signaling disciplines: signal and exit (SX), signal and wait (SW), and signal and urgent wait (SU). These differ from signal and continue, in that control is transferred immediately to a delayed process. Thus, the monitor invariant might not be true at the time control is transferred.

6.7   Consider the following proposed solution to the shortest job next allocation problem (4.11):

```
monitor SJN
   var free := true, turn : cond

   procedure request(time : int)
      if not free → wait(turn, time) fi
      free := false
   end

   procedure release( )
      free := true; signal(turn)
   end
end
```

For each of the four explicit signaling disciplines—signal and continue, signal and exit, signal and wait, and signal and urgent wait—determine whether the solution is correct. Clearly explain your answers.

6.8   The **wait**(*cond*) and **signal**(*cond*) statements manipulate the queue associated with *cond*. This queue is an implicit part of the program statement. However, the wait and signal axioms in (6.4) and (6.5) do not take account of changes to this queue.

(a) Extend the wait and signal axioms to account for changes to the queue associated with *cond*. Assume **signal** has signal and continue semantics.

(b) Develop an axiom for the priority **wait** statement **wait**(*cond*, *rank*).

(c) Using your answers to (a) and (b), develop a proof outline for the monitor in Figure 6.2. Your proof outline should demonstrate that the monitor services requests in shortest-job-next order.

(d) Develop axioms for **wait** and **signal** for each of the preemptive signaling disciplines: signal and exit (SX), signal and wait (SW), and signal and urgent wait (SU). Again, account for changes to the queue associated with *cond*. In the case of SU, also account for changes to the urgent queue.

6.9 The following problems deal with the readers/writers monitor in Figure 6.4.

(a) Suppose there is no **signal_all** primitive. Modify the solution so that it uses only **signal.** Assume signal and continue semantics.

(b) Modify the solution to give writers preference instead of readers.

(c) Modify the solution so that readers and writers alternate if both are trying to access the database.

(d) Modify the solution so that readers and writers are given permission to access the database in FCFS order. Allow readers concurrent access when that does not violate the FCFS order of granting permission.

6.10 For the readers/writers proof outline in Figure 6.5, show the complete details of all four applications of Call Rule (6.10). Show what in the program corresponds to predicates IN, OUT, and PR. Also show the substitutions of actual parameters for formals in both IN and OUT.

6.11 Consider the following definition of semaphores [Habermann 1972]. Let na be the number of times a process has attempted a **P** operation, let np be the number of completed **P** operations, and let nv be the number of completed **V** operations. The semaphore invariant for this representation is:

$$np = min(na, nv)$$

In words, this invariant specifies that a process delayed in a **P** operation should be awakened and allowed to continue as soon as enough **V** operations have been executed.

(a) Develop a monitor that implements semaphores using this representation and invariant. Use the signal and continue discipline.

(b) Develop a monitor that implements semaphores using this representation and invariant. Use the preemptive signal and wait (SW) discipline.

6.12 *The One-Lane Bridge.* Cars coming from the north and the south arrive at a one-lane bridge. Cars heading in the same direction can cross the bridge at the same time, but cars heading in opposite directions cannot.

(a) Develop a solution to this problem. Model the cars as processes, and use a monitor for synchronization. First specify the monitor invariant, then derive the body of the monitor. Do not worry about fairness, and do not give preference to any one kind of car.

(b) Develop a complete proof outline. Then use (6.13) and (6.14) to demonstrate that your answer to (a) ensures mutual exclusion and avoids deadlock.

(c) Modify your answer to (a) to ensure fairness. (Hint: Allow at most C cars to cross in one direction if cars are waiting to cross in the other direction.)

6.13   *The Savings Account Problem.* A savings account is shared by several people (processes). Each person may deposit or withdraw funds from the account. The current balance in the account is the sum of all deposits to date minus the sum of all withdrawals to date. The balance must never become negative.

(a) Derive a monitor to solve this problem. The monitor should have two procedures: *deposit(amount)* and *withdraw(amount)*. First specify a monitor invariant. Assume the arguments to *deposit* and *withdraw* are positive.

(b) Modify your answer to (a) so that withdrawals are serviced FCFS. For example, suppose the current balance is $200, and one customer is waiting to withdraw $300. If another customer arrives, he must wait, even if he wants to withdraw at most $200. Assume there is a magic function *amount(cv)* that returns the value of the amount parameter of the first process delayed on *cv*.

(c) Suppose a magic *amount* function does not exist. Modify your answer to (b) to simulate it in your solution.

6.14   Develop a monitor that implements a counter barrier for n processes (see Section 3.5). The monitor should have one procedure, *arrive*, that a process calls when it reaches the barrier. The barrier should be reusable. First specify a monitor invariant, then derive the body of the monitor.

6.15   Two kinds of processes, A's and B's, enter a room. An A process cannot leave until it meets two B processes, and a B process cannot leave until it meets one A process. Either kind of process leaves the room—without meeting any other processes—once it has met the required number of other processes.

(a) Develop a monitor to implement this synchronization. First specify a monitor invariant, then derive the body of the monitor.

(b) Modify your answer to (a) so that the first of the two B processes that meets an A process does not leave the room until after the A process meets a second B process.

6.16   *Atomic Broadcast.* Assume that one producer process and n consumer processes share a bounded buffer having b slots. The producer deposits messages in the buffer; consumers fetch them. Every message deposited by the producer is to be received by all n consumers. Furthermore, each consumer is to receive the messages in the order they were deposited. However, different consumers can receive messages at different times. For example, one consumer could receive up to b more messages than another if the second consumer is slow.

Develop a monitor that implements this kind of interprocess communication. First specify a monitor invariant, then derive the body of the monitor.

6.17   (a) Develop a monitor to implement the synchronization in the dining philosophers problem (4.4). The monitor should have two operations: *getforks* and *relforks*. First specify a monitor invariant, then derive the body of the monitor. Your solution need not be fair.

(b) Develop a complete proof outline for your monitor and the five philosopher processes. Using (6.13) and (6.14), show that neighboring philosophers cannot eat at the same time and that your solution is deadlock-free. You will need to use auxiliary variables.

(c) Modify your answer to (a) so that it is fair; i.e., a philosopher who wants to eat eventually gets to.

6.18 *The Dining Savages.* A tribe of savages eats communal dinners from a large pot that can hold M servings of stewed missionary. When a savage wants to eat, he helps himself from the pot, unless it is empty. If the pot is empty, the savage wakes up the cook and then waits until the cook has refilled the pot. The behavior of the savages and cook is specified by the following processes:

> *Savage*[1:*n*]:: **do** true → get serving from pot; eat **od**
>
> *Cook*:: **do** true → sleep; put M servings in pot **od**

Develop code for the actions of the savages and cook. Use a monitor for synchronization. Your solution should avoid deadlock and awaken the cook only when the pot is empty.

6.19 *Search/Insert/Delete.* Three kinds of processes share access to a singly-linked list: searchers, inserters, and deleters. Searchers merely examine the list; hence they can execute concurrently with each other. Inserters add new items to the end of the list; insertions must be mutually exclusive to preclude two inserters from inserting new items at about the same time. However, one insert can proceed in parallel with any number of searches. Finally, deleters remove items from anywhere in the list. At most one deleter process can access the list at a time, and deletion must also be mutually exclusive with searches and insertions.

Derive a monitor to implement this kind of synchronization. First specify a monitor invariant, then develop a coarse-grained solution using **await**, and finally develop a fine-grained solution that uses condition variables.

6.20 *Memory Allocation.* Suppose there are two operations: *request*(*amount* : **int**) and *release*(*amount* : **int**). When a process calls *request*, it delays until at least *amount* free pages of memory are available. A process returns *amount* pages to the free pool by calling *release*. Pages may be released in different quantities than they are acquired.

(a) Develop a monitor that implements *request* and *release*. First specify a global invariant, then develop a coarse-grained solution, and finally develop a fine-grained solution that uses condition variables. Do not worry about the order in which requests are serviced. (Hint: Use a covering condition.)

(b) Modify your answer to (a) to use the shortest-job-next (SJN) allocation policy. In particular, smaller requests take precedence over larger ones.

(c) Modify your answer to (a) to use a first-come, first-served (FCFS) allocation policy. This means that a pending request might have to delay, even if there is enough memory available.

(d) Suppose *request* and *release* acquire and return contiguous pages of memory; i.e., if a process requests two pages, it delays until two adjacent pages are available. Develop a monitor that implements these version of *request* and *release*. First choose a representation for the status of memory pages, and specify a monitor invariant.

6.21   Suppose n processes $P[1:n]$ share three printers. Before using a printer, $P[i]$ calls *request(printer)*. This operation returns the identity of a free printer. After using that printer, $P[i]$ returns it by calling *release(printer)*.

(a) Develop a monitor that implements *request* and *release*. First specify a monitor invariant, then derive the bodies of the procedures.

(b) Assume each process has a priority that it passes to the monitor as an additional argument to *request*. Modify *request* and *release* so that a printer is allocated to the highest priority waiting process. If two processes have the same priority, their requests should be granted in FCFS order.

6.22   Suppose a computer center has two printers, A and B, that are similar but not identical. Three kinds of processes use the printers: those that must use A, those that must use B, and those that can use either A or B.

Develop code that each kind of process executes to request and release a printer, and develop a monitor to allocate the printers. Your solution should be fair, assuming that a process using a printer eventually releases it.

6.23   *The Roller Coaster Problem* [Herman 1989]. Suppose there are n passenger processes and one car process. The passengers repeatedly wait to take rides in the car, which can hold C passengers, $C < n$. However, the car can only go around the tracks when it is full.

(a) Develop code for the actions of the passenger and car processes, and develop a monitor to synchronize them. Specify an invariant for your monitor.

(b) Generalize your answer to (a) to employ m car processes, $m > 1$. Since there is only one track, cars cannot pass each other; i.e., they must finish going around the track in the order in which they started. Again, a car can only go around the tracks when it is full.

6.24   *File Buffer Allocation*. Many operating systems, such as UNIX, maintain a cache of file access buffers. Each buffer is the size of a disk block. When a user process wants to read a disk block, the file system first looks in the cache. If the block is there, the file system returns the data to the user. Otherwise, the file system selects the least recently used buffer, reads the disk block into it, then returns the data to the user.

Similarly, if a user process wants to write a disk block that is in the cache, the file system simply updates the block. otherwise, the file system selects the least recently used buffer and writes into that one. The file system keeps track of which buffers contain new data—i.e., which have been modified—and writes them to disk before letting them be used for a different disk block. (This is called a write-back cache policy.)

Develop a monitor to implement a buffer cache having the above specifications. Define the procedures you need and their parameters. Next specify a monitor invariant. Finally, derive the procedure bodies. Explain any additional mechanisms you need, e.g., a clock and a disk-access process.

6.25 In the barber shop monitor in Figure 6.12, some of the **do** loops can be replaced by **if** statements. Determine which ones, and modify the monitor appropriately.

6.26 The barber shop monitor in Figure 6.12 is programmed using the signal and continue (SC) discipline.

(a) Is the monitor, as given, correct for the signal and wait (SW) discipline? If so, give a convincing argument. If not, modify the monitor so that it is correct.

(b) Is the monitor, as given, correct for the signal and urgent wait (SU) discipline? If so, give a convincing argument. If not, modify the monitor so that it is correct.

(c) Modify the monitor to use the signal and exit (SX) discipline. You will need to use additional procedures.

6.27 The following problems deal with the disk-scheduling monitor in Figure 6.16.

(a) Modify the monitor to employ the elevator algorithm. First specify a monitor invariant, then develop a solution.

(b) Modify the monitor to employ the shortest-seek-time algorithm. First specify a monitor invariant, then develop a solution.

6.28 In the sleeping barber problem (6.16), suppose there are several barbers rather than just one. Derive a monitor to synchronize the actions of the customers and barbers. First specify a monitor invariant, then develop a coarse-grained solution using **await**, and finally develop a fine-grained solution using condition variables. The monitor should have the same procedures as in Figures 6.11 and 6.12. Be careful to ensure that *finished_cut* awakens the same customer that a barber rendezvoused with in *get_next_customer*.

6.29 The following problems deal with the disk interface monitor in Figure 6.19.

(a) Give the details of the monitor invariant, and give proof outlines for the procedure bodies.

(b) Modify *finished_transfer* so that the disk driver process does not wait for a user process to fetch its results. However, be careful that the disk driver does not overwrite the results area.

(c) Combine the two procedures, *get_next_request* and *finished_transfer*, that are called by the disk driver. Be careful about the initialization of the monitor's variables.

6.30 Figure 6.20 illustrates the use of a *Disk_Access* monitor, and the text outlines its implementation. Develop a complete implementation of *Disk_Access*. Use the SCAN (elevator) disk-scheduling strategy. First specify an appropriate monitor invariant, and then develop the body of procedure *doIO*. Do not worry about implementing the *Disk_Transfer* monitor; just shown the calls to it at appropriate points from within *Disk_Access* (and assume they are open calls).

6.31 Section 6.5 described how to simulate automatic signaling (AS) using signal and continue (SC), and vice versa. It also described how to simulate AS using signal and wait (SW), and vice versa.

For each of the following, define any additional variables you need, and give complete code segments that transform a monitor that uses one signaling discipline into a monitor that uses another.

(a) Show how to simulate SC using SW, and vice versa.

(b) Show how to simulate SC using signal and urgent wait (SU), and vice versa.

(c) Show how to simulate SW using SU, and vice versa.

(d) Show how to simulate SC using signal and exit (SX), and vice versa.

(e) Show how to simulate SW using SX, and vice versa.

6.32 Suppose you have a concurrent program that uses conditional critical regions. Describe how to change the program to use monitors instead of CCRs. In particular, show how to simulate CCRs using monitors.

6.33 The syntax of an open path expression [Campbell & Kolstad 1980] is defined by the following BNF grammar:

$$
\begin{array}{lll}
\text{path\_declaration} & ::= & \text{"\textbf{path}" list "\textbf{end}"} \\
\text{list} & ::= & \text{sequence \{ "," sequence \}} \\
\text{sequence} & ::= & \text{item \{ ";" item \}} \\
\text{item} & ::= & \text{bound ":" "(" list ")" | "[" list "]" |} \\
& & \text{"(" list ")" | identifier}
\end{array}
$$

Braces denote zero or more occurrences of the enclosed items, and quotes enclose literal items (non-terminals). In the choices for item, bound is a positive integer, and identifier is the name of a procedure.

The comma operator in a list imposes no synchronization constraints. The semicolon operator in a sequence imposes the constraint that one execution of the first item must complete before each execution of the second item, which must complete before each execution of the third item, and so on. The bound operator limits the number of elements of the enclosed list that can be active at a time. The bracket operator [...] allows any number of elements of the enclosed list to be active at once. For example, the following specifies that any number of instances of a or b can proceed in parallel but that a and b are mutually exclusive with respect to each other:

path 1 : ([a], [b]) **end**

Equations (6.20) and (6.21) give two additional examples.

(a) Give a path expression to express the synchronization for a bounded buffer with n slots. The operations on the buffer are *deposit* and *fetch*. They are to execute with mutual exclusion.

(b) Give a path expression to express the synchronization for a bounded buffer with n slots. Allow maximal parallelism; i.e., instances of *deposit* and *fetch* can execute in parallel, as long as they are accessing different slots.

(c) Give a path expression to express the synchronization for the dining philosophers problem (4.4). Explain your answer.

(d) Give a path expression to express the synchronization for the readers-writers problem (4.5). Explain your answer.

(e) Give a path expression to expression the synchronization for the sleeping barber problem (6.16). Explain your answer.

(f) Show how to implement path expressions using semaphores. In particular, suppose you are given a path expression that specifies the synchronization for a set of procedures. Show what code you would insert at the start and end of each procedure to enforce the specified synchronization. Start with some simple examples, and then generalize your solution.

6.34   Suppose input and output on a terminal are supported by two procedures:

> *getline*(**var** *str* : **string**(MAXLINE); **var** *count* : **int**)
> *putline*(*str* : **string**(MAXLINE))

An application process calls *getline* to receive the next line of input; it calls *putline* to send a line to the display. A call of *getline* returns when there is another line of input. Result argument *str* is set to the contents of the line, and *count* is set to its actual length. A line contains at most MAXLINE characters; it is terminated by a newline character, which is not part of the line itself.

Assume both input and output are buffered; i.e., up to *n* input lines can be stored waiting to be retrieved by *getline*, and up to *n* output lines can be stored waiting to be printed. Also assume that input lines are echoed to the display; i.e., each complete input line is also sent to the display. Finally, assume that input lines are "cooked;" i.e., backspace and line-kill characters are processed by *getline* and do not get returned to the application process.

Develop a monitor that implements *getline* and *putline*. Assume there are two device driver processes. One reads characters from the keyboard; the other writes lines to the display. Your monitor will need to have additional procedures that these processes call.

6.35   Figure 6.21 shows how to use semaphores to implement monitor entry, monitor exit, **wait**, and **signal** for the signal and continue (SC) discipline.

(a) Develop an implementation for signal and exit (SX).

(b) Develop an implementation for signal and wait (SW).

(c) Develop an implementation for signal and urgent wait (SU).

6.36   Figure 6.22 gives kernel primitives that implement monitor entry, monitor exit, **wait**, and **signal** for the signal and continue (SC) discipline.

(a) Develop kernel primitives for signal and exit (SX).

(b) Develop kernel primitives for signal and wait (SW).

(c) Develop kernel primitives for signal and urgent wait (SU).

## PART III

Message Passing

The synchronization constructs we have examined so far are all based on shared variables. Consequently, they are used in concurrent programs that execute on hardware in which processors share memory. However, *network architectures*, in which processors share only a communication network, have become increasingly common. Examples of such architectures are a network of workstations or a multicomputer such as a hypercube. In addition, hybrid combinations of shared-memory and network architectures are sometimes employed, e.g., a network of multiprocessor workstations or a network containing workstations and a multiprocessor. Even on shared memory architectures, it is often necessary or convenient for processes not to share variables; e.g., processes executing on behalf of different users usually have different protection requirements.

To write programs for a network architecture, it is first necessary to define the network interface, i.e., the primitive network operations. These could simply be read and write operations analogous to read and write operations on shared variables. However, this would mean that processes would have to employ busy-waiting synchronization. A better approach is to define special network operations that include synchronization, much as semaphore operations are special operations on shared variables. Such network operations are called *message-passing primitives*. In fact, message passing can be viewed as extending semaphores to convey data as well as to provide synchronization.

With message passing, processes share *channels*. A channel is an abstraction of a physical communication network; it provides a communication path between processes. Channels are accessed by means of two kinds of primitives: **send** and **receive.** To initiate a communication, a process sends a message to a channel; another process acquires the message by receiving from the channel. Communication is accomplished since data

339

flows from the sender to the receiver. Synchronization is accomplished since a message cannot be received until after it has been sent.

When message passing is used, channels are typically the only objects processes share. Thus, every variable is local to and accessible by only one process, its *caretaker*. This implies that variables are never subject to concurrent access, and therefore no special mechanism for mutual exclusion is required. The absence of shared variables also changes the way in which condition synchronization is programmed since only a caretaker process can examine the variables that encode a condition. This requires using programming techniques different from those employed with shared variables. The final consequence of the absence of shared variables is that processes need not execute on processors that share memory; in particular, processes can be distributed among processors. For this reason, concurrent programs that employ message passing are called *distributed programs*. Such programs can, however, be executed on centralized processors, just as any concurrent program can be executed on a single, multiplexed processor. In this case, channels are implemented using shared memory instead of a communication network.

All programming notations based on message passing provide channels and primitives for sending to and receiving from them. Several different notations have been proposed. These vary in the way channels are provided and named, the way channels are used, and the way communication is synchronized. For example, channels can be global to processes, be connected to receivers, or be connected to a single sender and receiver. Channels can also provide either one-way or two-way information flow. Finally, communication can be asynchronous (non-blocking) or synchronous (blocking).

In Part III, we describe the four general combinations of these design choices that have proved the most popular. Each is especially well suited to solving some programming problems, and each can be implemented with reasonable efficiency.

Chapter 7 examines a notation in which channels have effectively unbounded capacity. Hence, the **send** primitive does not cause a process to block. This is called *asynchronous message passing* since sending and receiving processes execute independently, and a message might be received arbitrarily long after it has been sent.

Chapter 8 examines a notation in which communication and synchronization are tightly coupled. In particular, each channel provides a direct link between two processes, and a process sending a message delays until the other process is ready to receive the message. This is called *synchronous message passing* since the exchange of a message represents a synchronization point between two processes. Moreover, a channel never needs to contain stored messages. (There is also *buffered message passing*, in which a channel has a fixed capacity; thus, **send** delays if the channel is full.)

Chapter 9 examines two additional notations: remote procedure call (RPC) and rendezvous. These combine aspects of monitors and synchronous message passing. As with monitors, a module or process exports operations, and the operations are invoked by a **call** statement. As with synchronous message passing, execution of **call** is synchronous—the calling process delays until the invocation has been serviced and any results have been returned. An operation is thus a two-way communication channel, from the caller to the process that services the invocation and then back to the caller. An invocation is serviced in one of two ways. One approach is to create a new process. This is called remote procedure call (RPC) since the servicing process is declared as a procedure and it might execute on a different processor than the calling process. The second approach is to *rendezvous* with an existing process. A rendezvous is serviced by means of an input (or accept) statement that waits for an invocation, processes it, then returns results.

As we shall see, all four approaches are equivalent, in the sense that a program written using one set of primitives can be rewritten using any of the others. However, each approach is better suited for solving some problems than others. Moreover, the mechanisms perform differently (see Section 10.6).

When processes interact using shared variables, each process directly accesses those variables it needs. Hence our main concern in Part II was synchronizing access to shared variables so as to provide mutual exclusion and condition synchronization. By contrast, with message passing, only channels are shared, so processes must communicate in order to interact. Hence our main concern in Part III is synchronizing interprocess communication. How this is done depends on the way in which processes interact with each other.

There are four basic kinds of processes in a distributed program: filters, clients, servers, and peers. A *filter* is a data transformer. It receives streams of data values from its input channels, performs some computation on those values, and sends streams of results to its output channels. Because of these attributes, we can design a filter independent of other processes. Moreover, we can readily connect filters into networks that perform larger computations. All that is required is that each filter produce output that meets the input assumptions of the filter(s) that consume that output. Many of the user-level commands in the UNIX operating system are filters, e.g., the text formatting programs *tbl*, *eqn*, and *troff*.

A *client* is a triggering process; a *server* is a reactive process. Clients make requests that trigger reactions from servers. A client thus initiates activity, at times of its choosing; it often then delays until its request has been serviced. A server waits for requests to be made, then reacts to them. The specific action a server takes can depend on the kind of request, parameters in the request message, and the server's state; the server might be able to respond to a request immediately, or it might have to save the request and respond later. A server is often a non-terminating process and often provides service to more than one client. For example, a file server in a distributed system typically manages a collection of files and services requests from any client that wants to access those files.

A *peer* is one of a collection of identical processes that interact to provide a service or to solve a problem. For example, two peers might each manage a copy of a replicated file and interact to keep the two copies consistent. Or several peers might interact to solve a parallel programming problem, with each solving a piece of the problem.

The examples in Part III illustrate many different kinds of filters, clients, servers, and peers. They also introduce several process-interaction patterns that occur in distributed programs. Each *interaction paradigm* is an example or model of a communication pattern and associated programming technique that can be used to solve a variety of interesting distributed programming problems. Because each paradigm is different, there is no single derivation method for distributed programs. However, each process is designed much like a sequential program. Moreover, the same key concepts that apply to shared-variable programs also apply to message-based programs. In particular, we will again use invariants to characterize both the states of individual process and the global state maintained by a collection of processes. When necessary, we will also guard the communication actions of processes to ensure that invariants are maintained. Because each process has direct access only to its own variables, one of the challenges of designing distributed programs is maintaining—or determining—a global state. The examples will show how to do this.

## CHAPTER 7

Asynchronous Message Passing

With asynchronous message passing, communication channels are unbounded queues of messages. A process appends a message to the end of a channel's queue by executing a **send** statement. Since the queue is (conceptually) unbounded, execution of **send** does not block the sender. A process receives a message from a channel by executing a **receive** statement. Execution of **receive** delays the receiver until the channel is non-empty; then the message at the front of the channel is removed and stored in variables local to the receiver.

Channels are like semaphores that carry data. Hence, the **send** and **receive** primitives are like the **V** and **P** operations, respectively. In fact, if a channel contains only null messages—i.e., ones without any data—then **send** and **receive** are just like **V** and **P**, with the number of queued "messages" being the value of the semaphore.

Asynchronous message-passing primitives have been included in several programming languages; they are also provided by several operating systems. Section 7.1 defines the specific programming notation we will employ. There are many variations on this notation; the Historical Notes and References describe these and give citations to relevant literature. Section 7.2 presents axioms and inference rules that enable one to prove partial correctness properties of message-based programs.

The next several sections examine different ways in which groups of processes can interact in distributed programs. These provide a number of useful techniques for designing distributed programs. We describe the following interaction paradigms:

- one-way data flow through networks of filters,
- requests and replies between clients and servers,
- back-and-forth (heartbeat) interaction between neighboring processes,
- probes and echoes in graphs,
- broadcasts between processes in complete graphs,
- token-passing along edges in a graph,
- coordination between decentralized server processes, and
- replicated workers sharing a bag of tasks.

We illustrate the paradigms by solving a variety of problems, including parallel sorting, disk scheduling, computing the topology of a network, distributed termination detection, replicated files, and parallel adaptive quadrature. Chapters 8 and 9 give additional examples, show how to program them using the other message-passing notations, and discuss the tradeoffs between the various notations.

The final section of this chapter shows how to implement asynchronous message passing. We first show how to extend a shared-memory kernel with message-passing primitives and then show how to implement a distributed kernel that uses a communications network.

7.1 Programming Notation

Many different notations have been proposed for asynchronous message passing. Here, we employ one that is representative and also simple.

With asynchronous message passing, a channel is a queue of messages that have been sent but not yet received. A channel declaration has the form:

$$\textbf{chan } ch(id_1 : type_1, ..., id_n : type_n)$$

Identifier *ch* is the channel's name. The id_i and $type_i$ are the names and types of the data fields in messages transmitted via the channel. The field names are optional; they will be used when it is helpful to document what each field represents. For example, the following declares two channels:

$$\textbf{chan } input(\textbf{char})$$
$$\textbf{chan } disk\_access(cylinder, block, count : \textbf{int}; buffer : \textbf{ptr } [*]\textbf{char})$$

The first, *input*, is used to transmit single-character messages. The second, *disk_access*, contains messages having four fields, with the field names indicating their roles. In many examples we will employ arrays of channels, as in:

> **chan** *result*[1:*n*](**int**)

A process sends a message to channel *ch* by executing

> **send** *ch*(*expr*$_1$, ..., *expr*$_n$)

The *expr*$_i$ are expressions whose types must be the same as those of the corresponding fields in the declaration of *ch*. The effect of executing **send** is to evaluate the expressions, then append a message containing these values to the end of the queue associated with channel *ch*. Because this queue is conceptually unbounded, execution of **send** never causes delay; hence **send** is a *non-blocking* primitive.

A process receives a message from channel *ch* by executing

> **receive** *ch*(*var*$_1$, ..., *var*$_n$)

The *var*$_i$ are variables whose types must be the same as those of the corresponding fields in the declaration of *ch*. The effect of executing **receive** is to delay the receiver until there is at least one message on the channel's queue. Then the message at the front of the queue is removed, and its fields are assigned to the *var*$_i$. Thus, in contrast to **send**, **receive** is a *blocking* primitive since it might cause delay. The **receive** primitive has blocking semantics so the receiving process does not have to busy-wait polling the channel if it has nothing else to do until a message arrives.

We assume that access to the contents of each channel is indivisible and that message delivery is reliable and error-free. Thus, every message that is sent to a channel is eventually delivered, and messages are not corrupted. Because each channel is also a first-in/first-out queue, messages will be received in the order in which they were appended to a channel. Hence, if a process sends a message to a channel and later sends a second to the same channel, they will be received in the order in which they were sent.

As a simple example, Figure 7.1 contains a process that receives a stream of characters from one channel, *input*, then assembles the characters into lines and sends the resulting lines to a second channel, *output*. The carriage-return character, CR, indicates the end of a line; a line is at most MAXLINE characters long. Both CR and MAXLINE are symbolic constants. This process is an example of a filter; it transforms a stream of characters into a stream of lines.

Channels will be declared global to processes, as in Figure 7.1, since they are shared by processes. Any process may send to or receive from any channel. When channels are used in this way they are sometimes called *mailboxes*. However, in many examples we will consider, each channel will have exactly one receiver, although it may have many senders. In this case, a channel is often called an *input port* since it provides a window (porthole) into

chan *input*(**char**), *output*([1:MAXLINE] **char**)
Char_to_Line:: **var** *line*[1:MAXLINE] : **char**, *i* : **int** := 1
        do true →
          receive *input*(*line*[*i*])
          do *line*[*i*] ≠ CR **and** *i* < MAXLINE →
              { *line*[1:*i*] contains last *i* input characters }
              i := *i* + 1; **receive** *input*(*line*[*i*])
          od
          send *output*(*line*); *i* := 1
        od

Figure 7.1. Filter process to assemble lines of characters.

---

the receiving process. If a channel has just one sender and one receiver, it is often called a *link* since it provides a direct path from the sending to the receiving process.

Usually a process will want to delay when it executes **receive**, but not always. For example, the process might have other useful work to do if a message is not yet available for receipt. Or, a process such as a scheduler may need to examine all queued messages in order to select the best one to service next (e.g., the disk scheduler in Section 7.4). To determine whether a channel's queue is currently empty, a process can call the boolean-valued function:

    empty(*ch*)

This function is true if channel *ch* contains no messages; otherwise, it is false. Unlike with the corresponding primitive on monitor condition variables, if a process calls **empty** and gets back true, there may in fact be queued messages by the time the process continues execution. Moreover, if a process calls **empty** and gets back false, there may not be any queued messages when the process tries to receive one. (This second situation cannot happen if the process is the only one to receive from the channel.) In short, **empty** is a useful primitive, but care needs to be taken when using it.

7.2 Formal Semantics

When processes interact using shared variables, two steps are required to construct a proof of a program. First, one develops a *sequential proof* for each process. Then, one establishes *non-interference* to ensure that assertions in the sequential proof of one process are not invalidated by execution of assignment actions in other processes.

When processes interact using message passing, there is an additional step: a *satisfaction proof*. In the absence of shared variables, the only way in which a process reveals information about its local state is by sending a message, and the only way a process learns about the state of another is by receiving a message. To construct a sequential proof of a process, we thus need to make assertions about the effects of sending and receiving messages. For example, we might need to assert that the value received in a message is positive or that messages are sorted. The purpose of a satisfaction proof is to establish that such assertions are valid.

Even when processes do not share program variables, they might interfere. This is because properties of distributed programs often depend on the global state, which consists of the contents of message queues and the states of individual processes. In addition, one often needs to use auxiliary variables to specify global properties. A non-interference proof ensures that no process interferes with a predicate about the global state. In fact, a satisfaction proof is essentially a special case of a non-interference proof that deals only with effects of message-passing statements.

In the remainder of this section, we extend Programming Logic *PL* to encompass the use of asynchronous message passing. We describe the semantics in terms of sequences of messages sent to and received from channels. We will employ the following operations on sequences:

$s + v$	append value v to sequence s
$s1 - s2$	delete sequence $s2$ from the beginning of sequence $s1$
$s1 \leq s2$	true if sequence $s1$ is a prefix of sequence $s2$
$first(s)$	first value of sequence s

We will also use $\varnothing$ to denote a sequence containing no elements. Finally, to simplify notation, let *exprs* stand for a vector of expressions $expr_1, ..., expr_n$ and let *vars* stand for a vector of variables $var_1, ..., var_n$.

The formal semantics of message passing are more complex than those of individual synchronization mechanisms that use shared variables. This is because the **send** and **receive** statements manipulate the contents of a channel and hence are more powerful than operations on semaphores or condition variables. However, the complexity of asynchronous message passing is no greater than the combination of a monitor that implements an unbounded buffer plus the calls of the monitor's procedures. As was the case with shared variables, using the formal logic in full detail is impractical for large programs. But the underlying concepts once again provide the basis for a disciplined approach to programming, in this case with message passing.

Axioms and Satisfaction Proofs

At any point in time, a channel contains messages that have been sent to the channel but not yet received. The messages in a channel form a sequence ordered by the time they were appended; i.e., the oldest message is at the front of the sequence and the youngest message is at the end.

The critical properties of a channel are that (1) messages are received in the order they were sent, and (2) they are not lost or duplicated. To specify these properties, we represent each channel *ch* by two unbounded sequences. Sequence *sent*[*ch*] contains all messages sent to the channel, in the order they were appended. Sequence *rec*[*ch*] contains all messages received from the channel, in the order they were received. Thus, *sent*[*ch*] and *rec*[*ch*] are auxiliary variables that record the hidden state of channel *ch*. Then we require that *rec*[*ch*] is always a prefix of *sent*[*ch*]. This following axiom expresses this:

(7.1)   **Channel Axiom:**   At all times, $rec[ch] \leq sent[ch]$

The contents of the channel at any point in time are $sent[ch] - rec[ch]$. This is what would actually be stored, as discussed in Section 7.10.

A process appends a message to a channel *ch* by executing **send** *ch*(*exprs*), where *exprs* is the value of the message. The effect of executing **send** is to append a message to sequence *sent*[*ch*]. This is an assignment, so we have the following axiom for **send**:

(7.2)   **Send Axiom:** $\{\, P^{sent[ch]}_{sent[ch]+exprs} \,\}$ **send** $ch(exprs)$ $\{\, P \,\}$

If *P* does not reference the auxiliary variable *sent*[*ch*], then the pre- and post-conditions will be the same. This reflects the fact that sending a message does not alter program variables, only the channel.

A process receives a message by executing **receive** *ch*(*vars*), where *ch* is the channel and *vars* is the set of variables into which the message is to be stored. If a process is delayed while executing **receive**, the values of its local variables will not change. However, the values of global variables, such as auxiliary variables, could change. In fact, *sent*[*ch*] must change or the process will deadlock. Thus, the program state will be different when **receive** returns. Moreover, the receiving process cannot in general know what the contents of the message will be and hence what values will be assigned to *vars*. In short, we cannot in general know how the pre- and post-conditions of **receive** are related. Thus, we allow anything to be asserted after **receive.**

(7.3)   **Receive Axiom:** $\{\, P \,\}$ **receive** $ch(vars)$ $\{\, Q \,\}$

Since this axiom imposes no constraint on the relation between P and Q, we could use anything for Q. For example, Q could be the predicate *false*, which would allow us to conclude anything after **receive.** This is necessary in a programming logic, however, or it would not be (relatively) complete. For example, if a process receives from an empty channel and no message is ever sent to the channel, the process will block forever. Hence, to construct a partial correctness proof of the process, we have to be able to conclude *false* in the postcondition of **receive.** This is because *false* characterizes no program state, in this case, an unreachable state. However, in the more realistic situation that a **receive** statement terminates, Q had better be a sound characterization of the program state. In particular, Q has to be related to P and to the value of the received message. The role of a satisfaction proof is to ensure this.

By examining the actions of **receive**, we can discern the requirements of a satisfaction proof. Assume the sequential proof of a process contains:

$$\{\,P\,\}\ \textbf{receive}\ ch(vars)\ \{\,Q\,\}$$

Suppose ch is represented by $sent[ch]$ and $rec[ch]$ and that these are shared variables. Then we can implement **receive** by:

$$\langle\ \textbf{await}\ (sent[ch] - rec[ch]) \neq \varnothing \rightarrow$$
$$vars := first(sent[ch] - rec[ch])$$
$$rec[ch] := rec[ch] + first(sent[ch] - rec[ch])\ \rangle$$

Thus, **receive** delays until there is a message available, then assigns the first such message to $vars$ and appends it to $rec[ch]$. Let B be the guard in the above **await** statement, and let S be the body as shown. Then for soundness of an application of Receive Axiom (7.3), we require that:

$$P \wedge B\ \Rightarrow\ wp(S, Q)$$

In short, when there is a message available for receipt, the precondition P had better be such that executing **receive** makes Q true. These observations yield the following satisfaction rule.

(7.4)   **Satisfaction Rule for Asynchronous Communication.** For every application of Receive Axiom (7.3):
$$(\ P \wedge (sent[ch] - rec[ch]) \neq \varnothing \wedge M = first(sent[ch] - rec[ch])\ )$$
$$\Rightarrow Q^{vars,rec[ch]}_{M,rec[ch]+M}$$

Above, M is the value of the received message. It is used to simplify the consequent; therefore the expression specifying its value is added as a conjunct to the antecedent. Shortly we will see how to use (7.4) and will describe a general technique—based on global invariants as usual—for ensuring it.

We can also discern the semantics of **empty** from the representation of channels. The effect of invoking **empty**(*ch*) within a boolean expression is the same as evaluating:

(7.5) $(sent[ch] - rec[ch]) = \varnothing$

As noted earlier, if **empty**(*ch*) is true, there may in fact be queued messages before the process invoking **empty** next executes. This is reflected in the fact that (7.5) can be interfered with by another process sending a message to *ch*. Thus, while it is sometimes useful to determine that a channel is temporarily empty, it is not safe to depend on that. By contrast, if **empty** is false and only one process receives from *ch*, then (7.5) is negated and hence not interfered with. This is because only the one receiver process causes *rec*[*ch*] to change.

Auxiliary Variables and Non-Interference

After developing sequential proofs for each process and establishing satisfaction, the remaining proof obligation is establishing non-interference. In message-passing programs, auxiliary variables are used for two purposes. As in shared-variable programs, they are used to record aspects of the hidden part of the program state, such as the values of program counters. In fact, the communication axioms themselves employ auxiliary variables to represent channels. Second, we will often need to make assertions about the relation between the states of different processes. In general, we have to use auxiliary variables for this since processes are often not allowed to share program variables in a distributed program.

Since we use auxiliary variables solely for the purpose of constructing a proof, they must not alter the behavior of the program. In programs that do not employ message passing, this is ensured by the Auxiliary Variable Restriction (2.21). With message passing, auxiliary variables can also be added to messages in existing **send** and **receive** statements. (New **send** and **receive** statements cannot be added, however, since that could change the flow of control.) In particular, we extend (2.21) as follows.

(7.6)   **Auxiliary Variable Restriction for Asynchronous Message Passing.** Auxiliary variables appear only in:

(1) expressions being assigned to auxiliary variables,

(2) the variable list in **receive** statements, or

(3) the expression list in **send** statements where the corresponding variable in a **receive** statement is an auxiliary variable.

Thus, auxiliary variables can appear both in direct assignments and in the indirect assignments that result from message passing.

As defined in (2.10), establishing non-interference requires showing that no assignment action a in one process interferes with any critical assertion C in another process. The critical assertions in a program that employs message passing are the same as those in a program that employs shared variables—the pre- and postconditions of each atomic action. However, the assignment actions include **send** and **receive** statements as well as regular assignment statements.

We will say that critical assertion C is *parallel* to statement S if C is in the proof of one process and S is in a different process. To show that an assignment or **send** action a cannot invalidate an assertion C that is parallel to a, it suffices as in (2.9) to prove that the following is a theorem in our programming logic:

(7.7) $NI(a, C)$: $\{ pre(a) \wedge C \} \ a \ \{ C \}$

However, with message passing we also have to show that no **receive** statement invalidates an assertion parallel to the **receive.** This is because **receive** is also an assignment action, in this case into the variables in the **receive** statement (which could be global auxiliary variables). Showing non-interference for **receive** introduces another proof obligation similar to satisfaction: If **receive** $ch(vars)$ is executed and terminates, then critical assertions in other processes must still be true after the received message is assigned to $vars$ and appended to $rec[ch]$. In particular, for every **receive** statement r and assertion C parallel to r, the following must be a theorem:

(7.8) $NIasynch(r, C)$: $(C \wedge pre(r) \ \wedge \ (sent[ch] - rec[ch]) \neq \varnothing \ \wedge$
$$M = first(sent[ch] - rec[ch])) \ \Rightarrow \ C_{M, rec[ch]+M}^{vars, rec[ch]}$$

Satisfaction Rule (7.4) deals with assertions in the receiving process; the above requirement deals with assertions in *other* processes. As long as each process only makes assertions about its local variables, interference cannot result since a process can only receive into its own variables. But when auxiliary variables are used to relate the states of processes to each other, one needs to be careful.

Putting (7.7) and (7.8) together, we have the full proof obligation for showing that a program that uses asynchronous message passing is interference-free.

(7.9)   **Interference Freedom for Asynchronous Communication.**
Theorems $\{ P_i \} \ S_i \ \{ Q_i \}$, $1 \leq i \leq n$, are interference-free if both of the following are true:

For all assignment and **send** actions a in the proof of S_i, $1 \le i \le n$,
   For all critical assertions C parallel to a: $NI(a, C)$.

For all **receive** statements r in the proof of S_i, $1 \le i \le n$,
   For all critical assertions C parallel to r: $NIasynch(r, C)$.

This definition looks quite forbidding and entails a large number of proof obligations. However, one can use the same techniques for avoiding interference that were described in Section 2.4: disjoint variables, weakened assertions, and global invariants. With message passing, processes typically do not share program variables, so assertions about these variables will typically be disjoint. Thus, we can meet the non-interference obligations if we use global invariants about shared auxiliary variables.

To summarize, developing a proof of a program that uses asynchronous message passing involves three tasks. First, construct proofs of individual processes. Then show that all applications of the Receive Axiom meet Satisfaction Rule (7.4). Finally show that the proofs of the processes are interference-free. The inference rule for concurrent execution is thus Concurrency Rule (2.11) augmented with the satisfaction requirement.

An Example

A simple example will help clarify these new axioms and proof obligations, especially the nature of a satisfaction proof. Consider the following program, in which *P1* sends a value x to *P2*, which increments it and sends it back to *P1*. Since x is initially 0, its final value is clearly 1. Our task is to prove this.

```
chan ch1(int), ch2(int)
P1::  var x : int := 0
      send ch2(x)
      R1:  receive ch1(x)
P2::  var y : int
      R2:  receive ch2(y)
      send ch1(y + 1)
```

The key to proving that the final value of x is 1 is to prove that the postcondition of statement *R1* is $x = 1$. This in turn requires proving that $y = 0$ is a valid postcondition for statement *R2*. In both cases, the assertions are valid as long as the corresponding satisfaction formula is true. Since a satisfaction proof requires reasoning about the contents of the channels, we augment the program with auxiliary variables to represent the channels. We also annotate the augmented program with assertions about these variables; these assertions reflect the implicit assignments that occur when **send** and **receive** are executed. This results in the annotated program:

chan *ch1*(**int**), *ch2*(**int**)
var *sent*[*ch1*], *rec*[*ch1*] : **sequence of int** := $\varnothing, \varnothing$
var *sent*[*ch2*], *rec*[*ch2*] : **sequence of int** := $\varnothing, \varnothing$
P1:: **var** x : **int** := 0 $\{ x = 0 \wedge sent[ch2] = \varnothing \wedge rec[ch1] = \varnothing \}$
       send *ch2*(x) $\{ x = 0 \wedge sent[ch2] = [0] \wedge rec[ch1] = \varnothing \}$
       R1: **receive** *ch1*(x) $\{ x = 1 \wedge sent[ch2] = [0] \wedge rec[ch1] = [1] \}$
P2:: **var** y : **int** $\{ sent[ch]1 = \varnothing \wedge rec[ch2] = \varnothing \}$
       R2: **receive** *ch2*(y) $\{ y = 0 \wedge sent[ch1] = \varnothing \wedge rec[ch2] = [0] \}$
       send *ch1*($y + 1$) $\{ y = 0 \wedge sent[ch1] = [1] \wedge rec[ch2] = [0] \}$

In this proof outline, brackets enclose the contents of non-empty sequences.

Since the assertions in the program follow from the communication axioms, the proof is valid as long as the satisfaction and non-interference obligations are met. Non-interference follows trivially from the fact that no assertion references a variable changed by the other process. Unfortunately, satisfaction cannot yet be proved. Consider the satisfaction formula for the triple containing **receive** statement *R1*:

$$(x = 0 \wedge sent[ch2] = (0) \wedge rec[ch1] = \varnothing \wedge$$
$$(sent[ch1] - rec[ch1]) \neq \varnothing \wedge M = first(sent[ch1] - rec[ch1]))$$
$$\Rightarrow (x = 1 \wedge sent[ch2] = [0] \wedge rec[ch1] = [1])^{x, rec[ch1]}_{M, rec[ch1]+M}$$

Performing the indicated substitution, then simplifying, the requirement is:

$$(rec[ch1] = \varnothing \wedge (sent[ch1] - rec[ch1]) \neq \varnothing \wedge$$
$$M = first(sent[ch1] - rec[ch1])) \Rightarrow (M = 1 \wedge (rec[ch1] + M) = [1])$$

This is true if—whenever *ch1* is not empty—the first message on the channel has a value of 1. Writing out and simplifying the satisfaction formula for the triple containing **receive** statement *R2* yields a similar requirement: whenever *ch2* is not empty, the first message on *ch2* must have a value of 0.

Although the required satisfaction requirements clearly hold in this program, our assertions are not yet strong enough to prove them. However, all that we need is a predicate indicating what each channel contains:

$$(sent[ch1] = \varnothing \vee sent[ch1] = [1]) \wedge (sent[ch2] = \varnothing \vee sent[ch2] = [0])$$

This predicate is true initially, preserved by the **send** statements, and not affected by the **receive** statements. Hence, it is a global invariant. By adding this predicate to every assertion, the satisfaction formulas can be proved. The resulting annotated program is also interference-free. Therefore, after removing the auxiliary variables, we have a proof that $x = 1$ in the final state of the original program.

To summarize, developing a proof requires using the communication axioms and sequential programming logic to develop sequential proofs of each process, then showing that the satisfaction and non-interference obligations are met. The key step is ensuring satisfaction. This is done as illustrated above. In particular, use the auxiliary variables that represent the channels, and have each assertion be the conjunction of predicates about local variables and a global invariant that relates the contents of the channels to each other. This approach is once again based on the fact that processes should be viewed as invariant maintainers with respect to synchronization.

Although we have emphasized the role of satisfaction—and included it in our logic—it is not actually a fundamental concept. In particular, since the Satisfaction Rule for Asynchronous Communication applies only to **receive** statements, we could have replaced the Receive Axiom by an inference rule in which the requirements of the Satisfaction Rule are the hypotheses and the Receive Axiom is the conclusion. However, we have separated out satisfaction since it depends on the contents of message queues and hence on the effect of **send** statements. This reflects the fact that the only way a process learns information in the absence of shared variables is by receiving messages. Hence, the key to understanding process interaction that is based on message passing is to understand communication assumptions.

Safety and Liveness Properties

As with concurrent programs that employ shared variables, there are three general properties of interest in concurrent programs that employ asynchronous message passing: mutual exclusion, absence of deadlock, and fairness. Even though a message-based program typically does not contain shared program variables, we still might be interested in ascertaining that code segments in different processes are mutually exclusive. For example, in a solution to the readers/writers problem, we might wish to prove that a reader and a writer cannot simultaneously communicate with a process that implements the database. For this, we can employ the method of Exclusion of Configurations (2.25).

Recall that a variation on Exclusion of Configurations is used with conditional critical regions or monitors. That was because processes themselves cannot make assertions about resource or monitor variables. In contrast, with asynchronous message passing, the program state is characterized completely by assertions within processes, with auxiliary variables being used to make assertions about message queues. Consequently, however, the programmer has to worry about potential interference, whereas interference is automatically precluded with CCRs and monitors.

Absence of deadlock in a message-based program can also be proved by the method of Exclusion of Configurations. With asynchronous message passing, a process is blocked only if it is executing **receive** and there are no available messages. In particular, if r is a statement that receives from channel ch, a process is blocked executing r only if the state satisfies:

$$pre(r) \wedge (sent[ch] - rec[ch]) = \emptyset$$

Predicates of this form thus characterize states in which processes are blocked. By considering all such states—and those in which some processes might have terminated—we can construct a predicate characterizing a global deadlock state. If that predicate is false, a program is deadlock-free.

Since **receive** is the only blocking primitive, liveness properties depend on the scheduling policy of **receive**, assuming of course that every non-blocked process periodically gets the chance to execute. If message queues are never empty, then a weakly fair scheduler would ensure that every process gets a chance to proceed. This is because the delay condition would always be true, and hence **receive** would never need to block. However, this assumption is not very realistic. Thus a strongly fair scheduler is required. Fortunately, such a scheduler is easy to implement: awaken processes waiting to receive from a channel in the order in which they blocked. This gives strongly fair scheduling since if the delay condition is infinitely often true—because new messages keep being sent to a channel—then every process will eventually get to proceed.

7.3 Filters: A Sorting Network

As noted earlier, the key to understanding message-based programs is to understand communication assumptions. Hence, the key to developing a process that employs message passing is first to specify the communication assumptions. Since the output of a filter process is a function of its input, the appropriate specification is one that relates the value of messages sent on output channels to the values of messages received on input channels. The actions the filter takes in response to receiving input must ensure this relation every time the filter sends output.

To illustrate how filters are derived and programmed, consider the problem of sorting a list of n numbers into ascending order. The most direct way to solve the problem is to write a single filter process, *Sort*, that receives the input from one channel, employs one of the standard sorting algorithms, then writes the result to another channel. Let *input* be the input channel, and let *output* be the output channel. Assume the n values to be sorted are sent to *input* by some unspecified process. Then the goal of the sorting process is to ensure that the values sent to *output* are ordered and are a permutation of the values received from *input*. Let *sent[i]* indicate the ith value sent to *output*. Then the goal is specified by the following predicate:

$SORT$: ($\forall i$: $1 \leq i < n$: $sent[i] \leq sent[i+1]$) $\wedge$ values sent to
output are a permutation of values received from *input*

An outline of the *Sort* process is:

Sort:: receive all numbers from channel *input*
sort the numbers
send the sorted numbers to channel *output*

Since **receive** is a blocking primitive, a practical concern is for *Sort* to determine when it has received all the numbers. One solution is for *Sort* to know the value of n in advance. A more general solution is for n to be the first input value and for the numbers themselves to be the next n input values. An even more general solution is to end the input stream with a *sentinel* value, which is a special value that indicates that all numbers have been received. This solution is the most general since the process producing the input does not itself need to know in advance how many values it will send to *input*. Assuming the ends of *input* and *output* are marked with sentinels, then the goal, $SORT$, is modified slightly by replacing n by $n+1$ to account for the two sentinels.

If processes are "heavyweight" objects, as they are in most operating systems, the above approach would often be the most efficient way to solve the sorting problem. However, a different approach—which is amenable to direct implementation in hardware—is to employ a network of small processes that execute in parallel and interact to solve the problem. (A hybrid approach would be to employ a network of medium-sized processes.) There are many kinds of sorting networks, just as there are many different internal sorting algorithms. Here we present a *merge network*.

The idea behind a merge network is to merge repeatedly—and in parallel—two sorted lists into a longer sorted list. The network is constructed out of *Merge* filters. Each *Merge* process receives values from two ordered input streams, *in1* and *in2*, and produces one ordered output stream, *out*. Assume that the ends of the input streams are marked by a sentinel, EOS, as discussed above. Also assume that *Merge* appends EOS to the end of the output stream. If there are n input values, not counting the sentinels, then when *Merge* terminates the following should be true:

$MERGE$: *in1* and *in2* are empty $\wedge$ $sent[n+1]$ = EOS $\wedge$
($\forall i$: $1 \leq i < n$: $sent[i] \leq sent[i+1]$) $\wedge$
data values sent to *out* are a permutation of
data values received from *in1* and *in2*

The first line of $MERGE$ says all input has been consumed and EOS has been appended to the end of *out*; the second line says the output is ordered; the

```
chan in1(int), in2(int), out(int)
Merge:: var v1, v2 : int
        receive in1(v1); receive in2(v2)
        do v1 ≠ EOS and v2 ≠ EOS →
            if v1 ≤ v2 → send out(v1); receive in1(v1)
            [] v2 ≤ v1 → send out(v2); receive in2(v2)
            fi
        [] v1 ≠ EOS and v2 = EOS →
            send out(v1); receive in1(v1)
        [] v1 = EOS and v2 ≠ EOS →
            send out(v2); receive in2(v2)
        od
        send out(EOS)  { MERGE }
```

Figure 7.2. A process that merges two input streams.

---

third line says all input data has been output.

One way to implement *Merge* is to receive all input values, merge them, then send the merged list to *out*. However, this requires storing all input values. Since the input streams are ordered, a much better way to implement *Merge* is repeatedly to compare the next two values received from *in1* and *in2* and to send the smaller to *out*. Let *v1* and *v2* be these values. This suggests the following process outline:

```
chan in1(int), in2(int), out(int)
Merge:: var v1, v2 : int
        receive in1(v1); receive in2(v2)
        do more input to process →
            send smaller value to out
            receive another value from in1 or in2
        od
        send out(EOS)  { MERGE }
```

As a special case, after *Merge* has received all values from one input stream, it can simply append the values from the other input stream to *out*.

We can get an appropriate loop invariant by the techniques of replacing a constant by a variable and deleting a conjunct, as described in Section 1.5. In particular, delete the first line of *MERGE*, and replace constant n in the second line by auxiliary variable *size*[*sent*[*out*] − 1]. Expanding the loop and handling the special cases, we have the final program shown in Figure 7.2.

To form a sorting network, we employ a collection of *Merge* processes and arrays of input and output channels. Assuming the number of input values n

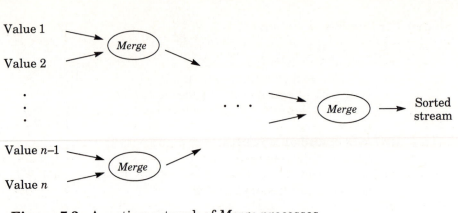

Figure 7.3. A sorting network of *Merge* processes.

is a power of 2, the processes and channels are connected so that the resulting communication pattern forms a tree, as depicted in Figure 7.3. Information in the sorting network flows from left to right. Each node at the left is given two input values, which it merges to form a stream of two sorted values. The next nodes form streams of four sorted values, and so on. The right-most node produces the final sorted stream. The sorting network contains $n - 1$ processes; the width of the network is $\log_2 n$.

To realize the sorting network in Figure 7.3, the input and output channels need to be shared. In particular, the output channel used by one instance of *Merge* needs to be the same as one of the input channels used by the next instance of *Merge* in the graph. This can be programmed in one of two ways. The first approach is to use *static naming*: declare all channels to be a global array, and have each instance of *Merge* receive from two elements of the array and send to one other element. This requires embedding the tree in an array so that the channels accessed by *Merge*$_i$ are a function of i. The second approach is to use *dynamic naming*: declare all channels to be global as above, parameterize the processes, and give each process three channels when it is created. This makes the programming of the *Merge* processes easier since each is textually identical. However, it requires having a main process that dynamically creates and passes channels to the *Merge* processes.

A key attribute of filters like *Merge* is that we can interconnect them in different ways. All that is required is that the output produced by one filter meet the input assumptions of another filter. An important consequence of this attribute is that, as long as the externally observable input and output behaviors are the same, we can replace one filter process—or a network of filters—by a different network. For example, we can replace the single *Sort* process described earlier by a network of *Merge* processes plus a process (or network) that distributes the input values to the merge network.

Networks of filters can be used to solve a variety of other parallel programming problems. Section 8.3 presents two additional examples: a prime number sieve and a matrix/vector multiplication network.

7.4 Clients and Servers

Recall that a server is a process that repeatedly handles requests from client processes. This section shows how to program servers and their clients. The first example shows how to turn monitors into servers and how to implement resource managers using message passing. It also points out the duality between monitors and message passing: each can directly simulate the other.

We then show how to implement a self-scheduling disk driver and a file server. The self-scheduling disk driver illustrates a third way to structure a solution to the disk-scheduling problem introduced in Section 6.4. The file server illustrates an important programming technique called *conversational continuity*. Both these examples also illustrate program structures that are directly supported by message passing, in the sense that they yield solutions that are more compact than is possible using any of the synchronization mechanisms of Part II.

Active Monitors

Recall that a monitor is a resource manager. It encapsulates permanent variables that record the state of the resource, and it provides a set of procedures that are called to access the resource. Moreover, the procedures execute with mutual exclusion and use condition variables for condition synchronization. Here we show how to simulate these attributes using server processes and message passing. In short, we show how to program monitors as active processes rather than as passive collections of procedures.

Assume for the moment that a monitor provides only one operation *op* and that it does not employ condition variables. Then the structure of the monitor is:

```
monitor Mname        # Invariant MI
    var permanent variables
    initialization code
    procedure op(formals)  body of op  end
end
```

As indicated, *MI* is the monitor invariant.

To simulate *Mname* using message passing, we employ one server process *Sname*. The permanent variables of *Mname* become *Sname*'s local variables; *Sname* is thus the caretaker for those variables. *Sname* first initializes the

chan *request*(**int**, types of value formals)
chan *reply*[1:*n*](types of result formals)

Sname:: **var** permanent variables
　　　　　var *index* : **int**, value formals, result formals
　　　　　initialization code
　　　　　do true → { loop invariant *MI* }
　　　　　　　　receive *request*(*index*, value formals)
　　　　　　　　body of *op*
　　　　　　　　# return reply to process that sent request
　　　　　　　　send *reply*[*index*](result formals)
　　　od
Client[*i*: 1..*n*]:: **send** *request*(*i*, value arguments)　　# "call" *op*
　　　　　　　　receive *reply*[*i*](result arguments)　　# wait for reply
　　　　...

Figure 7.4. Clients and server with one operation.

---

variables then executes a permanent loop in which it repeatedly services "calls" of *op*. A call is simulated by having a client process send a message to a request channel, then receive the result from a reply channel. The server thus repeatedly receives from the request channel and sends results to reply channels. The formal parameters in *Mname* become additional variables local to *Sname*. To avoid having one client see the result intended for another, each client needs its own private result channel. If these are declared as a global array, a client thus needs to pass the index of its private element of the result array to the server as part of the request message. (Some message-passing notations allow a receiving process to determine the identity of the sender.)

Figure 7.4 gives outlines for the server and its clients. Monitor invariant *MI* becomes the loop invariant of process *Sname*. It is true after the initialization code is executed and before and after each request is serviced. In particular, *MI* is true at all points at which *Sname* communicates with client processes. As shown in Figure 7.4, a client immediately waits for a reply after sending a request. However, the client could execute other actions before waiting if it has other work it could productively do. This is not often the case, but it is possible since a call is simulated by two distinct statements: **send**, and then later, **receive.**

The program in Figure 7.4 employs static naming since channels are global to the processes and are referenced directly. Consequently, each process must be coded carefully so that it uses the correct channels. For example, *Client*[*i*] must not use the reply channel of some other *Client*[*j*].

```
type op_kind = enum(op₁, ..., opₙ)
type arg_type = union(arg₁ : atype₁, ..., argₙ : atypeₙ)
type result_type = union(res₁ : rtype₁, ..., resₙ : rtypeₙ)
chan request(int, op_kind, arg_type)
chan reply[1:n](res_type)
```

Sname:: **var** permanent variables
        var *index* : **int**, *kind* : *op_kind*, *args* : *arg_type*, *results* : *res_type*
        initialization code
        do true → { loop invariant *MI* }
                receive *request(index, kind, args)*
                if *kind = op₁* → body of *op₁*
                [] ...
                [] *kind = opₙ* → body of *opₙ*
                fi
                send *reply[index](results)*
        od

Client[i: 1..n]:: **var** *myargs* : *arg_type*, *myresults* : *result_type*
        place value arguments in *myargs*
        send *request(i, opᵢ, myargs)*   # "call" *opᵢ*
        receive *reply[i](myresults)*   # wait for reply

        ...

Figure 7.5. Clients and server with multiple operations.

Alternatively, we could employ dynamic naming by having each client create a private reply channel, which it then passes to *Sname* as the first field of *request* in place of the integer index. This would ensure that clients could not access each other's reply channels. It would also permit the number of clients to vary dynamically. (In Figure 7.4, there is a fixed number *n* of clients.)

In general, a monitor has multiple procedures. To extend Figure 7.4 to handle this case, a client needs to indicate which operation it is calling. This is done by including an additional argument in request messages; the type of this argument is an enumeration type with one enumeration literal for each kind of operation. Since different operations will no doubt have different value and result formals, we also need to distinguish between them. This can be done by using a variant record or a union type. (Alternatively, we could make the argument parts of request and reply messages strings of bytes, and let clients and the server encode and decode these.)

Figure 7.5 gives outlines for clients and a server with multiple operations. The **if** statement in the server is like a case statement, with one branch for each different kind of operation. The body of each operation retrieves

```
monitor Resource_Allocator
    var avail : int := MAXUNITS, units : set of int := initial values
    var free : cond    # signaled when unit released and free not empty
    procedure acquire( res id : int )
        if avail = 0 → wait(free)
        [] avail > 0 → avail := avail − 1
        fi
        id := remove(units)
    end
    procedure release( id : int )
        insert(id, units)
        if empty(free) → avail := avail + 1
        [] not empty(free) → signal(free)
        fi
    end
end
```

Figure 7.6. Resource allocation monitor.

arguments from *args* and places result values in *results*. After the **if** statement terminates, *Sname* sends these results to the appropriate client.

So far we have assumed that *Mname* does not employ condition variables. Hence, *Sname* never needs to delay while servicing a request since the body of each operation will be a sequence of sequential statements. We now show how to handle the general case of a monitor with multiple operations and internal condition synchronization. (The clients do not change since they still just "call" an operation by sending a request and later receiving a reply; the fact that a request might not be serviceable immediately is transparent.)

To see how to translate a monitor with condition variables into a server process, we begin by considering a specific example and then describe how to generalize the example. In particular, consider the problem of managing a multiple unit resource—such as memory or file blocks. Clients acquire units of the resource, use them, and later release them back to the manager. For simplicity, clients acquire and release units one at a time. Figure 7.6 gives a monitor implementation of this resource manager. We use the method of passing the condition—as described in Section 6.3—since that program structure is most readily translated into a server process. The free units are stored in a set, which is accessed by *insert* and *remove* operations.

The resource allocation monitor has two operations, so the equivalent server process will have the general structure shown in Figure 7.5. One key difference is that, if no units are available, the server process cannot wait

```
type op_kind = enum(ACQUIRE, RELEASE)
chan request(index, op_kind, unitid : int)
chan reply[1:n](int)

Allocator::  var avail : int := MAXUNITS, units : set of int
             var pending : queue of int
             var index : int, kind : op_kind, unitid : int
             code to initialize units to appropriate values
             do true →
                 receive request(index, kind, unitid)
                 if kind = ACQUIRE →
                     if avail > 0 →    # honor request now
                         avail := avail − 1; unitid := remove(units)
                         send reply[index](unitid)
                     [] avail = 0 →    # remember request
                         insert(pending, index)
                     fi
                 [] kind = RELEASE →
                     if empty(pending) →    # return unitid
                         avail := avail + 1; insert(units, unitid)
                     [] not empty(pending) →    # allocate unitid
                         index := remove(pending)
                         send reply[index](unitid)
                     fi
                 fi
             od
Client[i: 1..n]::  var unitid : int
                   send request(i, ACQUIRE, 0)    # "call" request
                   receive reply[i](unitid)
                   # use resource unitid, and then release it
                   send release(i, RELEASE, unitid)
                   ...
```

Figure 7.7. Resource allocator and clients.

---

when servicing a request. It must save the request and defer sending a reply. Later, when a unit is released, the server needs to honor one saved request, if there is one, by sending the released unit to the requester.

Figure 7.7 gives an outline for the resource allocation server and its clients. The server now has nested **if** statements. The outer ones have branches for each kind of operation, and the inner ones correspond to the **if** statements in the monitor procedures. After sending a request message, a

Monitor-Based Programs	*Message-Based Programs*
permanent variables	local server variables
procedure identifiers	*request* channel and operation kinds
procedure call	**send** *request*; **receive** *reply*
monitor entry	**receive** *request*
procedure return	**send** *reply*
wait statement	save pending request
signal statement	retrieve and process pending request
procedure bodies	arms of case statement on operation kind

Table 7.1. Duality between monitors and message passing.

client waits to receive a unit. However, after sending a release message, the client does not wait for the message to be processed since there is no need to.

This example illustrates how to simulate a specific monitor by a server process. We can use the same basic pattern to simulate any monitor that is programmed using the technique of passing the condition. However, many of the monitors in Chapter 6 had **wait** statements embedded in loops or unconditionally executed **signal** statements. To simulate such **wait** statements, the server would need to save the pending request as in Figure 7.7 and would also need to record what actions should be taken when the request can be serviced. To simulate an unconditional **signal** statement, the server needs to check the queue of pending requests. If it is empty, the server does nothing; if there is a pending request, the server removes one from the queue and processes it *after* processing the operation containing the **signal.** The exact details depend on the monitor being simulated; several exercises explore specific examples.

The *Resource_Allocator* monitor in Figure 7.6 and the *Allocator* server in Figure 7.7 point out the duality between monitors and message passing: There is a direct correspondence between the various mechanisms in monitors and those in message passing. In particular, as shown in Table 7.1, the mechanisms in monitor-based programs serve the same purpose as do the ones listed opposite them in a message-based program.

Since the bodies of monitor procedures have direct duals in the arms of the server case statement, the relative performance of monitor-based versus message-based programs depends only on the relative efficiency of the implementation of the different mechanisms. On shared-memory machines, procedure calls and actions on condition variables tend to be more efficient than message-passing primitives. For this reason, most operating systems for such machines are based on a monitor-style implementation. On the other hand, most distributed systems are based on message passing since that is both efficient and the appropriate abstraction. It is also possible to combine aspects of both styles and implementations, as we will see in Chapter 9 when we discuss remote procedure call and rendezvous. In fact, this makes the duality between monitors and message passing even stronger.

A Self-Scheduling Disk Server

In Section 6.4 we considered the problem of scheduling access to a moving head disk. In that section we considered two different solution structures. In the first (Figure 6.14), the disk scheduler was a monitor separate from the disk. Thus clients first called the scheduler to request access, then used the disk, and finally called the scheduler to release access. In the second structure (Figure 6.17), the scheduler was an intermediary between clients and a disk server process. Thus clients had to call only a single monitor operation.

We can readily mimic both structures in a message-based program by implementing the monitor as a server using the techniques from the previous section. However, with message passing, an even simpler structure is possible. In particular, we can combine the intermediary and disk driver of Figure 6.17 into a single self-scheduling server process. (We cannot do this with monitors since we have to use a monitor to implement the communication path between clients and the disk driver.)

Figure 7.8 shows these three possible structures for a solution to the disk-scheduling problem. In all cases, we assume the disk is controlled by a server process that performs all disk accesses. The principal differences between the three structures are the client interface and the number of messages that must be exchanged per disk access.

When the scheduler is separate from the disk server, five messages must be exchanged per disk access: two to request scheduling and get a reply, two to request disk access and get a reply, and one to release the disk. A client is involved in all five communications. When the scheduler is an intermediary, four kinds of messages have to be exchanged: The client has to send a request and wait to receive a reply, and the disk driver has to ask the scheduler for the next request and get the reply. (The driver process can return the results of one disk access request when it asks for the next one.) As can be seen in Figure 7.8, a self-scheduling disk driver has the most attractive structure. In particular, only two messages need to be exchanged. The remainder of this section shows how to program the driver to implement this structure.

If the disk driver process did no scheduling—i.e., disk access were first come, first served—then it would have the structure of server *Sname* in Figure 7.7. In order to do scheduling, the driver must examine all pending requests, which means it must receive all messages that are waiting on the *request* channel. It does this by executing a loop that terminates when the *request* channel is empty and there is at least one saved request. The driver

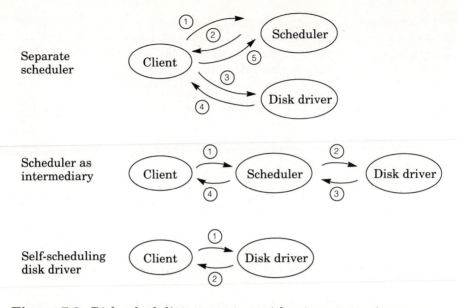

Figure 7.8. Disk scheduling structures with message passing.

then selects the best request, accesses the disk, and finally sends a reply to the client who sent the request. The driver can use any of the disk-scheduling policies described in Section 6.4.

Figure 7.9 outlines a disk driver that employs the shortest-seek-time (SST) scheduling policy. Hence, the driver stores pending requests in one of two ordered queues, *left* or *right*, depending on whether the request is to the left or right of the current position of the disk head. Requests in *left* are ordered by decreasing cylinder value; those is *right* are ordered by increasing cylinder value. The invariant for the outer loop of the driver process is:

> *SST*: *left* is an ordered queue from largest to smallest *cyl* $\wedge$
> all values of *cyl* in *left* are $\leq$ *headpos* $\wedge$
> *right* is an ordered queue from smallest to largest *cyl* $\wedge$
> all values of *cyl* in *right* are $\geq$ *headpos* $\wedge$
> (*nsaved* = 0) $\Rightarrow$ both *left* and *right* are empty

Variable *headpos* indicates the current head position; *nsaved* is a count of the number of saved requests.

In Figure 7.9, the **empty** primitive is used in the guard of the inner loop to determine whether there are more messages queued on the *request* channel. This is an example of the programming technique called *polling*. In this case, the disk driver process repeatedly polls the *request* channel to

```
chan request(index, cylinder: int; other argument types)
    # other arguments indicate read or write, block, buffer, etc.
chan reply[1:n](result types)

Disk_Driver::  var left, right :  ordered queue of (index : int, cyl : int, ...)
               var headpos : int := 1, nsaved := 0
               var index : int, cyl : int, args : other argument types
               do true → { SST }
                   do not empty(request) or nsaved = 0 →
                       # wait for first request or receive another one
                       receive request(index, cyl, args)
                       if cyl ≤ headpos := insert(left, (index, cyl, args))
                       [] cyl ≥ headpos := insert(right, (index, cyl, args))
                       fi
                       nsaved := nsaved + 1
                   od
                   # select best saved request from left or right
                   if size(left) = 0 → (index, cyl, args) := remove(right)
                   [] size(right) = 0 → (index, cyl, args) := remove(left)
                   [] size(right) > 0 and size(left) > 0 →
                       remove element from left or right depending
                       on which saved value of cyl is closer to headpos
                   fi
                   headpos := cyl; nsaved := nsaved − 1
                   access the disk
                   send reply[index](results)
               od
```

Figure 7.9. Self-scheduling disk driver.

---

determine if there are pending requests. If there are, the driver receives another one, so it has more requests to choose from. If there are not (at the time **empty** is evaluated), the driver services the best pending request. Polling is also useful in other situations and is often employed within hardware, e.g., to arbitrate access to a communication bus.

File Servers: Conversational Continuity

As a final example of client/server interaction, we present one way to implement file servers, which are processes that provide access to files on secondary storage, e.g., disk files. To access a disk file, a client first opens the file. If the open is successful—the file exists and the client has permission to access it—then the client makes a series of read and write requests.

Eventually the client closes the file.

Suppose that up to n files may be open at once and that access to each open file is provided by a separate file server process. Hence, there are n such processes. To open a file, a client needs to acquire a file server that is free to interact with it. If all file servers are identical, any free one will do.

We could allocate file servers to clients by using a separate allocator process. However, since all are identical and communication channels are shared, there is a much simpler approach. In particular, let *open* be a global channel. To acquire a file server, a client sends a request to *open*. When idle, file servers try to receive from *open*. A specific *open* request from a client will thus be received by one of the idle file servers. That server sends a reply to the client, then proceeds to wait for access requests. A client sends these to a different channel, *access*[i], where i is the index of the file server that allocated itself to the client. Thus, *access* is an array of n channels. Eventually the client closes the file, at which time the file server becomes idle so again waits for an open request.

Figure 7.10 gives outlines for the file servers and their clients. A client sends its file access requests—READ and WRITE—to the same server channel. This is necessary since the file server cannot in general know the order in which these requests will be made and hence cannot use different channels for each. For the same reason, when a client wants to close a channel, it sends a CLOSE request to the same access channel.

The interaction between a client and a server in Figure 7.10 is an example of *conversational continuity*. In particular, a client starts a "conversation" with a file server when that server receives the client's *open* request. The client then continues to converse with the same server. This is programmed by having the server first receive from *open*, then repeatedly receive from its element of *access*.

The program in Figure 7.10 illustrates one possible way to implement file servers. It assumes that *open* is a shared channel from which any file server can receive a message. If each channel can have only one receiver, then a separate file allocator process would be needed. That process would receive open requests and allocate a free server to a client; file servers would thus need to tell the allocator when they are free.

The solution in Figure 7.10 employs a fixed number n of file servers. In a language that supports dynamic process and channel creation, a better approach would be to create file servers and access channels dynamically as needed. This is better since at any point in time there would only be as many servers as are actually being used; more importantly, there would not be a fixed upper bound on the number of file servers. At the other extreme, there could simply be one file server per disk. In this case, however, either the file server or the client interface will be much more complex than shown in Figure 7.10. This is because either the file server has to keep track of the information associated with all clients who have files open or clients have to

```
type kind = enum(READ, WRITE, CLOSE)
chan open(fname : string[*], clientid : int)
chan access[1:n](kind : int, other types)     # buffer, number of bytes, etc.
chan open_reply[1:n](int)     # field is server index or error indication
chan access_reply[1:n](result types)     # file data, error flags, etc.

File_Server[i: 1..n]::  var fname : string[*], clientid : int
                        var k : kind, args : other argument types
                        var more : bool := false
                        var local buffer, cache, disk address, etc.
                        do true →
                            receive open(fname, clientid)
                            # open file fname; if successful then:
                            send open_reply[clientid](i); more := true
                            do more →
                                receive access[i](k, args)
                                if k = READ → process read request
                                [] k = WRITE → process write request
                                [] k = CLOSE → close file; more := false
                                fi
                                send access_reply[clientid](results)
                            od
                        od

Client[j: 1..m]::  send open("foo", j)          # open file "foo"
                   receive open_reply[j](serverid)  # get back server id
                   # use file then close it by executing the following
                   send access[serverid](access arguments)
                   receive access_reply[j](results)
                   ...
```

Figure 7.10. File servers and clients.

---

pass file state information with every request.

Yet another approach, which is used in the Sun Network File System (NFS), is to implement file access solely by means of remote procedures. Then, "opening" a file consists of acquiring a descriptor (called a file handle in NFS) and a set of file attributes. These are subsequently passed on each call to a file access procedure. Unlike the *File_Server* processes in Figure 7.10, the access procedures in NFS are themselves stateless—all information needed to access a file is passed as arguments on each call to a file access procedure. This increases the cost of passing arguments but greatly simplifies the handling of both client and server crashes. In particular, if a file server crashes, the client simply resends the request until a response is received. If a client crashes, the server need do nothing since it has no state information.

7.5 Heartbeat Algorithms

In a hierarchical system, servers at intermediate levels are often also clients of lower-level servers. For example, the file server in Figure 7.10 might well process read and write requests by communicating with a disk server such as the one in Figure 7.9.

In this and the next several sections, we examine a different kind of server interaction in which servers at the same level are peers that cooperate in providing a service. This type of interaction arises in distributed computations in which no one server has all the information needed to service a client request. In addition to examing several examples of such computations, we introduce several different programming paradigms that can be used to solve similar problems. We also introduce several techniques for developing solutions to distributed programming problems.

In this section, we consider the problem of computing the topology of a network. This problem is representative of a large class of distributed information-exchange problems that arise in networks. Given is a network of processors connected by bi-directional communication channels, as in Figure 7.11. Each processor can communicate only with its neighbors and knows only about the links to its neighbors. The problem is for each processor to determine the topology of the entire network, i.e., the entire set of links. (This information might then be used, for example, to make message routing decisions.)

Each processor is modeled by a process, and the communication links are modeled by shared channels. We solve this problem by first assuming that all processes have access to a shared memory, which is of course not realistic for this problem. Then we refine the solution into a distributed computation by replicating global variables and having neighboring processes interact to exchange their local information. In particular, each process executes a sequence of iterations. On each iteration, a process sends its local knowledge of the topology to all its neighbors, then receives their information and combines it with its own. The computation terminates when all processes have learned the topology of the entire network.

We call this type of process interaction a *heartbeat algorithm* since the actions of each node are like the beating of a heart: first expand, sending information out; then contract, gathering new information in. The same type of algorithm can be used to solve many other problems, especially those arising from parallel iterative computations. In the next two chapters we give three specific examples: parallel sorting, matrix multiplication, and an

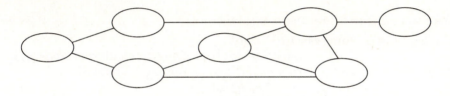

Figure 7.11. An example of a small network.

image-processing problem called region labeling. The Exercises contain additional examples.

Network Topology: Shared-Variable Solution

We begin as usual by specifying the network topology problem precisely. Given are n nodes, one per processor. Each node p can communicate only with its neighbors, and initially all it knows about the topology is its set of neighbors. We assume the neighbor relationship is symmetric: for each pair of nodes p and q, p is a neighbor of q if and only if q is a neighbor of p. The problem is to compute the set *top* of all links, namely all pairs (p, q) such that p is a neighbor of q. During the computation, we assume the topology of the network is static; i.e., links are not added or removed. (Exercise 7.21 explores the ramifications of relaxing this assumption.)

We will represent each node by a process *Node*[p: 1..n]. Within each process, we can then represent the neighbors of a node by a boolean (bit) vector *links*[1:n], with element *links*[q] being true in *Node*[p] if q is a neighbor of p. These vectors are assumed to be initialized to the appropriate values. The final topology *top* can then be represented by an adjacency matrix, with *top*[p, q] being true if p and q are neighboring nodes. Specifically, when the computation terminates, the following predicate is to be true:

$$TOPOLOGY:\ (\ \forall\, p, q:\ 1 \le p \le n, 1 \le q \le n:\ top[p, q] \Leftrightarrow links_p[q]\ )$$

Above, $links_p$ is the neighbor set of node p.

To solve the network topology problem, assume for now that *top* is global to all *Node* processes and that initially all elements of *top* are false. Then all that each process needs to do is store the value of its neighbor set in the appropriate row in *top*. In fact, since each process assigns to a different row of *top*, the assignments to *top* can execute in parallel without interference. This yields the shared-variable solution shown in Figure 7.12. When each node process *Node*[p] terminates, *top*[p, q] is true if q is a neighbor of p, and is false otherwise. The final state of the program is the union of the final state of each process; hence upon termination, *TOPOLOGY* is true as required.

var $top[1{:}n, 1{:}n]$: **bool** := $([n * n]$ false)

$Node[p{:}\ 1..n]$:: **var** $links[1{:}n]$: **bool**
>   # initially $links[q]$ true if q is a neighbor of $Node[p]$
>   **fa** $q := 1$ **to** n **st** $links[q] \rightarrow top[p, q] :=$ true **af**
>   { $top[p, 1{:}n] = links[1{:}n]$ }

Figure 7.12. Network topology using shared variables.

Network Topology: Distributed Solution

One way to turn the solution in Figure 7.12 into a distributed program that employs message passing is to have a single process T compute the topology. This would be done by having each node send its value of *links* to T, which would copy the message into the appropriate row of *top*. This approach uses a minimal number of messages $(2n)$, but it has a drawback: How does a node communicate with T if T is not one of its neighbors? We could have nodes who are neighbors of T forward messages from other nodes, but the resulting algorithm would be very asymmetric. A symmetric algorithm in which each node executes the same program is generally preferable since it is easier to develop and understand. Moreover, a symmetric algorithm is easier to modify to cope with potential failures of processors or communication links.

To get a symmetric, distributed algorithm to solve the network topology problem, we need a way for each node to compute for itself the entire topology *top*. Initially node p knows about the links to its neighbors. If it asks those nodes for their neighbor links—by sending a message to and receiving a reply from each—after one round of messages, p will have learned about the topology within two links of itself; i.e., it will know its links and those of its neighbors. If every node does the same thing, after one full round each node will know about the topology within two links of itself. If each node now executes another round in which it again exchanges what it knows with its neighbors, after two rounds each node will know about the topology within three links of itself. In general, after r rounds the following will be true in each node p:

$$ROUND:\ (\ \forall\, q{:}\ 1 \leq q \leq n{:}\ (dist(p, q) \leq r) \Rightarrow top[q, *]\ \text{filled in}\ )$$

Here $dist(p, q)$ is the distance from node p to node q, i.e., the length of the shortest path between them.

If each node executes an adequate number of rounds, then from *ROUND* we can conclude that each node will compute the entire topology. Assume for now that we know the *diameter* D of the network. This is the distance between the farthest pair of nodes; e.g., D is 4 for the network in Figure 7.11.

```
chan topology[1:n]([1:n, 1:n] bool)      # one private channel per node
Node[p: 1..n]::  var links[1:n] : bool
                    # initially links[q] true if q is a neighbor of Node[p]
                 var top[1:n, 1:n] : bool := ([n * n] false)     # known links
                 top[p, 1..n] := links    # fill in row for my neighbors
                 var r : int := 0
                 var newtop[1:n, 1:n] : bool
                 { top[p, 1:n] = links[1:n] ∧ r = 0 }  { ROUND }
                 do r < D →
                     # send local knowledge of topology to all neighbors
                     fa q := 1 to n st links[q] → send topology[q](top) af
                     # receive their local topologies and or it with top
                     fa q := 1 to n st links[q] →
                         receive topology[p](newtop)
                         top := top or newtop
                     af
                     r := r + 1
                 od
                 { ROUND ∧ r = D }  { TOPOLOGY }
```

Figure 7.13. Heartbeat algorithm for network topology, first refinement.

If we know the value of D, the program in Figure 7.13 solves the network topology problem. (For simplicity, the declarations of the communication channels in that program are to all the processes, although of course for this problem we assume that a node can communicate only with its neighbors.) As indicated, *ROUND* is the loop invariant in each node. It is made true initially by setting *top* to the node's neighbors and initializing local variable r to 0. It is preserved on each iteration since every node exchanges all its local information with its neighbors on each round. Logical **or** is used to union a neighbor's topology, which is received into *newtop*, with the local topology, which is stored in *top*. When a node terminates, it has executed D rounds. Since by definition of D no node is farther than D links away, *top* contains the entire topology.

There are two problems with the algorithm in Figure 7.13. First, we do not know the value of diameter D. Second, there is excessive message exchange. This is because nodes near the center of the network will know the entire topology as soon as they have executed enough rounds to have received information from nodes at the edges of the network. On subsequent rounds, these nodes will not learn anything new, yet they will continue to exchange information with every neighbor. As a concrete example, consider the network in Figure 7.11. The node in the center will have learned the topology after two rounds, but it takes four rounds before every node will have learned the topology.

Loop invariant *ROUND* and the above observations suggest how to overcome both problems. After r rounds, node p will know the topology within distance r of itself. In particular, for every node q within distance r of p, the neighbors of q will be stored in row q of *top*. Since the network is connected, every node has at least one neighbor. Thus, node p has executed enough rounds to know the topology as soon as every row in *top* has some true value. At this point, p needs to execute one last round in which it exchanges the topology with its neighbors; then p can terminate. This last round is necessary since p will have received new information on the previous round. It also avoids leaving unprocessed messages in message channels Since a node might terminate one round before (or after) a neighbor, each node also needs to tell its neighbors when it is terminating. To avoid deadlock, on the last round a node should exchange messages only with neighbors who did not terminate on the previous round.

Figure 7.14 gives the final program for the network topology problem. The comments indicate what is going on at each stage. In the program, r is now an auxiliary variable—it is used only to facilitate specification of predicate *ROUND*. The loop invariant is *ROUND* and a predicate specifying that *done* is true only if all rows in *top* have been filled in. Thus, when the loop terminates, a node has heard from every other process, so *top* contains the complete network topology.

The program in Figure 7.14 is deadlock-free since **send**s are executed before **receive**s and a node receives only as many messages on each round as it has active neighbors. The loop terminates in each node since the network is connected and information is propagated to each neighbor on every round. The final round of **send**s and **receive**s ensures that every neighbor sees the final topology and that no unreceived messages are left buffered. If the algorithm were only run once, this would probably not be a problem (depending on what the underlying implementation does about non-empty buffers.) However, an algorithm like this might well be run periodically on a real network since the topology invariably changes over time.

The centralized algorithm mentioned at the start of this section requires the exchange of $2n$ messages, one from each node to the central server and one in reply. The decentralized algorithm in Figure 7.14 requires the exchange of more messages. The actual number depends on the network topology since the number of rounds a node executes depends on its distance from the node farthest away from it. However, if m is the maximal number of neighbors any node has and D is the diameter of the network, the number of messages that are exchanged is bounded by $2n * m * (D + 1)$. This is because each of the n nodes executes at most $D + 1$ rounds during which it exchanges 2 messages with each of m neighbors. If m and D are relatively small compared with n, then the number of messages that are exchanged is not

chan *topology*[1:*n*](*sender* : **int**; *done* : **bool**; *top* : [1:*n*, 1:*n*] **bool**)

Node[*p*: 1..*n*]:: **var** *links*[1:*n*] : **bool**
           # initially *links*[*q*] true if *q* is a neighbor of *Node*[*p*]
        var *active*[1:*n*] : **bool** := *links*   # neighbors still active
        var *top*[1:*n*, 1:*n*] : **bool** := ([*n* * *n*] false)   # known links
        var *r* : **int** := 0, *done* : **bool** := *false*
        var *sender* : **int**, *qdone* : **bool**, *newtop*[1:*n*, 1:*n*] : **bool**
        top[*p*, 1..*n*] := *links*   # fill in row for my neighbors
        { *top*[*p*, 1:*n*] = *links*[1:*n*] $\wedge$ *r* = 0 $\wedge$ $\neg$*done*}
        { *ROUND* $\wedge$ *done* $\Rightarrow$ (all rows in *top* are filled in) }
        do not *done* $\rightarrow$
            # send local knowledge of topology to all neighbors
            fa *q* := 1 **to** *n* **st** *links*[*q*] $\rightarrow$
                send *topology*[*q*](*p*, false, *top*)
            af
            # receive their local topologies and or it with *top*
            fa *q* := 1 **to** *n* **st** *links*[*q*] $\rightarrow$
                receive *topology*[*p*](*sender*, *qdone*, *newtop*)
                top := *top* **or** *newtop*
                if not *qdone* $\rightarrow$ *active*[*sender*] := false **fi**
            af
            if all rows of *top* have a true entry $\rightarrow$ *done* := true **fi**
            r := *r* + 1
        od
        { *ROUND* $\wedge$ all rows in *top* filled in } { *TOPOLOGY* }
        # send topology to all neighbors who are still active
        fa *q* := 1 **to** *n* **st** *active*[*q*] $\rightarrow$
            send *topology*[*q*](*p*, *done*, *top*)
        af
        # receive one message from each to clear up channel
        fa *q* := 1 **to** *n* **st** *active*[*q*] $\rightarrow$
            receive *topology*[*p*](*sender*, *d*, *newtop*)
        af

Figure 7.14. Heartbeat algorithm for network topology, final version.

---

much greater than for the centralized algorithm. Moreover, these can be exchanged in parallel in many cases, whereas a centralized server sequentially waits to receive a message from every node before sending any reply.

The main loop in any heartbeat algorithm will have the same basic structure shown in Figures 7.13 and 7.14: send messages to all neighbors, then receive messages from them. What the messages contain and how they are processed of course depends on the application. For example, in a grid computation, nodes would exchange boundary values with their neighbors, and the computation in each round would be to compute new values for local grid points.

Another difference between instances of heartbeat algorithms is the termination criterion and how it is checked. For the network topology problem, each node can determine for itself when to terminate. This is because a node acquires more information on each round, and the information it already has does not change. In many grid computations, the termination criterion is also based on local information—e.g., the values of grid points after one round are within epsilon of their values after the previous round.

Termination cannot always be decided locally, however. For example, consider using a grid computation to label regions of an image, with each node in the grid being responsible for a block of the image. Since a region might "snake" across the image, a node cannot tell when it has all information from distant nodes; it might see no change on one round and get new information several rounds later. Such a computation can terminate only when there is no change anywhere after a round. Thus, the processes need to communicate with a central controller, exchange additional messages with each other, or execute the worst-case number of rounds. Later examples of heartbeat algorithms in Chapters 8 and 9 illustrate these techniques.

7.6 Probe/Echo Algorithms

Trees and graphs are used in many computing problems; e.g., game-playing, databases, and expert systems. They are especially important in distributed computing since the structure of many distributed computations is a graph in which processes are nodes and communication channels are edges.

Depth-first search (DFS) is one of the classic sequential programming paradigms for visiting all the nodes in a tree or graph. In a tree, the DFS strategy for each node is to visit the children of that node and then to return to the parent. This is called depth-first search since each search path reaches down to a leaf before the next path is traversed; e.g., the path in the tree from the root to the left-most leaf is traversed first. In a general graph—which may have cycles—the same approach is used, except we need to mark nodes as they are visited so that edges out of a node are traversed only once.

This section describes the probe/echo paradigm for distributed computations on graphs. A probe is a message sent by one node to its successor; an echo is a subsequent reply. Since processes execute concurrently, probes are sent in parallel to all successors. The probe/echo paradigm is thus the concurrent programming analog of DFS. We first illustrate the probe paradigm by showing how to broadcast information to all

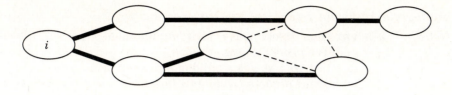

Figure 7.15. Example of a spanning tree.

nodes in a network. We then add the echo paradigm by developing a different algorithm for constructing the topology of a network.

Broadcast in a Network

Assume as in Section 7.5 that there is one node per processor and that each node can communicate only with its neighbors. Suppose one initiator node i wants to *broadcast* a message—i.e., to send some information to all other nodes. For example, i might be the site of the network coordinator, who wants to broadcast new status information to all other sites.

If every other node is a neighbor of i, broadcast would be trivial to implement: node i would simply send a message directly to every other node. However, in the more realistic situation in which only a small number of other nodes are neighbors of i, we need to have information forwarded by nodes until we are sure that all have seen it. In short, we need to send a probe to all nodes.

Assume that node i has a local copy *top* of the entire network topology, computed, for example, as shown in Figure 7.14. Then an efficient way for i to broadcast a message is first to construct a *spanning tree* of the network, with itself as the root of the tree. A spanning tree of a graph is a tree whose nodes are all those in the graph and whose edges are a subset of those in the graph. Figure 7.15 contains an example for the network given earlier in Figure 7.11; node i is on the left. Given spanning tree T, node i can then broadcast a message m by sending m together with T to all its children in T. Upon receiving the message, every node examines T to determine its children in the spanning tree, then forwards both m and T to all of them. The spanning tree is sent along with m since nodes other than i would not otherwise know what spanning tree to use.

The full algorithm is given in Figure 7.16. Since T is a spanning tree, eventually the message will reach every node; moreover, each node will receive it exactly once, from its parent in T. A separate process, *Initiator*, on node i initiates the broadcast. This makes the broadcast algorithm on each node symmetric.

chan *probe*[1:*n*](*span_tree* : [1:*n*, 1:*n*] **int**, message_type)

Node[*p*: 1..*n*]:: **var** *span_tree*[1:*n*, 1:*n*] : **int**, *m* : message_type
                receive *probe*[*p*](*span_tree*, *m*)
                fa *q* := 1 **to** *n* **st** *q* is a child of *p* in *span_tree* →
                    send *probe*[*q*](*span_tree*, *m*)
                af

Initiator:: **var** *i* : **int** := index of node that is to initiate broadcast
           var *top*[1:*n*, 1:*n*] : **int**   # initialized with network topology
           var *T*[1:*n*, 1:*n*] : **int**, *m* : message_type
           # compute spanning tree of *top* and store it in *T*
           m := message to be broadcast
           send *probe*[*i*](*T*, *m*)

Figure 7.16. Broadcast using a spanning tree.

The broadcast algorithm in Figure 7.16 assumes that the initiator node knows the entire topology, which it uses to compute a spanning tree that guides the broadcast. Suppose instead that each node knows only its neighbors. We can still broadcast a message *m* to all nodes as follows. First, node *i* sends *m* to all its neighbors. Upon receiving *m*, a node sends it along to all its other neighbors. If the links defined by the neighbor sets happen to form a tree rooted at *i*, the effect of this approach is the same as before. In general, however, the network will contain cycles. Thus, some node might receive *m* from two or more neighbors. In fact, two neighbors might send the message to each other at about the same time.

It would appear that all we need to do in the general case is ignore multiple copies of *m* that a node might receive. However, this leads to the following problem. After receiving *m* for the first time and sending it along, a node cannot know how many times to wait to receive *m* from a different neighbor. If the node does not wait at all, extra messages could be left buffered on some of the *probe* channels. If a node waits some fixed number of times, it might deadlock unless at least that many messages are sent; even so, there might be more.

The solution to the problem of unprocessed messages is to have a fully symmetric algorithm. In particular, let each node when it receives *m* for the first time send *m* to all its neighbors, including the one from whom it received *m*. Then the node receives redundant copies of *m* from all its other neighbors; these it ignores. The algorithm is given in Figure 7.17.

The broadcast algorithm using a spanning tree (Figure 7.16) causes *n* − 1 messages to be sent, one for each parent/child edge in the spanning tree. The algorithm using neighbor sets (Figure 7.17) causes two messages to be sent

chan *probe*[1:*n*](message_type)

Node[*p*: 1..*n*]::   **var** *links*[1:*n*] : **bool** := neighbors of node *p*
                          var *num* : **int** := number of neighbors
                          var *m* : message_type
                          receive *probe*[*p*](*m*)
                          # send *m* to all neighbors
                          fa *q* := 1 **to** *n* **st** *links*[*q*] → **send** *probe*[*q*](*m*) **af**
                          # receive *num* − 1 redundant copies of *m*
                          fa *q* := 1 **to** *num* − 1 → **receive** *probe*[*p*](*m*) **af**

Initiator::   **var** *i* : **int** := index of node that is to initiate broadcast
                      var *m* : message_type
                      m := message to be broadcast
                      send *probe*[*i*](*m*)

Figure 7.17. Broadcast using neighbor sets.

---

over every link in the network, one in each direction. The exact number depends on the topology of the network, but in general the number will be much larger than *n* − 1. For example, if the network topology is a tree rooted at the initiator process, $2(n - 1)$ messages will be sent; for a complete graph in which there is a link between every pair of nodes, $2n(n - 1)$ messages will be sent. However, the neighbor-set algorithm does not require that the initiator node know the topology and compute a spanning tree. In essence, the spanning tree is constructed dynamically; it consists of the links along which the first copies of *m* are sent. Also, the messages are shorter in the neighbor-set algorithm since the spanning tree (n^2 bits) need not be sent in each message.

Both broadcast algorithms assume that the topology of the network does not change. In particular, neither works correctly if there is a processor or communication link failure while the algorithm is executing. If a node fails, it cannot receive the message being broadcast. If a link fails, it might or might not be possible to reach the nodes connected by the link. The Historical Notes and References discuss papers that address the problem of implementing a fault-tolerant broadcast.

Network Topology Revisited

In Section 7.5, we derived a distributed algorithm for computing the topology of a network by first starting with a shared memory algorithm and then generating multiple copies of the shared data. Here we solve the same problem in a completely different manner. In particular, we have one initiator node gather the local topology data of every other node and then disseminate the full topology back to the other nodes. The topology is gathered in two phases. First, each node sends a probe to its neighbors, much as in Figure 7.17. Later, each node sends an echo containing local topology information back to the node from which it received the first probe. Eventually, the initiating node has gathered all the echoes. It can then compute a spanning tree for the network and broadcast the complete topology using the algorithm in either Figure 7.16 or 7.17.

Assume for now that the topology of the network is acyclic; since it is an undirected graph, this means the structure is a tree. Let node i be the root of this tree, and let i be the initiator node. Then we can gather the topology as follows. First i sends a probe to all its neighbors. When these nodes receive a probe, they send it to all their neighbors, and so on. Thus, probes propagate through the tree. Eventually they will reach leaf nodes. Since these have no other neighbors, they begin the echo phase. In particular, each leaf sends an echo containing its neighbor set to its parent in the tree. After receiving echoes from all of its children, a node combines them and its own neighbor set and echoes this information to its parent. Eventually the root node will receive echoes from all its children. The union of these will contain the entire topology since the initial probe will reach every node and every echo contains the neighbor set of the echoing node together with those of its descendants.

The full probe/echo algorithm for gathering the network topology in a tree is shown in Figure 7.18. The probe phase is essentially the broadcast algorithm from Figure 7.17, except that no message is broadcast; probe messages merely indicate the identity of the sender. The echo phase returns local topology information back up the tree. In this case, the algorithms for the nodes are not fully symmetric since the instance of *Node[p]* executing on node i needs to know to send its echo to the *Initiator*. After *Initiator* receives the final topology into *top*, it can compute a spanning tree and broadcast *top* back to the other nodes.

To compute the topology of a network that contains cycles, we generalize the above algorithm as follows. After receiving a probe, a node sends it on to all its other neighbors, then waits for an echo from each. However, because of cycles and because nodes execute concurrently, two neighbors might send each other probes at about the same time. Probes other than the first one can be echoed immediately. In particular, if a node receives a subsequent probe while waiting for echoes, it immediately sends an echo containing a null topology (this is sufficient since the local neighbor set of the node will be contained in the echo sent in response to the first probe). Eventually a node will receive an echo in response to every probe. At this point, it echoes the union of its neighbor set and the echoes it received.

The general probe/echo algorithm for computing the network topology is shown in Figure 7.19. Because a node might receive subsequent probes while waiting for echoes, the two types of messages have to be merged into one

```
const source = i     # index of node that initiates the algorithm
chan probe[1:n](sender : int)
chan echo[1:n](links[1:n, 1:n] : bool)     # part of the topology
chan finalecho[1:n](links[1:n, 1:n] : bool)     # final echo to Initiator

Node[p: 1..n]::  var links[1:n] : bool := neighbors of node p
                 var localtop[1:n, 1:n] : bool := ([n * n] false)
                 localtop[p, 1:n] := links
                 var newtop[1:n, 1:n] : bool
                 var parent : int    # node from whom probe is received
                 receive probe[p](parent)
                 # send probe to other neighbors, who are p's children
                 fa q := 1 to n st links[q] and q ≠ parent →
                     send probe[q](p)
                 af
                 # receive echoes and union them into localtop
                 fa q := 1 to n st links[q] and q ≠ parent →
                     receive echo[p](newto)
                     localtop := localtop or newtop
                 af
                 if p = source → send finalecho(localtop)   # node p is root
                 [] p ≠ source → send echo[parent](localtop)
                 fi

Initiator::  var top[1:n, 1:n] : bool
             send probe[source](source)  # start probe at local node
             receive finalecho(top)
```

Figure 7.18. Probe/echo algorithm for topology of a tree.

---

channel. (If they came in on separate channels, a node would have to use **empty** and polling to know when to receive from a channel.)

The correctness of the algorithm results from the following facts. Since the network is connected, every node eventually receives a probe. Deadlock is avoided since every probe is echoed—the first one just before a *Node* process terminates, others while it is waiting to receive echoes in response to its own probes (this avoids leaving messages buffered on the *probe_echo* channels). The last echo sent by a node contains its local neighbor set. Hence, the union of the neighbor sets eventually reaches *Node[i]*, which sends the topology on to the *Initiator*. As with the algorithm in Figure 7.17, the links along which first probes are sent form a dynamically computed spanning tree; the network topology is echoed back up this spanning tree, with the echo from a node containing the topology of the subtree rooted at that node.

```
const source = i     # index of node that initiates the algorithm
type kind = enum(PROBE, ECHO)
chan probe_echo[1:n](kind, sender : int, links[1:n, 1:n] int)
chan finalecho[1:n](links[1:n, 1:n] int)     # final echo to Initiator
Node[p: 1..n]::  var links[1:n] : bool := neighbors of node p
                 var localtop[1:n, 1:n] : bool := ([n * n] false)
                 localtop[p, 1:n] := links
                 var newtop[1:n, 1:n] : bool
                 var first : int     # node from whom first probe is received
                 var k : kind, sender : int
                 var need_echo : int := number of neighbors − 1
                 receive probe_echo[p](k, sender, newtop)   # get probe
                 first := sender
                 # send probe on to to all other neighbors
                 fa q := 1 to n st links[q] and q ≠ parent →
                     send probe_echo[q](PROBE, p, ∅)
                 af
                 do need_echo > 0 →
                     # receive echoes or probes from neighbors
                     receive probe_echo[p](k, sender, newtop)
                     if k = PROBE →
                         send probe_echo[sender](ECHO, p, ∅)
                     [] k = ECHO →
                         localtop := localtop or newtop
                         need_echo := need_echo − 1
                     fi
                 od
                 if p = source → send finalecho(localtop)
                 [] p ≠ source → send probe_echo[first](ECHO, p, localtop)
                 fi
Initiator::  var top[1:n, 1:n] : bool   # network topology
             send probe[source](PROBE, source, ∅)
             receive finalecho(top)
```

Figure 7.19. Probe/echo algorithm for topology of a network.

This probe/echo algorithm for computing the topology of a network requires fewer messages than the heartbeat algorithm in Figure 7.14. Two messages are sent along each link that is an edge in the spanning tree of first probes—one for the probe and another for the echo. Other links carry four messages—one probe and one echo in each direction. To disseminate the topology from the *Initiator* back to all nodes using the broadcast algorithm in Figure 7.16 would require another n messages. In any event, the number of messages is proportional to the number of links. For computations that disseminate or gather information on graphs, probe/echo algorithms are thus more efficient than heartbeat algorithms. In contrast, heartbeat algorithms are appropriate and necessary for many parallel iterative algorithms in which nodes repeatedly exchange information until they converge on an answer.

7.7 Broadcast Algorithms

In the previous section, we showed how to broadcast information in a network. In particular, we can use a probe algorithm to disseminate information and a probe/echo algorithm to gather or locate information.

In most local area networks, processors share a common communication channel such as an Ethernet or token ring. In this case, each processor is directly connected to every other one. In fact, such communication networks often support a special network primitive called **broadcast**, which transmits a message from one processor to all others. Whether supported by communication hardware or not, message broadcast provides a useful programming technique.

Let $P[1{:}n]$ be an array of processes, and let $ch[1{:}n]$ be an array of channels, one per process. Then a process $P[i]$ broadcasts a message m by executing

> **broadcast** $ch(m)$

Execution of **broadcast** places one copy of m on each channel $ch[i]$, including that of $P[i]$. The effect is thus the same as executing n **send** statements in parallel, with each sending m to a different channel. Process i receives a message from its channel by executing **receive** as usual. We do not assume that the **broadcast** primitive is indivisible, however. In particular, messages broadcast by two processes A and B might be received by other processes in different orders. (See the Historical Notes and References for papers that discuss how to implement reliable and totally ordered broadcasts.)

We can use broadcasts to disseminate or gather information; e.g., it is often used to exchange processor state information in local area networks. We can also use broadcasts to solve many distributed synchronization problems. This section illustrates the power of broadcasts by developing a distributed implementation of semaphores. The basis for distributed semaphores—and many other decentralized synchronization protocols—is a total ordering of communication events. We thus begin by showing how to implement logical clocks and then show how to use such clocks to order events.

Logical Clocks and Event Ordering

Processes in a distributed program execute local actions and communication actions. Local actions include such things as reading and writing local variables. They have no direct effect on other processes. Communication actions are sending and receiving messages. These affect the execution of other processes since they communicate information and are the basic synchronization mechanism. Communication actions are thus the significant *events* in a distributed program. Hence, we use the term *event* below to refer to execution of **send** and **receive** statements.

If two processes *A* and *B* are executing local actions, we have no way of knowing the relative order in which the actions are executed. However, if *A* sends a message to *B*, then the **send** action in *A* must happen before the corresponding **receive** action in *B*. If *B* subsequently sends a message to process *C*, then the **send** action in *B* must happen before the **receive** action in *C*. Moreover, since the **receive** action in *B* happens before the **send** action in *B*, there is a total ordering between the four communication actions: the **send** by *A* happens before the **receive** by *B*, which happens before the **send** by *B*, which happens before the **receive** by *C*. "Happens before" is thus a transitive relation between causally related events.

There is a total ordering between events that causally affect each other as described above. However, there is only a partial ordering between the entire collection of events in a distributed program. This is because unrelated sequences of events—for example, communications between different sets of processes—might occur before, after, or concurrently with each other.

If there were a single central clock, we could totally order communication actions by giving each a unique timestamp. In particular, when a process sends a message, it could read the clock and append the clock value to the message. When a process receives a message, it could read the clock and record the time at which the **receive** event occurred. Assuming the granularity of the clock is such that it "ticks" between any **send** and the corresponding **receive**, an event that happens before another will thus have an earlier timestamp. Moreover, if processes have unique identities, then we could induce a total ordering by, for example, using the smallest process identity to break ties if unrelated events in two processes happen to have the same timestamp.

Unfortunately, it is quite restrictive to assume the existence of a single, central clock. In a local area network, for example, each processor has its own clock. If these were perfectly synchronized, then we could use the local clocks for timestamps. However, physical clocks are never perfectly synchronized. Clock synchronization algorithms exist for keeping two clocks fairly close to each other, but perfect synchronization is impossible. Thus we need a way to simulate physical clocks.

A *logical clock* is a simple integer counter that is incremented when events occur. We assume that each process has a logical clock and that every message contains a timestamp. The logical clocks are then incremented according to the following rules.

(7.10) **Logical Clock Update Rules.** Let lc be a logical clock in process A.

(1) When A sends or broadcasts a message, it sets the timestamp of the message to the current value of lc and then increments lc by 1.

(2) When A receives a message with timestamp ts, it sets lc to the maximum of lc and $ts + 1$ and then increments lc by 1.

Since A increases lc after every event, every message sent by A will have a different, increasing timestamp. Since a **receive** event sets lc to be larger than the timestamp in the received message, the timestamp in any message subsequently sent by A will have a larger timestamp.

Using logical clocks, we can associate a clock value with each event as follows. For a **send** event, the clock value is the timestamp in the message, i.e., the local value of lc at the start of the send. For a **receive** event, the clock value is the value of lc after it is set to the maximum of lc and $ts + 1$ but before it is incremented by the receiving process. The above rules for updating logical clocks ensure that if event a happens before event b, then the clock value associated with a will be smaller than that associated with b. This induces a partial ordering on the set of causally related events in a program. If each process has a unique identity, then we can get a total ordering between all events by using the smaller process identity as a tie-breaker in case two events happen to have the same timestamp.

Distributed Semaphores

Semaphores are normally implemented using shared variables. However, we could implement them in a message-based program using a server process (active monitor), as shown in Section 7.4 (e.g., see Figure 7.6). We can also implement them in a distributed way without using a central coordinator. Here, we show how.

Recall the basic definition of semaphores (4.1): At all times, the number of completed **P** operations is at most the number of completed **V** operations plus the initial value. Thus, to implement semaphores, we need a way to count **P** and **V** operations and a way to delay **P** operations. Moreover, the processes that "share" a semaphore need to cooperate so that they maintain the semaphore invariant even though the program state is distributed.

We can meet these requirements by having processes broadcast messages when they want to execute **P** and **V** operations and by having them examine the messages they receive to determine when to proceed. In particular, each process has a local message queue *mq* and a logical clock *lc*. To simulate execution of a **P** or **V** operation, a process broadcasts a message to all the user processes, including itself. The message contains the sender's identity, a tag (P or V), and a timestamp. The timestamp in every copy of the message is the current value of *lc*, which is updated according to the rules in (7.10).

When a process receives a P or V message, it stores the message in its message queue *mq*. This queue is kept sorted in increasing order of the timestamps in the messages; sender identities are used to break ties. Assume for the moment that every process receives all messages that have been broadcast in the same order and in increasing order of timestamps. Then every process would know exactly the order in which P and V messages were sent. Thus, each could count the number of corresponding **P** and **V** operations and maintain the semaphore invariant.

Unfortunately, it is unrealistic to assume that **broadcast** is an atomic operation. Two messages broadcast by two different processes might be received by others in different orders. Moreover, a message with a smaller timestamp might be received after a message with a larger timestamp. However, different messages broadcast by one process will be received by the other processes in the order they were broadcast by the first process; these messages will also have increasing timestamps. This is because (1) execution of **broadcast** is the same as concurrent execution of **send**—which we assume provides ordered, reliable delivery—and (2) a process increases its logical clock after every communication event.

The fact that consecutive messages sent by every process have increasing timestamps gives us a way to make synchronization decisions. Suppose a process's message queue *mq* contains a message *m* with timestamp *ts*. Then, once the process has received a message with a larger timestamp from every other process, it is assured that it will never see a message with a smaller timestamp. At this point, message *m* is said to be *fully acknowledged*. Moreover, once *m* is fully acknowledged, then every other message in front of it in *mq* will also be fully acknowledged since they all have smaller timestamps. Thus, the part of *mq* containing fully acknowledged messages is a *stable prefix*: no new messages will ever be inserted into it.

Whenever a process receives a P or V message, we will have it broadcast an acknowledgement (ACK) message. Acknowledgements are broadcast so that every process sees the acknowledgement. The ACK messages have timestamps as usual, but they are not stored in the message queues and are not themselves acknowledged. They are used simply to determine when a regular message in *mq* has become fully acknowledged. (If we did not use ACK messages, a process could not determine that a message was fully acknowledged until it received a later P or V message from every other process; this would slow the algorithm down and would lead to deadlock if some user did not want to execute **P** or **V** operations.)

type *kind* = **enum**(V, P, ACK)
chan *semop*[1:*n*](*sender, kind, timestamp* : **int**), *go*[1:*n*](*timestamp* : **int**)

User[*i*: 1..*n*]::   **var** *lc* : **int** := 0   # logical clock
             var *ts* : **int**   # timestamp in *go* messages
             # execute a **V** operation
             broadcast *semop*(*i*, V, *lc*); *lc* := *lc* + 1

              ...
             # execute a **P** operation
             broadcast *semop*(*i*, P, *lc*); *lc* := *lc* + 1
             receive *go*[*i*](*ts*); *lc* := **max**(*lc*, *ts* + 1); *lc* := *lc* + 1

             ...

Helper[*i*: 1..*n*]::   **var** *mq* : **queue of** (**int**, *kind*, **int**)   # timestamp order
              var *lc* : **int** := 0   # logical clock
              var *sem* : **int** := initial value   # semaphore value
              var *sender* : **int**, *k* : *kind*, *ts* : *int*
              do true →   { *DSEM* }
                 receive *semop*[*i*](*sender, k, ts*)
                 lc := **max**(*lc*, *ts* + 1); *lc* := *lc* + 1
                 if *k* = P **or** *k* = V →
                     insert (*sender, k, ts*) at appropriate place in *mq*
                     broadcast *semop*(*i*, ACK, *lc*); *lc* := *lc* + 1
                 [] *k* = ACK →
                     record that another ACK has been seen
                     fa fully acknowledged V messages →
                         remove the message from *mq*; *sem* := *sem* + 1
                     af
                     fa fully acknowledged P messages **st** *sem* > 0 →
                         remove the message from *mq*; *sem* := *sem* − 1
                         if *sender* = *i* → **send** *go*[*i*](*lc*); *lc* := *lc* + 1 **fi**
                     af
                 fi
              od

Figure 7.20. Distributed semaphores algorithm.

To complete the implementation of distributed semaphores, each process simulates the semaphore operations. It uses a local variable *sem* to represent the value of the semaphore. When a process gets an ACK message, it updates the stable prefix of its message queue *mq*. For every V message, the process increments *sem* and deletes the V message. It then examines the P messages in timestamp order. If *sem* > 0, the process decrements *sem* and deletes the P message. In short, each process maintains the following predicate, which is its loop invariant:

$$DSEM: \; sem \geq 0 \; \wedge \; mq \text{ totally ordered by timestamps in messages}$$

The P messages are processed in the order in which they appear in the stable prefix so that every process makes the same decision about the order in which **P** operations complete. Even though the processes might be at different stages in handling P and V messages, each one will handle fully acknowledged messages in the same order.

The algorithm for distributed semaphores appears in Figure 7.20. The *User* processes initiate **V** and **P** operations by broadcasting messages on the *semop* channels. The *Helper* processes implement the **V** and **P** operations. There is one *Helper* for each *User*. Each *Helper* receives messages from its *semop* channel, manages its local message queue, broadcasts ACK messages, and tells its *User* process when to proceed after a **P** operation. As shown, every process maintains a logical clock, which it uses to place timestamps on messages.

We can use distributed semaphores to synchronize processes in a distributed program in essentially the same way we used regular semaphores in shared variable programs (Chapter 4). For example, we can use them to solve mutual exclusion problems, such as locking files or database records. We can also use the same basic approach—broadcasted messages and ordered queues—to solve additional problems. Section 7.9 describes how to coordinate the actions of replicated file servers. The Historical Notes and References and the Exercises consider additional applications.

When broadcast algorithms are used to make synchronization decisions, every process must participate in every decision. In particular, a process must hear from every other in order to determine when a message is fully acknowledged. This means that broadcast algorithms do not scale well to interactions among large numbers of processes. It also means that such algorithms must be modified to cope with failures.

7.8 Token-Passing Algorithms

This section illustrates yet another communication pattern: token-passing between processes. A token is a special kind of message that can be used either to convey permission to take an action or to gather global state information. We illustrate token-passing by presenting solutions to two additional synchronization problems. First we present a simple, distributed solution to the critical section problem. Then we develop two algorithms for detecting when a distributed computation has terminated. Token-passing is also the basis for several other algorithms; e.g., Section 7.9 describes how it can be used to synchronize access to replicated files (also see the Historical Notes and References and the Exercises).

Distributed Mutual Exclusion

Although the critical section problem arises primarily in shared-variable programs, it also arises in distributed programs whenever there is a shared resource that at most one process at a time can use. Moreover, the critical section problem is often a component of a larger problem, such as ensuring consistency in a distributed file or database system (see Section 7.9).

One way to solve the critical section problem is to employ an active monitor that grants permission to access the critical section. For many problems, such as implementing locks on non-replicated files, this is the simplest and most efficient approach. At the other extreme, the critical section problem can be solved using distributed semaphores, implemented as shown in the previous section. That approach yields a decentralized solution in which no one process has a special role, but it requires exchanging a large number of messages for each semaphore operation since each **broadcast** has to be acknowledged.

Here we solve the problem in a third way by using a token ring. The solution is decentralized and fair, like one using distributed semaphores, but it requires the exchange of far fewer messages. Moreover, the basic approach can be generalized to solve other synchronization problems that are not easily solved in other ways.

Let $P[1:n]$ be a collection of "regular" processes that contain critical and non-critical sections. As usual, we need to develop entry and exit protocols that these processes execute before and after their critical section. Also as usual, the protocols should ensure mutual exclusion, avoid deadlock and unnecessary delay, and ensure eventual entry (fairness).

Since the regular processes have other work to do, we do not want them also to have to circulate the token. Thus we will employ a collection of additional processes, *Helper*$[1:n]$, one per regular process. These helper processes form a ring, as shown in Figure 7.21. One token circulates between the helpers, being passed from *Helper*[1] to *Helper*[2] and so on to *Helper*[n], which passes it back to *Helper*[1]. When *Helper*[i] receives the token, it checks to see whether its client $P[i]$ wants to enter its critical section. If not, *Helper*[i] passes the token on. Otherwise, *Helper*[i] tells $P[i]$ it may enter its critical section, then waits until $P[i]$ exits; at this point *Helper*[i] passes the token on. Thus, the processes cooperate to ensure that the following predicate is always true:

DMUTEX: ($\forall i$: $1 \le i \le n$: $P[i]$ in its CS $\Rightarrow$ *Helper*[i] has token) $\wedge$
there is exactly one token

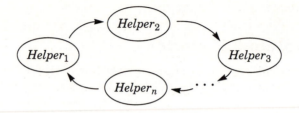

Figure 7.21. Token ring of helper processes.

The full solution is shown in Figure 7.22. The token ring is represented by an array of *token* channels, one per *Helper*. For this problem, the token itself carries no data, so it is represented by a null message. The other channels are used for communication between the clients $P[i]$ and their helpers. Each *Helper*[i] uses **empty** to determine whether $P[i]$ wishes to enter its critical section; if so, *Helper*[i] sends $P[i]$ a *go* message, and then waits to receive an *exit* message.

The solution in Figure 7.22 is fair—assuming as usual that processes eventually exit critical sections. This is because the token continuously circulates, and when *Helper* has it, $P[i]$ is permitted to enter if it wants to do so. As programmed, the token moves continuously between the helpers. This is in fact what happens in a physical token-ring network. In a software token ring, however, it is probably best to add some delay in each helper so that the token moves more slowly around the ring. (See Section 8.5 for another token-based mutual exclusion algorithm in which tokens do not circulate continuously.)

This algorithm again assumes that failures do not occur—the token must not be lost. Since control is distributed, however, it is possible to modify the algorithm to cope with failures. The Historical Notes and References describe algorithms for regenerating a lost token and for using two tokens that circulate in opposite directions.

Termination Detection in a Ring

It is trivial to detect when a sequential program has terminated. It is also simple to detect when a concurrent program has terminated on a single processor: Every process is blocked or terminated, and no I/O operations are pending, However, it is not at all easy to detect when a distributed program has terminated. This is because the global state is not visible to any one processor. Moreover, there may be messages in transit between processors.

chan *token*[1:*n*]( ), *enter*[1:*n*]( ), *go*[1:*n*]( ), *exit*[1:*n*]( )

Helper[*i*: 1..*n*]:: **do** true →   { *DMUTEX* }
　　　　　　　　　　receive *token*[*i*]( )　　　　# acquire token
　　　　　　　　　　if not(**empty**(*enter*[*i*])) →　# *P*[*i*] wants to enter
　　　　　　　　　　　　receive *enter*[*i*]( )
　　　　　　　　　　　　send *go*[*i*]( )
　　　　　　　　　　　　receive *exit*[*i*]( )
　　　　　　　　　　fi
　　　　　　　　　　send *token*[(*i* **mod** *n*) + 1]( ) # pass token on
　　　　　　　　od

P[*i*: 1..*n*]:: **do** true →
　　　　　　　　send *enter*[*i*]( )　　# entry protocol
　　　　　　　　receive *go*[*i*]( )
　　　　　　　　critical section
　　　　　　　　send *exit*[*i*]( )　　　# exit protocol
　　　　　　　　non-critical section
　　　　　　od

Figure 7.22. Mutual exclusion with a token ring.

The problem of detecting when a distributed computation has terminated can be solved in several ways. For example, we could use a probe/echo algorithm or use logical clocks and timestamps (see the Historical Notes and References). This section develops a token-passing algorithm, assuming that all communication between processes goes around a ring. The next section generalizes the algorithm for a complete communication graph. In both cases, token-passing is used to signify state changes.

Let *P*[1:*n*] be the processes in some distributed computation. For now, let *ch*[1:*n*] be an array of communication channels. For now, assume that the computation is such that the interprocess communication in the computation forms a ring. In particular, process *P*[*i*] receives messages only from channel *ch*[*i*] and sends messages only to channel *ch*[(*i* **mod** *n*) + 1]. Thus *P*[1] only sends messages to *P*[2], *P*[2] only sends to *P*[3], and so on, with *P*[*n*] sending messages to *P*[1]. As usual we also assume that messages from every process are received by its neighbor in the ring in the order in which they were sent.

At any point in time, each process *P*[*i*] is active or idle. Initially, every process is active. It is idle if it has terminated or is delayed at a **receive** statement. (If a process is temporarily delayed while waiting for an I/O operation to terminate, we consider it still to be active since it has not terminated and will eventually be awakened.) After receiving a message, an idle process becomes active. Thus, a distributed computation has terminated if the following two conditions hold:

> *DTERM*: every process is idle ∧ no messages are in transit

A message is in transit if it has been sent but not yet delivered to the destination channel. The second condition is necessary since when the message is delivered, it could awaken a delayed process.

Our task is to superimpose a termination-detection algorithm on an arbitrary distributed computation, subject only to the above assumption that the processes in the computation communicate in a ring. Clearly termination is a property of the global state, which is the union of the states of individual processes plus the contents of message channels. Thus, the processes have to communicate with each other in order to determine if the computation has terminated.

To detect termination, let there be one token, which is a special message that is not part of the computation proper. The process that holds the token passes it on when it becomes idle. (If a process has terminated its computation, it is idle with respect to the distributed computation but continues to participate in the termination-detection algorithm. In particular, the process passes the token on and ignores any regular messages it receives.)

Processes pass the token using the same ring of communication channels that they use in the computation itself. For example, $P[1]$ passes the token to $P[2]$ by sending a message to channel $ch[2]$. When a process receives the token, it knows that the sender was idle at the time it sent the token. Moreover, when a process receives the token, it has to be idle since it is delayed receiving from its channel and will not become active again until it receives a regular message that is part of the distributed computation. Thus, upon receiving the token, a process sends the token to its neighbor, then waits to receive another message from its channel.

The question now is how to detect that the entire computation has terminated. When the token has made a complete circuit of the communication ring, we know that every process was idle at some point. But how can the holder of the token determine if all other processes are still idle and that there are no messages in transit?

Suppose one process, $P[1]$ say, initially holds the token. When $P[1]$ becomes idle, it initiates the termination-detection algorithm by passing the token to $P[2]$. After the token gets back to $P[1]$, the computation has terminated if $P[1]$ has been *continuously idle* since it first passed the token to $P[2]$. This is because the token goes around the same ring that regular messages do, and messages are delivered in the order in which they are sent. Thus, when the token gets back to $P[1]$, there cannot be any regular messages either queued or in transit. In essence, the token has "flushed" the channels clean, pushing all regular messages ahead of it.

{ *RING*: $P[1]$ is blue $\Rightarrow$ ($P[1]$ ... $P[token + 1]$ are blue $\wedge$
$\quad\quad\quad\quad\quad\quad\quad\quad\quad ch[2]$ ... $ch[(token \bmod n) + 1]$ are empty) }

actions of $P[1]$ when it first becomes idle:
$\quad color[1] :=$ blue; $token := 0;$ **send** $ch[2](token)$

actions of $P[i: 1..n]$ upon receiving a regular message:
$\quad color[i] :=$ red

actions of $P[i: 2..n]$ upon receiving the token:
$\quad color[i] :=$ blue; $token := token + 1;$ **send** $ch[(i \bmod n) + 1](token)$

actions of $P[1]$ upon receiving the token:
$\quad$ **if** $color[1] =$ blue $\rightarrow$ announce termination and halt **fi**
$\quad color[1] :=$ blue; $token := 0;$ **send** $ch[2](token)$

Figure 7.23. Termination detection in a ring.

We can make the algorithm and its correctness more precise as follows. First, associate a color with every process: blue (cold) for idle and red (hot) for active. Initially all processes are active, so they are colored red. When a process receives the token, it is idle, so it colors itself blue and passes the token on. If the process later receives a regular message, it colors itself red. Thus, a process that is blue has become idle, passed the token on, and remained idle since passing the token.

Second, associate a value with the token indicating how many channels are empty if $P[1]$ is still idle. Let *token* be the value of the token. When $P[1]$ becomes idle, it colors itself blue, sets *token* to 0, and then sends *token* to $P[2]$. When $P[2]$ receives the token, it is idle and $ch[2]$ might be empty. Hence, $P[2]$ colors itself blue, increments *token* to 1, and sends the token to $P[3]$. Each process $P[i]$ in turn colors itself blue and increments *token* before passing it on.

These token-passing rules are listed in Figure 7.23. As indicated, the rules ensure that predicate *RING* is a global invariant. The invariance of *RING* follows from the fact that if $P[1]$ is blue, it has not sent any regular messages since sending the token, and hence there are no regular messages in any channel up to where the token resides. Moreover, all these processes have remained idle since passing the token on. Thus if $P[1]$ is still blue when the token gets back to it, all processes are blue and all channels are empty. Hence $P[1]$ can announce that the computation has terminated.

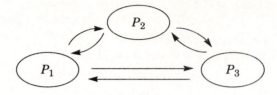

Figure 7.24. Complete communication graph.

Termination Detection in a Graph

In the previous section, we made a simplifying assumption: All communication goes around a ring. In general, the communication structure of a distributed computation will form an arbitrary directed graph. The nodes of the graph are the processes in the computation; the edges represent communication paths. There is an edge from one process to another if the first process sends to a channel from which the second receives.

Here we assume the communication graph is *complete*: there is one edge from every process to every other. In particular, there are n processes $P[1:n]$ and n channels $ch[1:n]$. Each process $P[i]$ receives from its private input channel $ch[i]$; every other process can send messages to $ch[i]$. With these assumptions, we can extend the previous termination-detection algorithm as described below. The resulting algorithm is adequate to detect termination in any network in which there is a direct communication path from each processor to every other. It can readily be extended to arbitrary communication graphs and multiple channels (see exercise 7.28).

Detecting termination in a complete graph is more difficult than in a ring since messages can arrive over any edge. For example, consider the complete graph of three processes shown in Figure 7.24. Suppose the processes pass the token only from $P[1]$ to $P[2]$ to $P[3]$ and back to $P[1]$. Suppose $P[1]$ holds the token and becomes idle; hence it passes the token to $P[2]$. When $P[2]$ becomes idle, it in turn passes the token to $P[3]$. But before $P[3]$ receives the token, it could send a regular message to $P[2]$. Thus, when the token gets back to $P[1]$, it cannot conclude that the computation has terminated even if it has remained continuously idle.

The key to the ring algorithm in Figure 7.23 is that all communication uses the same channels, and hence the token flushes out regular messages. In particular, the token traverses every edge of the ring. We can extend that algorithm to a complete graph by ensuring that the token traverses every edge of the graph, which means that it visits every process multiple times. If *every* process has remained continuously idle since it first saw the token, then we can conclude that the computation has terminated.

{ *GRAPH*: *token* has value T $\Rightarrow$
           (the last T channels token was received from were empty $\wedge$
              all $P[i]$ that passed it were blue when they passed it)

actions of $P[i: 1..n]$ upon receiving a regular message:
  $color[i]$:= red

actions of $P[i: 1..n]$ upon receiving the token:
  if *token* = *nc* $\rightarrow$ announce termination and halt **fi**
  if $color[i]$ = red $\rightarrow$ $color[i]$:= blue; *token* := 0
  [] $color[i]$ = blue $\rightarrow$ *token* := *token* + 1
  fi
  set j to the channel corresponding to the next edge to use in cycle c
  send $ch[j]$(*token*)

Figure 7.25. Termination detection in a complete graph.

As before, each process is colored red or blue, with all processes initially red. When a process receives a regular message, it colors itself red. When a process receives the token, it is blocked waiting to receive the next message on its input channel. Hence the process colors itself blue—if it is not already blue—and passes the token on. (Again, if a process terminates its regular computation, it continues to handle token messages.)

Any complete directed graph contains a cycle that includes every edge (some may need to be included more than once). Let c be a cycle in the communication graph, and let nc be its length. Each process keeps track of the order in which its outgoing edges occur in c. Upon receiving the token along one edge in c, a process sends it out over the next edge in c. This ensures that the token traverses every edge in the communication graph.

Also as before, the token carries a value indicating the number of times in a row the token has been passed by idle processes and hence the number of channels that might be empty. As the above example illustrates, however, in a complete graph a process that was idle might become active again, even if $P[1]$ remains idle. Thus, we need a different set of token-passing rules and a different global invariant that is sufficient to conclude termination.

The token starts at any process and initially has a value of 0. When that process becomes idle for the first time, it colors itself blue and then passes the token along the first edge in cycle c. Upon receiving the token, a process takes the actions shown in Figure 7.25. If the process is red when it receives the token—and hence was active since last seeing it—the process colors itself blue and sets the value of *token* to 0 before passing it along the next edge in c. This effectively reinitiates the termination-detection process. However, if the process is blue when it receives the token—and hence has been continuously idle since last seeing the token—the process increments the value of *token* before passing it on.

The token-passing rules ensure that predicate *GRAPH* is a global invariant. Once the value of *token* gets to *nc*, the length of cycle *c*, then the computation is known to have terminated. In particular, at that point the last *nc* channels the token has traversed were empty. Since a process only passes the token when it is idle—and since it only increases *token* if it has remained idle since last seeing the token—all channels are empty and all processes are idle. In fact, the computation had actually terminated by the time the token started its last circuit around the graph. However, no process could possibly know this until the token has made another complete cycle around the graph to verify that all processes are still idle and that all channels are empty. Thus, the token has to circulate a minimum of two times around the cycle after any activity in the computation proper: first to turn processes blue, and then again to verify that they have remained blue.

7.9 Replicated Servers

The final two process-interaction paradigms we will describe involve the use of replicated servers, i.e., multiple server processes that each do the same thing. Replication serves one of two purposes. First, we can increase the accessibility of data or services by having more than one process provide the same service. These decentralized servers interact to provide clients with the illusion there is just one centralized service. Second, we can sometimes use replication to speed up finding the solution to a problem by dividing the problem into subproblems and solving them concurrently. This is done by having multiple worker processes share a bag of subproblems. This section illustrates both of these applications by first showing how to implement a replicated file and then by developing an adaptive quadrature algorithm for numerical integration.

Replicated Files

A simple way to increase the likelihood that a critical data file is always accessible is to keep a back-up copy of the file on another disk, usually one that is attached to a different machine. The user can do this manually by periodically making a backup copy of a file. Or the file system could maintain the backup copy automatically. In either case, however, users wishing to access the file would have to know whether the primary copy was available and, if not, access the backup copy instead. (A related problem is bringing the primary copy back up to date when it becomes reaccessible.)

A third approach is for the file system to provide transparent replication. In particular, suppose there are *n* copies of a data file. Each copy is managed

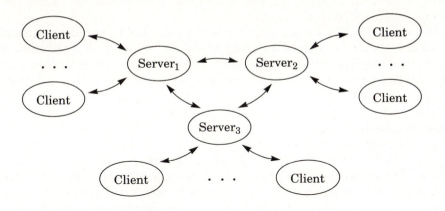

Figure 7.26. Replicated file server interaction pattern.

by a separate server process, which handles client requests to read from and write to the file. Each server provides an identical client interface such as that shown earlier in Figure 7.7. Thus, a client sends an open request to any server and subsequently continues to converse with that server, sending it read and write requests and eventually sending it a close request. The servers themselves interact to present clients with the illusion that there is a single copy of the file. Figure 7.26 shows the structure of this interaction pattern.

To present clients with the illusion that there is a single file, the file servers have to synchronize with each other. In particular, they have to solve the *file consistency* problem: the results of client read and write requests have to appear to be the same, independent of which copy of the file is accessed. File consistency is thus an instance of the readers/writers problem: two clients can read the file at the same time, but a client requires exclusive access when writing the file. There are several ways to implement file consistency, as described below. In this section, we assume that entire files are to be kept consistent. The same techniques can be used to ensure consistency at the level of records in files, which is more appropriate for database applications.

One way to solve the file consistency problem is to ensure that at most one client at a time can access any copy of the file. This can be implemented, for example, by the distributed solution to the critical section problem shown in Figure 7.22. When a client asks any one of the servers to open the file, that server first interacts with the other servers to acquire exclusive access. The server then processes the client's read and write requests. For a read request, the server reads the local copy of the file. For a write request, the server updates all copies of the file. When the client closes the file, the server releases exclusive control.

The above approach is of course more restrictive than necessary since only one client at a time can open any copy of the file. Suppose instead that when a client asks the server to open a file, it indicates whether it will be reading only or will be both reading and writing. To permit concurrent reading, the servers can employ a variation on the token-passing algorithm for mutual exclusion (Figure 7.17). In particular, let there be one token that has an initial value equal to the number ns of file servers. Then, when a client opens the file for reading, its server waits for the token, decrements it by one, sends it on to the next server (helper process, actually), and then handles the client's read requests. After the client closes the file, the server increments the value of the token the next time it comes around the ring. On the other hand, when a client opens the file for writing, its server waits for the token to have value ns and then holds on to the token while handling the client's read and write requests. After the client closes the file, the server updates all copies, then puts the token back into circulation.

The problem with the above token-passing scheme is that write requests will never get serviced if there is a steady stream of read requests. A somewhat different approach yields a fair solution. Instead of employing just one token, we can use ns tokens. Initially, each server has one token. When a client wants to read a file, its server must acquire one token; when a client wants to write a file, its server must acquire all ns tokens. Thus, when a server wants to write the file, it sends a message to all other servers requesting their tokens. Once it has gathered all the tokens, the server handles the write, propagating updates to the other servers as above. When a server wants to read the file, it can do so immediately if it holds a token. If not, it asks the other servers for one token.

This multiple-token scheme does, however, have two potential problems. First, two servers could at about the same time try to acquire all the tokens. If each is able to acquire some but not all, neither write will ever get executed. Second, while a server is acquiring all tokens preparatory to writing the file, another server might ask for a token so it can read the file. We can overcome both problems by using logical clocks to place timestamps on each request for a token. Then a server gives up a token if it receives a request with a timestamp earlier than the time at which it wanted to use the token. For example, if two servers want to write at about the same time, the one that initiated the write request earlier will be able to gather the tokens.*

---

*A variation on having ns tokens is to have ns read/write locks, one per copy of the file (see Section 9.4). To read from the file, a server acquires the read lock for its local copy. To write to the file, a server acquires the write locks for all copies. If every server acquires the locks in the same order—and if lock requests are handled in order of request—then the solution will be fair and deadlock-free. This use of locks avoids the need to put timestamps in messages.

An attractive attribute of using multiple tokens is that they will reside at active servers. For example, after a server gathers all tokens to perform a write, it can continue to process write requests until some other server requires a token. Thus, if the replicated file is being heavily written to by one client, the overhead of token-passing can be avoided. Similarly, if the file is mostly read from, and only rarely updated—which is quite commonly the case—the tokens will generally be distributed among the servers, and hence read requests will be able to be handled immediately.

A variation on the multiple-token scheme is *weighted voting*. In our example, a server requires one token to read but all *ns* to write. This in essence assigns a weight of 1 to reading and a weight of *ns* to writing. Instead, a different set of weights can be used. Let *rw* be the read weight and let *ww* be the write weight. Then if *ns* is 5, *rw* could be set to 2, and *ww* to 4. This means a server must hold at least 2 tokens to read from the file, and at least 4 tokens to write to the file. Any assignment of weights can be used as long as the following two requirements are met:

- *ww* > *ns*/2 (to ensure that writes are exclusive), and
- (*rw* + *ww*) > *ns* (to ensure that reads and writes exclude each other).

With weighted voting, not all copies of the file need to be updated when a write is processed. It is only necessary to update *ww* copies. However, then it is necessary to read *rw* copies. In particular, every write action must set a timestamp on the copies it writes to, and a read action must use the file with the most recent timestamp. By reading *rw* copies, a reader is assured of seeing at least one of the files changed by the most recent write action.

As mentioned at the start of this section, one of the rationales for replicating files is to increase availability. Yet each of the synchronization schemes above depends on every server being available and reachable. However, each scheme can be modified to be fault-tolerant (see the Historical Notes and References for details). If there is one circulating token that is lost, it can be regenerated. If there are multiple tokens and a server crashes, the other servers can interact to determine how many tokens were lost and then can hold an election to determine which one will get the lost tokens. Finally, with weighted voting, it is only necessary that *max(rw, ww)* copies of the file are accessible since only that many are needed to service any read or write.

Independent of the synchronization scheme, after recovery of a server or of a disk holding a copy of the file, the copy needs to be brought up to date before it is used. In essence, a recovered server needs to pretend it is a writer and gain write permission to the other copies of the file; it then reads an up-to-date copy into its local copy of the file and releases write permission. The server can then resume handling client requests.

Replicated Workers: Adaptive Quadrature

The previous section considered an example of data replication. Here we consider function replication. In particular, we present an adaptive, parallel solution to the quadrature problem for numerical integration. The solution illustrates how to parallelize any divide-and-conquer algorithm, subject only to the requirement that subproblems be independent. (See the Historical Notes and References and the Exercises for additional examples.)

The solution employs a shared channel, which contains a bag of tasks. Initially, there is one task corresponding the entire problem to be solved. Multiple worker processes take tasks from the bag and process them, often generating new tasks—corresponding to subproblems—that are put into the bag. The computation terminates when all tasks have been processed.

In the quadrature problem, we are given a continuous, non-negative function $f(x)$ and two endpoints l and r, with $l < r$. The problem is to compute the area bounded by $f(x)$, the x axis, and the vertical lines through l to r. Thus, we want to approximate the integral of $f(x)$ from l to r.

The typical way to approximate the area under a curve is to divide the interval $[l, r]$ into a series of subintervals and then to use a trapezoid to approximate the area of each subinterval. In particular, let $[a, b]$ be a subinterval. Then an approximation to the area under f from a to b is the area of the trapezoid with base $b - a$ and sides of height $f(a)$ and $f(b)$.

We can solve the quadrature problem either statically or dynamically. The static approach uses a fixed number of equal-sized intervals, computes the area of the trapezoid over each interval, and then sums the results. We repeat this process—typically by doubling the number of intervals—until two successive approximations are close enough to be acceptable.

The dynamic approach starts with one interval from l to r and computes the midpoint m between l and r. We then calculate the areas of the three trapezoids defined by l, m, r, and the value of f at these three points. Figure 7.27 illustrates this. Then we compare the area of the larger trapezoid with the sum of the areas of the two smaller ones. If these are sufficiently close, the area of the larger trapezoid is an acceptable approximation of the area under f. Otherwise, we solve the two subproblems of computing the area from l to m and from m to r. We repeat this process recursively until the solution to each subproblem is acceptable. We then sum the answers to each subproblem to yield the final answer.

The dynamic approach is called *adaptive quadrature* since the solution adapts itself to the shape of the curve. In particular, in places where the curve is flat, a wide trapezoid will closely approximate the area. Hence new subproblems will not be generated. However, in places where the curve is changing shape—and especially in places where the tangent of $f(x)$ is nearly vertical—smaller and smaller subproblems will continue to be generated as needed.

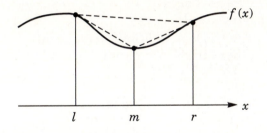

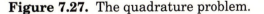

Figure 7.27. The quadrature problem.

With either the static or dynamic approach, every subproblem is independent of the others. Hence we can readily parallelize either algorithm. Here we present a parallel algorithm that employs adaptive quadrature since that approach is generally preferred.

The way to solve any parallel divide-and-conquer problem is to employ one *administrator* process and several *worker* processes. The administrator generates the first problem and gathers results. Workers solve subproblems, generating further subproblems when that is required. The workers share a single channel, *bag*, which contains the problems to be solved. In this case, a problem is characterized by five values: a left point a, a right point b, the values of $f(a)$ and $f(b)$, and the area from a to b. (The area is included to avoid recomputation.) When a worker computes an acceptable answer to a subproblem, it sends that answer to the administrator over channel *result*. The program terminates when the administrator detects that the area of the entire interval $[l, r]$ has been computed. (Or equivalently, when *bag* is empty and all workers are idle; however, this is difficult to detect.)

Figure 7.28 contains the algorithm for the adaptive quadrature problem. An especially interesting aspect of the algorithm is that there can be any number of worker processes! If there is only one, the algorithm is essentially an iterative, sequential algorithm. If there are more workers, subproblems can be solved in parallel. Thus, the number of workers can be tuned to match the hardware on which the algorithm executes.

The quadrature algorithm assumes that all workers can receive from the same channel, *bag*. In many distributed languages, a channel can have only one receiver. If this is the case, we have to implement the bag using a server process with which the workers communicate. In fact, the administrator itself can assume this role. The solution to the traveling salesman problem in Section 9.5 shows this.

chan *bag*(*a*, *b*, *fa*, *fb*, *area* : **real**)
chan *result*(*a*, *b*, *area* : **real**)
Administrator:: **var** *l*, *r*, *fl*, *fr*, *a*, *b*, *area*, *total* : **real**
                other variables to record finished intervals
                fl := *f*(*l*); *fr* := *f*(*r*)
                area := (*fl* + *fr*) * (*l* + *r*) / 2
                send *bag*(*l*, *r*, *fl*, *fr*, *area*)
                do entire area not yet computed →
                      receive *result*(*a*, *b*, *area*)
                      total := *total* + *area*
                      record that have completed interval [*a*, *b*]
                od
Worker[1:*n*]:: **var** *a*, *b*, *m*, *fa*, *fb*, *fm* : **real**
                var *larea*, *rarea*, *tarea*, *diff* : **real**
                do true →
                    receive *bag*(*a*, *b*, *fa*, *fb*, *tarea*)
                    m := (*a* + *b*) / 2; *fm* := *f*(*m*)
                    compute *larea* and *rarea* using trapezoids
                    diff := *tarea* − (*larea* + *rarea*)
                    if *diff* small → **send** *result*(*a*, *b*, *tarea*)
                    [] *diff* too large → **send** *bag*(*a*, *m*, *fa*, *fm*, *larea*)
                                  send *bag*(*m*, *b*, *fm*, *fb*, *rarea*)
                  fi
                od

Figure 7.28. Adaptive quadrature algorithm.

7.10 Implementations

In this section, we show how to implement asynchronous message passing. First we extend the shared-memory kernel of previous chapters to include message-passing primitives. This implementation is suitable for a single processor or a shared-memory multiprocessor. Then we show how to extend the shared-memory kernel into a distributed kernel. The distributed implementation is suitable for a multicomputer or a networked collection of separate machines.

Shared-Memory Kernel

To implement message passing, we need kernel primitives to create channels and to implement **send**, **receive**, and **empty**. Each channel in a program is represented by a channel descriptor in the kernel. An array of channels is represented by an array of descriptors. A channel descriptor contains the heads of two linked lists: a message list and a blocked list. The message list contains queued messages; the blocked list contains processes waiting to receive a message. At least one of these will always be empty. This is because a process is not blocked if there is an available message, and a message is not queued if there is a blocked process. If messages sent to the channel are of a fixed length, the channel descriptor might also record that length. (If messages can vary in size, each has to indicate its own length.)

A descriptor is created by means of the kernel primitive *create_chan*. This is called once for each **chan** declaration in a program, before any processes are created. An array of channels is created either by calling *create_chan* once for each element or by parameterizing *create_chan* with the array size and calling it just once. The *create_chan* primitive returns the name (index or address) of the descriptor.

The statement **send** *ch(expressions)* is implemented using the kernel's *send* primitive. First, the sending process evaluates the expressions and collects the values together into a single message, stored typically on the sending process's execution stack. Then *send* is called; its arguments are the channel name (returned by *create_chan*) and the message itself. The *send* primitive first finds the descriptor of *ch*. If there is a blocked process, one is removed from the blocked list, the message is copied into that process's address space, and the process's descriptor is inserted on the ready list. If there is no blocked process, the message has to be saved on the descriptor's message list. This is necessary since **send** is non-blocking, and hence the sender has to be allowed to continue executing.

Space for the saved message can be allocated dynamically from a single buffer pool, or there could be a communication buffer associated with each channel. However, asynchronous message passing raises an important implementation issue—what if there is no more kernel space? The kernel has two choices: halt the program due to buffer overflow or block the sender until there is enough buffer space. Halting the program is a drastic step since free space could soon become available. On the other hand, it gives definite feedback to the programmer that messages are being produced faster than they are being consumed, which often indicates an error on a single processor. Blocking the sender violates the non-blocking semantics of **send** and complicates the kernel somewhat since there is an additional cause of blocking. Then again, the writer of a concurrent program cannot assume anything about the rate at which or order in which processes execute. Operating system kernels block senders, and swap blocked processes out of memory if necessary, since they have to avoid crashing. However, halting the program is a reasonable choice for the kernel of a high-level programming language.

The statement **receive** *ch(vars)* is implemented by calling the kernel's *receive* primitive. Its arguments are the name of the channel and the address of a message buffer. The actions of *receive* are the dual of those of *send*. First the kernel finds the descriptor for *ch*, then it checks the message list. If the message list is not empty, the first message is removed and copied into the receiver's message buffer. If the message list is empty, the receiver is inserted on the blocked list. After receiving a message, the receiver unpacks the message from the buffer into the appropriate variables.

A fourth primitive, *empty*, is used to implement **empty**(*ch*). It simply finds the descriptor and checks whether the blocked list is empty. In fact, if the kernel data structures are not in a protected address space, a primitive is not needed; the executing process could simply check for itself whether the blocked list is empty. A critical section is not required since the executing process only needs to examine the head of the message list.

Figure 7.29 contains outlines of these four primitives. The actions of *send* and *receive* are very similar to the actions of *P* and *V* in the semaphore kernel in Figure 4.23. The main difference is that a channel descriptor contains a message list, whereas a semaphore descriptor merely contains the value of the semaphore.

The single-processor kernel in Figure 7.29 is turned into one for a shared-memory multiprocessor in the same way as before. In particular, kernel data structures are stored in memory accessible to all processors, and each processor uses critical sections to access data that might be interfered with.

Distributed Kernel

If all process interaction is by means of message passing, it is possible to execute a concurrent program on a distributed system such as a multi-computer or network of workstations. Here we show how to extend the shared-memory kernel to support distributed execution. The basic idea is to replicate the kernel—placing one copy on each machine—and to have the different kernels communicate with each other using network communication primitives.

In a distributed program, each channel is stored on some one machine. For now, assume that a channel can have any number of senders but that it has only one receiver. Then the logical place to put a channel's descriptor is on the machine on which the receiver executes. A process executing on that machine accesses the channel as in the shared-memory kernel. However, a process executing on another machine cannot access the channel directly. Instead, the kernels on the two machines need to interact. Below we describe how to change the shared-memory primitives and how to use the network to implement a distributed program.

Figure 7.30 illustrates the structure of a distributed kernel. The kernel on each machine contains descriptors for the channels stored on that machine and for the processes that execute on that machine. As before, each kernel has local interrupt handlers for supervisor calls (internal traps), timers, and

```
    procedure create_chan(msg_size : int) returns name : int
        get an empty channel descriptor and initialize it
        set name to the address of the descriptor
        call dispatcher( )
    end
    procedure send(chan : int; msg : string[∗])
        find descriptor of channel chan
        if blocked list empty → acquire buffer and copy msg into it
            insert buffer at end of message list
        [] blocked list not empty → 1remove process from blocked list
            copy msg into the process's address space
            insert the process at end of ready list
        fi
        call dispatcher( )
    end
    procedure receive(chan : int; res msg : string[∗])
        find descriptor of channel chan
        if message list empty → insert executing at end of blocked list
            store address of msg in executing's descriptor; executing := 0
        [] message list not empty → remove buffer from message list
            copy contents of buffer into msg
        fi
        call dispatcher( )
    end
    procedure empty(chan : int) returns result : bool
        find descriptor of channel chan
        if message list empty → result := true
        [] message list not empty → result := false
        fi
        call dispatcher( )
    end
```

Figure 7.29. Message-passing primitives for single processor.

---

input/output devices. The communication network is a special kind of
input/output device. Thus, each kernel has network interrupt handlers, and
each kernel contains routines that write to and read from the network.

As a concrete example, an Ethernet is typically accessed as follows. An
Ethernet controller has two independent parts, one for writing and one for
reading. Each part has an associated interrupt handler in the kernel. A
write interrupt is triggered when a write operation completes; the controller

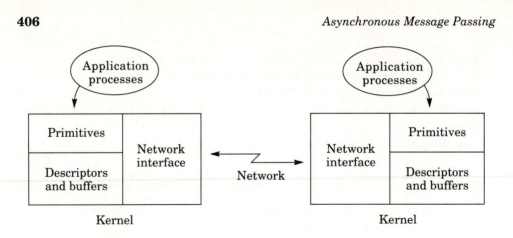

Figure 7.30. Distributed kernel structure and interaction.

itself takes care of network access arbitration. A read interrupt is triggered when a message for the processor arrives over the network.

When a kernel primitive—executing on behalf of an application process—needs to send a message to another machine, it calls kernel procedure *net_write*. This procedure has three arguments: a destination processor, a message kind (see below), and the message itself. First, *net_write* acquires a buffer, formats the message, and stores it in the buffer. Then, if the writing half of the network controller is free, an actual write is initiated. Otherwise the buffer is inserted on a queue of write requests. In either case *net_write* returns. Later, when a write interrupt occurs, the associated interrupt handler frees the buffer containing the message that was just written; if its write queue is not empty, the interrupt handler then initiates another network write.

Input from the network is typically handled in a reciprocal fashion. When a message arrives at a kernel, the network read interrupt handler is entered. It first saves the state of the executing process. Then it allocates a new buffer for the next network input message. Finally, the read handler unpacks the first field of the input message to determine the kind and then calls the appropriate kernel primitive.*

Figure 7.31 contains outlines for the network interface routines. These include the network interrupt handlers and the *net_write* procedure. The *net_read_handler* services three kinds of messages: SEND, CREATE_CHAN,

---

*An alternative approach to handling network input is to employ a daemon process that executes outside the kernel. In this case, the interrupt handler simply sends the message to a channel from which the daemon repeatedly receives. Using a daemon decreases execution time in the read interrupt handler but increases the time it takes to process network input. On the other hand, it simplifies the kernel since it removes the details of processing network messages.

type *mkind* = **enum**(SEND, CREATE_CHAN, CHAN_DONE)
var *writing* := false   # status of network write controller
var other variables for the write queue and transmission buffers

procedure *net_write*(*dest* : **int**, *kind* : *mkind*, *data* : **string**[*])
    acquire buffer; format message and store it in the buffer
    if *writing* → insert the message buffer on the write queue
    [] **not** *writing* → start transmitting the message on the network
    fi
end

net_write_handler: # entered with interrupts inhibited
    save state of *executing*
    free the current transmission buffer; *writing* := false
    if write queue not empty →
        remove first buffer from the queue
        writing := true; start transmitting the message
    fi
    call *dispatcher*( )

net_read_handler: # entered with interrupts inhibited
    save state of *executing*
    acquire new buffer; prepare network controller for next read
    unpack first field of input message to determine *kind*
    if *kind* = SEND → **call** *remote_send*(channel name, buffer)
    [] *kind* = CREATE_CHAN → **call** *remote_create*(creator)
    [] *kind* = CHAN_DONE → **call** *chan_done*(creator)
    fi

Figure 7.31. Network interface routines.

---

and CHAN_DONE. These are sent by one kernel and serviced by another, as described below. The kernel's *dispatcher* routine is called at the end of *net_write_handler* to resume execution of the interrupted process. However, the *dispatcher* is not called at the end of *net_read_handler* since that routine calls a kernel primitive—depending on the kind of input message—and that primitive in turn calls *dispatcher* (see Figure 7.32).

For simplicity, we assume that network transmission is error-free and hence that messages do not need to be acknowledged or retransmitted. We also ignore the problem of running out of buffer space for outgoing and incoming messages; in practice, the kernels would employ what is called *flow control* to limit the number of buffered messages. The Historical Notes and References cite literature that describes how to address these issues.

Since a channel can be stored either locally or remotely, a channel name now needs to have two fields: a machine number and an index or offset. The machine number indicates which machine the descriptor is stored on; the index indicates where to find the descriptor in that machine's kernel. We also need to augment the *create_chan* primitive so that it has an additional argument indicating the machine on which the channel is to be created. Within *create_chan*, the kernel checks this argument. If the creator and channel are on the same machine, the kernel creates the channel as in Figure 7.29. Otherwise the kernel blocks the executing process and transmits a CREATE_CHAN message to the remote machine. The message also contains the identity of the executing process. Eventually the local kernel will receive a CHAN_DONE message indicating that the channel has been created on the remote machine. This message contains the channel's name and indicates which process the channel was created for. As shown in Figure 7.31, when *net_read_handler* receives this message, it calls a new kernel primitive, *chan_done*, which unblocks the process that asked to have the channel created and returns the channel's name to it.

On the other side of the network, when a kernel daemon receives a CREATE_CHAN message, it calls the *remote_create* primitive. That primitive creates the channel then sends a CHAN_DONE message back to the first kernel. Thus, to create a channel on a remote machine, we have the following sequence of steps:

- An application process invokes the local *create_chan* primitive.
- Local kernel sends a CREATE_CHAN message to the remote kernel.
- Remote kernel's read interrupt handler receives the message and calls the remote kernel's *remote_create* primitive.
- Remote kernel creates the channel and then sends a CHAN_DONE message back to the local kernel.
- Local kernel's read interrupt handler receives the message and calls *chan_done*, which awakens the application process.

The *send* primitive also needs to be changed in a distributed kernel. However, *send* is much simpler than *create_chan* since the **send** statement is asynchronous. In particular, if the channel is on the local machine, *send* takes the same actions as before. If the channel is on another machine, *send* transmits a SEND message to that machine. At this point, the executing process can continue. When the message arrives at the remote kernel, that kernel calls the *remote_send* primitive, which takes essentially the same actions as the (local) *send* primitive. The only difference is that the incoming message is already stored in a buffer, and hence the kernel does not need to allocate a new one.

type *chan_name* = **rec**(*machine* : **int**; *addr* : **int**)

procedure *create_chan*(*machine* : **int**) **returns** *chan* : *chan_name*
    if *machine* = local →
        get an empty channel descriptor and initialize it
        chan := *chan_name*(local machine number, address of descriptor)
    [] *machine* ≠ local →
        call *net_write*(*machine*, CREATE_CHAN, *executing*)
        insert descriptor of *executing* on delay list; *executing* := 0
    fi
    call *dispatcher*( )
end

procedure *send*(*chan* : *chan_name*; *msg* : **string**[*])
    if *chan.machine* = local → same actions as in Figure 7.29
    [] *chan.machine* ≠ local → **call** *net_write*(*chan.machine*, SEND, *msg*)
    fi
    call *dispatcher*( )
end

procedure *remote_send*(*chan* : *chan_name*; *buffer* : **int**)
    find descriptor of channel *chan*
    if blocked list empty → insert *buffer* on message list
    [] blocked list not empty → remove process from blocked list
        copy message from *buffer* to process's address space
        insert the process at the end of the ready list
    fi
    call dispatcher( )
end

procedure *remote_create*(*creator* : **int**)
    var *chan* : *chan_name*
    get an empty channel descriptor and initialize it
    chan := *chan_name*(local machine number, address of descriptor)
    call *net_write*(*creator*, CHAN_DONE, *chan*)
    call *dispatcher*( )
end

procedure *chan_done*(*creator* : **int**)
    remove descriptor of process *creator* from the delay list
    insert the descriptor at the end of the ready list
    call *dispatcher*( )
end

Figure 7.32. Distributed kernel primitives.

Figure 7.32 contains outlines for the primitives of the distributed kernel. The *receive* and *empty* primitives are not shown since they do not change if each channel has only one receiver and the channel is stored on the same machine as the receiver. If this is not the case, then additional messages are needed to communicate between the machine on which a *receive* or *empty* primitive is invoked and the machine on which the channel is stored. This communication is analogous to that for creating a channel: The local kernel sends a message to the remote kernel, which executes the primitive and then sends the result back to the local kernel.

Historical Notes and References

The concept of message passing originated in the late 1960s. Even though general-purpose multiprocessors and computer networks did not exist at that time, some operating system designers realized that it would be attractive to organize an operating system as a collection of communicating processes. In particular, using message passing makes an operating system easier to understand and easier to get correct. This is because every process has a specific function, and one process cannot interfere with another since they do not share variables.

The multiprogramming nucleus developed by Per Brinch Hansen [1970] for the Danish RC 4000 computer was, in the author's opinion, the most elegant early message-passing proposal. Brinch Hansen's nucleus provides four primitives that support client/server communication using a shared pool of fixed-length buffers. A client initiates a conversation by calling **send_message**; this delays until there is a free buffer and then appends the buffer to the message queue of the named destination process. A server receives a message by calling **wait_message**; this delays until there is a message on the server's queue and then returns the buffer. After the server handles the request, it replies to the client by calling **send_answer**; the answer is returned in the same buffer that contained the request message. Finally, the client terminates a conversation by calling **wait_answer**, which delays until the answer arrives in the specified buffer and then returns the buffer to the pool. Brinch Hansen [1973a] later added two additional primitives—**wait_event** and **get_event**—to allow a server process to examine its message queue and answer buffers and receive specific messages or answers. This allows a server to engage in more than one conversation at a time.

Robert Balzer [1971] developed another early set of message-passing primitives and introduced the concept of communication ports. Shaw et al. [1975] describe a comprehensive operating system nucleus (kernel) that includes what are called resource classes. The primitives on resource classes support both interprocess communication and resource allocation. The textbook on operating systems by Bic and Shaw [1988] describes Brinch Hansen's original primitives (pp. 24-26) and the nucleus that includes resource classes (Chapter 3).

Because it is more efficient for processes to communicate using shared variables than message passing, most operating systems for single processors and shared memory multiprocessors use shared variables for process interaction within the operating system. However, these operating systems provide message-passing primitives so that processes can communicate with other machines on a network. For example, UNIX provides sockets and a variety of system calls for sending and receiving messages. Of necessity, operating systems for distributed memory multiprocessors provide and use message-passing primitives. For example, the NX/2 operating system for Intel's iPSC/2 multicomputer provides a variety of primitives. Athas and Seitz [1988] give a nice overview of multicomputer hardware and software.

Gypsy [Ambler et al. 1977] was one of the first programming languages to be based on message passing; it uses global channels (mailboxes) and buffered communication (hence **send** is not fully asynchronous). Gypsy was designed to support the specification and implementation of verifiable programs, and the designers were the first to develop an axiomatic semantics of message passing [Good et al. 1979].

PLITS, an acronym for Programming Language in the Sky, was another early language based on asynchronous message passing [Feldman 1979]. It provides a flexible set of options on **send** and **receive** statements. In PLITS, the **send** statement has the form:

> **send** *expressions* **to** *process* [**about** *key*]

The optional *key* is used to identify the kind of message; it obviates the need for putting kind fields in messages themselves. The **receive** statement in PLITS has the form:

> **receive** *variables* [**from** *process*] [**about** *key*]

If the optional *process* and *key* are omitted, the receiver waits for the next message. If *process* is included, the receiver waits for the next message from the named process. Finally, if *key* is included, the receiver waits for the next message having the specified key.

The Network Implementation Language, NIL, is another interesting language based on message passing [Parr & Strom 1983, Strom & Yemini 1983]. NIL provides output ports and input ports; a communication channel is formed by connecting an output port to an input port. An input port always has one owner at a time. However, the owner can pass an input port to another process; hence, communication paths can be dynamically configured. NIL supports both asynchronous and synchronous message passing. It also includes an interesting concept called the typestate, which captures both the type and initialization state of a variable [Strom & Yemini 1986]. The typestate mechanism is used to ensure that one process cannot affect the correctness of another by giving it bad data.

CONIC is a more recent distributed system that emphasizes support for dynamic configuration; i.e., being able to modify an executing program by replacing existing modules or adding new ones [Kramer & Magee 1985, Sloman & Kramer 1987]. The CONIC programming language is used to program modules; the CONIC configuration language is used to specify module interconnections. Channels in CONIC are entry and exit ports attached to modules. Entry ports support communication to a module; exit ports support communication from it. (Entry ports can also have result types, in which case the channel is bidirectional.) The CONIC configuration language provides a comprehensive set of primitives for creating, destroying, and modifying modules and links between ports.

Actors is a different kind of programming model and language that employs asynchronous message passing. The actor model was originally conceived as a way to view control structures in artificial intelligence applications [Hewitt 1977]. The various proposals for actor languages have consequently been variants of Lisp-like languages. An actor is essentially a process. Actor languages are related to object-oriented languages, but actors form dynamically changing hierarchies [Agha 1986, 1990]. The three actor primitives are **create**, which creates a new actor, **send to**, which sends a message to another actor, and **become**, which replaces the current behavior (program) of an actor by a new behavior.

Several additional languages are based on asynchronous message passing; see Tables 3 and 8 of the excellent survey paper by Bal et al. [1989]. In addition, SR (see Section 10.4) and StarMod [Cook 1980] provide asynchronous message passing as well as a variety of other communication primitives. Concurrent C [Gehani & Roome 1986] originally supported only synchronous communication; asynchronous communication was recently added for the reasons described in Gehani [1990a].

As mentioned, axioms for buffered message passing were first developed by the designers of Gypsy [Good et al. 1979]. Rick Schlichting and Fred Schneider [1984] developed the semantics presented in Section 7.2. Misra et al. [1982] describe a hierarchical proof technique that allows the specifications of processes to be combined to obtain a specification for a network of processes. We assume that the sender can continue as soon as its message has been buffered by the local kernel. Another possibility, first proposed by Art Bernstein [1987], is to delay the sender until the message has been queued at its ultimate destination; he calls this a *semi-synchronous* **send.** Bernstein's paper gives axiomatic semantics for semi-synchronous **send** and analyzes the differences between it and asynchronous send.

A book by Selim Akl [1985] describes numerous parallel sorting algorithms and sorting networks. Brinch Hansen [1989] analyzes the performance of a program that implements a merge network like that in Figure 7.3.

The duality between monitors and message passing was noticed and analyzed by Hugh Lauer and Roger Needham [1978]. Stroustrup [1982] reports on an experiment to evaluate the claim that performance would be identical; in most cases it was, but message passing occasionally led to slower response time. On the other hand, Reid [1980] and Gentleman [1981] show that monitors and message passing are typically used quite differently; the fact that they can simulate each other is beside the point. The examples in Chapters 6 and 7 indicate that the two programming styles are indeed quite different. Moreover, monitors do not directly support any of the process interaction paradigms except centralized servers.

At the end of Section 7.4, we briefly described how the Sun Network File System (NFS) implements access to remote files. See Sandberg et al. [1985] for details.

The idea of deriving a distributed algorithm by refining an algorithm that uses shared variables appears in Lamport [1982], which develops an algorithm for maintaining message-routing tables in a network. The derivation of the heartbeat algorithm for the network topology problem that we gave in Section 7.4 comes from Elshoff and Andrews [1988]. McCurley and Schneider [1986] derive essentially the same network topology algorithm directly as a distributed program. They call their solution a *wave algorithm* since for this specific problem topology information spreads out in waves from each node to others. We use the term *heartbeat algorithm* since that characterizes the actions of each process. Also, data in a heartbeat algorithm does not usually just get passed on in waves; e.g., in a grid computation, data from neighbors gets combined with local data on each iteration.

Both Lamport [1982] and Elshoff and Andrews [1988] show how to deal with a dynamic network in which processors and links might fail and then recover. See Afek et al. [1987] for a general discussion of dynamic network protocols.

Two recent books describe additional heartbeat algorithms. Fox et al. [1988] describe grid computations that arise in solving partial differential equations as well as matrix and sorting algorithms. Raynal [1990] gives additional examples.

The probe/echo paradigm was invented simultaneously by several people. Ernest Chang's Ph.D. dissertation [1979] and a later paper [Chang 1982] give probe/echo algorithms for a variety of graph problems, including sorting, computing bi-connected components, and knot (deadlock) detection. (Chang called them echo algorithms; we use the term *probe/echo* to indicate that there are two distinct phases.) Dijkstra and Scholten [1980] and Francez [1980] use the same paradigm—without giving it a name—to detect termination of a distributed program.

Several people have investigated the problem of providing reliable or fault-tolerant broadcast, which is concerned with ensuring that every functioning and reachable processor receives the message being broadcast and that all agree upon the same value. For example, Schneider et al. [1984] present an algorithm for fault-tolerant broadcast in a tree, assuming that a failed processor stops executing and that failures are detectable (i.e., that failures are fail stop [Schlichting & Schneider 1983]). On the other hand, Lamport et al. [1982] show how to cope with failures that can result in arbitrary behavior (i.e., so-called Byzantine failures). A recent paper [Kaashoek et al. 1989] presents an efficient, reliable broadcast protocol and reports on its performance.

Logical clocks were developed by Leslie Lamport [1978] in a now classic paper on how to order events in distributed systems. (Marzullo and Owicki [1983] describe the problem of synchronizing physical clocks.) Fred Schneider [1982] developed the implementation of distributed semaphores shown in Figure 7.20; that paper also shows how to modify this kind of algorithm to deal with failures. A paper that was written later but appeared earlier [Schneider 1980] shows how to use distributed semaphores to ensure consistency in a distributed database. The same basic approach—broadcasted messages and ordered queues—can also be used to solve additional problems. For example, Lamport [1978] presents an algorithm for distributed mutual exclusion, and Schneider [1982] presents a distributed implementation of the guarded input/output commands of CSP [Hoare 1978], the subject of Chapter 8. The algorithms in these papers do not assume that messages are totally ordered. For some problems, it helps if every process sees messages that have been broadcast in exactly the same order; Birman and Joseph [1987] give examples and show how to implement atomic broadcast.

Section 7.8 shows how to use token-passing to implement distributed mutual exclusion and termination detection and Section 7.9 describes how to use tokens to synchronize access to replicated files. Chandy and Misra [1984] describe how to use token-passing to achieve fair conflict resolution, and Chandy and Lamport [1985] show how to determine global states in a distributed computation.

The token-passing solution to the distributed mutual exclusion problem given in Figure 7.22 was developed by Gerard LeLann [1977]. That paper also shows how to bypass some node on the ring if it should fail and how to regenerate the token if it should become lost. LeLann's method requires knowing maximum communication delays and process identities. Jay Misra [1983] later developed an algorithm that overcomes these requirements by using two tokens that circulate around the ring in opposite directions. Additional token-passing algorithms for distributed mutual exclusion appear in Martin [1985], van de Snepshcheut [1987], and Raymond [1989].

The distributed mutual exclusion problem can also be solved using a broadcast algorithm. As mentioned in the text, one way is to use distributed semaphores. However, this requires exchanging a large number of messages since every message has to be acknowledged by every process. More efficient, broadcast-based algorithms are described in Lamport [1978], Ricart and Agrawala [1981], Maekawa [1985], and Suzuki and Kasami [1985]. These are also described and compared in books by Raynal [1986] and by Maekawa et al. [1987]. A recent paper [Goscinski 1990] presents yet another broadcast algorithm; it also uses priorities and is intended for real-time systems.

The token-passing algorithm for detecting termination in a ring is based on one in Dijkstra et al. [1983]. The algorithm for a complete communication graph first appeared in Misra [1983], which also describes how to modify the algorithm to detect termination in an arbitrary graph. The termination-detection problem can also be solved using other paradigms. For example, Dijkstra and Scholten [1980], Francez [1980], Misra and Chandy [1982], Francez and Rodeh [1982], and Mattern [1990] present probe/echo algorithms for different variations on the problem. Rana [1983] and Morgan [1985] show how to use logical clocks and timestamps. Chandrasekaran and Venkatesan [1990] present a message-optimal algorithm that combines the probe/echo and token-passing paradigms. See Raynal [1988b] for a description and comparison of several of these algorithms.

Deadlock detection in a distributed system is similar to termination detection. Several people have also developed probe/echo and token-passing algorithms for this problem. For example, Chandy et al. [1983] give a probe/echo algorithm. Knapp [1987] surveys that and other algorithms for deadlock detection in distributed database systems.

We developed an on-the-fly garbage collection algorithm in Section 3.7. An interesting paper by Tel et al. [1988] shows how to derive the algorithm for the marking phase of the collector process by transforming a token-passing solution to the distributed termination-detection problem! The reason the algorithms are similar is that both are concerned with examining a graph until it reaches a stable state. In the garbage-collection problem, the stable state is one in which all nodes have been marked and hence white nodes are garbage.

Section 7.9 described several techniques for implementing replicated files. Schneider [1980] shows how to use distributed semaphores; that approach can be made fault-tolerant using the techniques described in Schneider [1982]. The use of weighted voting is described in Gifford [1979], Maekawa [1985], and Thomas [1979]. Some of the algorithms use one token or lock per copy of the file. To make these algorithms fault-tolerant, one can regenerate the token or lock as described in LeLann [1977] and Misra [1983]. When there are multiple tokens and a server crashes, the other servers need to hold an election to determine which one will get the lost tokens. Numerous election algorithms are described in Garcia-Molina [1982], Schneider and Lamport [1985], and Raynal [1988b].

Grit and McGraw [1985] present two different parallel adaptive quadrature algorithms and analyzes their performance on a HEP supercomputer. The administrator/worker paradigm was introduced in Gentleman [1981]. The use of bags of tasks to implement parallel divide-and-conquer algorithms is described and illustrated in Carriero et al. [1986] and Carriero and Gelernter [1989b]. Finkel and Manber [1987] and Thomas and Crowther [1988] give additional examples and implementation techniques. The bag-of-tasks approach is also used in the implementation of the Multilisp language [Halstead 1985] and in the PTRAN system for parallelizing Fortran programs [Allen et al. 1988].

The problems and paradigms covered in this chapter were surveyed in Andrews [1991]. The problems continue to be studied, and the paradigms continue to be used to solve additional problems. Journals and proceedings of conferences on parallel and/or distributed computing often contain papers on these topics. For example, there are several papers in the proceedings of the Ninth International Conference on Distributed Computing Systems, which was held in 1989.

In the distributed kernel in Section 7.10, we assumed that network transmission was error free. Books on computer networks describe protocols for implementing reliable virtual circuits in real networks; e.g., see Tanenbaum [1988].

In this chapter, we have programmed the process-interaction paradigms using asynchronous message passing. The next two chapters will show how to program them using synchronous message passing, RPC, and rendezvous. Hence the programs are appropriate for execution on MIMD (multiple instruction, multiple data) machines. Some of the paradigms—such as networks of filters, heartbeat, broadcast, and replicated workers—are also applicable to programs that execute on SIMD (single instruction, multiple data) machines such as the Connection Machine [Hillis 1985]. Filters and heartbeat algorithms are also appropriate for systolic machines such as the WARP [Annaratone et al. 1986].

We have occasionally mentioned the issue of coping with failures, but a full treatment of fault-tolerant programming is beyond the scope of this book. Several of the above papers show how to extend specific algorithms to cope with failures. Kohler [1981] surveys synchronization and recovery techniques for decentralized systems that were known at that time. Lamport and Schneider [1985] give more recent information along with an excellent overview of fault-tolerant programming and several general solution paradigms.

Exercises

7.1   Suppose channels are bounded buffers—each has a fixed size that is specified when the channel is declared. Now **send** will need to delay if the channel is already full.

(a) Develop axioms for the channel, **send**, and **receive**, and develop a satisfaction rule for buffered communication.

(b) Modify the kernel in Figure 7.29 to implement buffered channels.

7.2   For the sorting network shown in Figure 7.3, suppose the merge processes are declared as an array *Merge*[1:*n*]. Give the declaration of the channels, and give the body of the array of *Merge* processes. Since the processes are to be identical, you will have to figure out how to embed the merge tree in an array.

7.3 Suppose there are four input values to a sorting network of three *Merge* processes (Figures 7.2 and 7.3). Using the axioms and proof rules in Section 7.2, develop a formal proof that the network will indeed sort the input values.

7.4 Given are two processes, *A* and *B*. *A* has a set of integers *S*, and *B* has a set of integers *T*. The two processes are to exchange values one at a time until all elements of *S* are less than all elements of *T*.

(a) Develop a program to solve this problem.

(b) Construct a complete proof outline for your program. Show that every application of Receive Axiom (7.3) meets the requirements of Satisfaction Rule (7.4). Finally show that your proof outline is interference-free (7.9).

7.5 Consider a filter process *Partition* having the following specifications. *Partition* receives unsorted values from one input channel *in* and sends the values it receives to one of two output channels, *out1* or *out2*. *Partition* uses the first value *v* it receives to partition the input values into two sets. It sends all values less than or equal to *v* to *out1*; it sends all values greater than *v* to *out2*. Finally, *Partition* sends *v* to *out1* and sends a sentinel EOS to both *out1* and *out2*. The end of the input stream is marked by a sentinel EOS.

(a) Develop an implementation of *Partition*. First give predicates specifying the contents of the channels, then develop the body of *Partition*.

(b) Show how to construct a sorting network out of *Partition* processes. Assume that there are *n* input values and that *n* is a power of 2. In the worst case, how big does the network have to be? (This is not a good way to do sorting; this is just an exercise!)

7.6 Modify the program in Figure 7.7 to allow clients to request and release more than one unit at a time.

7.7 Figure 7.7 shows how to simulate one specific monitor using a server process. Develop a simulation of an arbitrary monitor. In particular, show how you would simulate every monitor mechanism in Section 6.1—including **signal_all**, priority **wait**, and **empty.** Show the actions of the client processes as well as the server.

7.8 (a) Consider the dining philosophers problem (4.4). Develop a server process to synchronize the actions of the philosophers. Show the client (philosopher) interface to the server.

(b) Using the axioms and proof rules in Section 7.2, develop a formal proof of the correctness of your answer to (a). Prove that neighboring philosophers cannot eat at the same time and that the solution is deadlock-free.

7.9 Develop an implementation of a time-server process. The server provides two operations that can be called by client processes: one to get the time of day and one to delay for a specified interval. In addition, the time server receives periodic "tick" messages from a clock interrupt handler. Also show the client interface to the time server for the time of day and delay operations.

7.10 *The Savings Account Problem.* A savings account is shared by several people. Each person may deposit or withdraw funds from the account. The current balance in the account is the sum of all deposits to date minus the sum of all withdrawals to date. The balance must never become negative.

Develop a server to solve this problem, and show the client interface to the server. Clients make two kinds of requests: one to deposit *amount* dollars and one to withdraw *amount* dollars. Assume that *amount* is positive.

7.11 Two kinds of processes, *A*'s and *B*'s, enter a room. An *A* process cannot leave until it meets two *B* processes, and a *B* process cannot leave until it meets one *A* process. Each kind of process leaves the room—without meeting any other processes—once it has met the required number of other processes.

(a) Develop a server process to implement this synchronization. Show the interface of *A* and *B* processes to the server.

(b) Modify your answer to (a) so that the first of the two *B* processes that meets an *A* process does not leave the room until after the *A* process meets a second *B* process.

7.12 Suppose a computer center has two printers, A and B, that are similar but not identical. Three kinds of client processes use the printers: those that must use A, those that must use B, and those that can use either A or B.

Develop code that each kind of client executes to request and release a printer, and develop a server process to allocate the printers. Your solution should be fair assuming, a client using a printer eventually releases it.

7.13 *The Roller Coaster Problem* [Herman 89]. Suppose there are *n* passenger processes and one car process. The passengers repeatedly wait to take rides in the car, which can hold C passengers, C < *n*. However, the car can go around the tracks only when it is full.

(a) Develop code for the actions of the passenger and car processes. Use message passing for communication.

(b) Generalize your answer to (a) to employ *m* car processes, *m* > 1. Since there is only one track, cars cannot pass each other; i.e., they must finish going around the track in the order in which they started. Again, a car can go around the tracks only when it is full.

7.14 (a) Modify the self-scheduling disk driver in Figure 7.9 to use the CSCAN scheduling strategy that was employed in the monitor in Figure 6.16.

(b) Modify the self-scheduling disk driver in Figure 7.9 to use the SCAN (elevator) scheduling strategy described at the start of Section 6.4.

7.15 The following exercises deal with the file server program in Figure 7.10.

(a) In the program, the file servers share channel *open*; i.e., all of them receive from it. In many implementations of message passing, each channel can have only one receiver (but usually many senders). Modify the file server program so that it meets this restriction.

(b) In the program, each client process uses a different file server. Suppose there is only one file server. Modify the file server program so that all clients use the same server. Your solution should permit every client to have a file open at the same time.

(c) In the program, each client process uses a different file server. Suppose that clients that want to access the same file use the same file server. In particular, if a file is already open, the client should converse with the server that is managing that file; otherwise the client should start a conversation with a free file server. Modify the file server program to meet these requirements.

7.16 Figure 3.20 presents an algorithm for solving LaPlace's equation. That algorithm uses shared variables and barriers.

(a) Develop a heartbeat algorithm for solving LaPlace's equation. As in Figure 3.20, use one process for each of the n^2 grid points. Your program should terminate when the new value for each grid point is within EPSILON of its previous value.

(b) Modify your answer to (a) to use only m^2 processes, where m is a factor of n. For example, if n is 1024, m might be 8 or 16.

7.17 *Stable Marriage Problem.* Let *Man* and *Woman* each be arrays of n processes. Each man ranks the women from 1 to n and each woman ranks the men from 1 to n. A *pairing* is a one-to-one correspondence of men and women. A pairing is *stable* if, for two men m_1 and m_2 and their paired women w_1 and w_2, both of the following conditions are satisfied:

(1) m_1 ranks w_1 higher than w_2 or w_2 ranks m_2 higher than m_1; and

(2) m_2 ranks w_2 higher than w_1 or w_1 ranks m_1 higher than m_2.

Put differently, a pairing is unstable if a man and woman would both prefer each other to their current pair. A solution to the stable marriage problem is a set of n pairings, all of which are stable.

Write a program to solve the stable marriage problem. The processes should communicate using asynchronous message passing.

7.18 Given are three processes F, G, and H. Each has a local array of integers; all three arrays are sorted in non-decreasing order. At least one value is in all three arrays. Develop a program in which the three processes interact until each has determined the smallest common value. Give key assertions in each process. Messages should contain only one value at a time.

7.19 *Distributed Pairing* [Finkel et al. 1979]. Given are n processes, each corresponding to a node in a connected graph. Each node can communicate only with its neighbors. The problem is for each process to pair itself with one of its neighbors. When the processes finish pairing up, each process should be paired or single, and no two neighboring processes should be single.

Solve this problem using asynchronous message passing for communication. Every process is to execute the same algorithm. When the program terminates, every process should have stored in local variable *pair* the index of the neighbor it is paired with; *pair* should be i if process i is single. Your solution need not be optimal, in the sense of minimizing the number of single processes (that makes the problem *very* hard).

7.20 *Spanning Tree Construction* [Finkel et al. 1979]. Given are n processes, each corresponding to a node in a connected graph. Each node can communicate only with its neighbors. Recall that a spanning tree of a graph is a tree that includes every node of the graph and a subset of the edges.

Write a program to construct a spanning tree on the fly. Do not first compute the topology. Instead, construct the tree from the ground up by having the processes interact with their neighbors to decide which edges to put in the tree and which to leave out. You may assume processes have unique indexes.

7.21 (a) Extend the heartbeat algorithm for computing the topology of a network (Figure 7.14) to handle a dynamic topology. In particular, communication links might fail during the computation and later recover. (Failure of a processor can be modeled by failure of all its links.) Assume that when a link fails, it silently throws away undelivered messages.

Define any additional primitives you need to detect when a failure or recovery has occurred, and explain briefly how you would implement them. You might also want to modify the **receive** primitive so that it returns an error code if the channel has failed. Your algorithm should terminate, assuming that eventually failures and recoveries quit happening for a long enough interval that every node can agree on the topology.

(b) Repeat (a) for the probe/echo algorithm in Figure 7.19.

7.22 *Compare/Exchange Sorting*. Section 8.4 describes a heartbeat algorithm for parallel sorting.

(a) Program that algorithm using asynchronous message passing. Assume that there are n processes and n values, one per process.

(b) Modify your answer to (a) to use m processes, where m is a factor of n. Thus each process is responsible for m values.

7.23 Section 8.4 describes a broadcast algorithm for multiplying two $n \times n$ matrices using n^2 processes. Program that algorithm using asynchronous message passing. Do not assume you have a **broadcast** primitive; just use **send** and **receive.**

7.24 Given are n processes. Assume that the **broadcast** primitive sends a message from one process to all n processes and that **broadcast** is both reliable and totally ordered. That is, every process sees all messages that are broadcast and sees them *in the same order*.

Using this **broadcast** primitive (and **receive**, of course), develop a fair solution to the distributed mutual exclusion problem. In particular, devise entry and exit protocols that each process executes before and after a critical section. Do not use additional helper processes; the n processes should communicate directly with each other.

7.25   The solution to the distributed mutual exclusion problem in Figure 7.22 uses a token ring and a single token that circulates continuously. Assume instead that every *Helper* process can communicate with every other (i.e., the communication graph is complete). Design a solution that does not use circulating tokens. In particular, the *Helper* processes should be idle except when some process $P[i]$ is trying to enter or exit its critical section. Your solution should be fair and deadlock-free. Each *Helper* should execute the same algorithm, and the regular processes $P[i]$ should execute the same code as in Figure 7.22. (Hint: Associate a token with every pair of processes, i.e., with every edge of the communication graph.)

7.26   *Drinking Philosophers Problem* [Chandy & Misra 1984]. Consider the following generalization of the dining philosophers problem. Given is an undirected graph G. Philosophers are associated with nodes of the graph and can communicate only with neighbors. A bottle is associated with each edge of G. Each philosopher cycles between three states: tranquil, thirsty, and drinking. A tranquil philosopher may become thirsty. Before drinking, the philosopher must acquire the bottle associated with every edge connected to the philosopher's node. After drinking, a philosopher again becomes tranquil.

Design a solution to this problem that is fair and deadlock-free. Every philosopher should execute the same algorithm. Use tokens to represent the bottles. It is permissible for a tranquil philosopher to respond to requests from neighbors for any bottles the philosopher may hold.

7.27   Given is a collection of processes that communicate using asynchronous message passing. A *diffusing computation* is one in which one "main" process starts the computation by sending messages to one or more other processes [Dijkstra & Scholten 1980]. After first receiving a message, another process may send messages.

Design a signaling scheme that is superimposed on the computation proper and that allows the main process to determine when the computation has terminated. Use a probe/echo algorithm as well as ideas from Section 7.8. (Hint: Keep counts of messages and signals.)

7.28   The distributed termination detection algorithm in Figure 7.25 assumes that the graph is complete and that each process receives from exactly one channel. Solve the following exercises as separate problems.

(a) Extend the token-passing rules to handle an arbitrary connected graph.

(b) Extend the token-passing rules to handle the situation in which a process receives from multiple channels (one at a time, of course).

7.29   Consider the following variation on the token-passing rules for termination detection in a complete graph (Figure 7.25):

if *color*[i] = blue → *token* := blue [] *color*[i] = red → *token* := red **fi**
color[i] := blue
set j to the channel corresponding to the next edge to use in cycle c
send *ch*[j](*token*)

Using these rules, is there a way to detect termination? If so, explain when the computation is known to have terminated. If not, explain why the rules are insufficient.

7.30 Consider the replicated file server problem described in Section 7.9. Develop an implementation of the server processes. Also show the actions a client would take to open, access, and close a file. Assume there are *ns* copies of the file.

(a) In your solution, use *ns* tokens to ensure file consistency. Implement read operations by reading the local copy and write operations by updating all copies. When a client opens a file for reading, its server needs to acquire one token; for writing, the server needs all *ns* tokens. Your solution should be fair and deadlock-free.

(b) In your solution, use *ns* read locks and *ns* write locks to ensure file consistency. Implement read operations by reading from the local copy, and write operations by updating all copies. When a client opens a file for reading, its server needs to obtain the local read lock; for writing, the server needs to obtain all *ns* write locks. Your solution should be fair and deadlock-free.

(c) In your solution, use weighted voting to ensure file consistency. Use a read weight of *rw* and a write weight of *ww*. Your solution should be fair and deadlock-free.

(d) Compare your answers to (a), (b), and (c). For the different client operations, how many messages do the servers have to exchange in the different solutions? Consider the best case and the worst case.

7.31 The worker processes in the adaptive quadrature algorithm (Figure 7.28) all receive from the *bag* channel. In many implementations of message passing, each channel can have only one receiver (but usually many senders). Modify the algorithm so that it meets this restriction.

7.32 Develop a program to multiply two $n \times n$ matrices, a and b, using the replicated worker paradigm described in Section 7.9. Arrays a and b are initially local to an administrator process. Use w worker processes to compute the inner products and send them to the administrator. Do not use any shared variables; only channels may be shared. Explain your solution and justify your design choices, such as what you store in shared channels.

7.33 Gaussian elimination with partial pivoting is a method for reducing a non-singular real matrix $m[1{:}n, 1{:}n]$ to upper-triangular form. It involves iterating across the columns of m and zeroing out the elements in the column below the diagonal element $m[d, d]$. This is done by performing the following three steps for each column. First, select a pivot element, which is the element in column d having the largest absolute value. Second, swap row d and the row containing the pivot element. Finally, for each row r below the new diagonal row, subtract a multiple of row d from row r. The multiple to use for row r is $m[r, d]/m[d, d]$; subtracting this multiple of row d has the effect of setting $m[r, d]$ to zero.

(a) Write a distributed program to implement the above algorithm. Assign a process to each row, column, or point, and have them communicate with each other. Explain and justify your solution strategy.

(b) Solve this problem using a replicated worker algorithm and a shared bag of tasks. Use w worker processes.

(c) Compare your answers to (a) and (b). How many messages are exchanged in each algorithm? How much concurrency does each have?

7.34 Quicksort is a recursive sorting method that partitions an array into smaller pieces and then combines them (see exercise 2.18). Develop a program to implement quicksort using the replicated worker paradigm described in Section 7.9. Array $a[1:n]$ of integers is initially local to an administrator process. Use w worker processes to do the sorting. When your program terminates, the result should be stored back in administrator array a. Do not use any shared variables; only channels may be shared. Explain your solution and justify your design choices, such as what you store in shared channels.

7.35 The 8-queens problem is concerned with placing 8 queens on a chess board in such a way that none can attack another. Develop a program to generate all 92 solutions to the 8-queens problem using the replicated worker paradigm described in Section 7.9. Have an administrator process put 8 initial queen placements in a shared bag. Use w worker processes to extend partial solutions; when a worker finds a complete solution, it should send it to the administrator. The program should compute all solutions and terminate. Do not use any shared variables; only channels may be shared.

7.36 A replicated worker algorithm will have terminated when every worker is idle and the shared bag is empty. Design a termination detection protocol that could be superimposed on any replicated worker algorithm. Assume there is one shared channel that contains the bag of work. (In the adaptive quadrature program in Figure 7.28, using such a protocol would eliminate the need for the administrator process to keep track of which pieces of the area have been computed.)

7.37 Consider the distributed kernel in Figures 7.31 and 7.32.

(a) Extend the implementation to allow a channel to have multiple receivers. In particular, change the *receive* and *empty* primitives so that a process on one machine can access a channel stored on another machine.

(b) Modify the kernel so **send** is *semi-synchronous* [Bernstein 87]. In particular, when a process invokes **send**, it should delay until the message has been queued on the channel (or given to a receiver)—even if the channel is stored on another machine.

(c) Add termination detection code to the kernel. Ignore pending I/O; hence a computation has terminated when all ready lists are empty and the network is idle.

## CHAPTER 8

Synchronous
Message Passing

Since the **send** statement is non-blocking with asynchronous message passing, channels can contain an unbounded number of messages. This has three consequences. First, a sending process can get arbitrarily far ahead of a receiving process. If process A sends a message to process B and later needs to be sure B got it, A needs to wait to receive a reply from B. Second, message delivery is not guaranteed if failures can occur. If A sends a message to B and does not get a reply, A has no way of knowing whether the message could not be delivered, B crashed while acting on it, or the reply could not be delivered. Third, messages have to be buffered, yet buffer space is finite in practice. If too many messages are sent, either the program will crash or **send** will block; either consequence violates the semantics of asynchronous message passing.

Synchronous message passing avoids these consequences. In particular, both **send** and **receive** are blocking primitives. If a process tries to send to a channel, it delays until another process is waiting to receive from that channel. Thus, a sender and receiver synchronize at every communication point. If the sender proceeds, then the message was indeed delivered, and messages do not have to be buffered. In essence, the effect of synchronous communication is a distributed assignment statement, with the expression being evaluated by the sending process and then assigned to a variable in the receiving process.

There is thus a tradeoff between asynchronous and synchronous message passing. On the one hand, synchronous message passing simplifies solving some problems and does not require dynamic buffer allocation. On the other hand, it is more difficult, as we shall see, to program heartbeat and broadcast algorithms using synchronous message passing.

This chapter describes the syntax and semantics of synchronous message passing and presents numerous examples that illustrate its use. The programming notation is similar to that introduced by Hoare in 1978 in his seminal paper on Communicating Sequential Processes (CSP). One of the main concepts Hoare introduced in that paper is what we call *guarded communication* (it has also been called selective waiting). Guarded communication combines message passing with guarded statements to produce an elegant and expressive programming notation. We will illustrate guarded communication here with synchronous message passing. Guarded communication can also be used with rendezvous (see Section 9.2) or with asynchronous message passing (see Section 9.3).

8.1 Programming Notation

To avoid confusion with the **send** and **receive** primitives used in Chapter 7, we will use a different notation and terminology for synchronous message passing. Since process communication is tightly coupled, we will also use a direct channel-naming scheme. In particular, each channel will be a direct link between two processes rather than a global mailbox. This is not strictly necessary, but it is more efficient to implement.

In this section, we first describe and illustrate the two communication statements, output (send) and input (receive). Then we extend guarded statements to include communication statements.

Communication Statements

A process communicates with peripheral devices by means of input and output statements. Processes that share variables communicate with each other by means of assignment statements. Synchronous message passing combines these two concepts: input and output statements provide the sole means by which processes communicate, and the effect of communication is similar to the effect of an assignment statement.

Suppose process A wishes to communicate the value of expression e to process B. This is accomplished by the following program fragments:

(8.1) $A:: \ldots B \, ! \, e \ldots$

          $B:: \ldots A \, ? \, x \ldots$

$B \, ! \, e$ is an *output statement*. It names a destination process B and specifies an expression e whose value is to be sent to that process. $A \, ? \, x$ is an *input statement*. It names a source process A and specifies the variable x into which an input message from the source is to be stored. (The output operator ! is pronounced "shriek" or "bang;" the input operator ? is pronounced "query.")

Assuming the types of e and x are the same, the two statements above are said to *match*. An input or output statement delays the executing process until another process reaches a matching statement. The two statements are then executed simultaneously. The effect is to assign the value of the expression in the output statement to the variable in the input statement. Execution of matching communication statements can thus be viewed as a *distributed assignment* that transfers a value from one process to a variable in another. The two processes are synchronized while communication takes place, then each proceeds independently.

The above example employs the simplest forms of output and input statements. The general forms of these statements are:

$$Destination \ ! \ port(e_1, ..., e_n)$$

$$Source \ ? \ port(x_1, ..., x_n)$$

Destination and *Source* name a single process, as in (8.1), or an element of an array of processes. The *port* names a single communication channel in the destination process or an element of an array of ports in the destination process. The expressions e_i in an output statement are sent to the named port of the destination process. An input statement receives a message on the designated port from the source process and assigns the values to local variables x_i. Ports are used to distinguish between different kinds of messages that a process might receive. However, we will not explicitly declare port names; instead, we will simply introduce them when needed and give them unique names to avoid confusion with other identifiers. (The Occam language uses port declarations; see Section 10.2.)

Two processes communicate when they execute matching communication statements. Informally, an output and input statement match if all the pieces are compatible with each other. The formal definition follows.

(8.2)   **Matching Communication Statements.** An input statement and output statement match if all four of the following conditions hold:

(a) The output statement appears in the process named by the input statement.

(b) The input statement appears in the process named by the output statement.

(c) The port identifiers are the same, and, if present, the subscript values are the same.

(d) All the $x_i := e_i$ would be valid assignment statements, where the x_i are the variables in the input statement and the e_i are the expressions in the output statement.

We will employ two abbreviated forms of communication statements. First, we will omit the port when it is not important to distinguish between different kinds of messages. Second, if there is only one expression or variable and there is no port, we will omit the parentheses around the expression or variable. We employed both of these abbreviations in (8.1).

As a simple example, the following filter process repeatedly copies characters received from one process, *West*, to another process, *East*:

> *Copy*:: **var** *c* : **char**
> **do** true → *West* ? *c*; *East* ! *c* **od**

On each iteration, *Copy* inputs a character from *West*, then outputs the character to *East*. Either of these statements will delay if the other process is not yet ready to execute a matching statement.

As a second example, the following server process computes the greatest common divisor of two positive integers x and y:

> *GCD*:: **var** x, y : **int**
> **do** true → *Client* ? *args*(x, y)
> **do** $x \geq y → x := x - y$
> [] $x \leq y → y := y - x$
> **od**
> *Client* ! *result*(x)
> **od**

GCD waits to receive input on its *args* port from a single client process (below we extend this example to support multiple clients). *GCD* then computes the answer using Euclid's algorithm and sends the answer back to the client's *result* port. *Client* communicates with *GCD* by executing:

> ... *GCD* ! *args*$(v1, v2)$; *GCD* ? *result*(r) ...

Here the port names are not actually needed; however, they help indicate the role of each channel.

Guarded Communication

Communication statements enable processes to exchange values without employing shared variables. By themselves, however, they are somewhat limited. Often a process wishes to communicate with more than one other process—perhaps over different ports—yet does not know the order in which the other processes might wish to communicate with it. For example, consider extending the *Copy* process above so that up to, say, 10 characters are buffered. If more than 1 but fewer than 10 characters are buffered, *Copy* can either input another character from *West* or output another character to *East*. However, *Copy* cannot know which of *West* or *East* will next reach a matching statement. As a second example, in general a server process such as *GCD* above will have multiple clients. Again, *GCD* cannot know which client will next want to communicate with it.

Non-deterministic communication is elegantly supported by extending guarded statements to include communication statements. A *guarded communication statement* has the general form:

$$B; C \rightarrow S$$

Here B is an optional boolean expression, C is an optional communication statement, and S is a statement list. If B is omitted, it has the implicit value of true. If C is omitted, a guarded communication statement is simply a guarded statement.

Together, B and C comprise the guard. The guard *succeeds* if B is true and executing C would not cause a delay; i.e., some other process is waiting at a matching communication statement. The guard *fails* if B is false. The guard *blocks* if B is true but C cannot yet be executed without causing delay.

Guarded communication statements appear within **if** and **do** statements. An **if** statement is now executed as follows. If at least one guard succeeds, one of them is chosen non-deterministically. First the message passing statement in the guard is executed, and then the corresponding statement list is executed. If all guards fail, the **if** statement terminates. If no guard succeeds and some guards are blocked, execution delays until some guard succeeds. Since variables are not shared, the value of a boolean expression in a guard cannot change until the process executes further assignment statements. Thus, a blocked guard cannot succeed until some other process reaches a matching communication statement.

A **do** statement is executed in a similar way. The difference is that the above selection process is repeated until all guards fail.

Notice that both input and output statements can appear in guards. Also, there could be several matching pairs in different processes. In this case, any pair of guards that succeeds could be chosen. We give an example at the end of this section.

As a simple illustration of guarded communication, we can reprogram the previous version of *Copy* as follows:

```
Copy::  var c : char
        do West ? c → East ! c od
```

Here, the input statement is in the guard. The effect is the same as before: *Copy* delays until it receives a character from *West*, then outputs the character to *East*.

Using guarded communication, we can also reprogram *Copy* to implement a bounded buffer. For example, the following buffers up to 10 characters:

> *Copy*:: **var** *buffer*[1:10] : **char**
> **var** *front* := 1, *rear* := 1, *count* := 0
> **do** *count* < 10; *West* ? *buffer*[*rear*] →
>   *count* := *count* + 1; *rear* := (*rear* **mod** 10) + 1
> [] *count* > 0; *East* ! *buffer*[*front*] →
>   *count* := *count* − 1; *front* := (*front* **mod** 10) + 1
>   **od**

Notice that the interface to *West* (the producer) and *East* (the consumer) is unchanged. This version of *Copy* employs two guarded communication statements. The first succeeds if there is room in the buffer and *West* is ready to output a character; the second succeeds if the buffer contains a character and *East* is ready to input it. The **do** statement above never terminates since both guards never fail at the same time—at least one of the boolean expressions in the guards is always true.

The latter version of *Copy* illustrates the expressive power of guarded communication coupled with synchronous communication: It is not necessary for *East* to ask for a character since *Copy* can wait to give *East* one at the same time that it waits to receive another character from *West*. The solution also illustrates a fundamental tradeoff between asynchronous and synchronous communication: With asynchronous communication, processes like *West* and *East* can execute at their own rate since buffering is implicit; with synchronous communication, it is necessary to program an additional process to implement buffering if that is needed. Explicit buffering is generally much less efficient than implicit buffering since the additional process introduces additional context switching. However, buffering is often not needed. For example, a client often needs to wait for a reply from a server after sending a request; in this case, it does not matter whether the request is buffered in a channel or is just not delivered until the server wants it.

Often it will be useful to have several guarded communication statements that reference arrays of processes or ports and that differ only in the subscript they employ. In this case, we will precede a guard with a range specifying the values of the subscripts. For example, we can reprogram the server process *GCD* as follows so it can be used by any number of clients:

> *GCD*:: **var** *x, y* : **int**
>   **do** (*i*: 1..*n*) *Client*[*i*] ? *args*(*x, y*) →
>   **do** *x* ≥ *y* → *x* := *x* − *y* [] *x* ≤ *y* → *y* := *y* − *x* **od**
>   *Client*[*i*] ! *result*(*x*)
>   **od**

The range on the outer **do** loop is shorthand for a series of guarded communication statements, one for each value of i. GCD waits to receive input on its *args* port from any one of n clients. In the body of the outer **do** loop, i is the index of that client; GCD uses i to direct the result back to the appropriate client.

This program for GCD illustrates the differences between the notations we are using for asynchronous and synchronous message passing. There is a one-to-one correspondence between **receive** statements and input statements and between **send** statements and output statements. However, with asynchronous message passing, *args* and *results* would be arrays of global channels, and a client process would have to pass its index to GCD. Here channels are ports associated with processes, and the client index is set implicitly in the guarded statement. Also, the semantics of the two notations are different. As we shall see, these differences affect how proofs are developed and how programs are written.

As a final example, the following illustrates the non-deterministic choice that occurs when there is more than one pair of matching guards:

$A::$ **var** $x, y :$ **int**; **if** $B\,!\,x \to B\,?\,y$ [] $B\,?\,y \to B\,!\,x$ **fi**
$B::$ **var** $x, y :$ **int**; **if** $A\,!\,y \to A\,?\,x$ [] $A\,?\,x \to A\,!\,y$ **fi**

This causes A to send its value of x to B, and B to send its value of y to A, but it does not specify the order in which they communicate. Either A outputs to B and then inputs from B, or vice versa. We could of course program this exchange of values more simply by, for example, having A first send x to B and then receive y from B. However, the resulting algorithm would be asymmetric, whereas the above one is symmetric.

8.2 Formal Semantics

As with asynchronous message passing, there are three steps in constructing a proof of a program that employs synchronous message passing: construct a sequential proof for each process, show that these proofs do not interfere, and show that all communication assumptions are satisfied. As is to be expected, the details differ due to the synchronous versus asynchronous semantics of communication. On balance, however, the semantics of synchronous message passing are simpler since auxiliary variables are not needed to represent the hidden state of message buffers. Also, a predicate that is true in the precondition of an output statement will be true in the postcondition of a matching input statement if communication takes place—assuming the predicate is not interfered with. This is a direct consequence of communication being synchronous; it can often be used to simplify proofs.

In the remainder of this section, we extend Programming Logic *PL* with proof rules for synchronous communication and illustrate their use. For ease of comparison with the semantics of asynchronous message passing, the organization of this section is the same as that of Section 7.2.

Axioms, Inference Rules, and Satisfaction Proofs

Consider the communication statements:

$$out: \; Destination \,!\, port(e_1, ..., e_n)$$
$$in: \quad Source \,?\, port(x_1, ..., x_n)$$

If *out* and *in* are matching statements and are selected for execution, the effect is to assign the expressions to the variables. However, suppose the statements do not match each other or any other communication statements in a program. Then the processes containing *out* and *in* will deadlock if they reach these statements. (For example, consider the degenerate case of a single process that consists of a single communication statement.) In a programming logic, this means that anything can be asserted as the postcondition for either statement.

This effect is similar to the effect of **receive** in Section 7.2 and is handled in a similar way. In particular, the communication axioms allow anything to be asserted in the postconditions, but then a satisfaction rule is included in the proof system to ensure that the effect of executing matching statements is the same as executing an assignment statement. Thus, the axioms for the communication statements are:

(8.3)   **Output Axiom**: $\{P\} \; Destination \,!\, port(e_1, ..., e_n) \; \{U\}$

(8.4)   **Input Axiom**: $\{Q\} \; Source \,?\, port(x_1, ..., x_n) \; \{V\}$

As observed, a communication statement will not terminate if executed in isolation, so the axioms are sound for sequential proofs of individual processes. The purpose of a satisfaction proof is to impose restrictions on the postconditions so that soundness is preserved when communication statements do terminate.

To understand the obligations for establishing satisfaction, consider a matching pair of communication statements. Executing such statements is equivalent to executing an assignment statement and, according to the communication axioms, will leave the system in a state satisfying $U \wedge V$. Thus, it suffices for execution to be started in a state satisfying:

$$(P \wedge Q) \; \Rightarrow \; wp(x_1, ..., x_n := e_1, ..., e_n, U \wedge V)$$

$M::$ **var** $i, j :$ **int** $\{ i = I \wedge j = J \}$
  if $i \geq j \rightarrow \{ i = I \wedge j = J \wedge i \geq j \}$ $A \, ! \, i$ $\{ \text{true} \}$
  $[] \, j \geq i \rightarrow \{ i = I \wedge j = J \wedge j \geq i \}$ $A \, ! \, j$ $\{ \text{true} \}$
  fi
$A::$ **var** $m :$ **int** $\{ \text{true} \}$
  $M \, ? \, m$ $\{ m = max(I, J) \}$

Figure 8.1. Proof outline for a synchronous communication program.

These observations lead to the following:

(8.5) **Satisfaction Rule for Synchronous Communication.** Let *in* be an input statement in one process with precondition P and postcondition U. Let *out* be a matching output statement in another process with precondition Q and postcondition V. For all such matching pairs of communication statements and corresponding pre- and postconditions, show that:

$$(P \wedge Q) \implies (U \wedge V)^{x_1, \, ..., \, x_n}_{e_1, \, ..., \, e_n}$$

Every pair of matching statements must satisfy (8.5). However, it is sometimes the case that two statements match but can never be executed due to the logic of the program. This case is handled by having the preconditions of the communication statements be strong enough to ensure that the antecedent of (8.5) is false. This is another example of the use of Exclusion of Configurations (2.25) to show that two processes cannot simultaneously be in a certain state.

A simple example will illustrate the use of the communication axioms and satisfaction rule. Consider the program and proof outline in Figure 8.1, in which process M sends the maximum of two integer values to process A. The proof outline of each process follows directly from the semantics of **if** and application of the communication axioms. The postcondition in A is valid since the Satisfaction Rule holds. In particular, there are two cases to consider, one for each output statement in M matched with the input statement in A. For the first case, we have:

$$(i = I \wedge j = J \wedge i \geq j) \implies (m = max(I, J))^m_i$$

This is of course true. The second case is similar.

Communication statements can also appear in guards. This requires extending the inference rules for the **if** and **do** statements. Consider a guarded communication statement:

$$B; C \rightarrow S$$

Such a statement can be executed only if the guard succeeds. This in turn means that B is true, and executing C would not cause delay. If the guard succeeds, C is executed, and then S is executed. Thus, with respect to state changes, a guarded communication statement has the same effect as the corresponding guarded statement:

$$B \rightarrow C; S$$

For example, the following has the same effect as process M in Figure 8.1:

$$M':: \textbf{var } i, j : \textbf{int}$$
$$\textbf{if } i \geq j; A\,!\,i \rightarrow \textbf{skip}$$
$$[]\, j \geq i; A\,!\,j \rightarrow \textbf{skip}$$
$$\textbf{fi}$$

The difference between a guarded communication statement and the corresponding guarded statement is that the guarded statement is more prone to deadlock. In particular, even if B is true, C might not match another communication statement, and hence S might never be executed. However, deadlock is not directly reflected in inference rules in PL, so we can transform guarded communication statements into guarded statements for the purposes of constructing proofs. (Later we describe how to prove absence of deadlock.)

Let CIF and CDO stand for the following statements, each of which contains n guarded communication statements:

$$CIF\text{: } \textbf{if } B_1; C_1 \rightarrow S_1 \,[]\, ... \,[]\, B_n; C_n \rightarrow S_n \textbf{ fi}$$
$$CDO\text{: } \textbf{do } B_1; C_1 \rightarrow S_1 \,[]\, ... \,[]\, B_n; C_n \rightarrow S_n \textbf{ od}$$

Then, based on the above observations, the Alternative Rule (1.14) is extended to yield the following inference rule for CIF:

(8.6)   **Alternative Rule**: $P \wedge \neg(B_1 \vee ... \vee B_n) \Rightarrow Q$
$$\frac{\{P \wedge B_i\}\ C_i; S_i\ \{Q\}, 1 \leq i \leq n}{\{P\}\ CIF\ \{Q\}}$$

Iterative Rule (1.16) is extended similarly to yield an inference rule for CDO:

(8.7)   **Iterative Rule**: $\dfrac{\{I \text{ and } B_i\}\ C_i; S_i\ \{I\}, 1 \le i \le n}{\{I\}\ CDO\ \{I \wedge \neg B_1 \wedge \ldots \wedge \neg B_n\}}$

In both cases, the only change is to include communication statements in the hypotheses and in the bodies of the **if** and **do** statements.

Auxiliary Variables and Non-Interference

The third and final component of a proof system for synchronous message passing is a non-interference proof. In Figure 8.1, the two processes reference different variables; hence the processes are interference-free. However, if processes share auxiliary variables, they can interfere. As in any concurrent program, interference results if an assignment action in one process invalidates an assertion in another process. Interference can also result from executing communication statements since these are a form of assignment. In particular, when a matching pair of statements is executed by two processes, an assertion in a third process could be invalidated if the input statement assigns to an auxiliary variable referenced in the assertion. (The Satisfaction Rule ensures that the pre- and postconditions of the communication statements themselves are valid.)

Since auxiliary variables are added to a program solely for the purposes of constructing a proof, they must not influence the behavior of the program to which they are added. In programs that do not employ message passing, this is ensured by the Auxiliary Variable Restriction (2.21). With message passing, we can also allow auxiliary variables to appear in communication statements as long as they are only assigned to each other and do not change the sets of matching communication statements. Thus, we extend (2.21) to:

(8.8)   **Auxiliary Variable Restriction.** Auxiliary variables appear only:

> (a) as targets in assignment statements or in expressions in assignment statements as long as the corresponding target of assignment is an auxiliary variable; or
>
> (b) as variables in input statements or in expressions in output statements as long as the corresponding variable in every matching input statement is an auxiliary variable and the sets of matching communication statements are not affected by the presence of auxiliary variables.

To establish non-interference, it is necessary to show that each critical assertion C in the proof outline of one process is invariant with respect to execution of any action in another process. We shall say statement S is *parallel* to assertion C if S is contained in one process and C is contained in the proof outline of a different process. Similarly, we shall say matching communication statements are *parallel* to assertion C if they are both parallel to C; thus, C is in a process different from the two containing the communication statements.

To show that an assignment statement a cannot invalidate a parallel assertion C, it suffices as before to prove that the following is a theorem of Programming Logic *PL*:

$$NI(a, C): \{ pre(a) \wedge C \} \ a \ \{ C \}$$

For an input statement *in*, the proof that $NI(in, C)$ is a theorem follows trivially from the Input Statement Axiom since that axiom allows anything to appear in the pre- and postconditions. Similarly, $NI(out, C)$ is trivially a theorem for any output statement *out*. However, when a matching pair of communication statements is executed, an assignment takes place from the expressions e_i in *out* to the variables x_i in *in*. This assignment must not interfere with an assertion in a third process, i.e., one that is parallel to the matching statements. This will be the case if

$$NIsynch(in, out, C): \ (pre(in) \wedge pre(out) \wedge C) \ \Rightarrow C_{e_1, ..., e_n}^{x_1, ..., e_n}$$

is a theorem of *PL*. In words this says that if the program state is such that *in* and *out* are about to be executed and C is true, then this implies that C will be true if the communication statements are executed.

The full proof obligations for showing non-interference are captured by the following requirement.

(8.9)   **Interference Freedom for Synchronous Communication.**
Theorems $\{ P_i \} \ S_i \ \{ Q_i \}$, $1 \leq i \leq n$, are interference-free if both:

> For all assignment actions a in the proof of S_i, $1 \leq i \leq n$,
> For all critical assertions C parallel to a: $NI(a, C)$; and

> For all input statements *in* in S_i, $1 \leq i \leq n$,
> For all matching output statements *out* in S_j, $1 \leq j \leq n$, $i \neq j$,
> For all critical assertions C parallel to *in* and *out*:
> $NIsynch(in, out, C)$

Like the corresponding rule for asynchronous message passing, this rule looks forbidding. Again, however, the techniques of disjoint variables, weakened assertions, and global invariants can be used to simplify or eliminate the need for proving interference freedom. The example in the next section illustrates this.

```
C[1:n]::  do true → Sem ! P( )          # entry protocol
                    critical section
                    Sem ! V( )           # exit protocol
                    non-critical section
          od
Sem::  do (i: 1..n) C[i] ? P( ) →        # wait for P from any client
                    C[i] ? V( )          # wait for V from that client
       od
```

Figure 8.2. Critical section protocol.

An Example

To illustrate the various components of a proof of a program that uses synchronous message passing, consider again the critical section problem. (Recall that this problem often arises even in distributed programs, e.g., when implementing locks on shared files.) Let $C[1:n]$ be a set of processes that have critical sections of code. These client processes interact with a server, *Sem*, as shown in Figure 8.2.

As its name indicates, *Sem* implements a (binary) semaphore. It does so by alternately receiving a P signal from any client and then a V signal from the client that sent the P signal. The value of the semaphore does not need to be stored since there is only one semaphore and its value oscillates between 1 and 0. In fact, here all the input and output statements in the processes could be reversed! Because message passing is synchronous and the processes exchange only signals, not data, it does not matter in which direction the synchronization signals flow.

To prove that the program in Figure 8.2 solves the critical section problem, we need to add auxiliary variables to record when the $C[i]$ are inside and outside their critical sections. Let $in[1:n]$ be an array of such variables; $in[i]$ is to be 1 when process $p[i]$ is in its critical section, and 0 otherwise. Then, the solution is correct if the following predicate is a global invariant:

$$MUTEX: (\forall i: 1 \leq i \leq n: 0 \leq in[i] \leq 1) \wedge (in[1] + ... + in[n]) \leq 1$$

There is one remaining question, however: Where to put the assignments to the $in[i]$? With shared variables, we augmented **await** statements with assignments to auxiliary variables. We did this so that the assignments to auxiliary and program variables were coupled and hence the auxiliary variables accurately recorded control points. However, in Figure 8.2 there are no **await** statements. Instead, the atomic actions are the communication statements, and the two control points we want to record are the output statements in the clients. Thus, we add the auxiliary variables to the communication statements themselves, making sure that Auxiliary Variable Restriction (8.8) is followed.

Adding auxiliary variables as described, we get the proof outline shown in Figure 8.3. A client sends a 1 to *Sem* with the *P* message and sends a 0 with the *V* message. When *Sem* receives a message from *C*[*i*], it assigns the value to *in*[*i*]. Predicate *MUTEX* is a global invariant; it is included in all assertions. The other predicates in the clients specify the value of each client's element of *in*; the other predicates in *Sem* specify whether all values of *in*[*i*] are 0 or one of them is 1.

The proof outline for each process in Figure 8.3 is trivially true in isolation. This is because the only assignment actions are the communication statements and the axioms for these statements allow anything to be asserted. Thus, the validity of the proof outline depends upon meeting the requirements of the Satisfaction (8.5) and Interference Freedom (8.9) rules.

First consider satisfaction. There are two pairs of matching communication statements: the ones that use port *P* and the ones that use port *V*. For the pair that use port *P*, Satisfaction Rule (8.5) imposes the following proof obligation:

$$(\textit{MUTEX} \; \wedge \; in[i] = 0 \; \wedge \; (in[1] + ... + in[n]) = 0 \;) \; \Rightarrow$$
$$(\textit{MUTEX} \; \wedge \; in[i] = 1 \; \wedge (in[1] + ... + in[n]) = 1 \;)_1^{in[i]}$$

This is clearly true. The proof obligation for the other pair of communication statements is analogous and is also true.

The remaining proof obligation is showing that the proof outlines are interference-free. There are no assignment actions, so that part of (8.9) is trivial. Thus the only potential source of interference is between communication statements in two processes and an assertion in a third. Here, all communication is from clients to *Sem*. Consider the first output statement in one client *C*[*i*], the first input statement in *Sem*, and the first critical assertion in another client *C*[*j*]. Filling in *NIsynch*, we have the following proof obligation:

$$(\textit{MUTEX} \; \wedge (in[1] + ... + in[n]) = 0 \; \wedge \; in[i] = 0 \; \wedge in[j] = 0 \;) \; \Rightarrow$$
$$(\textit{MUTEX} \; \wedge \; in[j] = 0 \;)_1^{in[i]}$$

This is true since $i \neq j$. The other non-interference obligations are essentially identical. As in prior chapters, by factoring assertions into global invariants and assertions about local variables, non-interference follows. The essential difference between Figure 8.3 and earlier proof outlines for the critical section problem using shared variables is that the *in*[*i*] are assigned to by means of communication statements instead of by assignment statements.

var $in[1:n]$: **int** := ([n] 0)

{$MUTEX$: ($\forall$ i: $1 \le i \le n$: $0 \le in[i] \le 1$) $\wedge$ $(in[1] + ... + in[n]) \le 1$

$C[i:1..n]$:: **do** true $\rightarrow$
$\qquad\qquad$ { $MUTEX$ $\wedge$ $in[i] = 0$ }
$\qquad\qquad$ $Sem\ !\ P(1)$ $\qquad$ # entry protocol
$\qquad\qquad$ { $MUTEX$ $\wedge$ $in[i] = 1$ }
$\qquad\qquad$ critical section
$\qquad\qquad$ $Sem\ !\ V(0)$ $\qquad$ # exit protocol
$\qquad\qquad$ { $MUTEX$ $\wedge$ $in[i] = 0$ }
$\qquad\qquad$ non-critical section
$\qquad$ **od**

Sem:: { $MUTEX$ $\wedge$ $(in[1] + ... + in[n]) = 0$ }
$\qquad$ **do** $(i: 1..n)\ C[i]\ ?\ P(in[i]) \rightarrow$ $\qquad$ # wait for P signal
$\qquad\qquad$ { $MUTEX$ $\wedge$ $(in[1] + ... + in[n]) = 1$ }
$\qquad\qquad$ $C[i]\ ?\ V(in[i])$ $\qquad\qquad$ # wait for V signal
$\qquad\qquad$ { $MUTEX$ $\wedge$ $(in[1] + ... + in[n]) = 0$ }
$\qquad$ **od**

Figure 8.3. Critical section proof outline.

Safety and Liveness Properties

As usual, the method of Exclusion of Configurations (2.25) can be used to prove that two processes are not simultaneously in the same state. In Figure 8.3, for example, two clients $C[i]$ and $C[j]$ cannot be in their critical sections at the same time since:

$$(MUTEX\ \wedge\ in[i] = 1\ \wedge\ in[j] = 1\ \wedge i \ne j) = false$$

However, with synchronous message passing, it is more difficult to prove absence of deadlock or other properties that concern whether processes are blocked. This is because a process can block at both input and output statements. Thus, there are more configurations that have to be considered to determine whether a program is deadlock-free.

Recall that a program is deadlocked if every process is blocked or has terminated and if at least one process is blocked. A process is blocked if it is at a communication statement and no other process is at a matching statement. Thus, every communication statement is a potential source of permanent blocking. However, most of the time, blocking will only be temporary as the first process to arrive at a communication statement waits for another process to arrive at a matching statement.

For now, assume a program does not use guarded communication; hence, all input and output statements are unguarded. Also, for simplicity we will ignore the case in which some processes have terminated. A *potentially blocking configuration* is one in which each process is at a communication statement. In such a configuration, the preconditions of all the various communication statements would be true. If this state cannot exist, then the configuration is deadlock-free. Moreover, if a potentially blocking configuration contains a matching pair of communication statements, then the configuration is also deadlock-free. Thus, a sufficient condition for absence of deadlock is that every potentially blocking configuration be deadlock-free.

Consider again the program and proof outline in Figure 8.3. There are numerous potentially blocking configurations, but it is easy to show that none yields a deadlock state. One such configuration has all the $C[i]$ at their first output statement and *Sem* at the input statement in the guard of the **do** loop. This configuration is characterized by the predicate:

$$MUTEX \wedge (\forall i\colon 1 \le i \le n\colon in[i] = 0)$$

This predicate can be true since this is obviously a reasonable program state. However, it is one in which any of the $C[i]$ can communicate with *Sem* since there are n matching pairs of communication statements. Hence, this is not a deadlock state.

Another potentially blocking configuration is the one in which all the $C[i]$ are at their first output statement and *Sem* is at its second input statement. This configuration is characterized by:

$$MUTEX \wedge (\forall i\colon 1 \le i \le n\colon in[i] = 0) \wedge (in[1] + ... + in[n]) = 1$$

This predicate is false, which corresponds to the fact that *Sem* is waiting for a V signal only when one of the $C[i]$ is inside its critical section.

The other potentially blocking configurations are similar to the above two, and all are deadlock-free. Thus, the program in Figure 8.3 is deadlock-free.

The two blocking statements in a program that uses synchronous message passing are the input and output statements. Hence, the liveness properties of such a program depend on how input and output statements are scheduled. If two processes are waiting at matching communication statements, they can both make progress if the pair of statements is executed eventually. This requires an unconditionally fair scheduling policy. The reason is that, once the processes are at the matching statements, they will remain there until the statements are executed.

On the other hand, guarded communication statements in general require a strongly fair scheduling policy to ensure progress. The boolean expression in a guard can refer only to local variables; hence it remains true once it becomes true. However, whether the communication statement in a guard can be executed depends on the states of other processes. For example, suppose a process repeatedly executes a guarded communication statement that has two guards. Further suppose that both guards succeed infinitely often; e.g., infinitely often another process is at a matching statement. Then scheduling has to be strongly fair in order to ensure that one of the guarded statements eventually gets selected. On the other hand, only weakly fair scheduling is required for the guarded communication statement in process *Sem* in Figure 8.2.

8.3 Networks of Filters

Networks of filters are programmed using synchronous message passing in much the same way as they are using asynchronous message passing (see Section 7.3). In Section 8.1, we saw how to implement a simple *Copy* filter. In fact, such a filter could be interposed between any pair of output and input ports to simulate buffered message passing. Thus, the essential difference between using synchronous versus asynchronous message passing is the absence of implicit buffering. This can occasionally be used to good effect since the sender of a message knows when it has been received. The absence of buffering can also complicate some algorithms. For example, in a heart-beat algorithm, deadlock will result if two neighboring processes both first try to send to each other and then try to receive from each other. These points will be illustrated as we go along.

This section develops parallel solutions to two problems: prime number generation and matrix/vector multiplication. Both solutions employ networks of filters. The first algorithm uses an array of processes, with each process communicating with its two neighbors. The second algorithm uses a matrix of processes, with each communicating with all four of its neighbors. As is always the case with networks of filters, the output of each process is a function of its input. Also, data flows through the network. In particular, there is no feedback loop in which a process sends data to another process from which it might have received data. The next section presents several parallel programs in which processes exchange data.

Prime Number Generation: The Sieve of Eratosthenes

The sieve of Eratosthenes—named after the Greek mathematician who developed it—is a classic algorithm for determining which numbers in a given range are prime. Suppose we want to generate all the primes between 2 and n. First, write down a list with all the numbers:

$$2\ 3\ 4\ 5\ 6\ 7\ ...\ n$$

```
var num[2:n] : ([n − 1] 0)
var p := 2, i : int
{ I:  p is prime ∧
      ( ∀ j:  2 ≤ j ≤ (p − 1)²:  num[j] = 0 if and only if j is prime) }
do p * p ≤ n →
      fa i := 2 * p to n by p → num[i] := 1 af      # cross out multiples of p
      p := p + 1
      do num[p] = 1 → p := p + 1 od       # find next uncrossed-out number
od
```

Figure 8.4. Sieve of Eratosthenes: sequential algorithm.

Starting with the first uncrossed-out number in the list, 2, go through the list and cross out multiples of that number. If n is odd, this yields the list:

$$2 \ \ 3 \ \ \not{4} \ \ 5 \ \ \not{6} \ \ 7 \ ... \ n$$

At this point, crossed-out numbers are not prime; uncrossed-out numbers are still candidates for being prime. Now move to the next uncrossed-out number in the list, 3, and repeat the above process by crossing out multiples of 3. If we continue this process until every number has been considered, the uncrossed-out numbers in the final list will be all the primes between 2 and n. In essence, the primes form a sieve that prevents their multiples from falling through.

Figure 8.4 contains a sequential program that implements this algorithm. The list is represented by an array, $num[2:n]$. The entries in num are initially 0, to indicate that the numbers from 2 to n are not yet crossed out; a number i is crossed out by setting $num[i]$ to 1. The outer **do** loop iterates over primes p, which are elements of num that remain 0. The body of that loop first crosses out multiples of p and then advances p to the next prime. As indicated, the invariant for the outer loop says that if $num[j]$ is 0 and j is between 2 and $(p-1)^2$, then j is prime. The loop terminates when p^2 is larger than n, i.e., when p is larger than $sqrt(n)$. The upper bound for j in the invariant and the loop termination condition both follow from the fact that if a number i is not prime, it has a prime factor smaller than $sqrt(i)$.

Now consider how we might parallelize this algorithm. One possibility is to assign a different process to each possible value of p and to have each in parallel cross out multiples of p. However, this approach has two problems. First, since we assume in this chapter that processes can communicate only by exchanging messages, we would have to give each process a private copy of num, and we would have to use another process to combine the results. Second, we would have to employ more processes than primes (even if num

On every channel, the first number is a prime and all other numbers
are not a multiple of any prime smaller than the first number.
Sieve[1]:: **var** $p := 2, i$: **int**
           # pass odd numbers to *Sieve*[2]
           fa $i := 3$ **to** n **by** $2 \rightarrow$ *Sieve*[2] ! i **af**

Sieve[i: 2..L]: **var** p : **int**, *next* : **int**
           Sieve[$i - 1$] ? p # p is a prime
           do true $\rightarrow$
               # receive next candidate
               Sieve[$i - 1$] ? *next*
               # pass *next* on if it is not a multiple of p
               if *next* **mod** $p \neq 0 \rightarrow$ *Sieve*[$i + 1$] ! *next* **fi**
      od

Figure 8.5. Sieve of Eratosthenes: pipeline algorithm.

---

could be shared). In the sequential algorithm, the end of each iteration of the outer loop advances p to the next uncrossed-out number. At that point, p is known to be prime. However, if processes are executing in parallel, we have to make sure there is one assigned to every possible prime. We can quickly rule out all even numbers other than 2, but it is not possible to rule out many odd numbers without knowing in advance which are prime!

We can overcome both of these problems by parallelizing the sieve of Eratosthenes in a different way. In particular, we can employ a pipeline of filter processes. Each filter in essence executes the body of the outer loop in the sequential algorithm. In particular, each filter in the pipeline receives a stream of numbers from its predecessor and sends a stream of numbers to its successor. The first number a filter receives is the next largest prime; it passes on to its successor all numbers that are not multiples of the first.

Figure 8.5 contains the pipeline algorithm for prime number generation. The first process, *Sieve*[1], sends all the odd numbers from 3 to n to *Sieve*[2]. Every other process receives a stream of numbers from its predecessor. The first number p that process *Sieve*[i] receives is the ith prime. Each *Sieve*[i] subsequently passes on all other numbers it receives that are not multiples of its prime p. The total number L of *Sieve* processes must be large enough to guarantee that all primes up to n are generated. For example, there are 25 primes less than 100; the percentage decreases for increasing values of n.

The program in Figure 8.5 terminates in deadlock. We can easily modify it to terminate normally by using sentinels, as we did in the network of merge filters (Figure 7.2).

Matrix/Vector Multiplication

Consider now the problem of multiplying a matrix a by a vector b. For simplicity, we will assume a has n rows and n columns and hence that b has n elements. Our task is to compute the matrix/vector product:

$$x[1{:}n] := a[1{:}n, 1{:}n] \times b[1{:}n]$$

This requires computing n inner products, one for each row of a with vector b. In particular, the ith element of result vector x is to be:

$$x[i] := a[i, 1] * b[1] + \ldots + a[i, n] * b[n]$$

The standard sequential algorithm for solving this problem employs two loops. The outer loop ranges over rows of a; the inner loop computes the inner product of one row of a and vector b. The time complexity of this algorithm is $O(n^2)$ multiplications. However, the n inner products can be computed in parallel. This is because the elements of a and b are only read and the elements of x are disjoint; hence the processes computing the inner products will not interfere with each other. If variables are shared, we can thus employ the following parallel algorithm:

$$
\begin{aligned}
&\textbf{co } i := 1 \textbf{ to } n \rightarrow \\
&\quad x[i] := 0 \\
&\quad \textbf{fa } j := 1 \textbf{ to } n \rightarrow x[i] := x[i] + a[i, j] * b[i] \textbf{ af} \\
&\textbf{oc}
\end{aligned}
$$

Our task now is to develop a distributed algorithm for solving this problem using synchronous message passing. One approach would be to employ n independent processes, with each process executing the body of the **co** statement above. In this case, each process would have to have local variables that contain one row of a and a copy of of b.

A second approach is to employ a network of n^2 processes, connected as shown in Figure 8.6. Each process $P[i, j]$ has one element of a, namely $a[i, j]$. First, each process receives the value of $b[i]$ from its north neighbor and passes it on to its south neighbor. The process then receives a partial sum from its west neighbor, adds $a[i, j] * b[i]$ to it, and sends the result to its east neighbor. Thus, the processes execute the following:

$$
\begin{aligned}
(8.10) \quad &P[i{:}1..n, j{:}1..n]{::} \ \textbf{var } sum : \textbf{real} := 0, b : \textbf{real} \\
&\qquad\qquad P[i-1, j] \, ? \, b; P[i+1, j] \, ! \, b \\
&\qquad\qquad P[i, j-1] \, ? \, sum; P[i, j+1] \, ! \, (sum + a[i, j] * b)
\end{aligned}
$$

Not shown are processes on the border of the network. As illustrated in

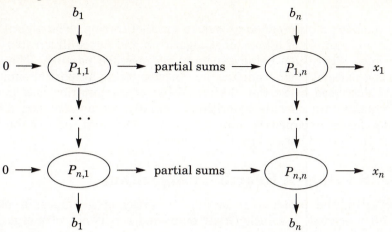

Figure 8.6. A matrix/vector multiplication network.

Figure 8.6, processes on the northern border send the elements of b, and processes on the western border send zeroes. The processes on the southern border merely receive the elements of b; processes on the eastern border receive the elements of result vector x. These processes are needed so that communication statements will not deadlock.

The processes in (8.10) do very little computation relative to the amount of communication. Thus, this algorithm would be very inefficient unless it were implemented directly in hardware. However, we can use the same process interaction pattern to perform full matrix/matrix multiplication (see exercise 8.9). Moreover, we can use the same basic approach with fewer processes (and processors) if we partition the matrix and vector into blocks. For example, if we have 16 processes and n is 1024, then we can partition a into 16 blocks of 256×256 elements. Each process would then receive 256 elements of b from its north neighbor and 256 partial sums from its west neighbor, compute 256 partial inner products, and send the elements of b to its south neighbor and the partial sums its east neighbor. With this change, each processes would do a lot more computation than those in (8.10). On the other hand, messages would be larger since 256 values would have to be transmitted over each channel.

8.4 Interacting Parallel Processes

In the parallel algorithms in the previous section, information flowed through a network of processes. In this section, we examine parallel algorithms in which processes exchange information until they have computed a solution.

First we consider a different approach to parallel sorting. The algorithm we present is an example of a heartbeat algorithm and hence illustrates how to program such algorithms using synchronous message passing. The second problem is a parallel prefix computation for computing all partial sums of an array. As described in Section 3.6, this kind of computation is a building-block for many data parallel algorithms. Finally, we present two different algorithms for matrix/matrix multiplication. The first uses a broadcast algorithm, the second uses a heartbeat algorithm.

Parallel Sorting: A Heartbeat Algorithm

Consider again the problem of sorting an array of n values in parallel. Section 7.3 presented a solution that employed a network of merge filters. Here we develop a different solution, in which neighboring processes repeatedly exchange information.

Assume that there are two processes, *P1* and *P2*, and that each process initially has an arbitrary $n/2$ of the values. (For simplicity, we assume n is even.) Then we can sort the entire collection of values into non-decreasing order by the following heartbeat algorithm. First, each process uses a sequential algorithm such as quicksort to sort its $n/2$ values. Then the processes repeatedly exchange values until *P1* has the $n/2$ smaller values and *P2* has the $n/2$ larger ones. In particular, on each step, *P1* gives *P2* a copy of its largest value, and *P2* gives *P1* a copy of its smallest value. Each process inserts the new value in the proper place in its sorted list of values, discarding the old value if necessary. The algorithm terminates when the largest value in *P1* is no larger than the smallest value in *P2*. The algorithm is guaranteed to terminate since each exchange—except the last—gets two more values to the correct process.

Figure 8.7 contains the program for this *compare and exchange* sorting algorithm. Notice how we have implemented the exchange steps. With asynchronous message passing, we could have each process execute a **send** followed by a **receive**. Since output and input statements are both blocking, however, we have used an asymmetric approach. To avoid deadlock, *P1* first executes an output statement and then an input statement; *P2* first executes an input statement and then an output statement. It is possible to use guarded communication to program such an exchange symmetrically. In particular, *P1* could execute:

do *P2* ? *new* → *P2* ! *a1*[*largest*] [] *P2* ! *a1*[*largest*] → *P2* ? *new* **od**

And *P2* could execute:

do *P1* ? *new* → *P1* ! *a2*[*smallest*] [] *P1* ! *a2*[*smallest*] → *P1* ? *new* **od**

Before each exchange, $a1$ and $a2$ are sorted.
$P1$ and $P2$ repeatedly exchange $a1[largest]$ and $a2[smallest]$
until $a1[largest] \leq a2[smallest]$.

$P1$:: **var** $a1[1:n/2]$: **int**   # initialized with $n/2$ values
        const $largest := n/2$; **var** new : **int**
        sort $a1$ into non-decreasing order
        $P2\ !\ a1[largest]$; $P2\ ?\ new$ # exchange values with $P2$
        do $a1[largest] > new \rightarrow$
                put new into proper place in $a1$, discarding old $a1[largest]$
                $P2\ !\ a1[largest]$; $P2\ ?\ new$ # exchange values with $P2$
        od

$P2$:: **var** $a2[1:n/2]$: **int**   # initialized with $n/2$ values
        const $smallest := 1$; **var** new : **int**
        sort $a2$ into non-decreasing order
        $P1\ ?\ new$; $P1\ !\ a2[smallest]$ # exchange values with $P1$
        do $a2[smallest] < new \rightarrow$
                put new into proper place in $a2$, discarding old $a2[smallest]$
                $P1\ ?\ new$; $P1\ !\ a2[smallest]$ # exchange values with $P1$
        od

Figure 8.7. Compare and exchange sorting between two processes.

Each process waits either to output a value or to input a value; depending on which communication takes place, the process then completes the exchange. This approach would be necessary if we could not impose a fixed order on the exchange. However, as we shall see in Section 8.6, the approach in Figure 8.7 is much more efficient since it is difficult and costly to implement guarded communication when both input and and output commands appear in guards.

In the best case, the processes in Figure 8.7 need exchange only one pair of values. This will happen if the smallest $n/2$ values are initially in $P1$ and the largest $n/2$ are initially in $P2$. In the worst case—which will happen if every value is initially in the wrong process—the processes will have to exchange $n/2 + 1$ values: $n/2$ to get each value to the correct process and one more to detect termination. (Actually, $n/2$ exchanges are sufficient, but it is not worth adding this special case to the algorithm.)

Now consider how we might effectively employ more than two processes. In particular, suppose we use k processes $P[1:k]$, e.g., because we have k processors. Initially, each process has n/k of the values. (Again, for simplicity assume that n is a multiple of k.) Assume that we arrange the processes in a linear sequence from $P[1]$ to $P[k]$ and that each process first sorts its n/k values. Then we can sort the n elements by using repeated parallel applications of the two-process compare and exchange algorithm (Figure 8.7).

Every process executes a series of *rounds*. In odd-numbered rounds, every odd-numbered process plays the role of *P1* from Figure 8.7, and every even-numbered process plays the role of *P2*. In particular, for all odd values of i, $P[i]$ exchanges values with $P[i + 1]$. (If k is odd, $P[k]$ does nothing in odd-numbered rounds.)

In even-numbered rounds, every even-numbered process plays the role of *P1* from Figure 8.7, and every odd-numbered process plays the role of *P2*. In this case, for all even values of i, $P[i]$ exchanges values with $P[i + 1]$. (In even-numbered rounds, $P[1]$ does nothing, and, if k is even, $P[k]$ also does nothing.)

To see how this algorithm works, assume both k and n are 4 and that the list to be sorted is (8, 7, 6, 5). On odd-numbered rounds, processes 1 and 2 exchange values, as do processes 3 and 4. On even-numbered rounds, just processes 2 and 3 exchange values. To sort the list, the processes need to execute four rounds:

round	$P[1]$	$P[2]$	$P[3]$	$P[4]$
0	8	7	6	5
1	7	8	5	6
2	7	5	8	6
3	5	7	6	8
4	5	6	7	8

Notice that after the first round the largest and smallest values have both moved toward their ultimate destination but that the other two values, 6 and 7, have temporarily moved in the wrong direction! However, no pair of values is ever exchanged in the wrong direction.

This algorithm is called an *odd/even exchange sort* (or an odd/even transposition sort). If the processes compare and exchange values as just described, after each round the lists in processes that just exchanged values will be sorted relative to each other. Moreover, every exchange makes progress toward a completely sorted list. A value might temporarily move in the wrong direction relative to where it belongs in the final state, but only if it is exchanged with a value that belongs on the other side of it. Thus, all values will be sorted eventually.

The question now is, how can the processes detect when the entire list is sorted? In the two-process algorithm, each process can readily determine when its half of the list is complete. The same is true for each pair of processes in each round of the k-process algorithm. But an individual process cannot detect that the entire list is sorted after a round since it knows only about two portions. In fact, a process could execute a few rounds without seeing any change, and then a new value could appear, having propagated from a process several links away in the chain.

One way to detect termination of the k-process algorithm is to employ a separate coordinator process. After each round, the k sorting processes tell the coordinator if they made any change to their portion of the list. If none did, then the list is sorted. The sorting processes then wait for the coordinator to tell them whether to terminate or to execute another round. This approach is effective but adds $2 * k$ messages of overhead to each round.

A second approach to termination is to have each process execute enough rounds to guarantee that the list will be sorted. In the two-process algorithm, only one round is required. However, in general, it is necessary to execute at least k rounds, as seen in the four-process example above. It is fairly complex to show that k rounds are sufficient since values can temporarily move away from their ultimate destination. But informally, after $k - 1$ rounds the smallest n/k values are ensured to get to $P[1]$, even if they all start out in $P[k]$. Similarly, $k - 1$ rounds are sufficient to ensure that the largest n/k values get to $P[k]$. During these $k - 1$ rounds, other values will get within one process of their ultimate destination. Thus, one more round is sufficient to ensure that all values are in the correct place.

As we have described the k-process algorithm, each of the k processes exchanges up to $n/k + 1$ messages on each round. Thus the entire algorithm requires up to $k^2 * (n/k + 1)$ message exchanges. A variation on the algorithm is the following. On each round, each pair of processes exchanges their entire sets of n/k values. The smaller numbered process then discards the n/k larger values, and the larger numbered process discards the n/k smaller values. This approach requires far fewer messages (k per round), but each message is much larger (n/k values), and each process requires twice as much local storage. Another variation—which has proved effective in practice—is to have each process first exchange half its values with its neighbor. If that is not sufficient, neighbors then exchange another quarter of their values, then an eighth, and so on.

Parallel Prefix Computations

As described in Section 3.6, it is frequently useful to apply an operation to all elements of an array. For example, to compute the average of an array of values $a[1{:}n]$, we first need to sum all the elements, then divide by n. Here we again consider the problem of computing in parallel the sums of all prefixes of an array. This illustrates how to program parallel prefix computations using message passing.

As before, we are given array $a[1{:}n]$ and are to compute $sum[1{:}n]$, where $sum[i]$ is to be the sum of the first i elements of a. To compute the sums of all prefixes in parallel, we can again use the technique of doubling the number of elements that have been added. First, set all the $sum[i]$ to $a[i]$. Then, in

$Sum[i: 1..n]::$ **var** $d := 1,\ sum := a[i],\ new : $**int**
$\qquad\qquad\quad \{SUM:\ sum = a[i - d + 1] + ... + a[i]\ \}$
$\qquad\qquad$ **do** $d < n \rightarrow$
$\qquad\qquad\qquad$ **if** $(i + d) \le n \rightarrow P[i + d]\ !\ sum$ **fi**
$\qquad\qquad\qquad$ **if** $(i - d) \ge 1 \rightarrow P[i - d]\ ?\ new;\ sum := sum + new$ **fi**
$\qquad\qquad\qquad d := 2 * d$
$\qquad\qquad$ **od**

Figure 8.8. Computing all partial sums using message passing.

---

parallel add $sum[i - 1]$ to $sum[i]$, for all $i > 1$. In particular, add elements that are distance 1 away. Now double the distance, adding $sum[i - 2]$ to $sum[i]$, in this case for all $i > 2$. If we continue to double the distance, then after $log(n)$ steps we will have computed all partial sums.

To implement this parallel prefix algorithm using message passing, we need n processes. Initially, each has one value of a. On each step, a process sends its partial sum to the process at distance d to the right (if there is one), then waits to receive a partial sum from the process at distance d to the left (again, if there is one). Processes that receive partial sums add them to $sum[i]$. Every process then doubles distance d. The full algorithm is shown in Figure 8.8. Loop invariant SUM specifies how much of the prefix of a each process has summed on each iteration.

The reader might be interested in comparing the algorithm in Figure 8.8 with the one in Figure 3.18. There are two essential differences. First, there are no shared variables, so processes use message passing to exchange values. Second, there is no need for barrier synchronization since the message passing statements enforce the required synchronization.

We can readily modify the algorithm in Figure 8.8 to use any associative binary operator. As in Figure 3.18, all that we need to change is the operator in the statement that modifies sum. (If the operator is not commutative, we would also need to put new on the left side of the operator and the partial result on the right.) We can also adapt this algorithm to use fewer than n processes. In this case, each process would have a slice of the array and would first need to compute the prefix sums of that slice before communicating these with the other processes. The process-interaction pattern would still be the same as in Figure 8.8.

Matrix Multiplication: Broadcast Algorithm

The network of filters in Figure 8.6 could be extended to multiply a matrix by a matrix. In this section and the next, we develop two additional matrix multiplication algorithms.

For simplicity, assume a and b are square matrices with n rows and n columns each. Our task is to compute the matrix product $c := a \times b$. This requires computing n^2 inner products, one for each combination of row and column. Since the inner products are disjoint, we can compute them in parallel. Thus, if a and b are shared, the following parallel algorithm will compute the matrix product:

> **co** $i := 1$ **to** $n, j := 1$ **to** $n \rightarrow$
> $\quad c[i,j] := 0$
> $\quad$ **fa** $k := 1$ **to** $n \rightarrow c[i,j] := c[i,j] + a[i,k] * b[k,j]$ **af**
> **oc**

If matrices a and b are not shared, we could multiply them using n^2 processes, as long as each has a copy of the appropriate row of a and column of b. However, suppose initially that a and b are fully distributed among the processes, with $a[i,j]$ and $b[i,j]$ being stored at $P[i,j]$. As above, each of the processes is to compute one inner product. But to do so, each $P[i,j]$ first needs to acquire the other elements of row i and column j. Stated differently, each $P[i,j]$ needs to send $a[i,j]$ to all processes in the same row of P and needs to send $b[i,j]$ to all processes in the same column of P. Thus, it needs to broadcast its values of a and b and receive values from other processes in the same row and column.

With asynchronous message passing, executing **broadcast** is equivalent to concurrently sending the same message to several channels. And **broadcast**, like **send**, is a non-blocking primitive. All the copies of the message get queued, and each copy can be received later by one of the participating processes. We could define a concept of **broadcast** for use with synchronous message passing. But in keeping with the blocking nature of output commands, a synchronous **broadcast** would have to block the sender until all recipients have received the message. This would not be very useful since processes that need to broadcast messages to others almost always also need to receive messages from others.

There are two ways to achieve the effect of **broadcast** with synchronous message passing. One way is to use a separate process to simulate a broadcast channel; i.e., clients would send broadcast messages to and receive them from this process. The second way is to to use guarded communication. When a process wants both to send and receive broadcast messages, it can use guarded communication with two guards. Each guard has a quantifier to enumerate the other partners. One guard outputs a message to all other partners; the other guard inputs a message from any other partner.

Figure 8.9 contains a distributed implementation of matrix multiplication. It uses the guarded-communication method of broadcasting messages. In particular, each process first sends its element of a to other processes in the same row and receives their elements of a. Each process then broadcasts its

$P[i: 1..n, j: 1..n]$::
  var aij, bij, cij : **real**
  var $row[1{:}n], col[1{:}n]$: **real**, k : **int**
  var $sent[1{:}n] := ([n] \text{ false})$, $recvd[1{:}n] := ([n] \text{ false})$
  $row[j] := aij; col[i] := bij$
  # broadcast aij and acquire other values of $a[i, *]$
  $sent[j] := \text{true}; recvd[j] := \text{true}$
  do $(k: 1..n)$ **not** $sent[k]; P[i, k] \: ! \: aij \rightarrow sent[k] := \text{true}$
   $[]$ $(k: 1..n)$ **not** $recvd[k]; P[i, k] \: ? \: row[k] \rightarrow recvd[k] := \text{true}$
  od
  # broadcast bij and acquire other values of $b[*, j]$
  $sent := ([n] \text{ false}); recvd := ([n] \text{ false})$
  $sent[i] := \text{true}; recvd[i] := \text{true}$
  do $(k: 1..n)$ **not** $sent[k]; P[k, j] \: ! \: bij \rightarrow sent[k] := \text{true}$
   $[]$ $(k: 1..n)$ **not** $recvd[k]; P[k, j] \: ? \: col[k] \rightarrow recvd[k] := \text{true}$
  od
  # now compute inner product of $a[i, *]$ and $b[*, j]$
  $cij := 0$
  fa $k := 1$ **to** $n \rightarrow cij := cij + row[k] * col[k]$ **af**

Figure 8.9. Matrix multiplication using a broadcast algorithm.

---

element of b to all processes in the same column and in turn receives their elements of b. (These two guarded communication statements could be combined into one with four guards.) Each process then computes one inner product. When the processes terminate, variable cij in process $P[i, j]$ contains result value $c[i, j]$.

In Figure 8.9, we have implemented the exchanges of values by using **do** statements that iterate until each process has sent a value to and received a value from $n - 1$ other processes. To know when to terminate each loop, we had to introduce additional boolean arrays, *sent* and *recvd*, to record which processes we have sent a value to and received a value from. This is necessary since we want to exchange values exactly once with every other process in the same row and column.

In general, **broadcast** has to be implemented as shown in Figure 8.9. For this specific problem, however, we could implement the message exchange more simply by having the processes circulate their values along rows and then columns. In particular, we could circulate all the aij around row i by having every $P[i, j]$ execute:

$$next := j; \, row[j] := aij$$
$$\textbf{fa } k := 1 \textbf{ to } n - 1 \rightarrow$$
$$\quad \textbf{if } P[i, j \ominus 1] \, ! \, row[next] \rightarrow P[i, j \oplus 1] \, ? \, row[next \oplus 1]$$
$$\quad [] \, P[i, j \oplus 1] \, ? \, row[next \oplus 1] \rightarrow P[i, j \ominus 1] \, ! \, row[next]$$
$$\quad \textbf{if}$$
$$\quad next := next \oplus 1$$
$$\textbf{af}$$

Again, $\oplus$ and $\ominus$ denote modular arithmetic. On the first iteration, $P[i, j]$ gives its element of a to its left neighbor and receives the right neighbor's element of a. On the next iteration, $P[i, j]$ passes that element to its left neighbor and receives another element from the right neighbor, which that neighbor in turn received from its right neighbor on the first iteration. The n elements in each row of a are thus shifted circularly to the left $n - 1$ times so that every process receives every value in its row. Values can be cycled along a column in a similar way.

Matrix Multiplication: Heartbeat Algorithm

Each process in Figure 8.9 sends and receives $2 * (n - 1)$ messages. However, each process stores an entire row of a and column of b. This section presents a matrix multiplication algorithm that requires two more messages per process, but each process has to store only one element of a and one of b at a time. The solution uses the shifting technique introduced at the end of the previous section. Again we assume that initially a and b are fully distributed so that each $P[i, j]$ has the corresponding elements of a and b.

To compute $c[i, j]$, process $P[i, j]$ needs to multiply every element in row i of a by the corresponding element in column j of b. But the order in which P performs these multiplications does not matter! This suggests that we can reduce the storage in each process to one element of a and one of b at a time if we can find a way to circulate the values among the processes so that each one gets a pair it needs at the right time.

First consider $P[1, 1]$. To compute $c[1, 1]$, it needs to get every element of row 1 of a and column 1 of b. Initially it has $a[1, 1]$ and $b[1, 1]$, so it can multiply them. If we then shift row 1 of a to the left 1 position and shift column 1 of b up one position, $P[1, 1]$ will have $a[1, 2]$ and $b[2, 1]$, which it can multiply and add to $c[1, 1]$. If we continue to shift $n - 1$ times, $P[1, 1]$ will see all the values it needs.

Unfortunately, this multiply and shift sequence will work only for processes on the diagonal. Other processes will see every value they need, but not in the right combinations. However, it is possible to rearrange a and b before we start the multiply and shift sequence. In particular, if we shift row i of a circularly left i positions and row j of b circularly up j positions, then every process will have corresponding pairs of values on each step. (It is

$P[i:1..n, j:1..n]$:: **var** aij, bij, cij : **real**
$\qquad\qquad\quad$ **var** new : **real**, k : **int**
$\qquad\qquad\quad$ # shift values in aij circularly left i columns
$\qquad\qquad\quad$ **if** $P[i, j \ominus i]\,!\,aij \rightarrow P[i, j \oplus i]\,?\,aij$
$\qquad\qquad\quad$ [] $P[i, j \oplus i]\,?\,new \rightarrow P[i, j \ominus i]\,!\,aij;\; aij := new$
$\qquad\qquad\quad$ **fi**
$\qquad\qquad\quad$ # shift values in bij circularly up j rows
$\qquad\qquad\quad$ **if** $P[i \ominus j, j]\,!\,bij \rightarrow P[i \oplus j, j]\,?\,bij$
$\qquad\qquad\quad$ [] $P[i \oplus j, j]\,?\,new \rightarrow P[i \ominus j, j]\,!\,bij;\; bij := new$
$\qquad\qquad\quad$ **fi**
$\qquad\qquad\quad$ $cij := aij * bij$
$\qquad\qquad\quad$ **fa** $k := 1$ **to** $n - 1 \rightarrow$
$\qquad\qquad\qquad\quad$ # shift aij left 1, bij up 1, then multiply
$\qquad\qquad\qquad\quad$ **if** $P[i, j \ominus 1]\,!\,aij \rightarrow P[i, j \oplus 1]\,?\,aij$
$\qquad\qquad\qquad\quad$ [] $P[i, j \oplus 1]\,?\,new \rightarrow P[i, j \ominus 1]\,!\,aij;\; aij := new$
$\qquad\qquad\qquad\quad$ **fi**
$\qquad\qquad\qquad\quad$ **if** $P[i \ominus 1, j]\,!\,bij \rightarrow P[i \oplus 1, j]\,?\,bij$
$\qquad\qquad\qquad\quad$ [] $P[i \oplus 1, j]\,?\,new \rightarrow P[i \ominus 1, j]\,!\,bij;\; bij := new$
$\qquad\qquad\qquad\quad$ **fi**
$\qquad\qquad\qquad\quad$ $cij := aij * bij$
$\qquad\qquad\quad$ **af**

Figure 8.10. Matrix multiplication using a heartbeat algorithm.

---

not at all obvious why this particular initial placement works; people came up with it by examining small matrices and then generalizing.) The following display illustrates the result of the initial rearrangement of the values of a and b for a 4×4 matrix:

$a[1,2], b[2,1]$	$a[1,3], b[3,2]$	$a[1,4], b[4,3]$	$a[1,1], b[1,4]$
$a[2,3], b[3,1]$	$a[2,4], b[4,2]$	$a[2,1], b[1,3]$	$a[2,2], b[2,4]$
$a[3,4], b[4,1]$	$a[3,1], b[1,2]$	$a[3,2], b[2,3]$	$a[3,3], b[3,4]$
$a[4,1], b[1,1]$	$a[4,2], b[2,2]$	$a[4,3], b[3,3]$	$a[4,4], b[4,4]$

Figure 8.10 gives an implementation of this matrix multiplication algorithm. Each process first sends its aij to the process i columns to its left and receives a new aij from the process i columns to the right. Then each process sends its bij to the process j rows above it and receives a new bij from the process j rows below it. All computations of row and column indices are done

modulo n using $\oplus$ and $\ominus$, so the shifts are circular.

After rearranging the *aij* and *bij*, the processes in Figure 8.10 set *cij* to *aij* * *bij*. Then they execute $n - 1$ heartbeat phases. In each, values in *aij* are shifted left by 1, values in *bij* are shifted up by 1, and then the new values are multiplied and added to *cij*.

Both this algorithm and the broadcast algorithm in Figure 8.9 can be adapted to work on partitions of matrices. In particular, we could divide large matrices into k square or rectangular blocks and could have one process compute the matrix product for each block. The processes would exchange data in the same way as in Figure 8.9 or 8.10.

8.5 Clients and Servers

Because communication flows in one direction, message passing is ideal for programming networks of filters and interacting peers. As discussed in Section 7.4, message passing can also be used to program the two-way information flow that occurs in client/server interactions.

This section examines several client/server problems and illustrates how to solve them using synchronous message passing. We first reprogram two examples from Section 7.4: the resource allocator and the file server. Both solutions illustrate the utility of guarded communication. Then we present two message-passing solutions to the dining philosophers problem: one with a centralized fork manager and one in which fork management is decentralized. The decentralized solution is an interesting instance of a token-passing algorithm.

Resource Allocation

Recall from Section 7.4 the problem of managing a multiple unit resource such as memory or file blocks. Clients request units of the resource from an allocator process, use them, then release them back to the allocator. Again we assume for simplicity that clients acquire and release units one at a time.

Such a resource allocator services two kinds of requests: acquire and release. With port naming, we can use a different port for each kind of request. In particular, when a client wants a unit, it sends a message to the *acquire* port. When the request can be satisfied, the server allocates a unit and returns it to the client. After using the resource, the client sends a message to the server's *release* port; this message contains the identity of the resource unit the client is releasing.

The resource allocator and client interface are shown in Figure 8.11. Here, we have been able to use guarded communication to greatly simplify the allocator, relative to the one in Figure 7.4. In particular, we have used two guarded communication statements with quantifiers. The first waits for

Allocator:: **var** *avail* := MAXUNITS, *units* : **set of int**, *unitid* : **int**
initialize *units* to appropriate values
do (*c*: 1..*n*) *avail* > 0; *Client*[*c*] ? *acquire*( ) →
        avail := *avail* − 1; *unitid* := *remove*(*units*)
        Client[*c*] ! *reply*(*unitid*)
[] (*c*: 1..*n*) *Client*[*c*] ? *release*(*unitid*) →
        avail := *avail* + 1; *insert*(*units*, *unitid*)
od

Client[*i*: 1..*n*]:: **var** *unitid* : **int**
      Allocator ! *acquire*( )   # ask for a unit
      Allocator ? *reply*(*unitid*)
      # use resource *unitid* and then later release it
      Allocator ! *release*(*unitid*)
      ...

Figure 8.11. Resource allocation using synchronous message passing.

---

acquire messages, which can be accepted as long as there are available units. The second waits for *release* messages, which can always be accepted. There is no need for merging these two kinds of messages. Moreover, the *Allocator* does not need to save pending requests. This is because it can use the boolean condition on the first guard, *avail* > 0, to defer accepting *acquire* messages when there are no free units.

As programmed, *Allocator* will accept *acquire* messages from clients in some arbitrary order. Most likely, this will be the order in which clients sent these messages. However, if *Allocator* wants to service client requests in some other order—e.g., by shortest resource usage time or by client priority, we would have to program *Allocator* as in Figure 7.4. We would have to make similar changes to handle requests for multiple units at a time. In both cases, the problem is that boolean conditions in guards cannot depend on the contents of a message; they can only reference local variables. Thus, if a server has to look at a message to determine whether it can be processed, the server has to save unprocessed requests.

In Figure 8.11, clients are an array of processes, and thus *Allocator* can use a client's index to direct reply messages to it. This is not very satisfactory in general, however, since it fixes both the number and names of all potential clients. A more flexible approach is to use some dynamic method of naming. One possibility is to have a data type for process identities and some function by which a process can determine its own identity. Another possibility is to have a data type for ports. In both cases, a client would pass a unique value of the appropriate type in *acquire* messages; the *Allocator* would then use this value to direct a reply back to the client.

File[*i*: 1..*n*]::   **var** *fname* : **string**, *args* : other argument types
                var *more* : **bool**
                var local buffer, cache, disk address, etc.
                do (*c*: 1..*m*) *Client*[*c*] ? *open*(*fname*) →
                    # open file *fname*; if successful then:
                    Client[*c*] ! *open_reply*( ); *more* := true
                    do *more* →
                        if *Client*[*c*] ? *read*(args) →
                            handle read; *Client*[*c*] ! *read_reply*(results)
                        [] *Client*[*c*] ? *write*(args) →
                            handle write; *Client*[*c*] ! *write_reply*(results)
                        [] *Client*[*c*] ? *close*( ) →
                            close file; *more* := false
                      fi
                  od
                od

Client[*j*: 1..*m*]::   **var** *server* : **int**
                do (*i*: 1..*n*) *File*[*i*] ! *open*("foo") →   # open file "foo"
                    server := *i*; *File*[*i*] ? open_reply(*serverid*)
                od
                # use and eventually close file; e.g., to read execute:
                File[*serverid*] ! *read*(access arguments)
                File[*serverid*] ? *read_reply*(results)
                ...

Figure 8.12. File servers and clients using synchronous message passing.

File Servers and Conversational Continuity

Consider again the interaction between clients and file servers described in Section 7.4. As before, up to *n* files may be open at once, and access to each open file is provided by a separate file server process. To use a file, a client first sends an open request to any one of the file servers and then waits for a response. Subsequently, the client engages in a conversation with the server that responded. During the conversation, the client sends read and write requests to the server. The client ends the conversation by sending a close request. The server is then free to start a conversation with another client.

Figure 8.12 shows how the file servers and clients can interact using synchronous message passing and guarded communication. An open request from a client is sent to any file server; one that is free receives the message and responds. Both the client and file server use the other's index for the remainder of the conversation.

The communication pattern in Figure 8.12 is identical to that in the asynchronous message passing solution in Figure 7.10. Messages are sent to ports rather than to global channels, but the message exchanges are the same. Also, the *File* processes are almost the same. The differences are that the input statement for *open* requests has been moved to the guard on the outer **do** loop and that guarded communication is used in the **if** statement that services other requests. These changes take advantage of guarded communication but are not necessary.

The fact that the communication patterns are identical in the programs in Figures 7.10 and 8.12 points out the similarity between asynchronous and synchronous message passing for client/server interaction. This similarity results from the fact that such interaction is inherently synchronous. Thus, the non-blocking semantics of asynchronous **send** do not yield any benefits in this case.

Centralized Dining Philosophers

In Chapters 4 and 5 we discussed how to solve the dining philosophers problem, first using semaphores and then using conditional critical regions. In this section and the next, we present two solutions that use message passing. We again represent the five philosophers by processes. But since the processes cannot share variables, we have to use one or more caretaker processes to manage the five forks.

One approach is to mimic the semaphore solution in Section 4.3. In particular, we would have one server process that implements five semaphores, one per fork. This server would be programmed like *Sem* in Figure 8.2. In this case—as in Figure 4.15—a philosopher would need to send two messages to request his forks and two messages to release them. Also, we would have to ensure that the philosophers did not all request the left (or right) fork first, or else deadlock could result.

A second approach is to mimic the CCRs solution in Section 5.2. In this case, we again use one server, but it keeps track of the status of each philosopher rather than the status of each fork. In particular, the server records whether or not each philosopher is eating. With this approach, a philosopher needs to send only one message to request or release both forks. It is also easy to avoid deadlock.

Figure 8.13 gives a message-passing solution using the second approach. To request permission to eat, a philosopher sends a message to the *Waiter*'s *getforks* port. By using a quantifier in the guarded communication statement that inputs *getforks* signals, the *Waiter* can postpone accepting a request from *Phil*[i] until neither neighbor is eating. Thus, the output statement to *getforks* in *Phil*[i] will block until the request can be honored. This obviates the need for an explicit reply message from *Waiter* telling the philosopher it can proceed. A philosopher releases its forks in much the same way, but in

Waiter:: **var** *eating*[1:5] := ([5] false)
　　　　{ *EAT*: (∀ *i*: 1 ≤ *i* ≤ 5: *eating*[*i*] ⇒ ¬(*eating*[*i*] ∨ *eating*[*i* ⊕ 1])) }
　　　　do (*i*: 1..5) **not** (*eating*[*i* ⊖ 1] **or** *eating*[*i* ⊕ 1]);
　　　　　　　　　Phil[*i*] ? *getforks*( ) → *eating*[*i*] := true
　　　[] (*i*: 1..5) *Phil*[*i*] ? *relforks*( ) → *eating*[*i*] := false
　　　　od
Phil[*i*: 1..5]:: **do** true →
　　　　　　Waiter ! *getforks*( )
　　　　　　eat
　　　　　　Waiter ! *relforks*( )
　　　　　　think
　　　　od

Figure 8.13. Centralized dining philosophers.

---

this case the input statement in *Waiter* need not be guarded. As shown in Figure 8.13, the *Waiter*'s loop invariant is the same as the CCRs resource invariant from Section 5.2. The invariant is ensured by the boolean expression in the guard that inputs *getforks* messages.

The solution in Figure 8.13 is not fair. In particular, a philosopher will starve if one neighbor is eating, then the other, and so on. To get a fair solution, we would have to do something like have the *Waiter* service *getforks* requests in first-come, first-served order. This requires changing the body of the *Waiter* and its interface with philosophers (see exercise 8.14).

Decentralized Dining Philosophers

The *Waiter* process in Figure 8.13 manages all five forks. In this section, we develop a decentralized solution in which there are five waiters, one per philosopher. The solution is another example of a token-passing algorithm. In this case, the tokens are the five forks. The structure of the process interaction pattern is much like that in the replicated file server example discussed in Chapter 7 (see Figure 7.26). The solution can be adapted to coordinate access to replicated files or to yield an efficient solution to the distributed mutual exclusion problem (see exercises 8.15 and 8.33).

Suppose there are five philosophers, five waiters, and five forks. The philosophers and waiters are represented by processes. The forks are tokens; each fork is shared by two waiters, one of whom holds it at a time. Each philosopher interacts with his own waiter. When a philosopher wants to eat, he asks his waiter to acquire two forks; that waiter interacts with neighboring waiters if necessary. The waiter then holds on to both forks while his philosopher eats.

As with replicated files, the key to a distributed solution is to manage the forks in such a way that deadlock is avoided. Ideally, the solution should also be fair. For this problem, deadlock could result if a waiter needs two forks and cannot get them. A waiter certainly has to hold on to both forks while his philosopher is eating. But when the philosopher is not eating, a waiter should be willing to give up his forks. However, we need to avoid passing a fork back and forth from one waiter to another without its being used. Hence we need a way for a waiter to decide whether to keep a fork or to give it up if his neighbor needs it.

One way for a waiter to decide whether to give up a fork or to keep it would be to use logical clocks and timestamps. In particular, waiters could record when their philosopher wants to eat, and these clock values could be used when neighboring waiters are competing for a fork. However, for this problem there is a much simpler approach.

The basic idea for avoiding deadlock is to have a waiter hold on to a fork if it is needed and has not yet been used; otherwise the waiter gives it up. Specifically, when a philosopher starts eating, his waiter marks both forks as "dirty." When another waiter wants a fork, if it is dirty and not currently being used, the first waiter cleans the fork and gives it up. The first waiter cannot get the fork back until it has been used since only dirty forks are passed between waiters. However, a dirty fork can be reused until it is needed by the other waiter.

This decentralized algorithm is given in Figure 8.14. (It is colloquially called the "hygienic philosophers" algorithm because of the way forks are cleaned and dirtied.) When a philosopher wants to eat, he sends a *hungry* message to his waiter, then waits for the waiter to send him an *eat* message. Neighboring waiters exchange *need* messages. When a philosopher is hungry and his waiter needs a fork, that waiter outputs a *need* message to the waiter who has the fork. The other waiter accepts the *need* message when the fork is dirty and is not being used. (With synchronous message passing, we do not need additional messages to pass forks between waiters.) Assertion *EAT* in *Waiter* indicates what is true when a philosopher is eating; it is the waiter's loop invariant.

As programmed in Figure 8.14, *Waiter*[1] initially has two forks, *Waiter*[5] has none, and the other waiters have one each. All forks are initially clean. It is imperative that either the forks be distributed asymmetrically as shown or that some be dirty and some clean. For example, if every philosopher initially has one fork and all are clean, then we could get deadlock if all waiters want two forks at the same time: Each would give up one and then wait forever to get it back.

The solution in Figure 8.14 is also fair, assuming as usual that a philosopher does not eat forever. In particular, if one waiter wants a fork that another holds, he will eventually get it. If the fork is dirty and in use, eventually the other philosopher will quit eating, and hence the other waiter

Waiter[*i*: 1..5]:: {*EAT*: (*eating* ⇒ *haveL* ∧ *haveR* ∧ *dirtyL* ∧ *dirtyR*) }
    var *eating* := false, *hungry* := false   # status of *Phil*[*i*]
    var *haveL*, *haveR* : **bool**   # status of forks
    var *dirtyL* := false, *dirtyR* := false
    if *i* = 1 → *haveL* := true; *haveR* := true
    [] *i* ≥ 2 **and** *i* ≤ 4 → *haveL* := false; *haveR* := true
    [] *i* = 5 → *haveL* := false; *haveR* := false
    fi
    do *Phil*[*i*] ? *hungry*( ) →
            hungry := true   # *Phil*[*i*] wants to eat
    [] *hungry* **and** *haveL* **and** *haveR* →
            hungry := false; *eating* := true   # *Phil*[*i*] may eat now
            dirtyL:= true; *dirtyR* := true; *Phil*[*i*] ! *eat*( )
    [] *hungry* **and not** *haveL*; *Waiter*[*i*⊖1] ! *need*( ) →
            haveL := true   # asked for left fork; now have it
    [] *hungry* **and not** *haveR*; *Waiter*[*i*⊕1] ! *need*( ) →
            haveR := true   # asked for right fork; now have it
    [] *haveL* **and not** *eating* **and** *dirtyL*; *Waiter*[*i*⊖1] ? *need*( ) →
            haveL := false; *dirtyL* := false   # give up left fork
    [] *haveR* **and not** *eating* **and** *dirtyR*; *Waiter*[*i*⊕1] ? *need*( ) →
            haveR := false; *dirtyR* := false   # give up right fork
    [] *Phil*[*i*] ? *full*( ) →
            eating := false   # *Phil*[*i*] done eating
    od
Phil[*i*: 1..5]:: **do** true →
            Waiter[*i*] ! *hungry*( ); *Waiter*[*i*] ? *eat*( );
            eat
            Waiter[*i*] ! *full*( )
            think
        od

Figure 8.14. Decentralized dining philosophers.

---

will give up the fork. If the fork is clean, it is because the other philosopher is hungry and the other waiter is waiting to get a second fork. By similar reasoning, the other waiter will eventually get the second fork, his philosopher will eat, and hence the waiter will give up the first fork. The other waiter will eventually get the second fork because there is no state in which every waiter holds one clean fork and wants a second. (This is another reason why asymmetric initialization is imperative.)

8.6 Implementations

This section presents two implementations of synchronous message passing. Both employ the asynchronous message primitives, which are in turn implemented as described in Section 7.10.

The first implementation employs a centralized server process, which coordinates the matching of input and output statements. This greatly simplifies the implementation—especially the handling of guarded communication—at the expense of having centralized control and a potential execution bottleneck. The second implementation is decentralized, with each process that wants to communicate interacting directly with others. As we shall see, the decentralized approach works well if guarded communication statements can contain input statements but not output statements. On the other hand, it is quite complex and costly if both input and output statements can appear in guards.

Centralized Clearing House

Assume that a program contains some number n of regular processes. The processes communicate and synchronize by executing input and output statements, as defined in Section 8.1 and illustrated by the examples throughout this chapter. Recall that two processes can communicate when they are ready to execute matching communication statements (8.2).

In the centralized implementation of synchronous message passing, we will use a "clearing house" process whose role is to pair up regular processes that want to execute matching communication statements. Suppose regular process P_i wants to execute an output statement with P_j as destination and that P_j wants to execute an input statement with P_i as source. Assume that the port name and message types also match. Then these processes interact with the clearing house and each other, as illustrated in Figure 8.15. First, each regular process sends a message to the clearing house. This message describes the desired communication, e.g., the source, destination, and port. The clearing house saves the first of these messages. When it receives the second, it finds the first and determines that these two processes want to execute matching statements. The clearing house then sends replies to both P_i and P_j. After getting the reply, P_i sends the expressions in its output statement to P_j, which receives them into the variables in its input statement. At this point, both processes resume executing their local code.

To develop programs that realize the interaction pattern in Figure 8.15, we need to design communication channels and message formats, data structures for the clearing house, and protocols for handling both unguarded and guarded communication. The first thing we need are channels for each communication path in Figure 8.15. We need one channel *match* for messages from regular processes to the clearing house. We need one reply

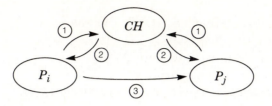

Figure 8.15. Interaction pattern with clearing-house process.

channel for each regular process; this will be used for messages back from the clearing house. And we need one data channel for each regular process that contains input statements; this will be used by other regular processes.

Let each regular process—including each element of an array of processes—have a unique identity that is an integer between 1 and n, the number of such processes. These will be used to index reply and data channels. The reply channels will be represented by an array *reply*[1:n]; these will carry reply messages from the clearing house. The data channels will also be represented by an array *data*[1:n]; these channels will in general have different types since regular processes communicate different kinds of messages. Rather than use a unique channel for each kind of message, however, we will assume that messages on data channels are self-describing; i.e., they contain tags that allow the receiver to determine the type of data in the message.

To pair matching communication statements, the clearing house needs descriptions of the statements. For this, we will use templates containing the following fields:

> direction, source, destination, port

The direction will be OUT for an output statement and IN for an input statement. Source and destination are the identities of the sender and intended receiver (for output) or intended sender and receiver (for input). The port is an integer that uniquely identifies the port and hence the data types in the input and output statements. There must be one of these for each different kind of port in the source program. This means every explicit port identifier needs to be assigned a unique integer value as does every anonymous port.

Figure 8.16 contains declarations of *template* data type and the *reply* and *data* channels. It also gives the protocols that regular processes execute when they reach output and input statements. For unguarded communication statements, a process *myid* sends a single template to the clearing house, then waits for a reply. The clearing house will send a reply when it

type *template* = **rec**(*direction* : (OUT, IN); *source, dest, port* : **int**)
chan *reply*[1:*n*](*direction* : (OUT, IN); *process* : **int**)
chan *data*[1:*n*](self describing data types)

output statement not in a guard:
    send *match*(*template*(OUT, *myid, destination, port*))
    receive *reply*[*myid*](*direction, process*)
    # *direction* will be OUT and *process* will be *destination*
    send *data*[*process*](expressions in output statement)

input statement not in a guard:
    send *match*(*template*(IN, *source, myid, port*))
    receive *reply*[*myid*](*direction, process*)
    # *direction* will be IN and *process* will be *myid*
    receive *data*[*myid*](variables in input statement)

guarded input or output statement:
    var *t* : **set of** *template* := ∅
    fa boolean expressions that are true →
        insert a template for the input or output statement into set *t*
    af
    send *match*(*t*)   # send set of possible matches to clearing house
    receive *reply*[*myid*](*direction, process*)
    use *direction* and *process* to determine which guarded communication
        statement was the one that matched
    if *direction* = IN → **receive** *data*[*myid*](variables in input stmt)
    [] *direction* = OUT → **send** *data*[*process*](expressions in output stmt)
    fi
    execute appropriate guarded statement *S*

Figure 8.16. Centralized protocols for regular processes.

---

finds a match, as discussed below. After getting its reply, the source process sends the expressions in the output statement to the destination process, which stores them in the variables in the input statement.

For guarded communication statements, a regular process needs to evaluate each guard. If a guard contains a range such as (*i*: 1..*n*), it is evaluated once for each different value in the range. For each guard that is true, the process constructs a template and inserts it into set *t*. After evaluating all guards, the process sends set *t* to the clearing house and then waits for a reply. When the process receives a reply, it will indicate which other process has been paired with this one and the direction in which communication is to occur. If the direction is OUT, the process sends a message to the other one; otherwise it waits to receive data from the other one. The

chan *match*(*t* : **set of** *template*)

CH:: **var** *pending*[1:*n*] : **set of** *template* := ([*n*] ∅)
{ (∀ *i*: 1 ≤ *i* ≤ *n*: *pending*[*i*] ≠ ∅ ⇒ process *i* blocked) }
var *t* : **set of** *template*
do true →
  receive *match*(*t*)
  look at some template in *t* to determine sender *s*
  fa templates in *t* →
    if there is a matching pair in some *pending*[*i*] →
      if *s* is the source → **send** *reply*[*s*](OUT, *i*)
                    send *reply*[*i*](IN, *s*)
      [] *s* is the destination → **send** *reply*[*s*](IN, *i*)
                      send *reply*[*i*](OUT, *s*)
      fi
      pending[*i*] := ∅
      exit   # get out of the for all loop
    fi
  af
  if no matching pair was found → *pending*[*s*] := *t* **fi**
od

Figure 8.17. Centralized clearing-house process.

---

process then selects the appropriate guarded statement and executes it. We assume that *direction* and *process* are sufficient to determine which guarded communication statement was the one matched by the clearing house; if this is not the case, the process needs to record additional information.

The protocol for guarded communication in Figure 8.16 does not handle the case that a guard does not contain a communication statement (e.g., as in the *Waiter* processes in Figure 8.14). If the guard is true in this case, a process can simply execute the body of that guarded statement; it is not necessary to communicate with the clearing house. The protocol also does not handle the case that all guards are false and hence that set *t* is empty after the guards have been evaluated. In this case, the enclosing **if** or **do** statement would simply terminate.

Figure 8.17 contains the clearing house process *CH* and its channel *match*. Array *pending* contains one set of templates for each regular process. If *pending*[*i*] is not empty, then regular process *i* is blocked waiting for a matching communication statement. When *CH* receives a new set *t*, it first looks at one of the templates to determine which process *s* sent *t*. (If the direction in a template is OUT, then the source is *s*; if the direction is IN, then the destination is *s*.) The clearing house then compares elements of *t* with templates in *pending* to see if there is a match. Because of the way we have constructed templates, two match if the directions are opposite, the ports are identical, and the source and destination are identical. If *CH* finds a match with some process *i*, it sends replies to both *s* and *i*; the replies tell each process the identity of the other and the direction in which they are to communicate. In this case, *CH* then clears *pending*[*i*] since process *i* is no longer blocked. If *CH* does not find a match for any template in *t*, it saves *t* in *pending*[*s*], where *s* is the sending process.

An example will help clarify how these protocols work. Suppose we have two processes *A* and *B* that want to exchange data by executing the following guarded communication statements:

$$A:: \ \textbf{do} \ B \ ! \ a1 \rightarrow B \ ? \ a2 \ [] \ B \ ? \ a2 \rightarrow B \ ! \ a1 \ \textbf{od}$$
$$B:: \ \textbf{do} \ A \ ! \ b1 \rightarrow A \ ? \ b2 \ [] \ A \ ? \ b2 \rightarrow A \ ! \ b1 \ \textbf{od}$$

When *A* starts executing its **do** statement, it builds a set with two templates (since both guards are true). These templates are:

$$(\text{OUT}, A, B, p2) \ \text{and} \ (\text{IN}, B, A, p1)$$

Here we assume that *p1* is the identity of *A*'s port and *p2* is the identity of *B*'s port. Process *A* then sends these templates to the clearing house.

Process *B* takes similar actions and sends the following two templates to the clearing house:

$$(\text{OUT}, B, A, p1) \ \text{and} \ (\text{IN}, A, B, p2)$$

When the clearing house gets the second set of templates, it sees that there are two possible matches. It picks one, sends replies to *A* and *B*, and then throws away both sets of templates. Processes *A* and *B* then execute the matching pair of guarded communication statements selected by the clearing house. *A* and *B* then go on to execute the unguarded communication statements. In this case, they send one template each to the clearing house, wait for replies, and then communicate with each other.

If the clearing house always searches for matching templates starting with process 1 (or any fixed starting point), some blocked processes might never get awakened, even if periodically there are matching templates. However, a simple strategy will provide fairness in the absence of deadlock. When *CH* receives a new set of templates, it should start searching for matches beginning with *pending*[*start*]. Once process *start* has gotten the chance to communicate, then *CH* should increment *start* to the next process whose pending set is not empty. In this way, *start* will continually cycle around the processes—assuming process *start* is not blocked forever—and thus each process will periodically get the chance to be checked first.

These protocols for synchronous message passing can be used in a distributed system, with asynchronous message passing being implemented by a distributed kernel as described in Section 7.10. The protocols can also be used on a single-processor system or a shared-memory multiprocessor, with asynchronous message passing being implemented by a shared-memory kernel. In the latter cases, however, it would be more efficient to put the data structures and actions of the clearing house process within the shared-memory kernel. Then regular processes would only have to make a single kernel call to check for a matching template. In addition, the kernel itself could perform the data transfer from output to input statements.

Decentralized Implementations

The main virtue of the centralized implementation is that the clearing-house process has a record of all pending communications. This makes it easy to check for matching communication statements. However, in a distributed system, the clearing house would most likely be executing on a machine different from at least many of the regular processes. This will add overhead to every communication between regular processes and the clearing house. Moreover, the clearing house could be an execution bottleneck. It would be ideal if regular processes could communicate directly with each other. This section presents such a decentralized implementation. But since the decentralized protocols are quite complex, we begin by making a simplifying assumption.

For now, assume that output statements do not appear in guarded statements.* Hence, only input statements can appear in guards. This restriction on output statements make some problems harder to solve and is not met by several of the examples in this chapter. However, it greatly simplifies a decentralized implementation of synchronous communication, as we shall see.

If an output statement cannot appear in a guard, a process executing an output statement has to block until another process reaches a matching input statement. This means that we can implement an output statement by simply sending a message to the destination process and then waiting for a reply from the destination. The reply will be sent when the destination has reached a matching input statement, which might be in a guard.

The implementation of input statements is more complicated, but not exceedingly so. The source of complication is that a process might have to check several output messages before it finds a matching one. The process

---

*Both the original proposal for CSP and the Occam language (Section 10.2) restrict output statements in these ways.

chan *match*[1:*n*](*sender, port* : **int**, *data* : self describing)
chan *reply*[1:*n*]( )

each process uses the following local variables:
    var *pending* : **set of** (*sender, port*: **int**, *data* : self describing) := ∅
    var *sender, port* : **int**, *data* : self describing

output statement not in a guard:
    send *match*[*destination*](*myid, port*, expressions in output statement)
    receive *reply*[*myid*]( )

input statement not in a guard:
    if there is some message in *pending* with the correct *port* →
        remove the message from *pending*
        store *data* in the variables in the input statement
        send *reply*[*sender*]( )
    fi
    do have not yet found a match →
        receive *match*[*myid*](*sender, port, data*)
        if *port* matches → store *data* in variables in input statement
                     send *reply*[*sender*]( )
        [] *port* does not match → insert (*sender, port, data*) in *pending*
        fi
    od

Figure 8.18 (a). Decentralized protocols: no output in guards.

also needs to save those that do not match since they might match a later input statement. For an unguarded input statement, a process first checks saved messages to see if there is a matching one. If so, the process removes the message from the set and sends a reply; if not, the process receives new messages and saves them until it finds a matching one. Input statements in guards are handled in a similar way. The only additional complexity is that there might be several input statements that could be matched.

Figure 8.18 gives the protocols for this restricted case where output statements cannot appear in guards. Only two messages need to be exchanged for any matching pair of communication statements: one from the process with the output statement to the destination and a reply back from the destination when the output statement has been matched with an input statement. The protocol, like that in Figure 8.17, does not need to employ busy waiting. Each process blocks until there are matching communication statements.

If output statements can appear in guards, a process needs to poll each possible destination, one at a time, to see if the destination is waiting to

guarded input statements:
    fa boolean expressions that are true →
        if there is some message in *pending* with the correct *port* →
            remove the message from *pending*
            store *data* in the variables in the input statement
            send *reply*[*sender*]( )
            execute the appropriate guarded statement
            exit   # get out of the for all loop
        fi
    af
    do have not yet found a match →
        receive *match*[*myid*](*sender*, *port*, *data*)
        if *port* matches some input statement with a true boolean →
            store *data* in the variables in the input statement
            send *reply*[*sender*]( )
            execute the appropriate guarded statement
        [] message does not match →
            insert (*sender*, *port*, *data*) in *pending*
        fi
    od

Figure 8.18 (b). Decentralized protocols: no output in guards.

---

execute a matching input statement. Polling is required because there may
be several communication statements that could succeed, and processes have
to query each other to determine if a pair of statements is acceptable. A
process needs to continue to poll—which is a form of busy waiting—until it
finds a match. In turn, destination processes need to answer every query
with a positive or negative reply. They cannot simply save *match* messages
as in Figure 8.18. Moreover, a process has to check periodically to see if it is
being polled since the process doing the polling has to block until it gets an
answer. (Alternatively, we could use helper processes to answer queries.)

As a specific example, consider the following three processes:

      A:: **if** *B* ! *a1* → **skip** [] *C* ? *a2* → **skip fi**
      B:: **if** *C* ! *b1* → **skip** [] *A* ? *b2* → **skip fi**
      C:: **if** *A* ! *c1* → **skip** [] *B* ? *c2* → **skip fi**

All three processes want to communicate with each other and there are three
matching pairs of communication statements. We need a protocol that selects
exactly one of the matching pairs. We also have to be careful to avoid

livelock. For example, suppose A polls B about its first guard about the same time that B polls C and C polls A. We have to avoid having all processes respond negatively, then poll about the second guards, respond negatively, and continue this pattern indefinitely.

We now develop protocols that support both input and output statements in guards. To simplify determining when two communication statements match and to avoid livelock, we will employ two kinds of asymmetry in the decentralized protocols. First, when a process wants to determine if an output statement matches an input statement, it will send a query to the destination. We will not send queries to inquire about input statements. This will cut down on the number of messages to determine matches and simplify deciding if there is a match. In addition, a process will make only one such query at a time; it will wait for a response before making another. This will avoid having to cancel outstanding queries in case there are multiple matches.

The second kind of asymmetry we will use is a priority ordering on the processes. Every process has a unique integer identity. To avoid livelock, we will give higher-numbered processes priority over lower-numbered processes in the following way. When a process makes a query, it waits to receive a response. While waiting, it might get queries from other processes. If the new query does not match an input statement that could be executed, the process will send a negative acknowledgement (NACK). If the query matches an input statement and is from a higher-priority process, the process will hold on to the query and answer it later (unless it is already holding one acceptable query, in which case the process will send a NACK). If the query is acceptable but is from a lower-priority process, the queried process will respond with a busy acknowledgement (BUSY). This use of BUSY precludes having a cycle of processes, each of which has made a query but is waiting to respond until it gets an answer to its query.

Figure 8.19 contains the decentralized protocols supporting both input and output statements in guards. Queries and responses are both sent to *request* channels. There are two kinds of queries—MUST and QUERY—and three kinds of responses—ACK, NACK, and BUSY. When a process executes an unguarded output statement, it sends a MUST query since it must wait until the destination process reaches a matching input statement. The destination thus saves the query in its local *pending* set until it is able to send an ACK. A destination process never sends a NACK or BUSY response to a MUST query.

When a process P reaches an output statement in a guard whose boolean part is true, P sends a QUERY message to the destination. In this case, P could get back any of the three responses. If P gets an ACK response, the query was accepted; hence, P sends the data in the output statement to the destination. If P gets a BUSY or NACK response, its query was not accepted. But while P was waiting for an answer, another process Q might have

type *request_kind* = (QUERY, MUST, ACK, NACK, BUSY)
chan *request*[1:*n*](*kind* : *request_kind*; *sender, port* : **int**)
chan *data*[1:*n*](self describing data types)

each process uses the following local variables:
    var *pending* : **set of** (*sender, port*: **int**) := ∅
    var *hold* : (*sender, port*), *hc* := 0
    var *kind* : *request_kind, sender, port* : **int**

output statement not in a guard:
    send *request*[*destination*](MUST, *myid, port*)
    do no match yet →
        receive *request*[*myid*](*kind, sender, port*)
        # cannot get NACK or BUSY responses to MUST messages
        if *kind* = ACK → **send** *data*[*sender*](expressions in output stmt)
        [] *kind* = MUST → insert (*sender, port*) in *pending*
        [] *kind* = QUERY → **send** *request*[*sender*](NACK, *myid*, 0)
        fi
    od

input statement not in guard:
    if there is some message in *pending* with the correct *port* →
        remove the message from *pending*
        send *request*[*sender*](ACK, *myid*, 0)
        receive *data*[*myid*](variables in input statement)
    fi
    do no match yet →
        receive *request*[*myid*](*kind, sender, port*)
        if (*kind* = QUERY **or** *kind* = MUST) **and** *port* matches →
            send *request*[*sender*](ACK, *myid*, 0)
            receive *data*[*myid*](variables in input statement)
        [] *kind* = QUERY **and** *port* does not match →
            send *request*[*sender*](NACK, *myid*, 0)
        [] *kind* = MUST **and** *port* does not match →
            insert (*sender, port, data*) in *pending*
        fi
    od

Figure 8.19 (a). Decentralized protocols: input and output in guards.

---

queried it. As described above, if the query is not acceptable—there is no matching input statement in one of the guards—then *P* sends a NACK. If the query is acceptable but *Q* is of lower priority, *P* sends a BUSY response. If the query is acceptable and *Q* is of higher priority, *P* saves the query in local variable *hold*. After P gets an answer to its query, it responds to the query it is holding (if any). If P got an ACK to its query, it sends a NACK response; otherwise it accepts the held query by sending an ACK response and then waiting for the data.

When a process is executing the guarded communication protocol in Figure 8.19, it continues to try output statements until it gets an ACK response or sends an ACK to another process. The process should try each output statement in turn and then might need to start over and try different output statements again. Even if one query receives a NACK response, a subsequent query to the same destination might receive an ACK response.

In addition to the actions shown in Figure 8.19, a process needs to respond to queries when it is not currently interested in communicating. In particular, it needs to send NACK responses to any such queries. This requires that a process periodically check to see if there are any pending messages on its *request* channel (or that such requests interrupt the process). Alternatively, each regular process could have a helper process that handles requests when the regular process does not wish to communicate.

To illustrate the protocols in Figure 8.19, consider again the example program given earlier:

$$A:: \textbf{if } B\,!\,a1 \to \textbf{skip } [] \ C\,?\,a2 \to \textbf{skip fi}$$
$$B:: \textbf{if } C\,!\,b1 \to \textbf{skip } [] \ A\,?\,b2 \to \textbf{skip fi}$$
$$C:: \textbf{if } A\,!\,c1 \to \textbf{skip } [] \ B\,?\,c2 \to \textbf{skip fi}$$

Assume that A is the lowest-priority process, that C is the highest, and that the processes start executing their guarded communication statements at about the same time. Then each process will send one query: A to B, B to C, and C to A. All three are acceptable since there is a matching input statement for each output statement. The processes handle these queries as follows:

> query from A to B — B replies BUSY since it has higher priority
> query from B to C — C replies BUSY since it has higher priority
> query from C to A — A holds on to query since it has lower priority

When A gets the BUSY response from B, it sends an ACK response to C. Process C then sends the value of $c1$ to A.

This use of priorities and BUSY responses avoids global livelock. In particular, if several processes are trying to select matching guarded communication statements—and there are matching pairs—at least some of the processes will succeed. However, the protocols do not avoid individual livelock (starvation). Consider the above example again, and change the **if** statements to **do** loops. If the processes execute at about the same rate, B

input and output statements in guards:
    # first check *pending* for an acceptable match, as in Figure 8.19 (a)
    do no match yet →
        pick next guard with an output statement and true boolean
        send *request*[*destination*](QUERY, *myid*, *port*)
        receive *request*[*myid*](*kind*, *sender*, *port*)
        # loop until get a response to the above query
        do *kind* = QUERY →
            if acceptable **and** *sender* < *myid* →
                send *request*[*sender*](BUSY, *myid*, 0)
            [] acceptable **and** *sender* > *myid* **and** *hc* = 0 →
                hold := (*sender*, *port*); *hc* := 1
            [] not acceptable **or** *hc* = 1 →
                send *request*[*sender*](NACK, *myid*, 0)
            fi
            receive *request*[*myid*](*kind*, *sender*, *port*)
        [] *kind* = MUST →
            insert (*sender*, *port*) in *pending*
            receive *request*[*myid*](*kind*, *sender*, *port*)
        od
        if *kind* = ACK →   # query accepted; transfer data
            if *hc* = 1 → **send**[*hold.sender*](NACK, *myid*, 0) **fi**
            send *data*[*sender*](expressions in output statement)
            execute the appropriate guarded statement
        [] (*kind* = BUSY **or** *KIND* = *NACK*) **and** *hc* = 0 →
            remember to try this output statement again later
        [] (*kind* = BUSY **or** *kind* = NACK) **and** *hc* = 1 →
            # an acceptable query came in before response
            send *request*[*hold.sender*](ACK, *myid*, 0)
            receive *data*[*myid*](variables in input statement)
            execute the appropriate guarded statement
        fi
        # if no match yet, again check *pending*
    od

Figure 8.19 (b). Decentralized protocols: input and output in guards.

---

might never get a chance to communicate. However, it is extremely unlikely that this will happen. In fact, the decentralized protocols are sufficient to avoid livelock in all of the programs in this chapter. There are fair, decentralized protocols, but they are either quite complex or require a large number of messages (see the Historical Notes and References).

To summarize, we have developed three different implementations of synchronous message passing. The first used a centralized clearing house. The second was a decentralized implementation in which output statements are not allowed in guards. The third was a decentralized implementation in which both input and output statements can appear in guards.

The second implementation is more complex than the centralized clearing house, but it is not too complex since processes executing output statements block. The third implementation, however, is quite complex since it requires the use of polling. This also affects performance. The programs in this chapter that employ output commands in guards could be reprogrammed to avoid them, but the resulting programs would in general require additional processes (see exercise 8.38). Thus, the combination of synchronous message passing plus guarded communication introduces a tradeoff between ease of programming and performance. As shown in Section 9.3, guarded communication can also be used with asynchronous message passing. However, since **send** is non-blocking, it is never necessary to put **send** statements in guards. Thus the combination of asynchronous message passing plus guarded communication does not introduce a tradeoff between ease of programming and performance.

Historical Notes and References

Synchronous communication was introduced by Tony Hoare [1978] in his now classic paper on communicating sequential processes (CSP). That paper, like Hoare's earlier paper on monitors [1974], is a model of clarity. The notation used in this chapter is essentially the same as that introduced in Hoare's paper. The major difference is that we allow output statements in guards. However, Hoare recognized the utility of this—and discusses the issue in Section 7.8 of his paper. In a later book on the semantics of CSP [Hoare 1985], he does in fact permit output statements in guards. The other difference between Hoare's notation and ours is that in Hoare [1978] an input statement in a guard fails if the source process has terminated; this has come to be called the distributed (or automatic) termination convention. Again, Hoare [1985] later abandoned this convention since it is difficult to define and implement.

CSP itself was not intended to be a full programming language. However, it has influenced several. Occam is the most important language based on synchronous message passing. (In fact, Hoare was a consultant to the language design team.) Section 10.2 describes Occam; the Historical Notes and References at the end of Chapter 10 gives citations to papers and books on the language.

Joyce is another major language based on CSP [Brinch Hansen 1987, 1989a, 1989b]. It is the most recent of three concurrent programming languages designed by Per Brinch Hansen. (Concurrent Pascal and Edison are the others.) Unlike Occam (or CSP), Joyce permits output commands in guards and supports dynamic process creation and recursive procedures. Several additional languages based on synchronous message passing are listed in Table 2 of Bal et al. [1989].

The semantics of synchronous communication presented in Section 8.2 were developed by Gary Levin in a Ph.D. dissertation supervised by David Gries [Levin

1980, Levin & Gries 1981]. The concept of a satisfaction proof is due to them. At about the same time, Krzysztof Apt, Nissim Francez, and Willem de Roever [1980] developed a different proof system. In their system, a satisfaction proof is subsumed by what they call a cooperation proof. In particular, one develops a proof of each process in isolation and then shows that the various proofs cooperate, in the sense that each meets the input/output assumptions of the others. The Apt et al. proof system also requires all auxiliary variables to be referenced only in a global invariant; this avoids the need for proving non-interference.

Several others have also examined aspects of the semantics of synchronous message passing. Misra and Chandy [1981] present a proof method for networks of processes. Soundararajan [1984] presents an axiomatic semantics in which the proof of each process can be developed in isolation; in particular, the axioms for input and output statements are stronger than those in Section 8.2 and obviate the need for a satisfaction (or cooperation) proof. Lamport and Schneider [1984] present a generalized "Hoare logic" based on invariant predicates and show how to apply it to programs that use shared variables and to programs that use synchronous message passing. Schlichting and Schneider [1984] examine the semantics of all the various kinds of message passing: asynchronous, synchronous, remote procedure call, and rendezvous. Prasad [1984] proposes a method for minimizing the amount of work required to prove non-interference in CSP; his method treats assignments to shared auxiliary variables as synchronization points. Finally, Hoare [1985] presents a thorough discussion of the mathematics of deterministic and non-deterministic processes. That book shows how to use traces to record the behavior of processes and shows how to decompose systems into concurrent subsystems.

Several people have also examined other, more pragmatic aspects of Hoare's original proposal and the use of synchronous message passing. Kieburtz and Silberschatz [1979] critique the absence of buffering, the distributed termination convention, and direct naming. Bernstein [1980] examines the non-determinism of guarded communication and the absence of output guards; that paper also proposes an implementation of output guards (see below for others). Misra and Chandy [1982] present a probe/echo algorithm for detecting termination of CSP programs. Hull and McKeag [1984a] show how to use CSP to design both centralized and distributed operating systems. The paper contains several client/server examples and also compares the use of monitors to synchronous message passing for structuring an operating system. Another paper by the same authors [1984b] shows how to implement different kinds of operating system queues in CSP. Hull [1984] presents a parallel algorithm for solving the stable marriage problem. Apt and Francez [1984] show how to model the distributed termination convention of CSP's guarded communication statements using other language constructs. De Carlini and Villano [1988] present an algorithm, programmed in Occam, for clock synchronization in networks. Finally, Huang [1990] presents a distributed deadlock detection algorithm for programs that use synchronous message passing.

The programs for the prime number sieve (Figure 8.5) and matrix/vector multiplication network (Figure 8.6) were adapted from ones in Hoare's original paper. The parallel algorithms developed in Section 8.4—as well as others—are discussed in Chapter 12 of Udi Manber's excellent book on algorithms [1989]. The algorithm for the decentralized dining philosophers (Figure 8.14) was first developed by Mani Chandy and Jay Misra [1984].

The centralized implementation of synchronous message passing (Figures 8.15 to 8.17) was developed by the author. Several people have developed decentralized implementations under a variety of assumptions. Silberschatz [1979] assumes processes form a ring. Van de Snepscheut [1981] considers hierarchical systems; his algorithm also preserves the non-determination present in the application program. Bernstein [1980] presents an implementation that works for any communication topology. Our decentralized algorithm (Figure 8.19) is quite similar to Bernstein's and, like his, can lead to individual starvation, as discussed at the end of Section 8.6. Schneider [1982] presents a broadcast algorithm that is simple and fair; it essentially replicates the pending sets of our clearing-house process (Figure 8.17). However, Schneider's algorithm requires a large number of messages since every process has to acknowledge every broadcast. Finally, Buckley and Silberschatz [1983] present a fair, decentralized algorithm that is a generalization of Bernstein's. It is more efficient than Schneider's but is much more complex. All these algorithms are discussed in Raynal's book [1988b] on distributed algorithms. A more recent paper, Bagrodia [1989], presents yet another algorithm that is simpler and more efficient than Buckley and Silberschatz's.

Exercises

8.1   Using the notation given in Section 8.1, write a server process that implements an array of n general semaphores. The server should be usable by any of an array of m clients.

8.2   (a) Write a program that copies array $a[1:m]$ from process *West* to array $b[1:m]$ of process *East* using an intermediate bounded buffer that holds up to n elements.

(b) Using the axioms and rules in Section 8.2, develop a proof outline that demonstrates the correctness of your program. Show all applications of Satisfaction Rule (8.5).

8.3   (a) Develop a centralized solution to the readers/writers problem using synchronous message passing. In particular, develop a program for a server process that grants permission to reader and writer processes. Also show the programs for the readers and writers.

(b) Using the axioms and rules in Section 8.2, develop a proof outline that demonstrates the correctness of your program. Show all applications of Satisfaction Rule (8.5). Using the method of Exclusion of Configurations (2.25), prove that readers and writers cannot access the database at the same time and that your solution is deadlock-free.

8.4   Given are two processes, A and B. A has a set of integers S, and B has a set of integers T. The two processes are to exchange values one at a time until all elements of S are less than all elements of T.

(a) Develop a program that uses synchronous message passing to solve this problem.

(b) Construct a complete proof outline for your program. Show that each pair of matching communication statements meets the requirements of Satisfaction Rule (8.5). Also show that your proof outline is interference-free (8.9).

8.5 Consider the following specification for a program to find the minimum of a set of integers [Levin & Gries 1981]. Given is an array of processes $Min[1{:}n]$. Initially, each process has one integer value. The processes repeatedly interact, with each one trying to give another the minimum of the set of values it has seen. If a process gives away its minimum, it terminates. Eventually, one process will be left, and it will know the minimum of the original set.

(a) Using synchronous message passing, develop a program to solve this problem.

(b) Develop a complete proof outline that demonstrates the correctness of your solution. Show all applications of Satisfaction Rule (8.5).

8.6 The pipeline algorithm for computing primes in Figure 8.5 terminates in deadlock. Modify the program so that every process terminates normally.

8.7 Figure 8.5 presents one algorithm for checking primality. A different approach is to use a bag of tasks and the replicated worker paradigm (Section 7.9). All odd numbers are put into a shared bag, in ascending order. Each of w worker processes removes the next candidate from the bag and determines if it is prime by dividing it by smaller primes up to the square root of the candidate. Initially, each worker knows that 2 is prime; it puts new primes into a second shared bag. When a worker needs to know about more primes in order to check a candidate, it takes additional primes out of the second bag (and puts them back so that other workers can get them too).

(a) Develop a program to solve this problem using synchronous message passing. Since processes cannot share a global channel, implement the two bags using a server process.

(b) Analyze the performance of your solution. How many communication statements get executed for w workers to check the primality of all odd numbers from 3 to n? Analyze the performance of the pipeline algorithm in Figure 8.5. How many communication statements does it execute to check the primality of all odd numbers from 3 to n?

8.8 It is possible to sort an array of n numbers using a pipeline of n filter processes $Sort[1{:}n]$. Initially, $Sort[1]$ has the entire array. It examines the elements one at a time, keeps the minimum it has seen, and passes the other on to $Sort[2]$. The other $Sort[i]$ receive values one at a time from $Sort[i \ominus 1]$, keep the smallest they have seen, and pass the others on to $Sort[i \oplus 1]$. $Sort[n]$ receives one value, which will be the largest in the original array.

(a) Develop a program to solve this problem using synchronous message passing.

(b) Analyze the performance of your solution. How many messages are sent to sort n values?

8.9   (a) Extend the matrix/vector multiplication network in Figure 8.6 to multiply two $n \times n$ matrices. Show the code executed by each process, including those on the border of the network.

(b) Compare the efficiency of your algorithm with those in Figures 8.9 and 8.10. How many messages are sent in each algorithm?

8.10   Section 8.4 describes a parallel algorithm for sorting n numbers by means of odd/even exchanges.

(a) Develop a complete program for that algorithm. Assume there is an array $P[1:n]$ of processes and that each initially has one number.

(b) Analyze the performance of your solution. How many messages are sent to sort n numbers?

(c) Modify your answer to (a) to use m processes, where m is a factor of n. How many messages are sent in this case?

8.11   Suppose n^2 processes are arranged in a square grid. In particular, each process can communicate only with its neighbors to the left, right, above, and below. (Processes on the corners have only two neighbors; others on the edges of the grid have three neighbors.) Every process has a local integer value v.

Write a heartbeat algorithm to compute the sum of the n^2 values. When your program terminates, each process should know the sum. Show the details for all processes, including those on the borders of the grid.

8.12   (a) Modify the resource allocation program in Figure 8.11 so that clients can request and release more than one unit at a time. Show the new allocator process and the client interface.

(b) Modify the resource allocation program in Figure 8.11 so that the allocator implements a shortest-job-next policy. In particular, when a client requests a unit, it indicates how long it will use the unit. If more than one client wants to acquire a free unit, the allocator gives it to the client that will use it for the shortest length of time.

8.13   Develop a complete proof outline for the centralized dining philosophers program in Figure 8.13. Show all applications of Satisfaction Rule (8.5). Using your proof outline and the method of Exclusion of Configurations (2.25), prove that neighboring philosophers cannot eat at the same time and that the program is deadlock-free.

8.14   Modify the centralized dining philosophers program in Figure 8.13 so that it is fair. In particular, if a philosopher wants to eat, eventually he is able to do so.

8.15   Extend the decentralized dining philosophers program in Figure 8.14 so that it implements distributed mutual exclusion. In particular, at most one philosopher at a time should be able to eat. Your solution should be fair.

8.16   Modify the decentralized dining philosophers program in Figure 8.14 to use asynchronous rather than synchronous message passing. Do not use guarded communication; use only the primitives defined in Section 7.1.

8.17 *The Savings Account Problem.* A savings account is shared by several people. Each person may deposit or withdraw funds from the account. The current balance in the account is the sum of all deposits to date minus the sum of all withdrawals to date. The balance must never become negative.

Using synchronous message passing for communication, develop a server to solve this problem and show the client interface to the server. Clients make two kinds of requests: one to deposit *amount* dollars and one to withdraw *amount* dollars. Assume that *amount* is positive.

8.18 Two kinds of processes, *A*'s and *B*'s, enter a room. An *A* process cannot leave until it meets two *B* processes, and a *B* process cannot leave until it meets one *A* process. Each kind of process leaves the room—without meeting any other processes—once it has met the required number of other processes.

(a) Develop a server process to implement this synchronization. Show the interface of *A* and *B* processes to the server. Use synchronous message passing.

(b) Modify your answer to (a) so that the first of the two *B* processes that meets an *A* process does not leave the room until after the *A* process meets a second *B* process.

8.19 Suppose a computer center has two printers, A and B, that are similar but not identical. Three kinds of client processes use the printers: those that must use A, those that must use B, and those that can use either A or B.

Using synchronous message passing, develop code that each kind of client executes to request and release a printer, and develop a server process to allocate the printers. Your solution should be fair, assuming a client using a printer eventually releases it.

8.20 *The Roller Coaster Problem* [Herman 1989]. Suppose there are *n* passenger processes and one car process. The passengers repeatedly wait to take rides in the car, which can hold C passengers, C < *n*. However, the car can go around the tracks only when it is full.

(a) Develop code for the actions of the passenger and car processes. Use synchronous message passing for communication.

(b) Generalize your answer to (a) to employ *m* car processes, *m* > 1. Since there is only one track, cars cannot pass each other; i.e., they must finish going around the track in the order in which they started. Again, a car can go around the tracks only when it is full.

8.21 Figure 3.20 presents an algorithm for solving LaPlace's equation. That algorithm uses shared variables and barriers.

(a) Develop a heartbeat algorithm for solving LaPlace's equation. Use synchronous message passing for communication. As in Figure 3.20, use one process for each of the n^2 grid points. Your program should terminate when the new value for each grid point is within EPSILON of its previous value.

(b) Modify your answer to (a) to use only m^2 processes, where *m* is a factor of *n*. For example, if *n* is 1024, *m* might be 8 or 16.

8.22 The following region-labeling problem arises in image processing. Given is integer array *image*[1:*n*, 1:*n*]. The value of each entry is the intensity of a pixel. The neighbors of a pixel are the four pixels that surround it, i.e., the elements of *image* to the left, right, above, and below it. Two pixels belong to the same region if they are neighbors and they have the same value. Thus, a region is a maximal set of pixels that are connected and that all have the same value.

The problem is to find all regions and assign every pixel in each region a unique label. In particular, let *label*[1:*n*, 1:*n*] be a second matrix, and assume that the initial value of *label*[i, j] is $n * i + j$. The final value of *label*[i, j] is to be the largest of the initial labels in the region to which pixel [i, j] belongs.

Using synchronous message passing, write a heartbeat algorithm to compute the final values of *label*. Your program should terminate when no *label* changes value on an iteration.

8.23 Using a grid computation to solve the region-labeling problem of the previous exercise requires worst case execution time of $O(n^2)$. This can happen if there is a region that "snakes" around the image. Even for simple images, the grid computation requires $O(n)$ execution time.

The region-labeling problem can be solved as follows in time $O(\log n)$. First, for each pixel, determine whether it is on the boundary of a region. Second, have each boundary pixel determine which neighbors are also on the boundary; in essence, for each region this produces a doubly linked list connecting all pixels that are on the boundary of that region. Third, using the lists, propagate the largest label of any of the boundary pixels to the others that are on the boundary. (The pixel with the largest label for any region will be on its boundary.) Finally, use a parallel prefix computation to propagate the label for each region to pixels in the interior of the region.

Using synchronous message passing, develop a parallel program that implements this algorithm. Analyze its execution time, which should be $O(\log n)$.

8.24 *Stable Marriage Problem.* Let *Man* and *Woman* each be arrays of *n* processes. Each man ranks the women from 1 to *n*, and each woman ranks the men from 1 to *n*. A *pairing* is a one-to-one correspondence of men and women. A pairing is *stable* if, for two men m_1 and m_2 and their paired women w_1 and w_2, both of the following conditions are satisfied:

(1) m_1 ranks w_1 higher than w_2 or w_2 ranks m_2 higher than m_1; and

(2) m_2 ranks w_2 higher than w_1 or w_1 ranks m_1 higher than m_2.

Put differently, a pairing is unstable if a man and woman would both prefer each other to their current pair. A solution to the stable marriage problem is a set of *n* pairings, all of which are stable.

(a) Write a program to solve the stable marriage problem. The processes should communicate using synchronous message passing.

(b) The stable roommates problem is a generalization of the stable marriage problem. In particular, there are 2*n* people. Each person has a ranked list of preferences for a roommate. A solution to the roommates problem is a set of *n* pairings, all of which are stable in the same sense as for the marriage problem.

Using synchronous message passing, write a program to solve the stable roommates problem.

8.25 Given are three processes *F*, *G*, and *H*. Each has a local array of integers; all three arrays are sorted in non-decreasing order. At least one value is in all three arrays. Develop a program in which the three processes interact until each has determined the smallest common value. Use synchronous message passing and give key assertions in each process. Messages should contain only one value at a time.

8.26 *Distributed Pairing* [Finkel et al. 1979]. Given are *n* processes, each corresponding to a node in a connected graph. Each node can communicate only with its neighbors. The problem is for each process to pair itself with one of its neighbors. When the processes finish pairing up, each process should be paired or single, and no two neighboring processes should be single.

Solve this problem using synchronous message passing and guarded communication. Every process is to execute the same algorithm. When the program terminates, every process should have stored in local variable *pair* the index of the neighbor it is paired with; *pair* should be *i* if process *i* is single. Your solution need not be optimal in the sense of minimizing the number of single processes (that makes the problem *very* hard).

8.27 *Spanning Tree Construction* [Finkel et al. 1979]. Given are *n* processes, each corresponding to a node in a connected graph. Each node can communicate only with its neighbors. Recall that a spanning tree of a graph is a tree that includes every node of the graph and a subset of the edges.

Using synchronous message passing, write a program to construct a spanning tree on the fly. Do not first compute the topology. Instead, construct the tree from the ground up by having the processes interact with their neighbors to decide which edges to put in the tree and which to leave out. You may assume processes have unique indexes.

8.28 Figure 7.28 contains a replicated worker program for implementing adaptive quadrature using asynchronous message passing. Rewrite the program using synchronous message passing. Explain your solution and justify your design choices, such as how you implement the bag of tasks.

8.29 Using synchronous message passing, develop a program to multiply two $n \times n$ matrices, *a* and *b*, using the replicated worker paradigm described in Section 7.9. Arrays *a* and *b* are initially local to an administrator process. Use *w* worker processes to compute the inner products and send them to the administrator. Do not use any shared variables. Explain your solution and justify your design choices, such as how you implement the bag of tasks.

8.30 Gaussian elimination with partial pivoting is a method for reducing a non-singular real matrix $m[1\!:\!n, 1\!:\!n]$ to upper-triangular form. It involves iterating across the columns of *m* and zeroing out the elements in the column below the diagonal element $m[d, d]$. This is done by performing the following three steps for each column. First, select a pivot element, which is the element in column *d* having the largest absolute value. Second, swap row *d* and the row containing the pivot element. Finally, for each row r below the new diagonal row, subtract a multiple of row d from row r. The multiple to use for row r is $m[r, d]/m[d, d]$; subtracting this multiple of row d has the effect of setting $m[r, d]$ to zero.

(a) Develop a program that implements the above algorithm. Assign a process to each row, column, or point, and have them communicate with each other using synchronous message passing. Explain and justify your solution strategy.

(b) Solve this problem using a replicated worker algorithm. Use w worker processes and synchronous message passing. Explain your solution and justify your design choices, such as how you implement the bag of tasks.

(c) Compare your answers to (a) and (b). How many messages are sent in each algorithm? How much concurrency does each have?

8.31 Quicksort is a recursive sorting method that partitions an array into smaller pieces and then combines them (see exercise 2.18). Using synchronous message passing, develop a program to implement quicksort using the replicated worker paradigm described in Section 7.9. Array $a[1{:}n]$ of integers is initially local to an administrator process. Use w worker processes to do the sorting. When your program terminates, the result should be stored back in administrator array a. Do not use any shared variables. Explain your solution and justify your design choices, such as how you implement the bag of tasks.

8.32 The 8-queens problem is concerned with placing 8 queens on a chess board in such a way that none can attack another. Using synchronous message passing, develop a program to solve the 8-queens problem using the replicated worker paradigm described in Section 7.9. Have an administrator process put 8 initial queen placements in a bag of tasks. Use w worker processes to extend partial solutions; when a worker finds a complete solution, it should send it to the administrator. The program should compute all solutions and terminate. Do not use any shared variables. Explain your solution and justify your design choices, such as how you implement the bag of tasks.

8.33 Consider the replicated file server problem described in Section 7.9. Develop an implementation of the server processes. Also show the actions a client would take to open, access, and close a file. Assume there are ns copies of the file. Use synchronous message passing for communication.

(a) In your solution, use ns tokens to ensure file consistency. Implement read operations by reading the local copy, and implement write operations by updating all copies. When a client opens a file for reading, its server needs to acquire one token; for writing, the server needs all ns tokens. Your solution should be fair and deadlock-free.

(b) In your solution, use ns read/write locks to ensure file consistency. Implement read operations by reading the local copy, and implement write operations by updating all copies. When a client opens a file for reading, its server needs to obtain the local read lock; for writing, the server needs to obtain all ns write locks. Your solution should be fair and deadlock-free.

(c) In your solution, use weighted voting to ensure file consistency. Use a read weight of *rw* and a write weight of *ww*. Your solution should be fair and deadlock-free.

(d) Compare your answers to (a), (b), and (c). For the different client operations, how many messages do the servers have to exchange in the different solutions? Consider the best case and the worst case.

8.34 Develop a kernel implementation of the synchronous message passing primitives defined in Section 8.1. First develop a single-processor kernel. Then extend your implementation to a distributed kernel having the structure shown in Figure 7.30.

8.35 The protocol in Figure 8.19b handles the general case in which both input and output statements appear in guards.

(a) Suppose a guarded communication statement does not contain output statements, only input statements. Simplify the protocol in Figure 8.19b to handle this case.

(b) Suppose a guarded communication does not contain input statements, only output statements. Simplify the protocol in Figure 8.19b to handle this case.

8.36 Suppose there are n processes $P[1:n]$ and that initially each has one value $a[i]$ of an array of n values. In the following program, each process sends its value to all the others; when the program terminates, every process thus has the entire array of values.

$$P[i: 1..n]::$$
$$\textbf{var}\ a[1:n] : \textbf{int} \quad \# a[i]\ \text{assumed to be initialized}$$
$$\textbf{var}\ sent[1:n] := ([n]\ \text{false}),\ recvd := 0$$
$$\textbf{do}\ (j: 1..n)\ i \neq j\ \textbf{and not}\ sent[j];\ P[j]\ !\ a[i] \rightarrow sent[j] := \text{true}$$
$$[]\ (j: 1..n)\ i \neq j\ \textbf{and}\ recvd < n-1;\ P[j]\ ?\ a[j] \rightarrow recvd := recvd + 1$$
$$\textbf{od}$$

(a) Give a trace of one possible sequence of messages that would be sent if this program is implemented using the centralized clearing house of Figure 8.17. Assume n is 4. Show the messages that would be sent by the processes and by the clearing house, and show the contents at each stage of the clearing house's pending set of templates.

(b) Give a trace of one possible sequence of messages that would be sent if this program is implemented using the decentralized protocols in Figure 8.19. Again assume n is 4. Also assume that $P[i]$ has priority i. Show the messages that would be sent by each process, and show the contents at each stage of the pending set in each process.

(c) Based on your answer to (b), determine bounds on the number of messages n processes would have to send if the above program is implemented using the decentralized protocols in Figure 8.19. What is the smallest possible number? What is the worst case?

8.37 The algorithm in Figure 7.20 gives a fair, decentralized implementation of semaphores. It uses **broadcast**, timestamps, and totally ordered message queues. Using the same kind of algorithm, develop a fair, decentralized implementation of synchronous message passing. Assume both input and output statements can appear in guards. (Hint: Generalize the centralized implementation in Section 8.6 by replicating the clearing house's pending set of templates.)

8.38 Suppose guarded communication statements can contain input statements but not output statements, as in the original CSP proposal. As described in the text (Section 8.6), this makes some programs harder to write but simplifies the implementation of guarded communication. For each of the following, reprogram the algorithm so that it does not use output statements in guards.

(a) The bounded buffer version of *Copy* in Section 8.1. Show the interface of the *East* process.

(b) The broadcast algorithm for matrix multiplication in Figure 8.9.

(c) The heartbeat algorithm for matrix multiplication algorithm in Figure 8.10.

(d) The file server and its clients in Figure 8.12.

(e) The decentralized dining philosophers in Figure 8.14.

8.39 Suppose an output statement does not need to name the destination and an input statement does not need to name the source. These versions of the statements have the forms !*port*(expressions) and ?*port*(variables) [Francez 1982]. They can be used to direct output to an unspecified destination process and to receive input from an source process.

(a) Define the semantics of these statements (in words, not formally). Then extend the rules for matching communication statements (8.2) to handle these forms as well as the other ones in Section 8.1.

(b) Consider all the programs in Chapter 8, and identify which ones would be simpler to program using these general forms of output and input. Show the changes you could make.

(c) Do these general forms of output and input add any power to the notation in Section 8.1? In particular, are there any problems you can solve using them that you cannot solve without them? What if guarded communication statements could not have quantifiers such as $(i: 1..n)$?

(d) Extend the centralized and decentralized implementations in Section 8.6 to support these additional forms of output and input statements. Explain the changes you need to make.

## CHAPTER 9

RPC and Rendezvous

Both asynchronous and synchronous message passing are powerful enough to program all four kinds of processes: filters, clients, servers, and peers. Since information flows through channels in one direction, both are ideally suited to programming filters and peers. However, the two-way information flow between clients and servers has to be programmed with two explicit message exchanges using two different message channels. Moreover, each client needs a different reply channel; this leads to a large number of channels.

This chapter examines two additional programming notations—remote procedure call (RPC) and rendezvous—that are ideally suited to programming client/server interactions. Both combine aspects of monitors and synchronous message passing. As with monitors, a module or process exports operations, and the operations are invoked by a **call** statement. As with the output statement in synchronous message passing, execution of **call** delays the caller. The novelty of RPC and rendezvous is that an operation is a two-way communication channel from the caller to the process that services the call and then back to the caller. In particular, the caller delays until the called operation has been executed to completion and any results have been returned.

The difference between RPC and rendezvous is the way in which invocations of operations are serviced. One approach is to declare a procedure for each operation and to create a new process (at least conceptually) to handle each call. This is called *remote procedure call* since the caller and procedure body may be on different machines. The second approach is to *rendezvous* with an existing process. A rendezvous is serviced by means of an input (or accept) statement that waits for an invocation, processes it, then returns results. (This is sometimes called an extended rendezvous to contrast it with the simple rendezvous between matching communication statements in synchronous message passing.)

This chapter describes representative programming notations for RPC and rendezvous and illustrates their use. As mentioned, each facilitates programming client/server interactions. Each can also be used to program filters and interacting peers. However, we will see that programming filters and peers is often cumbersome since neither RPC nor rendezvous supports asynchronous communication. Fortunately, we can overcome this problem by combining RPC, rendezvous, and asynchronous message passing into a powerful yet quite simple language, which we introduce in Section 9.3.

We illustrate the use of these notations and the tradeoffs between them by means of several examples. Some examine problems we have solved previously and thus facilitate comparison of the various forms of message passing. Other examples solve interesting new problems, including a region labeling problem and a parallel branch-and-bound algorithm for solving the traveling salesman problem. Finally, the last section as usual shows how to implement the different language mechanisms.

9.1 Remote Procedure Call

In Chapter 6, we used two kinds of components in programs: processes and monitors. Monitors encapsulate shared variables; processes communicate and synchronize by calling monitor procedures. Also, the processes and monitors in a program are all assumed to be in the same shared address space.

With RPC, we will use one program component—the module—that contains both processes and procedures. Also, we will allow modules to reside in different address spaces, e.g., on different nodes in a network. Processes within a module can share variables and call procedures declared in that module.* However, a process in one module can communicate with processes in a second module only by calling procedures in the second module.

To distinguish between procedures that are local to a module and those that provide communication channels, a module has two parts. The specification part (spec, for short) contains headers of procedures that can be called from other modules. The body implements these procedures and optionally contains local variables, initialization code, and local procedures and processes. The form of a module is:

---

*Processes in the same address space are often called *lightweight threads*. The term *thread* indicates that each has a distinct thread of execution. The term *lightweight* comes from the fact that relatively little information needs to be saved on a context switch. This is in contrast to heavyweight processes—such as those in UNIX—that have their own address space. Switching context between heavyweight processes requires saving and loading memory management tables as well as registers.

> **module** *Mname*
>   headers of visible procedures
> **body**
>   variable declarations
>   initialization code
>   bodies of visible procedures
>   local procedures and processes
> **end**

We will also employ arrays of modules, which will be declared by appending range information to a module's name.

The header of a visible procedure is specified by an operation declaration, which has the form:

> **op** *opname*(formals) **returns** result

The formals and optional returns part are specified in the same way as in a procedure declaration (see Section 1.1). The body of a visible procedure is contained in a **proc** declaration:

> **proc**(formal identifiers) **returns** result identifier
>   local variables
>   statements
> **end**

A **proc** is thus like a procedure, except the types of the parameters and result do not need to be specified.

As with monitors, a process (or procedure) in one module calls a procedure in another by executing:*

> **call** *Mname.opname*(arguments)

The implementation of an intermodule call is different than for a local call, however, since two modules can be in different address spaces. In particular, a new process services the call. The calling process delays while this server process executes the body of the procedure that implements *opname*. When the server returns from *opname*, it sends result arguments and any return value to the calling process, then the server terminates. After receiving results, the calling process continues. If the calling process and procedure are in the same address space, it is often possible to avoid creating a new process to service a remote call—the calling process can temporarily become

---

*For a local call, the module name can be omitted.

the server and execute the procedure body (see Section 9.7 for details). But in general, a call will be remote, so a server process must be created or allocated from a preexisting pool of available servers.

To help clarify the interaction between the calling process and the server process, the following diagram depicts their execution:

(9.1)

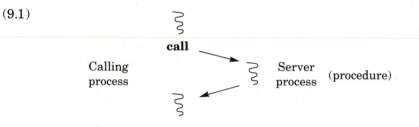

The squiggly lines indicate when a process is executing. When the calling process reaches a **call** statement, it delays while the server process executes the body of the called procedure. After the server returns results, the calling process continues.

Synchronization in Modules

By itself, RPC is purely a communication mechanism. Although a calling process and its server synchronize, the server's only role is to act on the caller's behalf. Conceptually, it is as if the calling process itself were executing the call, and thus the synchronization between the caller and server is implicit.

We also need some way for the processes in a module to synchronize with each other. These include both the server processes that are executing remote calls and other processes declared in the module. As usual, two kinds of synchronization arise: mutual exclusion and condition synchronization.

There are two approaches to providing synchronization in modules, depending on whether processes in the same module execute with mutual exclusion or execute concurrently. If processes execute with exclusion—i.e., at most one at a time is active—then shared variables are automatically protected against concurrent access. However, the processes need some way to program condition synchronization. For this we could use automatic signaling (**await** B) or condition variables, as described in Chapter 6.

If the processes in a module can execute concurrently (at least conceptually), we need mechanisms for programming both mutual exclusion and condition synchronization. In this case, each module is itself a concurrent program, so we could use any of the methods described earlier in the book. For example, we could use semaphores within modules or we could use local monitors. In fact, as we will see later in the chapter, we could also use rendezvous. (We could even use message passing.)

A program containing modules is executed by first executing the initialization code in every module. The initialization code in different modules can be executed concurrently, assuming this code does not make remote calls. Then the processes declared in each module begin executing. If exclusion is implicit, then one process at a time can execute in a module; when it delays or terminates, another can execute. If processes in modules execute concurrently, then all can begin execution at once.

If exclusion is implicit, modules are somewhat simpler to program than if processes can execute concurrently. This is because shared variables do not need to be protected against concurrent access. If a module executes on a single processor, the implementation can also be slightly more efficient if processes execute with exclusion. This is because context switching will occur only at entry, exit, or delay points in procedures or processes, not at arbitrary points where intermediate results of a computation might be in registers.

On the other hand, it is more general to assume that processes can execute concurrently. Concurrent execution can be much more efficient on a shared memory multiprocessor; such processors are increasingly common, and even multiprocessor workstations are becoming available. In addition, with the concurrent execution model we can implement timeslicing to divide execution time among processes and to gain control over runaway processes (i.e., ones in permanent loops). This is not possible with the exclusive execution model unless processes are certain to relinquish the processor in a reasonable amount of time. This is because, in that model, we can switch context only when the executing process reaches an exit or delay point. (If a compiler could tell for sure where non-critical sections of code are, it could put implicit kernel calls into such code sections; in general, however, this is an undecidable problem.)

Because it is more general, we will assume that processes within a module execute concurrently. (Exercise 9.3 explores the use and implementation of the exclusive execution model.) The next three sections present examples showing how to program a time server, distributed file system cache, and merge filter. For now, we use semaphores to program mutual exclusion and condition synchronization; we will add rendezvous and guarded communication in Section 9.3.

A Time Server

Consider the problem of implementing a time server, i.e., a module that provides timing services to client modules. Suppose the time server defines two visible operations: *get_time* and *delay(interval)*. A client process gets the time of day by calling *get_time*. A client calls *delay* to block for *interval* time units. The time server also contains an internal process that continuously starts a hardware timer, then increments the time of day when the timer interrupt occurs.

```
module TimeServer
  op get_time( ) returns time : int
  op delay( interval : int )
body

  var tod := 0        { tod ≥ 0 and increases monotonically }
  var m : sem := 1    { (m = 1) ⇒ ( ∀ napping processes:  tod < waketime) }
  var d[1:n] : sem := ([n] 0)        # private delay semaphores
  var napQ : queue of (waketime, process_id : int)

  proc get_time( ) returns time
      time := tod
  end

  proc delay(interval)        # assume interval > 0
      var waketime : int := tod + interval
      P(m)
      insert (waketime, myid) at appropriate place on napQ
      V(m)
      P(d[myid])        # wait to be awakened
  end

  Clock::  do true →
                start hardware timer; wait for interrupt
                P(m)
                tod := tod + 1
                do tod ≥ smallest waketime on napQ →
                    remove (waketime, id) from napQ; V(d[id])
                od
                V(m)
            od
end
```

Figure 9.1 A time server module.

Figure 9.1 contains the program for the time-server module. The time of day is stored in variable *tod*. Multiple clients can call *get_time* and *delay* at the same time, and hence several processes could be servicing these calls concurrently. Processes that service calls of *get_time* can execute concurrently since they merely read the value of *tod*. However, *delay* and *tick* need to execute with mutual exclusion when they are manipulating *napQ*, the queue of "napping" client processes. (In *delay*, the assignment to *wake_time* need not be in the critical section since *tod* is the only shared variable and it is merely read.) The value of *myid* in *delay* is assumed to be a unique value between 1 and *n*; it is used to indicate the private semaphore on which a client is waiting. After a clock interrupt, the *Timer* executes a loop to check the *napQ*; it signals the appropriate delay semaphore when a delay interval has transpired. A loop is used since more than one process may be waiting for the same wakeup time.

Caches in a Distributed File System

Now consider a simplified version of a problem that arises in most distributed file systems. Suppose application processes are executing on a workstation and that data files are stored on a file server. We will ignore how files are opened and closed and just focus on reading and writing them. When an application process wants to access a file, it calls a *read* or *write* procedure in a local module *FileCache*. Applications read and write arrays of characters (bytes). At times an application will read or write just a few characters; at other times it might read or write thousands.

Files are stored on the file server's disk in blocks, say, of 1024 bytes each. The *FileServer* module manages access to disk blocks. It provides two operations, *readblk* and *writeblk*, for reading and writing entire blocks.

The *FileCache* module maintains a cache of recently read data blocks. When an application asks to read a part of a file, *FileCache* first checks to see if the needed bytes are in its cache. If so, it can quickly satisfy the client's request. If not, it has to call the *readblk* procedure of the *FileServer* module to get the disk block(s) containing the data. (*FileCache* might also do read-ahead if it detects that a file is being accessed sequentially, which is often the case.)

Write requests are handled in a similar manner. When an application calls *write*, the data is stored in a block in the local cache. When a block is full or is needed to satisfy another request, *FileCache* calls the *writeblk* operation in *FileServer* to store the block on disk. (Or *FileCache* might use a write-through strategy, in which case it would call *writeblk* after every write request. Using write-through guarantees that the data is stored on disk when a *write* operation completes, but it slows down the operation.)

Figure 9.2 contains outlines of these modules. Each of course executes on a different machine. Application calls to *FileCache* are in fact local calls, but *FileCache* calls to *FileServer* are remote calls. The *FileCache* module is a server for application processes; the *FileServer* module is a server for several *FileCache* clients, one per workstation.

Assuming that there is one *FileCache* module per application process, *FileCache* does not need internal synchronization since at most one *read* or *write* call could be executing at a time. However, if application processes use the same *FileCache* module—or if the module contains a process that implements read-ahead—then *FileCache* would need to protect access to the shared cache.

```
module FileCache        # located on each diskless workstation
  op read(count : int; res buffer[1:*] : char)
  op write(count : int; buffer[1:*] : char)
body

  var cache of file blocks
  var variables to record file descriptor information
  var semaphores for synchronization of cache access (if needed)

  proc read(count, buffer)
      if needed data is not in cache →
          select cache block to use
          if necessary, call FileServer.writeblk( ... )
          call FileServer.readblk( ... )
      fi
      buffer := appropriate count bytes from cache block
  end
  proc write(count, buffer)
      if appropriate block not in cache →
          select cache block to use
          if necessary, call FileServer.writeblk( ... )
      fi
      cache block := count bytes from buffer
  end

end
```

Figure 9.2 (a). Distributed file system: file cache.

The *FileServer* module requires internal synchronization since it is shared by several *FileCache* modules and since it contains an internal *DiskDriver* process. In particular, servers handling calls to *readblk* and *writeblk* and the *DiskDriver* process need to synchronize with each other to protect access to the cache of disk blocks and to schedule disk access operations. Since Part II contains several examples illustrating how to program this kind of synchronization, Figure 9.2 does not contain the actual synchronization code.

A Sorting Network of Merge Filters

Although RPC provides good support for programming client/server interactions, it does not provide good support for programming filters or interacting peers. This section reexamines the problem of implementing a sorting network using merge filters, which was introduced in Section 7.3. It also introduces one way to support dynamic communication paths by means

```
module FileServer       # located on a file server
   op readblk(fileid, offset : int; res blk[1:1024] : char)
   op writeblk(fileid, offset : int; blk[1:1024] : char)
body
   var cache of disk blocks
   var queue of pending disk access requests
   var semaphores to synchronize access to the cache and queue
   proc readblk(fileid, offset, blk)
      if needed block not in the cache →
            store read request in disk queue
            wait for read operation to be processed
      fi
      blk := appropriate disk block
   end
   proc writeblk(fileid, offset, blk)
      select block from cache
      if necessary store write request in disk queue and
            wait for block to be written to disk
      cache block := blk
   end
   DiskDriver:: do true →
                  wait for a disk access request
                  start a disk operation; wait for interrupt
                  awaken process waiting for this request to complete
               od
end
```

Figure 9.2 (b). Distributed file system: file server.

---

of capabilities, which are pointers to operations in other modules.

Recall that a merge filter consumes two input streams and produces one output stream. Each input stream is assumed to be sorted; the task of the filter is to merge the values in the input streams to produce a sorted output stream. As in Section 7.3, we will assume that the end of an input stream is marked by a sentinel EOS.

One problem with using RPC to program a merge filter is that RPC does not support direct process-to-process communication. Instead, communication between processes has to be programmed indirectly using modules as communication buffers. In short, we need to implement interprocess communication explicitly in our program; it is not provided as a primitive as it is with asynchronous or synchronous message passing. The resulting program will execute approximately as efficiently, but the programmer has to write more.

Another problem we have to address is how to link instances of merge filters to each other. In particular, each filter needs to direct its output stream to one of the input streams of another filter. However, operation names—which provide the communication channels—are distinct identifiers. Thus, each input stream needs to be implemented by a distinct procedure. This makes it difficult to use static naming since a merge filter needs to know the literal name of the operation to call to give an output value to the next filter. A much better approach is to employ dynamic naming, in which each filter is passed a link to the operation to use for output. We will represent dynamic links by *capabilities*, which are essentially pointers to operations.

Figure 9.3 contains a module that implements one merge filter. The first line declares the type of the operations that are used for communication channels; in this case, each has one integer value. Each module provides two operations, *put1* and *put2*, that other modules call to produce the input streams. Each also has a third operation, *initial*, that a main module (not shown) would call to initialize capability *out*. For example, the main routine could give *Merge[i]* a capability for operation *put2* of *Merge[j]* by executing:

call *Merge[i].initial(Merge[j].put2)*

We assume that each module is initialized before any of them starts producing output.

The rest of the module is similar to the *Merge* process shown in Figure 7.2. Variables *in1* and *in2* correspond to the channels of the same name in Figure 7.2, and process *M* mimics the actions of the *Merge* process in Figure 7.2. However, *M* uses **call** to append the next smallest value to the appropriate output operation *out*. Also, process *M* uses semaphore operations to receive the next value from the appropriate input stream. Within the module, the implicit server processes that handle calls of *put1* and *put2* are producers; process *M* is a consumer. These processes synchronize in the same way as in Figure 4.9.

Formal Semantics

The semantics of modules and RPC are a straightforward combination of those of processes, procedures, and semaphores. Ignoring the procedures for a minute, the rest of a module contains processes, shared variables, and semaphores. Thus, to prove properties of a module, we would use the techniques of Chapter 4. As usual, it is important to identify and employ invariants to reduce or avoid interference. In this case, they would be called module invariants rather than global invariants since each module would have its own invariant specifying the stable state of its variables.

```
optype put(value : int)      # type of operations for data streams
module Merge[1:n]
  op put1 : put, put2 : put, initial(c : cap put)
body
  var in1, in2 : int      # input values from streams 1 and 2
  var out : cap put       # capability for output operation
  var empty1 : sem := 1, full1 : sem := 0
  var empty2 : sem := 1, full2 : sem := 0

  proc initial(c)      # called first to get output channel
      out := c
  end

  proc put1(v1)      # called to produce next value for stream 1
      P(empty1); in1 := v1; V(full1)
  end

  proc put2(v2)      # called to produce next value for stream 2
      P(empty2); in2 := v2; V(full2)
  end

  M::  P(full1); P(full2)
       do in1 ≠ EOS and in2 ≠ EOS →
           if in1 ≤ in2 → call out(in1); V(empty1); P(full1)
           [] in2 ≤ in1 → call out(in2); V(empty2); P(full2)
           fi
       []  in1 ≠ EOS and in2 = EOS →
           call out(in1); V(empty1); P(full1)
       []  in1 = EOS and in2 ≠ EOS →
           call out(in2); V(empty2); P(full2)
       od
       call out(EOS)
end
```

Figure 9.3. Merge-sort filters using RPC.

Procedures add some complexity but not much. A remote procedure call—like a local procedure call—passes value arguments to the procedure body, delays the caller until the procedure body has been executed, and then retrieves result arguments. The fact that there might be an implicit server process that executes the procedure body is transparent to the caller. Consequently, if parameters are passed by copying, the procedure call inference rule (6.10) still applies. And of course, it does not make sense to pass reference parameters between modules that are in different address spaces since the pointer would not have the same interpretation.

If at most one process at a time could be active in a module, then the internal semantics of a module would be like that of a monitor. In particular, the initialization code should make the module invariant true. Then each section of code between entry, exit, and delay points could assume that the module invariant was true at the start of execution of the section of code, as long as each section ensured that the module invariant was true at the end.

When processes in a module can execute concurrently, as we have assumed, synchronization has to be used to avoid interference within a module. In addition to considering potential interference between processes declared in each module, we have to worry about interference with implicit server processes. And there may be more than one instance of each procedure body that is active at a time.

With procedures in monitors, we could assume that the monitor invariant was true in the precondition of the procedure body. However, we cannot assume that a module invariant is true when a server process starts executing a procedure body. All such a process knows about are the arguments and local variables of the procedure. The shared variables in the module could be in any state. However, by using semaphores to implement mutual exclusion and condition synchronization, we can relate the local states of processes to the state of shared variables. For example, Figure 9.1 contains an assertion to specify that a process should not nap longer than necessary:

$$(m = 1) \Rightarrow (\forall \text{ napping processes: } tod < waketime)$$

Semaphore m provides mutually exclusive access to the queue of napping processes. Chapter 4 contains additional examples.

9.2 Rendezvous

As noted, RPC by itself provides only an intermodule communication mechanism. Within a module, we still need to program synchronization. And we often need to write other processes to manipulate the data communicated by means of RPC.

Rendezvous combines the actions of servicing a call with other processing of the information conveyed by the call. With rendezvous, a process exports operations that can be called by others. In this section, a process declaration will have the following form:

> *pname*:: operation declarations
> variable declarations
> statements

Operation declarations have the same form as in modules; they specify the headers of operations serviced by the process. We will also employ arrays of operations, which as usual are indicated by including range information in the declaration.

As with RPC, a process invokes an operation by means of a call statement, which in this case names another process and an operation in that process. But in contrast to RPC, an operation is serviced by the one process that exports it. Hence, operations are serviced one at a time rather than concurrently.

If a process exports operation *op*, it can rendezvous with a caller of *op* by executing:

$$\textbf{in } op(\text{formals}) \rightarrow S \textbf{ ni}$$

We will call the parts between the keywords a *guarded operation*. The guard names an operation and its formal parameters; the body contains a statement list *S*. The scope of the formals is the entire guarded operation.

This kind of input statement is more powerful than the input statement of synchronous message passing. In particular, **in** delays the servicing process until there is at least one pending call of *op*. It then selects the oldest pending call, copies the value arguments into the value formals, executes *S*, and finally returns the result parameters to the caller. At that point, both the process executing **in** and the process that called *op* can continue execution.

The following diagram depicts the relation between the calling process and the server process executing **in.** Again, squiggly lines indicate when a process is executing.

(9.2)

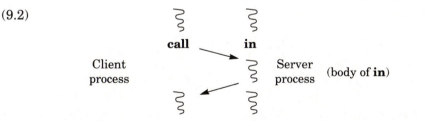

Just as with RPC, the calling process delays when it reaches a **call** statement; it continues after the server process executes the called operation. However, with rendezvous the server is an active process that executes both before and after servicing a remote invocation. As indicated above, the server will also delay if it reaches the **in** statement and there are no pending invocations. The reader might find it useful to compare this diagram with the corresponding one for RPC (9.1).

The basic form of **in** above services a single operation. As we saw in Chapter 8, guarded communication is very useful since it allows a process to choose non-deterministically from among a set of alternatives. To combine guarded communication with rendezvous, we will generalize the **in** statement as follows:

$$\textbf{in } op_1 \textbf{ and } B_1 \textbf{ by } e_1 \rightarrow S_1$$
$$[] \ ...$$
$$[] \ op_n \textbf{ and } B_n \textbf{ by } e_n \rightarrow S_n$$
$$\textbf{ni}$$

Each guarded operation again names an operation and its formals, and it contains a statement list. However, the guard can also contain two optional parts. The second part is a synchronization expression (**and** B_i); if omitted, B_i is assumed to be true. The third part of a guard is a scheduling expression (**by** e_i); its effect is described below.*

A guard in a guarded operation succeeds when (1) the operation has been called and (2) the corresponding synchronization expression is true. Since the scope of the formal parameters is the entire guarded operation, the synchronization expression can depend on the values of the formals and hence on the values of the arguments in a call. Thus, one call of an operation might make the guard succeed, but another call of the same operation might not.

Execution of **in** delays until some guard succeeds. As usual, if more than one guard succeeds, one of them is chosen non-deterministically. If there is no scheduling expression, the **in** statement services the oldest invocation that makes the guard succeed. In particular, the arguments of that call are copied into the formal parameters, and then the corresponding statement list is executed. When the statement list terminates, result formals and the return value (if any) are sent back to the process that called the operation. At that point, both the **call** and **in** statements terminate.

A scheduling expression is used to alter the default, oldest-invocation-first order of servicing invocations. In particular, if there is more than one invocation that makes a particular guard succeed, then the invocation that minimizes the value of the scheduling expression is serviced first. As with a synchronization expression, a scheduling expression can refer to formals in the operation and hence to the actual values in a **call.** In fact, if a scheduling

---

* The Ada programming language (Section 10.3) supports rendezvous by means of the **accept** statement and supports guarded communication by means of the **select** statement. The **accept** statement is like the basic form of **in**, but the **select** statement is less powerful than the general form of **in**. This is because **select** cannot reference arguments to operations or contain scheduling expressions. The ramifications of these differences are discussed later in this chapter and also in Section 10.3.

Buffer:: **op** *deposit*(*data* : *T*), *fetch*(**var** *result* : *T*)
      var *buf*[1:*n*] : *T*
      var *front* := 1, *rear* := 1, *count* := 0
      do true → { loop invariant *BUFFER*; see Figure 6.1 }
          in *deposit*(*data*) **and** *count* < *n* →
              buf[*rear*] := *data*
              rear := *rear* **mod** *n* + 1; *count* := *count* + 1
        [] *fetch*(*result*) **and** *count* > 0 →
              result := *buf*[*front*]
              front := *front* **mod** *n* + 1; *count* := *count* − 1
        ni
      od

Figure 9.4. Rendezvous implementation of a bounded buffer.

---

expression refers only to local variables, it will have no effect since its value
will not change during execution of an input statement.

    Both synchronization expressions and scheduling expressions—as defined
above—are useful, as we shall see. However, they are not fundamentally tied
to the use of rendezvous. They could also be used with asynchronous and
synchronous message passing. For example, we could have allowed **receive**
statements to look at their parameters.

Client/Server Examples

This section presents a series of client/server examples that illustrate the use
of input statements. For now, we assume that a program contains independent processes that do not share variables. In Section 9.3, we will combine
rendezvous with modules and RPC.

    Consider again the problem of implementing a bounded buffer. In
particular, we want a process that exports two operations: *deposit* and *fetch*.
Internally, the buffer process contains a buffer of up to *n* data items. A
producer process deposits an item into the buffer by calling the *deposit*
operation; a consumer process retrieves an item by calling the *fetch* operation.
As usual, *deposit* must delay if there are already *n* items in the buffer, and
fetch must delay until there is at least one item in the buffer.

    Figure 9.4 contains a server process that implements a bounded buffer.
This *Buffer* process declares local variables to represent the buffer, then
repeatedly executes an input statement. On each iteration, *Buffer* waits for a
call of *deposit* or *fetch*. The synchronization expressions in the guards ensure
that calls of *deposit* and *fetch* delay as necessary.

```
Waiter::  op getforks(i : int), relforks(i : int)
          var eating[1:5] := ([5] false)
          { EAT: ( ∀ i: 1 ≤ i ≤ 5: eating[i] ⇒ ¬(eating[i ⊖ 1] ∨ eating[i ⊕ 1]) }
          do true →
              in getforks(i) and
                      not (eating[i ⊖ 1] or eating[i ⊕ 1]) → eating[i] := true
              [] relforks(i) → eating[i] := false
              ni
          od
Phil[i: 1..5]::  do true →
                      call Waiter.getforks(i)
                      eat
                      call Waiter.relforks(i)
                      think
                 od
```

Figure 9.5. Centralized dining philosophers using rendezvous.

The reader should compare the *Buffer* process with the monitor in Figure 6.1. The interface to client processes is the same—and the effects of calling *deposit* and *fetch* are the same—but the implementation is different. In particular, the procedure bodies in the monitor implementation become the statement lists in an input statement. Also, condition synchronization is expressed using boolean synchronization expressions rather than condition variables. This is more like the way condition synchronization is programmed using CCRs (see Figure 5.5). Finally, the monitor invariant *BUFFER* becomes the loop invariant in the *Buffer* process.

As a second example, Figure 9.5 contains a server process that implements a centralized solution to the dining philosophers problem. The structure of *Waiter* is identical to that of *Buffer*. In this case, a call of *getforks* can be serviced when neither neighbor is eating; a call of *relforks* can always be serviced. A philosopher passes its index *i* to the *Waiter*, which uses this in the synchronization expression in the guard for *getforks*.

The reader should compare the program in Figure 9.5 with the quite similar one using synchronous message passing in Figure 8.13. The main difference between the two programs is that the above *Waiter* has single *getforks* and *relforks* operations, whereas the *Waiter* in Figure 8.13 uses arrays of operations. With synchronous message passing, as we defined it, arrays of operations were required since that was the only way a philosopher could identify itself to the waiter. We could have used arrays of operations in Figure 9.5, but we did not need to since an input statement can examine its parameters in synchronization expressions. Being able to examine param-

TimeServer:: **op** *get_time*( ) **returns** *time* : **int**
          op *delay*(*waketime* : **int**)
          op *tick*( )   # called by clock interrupt handler
          var *tod* := 0
          do true →
                  in *get_time*( ) **returns** time → *time* := *tod*
                  [] *delay*(*waketime*) **and** *waketime* ≤ *tod* → **skip**
                  [] *tick*( ) → *tod* := *tod* + 1; restart clock
                ni
          od

Figure 9.6. A time server using rendezvous.

SJN_Allocator:: **op** *request*(*time* : **int**), *release*( )
          var *free* := true
          do true →
                  in *request*(*time*) **and** *free* **by** *time* → *free* := false
                  [] *release*( ) → *free* := true
                ni
          od

Figure 9.7. Shortest-job-next allocator using rendezvous.

---

eters provides a powerful synchronization tool since we can synchronize based on an arbitrary value. The next example shows this.

Figure 9.6 contains a time-server process similar in functionality to the time server module in Figure 9.1. The process exports *get_time* and *delay* operations for clients; it also exports a *tick* operation that is assumed to be called by the clock interrupt handler. In Figure 9.6, the argument to *delay* is the actual time that a client process wants to be awakened. This is a slightly different client interface than in Figure 9.1; it avoids the need for the server to maintain a queue of napping processes. The napping processes are simply the ones whose wakeup times have not yet been reached.

The final example uses a scheduling expression as well as a synchronization expression. Figure 9.7 contains a shortest-job-next allocator process. The client interface in this case is the same as that in the monitor in Figure 6.2. But, as in the time-server process, this allocator does not need to maintain internal queues. Instead it merely delays accepting calls of *request* until the resource is free, and then it accepts the call with the smallest argument for *time*.

A Sorting Network of Merge Filters

Consider again the problem of implementing a sorting network using merge filters. Here we want to solve the problem using rendezvous. There are two approaches we could take. The first mimics asynchronous message passing, the second synchronous message passing.

With asynchronous message passing, channels are message buffers. There is no implicit buffering with rendezvous. But we can program a network of filters by using two kinds of processes: one to implement the filters and one to implement communication buffers. In particular, place a buffer process—implemented as in Figure 9.4—between each pair of filters. To receive new input, a filter process would call the buffer between it and the previous filter in a network; to send output along, it would call the buffer between it and the next filter in the network.

Networks of filters are implemented in essentially this way in UNIX, with buffers being provided by what UNIX calls pipes. A filter receives input by reading from an input pipe (or file); it sends results to an output pipe (or file). Pipes are not actually implemented by processes—they are more like monitors—but filters use them in the same way.

With the first approach, a filter process makes calls both to receive input and to send output. We can also program filters using a second approach, in which a filter uses an input statement to receive input and a **call** statement to send output. In this case, filters communicate directly with each other in a manner analogous to using synchronous message passing.

Figure 9.8 contains an array of filters for merge sorting, programmed this time using rendezvous. As in Figure 9.3, each filter receives values from operations *put1* and *put2* and sends results to operation *out*. Also, we have again used dynamic naming to give each process, through operation *initial*, a capability for the output stream it should use. Other than these similarities, however, the two programs are quite different. This is because rendezvous supports direct process-to-process communication, whereas RPC does not. This makes rendezvous easier to use for programming filter processes.

Except for the syntax of communication statements and the use of dynamic naming, the program in Figure 9.8 is identical to what could be used with synchronous message passing. In particular, the **call** statements are analogous to output commands (! statements), and the input statement are analogous to input commands (? statements). This is because the **call** statements merely transfer their arguments to another process, and the input statements merely assign the arguments to local variables.

The program in Figure 9.8 is also nearly identical to the merge filter in Figure 7.2, which uses asynchronous message passing. Again, the communication statements are programmed differently, but they are in exactly the same places. However, **call** statements delay, whereas **send** statements do not. Thus, process execution is much more tightly coupled with rendezvous

```
optype put(value : int)     # type of operations for data streams
Merge[1:n]::  op put1 : put, put2 : put, initial(c : cap put)
              var in1, in2 : int
              var out : cap put     # capability for output stream
              in initial(c) → out := c ni     # get output capability
              in put1(v) → in1 := v ni     # get two input values
              in put2(v) → in2 := v ni
              do in1 ≠ EOS and in2 ≠ EOS →
                   if in1 ≤ in2 → call out(in1)
                                   in put1(v) → in1 := v ni
                   [] in2 ≤ in1 → call out(in2)
                                   in put2(v) → in2 := v ni
                   fi
              [] in1 ≠ EOS and in2 = EOS →
                   call out(in1)
                   in put1(v) → in1 := v ni
              [] in1 = EOS and in2 ≠ EOS →
                   call out(in2)
                   in put2(v) → in2 := v ni
              od
              call out(EOS)
end
```

Figure 9.8. Merge sort filters using rendezvous.

---

or synchronous message passing than with asynchronous message passing.

Formal Semantics

The merge filter in Figure 9.8 illustrates how similar rendezvous is to synchronous message passing when information flows in one direction. It is also similar when a call returns results. In this case, a call is essentially the composition of an output command to send value arguments followed by an input command to receive result arguments. Similarly, an input statement is very similar to an input command to acquire value formals followed by an output command to return result formals, with an intervening statement list.

In this section we develop axioms and inference rules for rendezvous by simulating **call** and **in** using synchronous message passing. Since a **call** statement is much like a conventional procedure call, there is also similarity to the proof rules for procedures (Section 6.2). And since an input statement has aspects in common with an **if** statement—guarded operations, one of which is executed—there is also similarity to the alternative rule (1.14). We do not, however, consider the effects of scheduling expressions; they affect the order in which invocations are serviced but do not cause state changes (since we assume expression evaluation has no side-effects).

Suppose we have an operation declared as follows:

(9.3)   **op** *op*(**val** $x : T1$; **var** $y : T2$; **res** $z : T3$)

As in Section 6.2, x and y are value formals since they acquire values on a call; similarly, y and z are results formals, whose values are returned when a call completes. The Ti are some data types. For simplicity, we will assume that every operation has exactly three formal parameters, as above. The proof rules we develop below can readily be generalized to handle the general case and to include functions with return clauses.

A call to an operation serviced by an input statment is different from a call to a monitor procedure or to a remote procedure. In particular, with rendezvous, a call has to wait for the process that services the call to reach an appropriate input statement; value arguments are not transmitted until this occurs. On the other hand, with monitors and RPC, a call always gets started, and it is as if the calling process is executing the procedure body. The caller may delay due to synchronization in the called monitor or module, but the value arguments get transmitted as soon as a call is executed.

As noted above, the effect of a rendezvous call is essentially the composition of an output command followed by an input command. Given operations declared as in (9.3), **call** statements have the form:

call $op(a, b, c)$

As in Section 6.2, a and b are the value arguments and b and c are the result arguments. Using synchronous message passing, we can simulate such a call as follows:

(9.4)   *Server* ! *op*(a, b); *Server* ? *res*(b, c)

Here, *op* is an input port in the process *Server* that declares *op*, and *res* is a result port in the calling process *Caller*.

Recall the axioms for output (8.3) and input (8.4) commands. Each allows anything to appear in the postcondition since each in isolation can block forever. The same is true above; a **call** statement might never get even as far as transferring its value arguments to the process that services the operation. Thus we will permit a "miracle" to appear in the postcondition of the axiom for a rendezvous call.

(9.5)   **Rendezvous Call Axiom**: $\{ U \}$ **call** $op(a, b, c)$ $\{ W \}$

As with asynchronous and synchronous message passing, we will later define a satisfaction rule to ensure that uses of this axiom are sound.

Now consider servicing an operation. First, assume we have an input statement with one guarded operation and no synchronization expression:

$$\textbf{in } op(x, y, z) \rightarrow S \textbf{ ni}$$

Assuming that a call of op is simulated as in (9.4), this input statement can be simulated using synchronous message passing as follows:

$$Caller ? op(x, y); S; Caller ! res(y, z)$$

Since x, y, and z represent the formal parameters of the input statement, they cannot be accessed except within S.

Let P be the precondition of the input statement, and let Q be the post-condition. Then we have the following proof outline for the simulation of **in**:

(9.6) $\{ P \}$ $Caller ? op(x, y)$ $\{ R \}$ S $\{ T \}$ $Caller ! res(y, z)$ $\{ Q \}$

From the input and output command axioms, the two intermediate assertions R and T could be arbitrary ones. However, the local state of a process does not change while it is waiting for an invocation of op, nor does it change while the process sends results back to the caller. The satisfaction rule for rendezvous will ensure that P is related to R and that T is related to Q.

In general, an input statement will contain several guarded operations. In this case, it is like the **if** statement of Chapter 8, assuming that only input commands appear in guards. One difference is that the synchronization expressions in input statements can reference formals, and hence input values, whereas those in Chapter 8 did not. However, we can model this as in a conventional **if** statement: when the body of a guarded operation begins execution, synchronization expression B is true. The second difference is that **in** delays until a guard succeeds, whereas an **if** statement with guarded input commands terminates if all guards fail. From these observations and (9.6), we have the following inference rule for input statements.

(9.7)   **Input Rule:**
$$\frac{\{ R_i \wedge B_i \} \ S_i \ \{ T_i \}, 1 \leq i \leq n}{\begin{array}{l} \{ P \} \ \textbf{in } op_1(x_1, y_1, z_1) \textbf{ and } B_1 \rightarrow S_1 \\ \quad [] \ \ldots \\ \quad [] \ op_{n1}(x_n, y_n, z_n) \textbf{ and } B_n \rightarrow S_n \\ \textbf{ni} \ \{ Q \} \end{array}}$$

The rendezvous call axiom allows anything to be asserted after a **call** statement. The input rule imposes no constraint on the relations between P

and R_i or between T_i and Q. The role of the satisfaction rule for rendezvous is to ensure that uses of the axiom and inference rule are valid.

The simulations of rendezvous call and of input statements in terms of synchronous message passing reveal the satisfaction obligations. Taking an instance of the rendezvous call axiom (9.5) and simulating it as in (9.4), we have the following proof outline for the caller:

(9.8) $\{\,U\,\}$ *Server* $!\,op(a, b)$ $\{\,V\,\}$ *Server* $?\,res(b, c)$ $\{\,W\,\}$

Predicates U and W come from the axiom. Predicate V specifies the intermediate state in the simulation. Its purpose is to carry along properties of the local state of the caller.

From the hypotheses of the input rule and the simulation of an input statement as in (9.6), we have the following proof outline to capture the effect of executing an operation guarded by boolean expression B:

(9.9) $\{\,P\,\}$ *Caller* $?\,op(x, y)$ $\{\,R \wedge B\,\}$ S $\{\,T\,\}$ *Caller* $!\,res(y, z)$ $\{\,Q\,\}$

There are two matching pairs of communication statements in (9.8) and (9.9). Both must obey the requirements of the satisfaction rule for synchronous communication (8.5). In addition, since predicate V in (9.8) would not actually appear in the proof of the caller—and since all that happens between states U and V is assignment to the formals in (9.9)—we require that U implies that V is true after substitution of the value arguments for the value formals. Putting these three requirements together, we have the satisfaction rule for rendezvous.

(9.10)   **Satisfaction Rule for Rendezvous.** Let *call* be a **call** statement with precondition T and postcondition V as in the rendezvous call axiom. Let *in* be a guarded operation in an input statement with assertions P, R, B, T, and Q as in the input rule. Finally, let V be a predicate such that $U \Rightarrow V_{a,\,b}^{x,\,y}$. For every pair $(call, in)$ that name the same operation, show that:

$$(U \wedge P) \Rightarrow (R \wedge B)_{a,\,b}^{x,\,y} \ \wedge \ (V \wedge T) \Rightarrow (W \wedge Q)_{y,\,z}^{b,\,c}$$

A proof of a program employing rendezvous will often need to contain auxiliary variables. As always, these have to be used in such a way that they do not affect the flow of control in the program. The restrictions on the use of auxiliary variables are analogous to those in (8.8) for synchronous message passing.

Since auxiliary variables are typically used to record global states, their presence also introduces the possibility of interference. The requirements for interference freedom are also analogous to those for synchronous message

Buffer:: **op** *deposit*(**val** v : **int**), *fetch*(**res** r : **int**)
   var *buf* : **int**
   do true → **in** *deposit*(v) → *buf* := v **ni**
            in *fetch*(r) → r := *buf* **ni**
   od

Producer:: **var** p := 1, $a[1{:}n]$: **int** := initial values
      do $p \leq n$ → **call** *deposit*($a[p]$); p := $p + 1$ **od**

Consumer:: **var** c := 1, $b[1{:}n]$: **int**
      do $c \leq n$ → **call** *fetch*($b[c]$); c := $c + 1$ **od**

Figure 9.9. Producer/consumer program.

---

passing (8.9). However, there is one important difference: The body of an input statement cannot interfere with assertions in the proof of the process that called the operation that is being serviced. This is because that process is blocked while the body of the input statement is executed. The body of an input statement could, however, interfere with parallel assertions in a process other than the caller.

An Example Proof

A simple example will illustrate the use of the proof rules for rendezvous. Figure 9.9 contains a producer/consumer program. The producer process repeatedly deposits elements of array a in a buffer; the consumer process repeatedly fetches elements from the buffer and stores them in array b. The buffer process implements a single-slot buffer by alternately accepting a *deposit* call, then a *fetch* call. When the program terminates, a has been copied to b.

To prove formally that b is identical to a when *Consumer* terminates, we have to relate the states of the processes to each other. In particular, we need to know what the producer deposits in the buffer and hence what the consumer fetches. When the *Producer* call of *deposit* returns, *buf* contains $a[p]$. But then *Producer* increments p, so *buf* contains $a[p - 1]$. In order to be able to assert in *Buffer* exactly what *buf* contains, we need to use an auxiliary variable *in* to count the number of times *Producer* has called *deposit*. Using *in*, when the input statement that accepts *deposit* returns, we can assert that *buf* contains $a[in]$.

For similar reasons, we also need an auxiliary variable *out* to count the number of times *Consumer* has called *fetch*. We use two separate auxiliary variables rather than one in order to avoid interference. In particular, *deposit* increments *in*, and hence changes to *in* cannot interfere with

Producer assertions. Similarly, *fetch* increments *out*, so changes to *out* cannot interfere with *Consumer* assertions.

A proof outline for the producer/consumer program appears in Figure 9.10. Within each process, the postconditions of assignment statements clearly follow from their preconditions. Thus, to show that the proof outline is valid, we have to show that the call and input statments meet the requirements of satisfaction rule (9.10). We also have to show that the proofs are interference-free.

First consider the call of *deposit* in *Producer* and the corresponding input statement in *Buffer*. From the proof outlines, the parts of the first conjunct in satisfaction rule (9.10) are:

$$U:\ p = in + 1$$
$$P:\ in = out$$
$$R:\ in = out \wedge v = a[p] \wedge p = in + 1$$

Since the input statement that services *deposit* does not contain a synchronization expression, *B* is implicitly true. From (9.10), we have to show that the following predicate is true:

$$(p = in + 1 \wedge in = out) \Rightarrow (in = out \wedge v = a[p] \wedge p = in + 1)_{a[p]}^{v}$$

This is trivially true since the antecedent and consequent are the same.

For the call of *deposit*, the parts of the second conjunct in satisfaction rule (9.10) are:

$$V:\ true$$
$$W:\ p = in$$
$$T:\ in = out + 1 \wedge buf = a[in] \wedge p = in$$
$$Q:\ in = out + 1 \wedge buf = a[in]$$

We use *true* for *V* since in *Producer* we only care about the relation between p and *in*, which is affected by the call itself. From (9.10), we have to show that $T \Rightarrow (W \wedge Q)$. Again, this is trivially true since the predicates are the same. (There is no substitution in this case since *deposit* does not have any result parameters.)

The call of *fetch* in *Consumer* and the other input statement in *Buffer* also meet the satisfaction requirements. We leave it to the reader to verify this. One difference from the above is that *fetch* has a result parameter but no value parameter. The second difference is that we use *CONS* for *V* in (9.10) in order to carry the local state of the *Consumer* from the precondition to the postcondition of the call to *fetch*.

var $in := 0, out := 0$ # auxiliary variables

Buffer:: **op** *deposit*(**val** v : **int**), *fetch*(**res** r : **int**)
        var buf : **int**
        do true $\rightarrow$ { $in = out$ }
                    in *deposit*(v) $\rightarrow$ { $in = out \wedge v = a[p] \wedge p = in + 1$ }
                            $buf := v; in := in + 1$
                            { $in = out + 1 \wedge buf = a[in] \wedge p = in$ }
                ni
                { $in = out + 1 \wedge buf = a[in]$ }
                in *fetch*(r) $\rightarrow$ { $in = out + 1 \wedge buf = a[in] \wedge c = out + 1$ }
                            $r := buf; out := out + 1$
                            { $in = out \wedge r = a[out] \wedge c = out$ }
                ni
        od
Producer:: **var** $p := 1, a[1{:}n]$: **int** := initial values
        do $p \leq n \rightarrow$ { $p = in + 1$ }
                    call *deposit*($a[p]$)
                    { $p = in$ }
                    $p := p + 1$
        od
Consumer:: **var** $c := 1, b[1{:}n]$: **int**
        { *CONS*: ($\forall i$: $1 \leq i < c$: $b[i] = a[i]$) $\wedge c \leq n + 1$ }
        do $c \leq n \rightarrow$ { *CONS* $\wedge c = out + 1$ }
                    call *fetch*($b[c]$)
                    { *CONS* $\wedge b[c] = a[c] \wedge c = out$ }
                    $c := c + 1$
        od
        { *CONS* $\wedge c = n + 1$ } { $b[1{:}n] = a[1{:}n]$ }

Figure 9.10. Producer/consumer proof outline.

Finally, we have to show that the proof outline in Figure 9.10 is inter-ference-free. *Producer* does not interfere with *Consumer* since a is not changed and the other variables in the two processes are disjoint. *Producer* and *Buffer* do not interfere with each other since (1) the only assertions about p in *Buffer* are within the body of *deposit*, and (2) *in* is changed only within the body of *deposit*. Since *Producer* is the only process that calls *deposit*, the *Producer* cannot be executing when *Buffer* is executing the body of *deposit*. *Consumer* and *Buffer* do not interfere for similar reasons. Hence the proof outline is also interference-free.

Safety and Liveness Properties

Again, the method of Exclusion of Configurations (2.25) can be used to prove that processes are not simultaneously in the same state. For example, we could add assertions to the dining philosophers solution in Figure 9.5 to record when each philosopher is eating. These, together with global invariant *EAT*, could be used to conclude that neighboring philosophers cannot eat at the same time.

To prove absence of deadlock, we have to consider all possible ways in which processes could block. With rendezvous, there are two blocking statements: **call** and **in.** If there is no synchronization expression in a guarded operation, an invocation of that operation can always be serviced. This is the case, for example, in the producer/consumer program in Figures 9.9 and 9.10. That program does not deadlock since the producer and the consumer both call *deposit* and *fetch* the same number of times. (Upon termination, the *Buffer* process is blocked, but that is not a deadlock state since servers typically execute forever.) However, if either the producer or consumer executed different numbers of calls, deadlock would result.

When a guarded operation contains a synchronization expression, that expression must of course be true for the guard to succeed. For example, in the first guard in the bounded buffer in Figure 9.4, an invocation of *deposit* can succeed only if *count* < *n*. Again, however, deadlock will not occur if *deposit* and *fetch* are called the same number of times in a program.

Liveness properties such as absence of starvation depend as usual on the underlying scheduling policy. If an input statement contains one guarded operation and no synchronization expression—as in the producer/consumer program in Figure 9.9—then an unconditionally fair scheduling policy is sufficient to ensure progress in the absence of deadlock. Either a **call** statement or an input statement will delay until the other is executed, but as soon as both have been executed the guard will succeed.

If an input statement contains a single guarded operation with a synchronization expression—and if the synchronization expression for a specific invocation remains true if it becomes true—then a weakly fair scheduling policy is sufficient to ensure that the invocation gets serviced. This is because we assume that invocations are serviced in first-come, first-served order in the absence of a scheduling expression. In general, however, a strongly fair scheduling policy is required. For example, in the time-server example in Figure 9.6, a strongly fair policy is required to ensure that invocations of the different operations are eventually serviced.

On the other hand, no scheduling policy can guarantee progress if an input statement contains a scheduling expression, as in the shortest-job-next allocator in Figure 9.7. In that case, a call of *request* could delay forever if there is a continual stream of higher priority requests. This is similar to what can happen with priority wait statements in monitors. Scheduling expressions are very useful, but one has to consider whether theoretically possible starvation is acceptable.

9.3 A Multiple Primitives Notation

With both RPC and rendezvous, a process initiates communication by executing a **call** statement, and execution of **call** block the caller. This makes it difficult to program algorithms in which peer processes exchange information. For example, in a heartbeat algorithm, neighboring processes repeatedly exchange information and then update their local state. This is easy to program with asynchronous message passing since we can have each process first execute **send** then **receive.** We can also program the exchange using synchronous message passing—although not as easily or efficiently—by using guarded communication with both input and output commands in guards.

To program an exchange with RPC, a process in one module would first call remote procedures in neighboring modules to store its information in the other modules. The process would then use local synchronization to delay until information from all neighbors has been received. This indirect approach is needed since, as noted before, processes cannot communicate directly using RPC.

The situation is no better with rendezvous. Even though processes can communicate directly, a process cannot simultaneously execute **call** and an input statement. To exchange information, neighbor processes thus either have to execute asymmetric algorithms or have to employ helper processes. In the first case, we would have some processes first execute **call** and then **in** and have the other processes execute these statements in the other order. In the second case, a regular process would first call its neighbors' helpers and then accept input from its own helper. (We could have allowed **call** statements in guards of input statements, but no language has done so since this is difficult to implement and inefficient.)

The remainder of this section presents a programming notation that combines RPC, rendezvous, and asynchronous message passing into one coherent package. This multiple primitives notation provides a great deal of expressive power since it combines the advantages of the three component notations and provides additional power as well. It will be used in the examples in the remainder of this chapter.

Invoking and Servicing Operations

As with RPC, we will structure programs as collections of modules. Each module has the same form as before in Section 9.1:

```
        module Mname
            declarations of visible operations
        body
            variable declarations
            initialization code
            procedure declarations
            process declarations
        end
```

Visible operations are specified by **op** declarations, which have the form used earlier in this chapter. A module can also contain local operations. Again, we will also employ arrays of modules. A visible operation can be invoked by a process or procedure in any module; however, it can be serviced only by the module that declares it. A local operation can be invoked and service only by the module that declares it.

Now we will allow an operation to be invoked by synchronous **call** or asynchronous **send.** The invocation statements have the forms:

> **call** *Mname.op*(arguments)
> **send** *Mname.op*(arguments)

As with RPC and rendezvous, a **call** statement terminates when the operation has been serviced and result arguments have been returned. As with asynchronous message passing, a send statement terminates as soon as the arguments have been evaluated. If an operation returns results, it can be invoked within an expression; in this case the **call** keyword is omitted. (If an operation has result parameters and is invoked by **send**—or if a function is invoked by **send** or is not in an expression—any return values are ignored.)

In the multiple primitives notation, we will also allow an operation to be serviced either by a procedure (**proc**) or by rendezvous (**in** statements). The choice is up to the programmer of the module that declares the operation. It depends upon whether the programmer wants each invocation to be serviced by a different process or whether it is more appropriate to rendezvous with an existing process. Later examples will discuss this tradeoff.

When an operation is serviced by a **proc**, a new process services the invocation. If the operation was called, the effect is the same as with RPC. If the operation was invoked by **send**, the effect is dynamic process creation since the invoker proceeds asynchronously with the process that services the invocation. In both cases there is never a queue of pending invocations since each can be serviced immediately.

The other way to service operations is by using input statements, which have the form given in Section 9.2. In this case, there is a queue of pending invocations associated with each operation; access to the queue is atomic. An operation is selected for service according to the semantics of input statements. If such an operation is called, the effect is a rendezvous since the caller delays. If such an operation is invoked by **send**, the effect is similar to asynchronous message passing since the sender continues.

In summary, there are two ways to invoke an operation—**call** and **send**—and two ways to service an invocation—**proc** and **in.** These four combinations have the following effects:

(9.11) *invocation*   *service*   *effect*

call	**proc**	procedure call
call	**in**	rendezvous
send	**proc**	dynamic process creation
send	**in**	asynchronous message passing

A procedure call will be local if the caller and **proc** are in the same module; otherwise it will be remote. An operation cannot be serviced by both a **proc** and input statements since the meaning would be unclear. (Is the operation serviced immediately or is it queued?) However, an operation can be serviced by more than one input statement, and these can be in more than one process in the module that declares the operation. In this case, the processes share the queue of pending invocations (and they access it atomically).

With monitors and asynchronous message passing, we defined an **empty** primitive to determine whether a condition variable or message channel was empty. In this chapter we will use a similar but slightly different primitive. In particular, if *op* is an operation name, then ?*op* is a function that returns the number of pending invocations of *op*.* This is often useful in input statements. For example, the following gives priority to *op1* over *op2*:

$$\textbf{in } op1(...) \rightarrow S1 \;\; [] \;\; op2(...) \textbf{ and } ?op1 = 0 \rightarrow S2 \textbf{ ni}$$

The synchronization expression in the second guarded operation allows *op2* to be selected only if there are no invocations of *op1* at the time ?*op1* is evaluated.

Examples

Three small, closely related examples will illustrate various ways operations can be invoked and serviced. First consider the implementation of a queue shown in Figure 9.11. When *deposit* is invoked, a new item is stored in *buf*. If *deposit* is called, the invoker waits; if *deposit* is invoked by **send**, the invoker continues before the item is actually stored (in which case the

---

*Although the notation is similar, the ?*op* function is not to be confused with the input command of synchronous message passing.

```
module Queue
   op deposit(item : T), fetch(res item : T)
body
   var buf[1:n] : T, front := 1, rear := 1, count := 0
   proc deposit(item)
      if count < n → buf[rear] := item
                     rear := rear mod n + 1; count := count + 1
      [] count = n → take actions appropriate for overflow
      fi
   end
   proc fetch(item)
      if count > 0 → item := buf[front]
                     front := front mod n + 1;  count := count − 1
      [] count = 0 →  take actions appropriate for underflow
      fi
   end
end
```

Figure 9.11. A sequential queue.

---

invoker had better be sure overflow will not occur). When *fetch* is invoked, an item is removed from *buf*; in this case, *fetch* needs to be invoked by a **call** statement, or the invoker will not receive the result.

The *Queue* module is suitable for use by a single process in another module. It cannot be shared by more than one process since the implementation does not employ any synchronization. In particular, interference could result if the operations are invoked concurrently. If we need a "synchronized queue" instead, we can change the *Queue* module into one that implements a bounded buffer.

Figure 9.12 gives a bounded buffer module. The visible operations are the same as those in *Queue*. However, the operations are serviced by an input statement in a single process, in the same way as in Figure 9.4. Thus, invocations are serviced one at a time. Also, synchronization expressions are used to delay servicing *deposit* until there is room in *buf* and to delay servicing *fetch* until *buf* contains an item. Again, *fetch* should be invoked by a **call** statement, but now it is perfectly safe to invoke *deposit* by a send statement (unless there are so many pending invocations of *deposit* that all kernel buffers become used up). This is because *deposit* does not return results.

The modules in Figures 9.11 and 9.12 illustrate two different ways to implement the same interface. The choice is up to the programmer and

```
module BoundedBuffer
  op deposit(item : T), fetch(res item : T)
body
  var buf[1:n] : T, front := 1, rear := 1, count := 0
  Buffer:: do true →
              in deposit(item) and count < n →
                  buf[rear] := item; rear := rear mod n + 1
                  count := count + 1
              [] fetch(item) and count > 0 →
                  item := buf[front]; front := front mod n + 1
                  count := count - 1
              ni
          od
end
```

Figure 9.12. A bounded buffer (synchronized queue).

---

depends on how the queue will be used. In fact, there is also another way to implement a bounded buffer that illustrates yet another combination of the various ways to invoke and service operations in the multiple primitives notation.

Consider the following input statement, which waits for an invocation, then assigns the parameters to variables in the process or module that executes the statement:

$$\textbf{in } op(f1, ..., fn) \rightarrow v1 := f1; ...; vn := fn \textbf{ ni}$$

This form of **in** is identical to the **receive** statement of Chapter 7:

$$\textbf{receive } op(v1, ..., vn)$$

Since **receive** is just an abbreviation for a special case of **in**, we will use **receive** when that is how we want to service an invocation.

Now consider an operation that has no arguments and that is invoked by **send** and serviced by **receive** (or the equivalent **in** statement). In this case, the operation is equivalent to a semaphore, with **send** being a **V**, and **receive** being a **P**. The initial value of the semaphore is zero; its current value is the number of "null" messages that have been sent to the operation, minus the number that have been received.

Figure 9.13 gives a second implementation of *BoundedBuffer* that uses semaphores for synchronization. The *deposit* and *fetch* operations are

```
module BoundedBuffer
  op deposit(item : T), fetch(res item : T)
body

  var buf[1:n] : T, front := 1, rear := 1
  # local operations used to simulate semaphores as in Figure 4.12
  op empty( ), full( ), mutexD( ), mutexF( )
  send mutexD( ); send mutexF( )        # initialize the semaphores
  fa i := 1 to n → send empty( ) fa

  proc deposit(item)
    receive empty( ); receive mutexD( )
    buf[rear] := item; rear := rear mod n + 1
    send mutexD( ); send full( )
  end
  proc fetch(item)
    receive full( ); receive mutexF( )
    item := buf[front]; front := front mod n + 1
    send mutexF( ); send empty( )
  end
end
```

Figure 9.13. A bounded buffer using semaphore operations.

serviced by procedures as in Figure 9.11. Hence, there could be more than one instance of these procedures active at a time. However, here we use semaphore operations to implement the synchronization required by a bounded buffer. The semaphores implement mutual exclusion and condition synchronization as in Figure 4.12. The structure of this module is like that of a monitor (see Figure 6.1), but synchronization is implemented using semaphores rather than implicit exclusion and explicit condition variables.

The two implementations of a bounded buffer illustrate an important parallel between synchronization expressions in input statements and explicit synchronization in procedures. They are often used for the same purposes. Also, since synchronization expressions in input statements can depend on arguments of pending invocations, the two synchronization techniques are equally powerful. However, unless one needs the concurrency provided by multiple invocations of procedures, it is more efficient to have clients rendezvous with a single process than to have have each of their server processes synchronize with each other. This is because process creation takes time, and processes consume more space than message queues.

Formal Semantics

Since the multiple primitives notation combines RPC, rendezvous, and asynchronous message passing, the formal semantics of the notation combine those of the components. As shown in (9.11), there are four combinations of ways to invoke and service operations. To reduce the number of combinations that have to be considered, we can first model remote procedures as follows. Replace each **op** that is serviced by a **proc** by an array of operations, one per invoking process. Then replace each **proc** by an array of server processes, again, one per process that invokes the operation. Each server executes a permanent loop with an input statement that services invocations of one element of the array of operations. Thus, each invoker of a **proc** has its own private server.

By modeling procedures as above, all invocations are serviced by means of input statements. Thus, if an operation is called, the semantics are specified by the Call Axiom (9.5), Input Rule (9.7), and Satisfaction Rule for Rendezvous (9.10) given in Section 9.2.

If an operation is invoked by **send**, we can use auxiliary variables as in Section 7.2 to represent the queue of pending invocations. A **send** invocation would append a message to this queue as in Send Axiom (7.2). And, every input statement that services the operation would have to obey a satisfaction rule similar to the Satisfaction Rule for Asynchronous Message Passing (7.4). In particular, the arguments in any invocation queued by **send** would have to ensure that the precondition of the body of the guarded operation in an input statement be true. Since **send** is asynchronous, the only satisfaction obligation for the postcondition is that the postcondition of the body of a guarded operation imply the post-condition of the input statement.

9.4 Clients and Servers

With the multiple primitives notation, we can use asynchronous message passing to program filters almost exactly as in Chapter 7. The main difference is cosmetic: Processes are encapsulated by modules. Since the notation includes both RPC and rendezvous, we can also program clients and servers as in either Section 9.1 or 9.2. But the new notation provides additional flexibility, which we now illustrate. First we develop another solution to the readers/writers problem (4.5); unlike previous ones, this solution encapsulates access to the database. Then we give an implementation of replicated files, which were discussed in Section 7.9. Finally, we describe two additional ways to program a probe/echo algorithm for solving the network topology problem introduced in Section 7.5.

Readers/Writers Revisited: Encapsulated Access

Recall that, in the readers/writers problem, two kinds of processes share a database (or file). Readers examine the database and may do so concurrently; writers modify the database, so they need exclusive access. In earlier solutions—such as the monitor solution in Figure 6.4—processes had to be trusted to follow the protocol of requesting permission before accessing the database, then releasing control when finished. A monitor cannot encapsulate the access itself since only one process at a time can execute within a monitor, and hence readers cannot execute concurrently.

Figure 9.14 presents a solution in which a single module encapsulates access to the database. Client processes simply call the *read* or *write* operation; the module hides how these calls are synchronized. The module uses both RPC and rendezvous. The *read* operation is implemented by a **proc**, so multiple readers can execute concurrently. On the other hand, the *write* operation is implemented by rendezvous with the *Writer* process; this ensures that writes are serviced one at a time. The module also contains two local operations, *startread* and *endread*, which are used to ensure that *read*s and *write*s are mutually exclusive. The *Writer* process also services these, so it can keep track of the number of active readers and delay *write* as necessary.

The solution in Figure 9.14 gives priority to readers. Using the ? function, we can change the input statement as follows to give priority to writers:

> **in** *startread*( ) **and** ?*write* = 0 → *nr* := *nr* + 1
> [] *endread*( ) → *nr* := *nr* − 1
> [] *write*(values) **and** *nr* = 0 → write the database
> **ni**

This delays service to invocations of *startread* whenever there are pending invocations of *write*. We leave developing a fair solution to the reader (see exercise 9.11).

The program in Figure 9.14 "locks" the entire database for readers or for a writer. This is usually satisfactory for small data files. However, database transactions typically need to lock individual records as they proceed. This is because a transaction does not know in advance what records it will access; e.g., it has to examine some record before it knows what to examine next. To implement this kind of dynamic locking, we could employ multiple modules, one per database record. However, this would not encapsulate access to the database. Alternatively, we could employ a more elaborate and finer-grained locking scheme within the *ReadersWriters* module. For example, each *read* and *write* could acquire the locks it needs. Database management systems typically use the latter approach.

```
    module ReadersWriters
       op read(res results), write(new values)
    body

       op startread( ), endread( )
       var storage for the database or file transfer buffers

       proc read(results)
          call startread( )
          read the database
          send endread( )
       end
    Writer::  var nr := 0
              do true →
                 in startread( ) → nr := nr + 1
                 [] endread( ) → nr := nr − 1
                 [] write(values) and nr = 0 → write the database
                 ni
              od
```

Figure 9.14. Readers and writers with encapsulated database.

Replicated Files

In Section 7.9, we described the problem of implementing replicated files. Assume again that there are n copies of a file and that they are to be kept consistent. In Section 7.9, we described ways to use tokens to ensure consistency. Here we present a solution that uses locking.

Suppose there are n server modules and any number of client processes. Each server module provides access to one copy of the file. Each client interacts with one of the server modules, e.g., one executing on the same processor as the client.

When a client wants to access the file, it calls its server's *open* operation and indicates whether the file will be read or written. After opening a file, a client accesses the file by calling its server's *read* or *write* operations. If the file was opened for reading, only *read* may be used; otherwise both *read* and *write* may be used. When a client finishes accessing the file, it calls its server's *close* operation.

The file servers interact to ensure that copies of the file are kept consistent and that at most one client at a time is permitted to write into the file. Each instance of *RepFile* has a local lock manager process that implements a solution to the readers/writers problem. When a client opens a file for reading, the *open* operation calls the *startread* operation of the local lock manager. However, when a client opens a file for writing, the *open* operation

```
module RepFile[myid: 1..n]
   type mode = (READ, WRITE)
   op open(m : mode), close( ),                    # client operations
       read(res results), write(values)
   op remote_write(values), startwrite( ), endwrite( )   # server operations
body
   op startread( ), endread( )        # local operations
   var file buffers, use : mode

   proc open(m)
      if m = READ → call startread()    # get local read lock
                     use := READ
      [] m = WRITE → # get write locks for all copies of the file
                     fa i := 1 to n → call RepFile[i].startwrite( ) af
                     use := WRITE
      fi
   end

   proc close( )
      if use = READ → # release local read lock
                     send endread( )
      [] use = WRITE → # release all write locks
                     co i := 1 to n → send RepFile[i].endwrite( ) oc
      fi
   end
```

Figure 9.15 (a). Replicated files using one lock per copy.

---

calls the *startwrite* operation of all *n* lock managers.

Figure 9.15 contains the replicated file module. There are several interesting aspects of the implementation.

- Each *RepFile* module exports two sets of operations: ones called by its clients and others called by other *RepFile* modules. The *open*, *close*, and access operations are implemented by procedures, although only *read* has to be to permit concurrency. The locking operations are implemented by rendezvous with the lock manager.

- Each module keeps track of the current access mode, i.e., the last way in which the file was opened. It uses *use* to ensure that the file is not written to if it was opened for reading and to determine what actions to take when the file is closed. However, a module does not protect itself from a client that accesses a file without first opening it. This can be solved using dynamic naming or authentication.

```
      proc read(results)
         read from local copy of file and return results
      end
      proc write(values)
         if use = READ → error: file was not opened for writing fi
         write values into local copy of file
         # concurrently update all remote copies
         co i := 1 to n st i ≠ myid → call RepFile[i].remote_write(values) oc
      end
      proc remote_write(values)        # called by other file servers
         write values into local copy of file
      end
Lock::  var nr := 0, nw := 0
         do true →      { RW: (nr = 0 ∨ nw = 0) ∧ nw ≤ 1 }
            in startread( ) and nw = 0 → nr := nr + 1
            [] endread( ) → nr := nr − 1
            [] startwrite( ) and nr = 0 → nw := nw + 1
            [] endwrite( ) → nw := nw − 1
            ni
         od
end RepFile
```

Figure 9.15 (b). Replicated files using one lock per copy.

- Within the *write* procedure, a module first updates its local copy of the file and then concurrently updates every remote copy. An alternative approach is to update only the local copy in *write* and then to update all remote copies when the file is closed. This is analogous to using a write-back cache policy as opposed to a write-through policy.

- Clients acquire write permission from lock processes one at a time and in the same order. This avoids the deadlock that could result if two clients acquired write permission in different orders. However, clients release write permission concurrently and use **send** rather than **call** since there is no need to delay in this case.

- The lock manager process implements the classic solution to the readers/writers problem. It is an active monitor, so its loop invariant is the same as the monitor invariant in Figure 6.4.

```
module Node[p: 1..n]
   op probe(parent : int) returns topology[1:n, 1:n] : bool
body

   var N[1:n] : bool    # initialized so N[q] true if q is a neighbor of p
   var seen := false, mutex : sem := 1

   proc probe(parent) returns topology
      var newtop[1:n, 1:n] : bool
      var first : bool
      P(mutex); first := not seen; seen := true; V(mutex)
      if not first → topology := ∅       # have already seen probe
      [] first → topology := ([n∗n] false)   # initialize topology
                 topology[p, 1:n] := N         # add neighbor set
                 # probe all other neighbors and gather their topologies
                 co q := 1 to n st N[q] and q ≠ parent →
                     newtop := Node[q].probe(p)
                     topology := topology or newtop
          oc
      fi
   end
end
```

Figure 9.16. Network topology using RPC.

Network Topology Using Probe/Echo Algorithms

As a final client/server example, consider again the network topology problem
introduced in Section 7.5. Recall that in this problem there is a connected
network of nodes, each of which knows about links to its neighbors. The goal
is for one node to determine the topology of the entire network. As before, we
assume that there is at most one topology computation going on at a time and
that nodes and links do not fail during the computation.

To solve the network topology problem using a sequential algorithm, we
could employ depth-first search and backtracking. Such an algorithm could
be programmed directly using RPC. We can also readily adapt the sequential
algorithm to send probes in parallel.

Figure 9.16 contains a concurrent probe/echo algorithm programmed
using RPC. The computation is initiated by having some process (not shown)
call the *probe* operation of one of the nodes. That node in turn calls the *probe*
operation of all its neighbors, and so on. Since a network will usually contain
cycles, a node will receive probes from—and send probes to—every neighbor.
It passes the first probe on. But, as in Section 7.6, a node immediately
answers subsequent probes by returning an empty topology. Since the *probe*

```
module Node[p: 1..n]
   op probe(parent : int)
   op echo(topology : [1:n, 1:n] bool)
   op initiate(res topology : [1:n, 1:n] : bool)
body
   op finalecho(topology : [1:n, 1:n] bool)

   proc initiate(topology)
      send probe(p)
      receive finalecho(topology)
   end

Worker::  var N[1:n] : bool
          # initialize N so N[q] is true if q is a neighbor of p
          var localtop[1:n, 1:n] : bool := ([n * n] false)
          localtop[p, 1:n] := N      # put neighbor set in localtop
          do true →
            in probe(parent) →   # first probe
                var need_echo : int := number of neighbors − 1
                # send probe on to to all other neighbors
                fa q := 1 to n st N[q] and q ≠ parent →
                    send probe[q](p)
                af
                do need_echo > 0 →
                    # receive echoes or probes from neighbors
                    in probe(sender) → send Node[sender].echo(∅)
                    [] echo(newtop) → localtop := localtop or newtop
                                      need_echo := need_echo − 1
                    ni
                od
                if parent = p → send finalecho(localtop)
                [] parent ≠ p → send Node[parent].echo(localtop)
                fi
            ni
          od
end
```

Figure 9.17. Network topology using multiple primitives.

operation of a node might be called concurrently by more than one other node, a shared variable is needed to record whether the probe was the first one the node has seen. This variable has to be examined and altered in a critical section, so a shared semaphore is also needed for mutual exclusion.

Using the multiple primitives notation introduced in Section 9.3, we can also solve the network topology problem using the algorithm given in Figure 7.19. However, we can package that algorithm more cleanly by exploiting the encapsulation mechanism of modules and the guarded communication of input statements. Figure 9.17 contains a solution using these primitives.

When a process wants to initiate the computation, it calls the *initiate* procedure of some node. That procedure sends a probe to the local worker process, then waits for an echo from that process. As in the solution using asynchronous message passing, after receiving the first probe, a worker sends probes to all its other neighbors. It then waits to receive echoes from each of its probes. But while waiting for echoes, a worker will also receive probes from its other neighbors. Here we can use an input statement with two guarded operations, one for *probe* messages, the other for *echo* messages. This avoids the need for the message *kind* field and **if** statement that were required in Figure 7.19.

The solution in Figure 9.17 uses a nested input statement. In particular, the outer input statement receives the first probe, and the nested one receives echoes and other probes. This is not necessary in this problem, but it avoids having to save the identity of the sender of the first probe in a local variable.

Although we can readily solve the network topology problem using RPC, asynchronous message passing, or multiple primitives, the problem is difficult to solve using rendezvous alone (unless we were to allow **call** in guards). This is because both **call** and **in** are blocking primitives. To program a probe/echo algorithm directly, a node needs to be able both to initiate probes and respond to them. This requires some form of asynchrony since probes and echoes can arrive in any order. RPC supports asynchrony since multiple instances of a **proc** can execute concurrently. Asynchronous message passing and the combined notation both provide an asynchronous invocation primitive, i.e., **send.** Rendezvous alone does not provide either of these directly. Instead, one has to program asynchronous interaction explicitly by means of buffer processes, one per node (see exercise 9.7). This doubles the number of processes and hence leads to a much less compact solution. The solution would also be much less efficient since it requires more context switching and more message copying.

9.5 Parallel Algorithms

In this section, we develop parallel algorithms for two new problems. The first, region labeling, arises in image processing. We solve the problem using a heartbeat algorithm. The second example is the classic traveling salesman problem. This we solve using replicated worker processes. The solutions employ the multiple primitives notation introduced in Section 9.3.

Region Labeling: A Heartbeat Algorithm

An image consists of a matrix of pixels. Each pixel has a value that represents its light intensity. A common image-processing problem is to identify regions consisting of neighboring pixels having the same value. This is called the region-labeling problem since the goal is to identify and assign a unique label to each region.

To make the problem more precise, assume that the pixel values are stored in matrix *image*[1:n, 1:n]. The neighbors of a pixel are the four pixels that surround it. (Pixels on the borders of the image have fewer neighbors, of course.) Two pixels belong to the same region if they are neighbors and they have the same value. Thus, a region is a maximal set of pixels that are connected and have the same value.

The label of each pixel is stored in a second matrix *label*[1:n, 1:n]. Initially, each point is given a unique label, e.g., its coordinates $n * i + j$. The final value of *label*[i, j] is to be the largest of the initial labels in the region to which pixel [i, j] belongs.

The natural way to solve this problem is by means of an iterative algorithm. On each iteration, we examine every pixel and its neighbors. If the pixel and a neighbor have the same value, then we set its label to the maximum of its current label and that of its neighbor. We can do this in parallel for every pixel, assuming we store new labels in a separate matrix.

The algorithm terminates if no label changes during an iteration. If regions are fairly compact, the algorithm will terminate after about $O(n)$ iterations. However, in the worst case, $O(n^2)$ iterations will be required since there could be a region that "snakes" around the image.

Although n^2 parallel tasks could be employed in this problem, each is too small to be efficient. Moreover, n is apt to be large (e.g., 1024), so the number of tasks will typically be much, much larger than the number of available processors. Suppose that we have m^2 processors and that n is a multiple of m. Then a good way to solve the region-labeling problem is to partition the image into m^2 blocks and to employ one process for each block.

Each process computes the labels for the pixels in its block. If *image* and *label* are stored in shared memory, then each process can execute a parallel iterative algorithm and use barrier synchronization at the end of each iteration, as described in Section 3.4. However, here we will assume that processes cannot share variables. Hence, *image* and *label* need to be distributed among the processes.

Since regions can span block boundaries, each process needs to interact with its neighbors on each iteration. This leads to a heartbeat algorithm. In particular, on each iteration a process exchanges the labels of pixels on the boundary of its block with its four neighboring processes. Then it computes new labels.

```
module Block[i: 1..m, j: 1..m]
    const p := n/m
    op north(border[1:p] : int), south(border[1:p] : int)
    op east(border[1:p] : int), west(border[1:p] : int)
    op answer(change : bool)
body
    B::  var image[0 : p + 1, 0 : p + 1] : int    # initialized with pixel values
         var label[0 : p + 1, 0 : p + 1] : int    # initialized with unique labels
         var change := true
         do change →
              exchange labels of borders with neighbors
              change := false
              update label, setting change true if any label changes
              send Coordinator.result(change)
              receive answer(change)
         od
end
```

Figure 9.18 (a). Region labeling: main computation.

Figure 9.18 (a) contains an outline of the modules that handle each block. Each module calculates labels for its portion of the image. Each also stores the values and labels of pixels on the boundaries of neighboring blocks of the image. Neighboring modules use the operations *north*, *south*, *east*, and *west* to exchange boundary labels. We leave it to the reader to fill in the details of how *Block* uses these operations and computes new labels.

The *Block* module also exports an operation, *answer*, that is used to determine when to terminate. In the heartbeat algorithm for the network topology problem (Figure 7.14), a process could terminate when it received no new topology information on an iteration. Here, however, a process cannot determine by itself when to terminate. Even if there is no local change on an iteration, some label in another block could have changed, and that pixel could belong to a region that spans more than one block.

One way to detect global termination is to have each block execute the worst-case number of iterations. For this problem, however, that is much more than would typically be required. Consequently, we use a coordinator module to detect termination. This module is shown in Figure 9.18 (b). At the end of each iteration, every block tells the coordinator if any of its labels changed value. The coordinator collects these messages and then informs every block whether there was any change. If so, the blocks execute another iteration; if not, they terminate.

```
module Coordinator
    op result(localchange : bool)
body
    Check:: var change : bool := true
            do change →
                change := false
                # see if there has been a change in any block
                fa i := 1 to m, j := 1 to m →
                    in result(ch) → change := change or ch ni
                af
                # broadcast result to every block
                co i := 1 to m, j := 1 to m →
                    send Partition[i, j].answer(change)
                oc
            od
end
```

Figure 9.18 (b). Region labeling: termination detection.

Using a central coordinator adds $2m^2$ overhead messages to each round. As programmed in Figure 9.18, the single coordinator collects all *result* messages, and it collects them one at a time. Although this many messages have to be collected, we could employ multiple coordinator processes to collect them in parallel. For example, we could use m coordinators—one per row, say—to collect results for each row, and then use one more coordinator to collect the results from the other coordinators (see exercise 9.17).

The main computation in Figure 9.18 (a) uses asynchronous message passing to communicate with the coordinator. If the coordinator could respond to invocations in a different order than it receives them, the processes in the main computation could simply execute:

$$change := Coordinator.result(change)$$

They would not have to execute **send** and then **receive**. Some languages support this functionality. For example, SR (Section 10.4) has a **forward** statement, which takes an invocation that is being serviced and forwards it to another operation without replying to it yet. The caller unblocks when the invocation of the second operation is serviced (unless it too uses **forward**).

Using **forward**, we could reprogram the *Coordinator* module in Figure 9.18 (b) as follows. First, change operation *result* to a function that returns a boolean value. Second, declare a local operation *hold* that also returns a boolean value; invocations of *result* will be examined and then forwarded to *hold.* Third, reprogram the body of the loop in *Check* as follows:

> *change* := false
> **fa** $i := 1$ **to** $m, j := 1$ **to** $m \to$ # acquire results
>   **in** *result(ch)* $\to$ *change* := *change* **or** *ch*; **forward** *hold( )* **ni**
> **af**
> **fa** $i := 1$ **to** $m, j := 1$ **to** $m \to$ # respond to calls of *result*
>   **in** *hold( )* **returns** *answer* $\to$ *answer* := *change* **ni**
> **af**

The **forward** statement defers replying to invocations of *result* by saving them in local operation *hold*. After *Check* has received all m^2 invocations of *result*, it then services the m^2 invocations that have been forwarded to *hold*. The second loop thus returns the value of *change* to all the region-labeling processes.

The Traveling Salesman Problem: Replicated Workers

This section presents a parallel algorithm for solving the classic traveling salesman problem. The solution employs the replicated workers paradigm introduced in Section 7.9. It illustrates one way to implement branch-and-bound algorithms, which arise in many combinatorial search problems.

Given are n cities and a symmetric matrix $dist[1{:}n, 1{:}n]$. The value in $dist[i, j]$ is the distance from city i to city j, e.g., the airline miles. We assume there is a path from each city to every other and that $dist[i, i]$ is 0 for all i.

A salesman starts in city 1 and wishes to visit every city exactly once, ending back in city 1. The problem is to determine a path that minimizes the distance the salesman must travel. The result is to be stored in a vector *bestpath*$[1{:}n]$. The value of *bestpath* is to be a permutation of integers 1 to n such that the sum of the distances between adjacent pairs of cities—plus $dist[path[n], 1]$—is minimized.

For n cities, there are $(n - 1)!$ different paths starting and ending in city 1. Unless n is small, this is, of course, a very large number. Thus, we need to look for ways to cut down on the amount of computation that has to be performed and for ways to use parallelism to speed up the computation.

Suppose *bestlength* is the length of the best path that has been found so far. Then any partial or full path whose length is at least as long as *bestlength* cannot be a solution. Thus, as we enumerate paths we can discard those that are too long.

Since paths are independent, we could evaluate all of them in parallel. But since there are so many, this will result in far more concurrency than we could efficiently employ on most machines. Hence we will employ the technique of replicated workers that share a bag of chores. In this case, each chore will be a partial path and the length of that path. Initially, the bag

```
const dist[1:n, 1:n] := distances between pairs of cities
module Manager
    op bag(path[1:n], hops, length : int)      # partial tours
    op getjob(res path[1:n], hops, length : int)
    op newmin(path[1:n], length : int)
body
    var bestpath[1:n] : int, bestlength := MAXINT    # best tour so far

    M:: # generate first set of partial tours and put them into bag
        fa i := 2 to n → send bag( (1, i, [n – 2] 0), 2, dist[1,i]) af
        do true →
            in getjob(path, hops, length) →
                    # get another job from bag and return it to caller
                    receive bag(path, hops, length)
            [] newmin(path, length) by length →
                    if length < bestlength →
                        bestpath := path; bestlength := length
                        co i := 1 to w →    # broadcast new minimum
                            send Worker[i].updatemin(length)
                        oc
                    fi
            ni
        od
end
```

Figure 9.19 (a). Traveling salesman problem: manager module.

---

contains $n - 1$ chores, representing the $n - 1$ different tours starting at city 1. Each worker repeatedly takes a chore from the bag and extends the path with a city that has not yet been visited. If the path is not yet complete and the length is less than that of the best complete path found so far, the worker puts the new path and length in the bag of chores. If the path is complete and better than the best one found so far, we update *bestpath* and *bestlength*. If the path is too long, the worker discards it.

Figure 9.19 contains the solution programmed using the multiple primitives notation. The solution employs m worker modules and a manager module. The manager implements the bag. This is necessary here since operations cannot be global; instead, only the module that declares an operation can service it. Workers can send new chores to *bag*, but only the manager can receive from *bag*. It does so when a worker calls the *getjob* operation. (For maximum concurrency, m should be less than n; if m is larger, the manager should initialize the bag with more than m chores.)

```
module Worker[1:m]
  op updatemin(length : int)
body
  W::  var path[1:n], hops, length : int
       var shortest : int := MAXINT   # shortest tour this worker knows about
       do true →
           # first see if there is a better global minimum length tour
           do ?updatemin > 0 →      # is there a better shortest tour?
               receive updatemin(shortest); shortest := min(shortest, length)
           od
           # next get a job and process it
           call Manager.getjob(path, hops, length)
           extend path by 1 city that hasn't yet been visited
           update hops and length
           if hops < n and length < shortest →
               # put partial tour back into bag for further processing
               send Manager.bag(path, hops, length)
           [] hops = n and length < shortest →
               # account for distance back to starting city
               length := length + dist[path[n], 1]
               # if this tour is possibly the best, let manager know
               if length < shortest →      # tell manager
                   send Manager.newmin(path, length)
                   shortest := length
               fi
           fi
       od
  end
```

Figure 9.19 (b). Traveling salesman problem: worker modules.

The manager also maintains the values of *bestpath* and *shortest*. This is necessary since modules cannot share variables. (The distance matrix is constant, so it can be replicated in every module.)

When a worker finds a path that might be the best, it invokes the manager's *newmin* operation. Since workers execute concurrently, two might at about the same time find paths that both think are the best so far. Thus, when manager accepts a *newmin* invocation, it checks to see if it is indeed better. If it is better, the manager updates *bestpath* and *shortest* and then broadcasts the new value for *shortest* to all the workers. The manager accepts invocations of *newmin* in increasing order of *length* so that it accepts the shortest path first. This can decrease the number of times that the manager needs to broadcast a new *shortest* to the workers.

Workers on each iteration check *?updatemin* to see if they should update their local approximation of the global minimum. Each worker receives these messages in the order they are sent by the manager since as usual we assume that messages from one process to another arrive in the order they were sent. Consequently, each worker receives new values for *shortest* in strictly decreasing order. A worker might on one iteration have an outdated value for *shortest*. (A new value could arrive just after the worker checks *?updatemin.*) But this does not affect the correctness of the algorithm; at worst it might cause the worker to generate a new chore that is later discarded.

The traveling salesman solution is an example of what is called a branch-and-bound algorithm. The term comes from the fact that the collection of possible paths forms a tree, the leaves of which are complete paths. The bound, in this case *shortest*, is used to prune the tree so that only plausible paths are examined. This type of algorithm arises in many applications, such as searching game trees and solving optimization problems.

9.6 Implementations

This section describes ways to implement the programming notations introduced in this chapter. First we develop a kernel implementation of RPC. Then we show how to implement rendezvous using asynchronous message passing. Finally, we give a kernel implementation of the multiple primitives notation. Parts of this kernel give an alternative way to implement rendezvous.

Throughout this section, we assume that programs execute on a distributed memory multiprocessor. Each processor has its own local memory and its own local kernel. The different kernels interact as illustrated in Figure 7.30. The implementations can readily be adapted to a network of one or more shared memory multiprocessors using techniques described earlier.

RPC in a Kernel

Since RPC supports only communication, not synchronization, it has the simplest implementation. Recall that, with RPC, a program consists of a collection of modules that contain procedures and processes. The procedures (operations) declared in the specification part of a module can be invoked by processes executing in other modules. All parts of a module reside on the same machine. But different modules can reside on different machines. (We are not concerned here with how a programmer specifies where a module is located; one such mechanism is described in Section 10.4.)

Processes executing in the same module interact by means of shared variables; they synchronize using semaphores. We assume each machine has a local kernel that implements processes as described in Section 3.6 and semaphores as described in Section 4.6. We also assume the kernels contain the network interface routines given in Figure 7.31. Our task here is to add kernel primitives and routines to implement RPC.

There are three possible relations between a caller and a procedure:

- the caller and procedure are in the same module;
- the caller and procedure are in different modules but are on the same machine; or
- the caller and procedure are on different machines.

In the first case, we can use a conventional procedure call. There is no need to enter a kernel if we know at compile time that the procedure is local. The calling process can simply push value arguments on its stack and jump to the procedure; when the procedure returns, the calling process can pop results off the stack and continue.

A call to a procedure in another module specifies both the name of the module and the name of the procedure. We can uniquely identify each procedure by a (*machine*, *address*) pair, where *machine* indicates which machine the procedure body is stored on and *address* is the entry point of the procedure. Given this representation, we can implement intermodule call statements as follows:

> **if** *machine* local → execute a conventional call to *address*
> [] *machine* remote → **call** *rpc*(*machine*, *address*, value arguments)
> **fi**

When a procedure is on the same machine as the caller, we can use a conventional procedure call if the procedure is guaranteed to exist. This will be the case if all modules are created before any of them begin execution and if modules cannot be destroyed dynamically. However, if modules can be created and destroyed dynamically, we would have to enter the local kernel to ascertain that a module still exists before making a conventional call to a procedure in that module.

To execute a remote call, the calling process needs to send value arguments to the remote machine, then block until results are returned. When the remote machine receives a call message, it needs to create a process to execute the procedure body. When that process terminates, it in turn calls a primitive in the remote kernel, which then sends results back to the first machine.

var network buffers, free descriptors, and delay list

net_read_handler: # entered with interrupts inhibited
    save state of *executing*
    acquire new buffer; prepare network controller for next read
    unpack first field of input message to determine *kind*
    if *kind* = CALL → **call** *handle_rpc(caller, address, values)*
    [] *kind* = RETURN → **call** *handle_return(caller, results)*
    fi

procedure *rpc(machine, address* : **int**; *values* : **string**[*])
    call *net_write*(machine, CALL, (*executing, address, values*))
    insert descriptor of *executing* on delay list
    call *dispatcher*( )
end

procedure *handle_rpc(caller, address* : **int**; *values* : **string**[*])
    acquire free process descriptor; save identity of *caller* in it
    put *address* in a register for the process
    push *value* onto the stack of the process
    insert process descriptor on ready list
    call *dispatcher*( )
end

procedure *rpc_return(results* : **string**[*])
    retrieve identity of *caller* from descriptor of *executing*
    call *net_write*(*caller*'s machine, RETURN, (*caller, results*))
    put descriptor of *executing* back on free descriptor list
    call *dispatcher*( )
end

procedure *handle_return(caller* : **int**; *results* : **string**[*])
    remove descriptor of *caller* from delay list
    put *results* on *caller*'s stack
    insert descriptor of *caller* on ready list
    call *dispatcher*( )
end

Figure 9.20. Kernel routines for implementing RPC.

Figure 9.20 contains kernel primitives for implementing RPC; it also shows the network read interrupt handler. These routines use the *net_write* procedure of the distributed kernel for asynchronous message passing (Figure 7.31), which in turn interacts with the associated interrupt handler. The following events occur in processing a remote call:

- The caller invokes the *rpc* primitive, which sends the caller's identity, procedure address, and value arguments to the remote machine.

- The remote kernel's read interrupt handler receives the message and calls *handle_rpc*, which creates a process to service the call.

- The server process executes the body of the procedure, then invokes *rpc_return* to send results back to the caller's kernel.

- The read interrupt handler in the caller's kernel receives the return message and calls *handle_return*, which unblocks the caller.

In the *handle_rpc* primitive, we assume that there is a list of already created descriptors for processes that will service calls. This speeds up handling a remote call since it avoids the overhead of dynamic storage allocation and descriptor initialization. We also assume that each server process is set up so that its first action is to jump to the appropriate procedure and its last action is to call kernel primitive *rpc_return*.

Rendezvous Using Asynchronous Message Passing

Now we turn attention to implementing rendezvous. We can do so using a kernel (see next section), but here we show how to do so using asynchronous message passing. Recall that there are two partners in a rendezvous: the caller, which invokes an operation using a **call** statement, and the server, which services the operation using an input statement. In Section 7.4 we showed how to simulate a caller (client) and server using asynchronous message passing (see Figures 7.4 and 7.5). Here we extend that simulation to implement rendezvous.

The key to implementing rendezvous is implementing input statements. Recall that an input statement contains one or more guarded operations. Execution of **in** delays a process until there is an acceptable invocation—one that is serviced by the input statement and for which the corresponding synchronization expression is true. For now we will ignore scheduling expressions.

Recall that an operation can be serviced only by the process that declares it. Hence we can store pending invocations in that process. There are two basic ways we could store pending invocations: have one queue per operation or have one queue per process. (There is in fact a third choice that we will use in the next section for reasons that are explained there.) We will employ one queue per process since that leads to a simpler implementation. Also, many of the examples in this chapter employ a single input statement per server process. However, a server might use more than one input statement, and these might service different operations. In this case, we might have to look at invocations that could not possibly be selected by a given input statement.

chan *calls*[1:*n*](*caller*, *opid* : **int**; *values* : **string**[*])
chan *replies*[1:*n*](*results* : **string**[*])

call statement in process *C* to operation serviced by process *S*:
   send *S.calls*(*C*, *opid*, value arguments)
   receive *reply*(result variables)

input statement in process *S*:
   do invocation not yet selected →
     examine next invocation in *pending*
     if the invocation is acceptable →
        remove the invocation message from *pending*
        execute the appropriate guarded operation
        send *reply*[*caller*](result formals)
    fi
   od
   do invocation not yet selected →
     receive *calls*[*S*](*caller*, *opid*, *values*)
     if this invocation is acceptable →
        execute the appropriate guarded operation
        send *reply*[*caller*](result formals)
     [] invocation not acceptable →
        insert (*caller*, *opid*, *values*) in *pending*
    fi
   od

Figure 9.21. Rendezvous using asynchronous message passing.

A **call** statement is quite similar to an output command that names a specific destination. And an input statement is quite similar to a guarded communication statement that contains only input commands. The main differences are that (1) the synchronization expression in a guarded operation can depend on the values of the formal parameters, (2) a guarded operation can contain a scheduling expression, and (3) the caller of an operation delays until the body of the guarded operation has been executed and results have been returned. Because of the similarity, however, we can implement rendezvous by adapting the decentralized implementation of synchronous communication given in Figure 8.18.

Figure 9.21 gives an implementation of rendezvous using asynchronous message passing. Each process *C* that executes **call** statements has a *reply* channel, from which it receives results from calls. Each process *S* that executes input statements has a *calls* channel, from which it receives invocations. *S* also has a local queue, *pending*, that contains invocations that have not yet been serviced. Each invocation identifies the caller and the operation being called and contains value arguments from the **call** statement.

To implement an input statement, server process S first looks through invocation messages in *pending*. If it finds one that is acceptable—the invocation statement services that operation and the synchronization expression is true—then S removes the invocation from *pending*, executes the body of the guarded operation, and finally sends a reply to the caller. If *pending* does not contain an acceptable invocation, server S receives a new invocation from *call*. If it is acceptable, S services the invocation; otherwise S saves it in *pending* and waits for another invocation.

Recall that a scheduling expression affects which invocation is selected if more than one is acceptable. We can implement scheduling expressions by extending the implementation in Figure 9.21 as follows. First, a server process needs to know about all pending invocations in order to schedule them. These are the invocations in *pending* and others that might be queued in the *calls* channel. So, before looking at *pending*, server S needs to execute:

> **do not empty**(*calls*[S]) $\rightarrow$
>   **receive** *calls*[S](*caller*, *opid*, *values*)
>   insert (*caller*, *opid*, *values*) in *pending*
> **od**

Second, if the server finds an acceptable invocation in the first loop in Figure 9.21, it needs to look through the rest of *pending* to see if there is another invocation of the same operation that is also acceptable and that minimizes the value of the scheduling expression. If so, it removes that invocation from *pending* and services it instead of the first one it found. The second loop in Figure 9.21 does not need to change since inside that loop *pending* does not contain any acceptable invocation, and hence the first one the server receives is trivially the one that minimizes the scheduling expression.

Multiple Primitives in a Kernel

We now develop a kernel implementation of the multiple primitives notation of Section 9.3. This combines aspects of the distributed kernels for asynchronous message passing and RPC and the implementation of rendezvous using asynchronous message passing. It also illustrates one way to implement rendezvous in a kernel.

With the multiple primitives notation, operations can be invoked in two ways: by synchronous **call** statements or by asynchronous **send** statements. Operations can also be serviced in two ways: by procedures or by input statements (but not both). Thus, the kernels need to know how each operation is invoked and serviced. During execution of a program, we will assume that each reference to an operation is a record with three fields:

type *op_reference* = **rec**(*kind* : (PROC, IN); *machine*, *opid* : **int**)

The first field indicates how the operation is serviced. The second identifies the machine on which the operation is serviced. For an operation serviced by a **proc**, the third field gives the entry point of the procedure as in the kernel for RPC. For an operation serviced by input statements, the third field gives the address of an operation descriptor (see below).

With rendezvous, each operation is serviced by the process that declares it. Hence in the implementation of rendezvous we employed one set of pending invocations per server process. With the multiple primitives notation, however, an operation can be serviced by input statements in more than one process in the module that declares it. Thus, server processes in the same module potentially need to share access to pending invocations. We could employ one pending set per module, but then all processes in the module would compete for access to the set even if they do not service the same operation. This would lead to delays waiting to access the set and to unnecessary overhead examining invocations that could not possibly be acceptable to a given input statement. Consequently, we will employ multiple sets of pending invocations, one per operation class as defined below.

Here we will group operations into *operation classes*. Two operations are in the same class if they are serviced by the same input statement. In particular, an operation class is an equivalence class of the transitive closure of the relation "serviced by the same input statement." For example, if operations a and b appear in an input statement, they are in the same class. If a and c appear in a different input statement—which would have to be in the same module—then c is also in the same class. In the worst case, every operation in a module is in the same class; in the best case, every operation could be in a class by itself (e.g., if each is serviced by receive statements).

A reference to an operation that is serviced by input statements contains a pointer to an operation descriptor. This in turn contains a pointer to an operation-class descriptor. Both descriptors are stored on the machine on which the operation is serviced. The address of an operation descriptor uniquely identifies the operation. The class descriptor contains the following information:

> a lock
> pending invocations of operations in the class
> new invocations that arrive while the class is locked
> access list — processes waiting for the lock
> waiting list — processes waiting for new invocations to arrive

The lock is used to ensure that at most one process at a time is examining pending invocations. The other fields are used as described below.

procedure *invoke*(*kind* : (CALL, SEND);
                        opref : *op_reference*; *values* : **string**[∗])
  if *kind* = CALL → insert *executing* on call delay list **fi**
  if *opref.machine* local →
      call *local_invoke*(*executing*, *kind*, *opref*, *values*)
  [] *opref.machine* remote →
      call *netwrite*(*opref.machine*, INVOKE,
                     (*executing*, *kind*, *opref*, *values*))
      call *dispatcher*( )
  fi
end

procedure *local_invoke*(*caller* : **int**; *kind* : (CALL, SEND);
                         opref : *op_reference*; *values* : **string**[∗])
  if *opref.kind* = PROC →
      get free process descriptor
      if *kind* = CALL → save identity of *caller* in the descriptor
      [] *kind* = SEND → record that there is no caller (caller = 0)
      fi
      set program counter for the process to *opref.address*
      push *values* onto process stack; insert descriptor on ready list
  [] *opref.kind* = IN →
      look up operation descriptor stored at *opref.address*
      if *kind* = CALL → **call** *append*(opclass, (*caller*, *opref.opid*, *values*))
      [] *kind* = SEND → **call** *append*(opclass, (0, *opref.opid*, *values*))
      fi
  fi
  call *dispatcher*( )
end

procedure *append*(*opclass* : **int**; *inv* : **rec**(*caller* : **int**;
                  kind : (CALL, SEND); *opid* : **int**; *values* : **string**[∗]))
  if *opclass* locked → insert *inv* in *opclass.new*
                 move processes from wait list to access list (if any)
  [] *opclass* not locked → insert *inv* in *opclass.pending*
                 if wait list not empty →
                     put first process on ready list
                     move other processes to access list
                     set the lock
                 fi
  fi
end

Figure 9.22. Invocation primitives.

procedure *proc_done*(*results* : **string**[*])
    put *executing* back on free descriptor list
    look up identity of caller in process descriptor
    if *caller* = 0 → **skip**   # the operation was invoked by **send**
    [] *caller* local → **call** *awaken_caller*(*caller*, *results*)
    [] *caller* remote →
        call *netwrite*(*caller*'s machine, RETURN, (*caller*, *results*))
    fi
    call *dispatcher*( )
end
procedure *awaken_caller*(*caller* : **int**; *results* : **string**[*])
    remove descriptor of *caller* from call delay list
    put *results* on *caller*'s stack; insert descriptor on ready list
end

Figure 9.23. Return primitives.

The **call** and **send** statements are implemented as follows. If an operation is serviced by a procedure on the same machine, then a **call** statement is turned into a direct procedure call. A process can determine this by looking at the fields of the operation reference defined above. If an operation is on another machine or it is serviced by input statements, then a **call** statement executes the *invoke* primitive on the local machine. Independently of how an operation is serviced, a **send** statement executes the *invoke* primitive.

Figure 9.22 contains the code for the *invoke* primitive and two other kernel routines it uses. The first argument indicates the kind of invocation. For a CALL invocation, the kernel blocks the executing process until the invocation has been serviced. Then the kernel determines whether the operation is serviced locally or on a remote machine. If it is serviced remotely, the kernel sends an INVOKE message to the remote kernel. The *local_invoke* routine gets executed by the kernel that services the operation.

The *local_invoke* routine checks to see if an operation is serviced by a procedure. If so, it grabs a free process descriptor and dispatches a server process to execute the procedure, just as in the RPC kernel. The kernel also records in the descriptor whether the operation was called. This information is used later to determine whether there is a caller that needs to be awakened when the procedure returns.

If an operation is serviced by an input statement, *local_invoke* examines the class descriptor. If the class is locked—because a process is executing an input statement and examining pending invocations—the kernel saves the invocation in the list of new invocations and moves any processes waiting for new invocations to the access list of the class. If the class is not locked, the

procedure *start_in*(*opclass* : **int**)
   if *opclass* locked → insert *executing* on access list for *opclass*
   [] *opclass* not locked → set the lock
   fi
   call *dispatcher*( )
end

procedure *wait_new*(*opclass*)
   if *opclass.new* not empty →   # new invocations have arrived
      move invocations from *opclass.new* to *opclass.pending*
   [] *opclass.new* empty →
      insert *executing* on wait list of *opclass*
      if *opclass* access list empty → clear the lock
      [] *opclass* access list not empty → move first process to ready list
      fi
   fi
   call *dispatcher*( )
end

procedure *in_done*(*opclass*, *caller* : **int**; *results* : **string**[∗])
   if *caller* = 0 → **skip**   # the operation was invoked by **send**
   [] *caller* local → **call** *awaken_caller*(*caller*, *results*)
   [] *caller* remote →
      call *netwrite*(*caller*'s machine, RETURN, (*caller*, *results*))
   fi
   if *opclass.new* not empty →
      move invocations from *new* to *pending*
      move processes from waiting list to access list (if any)
   fi
   if access list not empty → move first descriptor to ready list
   [] access list empty → clear the lock
   fi
   call *dispatcher*( )
end

Figure 9.24. Input statement primitives.

---

kernel saves the invocation in the pending set and then checks the waiting list. (The access list is empty whenever the class is not locked.) If some process is waiting for new invocations, one is awakened, the lock is set, and any other waiting processes are moved to the access list.

When a process finishes executing a procedure, it calls kernel primitive *proc_done*, shown in Figure 9.23. This primitive frees the process descriptor

call *start_in(opclass* : **int**)
do true →   # loop until find an acceptable invocation
    search *opclass.pending* for acceptable invocation
    if found one → **exit**
    [] did not find one → **call** *wait_new(opclass)*
    fi
od
remove the invocation from *opclass.pending*
execute the appropriate guarded operation
call *in_done(opclass, caller*, result formals)

Figure 9.25. Input statement code executed by a process.

---

and then awakens the caller if there is one. The *awaken_caller* routine is executed by the kernel on which the caller resides.

An input statement is implemented using the kernel routines shown in Figure 9.24. In particular, a process executes the code shown in Figure 9.25. First, the process acquires exclusive access to the class descriptor of the operation. Then it searches pending invocations for one that is acceptable. If no pending invocation is acceptable, the process calls *wait_new* to delay until there is a new invocation. This primitive might return immediately if a new invocation arrives while the process is searching *pending*, and hence the class descriptor is locked.

Once a process finds an acceptable invocation, it executes the appropriate guarded operation and then calls *in_done*. The kernel awakens the caller if there is one and then updates the class descriptor. If new invocations arrive while the input statement is executing, they are moved to the pending set, and any processes waiting for new invocations are moved to the access list. Then, if some process is waiting to access the class, one is awakened; otherwise, the lock is cleared.

This implementation of input statements handles the most general case. It can be optimized for some special cases that arise quite frequently.

- If all operations in a class are serviced by just one process, then the access list is not needed since the server will never have to wait to acquire the lock. (The lock itself is still needed, however, so that the *append* routine can determine whether to insert a new invocation in the new or pending list.)

- If an operation is in a class by itself and is serviced by receive statements or by input statements that do not contain synchronization or scheduling expressions, then pending invocations are serviced in FIFO order, just as with message passing. To handle this case, we could add a kernel primitive that delays the server until there is a pending invocation and then returns it to the server. There is no need for the server to lock the class and then search *pending*.

- If an operation is effectively a semaphore—it has no parameters or return value, is invoked by **send**, and is serviced by **receive**—then it can be implemented by a semaphore.

These optimizations lead to significant performance increases. This topic is discussed further in Section 10.6, where we examine the relative performance of various synchronization mechanisms.

Historical Notes and References

Both remote procedure call (RPC) and rendezvous originated in the late 1970s. In fact, since the invocation primitive is the same in both cases—i.e., the **call** statement—they have been viewed as two different ways to service remote operations [Andrews & Schneider 1983]. The terminology used in this chapter has, however, come to be more widely accepted and used. Namely, RPC refers to the combination of **call** plus procedures, which are executed by implicit server processes, whereas rendezvous refers to the combination of **call** plus an **accept** or input statement, which is executed explicitly by an existing process.

Early research on the semantics, use, and implementation of RPC occurred in the operating systems community and continues to be a major interest of that group. (For example, the most recent Symposium on Operating Systems Principles, held in 1989, had an entire session on the topic.) Much of the early work was conducted at Xerox's Palo Alto Research Center (PARC). Bruce Nelson did many of the early experiments and wrote an excellent dissertation on the topic [Nelson 1981]. While pursuing his Ph.D., Nelson also collaborated with Andrew Birrell at PARC; their paper [Birrell and Nelson 1984] is now viewed as a classic on how to implement RPC efficiently in an operating system kernel. Down the road from PARC at Stanford, Alfred Spector also wrote a dissertation on the semantics and implementation of RPC; Spector [1982] is a paper resulting from that work.

Stamos and Gifford [1990] present an interesting generalization of RPC called remote evaluation (REV). With RPC, a server module provides a fixed set of predefined services, namely, the procedures it exports. With REV, a client can include a program as an argument in a remote call; when the server receives the call, it executes the program and then returns results. This allows a server to provide an unlimited set of services. Their paper describes how REV can simplify the design of many distributed systems and describes the developers' experience with a prototype implementation.

Per Brinch Hansen [1978] developed the first programming language based on RPC. His language is called Distributed Processes (DP). Processes in DP can export procedures. When a procedure is called by another process, it is executed by a new thread of control. A process can also have one "background" thread, which is executed first and may continue to loop. Threads in a DP process execute with mutual exclusion. They synchronize using shared variables and the **when** statement, which is like the **region** statement of CCRs.

RPC has also been included in several other languages. The Cedar language [Lampson 1983]—a descendant of Mesa (see Chapter 6)—uses RPC within the Cedar environment [Swinehart et al. 1985]; RPC in Cedar is implemented using Birrell and Nelson's algorithm. The Eden Programming Language (EPL)—a modest extension of Concurrent Euclid (see Chapter 6)—was used to program the Eden distributed system; Black [1985] discusses experience with Eden's support for distributed applications, including an evaluation of the use of RPC. Emerald [Black et al. 1986, Black et al. 1987, Raj et al. 1991] is an outgrowth of EPL; it is an object-based language for constructing distributed applications. In Cedar, EPL, and Emerald, processes servicing calls execute concurrently and synchronize using monitors.

Additional languages based on RPC include Argus [Liskov & Scheifler 1983, Weihl & Liskov 1985, Weihl 1990], Aeolus [Wilkes & LeBlanc 1986], and Avalon [Detlefs et al. 1988]. All of these combine RPC with what are called *atomic transactions*. A transaction is a group of operations (procedures calls). It is atomic if it is both indivisible and recoverable. If a transaction *commits*, all the operations appear to have been executed exactly once each and as an indivisible unit. If a transaction *aborts*, it has no visible effect. Atomic transactions originated in the database community; they are used to program fault-tolerant distributed applications.

Rendezvous was developed simultaneously and independently in the summer of 1978 by Jean-Raymond Abrial of the Ada design team and by the author in the design of the SR language [Andrews 1981]. The term *rendezvous* was coined by the Ada designers, many of whom are French. Section 10.3 gives a summary of Ada and an example program; numerous references are given at the end of Chapter 10.

Concurrent C is another language based on rendezvous [Gehani & Roome 1986, 1989]. It extends C with processes, rendezvous using an **accept** statement, and guarded communication using a **select** statement. The **select** statement is like that in Ada, but the **accept** statement is more powerful. In particular, Concurrent C borrows two ideas from SR: synchronization expressions can reference parameters, and an **accept** statement can also contain a scheduling expression (**by** expression). Thus, the combination of **select** and **accept** in Concurrent C is very much like the **in** statement of Section 9.2. Gehani and Roome [1988a] compare the rendezvous facilities of Concurrent C and Ada. In [1988b], the same authors describe Concurrent C++, which combines Concurrent C with C++. Cmelik et al. [1989] report on experience with multiple processor versions of the language. The original version of Concurrent C provided only blocking invocations using **call** statements. Recently, asynchronous **send** was added for the reasons described in Gehani [1990a].

Several languages include multiple primitives. SR includes all those defined in Section 9.3 as well as some others. Section 10.4 describes SR; references are given in the Historical Notes at the end of Chapter 10.

StarMod [Cook 1980, LeBlanc et al. 1984] is an extension of Modula that—like SR—supports asynchronous message passing, RPC, rendezvous, and dynamic process creation. However, StarMod does not support guarded communication; the analog of SR's **in** statement cannot contain either synchronization or scheduling expressions. Processes within modules can share variables and execute concurrently; they synchronize using semaphores.

Lynx is a third language supporting multiple primitives [Scott 1987, 1991]. It was developed by Michael Scott in his Ph.D. dissertation at Wisconsin. A novel aspect of

Lynx is that it supports dynamic program reconfiguration and protection with what are called *links*. A link is a two-way channel that has one invoker (producer) and one servicer (consumer) at a time. The producer invokes a remote operation (entry) by connecting to a link; **connect** is like a **call** statement. An operation is serviced either by RPC or rendezvous. Within the servicing module, at most one process at a time is active; these threads synchronize by means of a CCR-like **await** statement. Links can be passed in messages; furthermore, the consumer's end can be dynamically bound to different remote operations. Recently, Scott and his colleagues have explored operating system support for multiple primitives and programming models [Scott et al. 1990].

As noted in the text, the semantics of RPC are essentially the same as those of conventional procedure calls. Several people have developed axiomatic semantics for rendezvous, especially the **accept** and **select** statements of Ada. Gerth [1982] gives a sound and complete proof system for a subset of Ada. Barringer and Mearns [1982] give axioms for a larger subset of Ada; see also Barringer [1985], which surveys a variety of proof techniques for concurrent programs. Schlichting and Schneider [1984] give axioms and inference rules for most of the message passing constructs described in Part III; the development in Section 8.2 of the semantics of rendezvous by simulating it using synchronous message passing is based on material in that paper. A recent paper [Dillon 1990] shows how to use symbolic execution to generate the conditions that have to be checked to verify programs written in a subset of Ada (the same subset studied by Gerth).

As mentioned in Section 9.1, many operating systems implement file caches on client workstations. The distributed file system outlined in Figure 9.2 is essentially identical to that in Amoeba. Tanenbaum et al. [1990] give an overview of Amoeba and describe experience with the system. Amoeba uses RPC as its basic communication system. Within a module, threads execute concurrently; they synchronize using "mutexes" (locks) and semaphores.

In the region-labeling example in Section 9.5, we showed how to use SR's **forward** statement to defer replying to a remote call. Communication Port [Mao & Yeh 1980] and NIL [Parr & Strom 1983, Strom & Yemini 1983] provide similar mechanisms.

In Section 9.2, we defined the semantics of guard selection in an input statment to be non-deterministic. In particular, if more than one guard succeeds, an arbitrary one is chosen. This is the semantics assumed by Ada. However, SR takes a different approach: Invocations are serviced in the order in which they arrive (assuming synchronization expressions are true). Thus, if two guards succeed, the one with the oldest invocation is selected. Olsson and McNamee [1991] explore the tradeoffs between these two approaches.

In Section 9.6, we presented direct implementations of rendezvous using first asynchronous message passing and then a kernel. The performance of rendezvous is in general quite poor relative to other synchronization mechanisms (see Section 10.6 for details). However, in many cases it is possible to transform programs so that rendezvous is replaced by less expensive mechanisms such as procedures and semaphores. Habermann and Nassi [1980] show how to transform some instances of Ada's rendezvous mechanisms. Roberts et al. [1981] consider a wider class of special cases. McNamee and Olsson [1990] present new transformations that significantly extend previous ones; they also analyze the speed-up that is gained, which is up to 95% in some cases.

Exercises

9.1 Modify the time server module in Figure 9.1 so that the clock process does not get awakened on every tick of the clock. Instead, the clock process should set the hardware timer to go off at the next interesting event. Assume that the time of day is maintained in milliseconds and that the timer can be set to any number of milliseconds. Also assume that processes can read how much time is left before the hardware timer will go off. Finally, assume that the timer can be reset at any time.

9.2 (a) Develop complete programs for the file cache and file server modules outlined in Figure 9.2. Develop implementations of the caches in each module, add synchronization code, etc.

(b) The distributed file system modules in Figure 9.2 are programmed using RPC. Reprogram the file system using the rendezvous primitives defined in Section 9.2. Give a level of detail comparable with that in Figure 9.2.

9.3 Assume modules have the form shown in Section 9.1 and that processes in different modules communicate using RPC. However, suppose that processes servicing remote calls execute with mutual exclusion (as in monitors). Condition synchronization is programmed using the statement **when** *B*. This delays the executing process until boolean expression *B* is true; *B* can reference any variables in the scope of the statement.

(a) Reprogram the time server module in Figure 9.1 to use these mechanisms.

(b) Reprogram the merge filter module in Figure 9.3 to use these mechanisms.

(c) Modify the kernel implementation of RPC (Figure 9.20) to implement these mechanisms. Design appropriate kernel data structures to implement implicit exclusion and **when** statements.

9.4 The *Merge* module in Figure 9.3 has three procedures and a local process. Change the implementation to get rid of process *M*. In particular, let the processes servicing calls to *put1* and *put2* take on the role of *M*.

9.5 Rewrite the *TimeServer* process in Figure 9.6 so that *delay* specifies an interval as in Figure 9.1 rather than an actual wakeup time. Use only the rendezvous primitives defined in Section 9.2. Hint: You will need one or more additional operations, and the client will not be able simply to call *delay*.

9.6 Consider a self-scheduling disk driver process as in Figure 7.9. Suppose the process exports one operation: *request(cylinder, ...)*. Show how to use rendezvous and an **in** statement to implement each of the following disk-scheduling algorithms: shortest seek time, circular scan, and elevator. (Hint: Use scheduling expressions.)

9.7 Ada provides rendezvous primitives similar to those defined in Section 9.2. However, in the Ada equivalent of the **in** statement, synchronization expressions cannot reference formal parameters of operations. Moreover, Ada does not provide scheduling expressions.

Using the rendezvous primitives of Section 9.2 and this restricted form of **in**, reprogram the following algorithms.

(a) The centralized dining philosophers in Figure 9.5.

(b) The time server in Figure 9.6.

(c) The shortest-job-next allocator in Figure 9.7.

(d) The network topology algorithm in Figure 9.17.

(e) The region labeling algorithm in Figure 9.18.

(f) The traveling salesman algorithm in Figure 9.19.

9.8   Develop a complete proof outline for the dining philosophers algorithm in Figure 9.5. Show that all matching **call** and **in** statements meet the requirements of the Satisfaction Rule for Rendezvous (9.10).

9.9   Develop a program and complete proof outline for the readers/writers problem. Give programs for reader processes, writer processes, and a central allocator (see Figure 9.14). Use only the language notation defined in Section 9.2. Show that all matching **call** and **in** statements meet the requirements of the Satisfaction Rule for Rendezvous (9.10).

9.10 Consider the following specification for a program to find the minimum of a set of integers. Given is an array of processes $Min[1{:}n]$. Initially, each process has one integer value. The processes repeatedly interact, with each one trying to give another the minimum of the set of values it has seen. If a process gives away its minimum value, it terminates. Eventually, one process will be left, and it will know the minimum of the original set.

(a) Using only the rendezvous primitives defined in Section 9.2, develop a program to solve this problem.

(b) Develop a complete proof outline that demonstrates the correctness of your solution. Show all applications of Satisfaction Rule (9.10).

9.11 The readers/writers algorithm in Figure 9.14 gives readers preference.

(a) Change the input statement in *Writer* to give writers preference.

(b) Change the input statement in *Writer* so that readers and writers alternate turns when both want to access the database.

9.12 The *RepFile* module in Figure 9.15 uses **call** to update remote copies. Suppose the **call** of *remote_write* is replaced by asynchronous **send.** Will the solution still work? If so, explain why. If not, explain what can go wrong.

9.13 In the RPC solution to the network topology problem (Figure 9.16), suppose the **co** statement is replaced by a **fa** loop.

(a) Is the solution correct? Explain.

(b) Is the *mutex* semaphore still needed? Explain.

9.14 (a) Modify the RPC solution to the network topology problem (Figure 9.16) to handle multiple, simultaneous probes.

(b) Modify the multiple primitive solution to the network topology problem (Figure 9.17) to handle multiple, simultaneous probes.

9.15 Using the multiple primitives notation, program a heartbeat algorithm to solve the network topology problem. Each node should have two visible operations: *topology* as in Figure 7.14 and *done*. A node uses the second operation to inform neighbors when it is about to terminate.

9.16 Suppose you have only the RPC language mechanisms defined in Section 9.1. Reprogram each of the following algorithms.

(a) The region labeling algorithm in Figure 9.18.

(b) The traveling salesman algorithm in Figure 9.19.

9.17 Change the program in Figure 9.18 to use $m + 1$ coordinators to detect termination. Use m coordinators to collect changes in each row (or column) and one more to collect and disseminate the combined result.

9.18 Modify the traveling salesman solution in Figure 9.19 so that every process terminates normally; i.e., without deadlocking.

9.19 Figure 8.5 presents one algorithm for checking primality using synchronous message passing. A second approach is to use a bag of tasks and the replicated worker paradigm (Section 7.9). All odd numbers are put into a shared bag, in ascending order. Each of w worker processes removes the next candidate from the bag and determines if it is prime by dividing it by smaller primes up to the square root of the candidate. Initially, each worker knows that 2 is prime; it puts new primes into a second shared bag. When a worker needs to know about more primes in order to check a candidate, it takes additional primes out of the second bag (and puts them back so that other workers can get them too).

(a) Reprogram the algorithm in Figure 8.5 to use the multiple primitives notation defined in Section 9.3.

(b) Develop a program for testing primality using the bag of tasks approach. Again, use the multiple primitives notation defined in Section 9.3.

(c) Compare the performance of your answers to parts (a) and (b). How many messages get sent to check the primality of all odd numbers from 3 to n? Count a **call** statement as two messages, even if no values are returned.

9.20 Section 8.4 describes a parallel algorithm for sorting n numbers by means of odd/even exchanges.

(a) Develop a complete program for that algorithm using only the rendezvous primitives defined in Section 9.2. Assume there is an array $P[1:n]$ of processes and that each initially has one number.

(b) Develop a complete program for that algorithm using the multiple primitives notation defined in Section 9.3.

(c) Compare the performance of your answers to parts (a) and (b). How many messages are sent to sort n numbers? Count a **call** statement as two messages, even if no values are returned.

9.21   Suppose n^2 processes are arranged in a square grid. In particular, each process can communicate only with its neighbors to the left, right, above, and below. (Processes on the corners have only two neighbors; others on the edges of the grid have three neighbors.) Every process has a local integer value v.

(a) Using only the rendezvous primitives defined in Section 9.2, write a heartbeat algorithm to compute the sum of the n^2 values. When your program terminates, each process should know the sum.

(b) Using the multiple primitives notation defined in Section 9.3, write a heartbeat algorithm to compute the sum of the n^2 values. When your program terminates, each process should know the sum.

9.22   *The Savings Account Problem.* A savings account is shared by several people. Each person may deposit or withdraw funds from the account. The current balance in the account is the sum of all deposits to date minus the sum of all withdrawals to date. The balance must never become negative.

Using the multiple primitives notation, develop a server to solve this problem and show the client interface to the server. Clients make two kinds of requests: one to deposit *amount* dollars and one to withdraw *amount* dollars. Assume that *amount* is positive.

9.23   Two kinds of processes, A's and B's, enter a room. An A process cannot leave until it meets two B processes, and a B process cannot leave until it meets one A process. Each kind of process leaves the room—without meeting any other processes—once it has met the required number of other processes.

(a) Develop a server process to implement this synchronization. Show the interface of A and B processes to the server. Use the multiple primitives notation.

(b) Modify your answer to (a) so that the first of the two B processes that meets an A process does not leave the room until after the A process meets a second B process.

9.24   Suppose a computer center has two printers, A and B, that are similar but not identical. Three kinds of client processes use the printers: those that must use A, those that must use B, and those that can use either A or B.

Using the multiple primitives notation, develop code that each kind of client executes to request and release a printer, and develop a server process to allocate the printers. Your solution should be fair, assuming a client using a printer eventually releases it.

9.25   *The Roller Coaster Problem* [Herman 1989]. Suppose there are n passenger processes and one car process. The passengers repeatedly wait to take rides in the car, which can hold C passengers, C < n. However, the car can go around the tracks only when it is full.

(a) Develop code for the actions of the passenger and car processes. Use the multiple primitives notation.

(b) Generalize your answer to (a) to employ m car processes, $m > 1$. Since there is only one track, cars cannot pass each other; i.e., they must finish going around the track in the order in which they started. Again, a car can go around the tracks only when it is full.

9.26 Figure 3.20 presents an algorithm for solving LaPlace's equation. That algorithm uses shared variables and barriers.

Develop a heartbeat algorithm for solving LaPlace's equation. Use only the rendezvous primitives defined in Section 9.2; i.e., do not use **send.** As in Figure 3.20, use one process for each of the n^2 grid points. Your program should terminate when the new value for each grid point is within EPSILON of its previous value.

9.27 The region-labeling algorithm in Figure 9.18 has worst case execution time of $O(n^2)$. This can happen if there is a region that "snakes" around the image. Even for simple images, the algorithm requires $O(n)$ execution time.

The region-labeling problem can be solved as follows in time $O(\log n)$. First, for each pixel, determine whether it is on the boundary of a region. Second, have each boundary pixel determine which neighbors are also on the boundary; in essence, for each region this produces a doubly linked list connecting all pixels that are on the boundary of that region. Third, using the lists, propagate the largest label of any of the boundary pixels to the others that are on the boundary. (The pixel with the largest label for any region will be on its boundary.) Finally, use a parallel prefix computation to propagate the label for each region to pixels in the interior of the region.

Using the multiple primitives notation, develop a parallel program that implements this algorithm.

9.28 *Stable Marriage Problem.* Let *Man* and *Woman* each be arrays of n processes. Each man ranks the women from 1 to n, and each woman ranks the men from 1 to n. A *pairing* is a one-to-one correspondence of men and women. A pairing is *stable* if, for two men m_1 and m_2 and their paired women w_1 and w_2, both of the following conditions are satisfied:

(1) m_1 ranks w_1 higher than w_2 or w_2 ranks m_2 higher than m_1; and

(2) m_2 ranks w_2 higher than w_1 or w_1 ranks m_1 higher than m_2.

Put differently, a pairing is unstable if a man and woman would both prefer each other to their current pair. A solution to the stable marriage problem is a set of n pairings, all of which are stable.

(a) Using the multiple primitives notation, write a program to solve the stable marriage problem.

(b) The stable roommates problem is a generalization of the stable marriage problem. In particular, there are $2n$ people. Each person has a ranked list of preferences for a roommate. A solution to the roommates problem is a set of n pairings, all of which are stable in the same sense as for the marriage problem. Using the multiple primitives notation, write a program to solve the stable roommates problem.

9.29 Figure 7.28 contains a replicated worker program for implementing adaptive quadrature using asynchronous message passing. Rewrite the program using the multiple primitives notation. Explain your solution and justify your design choices.

9.30 Figure 8.10 gives a heartbeat algorithm for multiplying two $n \times n$ matrices a and b. The algorithm uses n^2 processes; each initially has one value of a and one of b, and each computes one value of result matrix c.

(a) Reprogram the algorithm using the multiple primitives notation.

(b) A different way to multiply matrices a and b is to use the replicated worker paradigm described in Section 7.9. Arrays a and b are initially local to an administrator process; w worker processes compute the inner products and send them to the administrator. Using the multiple primitives notation, write a program to implement this replicated worker algorithm. Justify your design choices, such as what you store in the shared bag of tasks.

(c) Compare your answers to parts (a) and (b). How many messages are sent in each program? Count a **call** statement as two messages, even if there are no return values.

9.31 Figure 8.14 gives a decentralized algorithm for the dining philosophers problem. The algorithm is programmed using synchronous message passing. Reprogram the algorithm using the multiple primitives notation.

9.32 Gaussian elimination with partial pivoting is a method for reducing a non-singular real matrix $m[1{:}n, 1{:}n]$ to upper-triangular form. It involves iterating across the columns of m and zeroing out the elements in the column below the diagonal element $m[d, d]$. This is done by performing the following three steps for each column. First, select a pivot element, which is the element in column d having the largest absolute value. Second, swap row d and the row containing the pivot element. Finally, for each row r below the new diagonal row, subtract a multiple of row d from row r. The multiple to use for row r is $m[r, d]/m[d, d]$; subtracting this multiple of row d has the effect of setting $m[r, d]$ to zero.

(a) Using the multiple primitives notation, develop a program that implements the above algorithm. Assign a process to each row, column, or point, and have them communicate with each other using synchronous message passing. Explain and justify your solution strategy.

(b) Solve this problem using a replicated worker algorithm. Use w worker processes and again use the multiple primitives notation. Explain your solution and justify your design choices.

(c) Compare your answers to parts (a) and (b). How many messages are sent in each algorithm? How much concurrency does each have? Count a **call** statement as two messages, even if no value is returned.

9.33 The 8-queens problem is concerned with placing 8 queens on a chess board in such a way that none can attack another.

(a) Using the multiple primitives notation, develop a solution to this problem. Use recursive procedure calls.

(b) Develop a program to solve the 8-queens problem using the replicated worker paradigm described in Section 7.9. Again, use the multiple primitives notation. Have an administrator process put 8 initial queen placements in a bag of tasks. Use w worker processes to extend partial solutions; when a worker finds a complete solution it should send it to the administrator. The program should compute all solutions and terminate. Explain your solution and justify your design choices.

9.34   The kernel in Figures 9.22 to 9.25 implements the multiple primitives notation defined in Section 9.3.

(a) Suppose a language has just the rendezvous mechanisms defined in Section 9.2. In particular, operations are invoked only by **call** and serviced only by **in** statements. Also, each operation is serviced only by the one process that declares it. Simplify the kernel as much as possible so that it implements just this set of mechanisms.

(b) In Ada, the equivalent of the **in** statement is further restricted as follows: Synchronization expressions cannot reference formal parameters, and there are no scheduling expressions. Modify your answer to (a) to implement this restricted form of **in** statement.

## PART IV

Practice

The preceding chapters have described and illustrated the most common mechanisms for process synchronization. Figure IV.1 summarizes these and illustrates the historical and conceptual relationships among them. For example, monitors employ the explicit signaling of semaphores and the implicit mutual exclusion of CCRs, asynchronous message passing extends semaphores with data, and both RPC and rendezvous combine the procedural interface of monitors with synchronous message passing. As pictured, the mechanisms appear to form a closed circle. Indeed, there have not been any fundamentally new proposals in a decade. However, there have been some interesting offshoots and variations, as described in the next chapter and in the Historical Notes and References at the ends of previous chapters.

The synchronization techniques we have described fall into two broad categories: ones that use shared variables and ones that use message passing. These correspond to the two major categories of multiprocessor computers: ones in which processors can access shared memory and ones in which independent processors and memories are connected by a communication network. As we have shown, a program written using message passing can be executed on a shared-memory machine. There are also software systems that provide the illusion of a shared virtual memory and hence permit shared-variable programs to be executed on distributed-memory machines.

For many years, concurrent programming has been practiced only by system programmers building operating systems or database systems. But with the increasing prevalence of multiprocessor architectures, many application programmers now have the need—and opportunity—to write concurrent programs. This is especially true in the scientific computing community since parallelism is the only way to overcome the fundamental limitation the speed of light places on performance.

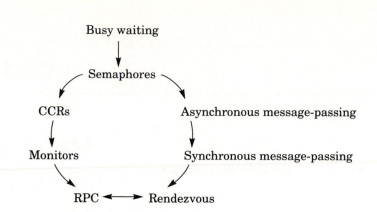

Figure IV.1. Major techniques for process interaction.

To facilitate writing concurrent programs, manufacturers of scientific workstations and of multiprocessors provide subroutine libraries supporting process creation and a subset of the synchronization mechanisms we have described. For example, the operating system for Sun workstations (SunOS) supports remote procedure call and asynchronous message passing (using what are called sockets). The Sequent parallel programming library supports spin locks, barriers, and semaphores. And the communication library for the Intel hypercube supports asynchronous and synchronous message passing. In all cases, the library routines available on a particular machine provide functionality appropriate for that architecture.

One can write a concurrent program for a specific machine by starting with a sequential program and then using a subroutine library for process creation, synchronization, and communication. Indeed, this is how many parallel applications are currently written. However, this approach is akin to programming in assembly language since the programmer has to deal with the machine architecture explicitly, package and unpackage messages, do intermachine type checking, and so on. Moreover, the resulting program is not portable since it uses the subroutine library of a specific machine and operating system.

A much more attractive approach is to employ a high-level concurrent programming language. The programmer can then concentrate on the logic of the application and let the implementors of the language worry about how to employ the low-level library routines of a specific machine. Numerous concurrent programming languages have been designed, and many of them have been implemented. In this final part of the book, we give synopses of five of the most important. We also discuss the tradeoffs among them and their relative performance.

## CHAPTER 10

Language
Overviews

There have long been programming languages with mechanisms for specifying concurrency, communication, and synchronization, e.g., PL/I and Algol 68. Early languages were, however, mostly intended for sequential programming, and the concurrency mechanisms were in essence add-ons. Only in the past two decades have we seen languages specifically intended for concurrent programming and in which the concurrency features play a central role.

Because there are several kinds of concurrent programming mechanisms—and several language designers who believe they have a better idea—there are numerous concurrent programming languages. Figure 10.1 lists those that, in the author's opinion, are the most widely known and important. Each of the communication and synchronization mechanisms we have described in this book has been included in one or more of the languages in Figure 10.1, as well as in others that are less well known. As the figure shows, many languages contain more than one mechanism.

There is also a large variation in the sequential component of concurrent programming languages. Some extend an existing sequential language, such as C or Pascal, whereas others are specially designed (although certainly influenced by other languages). Basing a concurrent language on a known sequential language has the benefit of greater familiarity. But it is often possible to provide a cleaner integration of the sequential and concurrent features of a language by designing them together.

No one concurrent programming language dominates the field or is it likely to. This is due to the variety of programming models, hardware architectures, and applications; it is also due to the newness of the field. In this chapter, we give synopses of five of the most important languages,

Language	*Synchronization Mechanism(s)*
Actors	asynchronous message passing (object oriented)
Ada	rendezvous
Argus	RPC + CCRs + atomic transactions
Concurrent C	rendezvous + asynchronous send
Concurrent Euclid	monitors (SW discipline)
Concurrent Pascal	monitors (SX discipline)
CONIC	asynchronous message passing
CSP	synchronous message passing
DP	RPC + CCRs
Edison	CCRs
Emerald	RPC + monitors (object oriented)
Gypsy	asynchronous message passing
Joyce	synchronous message passing
Linda	messages with shared tuple space
Lynx	RPC + rendezvous + CCRs
Mesa	RPC + monitors (SC discipline)
Modula	monitors (SW discipline)
Modula-3	package with coroutines + locks + monitors (SC)
NIL	asynchronous message passing + rendezvous
Occam	synchronous message passing
Pascal Plus	monitors (SU discipline)
Path Pascal	modules + path expressions
PLITS	asynchronous message passing
SR	multiple shared and message primitives
StarMod	multiple message primitives
Turing Plus	monitors (SC and SW disciplines)

Figure 10.1. Major concurrent programming languages.

including a complete program that solves one of the problems introduced earlier:

- Turing Plus — the most recent monitor-based language.

- Occam — a derivative of CSP and the systems language for transputer machines.

- Ada — the U.S. Department of Defense sponsored language for programming embedded systems.

- SR — a language with multiple primitives supporting both shared-memory and distributed programming.

- Linda — a collection of four basic primitives that can be added to any sequential programming language.

Each of these languages contains novel features, is in active use, and is available on several machines (see the Historical Notes and References). Collectively they illustrate the range of possibilities for communication and synchronization as well as for modularization, component naming, and component placement (i.e., mapping to hardware).

Section 10.6 briefly compares these five languages and then discusses some performance issues in concurrent programming, including the relative efficiency of different communication and synchronization mechanisms. See the Historical Notes and References for citations and information on how to acquire each language. The other languages in Figure 10.1 were summarized in the Historical Notes and References at the ends of previous chapters.

10.1 Turing Plus: Monitors

As indicated in Figure 10.1, there are several monitor-based concurrent programming languages. In fact, each of the five different monitor signaling disciplines has been incorporated into at least one language. This section describes Turing Plus, which is the most recent such language and quite representative of the others.

Turing is a sequential language developed in 1982-1983 for instructional computing. The designers' goal—like that of most language designers—was to create a language that is easy to learn and use, expressive, and efficient. In addition, they wanted a mathematically precise formal definition. Turing Plus was designed in the mid 1980s to support a greater range of applications, including systems programming. Turing Plus extends Turing with processes, monitors, and shared variables as well as with additional features such as separate compilation, exception handling, and device controller monitors.

Program Structure

A Turing program consists of a single compilation unit. Unlike in most other languages, there is no "packaging" around the program; it simply starts with a declaration or statement. For example, the following is a complete program:

> **put** "Hello world."

In Turing Plus, a program is composed from declarations, statements, subprograms (procedures and functions), processes, modules, and monitors.

A Turing Plus program can be compiled as a single unit. Alternatively, subprograms, modules, and monitors can be moved out of the main program and compiled separately. In this case, each such component in the main program is replaced by a child directive, which names the file in which the component was placed. In turn, the child component starts with a parent directive, which names the file containing the main component. Turing Plus also supports further parent/child nesting of components.

A module that is compiled as a single unit has a form similar to that introduced in Section 9.1:

> **module** *name*
>   **import** (global identifiers)
>   **export** (local identifiers)
>   declarations and statements
> **end** *name*

The import clause makes global declarations accessible to the module; these can include variables, subprograms, types, and so on. The export clause makes locally declared objects accessible outside the module; these can include subprograms, constants, and types. Modules cannot, however, export variables; this ensures that representation details are hidden.

When a module is separately compiled, it is separated into a stub and a body. The stub contains the import and export clauses and the declarations of exported objects; the stub contains only the headers of exported procedures or functions. The body of a module contains the implementation details, e.g., local variables and the bodies of subprograms.

Monitors are a special kind of module (see below). They can be compiled either as a single unit or separately with a stub and a body. The large example given later illustrates this.

Process declarations in Turing Plus have the basic form:

> **process** *name*(formals)
>   declarations and statements
> **end** *name*

Processes can be declared in the main component and in modules. They cannot, however, be declared within monitors since that would conflict with the implicit mutual exclusion assumed within monitors. Process declarations are patterns, as are procedure declarations. An instance of a process is created by means of the **fork** statement:

> **fork** *name*(actuals)

This creates a new instance of process *name* and passes the actual parameters to it. The new process then executes concurrently with the process that executes **fork.**

Turing Plus contains the usual kinds of declarations and statements. The syntax is basically a cleaned-up Pascal. The language does, however, contain four additional features that are related to program verification: **assert** B, **pre** B, **post** B, and **invariant** B. In each case, B is a boolean expression. The programmer can use these features to specify critical assertions. Moreover, if run-time checking is enabled, the assertions are checked during execution; if any assertion is false, program execution aborts.

The **assert** statement can be placed anywhere a normal statement can. The **pre** and **post** clauses can be placed at the start of a subprogram, module, or monitor. In a subprogram, **pre** specifies a precondition that must be true after every call; **post** specifies a postcondition that must be true before every return. In a module or monitor header, **pre** specifies what must be true at the start of initialization, and **post** specifies what must be true at the end of initialization. The invariant clause can be placed at the start of a module or monitor, in which case it specifies the module or monitor invariant. It can also be appended to the **loop** statement to specify a loop invariant.

Process Interaction

Processes in Turing Plus programs interact using global variables, monitors, or both. For this reason, programs can be executed on single processors—using multiplexing—or on shared-memory multiprocessors.

As mentioned, monitors are special kinds of modules. As usual, processes in monitors execute with mutual exclusion and use condition variables for condition synchronization. Turing Plus provides four kinds of condition variables: regular, deferred, priority, and timeout. Condition variables are accessed using **wait** and **signal** statements and an **empty** function.

Regular condition variables are FIFO queues of waiting processes with signal-and-wait (SW) semantics; i.e., **signal** is preemptive. Deferred condition variables are FIFO queues of waiting processes with signal-and-continue (SC) semantics. Priority condition variables provide priority wait plus SW signaling. Finally, timeout condition variables support interval timing. A process specifies a delay interval in the **wait** statement; it is awakened by an implicit, non-preemptive signal when that interval has expired.

For low-level systems programming, Turing Plus provides a special kind of monitor called a device monitor. As the name suggests, a device monitor is used to program the interface to a hardware device. Turing Plus implements mutual exclusion in device monitors by inhibiting hardware interrupts. Such monitors can also contain interrupt handling procedures, which are called when hardware interrupts occur. Other low-level mechanisms allow a Turing Plus program to access device registers.

All condition variables in device monitors must be deferred. This ensures that interrupt handling procedures do not get preempted when they signal regular processes. This makes interrupt handlers efficient. It also makes it much easier to implement mutual exclusion by means of interrupt inhibit.

Example: File Difference Checker

This section presents a complete Turing Plus program that examines two input files and reports lines that differ. The program is a simplified version of the UNIX *diff* command.

Input to the program consists of two data files; the names of the files are command line arguments. The program compares each pair of input lines and prints those that differ. If one file is longer than the other, the extra lines in the longer file are also printed.

The main component of the program is in Figure 10.2 (a). It first reads the command line arguments and opens the input files. Then the main component declares two processes, *input* and *output*. Finally, the main component forks two instances of *input* and one of *output*.

The input processes read lines from input files into array *line*. Each input process uses two elements of *line* for what is called double buffering. It reads into one, then calls the *putline* procedure in monitor *diff*. Once that call returns, the input process reads into its other element of *line*; the previous line remains accessible to the monitor and output process until it has been examined by them. The lines are stored in a global array to avoid copying. The grant directive after the declaration of *line* makes the array accessible to the monitor in the separately compiled child component. When an input process reaches the end of its input file, it calls *diff.stop*.

The output process repeatedly calls *diff.getline*. Each call returns when there are two lines that differ (or when both input processes have terminated). The output process then prints the lines. Result parameters *done1* and *done2* indicate when the input processes have terminated.

Figure 10.2 (b) contains the monitor. It implements both a barrier and a bounded buffer. It also contains the code that compares input lines. (The output process could do this, but then it would have to look at every pair of lines and hence make many more calls to *getline*.)

For every pair of input lines, the first input process to call *putline* delays on condition variable *barrier*. When the other input process calls *putline*, it compares the pair of lines. If they differ, the second input process deposits the line number in variable *lineout*. That process waits if necessary for the output process to have consumed the previous message; then it deposits the new message and signals the output process. The final action of the second input process is to awaken the first. The **if** statements in *putline* also handle the special case that one input process terminates before the other.

% read names of input files from command line and open them
var *name* : **array** 1..2 **of string**
var *infile* : **array** 1..2 **of int**
get : 1, *name*(1); **get** : 2, *name*(2)
open: *infile*(1), *name*(1), **get**; **open**: *infile*(2), *name*(2), **get**

var *line* : **array** 1..2, 0..1 **of string**   % input buffers, two per file
grant (*line*)   % let monitor access *line*

child "*synch.ch*"   % read in file containing stub for monitor *synch*

process *input*(*f* : **int**)   % read input lines from file *f*
  var *linenum* := 1
  loop
    exit when *eof*(*infile*(*f*))
    get : *infile*(*f*), *line*(*f*, *linenum* **mod** 2) : *   % read next line
    synch.putline(*f*, *linenum*)   % give it to monitor
    linenum += 1
  end loop
  synch.stop(*f*)   % tell monitor this file is empty
end *input*

process *output*   % print lines that differ on default output stream
  var *done1*, *done2* : **bool**
  var *linenum* : **int**
  loop
    synch.getline(*linenum*, *done1*, *done2*)   % get lines that differ
    exit when *done1* **or** *done2*   % at least one input file is empty
    put *name*(1), ":", *linenum*, ": ", *line*(1, *linenum* **mod** 2)
    put *name*(2), ":", *linenum*, ": ", *line*(2, *linenum* **mod** 2)
  end loop
  loop
    exit when *done1* **and** *done2*   % both input files empty
    if *done1* **then**
      put *name*(2), ":", *linenum*, ":", *line*(2, *linenum* **mod** 2)
    else
      put *name*(1), ":", *linenum*, ":", *line*(1, *linenum* **mod** 2)
    end if
    synch.getline(*linenum*, *done1*, *done2*)
  end loop
end *output*

fork *input*(1); **fork** *input*(2); **fork** *output*   % create the processes

Figure 10.2 (a). File differences in Turing Plus: processes.

```
parent "synch.t"      % file containing parent compilation unit
stub monitor synch
  import (line)
  export (putline, getline, stop)
  procedure putline(f, linenum : int)
  procedure getline(var linenum : int, var done1, done2 : bool)
  procedure stop(f : int)
end synch

body monitor synch
  var lnum : array 1..2 of int := init(0,0)
  var barrier, producer, consumer : cond
  var lineout : int; var full : bool := false
  var done : array 1..2 of boolean := init(false, false)

  body procedure putline
    lnum(f) := linenum
    if lnum(f) > lnum(3 – f) and not done(3 – f) then
      wait barrier    % wait for other input process to arrive
      return          % other input process will compare the lines
    end if
    if line(f, lnum(f) mod 2) not= line(3 – f, lnum(f) mod 2)
      or done(3 – f) then
        if full then  wait producer  end if
        lineout := lnum(f); full := true
        signal consumer     % awaken output process, if necessary
    end if
    signal barrier      % awaken other input process, if necessary
  end putline

  body procedure getline
    if not full then  wait consumer  end if
    linenum := lineout; done1 := done(1); done2 := done(2); full := false
    signal producer     % awaken input process, if necessary
  end getline

  body procedure stop
    done(f) := true
    if done(3 – f) then     % both input processes now done
      if full then  wait producer  end if
      full := true; signal consumer
    end if
  end stop
end synch
```

Figure 10.2 (b). File differences in Turing Plus: monitor.

The *getline* procedure implements a fetch operation. It delays the output process until there is a pair of lines that differ—or until both input processes have terminated.

The *stop* procedure provides the final bit of synchronization between the input processes (producers) and the output process (consumer). An input process calls *stop* when it reaches the end of its input file. It sets its value of *done* to true and then informs the output process if both input processes are now done.

The program in Figure 10.2 uses two coding techniques. First, array *line* is indexed by line numbers modulo 2. This avoids having to use additional variables to keep track of which element of *line* to use. Second, in the monitor, the input process reading file *f* uses $3 - f$ to reference the other input process's elements of *lnum* and *done*; since *f* is 1 or 2, the other value is $3 - f$.

10.2 Occam: Synchronous Message Passing

Occam is a distinctive language, more so than any other described in this chapter. It contains a very small number of mechanisms (hence the name, which comes from Occam's razor). It has a unique syntax. The most basic statements—assignment and communication—are themselves regarded as primitive processes. And an Occam program contains a static number of processes and static communication paths.

The CSP programming notation introduced synchronous message passing; however, CSP itself was never implemented. Occam is the derivative of CSP that is most widely known and used. The first version of Occam was designed in the mid 1980s. Here we described the latest version, Occam 2, which appeared in 1987. Although Occam is a language in its own right, it has always been closely associated with the *transputer*, a relatively inexpensive distributed memory multiprocessor implemented in VLSI. In fact, Occam is essentially the machine language of the transputer.

Program Structure

The basic units of an Occam program are declarations and three primitive "processes:" assignment, input, and output. An assignment process is simply an assignment statement. The input and output processes are essentially the input and output commands of Chapter 8. The main difference is that channels are declared global to processes—as in Chapter 7. However, each channel must have exactly one sender and one receiver.

Primitive processes are combined into conventional processes using what Occam calls constructors (i.e., structured statements). These include sequential constructors, a parallel constructor similar to the **co** statement, and a guarded communication statement. A constructor can be preceded by declarations of variables and channels; the scope of these items is the constructor. As we will see, Occam has a very distinctive syntax: each primitive process, constructor, and declaration occupies a line by itself; declarations have a trailing colon; and the language imposes an indentation convention.

Procedures and functions provide the only form of modularization in an Occam program. They are essentially parameterized processes and can share only channels and constants. Occam does not support recursion or any form of dynamic creation or naming. This makes many algorithms harder to program. However, it ensures that an Occam compiler can determine exactly how many processes a program contains and how they communicate with each other. This, and the fact that different constructors cannot share variables, makes it possible for a compiler to assign processes and data to processors on a distributed-memory machine such as a transputer.

Sequential and Parallel Constructors

In most languages, the default is to execute statements sequentially; the programmer has to say explicitly to execute statements concurrently. Occam takes a different approach: There is no default! Instead, Occam contains two basic constructors: SEQ for sequential execution and PAR for parallel execution. For example, the following program increments x, then y:

```
INT x, y :
SEQ
    x := x + 1
    y := y + 1
```

Since the two statements access different variables, they can, of course, be executed concurrently. This is expressed by:

```
INT x, y :
PAR
    x := x + 1
    y := y + 1
```

All that changes is the name of the constructor. However, PAR is not as powerful as the **co** statement since Occam processes are not permitted to share variables.

Occam contains a variety of other constructors. The IF constructor is used for alternation. It is similar to the guarded **if** statement used in this text, but there are two differences: the guards are evaluated in the order they are listed, and at least one guard must be true. The CASE constructor is a variant of IF that can be used for **case** statements. The WHILE constructor is one of the iteration mechanisms; it is like the **while** statement in Pascal.

Occam also contains an interesting mechanism called a replicator. It is similar to a quantifier and is used in similar ways. For example, the following declares an 11-element array a and iteratively assigns a value to each element:

```
[10]INT a :
SEQ i = 0 FOR 10
   a[i] := i
```

As shown, only the upper bound of an array is declared; the lower bound is implicitly 0 for all arrays. (Matrices are declared as arrays of arrays.)

A replicator adds no new functionality to the language; it is merely an abbreviation for a collection of components. Occam requires that the upper bound be a constant, and hence a replicator can always be expanded to yield an equivalent but longer program. In the above example, PAR can be used instead of SEQ since, if the replicator is expanded, the assignments will be textually distinct. In general, however, an Occam compiler will not be able to determine whether processes are distinct, e.g., if an array is indexed by other than the control variable in the replicator.

The processes specified using PAR execute with equal priority and on any processor. The PRI PAR constructor can be used to specify that the first process has the highest priority, the second has next highest, and so on, with the last process having the lowest priority. The PLACED PAR constructor can be used to specify explicitly where each process is to be placed and hence executed.

Since Occam requires that the upper bound of every replicator be a compile-time constant, a compiler can determine exactly how many processes a program contains. Unfortunately, this means that the amount of parallelism in a program cannot depend on input data. For example, if the programmer wants to experiment with different numbers of blocks in a grid computation—or different numbers of workers in a replicated worker algorithm—then the programmer has to write multiple, slightly different programs. Alternatively, one can write a single program for the largest case and use an IF constructor so that some of the processes do nothing; however, these processes will still get created.

Communication and Synchronization

As mentioned, statements in different Occam constructors cannot share variables. To communicate and synchronize, they must use channels. A channel declaration has the form:

CHAN OF protocol *name* :

The protocol defines the type of values that are transmitted over the channel. These can be basic types, fixed or variable length arrays, or fixed or variant records.

Channels are accessed by the primitive input (?) and output (!) processes. At most one composite process can output to a channel, and at most one can input from a channel. Since naming is static, an Occam compiler can enforce this requirement. Following is a simple program that echoes keyboard characters to a display:

```
WHILE TRUE
  BYTE ch :
  SEQ
    keyboard ? ch
    ch ! screen
```

Here *keyboard* and *screen* are channels that are assumed to be connected to peripheral devices. Although Occam does not define I/O mechanisms as part of the language, it provides mechanisms for binding I/O channels to devices. The transputer development system, for example, contains a library of I/O procedures.

The above program uses a single character buffer, *ch*. It can be turned into a concurrent program that uses double buffering by employing two processes, one to read from the keyboard and one to write to the screen. The process communicate using an additional channel *comm*; each has a local character *ch*.

```
CHAN OF BYTE comm :
PAR
  WHILE TRUE
    BYTE ch :
    SEQ
      keyboard ? ch
      comm ! ch
  WHILE TRUE
    BYTE ch :
    SEQ
      comm ? ch
      display ! ch
```

This program clearly indicates Occam's unique syntax. The requirement that every item be on a separate line leads to long programs, but the required indentation avoids the need for closing keywords.

The ALT constructor supports guarded communication. Each guard consists of an input process, a boolean expression and an input process, or a boolean expression and a SKIP (which reduces in essence to a pure boolean expression). A replicator may be used as an abbreviation, e.g., to wait to receive input from one of an array of channels. For example, the following implements a simple resource allocator:

```
ALT i = 0 FOR n
    avail > 0 & acquire[i] ? unitid
       SEQ
          avail := avail − 1          - - and select unit to allocate
          reply[i] ! unitid
    release[i] ? unitid
       avail := avail + 1             - - and return unit
```

Here *acquire*, *reply*, and *release* are arrays of channels, with one element for each client *i*. Arrays are needed since a channel can be used by only two processes. Occam also does not allow null messages (signals), so a value has to be sent across the *acquire* channel even though that value is not used.

Output processes are not allowed in guards in an ALT constructor. As mentioned in Chapter 8, this makes some algorithms harder to program, but it greatly simplifies the implementation. The latter is especially important since Occam is the machine language of the transputer.

The guards in an ALT constructor are evaluated in an undefined order. The PRI ALT constructor can be used to force the guards to be evaluated in the order in which they are textually listed.

Occam also contains a timer and alarm clock facility. A timer is a special kind of channel. A hardware process is always ready to output to any timer channel declared in a program. If a process declares timer channel *myclock*, it can read the time of day by executing:

> *myclock* ? *time*

The process can also delay until the clock reaches a certain value by executing:

> *myclock* ? *time* AFTER *value*

Here *value* is an absolute time, not an interval. A timer can also be used in a guard in an ALT constructor; this can be used to program an interval timer.

```
VAL INT n IS 50 :              -- number of primes to generate
VAL INT limit IS 1000 :        -- range of numbers to check
[n - 2]CHAN OF INT link :      -- links between filter processes
[n - 1]CHAN OF INT prime :     -- channels to Print process
CHAN OF INT display :          -- output display connected to device 1
PLACE display AT 1 :
PROC Starter(CHAN OF INT out, print)    -- generate odd numbers
  INT i :
  SEQ
    print ! 2
    i := 3
    WHILE i < limit
      SEQ
        out ! i
        i := i + 2 :
PROC Sieve(CHAN OF INT in, out, print)    -- filter out one prime
  INT p, next :
  SEQ
    in ? p        -- p is a prime
    print ! p
    WHILE TRUE
      SEQ
        in ? next
        IF
          (next/p) <> 0        -- this is evaluated first
            out ! next
          TRUE                 -- IF needs some true guard
            SKIP :
PROC Ender(CHAN OF INT in, print)    -- consume rest of numbers
  INT p :
  SEQ
    in ? p
    print ! p
    WHILE TRUE
      in ? p :
PROC Printer( [ ]CHAN OF INT value)    -- print each prime, in order
  INT p :
  SEQ i = 0 FOR SIZE value
    SEQ
      value[i] ? p
      display ! p :
```

```
PAR                         – – start execution of all the processes
   Starter(link[0], prime[0])
   PAR i = 1 FOR n – 2
      Sieve(link[i – 1], link[i], prime[i])
   Ender(link[n – 1], prime[n – 1])
   Printer(prime)
```

Figure 10.3. Prime number sieve in Occam.

Example: Prime Number Sieve

We now give a complete Occam program for generating the first n primes using the Sieve of Eratosthenes. As in Figure 8.5, the solution uses a pipeline of filter processes. It illustrates the use of Occam procedures (PROCs) to describe templates for the processes; the arguments to each process specify the channels that process is to use.

Figure 10.3 contains the program. The constant n specifies how many primes to generate; *limit* is a value at least as large as the nth prime. The procedures declare templates for the filter processes and printer process. The pipeline consists of one instance of *Starter*, $n – 2$ instances of *Sieve*, and one instance of *Ender*. Each process produces one prime. The $n – 1$ *link* channels are used to connect the pipeline of processes together. The n *print* channels are used to send primes to the *Printer* process. The *display* channel is used to print the primes on the standard output display, which by convention is physical device 1.

The initialization code at the end of the program starts the processes. The *Printer* process is passed an array of channels, one for each filter process. An array is needed since only two processes can use any one channel. The initialization code uses nested PAR constructors; this is done in order to use a replicator in the PAR constructor that activates the *Sieve* processes.

As programmed in Figure 10.3, the *Sieve* and *Ender* processes execute permanent loops. Hence, when the program as a whole terminates, these processes are blocked waiting for additional input. We can change the program to get every process to terminate normally by, for example, sending a sentinel value along each *in* channel (see Sections 7.3 and 8.3).

10.3 Ada: Rendezvous

Unlike the other languages described in this chapter, Ada is the result of an extensive international design competition. Consequently, Ada is the most widely known concurrent programming language. The concurrency features of Ada are an important part of the language—and are critical for its intended use in programming embedded systems that control aircraft, submarines, and so on. However, Ada also contains an incredibly large and rich set of mechanisms for sequential programming.

The initial version of Ada was designed in 1977-1978 and refined in 1978-1979. The design team consisted of several people; they received input from hundreds of others. The current version of Ada was standardized in 1983. With respect to concurrent programming, the main language mechanisms are tasks (processes) and rendezvous. Ada also contains timing mechanisms for writing real-time programs. Here we give an overview of the main concurrency mechanisms of the language; the example also illustrates some of the sequential and program structuring mechanisms. The reader should consult the Ada reference manual or any of the several books on the language for further information.

Program Components

An Ada program is constructed from subprograms, packages, and tasks. A subprogram is a procedure or function, a package is a collection of declarations, and a task is essentially a process. Each of these has a specification part and a body. The specification part declares visible objects; the body contains additional local declarations and statements. (The specification and body can be separately compiled.) Subprograms and packages can also be generic; i.e., they can be parameterized by data types.

The most common form of a task specification is:

```
task identifier is
    entry declarations
end;
```

The entry declarations are similar to **op** declarations (Chapter 9); they define operations serviced by the task. A task with no entry points has an abbreviated specification. The specification of a task that controls hardware devices can include what are called representation clauses, e.g., to map an entry to a hardware interrupt.

The most common form of a task body is:

```
task body identifier is
    local declarations
begin
    statements
end identifier;
```

The body can also contain exception handlers (see the language reference manual for details). The ending identifier is optional.

A task must be declared within a subprogram or package. The simplest concurrent program in Ada is thus a single procedure that contains task specifications and bodies:

> **procedure** identifier **is**
>   tasks and other declarations
> **begin**
>   sequential statements
> **end** identifier;

The declarations are *elaborated* one at a time, in the order in which they appear. Elaborating a task declaration creates an instance of the task. After all declarations are elaborated, the sequential statements in the subprogram begin execution as an anonymous task. Although Ada discourages the use of shared variables, they are permitted. If the sequential statements initialize these variables, the programmer has to ensure that other tasks delay until the shared variables have been initialized. The later example illustrates this.

A task specification defines a single task. One instance of the corresponding task body is created in the block in which the task is declared. Ada also supports arrays of tasks, but in a way that is different than in most other languages. In particular, the programmer first declares a task type and then declares an array of instances of that type. The programmer can also use task types in conjunction with pointers—which Ada calls access types—to create tasks dynamically. Ada does not, however, provide any mechanism for assigning tasks to processors and hence for controlling the layout of a distributed program; if this is needed, it has to be expressed in an implementation-specific configuration language.

Communication and Synchronization

Rendezvous is the sole synchronization mechanism in Ada; everything else, such as a bag of tasks or buffered communication, has to be programmed using it. Rendezvous is also the primary communication mechanism (tasks can also share variables). As mentioned, entry declarations are very similar to **op** declarations. They have the form:

> **entry** identifier(formals)

Entry parameters in Ada are passed by copy-in (**in**, the default), copy-out (**out**), or copy-in/copy-out (**in out**).* Ada also supports arrays of entries,

---

*An implementation can use call-by-reference for non-scalar parameters if the programmer cannot tell the difference.

which are called entry families.

If task T declares entry E, other tasks in the scope of the specification of T can invoke E by a **call** statement:

> **call** T.E(actuals)

As usual, execution of **call** delays the caller until operation E has terminated (or aborted or raised an exception).

The task that declares an entry services calls of that entry by means of the **accept** statement. This has the general form:

> **accept** E(formals) **do**
> statement list
> **end**;

Execution of **accept** delays the task until there is an invocation of E, copies input arguments into input formals, then executes the statement list. When the statement list terminates, output formals are copied to output arguments. At that point, both the caller and the executing process continue. An **accept** statement is thus like an input statement (Section 9.2) with one guard, no synchronization expression, and no scheduling expression.

To control non-determinism, Ada provides three kinds of **select** statements: selective wait, conditional entry call, and timed entry call. The selective wait statement supports guarded communication. The most common form of this statement is:

> **select when** B_1 $\Rightarrow$ accept statement; statements
> **or** ...
> **or**   **when** B_n $\Rightarrow$ accept statement; statements
> **end select**

Each line (except the last) is called an *alternative*. The B_i are boolean expressions, and the **when** clauses are optional. An alternative is said to be *open* if B_i is true or the **when** clause is omitted.

This form of selective wait delays the executing process until the **accept** statement in some open alternative can be executed, i.e., there is a pending invocation of the entry named in the **accept** statement. Since each guard B_i precedes an **accept** statement, it cannot reference the parameters of an entry call. Also, Ada does not provide scheduling expressions. As we discussed in Section 9.2 and will see in the example in the next section, this makes it difficult to solve many synchronization and scheduling problems.

The selective wait statement can contain an optional **else** alternative, which is selected if no other alternative can be. In place of the **accept** statement, the programmer can also use a **delay** statement or a **terminate** alternative. An open alternative with a **delay** statement is selected if the delay interval has transpired; this provides a timeout mechanism. The **terminate** alternative is selected essentially if all the tasks that rendezvous with this one have terminated or are themselves waiting at a **terminate** alternative (see the example in Figure 10.4).

These various forms of selective wait statements provide a great deal of flexibility, but they also result in a somewhat confusing number of different combinations. To make matters worse, there are two additional kinds of **select** statement.

A conditional entry call is used to if one task wants to poll another. It has the form:

> **select** entry call; statements
> **else**   statements
> **end select**

The entry call is selected if it can be executed immediately; otherwise, the **else** alternative is selected.

A timed entry call is used if a calling task wants to wait at most a certain interval of time. Its form is similar to that of a conditional entry call:

> **select** entry call; statements
> **or**   delay statement; statements
> **end select**

In this case, the entry call is selected if it can be executed before the delay interval expires. This statement thus supports timeout, in this case, of a **call** rather than an **accept.**

Ada provides a few additional mechanisms for concurrent programming. Tasks can share variables; however, they cannot assume that these variables are updated except at synchronization points (e.g., rendezvous statements). The **abort** statement allows one task to terminate another. There is a mechanism for setting the priority of a task. Finally, there are so-called attributes that enable one to determine whether a task is callable or has terminated or to determine the number of pending invocations of an entry.

Example: The Dining Philosophers

This section presents a complete Ada program for the dining philosophers problem (4.4). The program illustrates the use of tasks, rendezvous, separate compilation, input/output, declarations, and sequential statements. The solution is typeset in the Ada formatting convention, with keywords in lower-case bold and identifiers in upper-case Roman. For convenience in the program, we use $\oplus$ and $\ominus$ as before to indicate modular arithmetic; these operators are not part of Ada, however.

Figure 10.4 (a) contains the main procedure DINING_PHILOSOPHERS. Before the procedure are a **with** clause and a **use** clause. The **with** clause says this procedure depends on the objects in TEXT_IO, which is a predefined package. The **use** clause makes the names of the objects exported by that package directly visible (i.e., so they do not have to be qualified by the package name).

The main procedure first declares ID to be an integer range from 1 to 5, the indices of the 5 philosophers. The specification of the WAITER task declares three entries: NEED, PICKUP, and PUTDOWN. PICKUP is a family (array) of entries. Every philosopher calls NEED and PUTDOWN; each uses a different element of PICKUP to synchronize with the waiter. In this example, the body of WAITER is separately compiled; it is given in Figure 10.4 (b).

The specification of PHILOSOPHER is a task type so that we can declare an array DP of 5 such tasks. The body of each PHILOSOPHER is a loop that executes ROUNDS iterations. ROUNDS is a shared variable; the initialization code at the end of the main procedure calls the input procedure GET to assign a value to ROUNDS. Each philosopher has an entry, INIT, that the initialization code calls to pass the philosopher his index in the array of tasks. There is no way in Ada for an element of an array of tasks to determine its own index. However, this use of rendezvous ensures that the shared variable ROUNDS is not read until it has been initialized.

Figure 10.4 (b) contains the body of the WAITER task. The first line indicates that the specification of WAITER is contained in another compilation unit. The WAITER task is much more complicated than the *Waiter* process in Figure 9.5. This is because the **when** conditions in the Ada **select** statement cannot reference entry parameters. Consequently, a philosopher first has to call NEED to tell the waiter he wants to eat, then has to call his element of the array of PICKUP entries to wait to be granted permission to eat.

When WAITER accepts a call of NEED, it records who called and then ends the **accept** statement; this unblocks the calling philosopher so that he can call PICKUP(I). The WAITER then determines if the philosopher can eat now. If so, WAITER accepts the call of PICKUP(I); otherwise, WAITER records that philosopher I wants to eat. The PICKUP(I) entry is used only for synchronization, so the **accept** statement that services it has no associated statement list.

```
with TEXT_IO; use TEXT_IO;
procedure DINING_PHILOSOPHERS is
   subtype ID is INTEGER range 1..5;

   task WAITER is
      entry NEED(I : in ID);
      entry PICKUP(ID)( );     -- one entry per philosopher
      entry PUTDOWN(I : in ID);
   end
   task body WAITER is separate;   -- see Figure 10.4 (b)

   task type PHILOSOPHER is
      entry INIT(WHO : in ID);
   end;
   DP : array(ID) of PHILOSOPHER;   -- the 5 philosopher tasks

   ROUNDS : INTEGER;        -- the number of rounds to think and eat
   task body PHILOSOPHER
      MYID : ID;
   begin
      accept INIT(WHO);     -- get identity
         MYID := WHO;
      end
      for J in 1..ROUNDS loop
         -- "think"
         call WAITER.NEED(MYID);        -- first tell waiter I want to eat
         call WAITER.PICKUP(MYID)( );  -- now wait to get permission
         -- "eat"
         call WAITER.PUTDOWN(MYID);
      end loop;
   end PHILOSOPHER;
begin
   GET(ROUNDS);   -- read number of rounds from standard input file
   for J in 1..ID loop     -- give philosophers their index
      call DP(J).INIT(J);
   end loop;
end DINING_PHILOSOPHERS;
```

Figure 10.4 (a). Dining philosophers in Ada: main program.

```
separate (DINING_PHILOSOPHERS)
task body WAITER is
  WANT : array (ID) of BOOLEAN;        -- which waiters want to eat
  EATING : array (ID) of BOOLEAN;      -- which waiters are eating
  WHO : INTEGER
begin
  for J in ID loop                     -- initialize the arrays
    WANT(J) := FALSE; EATING(J) := FALSE;
  end loop;
  loop
    select
      accept NEED(I : in ID) do    -- philosopher I needs forks
        WHO := I;
      end;
      -- see whether philosopher I (WHO) may eat
      if not(EATING(WHO ⊖1) or EATING(WHO ⊕1)) then
        accept PICKUP(WHO)( );
        EATING(WHO) := TRUE;
      else
        WANT(WHO) := TRUE;
      end if;
    or
      accept PUTDOWN(I : in ID) do    -- philosopher I done eating
        EATING(I) := FALSE; WHO := I;
      end
      -- check neighbors to see if they want to and may eat
      if WANT(WHO ⊖1) and not EATING(WHO ⊖2) then
        accept PICKUP(WHO ⊖1)( );
        EATING(WHO ⊖1) := TRUE; WANT(WHO ⊖1) := FALSE;
      end if;
      if WANT(WHO ⊕1) and not EATING(WHO ⊕2) then
        accept PICKUP(WHO ⊕1)( );
        EATING(WHO ⊕1) := TRUE; WANT(WHO ⊕1) := FALSE;
      end if;
    or
      terminate;   -- quit when all philosophers have terminated
    end select;
  end loop;
end WAITER;
```

Figure 10.4 (b). Dining philosophers in Ada: waiter task.

After eating, a philosopher calls PUTDOWN. When WAITER accepts this call, it checks if either neighbor wants to eat and whether he may do so. In this case, the **accept** statement that services PUTDOWN could encompass the entire select alternative—i.e., the end of the **accept** could be after the two **if** statements. We have placed it earlier, however, since there is no need to delay the philosopher who called PUTDOWN.

For this problem, we could have serviced the PICKUP entries in five additional alternatives of the **select** statement, with each guarded by the appropriate condition. For example, one of these alternatives could be:

> **when not** (EATING(1) **or** EATING(3)) ⇒
> **accept** PICKUP(2)( ); EATING(2) := TRUE;

We would need to use five different alternatives since each guard is different and Ada does not provide something like quantifiers to simplify expressing closely related conditions.

10.4 SR: Multiple Primitives

The first version of SR (Synchronizing Resources) was designed in the late 1970s. The language has since evolved from a purely distributed language with multiple message passing primitives to one that also contains mechanisms for programming shared-memory computations. Consequently, SR can be used to implement directly almost all the algorithms in this book. In fact, the sequential and many of the concurrent programming notations used in this book are identical to those in SR. Although SR contains a large variety of mechanisms, they are based on a small number of orthogonal concepts. Also, the sequential and concurrent mechanisms are carefully integrated so that similar things are done in similar ways.

We have already discussed and illustrated many aspects of SR—without actually saying so. Therefore this section concentrates on additional aspects: program structure, dynamic naming, and dynamic creation and placement. As an example, we give a shared-variable version of the algorithm for the traveling salesman problem (Figure 9.19). The solution also illustrates how SR's finalization code mechanism can be used to print the results after the main algorithm terminates (in deadlock).

Program Components

An SR program is constructed from what are called resources and globals. A resource is a pattern for a module; its structure is quite similar to that of a **module** (Chapter 9):

```
resource name
    import specification
    operation and type declarations
body name(formals)
    variable and other local declarations
    initialization code
    procedures and processes
    finalization code
end name
```

Each resource is separately compiled; the specification and body of a single resource can also be separately compiled. A resource contains one or more import specifications if it makes use of the declarations exported from other resources or from globals. Declarations and initialization code in the body can be intermixed; this supports dynamic arrays and permits the programmer to control the order in which variables are initialized and processes are created.

Instances of resources are created dynamically by means of the **create** statement. For example, executing

$$rcap := \textbf{create } name(\text{actuals})$$

passes the actuals (by value) to an new instance of resource *name* and then executes that resource's initialization code. When the initialization code terminates, a *resource capability* is returned by **create** and assigned to variable *rcap*. This variable can subsequently be used to invoke operations exported by the resource or to destroy the instance. (SR also provides capabilities for individual operations.)

A global component is essentially a single unparameterized instance of a resource. It is used to declare things like types, variables, operations, and procedures that are shared by resources. One instance of a global is stored in each virtual machine (address space) that needs it. In particular, when a resource is created, any globals that it imports are created implicitly if they have not yet been created.

By default, execution of **create** places a new resource in the same virtual machine (address space) as that of the resource that created it. To construct a distributed implementation of a program, one can append "**on** *machine*" to the **create** statement; *machine* is either the symbolic name of another machine or a capability for a dynamically created virtual machine (which is in turn created in essentially the same way as a resource). Thus SR, unlike Ada, gives the programmer complete control over how resources are mapped to machines and this mapping can depend on input to the program.

An SR program always contains one distinguished main resource. Execution of a program begins with implicit creation of one instance of this resource. The initialization code in the main resource is then executed; it typically creates instances of other resources.

All resources are created dynamically. They can also be destroyed dynamically be means of the **destroy** statement. If *rcap* is a capability for an instance of a resource, execution of

> **destroy** *rcap*

stops any activity in that instance, executes the finalization code (if any), and then frees storage allocated to the instance.

An SR program terminates when every process has terminated or is blocked. (There is also an explicit **stop** statement.) At this point, the runtime system executes the finalization code (if any) in the main resource and then finalization code (if any) in globals. This provides a way for the programmer to regain control in order to print results and timing information. The later example will illustrate the utility of this.

Communication and Synchronization

The most distinguishing attribute of SR is its variety of communication and synchronization mechanisms. Processes in the same resource can share variables, as can resources in the same address space (through the use of globals). Processes can also communicate and synchronize using all the primitives described in Section 9.3: semaphores, asynchronous message passing, RPC, and rendezvous. Thus, SR can be used to implement concurrent programs for shared memory multiprocessors as well as for distributed systems.

Operations are declared in **op** declarations, which have the form given in Chapter 9. Such declarations can appear in resource specifications, in resource bodies, and even within processes. An operation declared within a process is called a *local operation*. The declaring process can pass a capability for a local operation to another process, which can then invoke the operation. This supports conversational continuity.

An operation is invoked using synchronous **call** or asynchronous **send.** To specify which operation to invoke, an invocation statement uses an operation capability or a field of a resource capability. Within the resource that declares it, the name of an operation is in fact a capability, so an invocation statement can use it directly. Resource and operation capabilities can be passed between resources, so communication paths can vary dynamically.

An operation is serviced either by a procedure (**proc**) or by input statements (**in**). A new process is created to service each remote call of a **proc**; calls from within the same address space are optimized so that the caller itself executes the procedure body. All processes in a resource execute concurrently, at least conceptually.

The input statement supports rendezvous. It has the form shown in Section 9.2 and can have both synchronization and scheduling expressions that depend on parameters. The input statement can also contain an optional **else** clause, which is selected if no other guard succeeds.

Several mechanisms in SR are abbreviations for common uses of operations. A **process** declaration is an abbreviation for an **op** declaration and a **proc** to service invocations of the operation. One instance of the process is created by an implicit **send** when the resource is created. The body of a **process** is often a permanent loop. (The programmer can also declare arrays of processes.) A **procedure** declaration is an abbreviation for an **op** declaration and a **proc** to service invocations of the operation.

Two additional abbreviations are the **receive** statement and semaphores. In particular, **receive** abbreviates an input statement that services one operation and that merely stores the arguments in local variables. A semaphore declaration (**sem**) abbreviates the declaration of a parameterless operation. The **P** statement is a special case of **receive**, and the **V** statement is a special case of **send.**

SR also provides a few additional statements that have proven useful. The **reply** statement is used by a **proc** to return values, such as communication links, to its caller and then continue execution. The **forward** statement can be used to pass an invocation on to another process for further service; in this case the caller remains blocked. (We defined and illustrated the use of SR's **forward** statement in the region-labeling algorithm in Section 9.5.) Finally, SR contains a restricted form of **co** that can be used to create resources or invoke operations in parallel.

Example: The Traveling Salesman Problem

As an example of an SR program, consider again the traveling salesman problem introduced in Section 9.5. There we developed a distributed algorithm (Figure 9.19). In particular, the bag of partial tours was stored in the manager module rather than being shared by the manager and workers.

The distributed algorithm in Figure 9.19 can be implemented in SR with only minor modifications. But SR can also be used to solve the problem using a shared bag of chores. Figure 10.5 contains a complete SR program, including input and output. The program is started by a UNIX command that has three arguments: the number of cities n, the number of workers w, and the name of a file *fname* that contains a distance matrix.

The SR program contains two global components. The first, *Arguments*, declares the three command-line arguments. The second global, *Shared*, declares the distance matrix and an operation that is used for the bag of tasks; these are declared in a global component so that they can be accessed by both the manager and the workers.

```
global Arguments      # command-line arguments to the program
   var n, w : int            # number of cities and workers
   var fname : string[20]      # name of distances file
body Arguments
   getarg(1, n); getarg(2, w); getarg(3, fname)
end

global Shared      # data shared by manager and workers
   import Arguments
   op bag(path[1:*], hops, length : int)      # partial tours
   var dist[1:n, 1:n] : int                  # distances
body Shared
   var fd : file; fd := open(fname, READ)
   fa i := 1 to n, j := 1 to n → read(fd, dist[i, j]) af   # read distances
end

resource Manager
   import Arguments, Shared, Worker
   op newmin(path[1:*], length : int)
body Manager( )

   var bestpath[1:n] : int, bestlength := 1000000      # best tour so far
   var cw[1:w] : cap Worker
   # create workers and give them capabilities for this resource
   fa i := 1 to w → cw[i] := create Worker(myresource( )) af

   process manager
      # generate first set of partial tours and put them into bag
      var path[1:n] : int := (1, [n − 1] 0)
      fa i := 2 to n → path[2] := i; send bag(path, 2, dist[1, i]) af
      do true →
         # wait for candidates for new shortest path
         in newmin(path, length) by length →
            if length < bestlength →
               bestpath := path; bestlength := length
               # broadcast new minimum to all workers
               co (i := 1 to w) send cw[i].updatemin(length) oc
            fi
         ni
      od
   end

   final
      write("length of best path: ", bestlength)
      writes("path:  "); fa i := 1 to n → writes(bestpath[i], ", ") af; write( )
   end

end Manager
```

```
resource Worker
   import Arguments, Shared, Manager
   op updatemin(length : int)
body Worker(cm : cap Manager)
   procedure extend_path(var path[1:*], hops, length : int)
      var visit[1:n] : bool := ([n] false)   # cities that have been visited
      fa i := 1 to hops → visit[path[i]] := true af
      var j := 1; do visit[j] → j + + od     # find unvisited city
      path[hops + 1] := j; length := length + dist[path[hops], j]; hops + +
   end

   process worker
      var path[1:n], hops, length : int
      var shortest : int := 1000000      # shortest tour known so far
      do true →
         do ?updatemin > 0 →     # is there a better shortest tour?
            receive updatemin(length); shortest := min(length, shortest)
         od
         receive bag(path, hops, length)   # get task and process it
         call extend_path(path, hops, length)
         if hops < n and length < shortest →
            send bag(path, hops, length)   # put back into bag
         [] hops = n and length < shortest →
            length := length + dist[path[n], 1]   # distance back to city 1
            if length < shortest →   # if might be best, tell manager
               send cm.newmin(path, length); shortest := length
            fi
         fi
      od
   end
end Worker
```

Figure 10.5. Traveling salesman solution in SR.

The *Manager* resource in Figure 10.5 is the main resource in this program. Since *Manager* imports *Arguments* and *Shared*, those globals are created before the manager executes. *Arguments* is created first since *Shared* imports it; the body of *Arguments* reads the command-line arguments. Then *Shared* is created; since variable n now has a value, the size of the distance matrix is determined at run-time. The body of *Shared* then reads in the distances.

At this point, the *Manager* resource begins execution. It creates *w* instances of the *Worker* resource. So that the workers can invoke the manager's *updatemin* operation, *Manager* passes a capability for itself to each worker. (The predefined function *myresource* produces this capability.) The background process, *manager*, now executes. The *manager* process initializes the bag with the first set of partial tours. The workers then take partial tours from the bag and extend them. When a worker finds a complete tour that it thinks might be best, it sends it to the manager. Whenever the manager gets a shorter-length tour, it broadcasts it to the workers. On each iteration of its main loop, a *worker* process uses *?updatemin* to see if there is a pending invocation of *updatemin*, which means there is a better shortest tour; if so, the worker receives the invocation.

The manager and workers in Figure 10.5 terminate in deadlock when all plausible tours have been examined. The workers are waiting to receive from *bag*, which is empty, and the manager is waiting to service *newmin*. When the SR run-time system detects termination (i.e., there is no pending I/O and all processes are blocked), it automatically activates the finalization code in *Manager*. That code prints the value of the best path; when that code terminates, the program as a whole terminates. This use of finalization code greatly simplifies the program. Without it, we would have to detect termination within the program, which is very difficult to do for this problem.

10.5 Linda: Distributed Data Structures

Linda embodies an approach to concurrent programming that is quite different from the others we have considered. First, Linda is not itself a language. Rather it is a small number of primitives that are used to access what is called tuple space. Any sequential programming language can be augmented with the Linda primitives to yield a concurrent programming variant of that language.

Second, Linda generalizes and synthesizes aspects of shared variables and asynchronous message passing. Tuple space (TS) is a shared, associative memory consisting of a collection of tagged data records called tuples. TS is like a single shared communication channel, except that tuples are unordered. The operation to deposit a tuple (**out**) is like a **send** statement, the operation to extract a tuple (**in**) is like a **receive** statement, and the operation to examine a tuple (**rd**) is like an assignment from shared to local variables. A fourth operation, **eval**, provides process creation. The two final operations, **inp** and **rdp**, provide non-blocking input and reading.

Although TS is logically shared by processes, it can be (and has been) implemented by distributing parts among processors in a multicomputer or network. Thus, TS can be used to store distributed data structures, and different processes can concurrently operate on different elements of the data structure. As the later example will show, this directly supports the replicated worker paradigm for process interaction. Linda also supports data parallel programming and message passing, although not as elegantly.

Linda was first conceived in the early 1980s. The initial proposal had three primitives; the others were added in the mid and late 1980s. Several languages have been augmented with the Linda primitives, including C and Fortran. In the examples, we use C-Linda.

Tuple Space and Process Interaction

Tuple space consists of an unordered collection of passive data tuples and active process tuples. Data tuples are tagged records that contain the shared state of a computation. Process tuples are routines that execute asynchronously. They interact by reading, writing, and generating data tuples. When a process tuple terminates, it turns into a data tuple.

Each data tuple in TS has the form:

$$(\text{"tag"}, value_1, ..., value_n)$$

The tag is a string literal that is used to distinguish between tuples representing different data structures. The $value_i$ are zero or more data values, e.g., integers, reals, or arrays.*

Linda defines three basic primitives for manipulating data tuples: **out**, **in**, and **rd.** All three are atomic; i.e., they appear to be indivisible operations. A process deposits a tuple in TS by executing:

$$\textbf{out}(\text{"tag"}, expr_1, ..., expr_n)$$

Execution of **out** terminates once the expressions have been evaluated and the resulting data tuple has been deposited in TS. The **out** operation is thus similar to a **send** statement, except the tuple is stored in unordered TS rather than appended to a specific channel.

A process extracts a data tuple from TS by executing:

$$\textbf{in}(\text{"tag"}, field_1, ..., field_n)$$

Each $field_i$ is either an expression or a formal parameter of the form ? *var* where *var* is a local variable in the executing process. The arguments to **in** are called a template. The process executing **in** delays until TS contains at least one tuple that matches the template, then removes one from TS.

---

*Other fields in a data tuple can also be type designators, but we will not consider that case here since it is not especially useful and is hard to implement in its most general form.

A template t matches a data tuple d if: (1) the tags are identical, and t and d have the same number of fields, (2) expressions in t are equal to the corresponding value in d, and (3) variables in t have the same type as the corresponding value in d. After a matching tuple is removed from TS, formal parameters in the template are assigned the corresponding values from the tuple. Thus, **in** is like a **receive** statement, with the tag and values in the template serving to identify the channel.

Two simple examples will help clarify these concepts. First, we can simulate a semaphore in Linda as follows. Let "sem" be the symbolic name of a semaphore. Then the **V** operation is simply **out**("sem"), and the **P** operation is simply **in**("sem"). The value of the semaphore is the number of "sem" tuples in TS. To simulate an array of semaphores, we would use an additional field to represent the array index, for example:

$$\textbf{out}(\text{"forks"}, i) \qquad \# \textbf{V}(forks[i])$$
$$\textbf{in}(\text{"forks"}, i) \qquad \# \textbf{P}(forks[i])$$

The template in the **in** statement matches any tuple having the same tag "forks" and the same value i.

The third basic data tuple primitive is **rd**, which is used to examine tuples. If t is a template, execution of **rd**(t) delays the process until TS contains a matching data tuple. As with **in**, variables in t are then assigned values from the corresponding fields of the data tuple. However, the tuple remains in TS.

There are also non-blocking variants of **in** and **rd**. Operations **inp** and **rdp** are predicates that return true if there is a matching tuple in TS, and return false otherwise. If they return true, they have the same effect as **in** and **rd**, respectively. These variants provide a way for a process to poll TS.

Using the three basic primitives, we can modify and examine a "global" variable. For example, we can implement a single counter barrier for n processes as follows. First, some process initializes the barrier by depositing a counter in TS:

$$\textbf{out}(\text{"barrier"}, 0)$$

When a process reaches a barrier synchronization point, it first increments the counter by executing:

$$\textbf{in}(\text{"barrier"}, ?\, counter) \qquad \# \text{ extract tuple and get value of counter}$$
$$\textbf{out}(\text{"barrier"}, counter + 1) \quad \# \text{ increment counter and put it back}$$

Then the process waits for all n processes to arrive by executing:

> **rd**("barrier", n)

This statement delays the process until the counter part of the barrier tuple is exactly n.

The sixth and final Linda primitive is **eval**, which creates a process tuple. This operation has the same form as **out**:

> **eval**("tag", $expr_1, ..., expr_n$)

The difference is that a process is forked to evaluate the expressions. One of the expressions is typically a procedure or function call. When the forked process terminates, the tuple becomes a passive data tuple.

The **eval** primitive provides the means by which concurrency is introduced into a Linda program. (Recall that the Linda primitives are added to a standard sequential language.) As a simple example, consider the following concurrent statement:

> **co** $i := 1$ **to** $n \rightarrow a[i] := f(i)$ **oc**

This statement evaluates n calls of f in parallel and assigns the results to shared array a. The corresponding C-Linda code is:

```
for ( i = 1; i ≤ n; i + +)
    eval( "a", i, f(i) );
```

This forks n process tuples; each evaluates one call of $f(i)$. When a process tuple terminates, it turns into a data tuple containing the array name, an index, and the value of that element of a.

TS can also be used to implement conventional point-to-point message passing. For example, a process can send a message to a channel ch by executing:

> **out**("ch", expressions)

Again, the name of a shared object is turned into a tag on a tuple. Another process can receive the message by executing:

> **in**("ch", variables)

However, this statement extracts any matching tuple. If it is important that messages be received in the order they are sent, we can use counters as follows. Assume that ch has one sender and one receiver. Then the sender can add an additional count field to every "ch" tuple; the value in this field is 1 for the first message, 2 for the second, and so on. The receiver then uses its own counter to match the first message, then the second, and so on. If the channel has multiple senders or receivers, the counters can themselves be stored in TS; they would be read and incremented like the barrier counter given earlier.

To summarize, TS contains data tuples that are produced by **out** and **eval** and examined by **in**, **rd**, **inp**, and **rdp.** Since TS is shared, all processes can examine it. Although each operation on TS must appear to be indivisible, different processes can examine different tuples concurrently. This supports both the data parallel and replicated worker programming styles. However, tuple space is unprotected—any process can extract or examine any tuple. Moreover, tags are linear strings of characters; there is no hierarchy to the name space and no sense of scoping. These attributes of TS are bad for abstraction and hinder the development of large programs.

Another disadvantage of tuple space is that the performance of TS operations is in general much worse than that of any of the shared variable or message-passing mechanisms described in Parts II and III. On a shared memory machine, TS can be stored in memory shared by all processors and hence all processes. However, tuples cannot be updated in place; they have to be extracted, modified, and then deposited back into TS. Moreover, implementing **rd** and **in** operations requires doing an associative lookup for a matching tuple. The situation is worse on a distributed memory machine since tuple space would likely be spread across machines. For example, an **out** or **eval** operation might place a tuple in the local memory; but then an **rd** or **in** operation would in general have to examine all memories. With hardware support for broadcast, it is, however, possible to get reasonable performance (see the Historical Notes and References).

Example: Prime Numbers with Replicated Workers

In Section 8.3, we showed how to generate prime numbers using the Sieve of Eratosthenes. In that approach, candidate numbers pass through a pipeline of filter processes. Each filter checks one prime factor.

We can also generate primes using the replicated worker paradigm. As usual, the workers share a bag of tasks. In this case, the bag contains the candidate numbers. Each worker repeatedly removes a candidate from the bag and determines whether it is prime. But to do so, the worker of course needs to know about all primes up to the square root of the candidate.

Since the workers are checking primality, how can they also acquire the primes they need? The answer is to check candidates in strictly increasing order. In this way, the prime factors needed to check a candidate will already have been generated before they are needed. A worker might have to delay—waiting for another worker to generate a smaller prime—but workers will not deadlock since all smaller primes will eventually be generated.

```
#include "linda.h"
#define LIMIT 1000
lmain(argc, argv)
  int argc;
  char *argv[ ];
{
  int primes[LIMIT] = { 2, 3 };      /* seed table with first two primes */
  int limit, num_workers, i, isprime, numprimes = 2, value = 5;
  limit = atoi(argv[1]);                        /* read command line arguments */
  num_workers = atoi(argv[2]);
  for ( i = 1; i ≤ num_workers; i + + )     /* create worker processes */
    eval("worker", worker( ));
  out("candidate", value);            /* put first candidate in TS */
  while ( numprimes < limit ) {
    /* get results from workers in increasing order of odd values */
    in("result", value, ? isprime);
    if ( isprime ) {         /* put value in table and TS */
      primes[numprimes] = value;
      out("prime", numprimes, value);
      numprimes + +;
    }
    value = value + 2;
  }
  out("stop");          /* tell workers to quit */
  for ( i = 0; i < limit; i + + )
    printf("%d\n", primes[i]);
}
```

Figure 10.6 (a). Prime number generation in C-Linda: manager.

Figure 10.6 contains a C-Linda program that generates the first *limit* primes using the replicated worker paradigm. The structure of a C-Linda program is essentially that of a C program. One difference is that the main routine is named *lmain* rather than *main*. The second difference is that the program employs the Linda tuple-space primitives.

The main routine executes first as a single process. In Figure 10.6 (a), *lmain* first reads command line arguments to determine how many primes to generate and how many workers to use. It then uses **eval** to fork the worker processes and uses **out** to deposit the first candidate, 5, in TS.

The main routine then assumes the role of the manager process. In particular, it waits to get the results from workers. It uses **in** to receive the results, in order from the smallest to largest candidate. Results are received

```
worker( )
{
    int primes[LIMIT] = { 2, 3 };      /* local table of primes */
    int numprimes = 1, i, candidate, isprime;
    while ( 1 ) {
        if ( rdp("stop") )    /* check for termination */
            return;
        in("candidate", ? candidate);    /* get next candidate */
        out("candidate", candidate + 2);
        i = 1; isprime = 1;
        while ( primes[i] * primes[i] < candidate ) {
            if ( candidate % primes[i] = = 0 ) {    /* not a prime */
                isprime = 0;
                break;
            }
            i + +;
            if ( i > numprimes ) {      /* need another prime */
                numprimes + +;
                rd("prime", numprimes, ? primes[numprimes]);
            }
        }
        out("result", candidate, isprime);   /* tell manager the result */
    }
}
```

Figure 10.6 (b). Prime number generation in C-Linda: workers.

---

in order so that primes can be counted. When *lmain* receives a prime, it deposits it value and its number, *numprimes*, into TS and updates its local table. For example, 5 is the 3rd prime, 7 is the 4th, and so on. The main routine deposits primes in TS so that workers can see them.

The program terminates when *lmain* has computed *limit* primes. It first tells the workers to stop by depositing a "stop" token in TS. Then *lmain* prints the primes stored in its local table. It could read them back in from TS, but it is much more efficient to access local variables than TS.

The worker processes are shown in Figure 10.6 (b). Each worker repeatedly gets a candidate number from TS, checks its primality and sends the result to the manager by depositing the result in TS. After a worker extracts a candidate number using **in**, it deposits the next odd candidate into TS. Thus there is at most one candidate number in TS at a time, and the candidates are increasing odd integers.

To minimize reads from TS, each worker keeps a local table of prime factors. It extends this table when it needs another prime factor to check a candidate number. It gets the prime by reading it from TS. To avoid deadlock, workers read primes in strictly increasing order.

On each iteration, a worker uses the conditional read primitive, **rdp**, to see if it should stop. This primitive returns true if there is a "stop" tuple in TS; otherwise it returns false. Since the workers will not see the "stop" tuple until after the manager has acquired *limit* primes, more candidates than necessary will be checked. This is hard to avoid without having the processes exchange many more messages.

The program in Figure 10.6 is not the most efficient one we could devise. This is because each candidate is deposited and extracted twice—once in a "candidate" tuple and then in a "result" tuple. Accessing TS is much less efficient than accessing local variables. To increase the use of local variables, we could have the manager deposit ranges of candidates—say 10 or 20 numbers at a time—and have the workers compute all primes in a given range then send the collective result to the manager. We could also seed the tables of primes in the manager and workers with more of the small primes.

10.6 Comparison and Performance

Previous chapters examined several mechanisms for process communication and synchronization. This chapter has surveyed five languages that illustrate different combinations of these mechanisms. The five languages also have many other differences.

- Occam is a very Spartan language with a peculiar syntax; Ada is extremely verbose.

- Turing Plus supports shared memory computations; Occam, Ada, and Linda support distributed computations; SR supports both.

- Occam has a static number of processes; Turing Plus, SR, and Linda support dynamic process creation; Ada is in between (tasks are static, but pointers can be used to create instances of task types).

- Linda has a very small number of primitives; SR has many (but all are variations on ways to invoke and service operations).

- Turing Plus, Ada, and SR separate the specification of a component from its implementation; Occam and Linda do not.

- SR gives the programmer control over where components of a distributed computation are placed; the other languages do not.

What is perhaps not so obvious is that the different communication and synchronization mechanisms also have major differences in performance. Naturally, it takes much longer to communicate using message passing—especially across a network—than it does using shared variables. But there are also major performance differences between the various message passing mechanisms. This in turn affects the performance of applications.

This section describes experiments we conducted to measure the performance of several process-interaction mechanisms: procedure call, semaphores, process creation, asynchronous and synchronous message passing, RPC, and rendezvous. We first describe how the experiments were conducted. Then we present and interpret the results.

Performance Experiments

We used the SR language for the experiments since SR includes all these mechanisms (not to mention that the author has ready access to the SR implementation!). Others have independently shown that the performance of each mechanism in SR is comparable with that in languages that contain only a subset of SR's mechanisms (see the Historical Notes and References).

In order to provide a basis for interpreting the results, we first summarize how SR is implemented. The SR implementation is built on top of UNIX. It has three major components: the compiler, linker, and run-time system (RTS). The SR compiler generates C code, which is passed through a C compiler to produce machine code. The SR linker combines machine code from different resources, standard libraries, the RTS, and a remote execution manager (if needed) to produce an executable program.

During execution, an SR program consists of one or more virtual machines (address spaces). Each virtual machine executes within a single UNIX process; it contains storage for program variables, sequential code, and one instance of the RTS. The RTSs in different virtual machines interact using UNIX sockets, which in turn use a communication network if the virtual machines are located on different physical machines. The overall structure of an executing SR program is thus like that depicted in Figure 7.30.

The RTS is a collection of primitives that implement processes and the various SR process interaction mechanisms. It is quite similar to the multiple primitives kernel presented in Figures 9.22 to 9.24. In particular, the RTS contains descriptors for processes and operation classes and primitives for invoking and servicing operations. The RTS also contains resource descriptors and additional primitives for memory management, resource management, semaphores, virtual machines, and input/output.

For the most part, each process interaction mechanism in SR has its own set of RTS primitives. This makes the RTS somewhat large in terms of code size, but it permits each language feature to be implemented quite efficiently. For example, SR's implementation of rendezvous is only slightly less efficient

```
resource rendezvous( )
    const TRIALS := 10
    var num : int
    op dummy( )
    initial
        getarg(1, num)        # read command line argument
    end
    process server
        do true →
            in dummy( ) → skip ni
        od
    end
    process main
        var start, finish : int, total := 0
        fa t := 1 to TRIALS →
            start := age( )
            fa i := 1 to num → call dummy( ) af
            finish := age( )
            write("elapsed time: ", finish − start)
            total := total + (finish − start)
        af
        write("average time per test: ", total/TRIALS)
    end
end
```

Figure 10.7. Test program for rendezvous.

than the best implementations of Ada rendezvous. This is despite the fact that SR contains a more powerful rendezvous mechanism.

We developed and executed test programs for each of SR's process interaction mechanisms; we also measured the effect of context-switching time. Each test program ran in a single virtual machine and exercised a single combination of primitives. For example, Figure 10.7 contains the program that was run to determine the cost of a rendezvous with no arguments. The initial code in that program reads a command line argument *num*, which specifies how many times to repeat the test, and then implicitly creates both processes. The *main* process contains two loops. The inner loop makes *num* calls of operation *dummy*, which is serviced by an input statement in process *server*. The outer loop repeats the test ten times. The SR *age* function is called before and after the inner loop; it returns the elapsed time, in milliseconds, that the SR program has been executing.

local call	2
semaphore pair	5
interresource call	75
asynchronous send/receive	105
context switch, semaphores	130
context switch, message passing	180
synchronous send/receive	290
process create/destroy	350
rendezvous	470
RPC with new process	700

Figure 10.8.   Performance measurements (in microseconds).

Interpretation of Results

Figure 10.8 lists the execution time, in microseconds, of different combinations of process interaction mechanisms. Each test program was executed several times on an unloaded Sun SPARCstation 1+. The command-line argument *num* was varied from 10,000 to a million to ensure that results were consistent. There were occasional perturbations—e.g., due to the arrival of an electronic mail message—but each test produced quite consistent results. The numbers in Figure 10.8 are the median values, with the larger values rounded to the nearest 5 microseconds; these values were produced by well over 75% of the tests. The numbers include loop overhead, which was measured to be a trivial 1.1 microseconds per iteration.

A local call is extremely fast. It is not, however, quite as fast as a null C procedure call since an SR call contains four hidden arguments that are used to address global variables and to handle the general case that a call might be remote.

The semaphore test program did repeated **V** and **P** operations, in that order, so that the main process never blocked. As a result, semaphore operations are also extremely fast.

The SR compiler optimizes calls to procedures in the same resource. Since it compiles resources separately, however, it cannot optimize interresource calls. In fact, the compiler cannot in general know whether an operation in another resource is serviced by a procedure or by rendezvous or whether an instance of another resource will be in the same address space. Thus, a call to a non-local operation has to be handled by the RTS. If the RTS determines that the operation is serviced by a procedure and is in the same address space, then the RTS simply jumps to the procedure. An interresource call takes 75 microseconds due to this overhead of entering the RTS and due to the need to allocate storage for the arguments. (Storage allocation is required since the call might be to a remote operation.)

Asynchronous message passing is much more costly than semaphores since the RTS has to manipulate message queues. It is also more costly than an interresource procedure call since the message has to be copied into the receiver's address space. The time listed in Figure 10.8 is the cost of a pair of **send** and **receive** operations, not including any potential context-switching time. In particular, the test program was constructed so that **receive** never blocked.

The next two times listed in Figure 10.8 are the costs of context switches. These were measured using two programs that forced a context switch at every synchronization point. One program used semaphores; the other used asynchronous message passing. (The times listed are total execution time minus synchronization time.) Context switching is expensive on the SPARC architecture since many registers have to be saved. In the SR implementation, context switching is faster with semaphores than with message passing since less SR-related state information has to be saved.

With asynchronous message passing, in the best case neither process will block, and hence there will be no context switch. With synchronous message passing, however, at least one of the processes has to block. Hence the cost of synchronous message passing is the cost of a **send/receive** pair plus a general context switch.

The process creation/destruction time listed in Figure 10.8 is the time it takes the RTS to fork a new process plus the time it takes to destroy that process when it terminates. The listed time does not include the context-switching overhead.

Rendezvous is much more costly than message passing. This is because communication is two-way, and because there have to be two context switches to complete a rendezvous. The measured time for rendezvous was 470 microseconds. This is indeed the time for synchronous message passing plus a second general context switch. This time also happens to be the sum of two **send/receive** exchanges plus two semaphore context switches (although in fact the caller does not actually execute **send** then **receive**, and the context-switching time is somewhat higher).

In SR, the most expensive process interaction mechanism is RPC whenever a new process has to be created to service the call. The measured time was 700 microseconds. This is approximately the cost of creating and destroying a process plus two general context switches; in fact, the context-switching time is somewhat less, but there is overhead to return result parameters to the caller.

SR does not directly support CCRs or monitors. However, these can be simulated by procedures and semaphores, so we can approximate their performance from the costs of semaphore operations and semaphore context switches (see the Exercises).

These test programs have also been run on several other architectures, including DEC Vaxes, a DECstation 3100 (MIPS architecture), Sun 2s and 3s, HP workstations, a Silicon Graphics workstation, and Encore and Sequent multiprocessors. Naturally, performance is better on faster machines. However, the relative differences are the same. Also, the ratios are approximately the same.

We have also run the message-passing tests on our local network, with the main process executing on one workstation and the server process on another. When the test program executes on top of UNIX, communication is about an order of magnitude slower; e.g., RPC takes about 6.4 milliseconds instead of 700 microseconds. However, there is also a stand-alone implementation of SR that employs a customized communication kernel. In this case, remote RPC takes only about 1.3 milliseconds.

A major factor affecting relative performance is context-switching overhead. On the SPARC architecture, a context switch takes approximately ten times longer than on the MIPS architecture. Thus, synchronous message passing, rendezvous, and RPC with a new process are much faster than shown in Figure 10.8. However, they still remain much more expensive than the other mechanisms.

To summarize, using shared variables is always less expensive than using message passing. This is hardly surprising since it takes less time to write into shared variables than it does to allocate a message buffer, fill it, and pass it on to another process. Thus, on a shared memory machine, the programmer would be well advised not to use message passing unless that is the most natural way to structure the solution to a problem.

On a distributed memory architecture, message passing of some form has to be used, either explicitly or implicitly. In this case, if information flow is one-way—e.g., in a network of filters—then asynchronous message passing is the most efficient mechanism. Asynchronous message passing is also the most efficient, as well as the easiest to use, for interacting peers (e.g., in heartbeat algorithms.) For client/server interaction, however, rendezvous is slightly less expensive than using two explicit **send/receive** pairs. In this case, rendezvous and RPC are also more convenient to use. Moreover, RPC can be—and has been—implemented quite efficiently by employing pools of precreated processes and preallocated message buffers. RPC also has the advantage of being easy for the programmer to learn since it is a straightforward extension of conventional procedure call.

Historical Notes and References

As mentioned in the Historical Notes and References for Chapter 6, Turing Plus is the latest in a series of monitor-based programming languages designed by Ric Holt and his colleagues at the University of Toronto. (Concurrent SP/k and Concurrent Euclid were the first two.) The language—like many others—is named after a major historical figure who influenced computer science, in this case, English mathematician Alan M. Turing. Turing Plus is used by a number of universities to give a taste of concurrent programming and to write operating systems for shared-memory multiprocessors. It is also used for commercial work, such as a special purpose system for signal processing. The Turing subset is also used in high schools and universities for introductory computing courses.

Holt and Cordy [1988] provides an excellent introduction to Turing and the Turing Plus extension; that paper also summarizes the historical development of the language. Earlier information on the origins of the language appears in Holt [1984]. The Turing language is described in detail in Holt et al. [1987]; the Turing Plus extension is defined in Holt and Cordy [1985]. The implementation of Turing includes an interactive programming environment, which Ric Holt used to test the program in Figure 10.2. For information on the Turing Plus distribution, contact Ms. Chris Stephenson, Holt Software Associates, Inc., 203 College Street, Suite 305, Toronto, Canada M5T 1P9.

Occam was developed by David May and colleagues at the British computer firm INMOS Ltd.; that company also developed the transputer machine. The first versions were designed in the early 1980s. As noted in the text, Occam is a derivative of CSP; Tony Hoare, the designer of CSP, was a consultant to May's group. May [1983] gives an overview of what is now called Occam 1 (there was also a preliminary version); Occam 1 is described in detail in INMOS [1984]. Occam 2 was released in 1987 [May 1987]. It adds several features that were lacking in Occam 1: floating point numbers, multi-dimensional arrays, records, multiple value messages, functions, and access to a real-time clock. Occam and the transputer development system are distributed by INMOS and its representatives.

A book by Alan Burns [1988] gives a thorough overview of Occam 2 and the transputer machine and compares Occam 2 with Ada; the prime number sieve in Figure 10.3 was adapted from one in that book. Hull [1987] summarizes the main features of the language and gives several sample programs. Fisher [1986] describes a multiprocessor implementation. Fisher [1988] critiques Occam's channel types and proposes an alternative type system in which the programmer can specify the number of messages that can be sent to a channel as well as their data types. Finally, Wilson [1989] proposes adding generic parameterization to Occam procedures (the standard library of I/O routines includes 28 different read and write functions, one for each kind of data type).

In response to the growing development and maintenance costs of software, the U.S. Department of Defense (DoD) began the "common higher order language" program in 1974. The early stages of the program produced a series of requirements documents that culminated in what were called the Steelman specifications. Four industrial/university design teams submitted language proposals in the spring of 1978. Two—code named Red and Green—were selected for the final round and given several months to respond to comments and to refine their proposals.

The Red design team was led by Intermetrics, the Green team by Cii Honeywell Bull; both teams were assisted by numerous outside experts. The Green design was selected in the spring of 1979. The DoD named the language Ada, in honor of Augusta Ada Lovelace, daughter of the poet Lord Byron and assistant to Charles Babbage, the inventor of the Analytical Engine. In response to additional comments and early experience, Ada was refined further and then standardized in February of 1983 [Dept.

of Defense 1983]. Interestingly, the initial Green proposal was based on synchronous message passing for communication and synchronization. The design team changed to rendezvous in the summer and fall of 1978.

Because the DoD has mandated the use of Ada for programming its embedded computer systems, several companies market Ada implementations and programming environments for a variety of machines. In addition, there are numerous books that describe the language. One by Gehani [1983] emphasizes the advanced features, including concurrency; the dining philosophers algorithm in Figure 10.4 was adapted from that book. An early paper by one of the members of the Ada design team [Barnes 1980] gives a good overview of the language and its historical and technical background.

When a programming language is destined from the start to be widely used, it invites critical evaluation. Although Ada has many attractive attributes, others are less so. One of the major criticisms is the sheer complexity of the language, which is an inevitable consequence of the numerous requirements the designers had to meet. Tony Hoare [1981] addressed this issue in his Turing Award lecture; that paper is must reading for anyone interested in programming language design.

Several people have examined Ada's concurrency mechanisms. Welsh and Lister [1981] compare Ada with CSP and DP and conclude that, although Ada's tasking and rendezvous mechanisms have significant advantages in some cases, they have significant disadvantages in others. Wegner and Smolka [1983] compare Ada with CSP and monitors and reach many of the same conclusions. Liskov et al. [1986] analyze the concurrency requirements of distributed programs and conclude that the combination of synchronous communication and a static process structure—which is all Ada provides—leads to complex solutions to common problems. Gehani and Roome [1988a] compare the rendezvous facilities of Ada with those of Concurrent C (which borrowed SR's functionality) and show that Ada programs can become convoluted since Ada does not directly support synchronization or scheduling that depends on parameters to operations.

Additional papers have explored other aspects of Ada. In Ada, program components can be arbitrarily nested within each other; Clarke et al. [1980] examine this and conclude that "nesting in Ada is for the birds." Roberts et al. [1981] evaluate the applicability of Ada's task management facilities for real-time multiprocessors and conclude that Ada does not meet the needs of real-time embedded systems. Krogdahl and Olsen [1986] compare Ada's abstraction mechanisms with those in Simula and point out advantages and disadvantages of having several different mechanisms (records, packages, tasks, etc.). Finally, Volz et al. [1989] examine issues related to executing Ada on distributed systems and question whether distributed Ada programs are really Ada since the language itself does not provide mechanisms to specify where tasks are located.

The basic ideas in SR—resources, operations, input statements, and asynchronous (**send**) and synchronous (**call**) invocation—were conceived by the author in 1978 and written up in early 1979; that paper eventually appeared in late 1981 [Andrews 1981]. The initial version of a full SR language was defined in the early 1980s and implemented by the author and several graduate students [Andrews 1982]. That version is now called SR_0 ("SR naught"). Based on local experience with SR_0, the author and Ron Olsson—one of the implementors of SR_0—designed a new version in the mid 1980s; it added RPC, semaphores, early reply, and several additional mechanisms. Andrews and Olsson [1986] describe the evolution of SR, explaining what was changed and why, as well as what was not changed and why not (also see Olsson's Ph.D. dissertation [1986]). After using and testing the new version locally, we began distributing SR in March 1988. Andrews et al. [1988] describe version 1.0 of SR, explains the implementation, and compares SR with other languages.

Feedback from users of SR 1.0—and contributions from many of them—led to version 1.1, which was released in May 1989 [Andrews and Olsson 1989]. Further experience, plus the desire to provide better support for parallel programming using shared variables and operations, led to the design of version 2.0. That is the version of SR described in Section 10.4. Andrews and Olsson [1992] give a complete description of SR 2.0, including numerous examples. The new implementation will be distributed beginning in late 1991. For details, contact the SR Project, Department of Computer Science, University of Arizona, Tucson, AZ 85721.

Several papers evaluate aspects of SR and report on experiences using SR for various applications. Atkins [1988] describes experiments using different upcall program structures for implementing network communications software. Coffin and Olsson [1989] show how to use SR to program multiway rendezvous, which is a generalization of rendezvous in which more than two processes participate. Olsson and Whitehead [1989] describe the **srm** tool for generating "makefiles" for SR programs and show how their techniques can automate—and avoid unnecessary—recompilation in any modular language. Huang and Olsson [1990] defines an exception-handling mechanism for the language. Olsson [1990] shows how to use SR to implement discrete event simulation and contrasts the SR solution to an Ada solution for the same problem. Bal [1990a] evaluates the design of SR based on experience using SR to implement several parallel algorithms. Finally, McNamee and Olsson [1990] present a collection of program transformations that improve the performance of rendezvous. The transformations are illustrated using SR; they use the technique of passing the baton that we described in Chapter 4.

Linda was developed by David Gelernter in a Ph.D. dissertation supervised by Art Bernstein [Gelernter & Bernstein 1982]. The journal paper that introduced the Linda primitives is Gelernter [1985]. As Gelernter says in that paper, Linda's support for "generative communication" is sufficiently different from either shared variables or message passing to constitute a different programming model. Generative communication is like message passing, in that tuples are deposited into and extracted from tuple space, but it is also somewhat like using shared variables since tuple space is logically shared even if physically distributed.

The original proposal for Linda had only three primitives: **out**, **in**, and **rd**. The **eval** primitive was added in the mid 1980s; the predicate variants of **in** and **rd** were added later still. Carriero et al. [1986] describe how Linda can be used to implement distributed data structures and the bag of tasks programming paradigm. Ahuja et al. [1986] give an overview of how Linda can be used for parallel programming and summarize how it can be implemented. Carriero and Gelernter [1986] give a detailed description of one Linda implementation. Ahuja et al. [1988] describe a special purpose parallel computer, the Linda Machine, designed specifically to support efficient execution of Linda programs. A recent paper [Carriero & Gelernter 1989a] summarizes the current status of Linda and compares Linda with message passing, concurrent objects, concurrent logic programming, and functional programming; the bibliography in that paper includes several papers that describe specific applications of Linda. The replicated worker algorithm for the prime number program in Figure 10.6 is adapted from that paper. Finally, a recent survey paper [Carriero & Gelernter 1989b] describes three methods for parallel programming—which they call result parallelism, agenda parallelism, and specialist parallelism—and shows how each method can be implemented in Linda.

The Linda primitives have been added to several sequential languages, and Linda implementations exist for several different workstations and multiprocessors. Linda is distributed by Scientific Computing Associates, 246 Church Street, Suite 307, New Haven, CT 06510.

Tuple space is used to implement distributed data structures. Orca and Ease are two recent languages that are also based on the use of distributed data structures. Orca was developed by Henri Bal in a Ph.D. dissertation supervised by Andy Tanenbaum [Bal 1990b] (see also Bal et al. [1989]). In Orca, processes can share instances of user-defined data types; operations on these types are executed atomically. Ease was developed by Steven Ericsson Zenith in a Ph.D. dissertation at Yale [Zenith 1990]. Given its roots at Yale, Ease is heavily influenced by Linda. However, shared data structures are specified differently in Ease, and Ease provides a richer set of primitives than does Linda. One benefit of these differences is that Ease can be implemented more efficiently than Linda on a shared memory machine (fewer copy operations are required to exchange data).

Most papers that describe the implementation of a concurrent programming language include performance figures. There have also been several other performance studies. For example, Clapp et al. [1986] describe benchmarks that were developed to measure the performance of Ada and reports on the results. Atkins and Olsson [1988] describe experiments to measure the performance of SR's concurrency, communication, and synchronization mechanisms; they compare the results with those in Clapp et al. [1986]. Scott and Cox [1987] give an empirical study of message passing overhead in an implementation of the Lynx language on the BBN Butterfly multiprocessor; these authors also explain how their results and lessons apply to other message-passing systems.

Several of the above papers evaluate the synchronization mechanisms in a specific language and compare them with those in other languages. Bloom [1979] presents a general methodology for evaluating synchronization constructs. Bloom examines three areas: modularity, expressive power, and ease of use. With respect to synchronizing access to a shared resource, she identifies five kinds of information that can be required to specify exclusion and priority constraints: (1) the name of the operation being requested, (2) the order in which requests are made, (3) parameters of the requests, (4) the current state of the resource, and (5) history information (i.e., a record of past actions). Monitors permit access to all this information, as does the SR **in** statement defined in Section 9.2. On the other hand, an Ada task cannot access parameters of entry calls or control the order in which they are serviced.

This text has focused on *explicit* concurrent programming in which the programmer specifies the processes and explicitly programs communication and synchronization using shared variables or message passing. The vast majority of work on concurrent programming has been concerned with this approach, but there are other approaches to concurrency. At the other extreme are parallelizing compilers, which take a sequential program, infer what concurrency they can, and generate code to create processes and synchronize their execution.

In between these two extremes are concurrent variants of functional and logic programming languages. In these, at least one of concurrency, communication, or synchronization is implicit. For example, Multilisp [Halstead 1985] provides parallel function calls and what are called *futures*, but it provides no explicit synchronization. Instead, when a process needs the value of an expression that another process is evaluating as a future, the first process implicitly delays. (This is essentially the dual of lazy evaluation; with lazy evaluation, an expression is not evaluated until it is needed; with futures, an expression is evaluated ahead of time in the hope that its value will be computed by the time it is needed.) The September 1989 issue of *ACM Computing Surveys* contains three papers that consider this class of languages: Bal et al. [1989] survey concurrent functional and logic languages as well as those based on explicit message passing, Hudak [1989] surveys functional languages (one section considers concurrency), and Shapiro [1989] surveys the family of concurrent logic languages.

Exercises

10.1 This chapter gives five complete programs (Figures 10.2 to 10.6), one in each of the different languages. Rewrite each program in the other four languages.

10.2 The following refer to the prime number generator program written in Occam (Figure 10.3).

(a) Change the program so that n, the number of primes to generate, is an input value between 1 and 100.

(b) Change the program so that every process terminates. (The program in Figure 10.3 terminates in deadlock.)

10.3 Change the WAITER process in the dining philosophers program in Ada (Figure 10.4) so that it services *all* entry calls in the one **select** statement.

10.4 Implement a shortest-job-next scheduler in Ada. (Hint: Use multiple entries, including an array.)

10.5 (a) Simulate CCRs using the mechanisms in SR; do not use semaphores. (Hint: Use a caretaker process per shared variable, and turn region statements into operations.)

(b) Using the performance numbers in Figure 10.8 and your answer to (a), estimate the performance of CCRs.

(c) Using the performance numbers in Figure 10.8, estimate the performance of CCRs if they are implemented using semaphores and Rem's algorithm (Figure 5.8).

(d) Compare your answers to (b) and (c).

10.6 (a) Develop a simulation of monitors using SR. Each monitor should be in a resource; use semaphores to implement mutual exclusion and condition variables. Assume that condition variables have signal-and-continue (SC) semantics.

(b) Using the performance numbers in Figure 10.8 and your answer to (a), estimate the performance of monitor entry and exit and of operations on condition variables (**wait** and **signal**).

10.7   Develop a simulation of tuple space and the Linda operations in SR. Assume that all SR processes execute in the same virtual machine (address space). (Hint: Use shared operations.)

10.8   Develop a distributed implementation of tuple space and the Linda operations. Program your implementation in SR or the asynchronous message passing primitives defined in Chapter 7. Justify your design choices, such as where you store tuples and how you implement the Linda operations.

10.9   Write a program in Turing Plus to solve each of the problems considered in Chapter 6 (monitors).

10.10   Write a program in Occam to solve each of the problems considered in Chapter 8 (synchronous message passing). Since Occam does not allow output commands in guards of ALT constructors, many problems will be harder to solve.

10.11   Write a program in Ada to solve each of the problems considered in Chapter 9 (RPC and rendezvous). Since Ada does not allow **select** or **accept** statements to reference arguments of entry calls, many problems will be harder to solve.

10.12   (a) Write a program in Linda to solve any six different problems in Chapters 6 to 9. Pick at least one problem from each of these chapters, and pick ones that use different programming techniques.

        (b) Compare the Linda programs with those in the text. For each problem, which program is clearer and easier to write? Explain your answers.

10.13   This chapter gave synopses of five of the languages listed in Figure 10.1. Pick another one of those languages, and write a synopsis with a comparable level of detail. In particular, give a brief history of the language, describe the main program components, describe the communication and synchronization mechanisms, and give a complete program that solves one of the larger problems given earlier in the book. In addition, give a critical evaluation of the language. What are its attractive attributes? What are its limitations?

10.14   Section 10.6 described performance experiments and results for the SR language. For some other concurrent programming language that you have access to, conduct a similar set of experiments to measure the performance of the concurrency mechanisms in that language. Compare your results with those in Figure 10.8. Explain similarities and differences.

10.15   Write a synopsis of a concurrent functional or logic programming language such as Multilisp, PARLOG, or Concurrent Prolog. Give a level of detail comparable to the synopses of the five languages given in this chapter. Include examples of small and large programs. In addition, give a critical evaluation of the language. What are its attractive attributes? What are its limitations? What can you say about its performance?

10.16   Design, implement, and document a parallel or distributed program that makes creative use of several processes. If you have access to one or more concurrent programming languages, use one of them. If not, use the system call library of the host operating system.

Following is a list of possible projects. Either pick one of these or design your own project having a comparable level of difficulty. Provide your instructor with a brief description of your project before you begin, and demonstrate your program when the project is completed.

(a) Take some problem that could be parallelized or distributed in different ways—e.g, sorting, prime number generation, traveling salesman, matrix multiplication. Develop different algorithms to solve the problem, and perform a series of experiments to determine which approach works best under different assumptions. Ideally, perform experiments on both shared-memory and distributed-memory multiprocessors.

(b) Construct an automated teller system having several customer "terminals" and a centralized or, better yet, distributed database of accounts. Your program should implement several kinds of user transactions, such as deposits, withdrawals, and balance inquiries. Ideally, construct a user interface that looks like a teller machine.

(c) Construct an airline reservation system that allows users to ask about flights and to reserve and cancel seats. Support multiple reservation agents. This project is similar to implementing an automated teller system.

(d) Develop a program that plays some game and employs several displays, either to show the results for different players or to enable several players to play against each other and perhaps "the machine." If you choose this project, keep the game relatively simple so that you do not get bogged down just getting the game itself programmed. For example, implement a simple card game such as blackjack or a simple video game.

(e) Construct a mail system that enables users to communicate, even if they log on at different terminals at different times. To make the system interesting, it would be nice if a user could send and receive mail if *any* machine in the network is operational.

(f) Implement a UNIX-like command language that allows users to invoke commands that are optionally executed in the background. You will probably need to program the commands themselves in the language you are using. Support I/O redirection and pipes.

(g) Implement a "talk" command that allows users on different terminals to converse with each other. Support both person-to-person and conference calls. Allow a person to join a conversation that is already in progress.

(h) Implement a distributed file system. In particular, allow a user on one machine to read and write files stored on other machine. Employ file caches as outlined in Figure 9.2. Do not use an underlying network file system that trivializes this problem; instead, figure out how to solve it yourself.

(i) Implement a replicated file system. This is a generalization of the previous problem.

(j) Using a concurrent programming language you have access to, develop a simulation of a different language. (For example, write an SR program to simulate Occam or CSP programs.) Write a preprocessor to convert source programs written in the language being simulated into programs in the simulation language, then compile and execute the resulting program.

(k) Develop a discrete-event simulation of some physical system. For example, simulate an elevator with customers getting on and off at various floors, or simulate traffic at an intersection with a traffic light. Implement the various entities in the simulation as processes that react to and generate events. You will also need a scheduler process to manage the simulation, e.g., to keep track of the event list and update the simulation clock.

Glossary

Assertion. A predicate that characterizes a program state. When an assertion is placed before a statement in a program, it specifies that the predicate must be true every time the statement starts to execute.

At-Most-Once Property. An expression or assignment statement satisfies this property if it contains at most one reference to a variable changed by another process. If this is the case, the expression or statement will execute as an atomic action.

Atomic Action. A sequence of one or more statements that appears to be indivisible; i.e., no other process can see an intermediate state. A fine-grained atomic action is one that can be implemented directly by an indivisible machine instruction. A coarse-grained atomic action is a sequence of fine-grained actions that appear to be indivisible.

Auxiliary Variable. A variable that is added to a program to record aspects of the hidden state, e.g., the program counter in a process. An auxiliary variable is used in order to prove safety and liveness properties.

Axiom. A formula in a logical system that is assumed to be true.

Bound Variable. A variable introduced in an existential ($\exists$) or universal ($\forall$) quantifier.

Bounding Expression. An integer valued expression that is non-negative and that decreases every time a loop is executed. It is used to prove that a loop terminates.

Busy Waiting. A process is busy waiting (spinning) if it is executing a loop waiting for a condition to be true, e.g., **do** $B \rightarrow$ **skip od.**

Completeness. A formal logic is complete if it is possible to construct a proof for every formula whose interpretation is true.

Condition Synchronization. A synchronization technique that involves delaying a process until the state satisfies some boolean condition B.

Conditional Atomic Action. An atomic action that must delay until the state satisfies some boolean condition B.

Critical Assertion. The critical assertions in a process are the preconditions of each statement in the process and the postcondition; see also **Non-Interference.**

Critical Section. A sequence of statements that must be executed with mutual exclusion with respect to critical sections in other processes that reference the same shared variables.

Deadlock. A process is in a deadlock state if it is blocked waiting for a condition that will never become true.

Eligible Action. An atomic action in a process is eligible if it is the next action the process wants to execute and if any delay condition in the action is true.

Exclusion of Configurations. A method for proving safety properties, such as mutual exclusion and absence of deadlock. Process P_1 cannot be in a state satisfying assertion A_1 at the same time process P_2 is in a state satisfying A_2 if $(A_1 \wedge A_2) = \textit{false}$.

Fairness. Guaranteeing that every delayed process gets a chance to proceed; see also **Scheduling Policy.**

Free Variable. A variable that is not a bound variable, e.g., a program variable.

Global Invariant. A predicate that is true in every visible program state, i.e., between every pair of atomic actions.

Guard and Guarded Statement. A guard is a boolean condition in a statement such as **if**, **do**, or **await**. A guarded statement has the form $B \rightarrow S$ where B is the guard and S is a statement list; S is executed only if B is true.

History. The sequence of states, or actions, resulting from one execution of a program; also called a trace.

Inference Rule. In a formal logic, an inference rule is used to conclude that a new formula is true. It has hypotheses and a conclusion. If the hypotheses are true, then an inference rule says that the conclusion is also true.

Interference Freedom. Given proofs for a collection of processes, the proofs are interference-free if no assignment action interferes with a critical assertion in another process; see also **Non-Interference.**

Interpretation of a Logic. A decision procedure that specifies whether a given formula is true or false.

Livelock. A process is livelocked if it is spinning while waiting for a condition that will never become true. This is the busy-waiting analog of deadlock.

Liveness Property. A program satisfies a liveness property if every execution of the program eventually reaches a good state. Termination and eventual entry into a critical section are examples of liveness properties.

Logical Variable. A special variable in a predicate that stands for the value of a program variable without specifying what that value is. For example, $(a = A)$ specifies that program variable a has some value A.

Loop Invariant. A predicate that is true before and after every execution of the statements in a loop.

Mutual Exclusion. Two statements in different processes execute with mutual exclusion if they cannot both execute at the same time.

Non-Interference. An atomic action a in one process does not interfere with a critical assertion C in another process if the following triple is a theorem: $\{\,pre(a) \wedge C\,\}\, a\, \{\,C\,\}$. In words, this says that if a is about to execute, hence $pre(a)$ is true, and if C is true, then executing a will leave C true.

Partial Correctness. A program is partially correct if it computes the desired result, assuming it terminates.

Postcondition. The postcondition of a statement S, denoted $post(S)$, is an assertion that is true when S finishes execution.

Precondition. The precondition of a statement S, denoted $pre(S)$, is an assertion that is true when S starts execution.

Proof Outline. A program interspersed with assertions. It should contain enough assertions to convince the reader that the program is correct. A complete proof outline has an assertion before and after every statement.

Safety Property. A program satisfies a safety property if it never enters a bad state. Partial correctness, mutual exclusion, and absence of deadlock are examples of safety properties.

Scheduling Policy. A scheduling policy determines which eligible action gets to execute next, i.e., the order in which processes execute. A scheduling policy is unconditionally fair if unconditional atomic actions eventually get to execute. It is weakly fair if conditional atomic actions eventually get to execute if the delay condition becomes true and remains true. It is strongly fair if conditional atomic actions eventually get to execute if the delay condition is infinitely often true.

Soundness. A formal logic is sound if it is not possible to construct a proof for a formula whose interpretation is false.

Spin Lock. A spin lock is a boolean variable that is used in conjunction with busy waiting; in particular, a process spins until the lock is set.

State of a Program. The value of every program variable.

Textual Substitution. Textual substitution, denoted P_e^x, means replace all free occurrences of variable x by expression e.

Total Correctness. A program is totally correct if it computes the desired result and it terminates.

Triple. A programming logic formula having the form $\{\,P\,\}\, S\, \{\,Q\,\}$. P and Q are predicates; S is a statement list. The interpretation is: If execution of S starts in a state satisfying P, and if S terminates, then the final state will satisfy Q.

Unconditional Atomic Action. An atomic action that does not have a delay condition; i.e., if it is eligible, it can be selected for execution.

Valid Formula. A formula in a logic that is true in every state, i.e., for every possible value of the variables; also called a tautology.

Weakest Precondition. The weakest precondition of statement list S and predicate Q, denoted $wp(S, Q)$, is a predicate that characterizes all states such that, if execution of S is begun in one of those states, S will terminate in a state satisfying Q.

Bibliography

Afek, Y., Awerbuch, B., and Gafni, E. 1987. Applying static network protocols to dynamic networks. *Proc. 28th Symp. on Foundations of Computer Science*, October, 358-370.

Agha, G. 1986. *Actors: A Model of Concurrent Computation in Distributed Systems.* MIT Press, Cambridge, MA.

Agha, G. 1990. Concurrent object-oriented programming. *Comm. ACM 33*, 9 (September), 125-141.

Ahuja, S., Carriero, N., and Gelernter, D. 1986. Linda and friends. *IEEE Computer 19*, 8 (August), 26-34.

Ahuja, S., Carriero, N.J, Gelernter, D.H., and Krishnaswamy, V. 1988. Matching language and hardware for parallel computation in the Linda Machine. *IEEE Trans. on Computers 37*, 8 (August), 921-929.

Akl, Selim G. 1985. *Parallel Sorting Algorithms.* Academic Press, Orlando, FL.

Allen, F., Burke, M., Charles, P., Cytron, R., and Ferrante, J. 1988. An overview of the PTRAN analysis system. *Journal of Parallel and Distributed Computing 5*, 5 (October), 617-640.

Almasi, G.S., and Gottlieb, A. 1989. *Highly Parallel Computing.* Benjamin/Cummings, Redwood City, CA.

Ambler, A.L., Good, D.I., Browne, J.C., Burger, W.F., Cohen, R.M., Hoch, C.G., and Wells, R.E. 1977. Gypsy: a language for specification and implementation of verifiable programs. *Proc. ACM Conference on Language Design for Reliable Software, SIGPLAN Notices 12*, 3 (March), 1-10.

Anderson, T.E. 1989. The performance implications of spin-waiting alternatives for shared-memory multiprocessors. *Proc. 1989 Int. Conf. on Parallel Processing*, Vol. II, August, 170-174.

Andler, S. 1979. Predicate path expressions. *Proc. Sixth ACM Symp. on Principles of Prog. Languages*, January, 226-236.

Andrews, G.R. 1979. The design of a message switching system: an application and evaluation of Modula. *IEEE Trans. on Software Engr. SE-5*, 2 (March), 138-147.

Andrews, G.R. 1981. Synchronizing resources. *ACM Trans. on Prog. Languages and Systems 3*, 4 (October), 405-430.

Andrews, G.R. 1982. The distributed programming language SR—mechanisms, design, and implementation. *Software—Practice and Experience 12*, 8 (August), 719-754.

Andrews, G.R. 1989. A method for solving synchronization problems. *Science of Computer Prog. 13*, 4 (December), 1-21.

Andrews, G.R. 1991. Paradigms for process interaction in distributed programs. *ACM Computing Surveys 23*, 1 (March), in press.

Andrews, G.R., and McGraw, J.R. 1977. Language features for process interaction. *Proc. ACM Conference on Language Design for Reliable Software, SIGPLAN Notices 12*, 3 (March), 114-127.

Andrews, G.R., and Olsson, R.A. 1986. The evolution of the SR language. *Distributed Computing 1*, 3 (July), 133-149.

Andrews, G.R., and Olsson, R.A. 1989. Report on the SR programming language, version 1.1. TR 89-6, Dept. of Computer Science, University of Arizona, May.

Andrews, G.R. and Olsson, R.A. 1992. *Concurrent Programming in SR*. Benjamin/-Cummings, Redwood City, CA.

Andrews, G.R., Olsson, R.A., Coffin, M., Elshoff, I., Nilsen, K., Purdin, T., and Townsend, G. 1988. An overview of the SR language and implementation. *ACM Trans. on Prog. Languages and Systems 10*, 1 (January), 51-86.

Andrews, G.R., and Schneider, F.B. 1983. Concepts and notations for concurrent programming. *ACM Computing Surveys 15*, 1 (March), 3-43.

Annaratone, M, Arnould, E., Gross, T., Kung, H.T., Lam, M.S, Mezilcioglu, O., Sarocky, K., and Webb, J.A. 1986. Warp architecture and implementation. *Proc. 13th Int. Symp. on Computer Architecture*, 346-356.

Appel, A.W., Ellis, J.R., and Li, K. 1988. Real-time concurrent collection on stock multiprocessors. *Proc. SIGPLAN '88 Conf. on Prog. Language Design and Implementation*, June, 11-20.

Apt, K.R., and Francez, N. 1984. Modeling the distributed termination convention of CSP. *ACM Trans. on Prog. Languages and Systems 6*, 3 (July), 370-379.

Apt, K.R., Francez, N., and de Roever, W.P. 1980. A proof system for communicating sequential processes. *ACM Trans. on Prog. Languages and Systems 2*, 3 (July), 359-385.

Ashcroft, E. 1975. Proving assertions about parallel programs. *Journal of Computer and Systems Sciences 10*, 1 (January), 110-135.

Ashcroft, E. 1976. Program verification tableaus. Report CS-76-01, University of Waterloo, Waterloo, Ontario, January.

Ashcroft, E., and Manna, Z. 1971. Formalization of properties of parallel programs. *Machine Intelligence 6*, 17-41.

Athas, W.C., and Seitz, C.L. 1988. Multicomputers: Message-passing concurrent computers. *IEEE Computer 12*, 8 (August), 9-24.

Atkins, M.S. 1988. Experiments in SR with different upcall program structures. *ACM Trans. on Computer Systems 6*, 9 (November), 365-392.

Atkins, M.S., and Olsson, R.A. 1988. Performance of multi-tasking and synchronization mechanisms in the programming language SR. *Software—Practice and Experience 18*, 9 (September), 879-895.

Atwood, J.W. 1976. Concurrency in operating systems. *IEEE Computer 9*, 10 (October), 18-26.

Bagrodia, R. 1989. Synchronization of asynchronous processes in CSP. *ACM Trans. on Prog. Languages and Systems 11*, 4 (October), 585-597.

Bal, H.E. 1990a. An evaluation of the SR language design. Report IR-219, Dept. of Mathematics and Computer Science, Vrije Universiteit, Amsterdam, August.

Bal, H.E. 1990b. *The Shared Data-Object Model as a Paradigm for Programming Distributed Systems.* Silicon Press, Summit, NJ.

Bal, H.E., Steiner, J.G., and Tanenbaum, A.S. 1989. Programming languages for distributed computing systems. *ACM Computing Surveys 21*, 3 (September), 261-322.

Balzer, R.M. 1971. PORTS—a method for dynamic interprogram communication and job control. *Proc. AFIPS SJCC Computer Conf. 39*, 485-489.

Barnes, J.G.P. 1980. An overview of Ada. *Software—Practice and Experience 10*, 851-887.

Barringer, H. 1985. *A Survey of Verification Techniques for Parallel Programs.* Lecture Notes in Computer Science Vol. 191, Springer-Verlag, New York.

Barringer, H., and Mearns, I. 1982. Axioms and proof rules for Ada tasks. *IEE Proc. 129*, Part E, No. 2 (March), 38-48.

Ben-Ari, M. 1982. *Principles of Concurrent Programming.* Prentice-Hall Int., Englewood Cliffs, NJ.

Ben-Ari, M. 1984. Algorithms for on-the-fly garbage collection. *ACM Trans. on Prog. Languages and Systems 6*, 3 (July), 333-344.

Bernstein, A. J. 1966. Analysis of programs for parallel processing. *IEEE Trans. on Computers EC-15*, 5 (October), 757-762.

Bernstein, A.J. 1980. Output guards and non-determinism in CSP. 1980. *ACM Trans. on Prog. Languages and Systems 2*, 2 (April), 234-238.

Bernstein, A.J. 1987. Predicate transfer and timeout in message passing systems. *Information Processing Letters 24*, 1 (January), 43-52.

Bernstein, A.J., and Ensor, J.R. 1981. A Modula based language supporting hierarchical development and verification. *Software—Practice and Experience 11*, 237-255.

Bic, L., and Shaw, A.C. 1988. *The Logical Design of Operating Systems*, Second Edition. Prentice-Hall, Englewood Cliffs, NJ.

Birman, K. P., and Joseph, T.A. 1987. Reliable communication in the presence of failures. *ACM Trans. on Computer Systems 5*, 1 (February), 47-76.

Birrell, A.D., and Nelson, B.J. 1984. Implementing remote procedure calls. *ACM Trans. on Computer Systems 2*, 1 (February), 39-59.

Black, A.P. 1985. Supporting distributed applications: experience with Eden. *Proc. 10th Symp. on Operating Systems Principles*, December, 181-193.

Black, A., Hutchinson, N., Jul, E., and Levy, H. 1986. Object structure in the Emerald system. *ACM 1986 OOPSLA Proceedings*, September, 78-86.

Black, A., Hutchinson, N., Jul, E., Levy, H., and Carter, L. 1987. Distribution and abstract types in Emerald. *IEEE Trans. Soft. Engr. SE-13*, 1 (January), 65-76.

Block, K., and Woo, Tai-Kuo. 1990. A more efficient generalization of Peterson's mutual exclusion algorithm. *Information Processing Letters 35*, August, 219-222.

Bloom, T. 1979. Evaluating synchronization mechanisms. *Proc. Seventh Symp. on Operating Systems Principles*, December, 24-32.

Brinch Hansen, P. 1970. The nucleus of a multiprogramming system. *Comm. of the ACM 13*, 4 (April), 238-241.

Brinch Hansen, P. 1972a. A comparison of two synchronizing concepts. *Acta Informatica 1*, 190-199.

Brinch Hansen, P. 1972b. Structured multiprogramming. *Comm. ACM 15*, 7 (July), 574-578.

Brinch Hansen, P. 1973a. *Operating System Principles*. Prentice-Hall, Englewood Cliffs, NJ.

Brinch Hansen, P. 1973b. Concurrent programming concepts. *ACM Computing Surveys 5*, 4 (December), 223-245.

Brinch Hansen, P. 1975. The programming language Concurrent Pascal. *IEEE Trans. on Software Engr. SE-1*, 2 (June), 199-206.

Brinch Hansen, P. 1976a. The Solo operating system: job interface. *Software—Practice and Experience 6*, 151-164.

Brinch Hansen, P. 1976b. The Solo operating system: processes, monitors, and classes. *Software—Practice and Experience 6*, 165-200.

Brinch Hansen, P. 1977. *The Architecture of Concurrent Programs*. Prentice-Hall, Englewood Cliffs, NJ.

Brinch Hansen, P. 1978. Distributed processes: A concurrent programming concept. *Comm. ACM 21*, 11 (November), 934-941.

Brinch Hansen, P. 1981a. Edison: a multiprocessor language. *Software—Practice and Experience 11*, 4 (April), 325-361.

Brinch Hansen, P. 1981b. The design of Edison. *Software—Practice and Experience*, (April), 363-396.

Brinch Hansen, P. 1987. Joyce—a programming language for distributed systems. *Software—Practice and Experience 17*, 1 (January), 29-50.

Brinch Hansen, P. 1989a. The Joyce language report. *Software—Practice and Experience 19*, 6 (June), 553-578.

Brinch Hansen, P. 1989b. A multiprocessor implementation of Joyce. *Software—Practice and Experience 19*, 6 (June), 579-592.

Brinch Hansen, P. 1989c. Analysis of a parallel mergesort. Report CIS 89-3, School of Computer and Information Science, Syracuse University, July.

Brooks, E.D., III. 1986. The butterfly barrier. *Int. Journal of Parallel Prog. 15*, 4 (August), 295-307.

Buckley, G.N., and Silberschatz, A. 1983. An effective implementation for the generalized input-output construct of CSP. *ACM Trans. on Prog. Languages and Systems 5*, 2 (April), 223-235.

Burns, A. 1988. *Programming in occam 2*. Addison-Wesley, Reading, MA.

Burns, J.E. 1981. Symmetry in systems of asynchronous processes. *Proc. 22nd Symp. on Foundations of Computer Science*, October, 169-174.

Bustard, D., Elder, J, and Welsh, J. 1988. *Concurrent Program Structures*. Prentice-Hall Int., Englewood Cliffs, NJ.

Campbell, R.H., and Habermann, A.N. 1974. The specification of process synchronization by path expressions. *Lecture Notes in Computer Science 16*, Springer-Verlag, Heidelberg, 89-102.

Campbell, R.H., and Kolstad, R.B. 1979. Path expressions in Pascal. *Proc. Fourth Int. Conf. on Software Engr.*, September, 17-19.

Campbell, R.H., and Kolstad, R.B. 1980. An overview of Path Pascal's design, and Path Pascal user manual. *SIGPLAN Notices 15*, 9 (September), 13-24.

Cardelli, L., Donahue, J., Glassman, L., Jordan, M., Kalsow, B., and Nelson, G. 1989. *Modula-3 Report* (revised). Report 52, DEC Systems Research Center, November.

Carriero, N., and Gelernter, D. 1986. The S/Net's Linda kernel. *ACM Trans. Computer Systems 4*, 2 (May), 110-129.

Carriero, N., and Gelernter, D. 1989a. Linda in Context. *Comm. ACM 32*, 4 (April), 444-458.

Carriero, N., and Gelernter, D. 1989b. How to write parallel programs: a guide to the perplexed. *ACM Computing Surveys 21*, 3 (September), 323-358.

Carriero, N., Gelernter, D., and Leichter, J. 1986. Distributed data structures in Linda. *Thirteenth ACM Symp. on Principles of Prog. Langs.*, January, 236-242.

Chandrasekaran, S., and Venkatesan, S. 1990. A message-optimal algorithm for distributed termination detection. *Journal of Parallel and Distributed Computing 8*, 245-292.

Chandy, K.M., Haas, L.M., and Misra, J. 1983. Distributed deadlock detection. *ACM Trans. on Computer Systems 1*, 2 (May), 144-156.

Chandy, K.M., and Lamport, L. 1985. Distributed snapshots: Determining global states of distributed systems. *ACM Trans. on Computer Systems 3*, 1 (February), 63-75.

Chandy, K.M., and Misra, J. 1984. The drinking philosophers problem. *ACM Trans. on Prog. Languages and Systems 6*, 4 (October), 632-646.

Chandy, K.M., and Misra, J. 1988. *Parallel Program Design: A Foundation*. Addison-Wesley, Reading, MA.

612

Chang, E.J.-H. 1979. Decentralized Algorithms in Distributed Systems. TR CSRG-103. Doctoral dissertation, Computer Systems Research Group, University of Toronto, October.

Chang, E.J.-H. 1982. Echo algorithms: depth parallel operations on general graphs. *IEEE Trans. on Software Engr. 8*, 4 (July), 391-401.

Clapp, R.M., Duchesneau, L., Volz, R.A., Mudge, T.N., and Schultze, T. 1986. Toward real-time performance benchmarks in Ada. *Comm. ACM 29*, 8 (August), 760-778.

Clarke, L.A., Wileden, J.C., and Wolf, A.L. 1980. Nesting in Ada programs is for the birds. *Proc. SIGPLAN Symp. on the Ada Prog. Language*, December, 139-145.

Clint, M. 1973. Program proving: coroutines. *Acta Informatica 2*, 50-63.

Cmelik, R.F., Gehani, N.H., and Roome, W.D. 1989. Experience with multiple processor versions of concurrent C. *IEEE Trans. on Software Engr. 15*, 3 (March), 335-344.

Coffin, M., and Olsson, R.A. 1989. An SR approach to multiway rendezvous. *Computer Languages 14*, 4, 255-262.

Cohen, J. 1981. Garbage collection of linked data structures. *ACM Computing Surveys 13*, 3 (September), 341-368.

Constable, R.L., and O'Donnell, M.J. 1978. *A Programming Logic*. Winthrop Publishers, Cambridge, MA.

Cook, R.P. 1980. StarMod—A language for distributed programming. *IEEE Trans. on Software Engr. SE-6*, 6 (November), 563-571.

Courtois, P.J., Heymans, F., and Parnas, D.L. 1971. Concurrent control with "readers" and "writers." *Comm. ACM 14*, 10 (October), 667-668.

Courtois, P.J., Heymans, F., and Parnas, D.L. 1972. Comments on "A comparison of two synchronizing concepts" by P.B. Hansen. *Acta Informatica 1*, 375-376.

Dahl, O.J. 1972. Hierarchical program structures. In *Structured Programming*, Dahl, O.-J., Dijkstra, E.W., and Hoare, C.A.R. (Eds.), Academic Press, New York.

de Bakker, J.W., de Roever, W.P, and Rozenberg, G. (Eds.) 1986. *Current Trends in Concurrency*. Lecture Notes in Computer Science Vol. 224, Springer-Verlag, New York.

deBruijn, N.G. 1967. Additional comments on a problem in concurrent programming control. *Comm. ACM 10*, 3 (March), 137-138.

De Carlini, U., and Villano, U. 1988. A simple algorithm for clock synchronization in transputer networks. *Software—Practice and Experience 18*, 4 (April), 331-347.

Dennis, J.B., and Van Horn, E.C. 1966. Programming semantics for multi-programmed computations. *Comm. ACM 9*, 3 (March), 143-155.

Dept. of Defense. 1983. *Reference Manual for the Ada Programming Language*. Springer-Verlag, New York.

Detlefs, D.L., Herlihy, M.P., and Wing, J.M. 1988. Inheritance of synchronization and recovery properties in Avalon / C + +. *IEEE Computer 21*, 12 (December), 57-69.

Dijkstra, E.W. 1965. Solution of a problem in concurrent programming control. *Comm. ACM 8*, 9 (September), 569.

Dijkstra, E.W. 1968a. The structure of the "THE" multiprogramming system. *Comm. ACM 11*, 5 (May), 341-346.

Dijkstra, E.W. 1968b. Cooperating sequential processes. In *Programming Languages*, F. Genuys (ed.), Academic Press, New York, 43-112.

Dijkstra, E.W. 1972. Hierarchical ordering of sequential processes. In *Operating Systems Techniques*, Hoare, C.A.R., and Perrott, R.H. (Eds.), Academic Press, New York.

Dijkstra, E.W. 1975. Guarded commands, nondeterminacy, and formal derivation of programs. *Comm. ACM 18*, 8 (August), 453-457.

Dijkstra, E.W. 1976. *A Discipline of Programming*. Prentice-Hall, Englewood Cliffs, NJ.

Dijkstra, E.W. 1977. On making solutions more and more fine-grained. EWD 629, reprinted in Dijkstra, E.W., *Selected Writings on Computing: A Personal Perspective*, Springer-Verlag, New York, 1982, 313-318.

Dijkstra, E.W. 1979. A tutorial on the split binary semaphore. EWD 703, Neunen, The Netherlands, March.

Dijkstra, E.W. 1980. The superfluity of the general semaphore. EWD 734, Neunen, The Netherlands, April.

Dijkstra, E.W., Feijen, W.H.J., and van Gasteren, A.J.M. 1983. Derivation of a termination detection algorithm for distributed computation. *Information Processing Letters 16*, 5 (June), 217-219.

Dijkstra, E.W., Lamport, L., Martin, A.J., Scholten, C.S., and Steffens, E.M.F. 1978. On-the-fly garbage collection: an exercise in cooperation. *Comm. ACM 21*, 11 (November), 966-975.

Dijkstra, E.W., and Scholten, C.S. 1980. Termination detection in diffusing computations. *Information Processing Letters 11*, 1 (August), 1-4.

Dillon, L.K. 1990. Using symbolic execution for verification of Ada tasking programs. *ACM Trans. on Prog. Languages and Systems 12*, 4 (October), 643-669.

Eggers, S.J., and Katz, R.H. 1989. The effect of sharing on the cache and bus performance of parallel programs. *Third Int. Conf. on Architectural Support for Prog. Languages and Operating Systems*, April, 257-270.

Eisenberg, M.A., and McGuire, M.R. 1972. Further comments on Dijkstra's concurrent programming control problem. *Comm. ACM 15*, 11 (November), 999.

Elshoff, I.J.P., and Andrews, G.R. 1988. The development of two distributed algorithms for network topology. TR 88-13, Dept. of Computer Science, University of Arizona, March.

Faulk, S.R., and Parnas, D.L. 1988. On synchronization in hard-real-time systems. *Comm. ACM, 31*, 3 (March), 274-287.

Feldman, J.A. 1979. High level programming for distributed computing. *Comm. ACM 22*, 6 (June), 353-368.

Fillman, R.E., and Friedman, D.P. 1983. *Coordinated Computing: Tools and Techniques for Distributed Software*. McGraw-Hill, New York.

Finkel, R.A., Solomon, M., and Horowitz, M.L. 1979. Distributed algorithms for global structuring. *AFIPS Conference Proceedings, 1979 National Computer Conference*, , 455-460.

Finkel, R., and Manber, U. 1987. DIB—a distributed implementation of backtracking. *ACM Trans. on Prog. Languages and Systems 9*, 2 (April), 235-256.

Fisher, A.J. 1986. A multiprocessor implementation of occam. *Software—Practice and Experience 16*, 10 (October), 857-892.

Fisher, A.J. 1988. A critique of occam channel types. *Computer Languages 13*, 2, 95-105.

Floyd, R.W. 1967. Assigning meanings to programs. *Proc Amer. Math. Society Symp. in Applied Mathematics 19*, 19-31.

Fox, G.C., Johnson, M.A., Lyzenga, G.A., Otto, S.W., Salmon, J.K., and Walker, D.W. 1988. *Solving Problems on Concurrent Processors, Volume I: General Techniques and Regular Problems*. Prentice-Hall, Englewood Cliffs, NJ.

Francez, N. 1980. Distributed termination. *ACM Trans. on Prog. Languages and Systems 2*, 1 (January), 42-55.

Francez, N. 1982. Extending naming conventions for communicating processes. *Proc. Ninth ACM Symp. on Principles of Prog. Languages*, January, 40-45.

Francez, N. 1986. *Fairness*. Springer-Verlag, New York.

Francez, N., and Rodeh, M.. 1982. Achieving distributed termination without freezing. *IEEE Trans. on Software Engineering SE-8*, 3 (May), 287-292.

Gallier, J.H. 1986. *Logic for Computer Science: Foundations of Automatic Theorem Proving*. Harper & Row, New York.

Garcia-Molina, H. 1982. Elections in a distributed computing system. *IEEE Trans. on Computers C-31*, 1 (January), 48-59.

Gehani, N.H. 1990a. Message passing in Concurrent C: synchronous versus asynchronous. *Software—Practice and Experience 20*, 6 (June), 571-592.

Gehani, N.H. 1990b. Capsules: A shared memory access mechanism for Concurrent C/C++. *AT&T Bell Labs Technical Memo*, August.

Gehani, N.H., and McGettrick, A. D. 1988. *Concurrent Programming*. Addison-Wesley, Reading, MA.

Gehani, N.H., and Roome, W.D. 1986. Concurrent C. *Software—Practice and Experience 16*, 9 (September), 821-844.

Gehani, N.H., and Roome, W.D. 1988a. Rendezvous facilities: Concurrent C and the Ada language. *IEEE Trans. on Software Engr. 14*, 11 (November), 1546-1553.

Gehani, N.H. and Roome, W.D. 1988b. Concurrent C++: concurrent programming with class(es). *Software—Practice and Experience 18*, 12 (December), 1157-1177.

Gehani, N.H., and Roome, W.D. 1989. *The Concurrent C Programming Language*. Silicon Press, Summit, NJ.

Geist, R., and Daniel, S. 1987. A continuum of disk scheduling algorithms. *ACM Trans. on Computer Systems 5*, 1 (February), 77-92.

Gelernter, D. 1985. Generative communication in Linda. *ACM Trans. on Prog. Languages and Systems 7*, 1 (January), 80-112.

Gelernter, D., and Bernstein, A.J. 1982. Distributed communication via global buffer. *Proc. Symp. on Principles of Distributed Computing*, August, 10-18.

Gentleman, W.M. 1981. Message passing between sequential processes: the reply primitive and the administrator concept. *Software—Practice and Experience 11*, 435-466.

Gerth, R. 1982. A sound and complete Hoare axiomatization of the Ada-rendezvous. *Proc. Ninth Int. Colloquium on Automata, Languages and Prog., Lecture Notes in Computer Science, Vol. 140*, Springer-Verlag, Heidelberg, 252-264.

Gifford, D.K. 1979. Weighted voting for replicated data. *Proc. Seventh Symp. on Operating Systems Principles*, December, 150-162.

Good, D.I, Cohen, R.M., and Keeton-Williams, J. 1979. Principles of proving concurrent programs in Gypsy. *Proc. Sixth ACM Symp. on Principles of Prog. Languages*, January, 42-52.

Goodman, J.R., Vernon, M.K., and Woest, P.J. 1989. Efficient synchronization primitives for large-scale cache-coherent multiprocessors. *Third Int. Conf. on Architectural Support for Prog. Languages and Operating Systems*, April, 64-75.

Goscinski, A. 1990. Two algorithms for mutual exclusion in real-time distributed computer systems. *Journal of Parallel and Distributed Computing 9*, 77-82.

Gottlieb, A., Lubachevsky, B.D., and Rudolph, L. 1983. Basic techniques for the efficient coordination of very large numbers of cooperating sequential processors. *ACM Trans. on Prog. Languages and Systems 5*, 2 (April), 164-189.

Gries, D. 1977a. An exercise in proving parallel programs correct. *Comm. ACM 20* 12 (December), 921-930.

Gries, D. 1977b. A proof of correctness of Rem's semaphore implementation of the with-when statement. TR 77-314, Dept. of Computer Science, Cornell University.

Gries, D. 1981. *The Science of Programming*. Springer-Verlag, New York.

Gries, D., and Levin, G.M. 1980. Assignment and procedure call proof rules. *ACM Trans. on Prog. Languages and Systems 2*, 4 (October), 564-579.

Grit, D.H., and McGraw, J.R. 1985. Programming divide and conquer on a MIMD machine. *Software—Practice and Experience 15*, 1 (January), 41-53.

Gupta, R. 1989. The fuzzy barrier: a mechanism for high speed synchronization of processors. *Third Int. Conf. on Architectural Support for Prog. Languages and Operating Systems*, April, 54-63.

Habermann, A.N. 1972. Synchronization of communicating processes. *Comm. ACM 15*, 3 (March), 171-176.

Habermann, A.N., and Nassi, I.R. 1980. Efficient implementation of Ada tasks. Technical Report CMU-CS-80-103, Carnegie-Mellon University, January.

Haddon, B.K. 1977. Nested monitor calls. *Operating Systems Review 11*, 4 (October), 18-23.

Halstead, R.H. 1985. Multilisp: A language for concurrent symbolic computation. *ACM Trans. on Prog. Languages and Systems 7*, 4 (October), 501-538.

Hehner, E.C.R. 1984. *The Logic of Programming*. Prentice-Hall Int., Englewood Cliffs, NJ.

Hensgen, D., Finkel, R., and Manber, U. 1988. Two algorithms for barrier synchronization. *Int. Journal of Parallel Prog. 17*, 1 (January), 1-17.

Herlihy, M.P. 1990. A methodology for implementing highly concurrent data structures. *Proc. Second ACM Symp. on Principles & Practice of Parallel Prog.*, March, 197-206.

Herlihy, M.P. 1991. Wait-free synchronization. *ACM Trans. on Prog. Languages and Systems 11*, 1 (January), 124-149.

Herlihy, M.P., and Wing, J.M. 1990. Linearizability: a correctness condition for concurrent objects. *ACM Trans. on Prog. Languages and Systems 12*, 3 (July), 463-492.

Herman, J.S. 1989. A comparison of synchronization mechanisms for concurrent programming. Master's thesis, CSE-89-26, University of California at Davis, September.

Hewitt, C. 1977. Viewing control structures as patterns on passing messages. *Journal Artificial Intelligence 8*, 3 (June), 323-364.

Hill, M.D., and Larus, J.R. 1990. Cache considerations for multiprocessor programmers. *Comm. ACM 33*, 8 (August), 97-102.

Hillis, W.D. 1985. *The Connection Machine*. MIT Press, Cambridge, MA.

Hillis, W.D., and Steele, G.L., Jr. 1986. Data parallel algorithms. *Comm. ACM 29*, 12 (December), 1170-1183.

Hoare, C.A.R. 1969. An axiomatic basis for computer programming. *Comm. ACM 12*, 10 (October), 576-580, 583.

Hoare, C.A.R. 1972. Towards a theory of parallel programming. In *Operating Systems Techniques*, Hoare, C.A.R., and Perrott, R.H. (Eds.), Academic Press, New York.

Hoare, C.A.R. 1973. A structured paging system. *Computer Journal 16*, 3, 209-215.

Hoare, C.A.R. 1974. Monitors: an operating system structuring concept. *Comm. ACM 17*, 10 (October), 549-557.

Hoare, C.A.R. 1975. Parallel programming: an axiomatic approach. *Computer Languages 1*, 151-160.

Hoare, C.A.R. 1978. Communicating sequential processes. *Comm. ACM 21*, 8 (August), 666-677.

Hoare, C.A.R. 1981. The emperor's old clothes. *Comm. ACM 24*, 2 (February), 75-83.

Hoare, C.A.R. 1985. *Communicating Sequential Processes*. Prentice-Hall Int., Englewood Cliffs, NJ.

Hoare, C.A.R., and Wirth, N. 1973. An axiomatic definition of the programming language Pascal. *Acta Informatica 2*, 335-355.

Hofstadter, D.J. 1979. *Gödel, Escher, Bach: An Eternal Golden Braid*. Vintage Books, New York.

Holden, J., and Wand, I.C. 1980. An assessment of Modula. *Software—Practice and Experience 10*, 593-621.

Holt, R.C. 1983. *Concurrent Euclid, The UNIX System, and Tunis*. Addison-Wesley, Reading, MA.

Holt, R.C. 1984. TURING: an inside look at the genesis of a programming language. *Computerworld 18*, 20 (May).

Holt, R.C., and Cordy, J.R. 1985. The Turing Plus report. Tech. Memo, Computer Systems Research Institute, University of Toronto.

Holt, R.C., and Cordy, J.R. 1988. The Turing programming language. *Comm. ACM 31*, 12 (December), 1410-1423.

Holt, R.C., Graham, G.S., Lazowska, E.D., and Scott, M.A. 1978. *Structured Concurrent Programming with Operating System Applications*. Addison-Wesley, Reading, MA.

Holt, R.C., Matthews, P.A., Rosselet, J.A., and Cordy, J.R. 1987. *The TURING Programming Language: Design and Definition*. Prentice-Hall, Englewood Cliffs, NJ.

Horning, J.J., and Randell, B. 1973. Process structuring. *ACM Computing Surveys 5*, 1 (March), 5-30.

Howard, J.H. 1976a. Proving monitors. *Comm. ACM 19*, 5 (May), 273-279.

Howard, J.H. 1976b. Signaling in monitors. *Proc. 2nd Int. Conference on Software Engr.*, October, 47-52.

Huang, D.T., and Olsson, R.A. 1990. An exception handling mechanism for SR. *Computer Languages 15*, 3, 163-176.

Huang, S.-T. 1990. A distributed deadlock detection algorithm for CSP-like communication. *ACM Trans. on Prog. Languages and Systems 12*, 1 (January), 102-122.

Hudak, P. 1989. Conception, evolution, and application of functional programming languages. *ACM Computing Surveys 21*, 3 (September), 359-411.

Hull, M.E.C. 1984. A parallel view of stable marriages. *Information Processing Letters 18*, 2 (February), 63-66.

Hull, M.E.C. 1987. Occam—a programming language for multiprocessor systems. *Computer Languages 12*, 1, 27-37.

Hull, M.E.C., and McKeag, R.M. 1984a. Communicating sequential processes for centralized and distributed operating system design. *ACM Trans. on Prog. Languages and Systems 6*, 2 (April), 175-191.

Hull, M.E.C., and McKeag, R.M. 1984b. A general approach to queuing in CSP. *Software—Practice and Experience 14*, 8 (August), 769-773.

INMOS Limited. 1984. *Occam Programming Manual.* Prentice-Hall Int., Englewood Cliffs, NJ.

Jones, A.K., and Schwarz, P. 1980. Experience using multiprocessor systems—a status report. *ACM Computing Surveys 12*, 2 (June), 121-165.

Jordan, H.F. 1978. A special purpose architecture for finite element analysis. *Proc. 1978 Int. Conf. on Parallel Processing*, 263-266.

Joseph, M., Prasad, V.R., and Natarajan, N. 1984. *A Multiprocessor Operating System.* Prentice-Hall Int., Englewood Cliffs, NJ.

Kaubisch, W.H., Perrott, R.H., and Hoare, C.A.R. 1976. Quasiparallel programming. *Software—Practice and Experience 6*, 341-356.

Keedy, J.L. 1978. On structuring operating systems with monitors. *The Australian Computer Journal 10*, 1 (February), 23-27. Reprinted in *Operating Systems Review 13*, 1 (January 1979), 5-9.

Kessels, J.L.W. 1977. An alternative to event queues for synchronization in monitors. *Comm. ACM 20*, 7 (July), 500-503.

Kessels, J.L.W., and Martin, A.J. 1979. Two implementations of the conditional critical region using a split binary semaphore. *Information Processing Letters 8*, 2 (February), 67-71.

Kieburtz, R.B., and Silberschatz, A. 1979. Comments on "Communicating Sequential Processes." *ACM Trans. on Prog. Languages and Systems 1*, 2 (October), 218-225.

Kieburtz, R.B., and Silberschatz, A. 1983. Access-right expressions. *ACM Trans. on Prog. Languages and Systems 5*, 1 (January), 78-96.

Knapp, E. 1987. Deadlock detention in distributed databases. *ACM Computing Surveys 19*, 4 (December), 303-328.

Knuth, D.E. 1966. Additional comments on a problem in concurrent programming control. *Comm. ACM 9*, 5 (May), 321-322.

Kohler, W.H. 1981. A survey of techniques for synchronization and recovery in decentralized computer systems. *ACM Computing Surveys 13*, 2 (June), 149-183.

Kramer, J., and Magee, J. 1985. Dynamic configuration for distributed systems. *IEEE Trans. on Software Engr. SE-11*, 4 (April), 424-436.

Krogdahl, S., and Olsen, K.A. 1986. Ada, as seen from Simula. *Software—Practice and Experience 16*, 8 (August), 689-700.

Kung, H.T., and Song, S.W. 1977. An efficient parallel garbage collection system and its correctness proof. *18th Annual Symp. on Foundations of CS (FOCS)*, October, 120-131.

Lamport, L. 1974. A new solution of Dijkstra's concurrent programming problem. *Comm. ACM 17*, 8 (August), 453-455.

Lamport, L. 1977a. Proving the correctness of multiprocess programs. *IEEE Trans. on Software Engr. SE-3*, 2 (March), 125-143.

Lamport, L. 1977b. Concurrent reading and writing. *Comm. ACM 20*, 11 (November), 806-811.

Lamport, L. 1978. Time, clocks, and the ordering of events in distributed systems. *Comm. ACM 21*, 7 (July), 558-565.

Lamport, L. 1979. A new approach to proving the correctness of multiprocess programs. *ACM Trans. on Prog. Languages and Systems 1*, 1 (July), 84-97.

Lamport, L. 1980. The "Hoare logic" of concurrent programs. *Acta Informatica 14*, 21-37.

Lamport, L. 1982. An assertional correctness proof of a distributed algorithm. *Science of Computer Prog. 2*, 3 (December), 175-206.

Lamport, L. 1987. A fast mutual exclusion algorithm. *ACM Trans. on Computer Systems 5*, 1 (February), 1-11.

Lamport, L. 1988. Control predicates are better than dummy variables for reasoning about program control. *ACM Trans. on Prog. Lang. and Systems 10*, 2 (April), 267-281.

Lamport, L. 1990. *win* and *sin*: predicate transformers for concurrency. *ACM Trans. on Prog. Languages and Systems 12*, 3 (July), 396-428.

Lamport, L., and Schneider, F.B. 1984. The "Hoare Logic" of CSP and all that. *ACM Trans. on Prog. Languages and Systems 6*, 2 (April), 281-296.

Lamport, L., Shostak, R., and Pease, M. 1982. The Byzantine generals problem. *ACM Trans. on Prog. Languages and Systems 3*, 3 (July), 382-401.

Lampson, B.W. 1983. A description of the Cedar language. Technical Report CSL-83-15, Xerox Palo Alto Research Center, December.

Lampson, B.W., Horning, J.J., London, R.L., Mitchell, J.G., and Popek, G.J. 1977. Report on the programming language Euclid. *SIGPLAN Notices 12*, 2 (February), 1-79.

Lampson, B.W., and Redell, D.D. 1980. Experience with processes and monitors in Mesa. *Comm. ACM 23*, 2 (February), 105-117.

Lauer, H.C., and Needham, R.M. 1978. On the duality of operating system structures. *Proc. Second Int. Symp. on Operating Systems*, October; reprinted in *Operating Systems Review 13*, 2 (April 1979), 3-19.

LeBlanc, T.J., Gerber, R.H., and Cook, R.P. 1984. The StarMod distributed programming kernel. *Software—Practice and Experience 14*, 12 (December), 1123-1139.

Lehman, D., Pnueli, A., and Stavii, J. 1981. Impartiality, justice, and fairness: the ethics of concurrent termination. *Proc. Eighth Colloq. on Automata, Languages, and Prog.*, Lecture Notes in Computer Science Vol. 115, Springer-Verlag, New York, 264-277.

Lehmann, D., and Rabin, M.O. 1981. A symmetric and fully distributed solution to the dining philosophers problem. *Proc. Eighth ACM Symp. on Principles of Prog. Languages*, January, 133-138.

LeLann, G. 1977. Distributed systems: Towards a formal approach. *Proc. Information Processing 77*, North-Holland, Amsterdam, 155-160.

620

Levin, G.M., and Gries, D. 1981. A proof technique for communicating sequential processes. *Acta Informatica 15*, 281-302.

Levitt, K.N. 1972. The application of program-proving techniques to the verification of synchronization processes. *Proc. AFIPS Fall Joint Computer Conf.*, AFIPS Press, 33-47.

Liskov, B., Herlihy, M., and Gilbert, L. 1986. Limitations of remote procedure call and static process structure for distributed computing. *Proc. 13th ACM Symp. on Principles of Prog. Languages*, January, 150-159.

Liskov, B., and Scheifler, R. 1983. Guardians and actions: linguistic support for robust, distributed programs. *ACM Trans. of Prog. Languages and Systems 5*, 3 (July), 381-404.

Lister, A. 1977. The problem of nested monitor calls. *Operating Systems Review 11*, 3 (July), 5-7.

Loehr, K-P. 1977. Beyond Concurrent Pascal. *Proc. of Sixth ACM Symp. on Operating Systems Principles*, November, 173-180.

Lubachevsky, B. 1984. An approach to automating the verification of compact parallel coordination programs. *Acta Informatica 14*, 125-169.

Maekawa, M. 1985. A $\sqrt{N}$ algorithm for mutual exclusion in decentralized systems. *ACM Trans. on Computer Systems 3*, 2 (May), 145-159.

Maekawa, M., Oldehoeft, A.E., and Oldehoeft, R.R. 1987. *Operating Systems: Advanced Concepts*. Benjamin/Cummings, Redwood City, CA.

Manber, U. 1989. *Introduction to Algorithms: A Creative Approach*. Addison-Wesley, Reading, MA.

Manna, Z., and Waldinger, R. 1985. *The Logical Basis for Computer Programming*. Addison-Wesley, Reading, MA.

Mao, T.W., and Yeh, R.T. 1980. Communication port: a language concept for concurrent programming. *IEEE Trans. on Software Engr. SE-6*, 2 (March), 194-204.

Martin, A.J. 1985. Distributed mutual exclusion on a ring of processes. *Science of Computer Programming 5*, 265-276.

Martin, A.J., and Burch, A.J. 1985. Fair mutual exclusion with unfair P and V operations. *Information Processing Letters 21*, 2 (August), 97-100.

Marzullo, K., and Owicki, S.S. 1983. Maintaining the time in a distributed system. *Proc. Second ACM Symp. on Principles of Distr. Computing*, August, 295-305.

Mattern, F. 1990. Asynchronous distributed termination—parallel and symmetric solutions with echo algorithms. *Algorithmica 5*, 325-340.

May, D. 1983. OCCAM. *SIGPLAN Notices 18*, 4 (April), 69-79.

May, D. 1987. *Occam 2 Language Definition*. Inmos Ltd., Bristol, United Kingdom.

McCurley, E.R. 1989. Auxiliary variables in partial correctness programming logics. *Information Processing Letters 33*, 3 (November), 131-133.

McCurley, E.R., and Schneider, F.B. 1986. Derivation of a distributed algorithm for finding paths in directed networks. *Science of Computer Prog. 6*, 1 (January), 1-9.

McNamee, C.M., and Olsson, R.A. 1990. Transformations for optimizing interprocess communication and synchronization mechanisms. *Int. Journal of Parallel Programming 19*, 5 (October), in press.

Mellor-Crummey, J.M., and Scott, M.L. 1991. *ACM Trans. on Computer Systems*, in press.

Misra, J. 1983. Detecting termination of distributed computations using markers. *Proc. Second ACM Symp. on Principles of Distr. Computing*, August, 290-294.

Misra, J., and Chandy, K.M. 1981. Proofs of networks of processes. *IEEE Trans. on Software Engr. SE-7*, 4 (July), 417-426.

Misra, J., and Chandy, K.M. 1982. Termination detection of diffusing computations in communicating sequential processes. *ACM Trans. on Prog. Languages and Systems 4*, 1 (January), 37-43.

Misra, J., Chandy, K.M., and Smith, T. 1982. Proving safety and liveness of communicating processes with examples. *Proc. ACM Symp. on Principles of Distributed Computing*, August, 201-208.

Mitchell, J.G., Maybury, W., and Sweet, R. 1979. Mesa language manual, version 5.0. Xerox Palo Alto Research Center Report CSL-79-3, April.

Morgan, C. 1985. Global and logical time in distributed algorithms. *Information Processing Letters 20*, 4 (May), 189-194.

Morris, J.M. 1979. A starvation-free solution to the mutual exclusion problem. *Information Processing Letters 8*, 2 (February), 76-80.

Naur, P. 1966. Proof of algorithms by general snapshots. *BIT 6*, 4, 310-316.

Nelson, B.J. 1981. Remote procedure call. Doctoral dissertation, Dept. of Computer Science Report CMU-CS-81-119, Carnegie-Mellon University, May.

Olsson, R.A. 1986. Issues in distributed programming languages: the evolution of SR. TR 86-21. Doctoral dissertation, Dept. of Computer Science, The University of Arizona, August.

Olsson, R.A., and McNamee C.M. 1991. Inter-entry selection: non-determinism and explicit control mechanisms. *Computer Languages 16*, in press.

Olsson, R.A., and Whitehead, G.R. 1989. A simple technique for automatic recompilation in modular programming languages. *Software—Practice and Experience 19*, 8 (August), 757-773.

Owicki, S.S. 1975. Axiomatic proof techniques for parallel programs. TR 75-251. Doctoral dissertation, Dept. of Computer Science, Cornell University, Ithaca NY.

Owicki, S.S., and Gries, D. 1976a. An axiomatic proof technique for parallel programs. *Acta Informatica 6*, 319-340.

Owicki, S.S., and Gries, D. 1976b. Verifying properties of parallel programs: an axiomatic approach. *Comm. ACM 19*, 5 (May), 279-285.

Owicki, S., and Lamport, L. 1982. Proving liveness properties of concurrent programs. *ACM Trans. on Prog. Languages and Systems 4*, 3 (July), 455-495.

Parnas, D.L. 1975. On a solution to the cigarette smoker's problem (without conditional statements). *Comm. ACM 18*, 3 (March), 181-183.

Parnas, D.L. 1978. The non-problem of nested monitor calls. *Operating Systems Review 12*, 1 (January), 12-14.

Parr, F.N., and Strom, R.E. 1983. NIL: A high-level language for distributed systems programming. *IBM Systems Journal 22*, 1-2, 111-127.

Patil, S.S. 1971. Limitations and capabilities of Dijkstra's semaphore primitives for coordination among processes. MIT Project MAC Memo 57, February.

Perrott, R.H. 1987. *Parallel Programming*. Addison-Wesley, Reading, MA.

Peterson, G.L. 1981. Myths about the mutual exclusion problem. *Information Processing Letters 12*, 3 (June), 115-116.

Peterson, G.L. 1983a. Concurrent reading while writing. *ACM. Trans. on Prog. Languages and Systems 5*, 1 (January), 46-55.

Peterson, G.L. 1983b. A new solution to Lamport's concurrent programming problem using small shared variables. *ACM Trans. on Prog. Languages and Systems 5*, 1 (January), 56-65.

Pnueli, A. 1977. The temporal logic of programs. *Proc. 18th Symp. on the Foundations of Computer Science*, November, 46-57.

Prasad, V.R. 1984. Interference-freedom in proofs of CSP program. *Fourth Int. Conf. on Dist. Computing Systems*, May, 79-86.

Presser, L. 1975. Multiprogramming coordination. *ACM Computing Surveys 7*, 1 (March), 149-167.

Raj, R.K., Tempero, E., Levy, H.M., Black, A.P., Hutchinson, N.C., and Jul, E. 1991. Emerald: a general purpose programming language. *Software—Practice and Experience 21*, 1 (January), 91-118.

Rana, S.P. 1983. A distributed solution of the distributed termination problem. *Information Processing Letters 17*, 1 (July), 43-46.

Raymond, K. 1989. A tree-based algorithm for distributed mutual exclusion. *ACM Trans. on Computer Systems 7*, 1 (February), 61-77.

Raynal, M. 1986. *Algorithms for Mutual Exclusion*. MIT Press, Cambridge, MA.

Raynal, M. 1988a. *Networks and Distributed Computation*. MIT Press, Cambridge, MA.

Raynal, M. 1988b. *Distributed Algorithms and Protocols*. John Wiley & Sons, New York.

Raynal, M., and Helary, J.M. 1990. *Control and Synchronisation of Distributed Systems and Programs*. John Wiley & Sons, Chichester, West Sussex, England.

Reed, D.P., and Kanodia, R.K. 1979. Synchronization with eventcounts and sequencers. *Comm. ACM 22*, 2 (February), 115-123.

Reid, L.G. 1980. Control and communication in programmed systems. Doctoral dissertation, Dept. of Computer Science Report CMU-CS-80-142, Carnegie-Mellon University, September.

Ricart, G., and Agrawala, A.K. 1981. An optimal algorithm for mutual exclusion. *Comm. ACM 24*, 1 (January), 9-17.

Ritchie, D.M., and Thompson, K. 1974. The UNIX timesharing system. *Comm. ACM 17*, 7 (July), 365-375.

Roberts, E.S., Evans, A., Morgan, C.R., and Clarke, E.M. 1981. Task management in Ada—a critical evaluation for real-time multiprocessors. *Software—Practice and Experience 11*, 1019-1051.

Sandberg, R., Goldberg, D., Kleiman, S., Walsh, D., and Lyon, B. 1985. Design and implementation of the Sun network filesystem. *Proc. of the Usenix Conference*, June, 119-130.

Schlichting, R.D., and Schneider, F.B. 1983. Fail-stop processors: An approach to designing fault-tolerant computing systems. *ACM Trans. on Computer Systems 1*, 3 (August), 222-238.

Schlichting, R.D., and Schneider, F.B. 1984. Using message passing for distributed programming: proof rules and disciplines. *ACM. Trans. on Prog. Languages and Systems 6*, 3 (July), 402-431.

Schmid, H.A. 1976. On the efficient implementation of conditional critical regions and the construction of monitors. *Acta Informatica 6*, 227-279.

Schneider, F.B. 1980. Ensuring consistency in a distributed database system by use of distributed semaphores. *Proc. of Int. Symp. on Distributed Databases*, March, 183-189.

Schneider, F.B. 1982. Synchronization in distributed programs. *ACM Trans. on Prog. Languages and Systems 4*, 2 (April), 125-148.

Schneider, F.B. 1987. Decomposing properties into safety and liveness using predicate logic. Dept. of Computer Science, Cornell University (October).

Schneider, F.B., and Andrews, G.R. 1986. Concepts for concurrent programming. In *Current Trends in Concurrency*, Lecture Notes in Computer Science Vol. 224, Springer-Verlag, New York, 669-716.

Schneider, F.B., and Bernstein, A.J. 1978. Scheduling in Concurrent Pascal. *Operating Systems Review 12*, 2 (April), 15-20.

Schneider, F.B., Gries, D., and Schlichting, R.D. 1984. Fault-tolerant broadcasts. *Science of Computer Prog. 4*, 1-15.

Schneider, F.B., and Lamport, L. 1985. Paradigms for distributed programs. In *Distributed Systems: Methods and Tools for Specification, An Advanced Course*, Lecture Notes in Computer Science, Vol. 190, Springer-Verlag, Berlin.

Schwartz, J.T. 1980. Ultracomputers. *ACM Trans. on Prog. Languages and Systems 2*, 4 (October), 484-521.

Scott, M.L. 1987. Language support for loosely coupled distributed programs. *IEEE Trans. Software Engr. SE-13*, 1 (January), 88-103.

Scott, M.L. 1991. The Lynx distributed programming language: motivation, design, and experience. *Computer Languages 16*, in press.

Scott, M.L., and Cox, A.L. 1987. An empirical study of message-passing overhead. *Proc. Seventh Int. Conf. on Distributed Computing Systems*, September, 536-543.

624

Scott, M.L., LeBlanc, T.J., and Marsh, B.D. 1990. Multi-model parallel programming in Psyche. *Proc. Second ACM Symp. on Principles & Practice of Parallel Prog.*, March, 70-78.

Shapiro, E. 1989. The family of concurrent logic programming languages. *ACM Computing Surveys 21*, 3 (September), 412-510.

Shaw, A., Weiderman, N., Andrews, G., Felcyn, M., Rieber, J., and Wong, G. 1975. A multiprogramming nucleus with dynamic resource facilities. *Software—Practice and Experience 5*, 245-267.

Silberschatz, A. 1979. Communication and synchronization in distributed programs. *IEEE Trans. on Software Engr. SE-5*, 6 (November), 542-546.

Silberschatz, A., Kieburtz, R.B., and Bernstein, A.J. 1977. Extending Concurrent Pascal to allow dynamic resource management. *IEEE Trans. on Software Engr. SE-3*, 3 (May), 210-217.

Skillicorn, D.B., and Barnard, D.B. 1989. Parallel parsing on the Connection Machine. *Information Processing Letters 31*, 3 (May), 111-118.

Sloman, M., and Kramer, J. 1987. *Distributed Systems and Computer Networks.* Prentice-Hall, Englewood Cliffs, NJ.

Soundararajan, N. 1984. Axiomatic semantics of communicating sequential processes. *ACM Trans. on Prog. Languages and Systems 6*, 4 (October), 647-662.

Spector, A.Z. 1982. Performing remote operations efficiently on a local computer network. *Comm. ACM 25*, 4 (April), 246-260.

Stamos, J.W, and Gifford, D.K. 1990. Remote evaluation. *ACM Trans. on Prog. Languages and Systems 12*, 4 (October), 537-565.

Steele, G.L., Jr. 1975. Multiprocessing compactifying garbage collection. *Comm. ACM 18*, 9 (September), 495-508.

Strom, R.E., and Yemini, S. 1983. NIL: An integrated language and system for distributed programming. *SIGPLAN Notices 18*, 6 (June), 73-82

Strom, R.E., and Yemini, S. 1986. Typestate: a programming language concept for enhancing software reliability. *IEEE Trans. on Software Engr SE-12*, 1 (January), 157-171.

Stroustrup, B. 1982. An experiment with the interchangeability of processes and monitors. *Software—Practice and Experience 12*, 1011-1025.

Suzuki, I., and Kasami, T. 1985. A distributed mutual exclusion algorithm. *ACM Trans. on Computer Systems 3*, 4 (November), 344-349.

Swinehart, D.C., Zellweger, P.T., and Hagmann, R.B. 1985. The structure of Cedar. *Proc. ACM SIGPLAN 85 Symp. on Language Issues in Programming Environments*, July, 230-244.

Tanenbaum, A.S. 1988. *Computer Networks*, Second Edition. Prentice-Hall, Englewood Cliffs, NJ.

Tanenbaum, A.S, van Renesse, R., van Staveren, H., Sharp, G.J., Mullender, S.J., Jansen, J., and van Rossum, G. 1990. Experiences with the Amoeba distributed operating system. *Comm. ACM 33*, 12 (December), 46-63.

Tel, G., Tan, R.B., and van Leeuwen, J. 1988. The derivation of graph marking algorithms from distributed termination detection protocols. *Science of Computer Prog. 10*, 107-137.

Teorey, T.J., and Pinkerton, T.B. 1972. A comparative analysis of disk scheduling policies. *Comm. ACM 15*, 3 (March), 177-184.

Thomas, R.H. 1979. A majority consensus approach to concurrency control in multiple copy databases. *ACM Trans. on Database Systems 4*, 2 (June), 180-209.

Thomas, R.H., and Crowther, W. 1988. The uniform system: an approach to runtime support for large scale shared memory parallel processors. *Proc. 1988 Int. Conf. on Parallel Processing*, August, 245-254.

Thompson, K. 1978. UNIX implementation. *The Bell System Technical Journal 57*, 6, part 2 (July-August), 1931-1946.

Tucker, A., and Gupta, A. 1989. Process control and scheduling issues for multi-programmed shared-memory multiprocessors. *Proc. Twelfth ACM Symp. on Operating Systems Principles*, December, 159-166.

Tucker, L.W., and Robertson, G.G. 1988. Architecture and applications of the Connection Machine. *IEEE Computer 21*, 8 (August), 26-38.

Udding, J. 1986. Absence of individual starvation using weak semaphores. *Information Processing Letters 23*, 3 (October), 159-162.

van de Snepscheut, J.L.A. 1981. Synchronous communication between asynchronous components. *Information Processing Letters 13*, 3 (December), 127-130.

van de Snepscheut, J.L.A. 1987. Fair mutual exclusion on a graph of processes. *Distributed Computing 2*, 2, 113-115.

van Wijngaarden, A., Mailloux, B.J., Peck, J.L., Koster, C.H.A., Sintzoff, M., Lindsey, C.H., Meertens, L.G.L.T., and Fisker, R.G. 1975. Revised report on the algorithmic language ALGOL 68. *Acta Informatica 5*, 1-3, 1-236.

Volz, R.A., Mudge, T.N., Buzzard, G.D., and Krishnan, P. 1989. Translation and execution of distributed Ada programs: is it still Ada? *IEEE Trans. on Software Engr. SE-15*, 3 (March), 281-292.

Wegner, P., and Smolka, S.A. 1983. Processes, tasks and monitors: a comparative study of concurrent programming primitives. *IEEE Trans. on Software Engr. SE-9*, 4(July), 446-462.

Weihl, W.E. 1990. Linguistic support for atomic data types. *ACM Trans. on Prog. Languages and Systems 12*, 2 (April), 178-202.

Weihl, W., and Liskov, B. 1985. Implementation of resilient, atomic data types. *ACM Trans. on Prog. Languages and Systems 7*, 2 (April), 244-269.

Welsh, J., and Bustard, D.W. 1979. Pascal-Plus—another language for modular multiprogramming. *Software—Practice and Experience 9*, 947-957.

Welsh, J., and Lister, A. 1981. A comparative study of task communication in Ada. *Software—Practice and Experience 11*, 257-290.

Welsh, J., and McKeag, M. 1980. *Structured System Programming*. Prentice-Hall Int., Englewood Cliffs, NJ.

Wettstein, H. 1978. The problem of nested monitor calls revisited. *Operating Systems Review 12*, 1 (January), 19-23.

Whiddet, R.J. 1987. *Concurrent Programming for Software Engineering*. John Wiley & Sons, New York.

Wilkes, C.T., and LeBlanc, R.J. 1986. Rationale for the desing of Aeolus: a systems programming language for the action/object system. *Proc. 1986 IEEE Int. Conf. on Computer Languages*, October, 107-122.

Wilson, G.A. 1989. Generic parameters in occam. *Software—Practice and Experience 19*, 11 (November), 1057-1064.

Wirth, N. 1977a. Modula: a language for modular multiprogramming. *Software—Practice and Experience 7*, 3-35.

Wirth, N. 1977b. The use of Modula. *Software—Practice and Experience 7*, 37-65.

Wirth, N. 1977c. Design and implementation of Modula. *Software—Practice and Experience 7*, 67-84.

Wirth, N. 1977d. Towards a discipline of real-time programming. *Comm. ACM 20*, 8 (August), 577-583.

Yew, P.-C., Tzeng, N.-F., and Lawrie, D.H. 1987. Distributing hot-spot addressing in large-scale multiprocessors. *IEEE Trans. on Computers C-36*, 4 (April), 388-395.

Young, M., Tevanian, A., Rashid, R., Golub, D., Eppinger, J., Chew, J., Boloshky, W., Black, D., and Baron, R. 1987. The duality of memory and communication in the implementation of a multiprocessor system. *Proc. Eleventh ACM Symp. on Operating Systems Principles*, November, 63-76.

Zenith, S.E. 1990. Programming with Ease: a semiotic definition of the language. Research Report RR809, Dept. of Computer Science, Yale University, New Haven, CT, July.

Index